Ford Taurus & Mercury Sable Automotive Repair Manual

by Bob Henderson and John H Haynes

Member of the Guild of Motoring Writers

Models covered:
Ford Taurus & Mercury Sable
1986 through 1990

(11R1–1421)

ABCDE
FGHIJ
KLMNO
PQ

Haynes Publishing Group
Sparkford Nr Yeovil
Somerset BA22 7JJ England

Haynes Publications, Inc
861 Lawrence Drive
Newbury Park
California 91320 USA

Acknowledgements

We are grateful for the help and cooperation of the Ford Motor Company for their assistance with technical information, certain illustrations and vehicle photos, and the Champion Spark Plug Company who supplied the illustrations of various spark plug conditions. Technical writers who contributed to this project include Larry Warren, Mike Stubblefield and Ken Freund.

© **Haynes Publishing Group 1988, 1990**

A book in the **Haynes Automotive Repair Manual Series**

Printed by J.H. Haynes & Co., Ltd. Sparkford Nr. Yeovil, Somerset BA22 7JJ, England

ISBN 1 85010 709 2

Library of Congress Catalog Card Number 88-83176

Contents

1986 Ford Taurus four-door sedan

1986 Ford Taurus station wagon

About this manual

Its purpose

The purpose of this manual is to help you get the best value from your vehicle. It can do so in several ways. It can help you decide what work must be done, even if you choose to have it done by a dealer service department or a repair shop; it provides information and procedures for routine maintenance and servicing; and it offers diagnostic and repair procedures to follow when trouble occurs.

It is hoped that you will use the manual to tackle the work yourself. For many simpler jobs, doing it yourself may be quicker than arranging an appointment to get the vehicle into a shop and making the trips to leave it and pick it up. More importantly, a lot of money can be saved by avoiding the expense the shop must pass on to you to cover its labor and overhead costs. An added benefit is the sense of satisfaction and accomplishment that you feel after having done the job yourself.

Using the manual

The manual is divided into Chapters. Each Chapter is divided into numbered Sections, which are headed in bold type between horizontal lines. Each Section consists of consecutively numbered paragraphs.

At the beginning of each numbered section you will be referred to any illustrations which apply to the procedures in that section. The reference numbers used in illustration captions pinpoint the pertinent Section and the Step within that section. That is, illustration 3.2 means the illustration refers to Section 3 and Step (or paragraph) 2 within that Section.

Procedures, once described in the text, are not normally repeated. When it is necessary to refer to another Chapter, the reference will be given as Chapter and Section number i.e. Chapter 1/16). Cross references given without use of the word "Chapter" apply to Sections and/or paragraphs in the same Chapter. For example, "see Section 8" means in the same Chapter.

Reference to the left or right side of the vehicle is based on the assumption that one is sitting in the driver's seat, facing forward.

Even though extreme care has been taken during the preparation of this manual, neither the publisher nor the author can accept responsibility for any errors in, or omissions from, the information given.

NOTE

A Note provides information necessary to properly complete a procedure or information which will make the steps to be followed easier to understand.

CAUTION

A Caution indicates a special procedure or special steps which must be taken in the course of completing the procedure in which the **Caution** is found which are necessary to avoid damage to the assembly being worked on.

WARNING

A Warning indicates a special procedure or special steps which must be taken in the course of completing the procedure in which the **Warning** is found which are necessary to avoid injury to the person performing the procedure.

Introduction to the Ford Taurus/Mercury Sable

The Ford Taurus/Mercury Sable features front wheel drive and is available in four door sedan and station wagon body styles.

Transversely-mounted inline four-cylinder and V6 engines equipped with fuel injection are used to power these models.

The engine drives the front wheels through either a five-speed manual or four-speed automatic transaxle and driveaxles incorporating constant velocity joints.

Suspension is handled by independent coil springs at all four wheels. Rack and pinion steering, mounted behind the engine, is used with power assist standard.

The brakes on most models are disc-type at the front and drums at the rear with vacuum assist standard. Some later models are equipped with rear disc brakes and an Anti-Lock Brake System (ABS).

Vehicle identification numbers

Modifications are a continuing and unpublicized process in automotive manufacturing. Because spare parts manuals and lists are compiled on a numerical basis, the individual vehicle numbers are essential to correctly identify the component required.

Vehicle identification number (VIN)

The VIN number is very important because it is used for title and registration purposes. The VIN number is stamped on a metal plate fastened to the instrument panel close to the windshield on the driver's side (see illustration). The 17-character Vehicle Identification Number is used for warranty identification of the vehicle and indicates such things as manufacturer, type of restraint system, line, series, body type, engine, model year and consecutive unit number.

Vehicle Certification Label

The Vehicle Certification Label (VC Label) is affixed to the left front door lock panel or door pillar (see illustration). The upper half of the label contains the name of the manufacturer, the month and year of manufacture, the Gross Vehicle Weight Rating (GVWR), the Gross Axle Weight Rating (GAWR) and the certification statement.

Engine identification number

For quick engine identification, refer to the VIN, which lists the engine code in position number 8. Find the engine code (letter or number), then refer to the engine identification chart (see illustrations) to determine the engine type and size.

Transaxle identification number

The transaxle identification number is located on a tag (see illustration) attached to the housing.

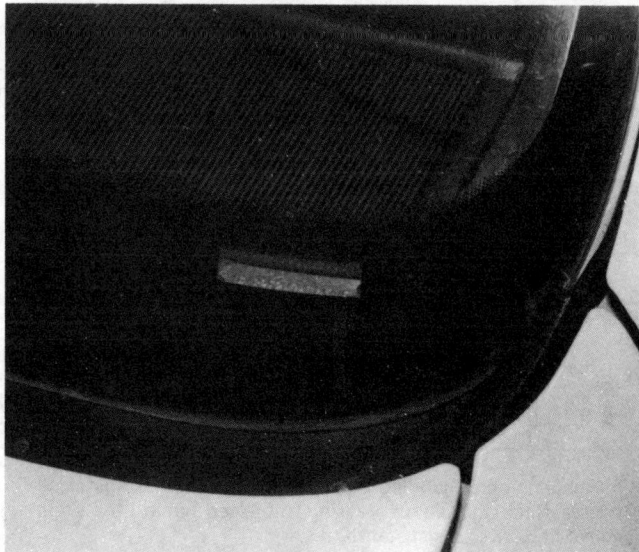

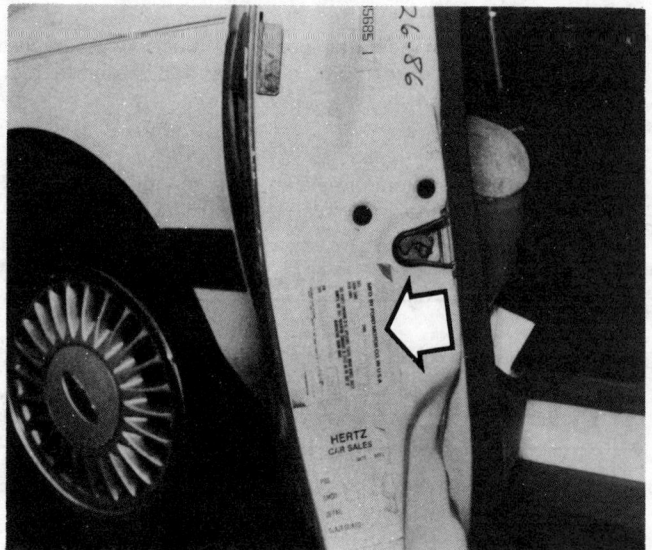

The Vehicle Identification Number (VIN), stamped on a metal plate fastened to the top of the dashboard on the driver's side, is clearly visible through the windshield

The Vehicle Certification label (VC label) is on the left front door lock panel or the door pillar

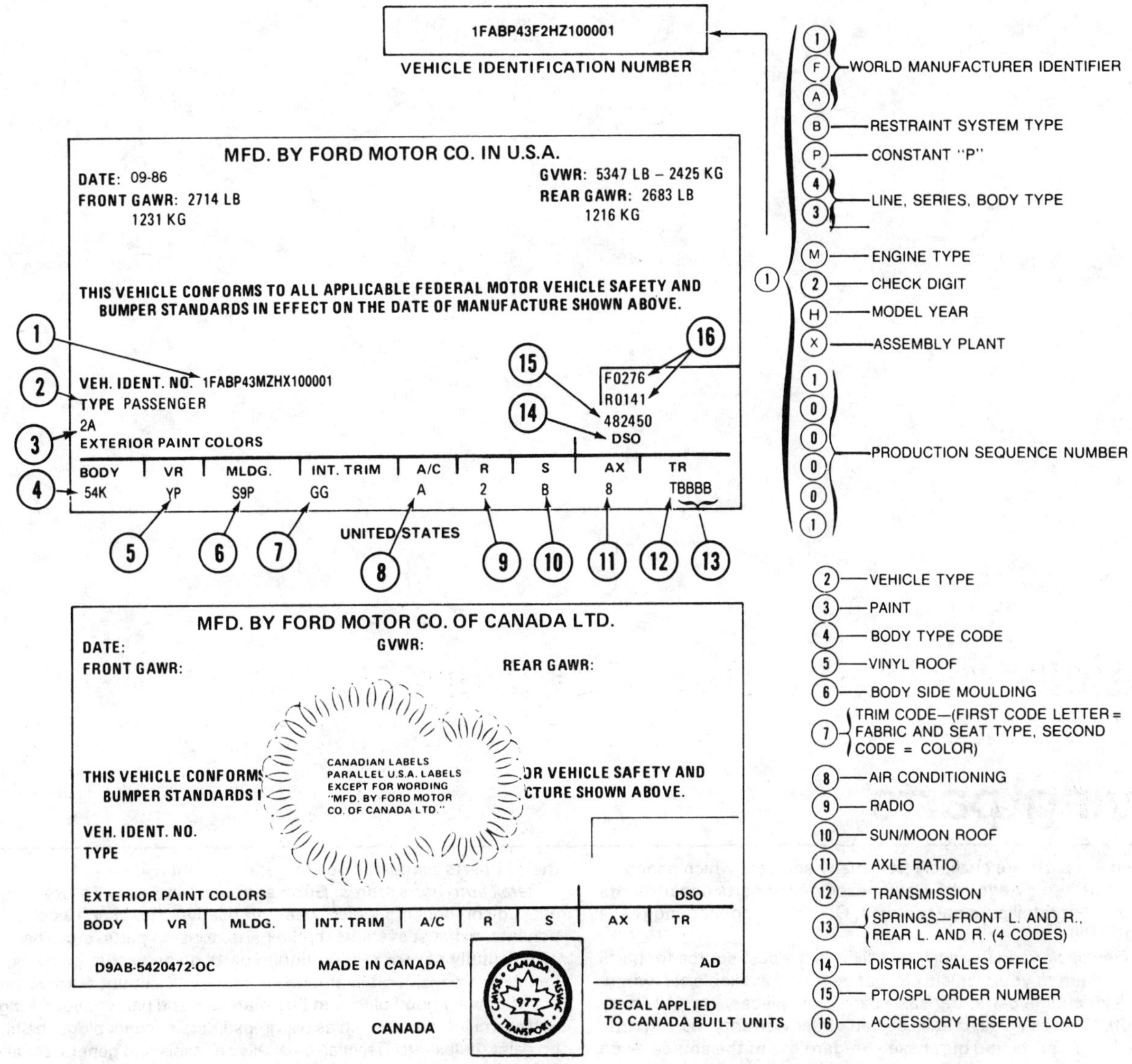

1FABP43F2HZ100001

VEHICLE IDENTIFICATION NUMBER

MFD. BY FORD MOTOR CO. IN U.S.A.

DATE: 09-86

GVWR: 5347 LB – 2425 KG

FRONT GAWR: 2714 LB
1231 KG

REAR GAWR: 2683 LB
1216 KG

THIS VEHICLE CONFORMS TO ALL APPLICABLE FEDERAL MOTOR VEHICLE SAFETY AND
BUMPER STANDARDS IN EFFECT ON THE DATE OF MANUFACTURE SHOWN ABOVE.

① VEH. IDENT. NO. 1FABP43MZHX100001

② TYPE PASSENGER

③ 2A
EXTERIOR PAINT COLORS

F0276
R0141
482450
DSO

BODY	VR	MLDG.	INT. TRIM	A/C	R	S	AX	TR
54K	YP	S9P	GG	A	2	B	8	TBBBB

④ ⑤ ⑥ ⑦ UNITED STATES ⑧ ⑨ ⑩ ⑪ ⑫ ⑬ ⑭ ⑮ ⑯

MFD. BY FORD MOTOR CO. OF CANADA LTD.

DATE:

GVWR:

FRONT GAWR:

REAR GAWR:

CANADIAN LABELS PARALLEL U.S.A. LABELS EXCEPT FOR WORDING "MFD. BY FORD MOTOR CO. OF CANADA LTD."

THIS VEHICLE CONFORMS ... OR VEHICLE SAFETY AND
BUMPER STANDARDS I ... CTURE SHOWN ABOVE.

VEH. IDENT. NO.
TYPE

EXTERIOR PAINT COLORS

DSO

BODY	VR	MLDG.	INT. TRIM	A/C	R	S	AX	TR

D9AB-5420472-OC

MADE IN CANADA

AD

CANADA

CANADA 977 TRANSPORT

DECAL APPLIED
TO CANADA BUILT UNITS

① WORLD MANUFACTURER IDENTIFIER
(F)(A)

(B) RESTRAINT SYSTEM TYPE

(P) CONSTANT "P"

(4)(3) LINE, SERIES, BODY TYPE

(M) ENGINE TYPE

(2) CHECK DIGIT

(H) MODEL YEAR

(X) ASSEMBLY PLANT

(1)(0)(0)(0)(0)(1) PRODUCTION SEQUENCE NUMBER

② VEHICLE TYPE
③ PAINT
④ BODY TYPE CODE
⑤ VINYL ROOF
⑥ BODY SIDE MOULDING
⑦ TRIM CODE—(FIRST CODE LETTER = FABRIC AND SEAT TYPE, SECOND CODE = COLOR)
⑧ AIR CONDITIONING
⑨ RADIO
⑩ SUN/MOON ROOF
⑪ AXLE RATIO
⑫ TRANSMISSION
⑬ SPRINGS—FRONT L. AND R., REAR L. AND R. (4 CODES)
⑭ DISTRICT SALES OFFICE
⑮ PTO/SPL ORDER NUMBER
⑯ ACCESSORY RESERVE LOAD

Ford Vehicle Certification label codes

1FABP18 ④ 2JZ100001

VIN CODE	DISPLACEMENT		CYLINDERS	FUEL	MANUFACTURER
	LITER	CID			
D	2.5 HSC CFI	153	4	Gasoline	Ford
U	3.0 EFI	182	6	Gasoline	Ford
4	3.8 EFI	232	6	Gasoline	Ford

Engine identification chart (VIN position 8)

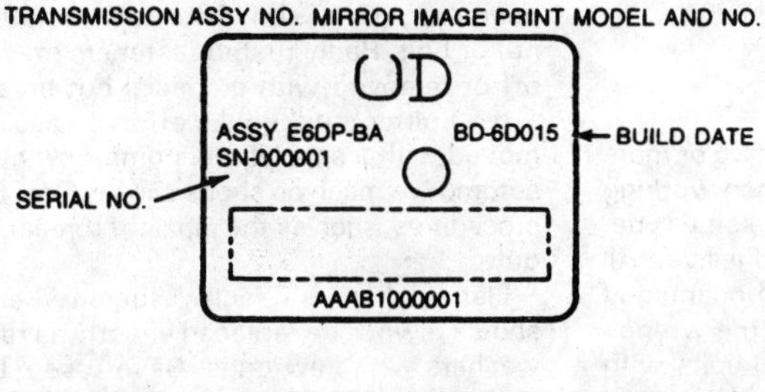

TRANSMISSION ASSY NO. MIRROR IMAGE PRINT MODEL AND NO.

UD

ASSY E6DP-BA   BD-6D015 ← BUILD DATE
SN-000001

SERIAL NO.

AAAB1000001

Automatic transaxle
identification tag

Buying parts

Replacement parts are available from many sources, which generally fall into one of two categories — authorized dealer parts departments and independent retail auto parts stores. Our advice concerning these parts is as follows:

Authorized dealer parts department: This is the best source for parts which are unique to your vehicle and not generally available elsewhere such as major engine parts, transaxle parts, trim pieces, etc. *Warranty information:* If your vehicle is still covered under warranty, be sure that any replacement parts you purchase — regardless of the source — do not invalidate your warranty! To be sure of obtaining the correct parts, have your engine and chassis numbers available and, if possible, take the old parts along for positive identification.

Retail auto parts stores: Good auto parts stores will stock frequently needed components which wear out relatively fast such as clutch components, exhaust systems, brake parts, tune-up parts, etc. These stores often supply new or reconditioned parts on an exchange basis, which can save a considerable amount of money. Discount auto parts stores are often very good places to buy materials and parts needed for general vehicle maintenance such as oil, grease, filters, spark plugs, belts, touch up paint, bulbs, etc. They also usually sell tools and general accessories, have convenient hours, charge lower prices, and can often be found not far from your home.

Maintenance techniques, tools and working facilities

Maintenance techniques

There are a number of techniques involved in maintenance and repair that will be referred to throughout this manual. Application of these techniques will enable the home mechanic to be more efficient, better organized and capable of performing the various tasks properly, which will ensure that the repair job is thorough and complete.

Fasteners

Fasteners are nuts, bolts, studs and screws used to hold two or more parts together. There are a few things to keep in mind when working with fasteners. Almost all of them use a locking device of some type, either a lockwasher, locknut, locking tab or thread adhesive. All threaded fasteners should be clean and straight, with undamaged threads and undamaged corners on the hex head where the wrench fits. Develop the habit of replacing all damaged nuts and bolts with new ones. Special locknuts with nylon or fiber inserts can only be used once. If they are removed, they lose their locking ability and must be replaced with new ones.

Rusted nuts and bolts should be treated with a penetrating fluid to ease removal and prevent breakage. Some mechanics use turpentine in a spout-type oil can, which works quite well. After applying the rust penetrant, let it work for a few minutes before trying to loosen the nut or bolt. Badly rusted fasteners may have to be chiseled or sawed off or removed with a special nut breaker, available at tool stores.

If a bolt or stud breaks off in an assembly, it can be drilled and removed with a special tool commonly available for this purpose. Most automotive machine shops can perform this task, as well as other repair procedures, such as the repair of threaded holes that have been stripped out.

Flat washers and lockwashers, when removed from an assembly, should always be replaced exactly as removed. Replace any damaged washers with new ones. Never use a lockwasher on any soft metal surface (such as aluminum), thin sheet metal or plastic.

Fastener sizes

For a number of reasons, automobile manufacturers are making wider and wider use of metric fasteners. Therefore, it is important to be able to tell the difference between standard (sometimes called U.S. or SAE) and metric hardware, since they cannot be interchanged.

All bolts, whether standard or metric, are sized according to diameter, thread pitch and length. For example, a standard 1/2 — 13 x 1 bolt is 1/2 inch in diameter, has 13 threads per inch and is 1 inch long. An M12 — 1.75 x 25 metric bolt is 12 mm in diameter, has a thread pitch of 1.75 mm (the distance between threads) and is 25 mm long. The two bolts are nearly identical, and easily confused, but they are not interchangeable.

In addition to the differences in diameter, thread pitch and length, metric and standard bolts can also be distinguished by examining the bolt heads. To begin with, the distance across the flats on a standard bolt head is measured in inches, while the same dimension on a metric bolt is sized in millimeters (the same is true for nuts). As a result, a standard wrench should not be used on a metric bolt and a metric wrench should not be used on a standard bolt. Also, most standard bolts have slashes radiating out from the center of the head to denote the grade or strength of the bolt, which is an indication of the amount of torque that can be applied to it. The greater the number of slashes, the greater the strength of the bolt. Grades 0 through 5 are commonly used on automobiles. Metric bolts have a property class (grade) number, rather than a slash, molded into their heads to indicate bolt strength. In this case, the higher the number, the stronger the bolt. Property class numbers 8.8, 9.8 and 10.9 are commonly used on automobiles.

Strength markings can also be used to distinguish standard hex nuts from metric hex nuts. Many standard nuts have dots stamped into one side, while metric nuts are marked with a number. The greater the number of dots, or the higher the number, the greater the strength of the nut.

Metric studs are also marked on their ends according to property class (grade). Larger studs are numbered (the same as metric bolts),

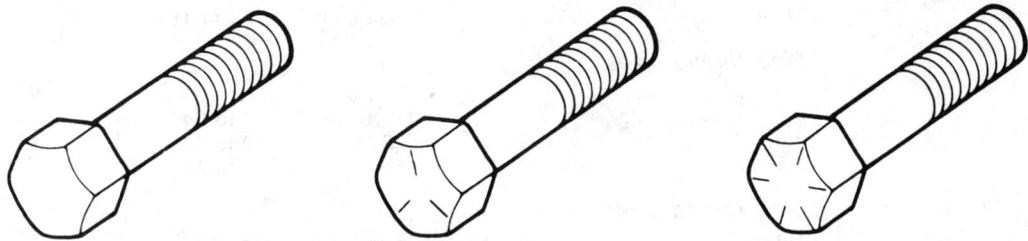

Grade 1 or 2   Grade 5   Grade 8

4.6   4.8   5.8   8.8   9.8   10.9

Bolt strength markings (top — standard/SAE/USS; bottom — metric)

Grade	Identification
Hex Nut Grade 5	3 Dots
Hex Nut Grade 8	6 Dots

Standard hex nut strength markings

Class	Identification
Hex Nut Property Class 9	Arabic 9
Hex Nut Property Class 10	Arabic 10

Metric hex nut strength markings

CLASS 10.9   CLASS 9.8   CLASS 8.8

Metric stud strength markings

while smaller studs carry a geometric code to denote grade.

It should be noted that many fasteners, especially Grades 0 through 2, have no distinguishing marks on them. When such is the case, the only way to determine whether it is standard or metric is to measure the thread pitch or compare it to a known fastener of the same size.

Standard fasteners are often referred to as SAE, as opposed to metric. However, it should be noted that SAE technically refers to a non-metric *fine thread* fastener only. Coarse thread non-metric fasteners are referred to as USS sizes.

Since fasteners of the same size (both standard and metric) may have different strength ratings, be sure to reinstall any bolts, studs or nuts removed from your vehicle in their original locations. Also, when replacing a fastener with a new one, make sure that the new one has a strength rating equal to or greater than the original.

Tightening sequences and procedures

Most threaded fasteners should be tightened to a specific torque value (torque is the twisting force applied to a threaded component such as a nut or bolt). Overtightening the fastener can weaken it and cause it to break, while undertightening can cause it to eventually come loose. Bolts, screws and studs, depending on the material they are made of and their thread diameters, have specific torque values, many of which are noted in the Specifications at the beginning of each Chapter. Be sure to follow the torque recommendations closely. For fasteners not assigned a specific torque, a general torque value chart is presented here as a guide. These torque values are for dry (unlubricated) fasteners threaded into steel or cast iron (not aluminum). As was previously mentioned, the size and grade of a fastener determine the amount of torque that can safely be applied to it. The figures listed here are approximate

Metric thread sizes	Ft-lb	Nm/m
M-6	6 to 9	9 to 12
M-8	14 to 21	19 to 28
M-10	28 to 40	38 to 54
M-12	50 to 71	68 to 96
M-14	80 to 140	109 to 154
Pipe thread sizes		
1/8	5 to 8	7 to 10
1/4	12 to 18	17 to 24
3/8	22 to 33	30 to 44
1/2	25 to 35	34 to 47
U.S. thread sizes		
1/4 — 20	6 to 9	9 to 12
5/16 — 18	12 to 18	17 to 24
5/16 — 24	14 to 20	19 to 27
3/8 — 16	22 to 32	30 to 43
3/8 — 24	27 to 38	37 to 51
7/16 — 14	40 to 55	55 to 74
7/16 — 20	40 to 60	55 to 81
1/2 — 13	55 to 80	75 to 108

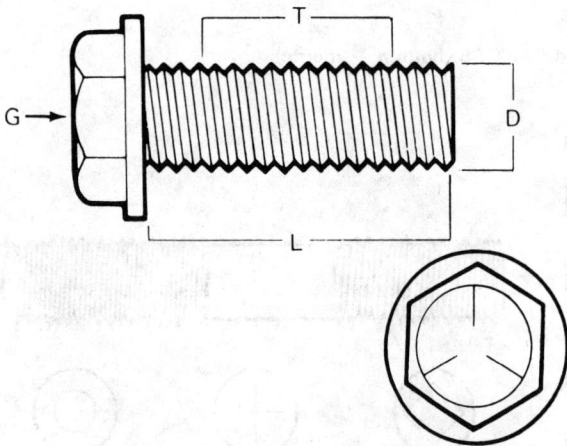

Standard (SAE and USS) bolt dimensions/grade marks

G Grade marks (bolt strength)
L Length (in inches)
T Thread pitch (number of threads per inch)
D Nominal diameter (in inches)

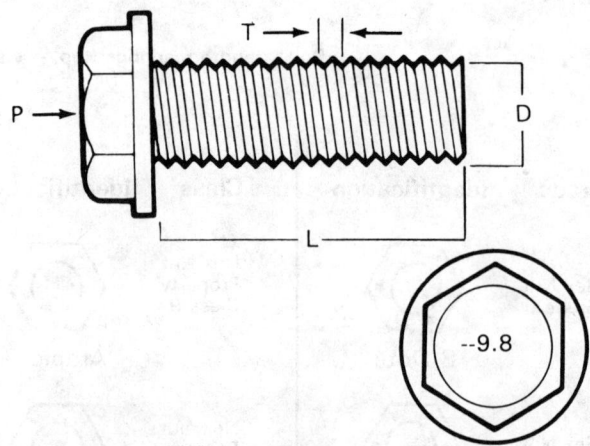

Metric bolt dimensions/grade marks

P Property class (bolt strength)
L Length (in millimeters)
T Thread pitch (distance between threads in millimeters)
D Diameter

for Grade 2 and Grade 3 fasteners. Higher grades can tolerate higher torque values.

Fasteners laid out in a pattern, such as cylinder head bolts, oil pan bolts, differential cover bolts, etc., must be loosened or tightened in sequence to avoid warping the component. This sequence will normally be shown in the appropriate Chapter. If a specific pattern is not given, the following procedures can be used to prevent warping.

Initially, the bolts or nuts should be assembled finger-tight only. Next, they should be tightened one full turn each, in a criss-cross or diagonal pattern. After each one has been tightened one full turn, return to the first one and tighten them all one-half turn, following the same pattern. Finally, tighten each of them one-quarter turn at a time until each fastener has been tightened to the proper torque. To loosen and remove the fasteners, the procedure would be reversed.

Component disassembly

Component disassembly should be done with care and purpose to help ensure that the parts go back together properly. Always keep track of the sequence in which parts are removed. Make note of special characteristics or marks on parts that can be installed more than one way, such as a grooved thrust washer on a shaft. It is a good idea to lay the disassembled parts out on a clean surface in the order that they were removed. It may also be helpful to make sketches or take instant photos of components before removal.

When removing fasteners from a component, keep track of their locations. Sometimes threading a bolt back in a part, or putting the washers and nut back on a stud, can prevent mix-ups later. If nuts and bolts cannot be returned to their original locations, they should be kept in a compartmented box or a series of small boxes. A cupcake or muffin tin is ideal for this purpose, since each cavity can hold the bolts and nuts from a particular area (i.e. oil pan bolts, valve cover bolts, engine mount bolts, etc.). A pan of this type is especially helpful when working on assemblies with very small parts, such as the carburetor, alternator, valve train or interior dash and trim pieces. The cavities can be marked with paint or tape to identify the contents.

Whenever wiring looms, harnesses or connectors are separated, it is a good idea to identify the two halves with numbered pieces of masking tape so they can be easily reconnected.

Gasket sealing surfaces

Throughout any vehicle, gaskets are used to seal the mating surfaces between two parts and keep lubricants, fluids, vacuum or pressure contained in an assembly.

Many times these gaskets are coated with a liquid or paste-type gasket sealing compound before assembly. Age, heat and pressure can sometimes cause the two parts to stick together so tightly that they are very difficult to separate. Often, the assembly can be loosened by striking it with a soft-face hammer near the mating surfaces. A regular hammer can be used if a block of wood is placed between the hammer and the part. Do not hammer on cast parts or parts that could be easily damaged. With any particularly stubborn part, always recheck to make sure that every fastener has been removed.

Avoid using a screwdriver or bar to pry apart an assembly, as they can easily mar the gasket sealing surfaces of the parts, which must remain smooth. If prying is absolutely necessary, use an old broom handle, but keep in mind that extra clean up will be necessary if the wood splinters.

After the parts are separated, the old gasket must be carefully scraped off and the gasket surfaces cleaned. Stubborn gasket material can be soaked with rust penetrant or treated with a special chemical to soften it so it can be easily scraped off. A scraper can be fashioned from a piece of copper tubing by flattening and sharpening one end. Copper is recommended because it is usually softer than the surfaces to be scraped, which reduces the chance of gouging the part. Some gaskets can be removed with a wire brush, but regardless of the method used, the mating surfaces must be left clean and smooth. If for some reason the gasket surface is gouged, then a gasket sealer thick enough to fill scratches will have to be used during reassembly of the components. For most applications, a non-drying (or semi-drying) gasket sealer should be used.

Hose removal tips

Warning: *If the vehicle is equipped with air conditioning, do not disconnect any of the A/C hoses without first having the system depressurized by a dealer service department or an air conditioning specialist.*

Hose removal precautions closely parallel gasket removal precautions. Avoid scratching or gouging the surface that the hose mates against or the connection may leak. This is especially true for radiator hoses. Because of various chemical reactions, the rubber in hoses can bond itself to the metal spigot that the hose fits over. To remove a hose, first loosen the hose clamps that secure it to the spigot. Then, with slip-joint pliers, grab the hose at the clamp and rotate it around the spigot. Work it back and forth until it is completely free, then pull it off. Silicone or other lubricants will ease removal if they can be applied between the hose and the outside of the spigot. Apply the same lubricant to the inside of the hose and the outside of the spigot to simplify installation.

As a last resort (and if the hose is to be replaced with a new one anyway), the rubber can be slit with a knife and the hose peeled from the spigot. If this must be done, be careful that the metal connection is not damaged.

If a hose clamp is broken or damaged, do not reuse it. Wire-type clamps usually weaken with age, so it is a good idea to replace them with screw-type clamps whenever a hose is removed.

Tools

A selection of good tools is a basic requirement for anyone who plans to maintain and repair his or her own vehicle. For the owner who has few tools, the initial investment might seem high, but when compared to the spiraling costs of professional auto maintenance and repair, it is a wise one.

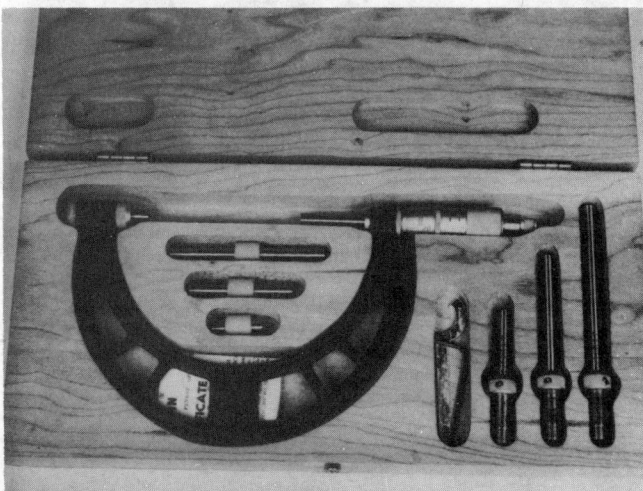

Micrometer set

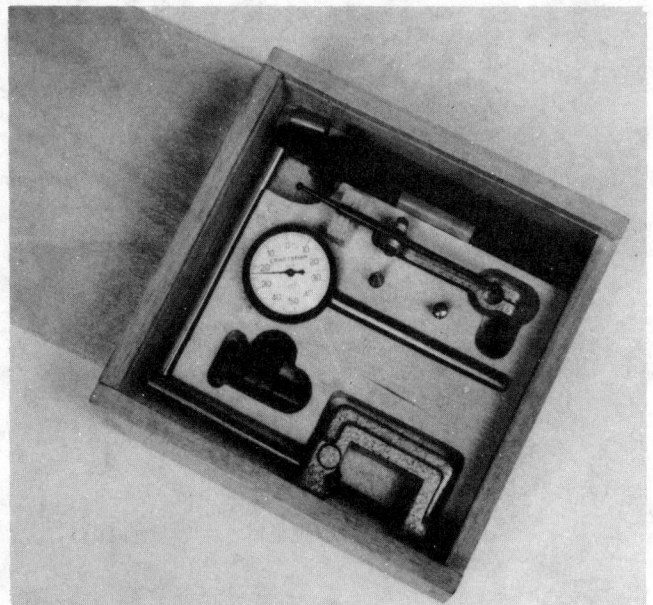

Dial indicator set

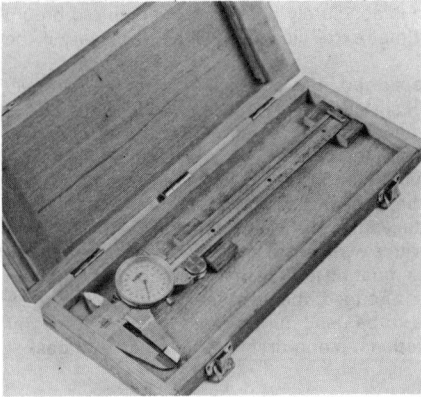

Dial caliper

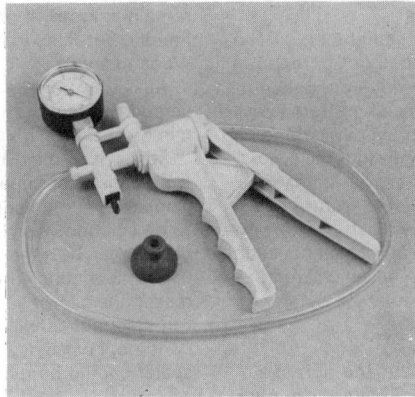

Hand-operated vacuum pump

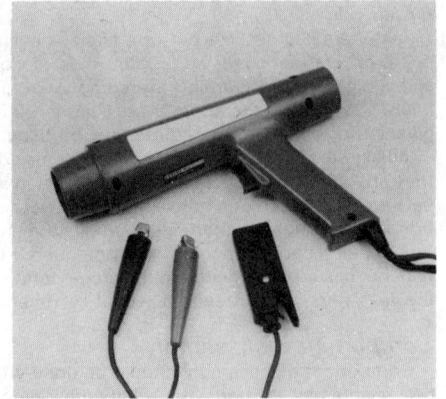

Timing light

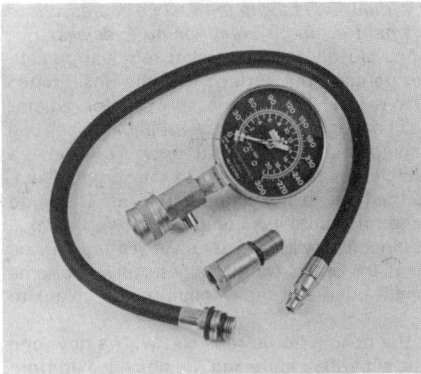

Compression gauge with spark plug
hole adapter

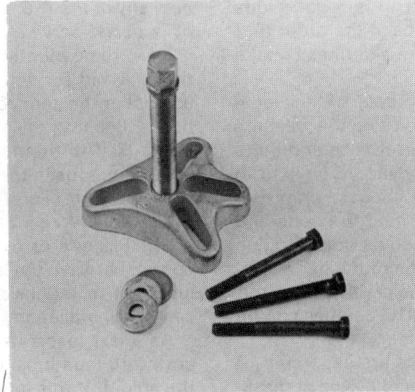

Damper/steering wheel puller

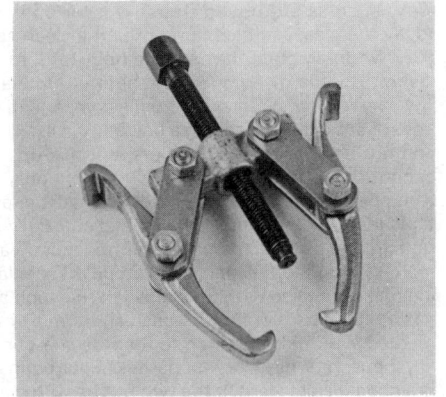

General purpose puller

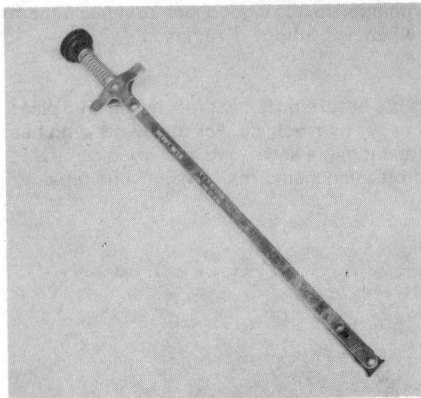

Hydraulic lifter removal tool

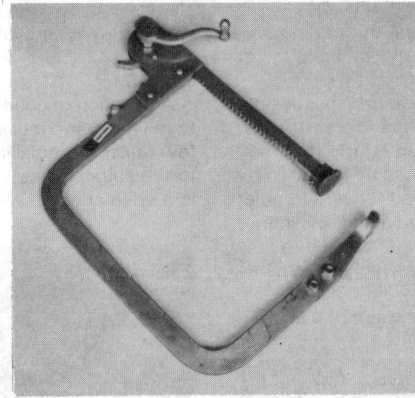

Valve spring compressor

Valve spring compressor

Ridge reamer

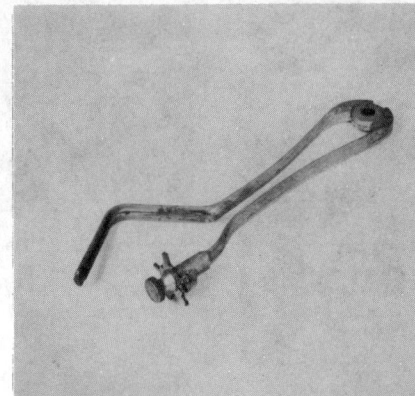

Piston ring groove cleaning tool

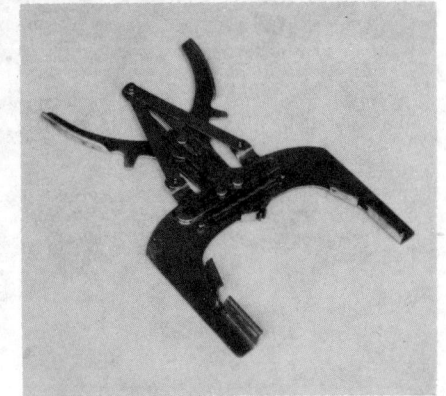

Ring removal/installation tool

Ring compressor

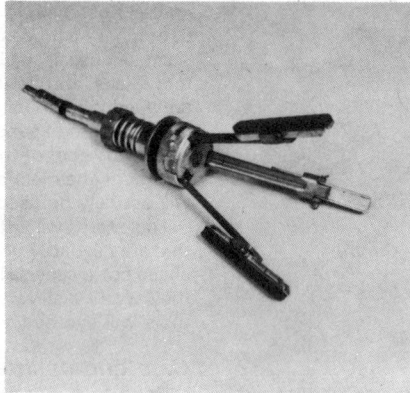
Cylinder hone

Brake hold-down spring tool

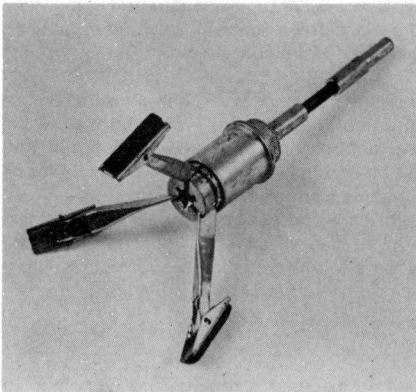
Brake cylinder hone

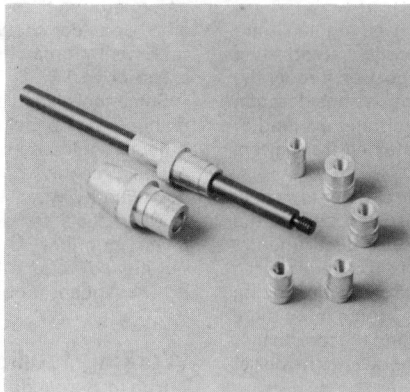
Clutch plate alignment tool

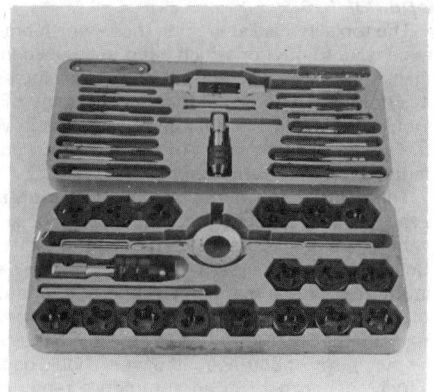
Tap and die set

To help the owner decide which tools are needed to perform the tasks detailed in this manual, the following tool lists are offered: *Maintenance and minor repair*, *Repair/overhaul* and *Special*.

The newcomer to practical mechanics should start off with the maintenance and minor repair tool kit, which is adequate for the simpler jobs performed on a vehicle. Then, as confidence and experience grow, the owner can tackle more difficult tasks, buying additional tools as they are needed. Eventually the basic kit will be expanded into the repair and overhaul tool set. Over a period of time, the experienced do-it-yourselfer will assemble a tool set complete enough for most repair and overhaul procedures and will add tools from the special category when it is felt that the expense is justified by the frequency of use.

Maintenance and minor repair tool kit

The tools in this list should be considered the minimum required for performance of routine maintenance, servicing and minor repair work. We recommend the purchase of combination wrenches (box-end and open-end combined in one wrench). While more expensive than open end wrenches, they offer the advantages of both types of wrench.

Combination wrench set (1/4-inch to 1 inch or 6 mm to 19 mm)
Adjustable wrench, 8 inch
Spark plug wrench with rubber insert
Spark plug gap adjusting tool
Feeler gauge set
Brake bleeder wrench
Standard screwdriver (5/16-inch x 6 inch)
Phillips screwdriver (No. 2 x 6 inch)
Combination pliers — 6 inch
Hacksaw and assortment of blades
Tire pressure gauge
Grease gun
Oil can
Fine emery cloth
Wire brush

Battery post and cable cleaning tool
Oil filter wrench
Funnel (medium size)
Safety goggles
Jackstands (2)
Drain pan

Note: *If basic tune-ups are going to be part of routine maintenance, it will be necessary to purchase a good quality stroboscopic timing light and combination tachometer/dwell meter. Although they are included in the list of special tools, it is mentioned here because they are absolutely necessary for tuning most vehicles properly.*

Repair and overhaul tool set

These tools are essential for anyone who plans to perform major repairs and are in addition to those in the maintenance and minor repair tool kit. Included is a comprehensive set of sockets which, though expensive, are invaluable because of their versatility, especially when various extensions and drives are available. We recommend the 1/2-inch drive over the 3/8-inch drive. Although the larger drive is bulky and more expensive, it has the capacity of accepting a very wide range of large sockets. Ideally, however, the mechanic should have a 3/8-inch drive set and a 1/2-inch drive set.

Socket set(s)
Reversible ratchet
Extension — 10 inch
Universal joint
Torque wrench (same size drive as sockets)
Ball peen hammer — 8 ounce
Soft-face hammer (plastic/rubber)
Standard screwdriver (1/4-inch x 6 inch)
Standard screwdriver (stubby — 5/16-inch)
Phillips screwdriver (No. 3 x 8 inch)
Phillips screwdriver (stubby — No. 2)

Pliers — vise grip
Pliers — lineman's
Pliers — needle nose
Pliers — snap-ring (internal and external)
Cold chisel — 1/2-inch
Scribe
Scraper (made from flattened copper tubing)
Centerpunch
Pin punches (1/16, 1/8, 3/16-inch)
Steel rule/straightedge — 12 inch
Allen wrench set (1/8 to 3/8-inch or 4 mm to 10 mm)
A selection of files
Wire brush (large)
Jackstands (second set)
Jack (scissor or hydraulic type)

Note: *Another tool which is often useful is an electric drill motor with a chuck capacity of 3/8-inch and a set of good quality drill bits.*

Special tools

The tools in this list include those which are not used regularly, are expensive to buy, or which need to be used in accordance with their manufacturer's instructions. Unless these tools will be used frequently, it is not very economical to purchase many of them. A consideration would be to split the cost and use between yourself and a friend or friends. In addition, most of these tools can be obtained from a tool rental shop on a temporary basis.

This list primarily contains only those tools and instruments widely available to the public, and not those special tools produced by the vehicle manufacturer for distribution to dealer service departments. Occasionally, references to the manufacturer's special tools are inluded in the text of this manual. Generally, an alternative method of doing the job without the special tool is offered. However, sometimes there is no alternative to their use. Where this is the case, and the tool cannot be purchased or borrowed, the work should be turned over to the dealer service department or an automotive repair shop.

Valve spring compressor
Piston ring groove cleaning tool
Piston ring compressor
Piston ring installation tool
Cylinder compression gauge
Cylinder ridge reamer
Cylinder surfacing hone
Cylinder bore gauge
Micrometers and/or dial calipers
Hydraulic lifter removal tool
Balljoint separator
Universal-type puller
Impact screwdriver
Dial indicator set
Stroboscopic timing light (inductive pick-up)
Hand operated vacuum/pressure pump
Tachometer/dwell meter
Universal electrical multimeter
Cable hoist
Brake spring removal and installation tools
Floor jack

Buying tools

For the do-it-yourselfer who is just starting to get involved in vehicle maintenance and repair, there are a number of options available when purchasing tools. If maintenance and minor repair is the extent of the work to be done, the purchase of individual tools is satisfactory. If,

on the other hand, extensive work is planned, it would be a good idea to purchase a modest tool set from one of the large retail chain stores. A set can usually be bought at a substantial savings over the individual tool prices, and they often come with a tool box. As additional tools are needed, add-on sets, individual tools and a larger tool box can be purchased to expand the tool selection. Building a tool set gradually allows the cost of the tools to be spread over a longer period of time and gives the mechanic the freedom to choose only those tools that will actually be used.

Tool stores will often be the only source of some of the special tools that are needed, but regardless of where tools are bought, try to avoid cheap ones, especially when buying screwdrivers and sockets, because they won't last very long. The expense involved in replacing cheap tools will eventually be greater than the initial cost of quality tools.

Care and maintenance of tools

Good tools are expensive, so it makes sense to treat them with respect. Keep them clean and in usable condition and store them properly when not in use. Always wipe off any dirt, grease or metal chips before putting them away. Never leave tools lying around in the work area. Upon completion of a job, always check closely under the hood for tools that may have been left there so they won't get lost during a test drive.

Some tools, such as screwdrivers, pliers, wrenches and sockets, can be hung on a panel mounted on the garage or workshop wall, while others should be kept in a tool box or tray. Measuring instruments, gauges, meters, etc. must be carefully stored where they cannot be damaged by weather or impact from other tools.

When tools are used with care and stored properly, they will last a very long time. Even with the best of care, though, tools will wear out if used frequently. When a tool is damaged or worn out, replace it. Subsequent jobs will be safer and more enjoyable if you do.

Working facilities

Not to be overlooked when discussing tools is the workshop. If anything more than routine maintenance is to be carried out, some sort of suitable work area is essential.

It is understood, and appreciated, that many home mechanics do not have a good workshop or garage available, and end up removing an engine or doing major repairs outside. It is recommended, however, that the overhaul or repair be completed under the cover of a roof.

A clean, flat workbench or table of comfortable working height is an absolute necessity. The workbench should be equipped with a vise that has a jaw opening of at least four inches.

As mentioned previously, some clean, dry storage space is also required for tools, as well as the lubricants, fluids, cleaning solvents, etc. which will soon become necessary.

Sometimes waste oil and fluids, drained from the engine or cooling system during normal maintenance or repairs, present a disposal problem. To avoid pouring them on the ground or into a sewage system, pour the used fluids into large containers, seal them with caps and take them to an authorized disposal site or recycling center. Plastic jugs, such as old antifreeze containers, are ideal for this purpose.

Always keep a supply of old newspapers and clean rags available. Old towels are excellent for mopping up spills. Many mechanics use rolls of paper towels for most work because they are readily available and disposable. To help keep the area under the vehicle clean, a large cardboard box can be cut open and flattened to protect the garage or shop floor.

Whenever working over a painted surface, such as when leaning over a fender to service something under the hood, always cover it with an old blanket or bedspread to protect the finish. Vinyl covered pads, made especially for this purpose, are available at auto parts stores.

Booster battery (jump) starting

Certain precautions must be observed when using a booster battery to start a vehicle.

  a) Before connecting the booster battery, make sure the ignition switch is in the Off position.

  b) Turn off the lights, heater and other electrical loads.

  c) Your eyes should be shielded. Safety goggles are a good idea.

  d) Make sure the booster battery is the same voltage as the dead one in the vehicle.

  e) The two vehicles MUST NOT TOUCH each other!

  f) Make sure the transmission is in Neutral (manual) or Park (automatic).

  g) If the booster battery is not a maintenance-free type, remove the vent caps and lay a cloth over the vent holes.

Connect the red jumper cable to the *positive* (+) terminals of each battery.

Connect one end of the black jumper cable to the *negative* (–) terminal of the booster battery. The other end of this cable should be connected to a good ground on the vehicle to be started, such as a bolt or bracket on the engine block **(see illustration)**. Use caution to ensure that the cable will not come into contact with the fan, drivebelts or other moving parts of the engine.

Start the engine using the booster battery, then, with the engine running at idle speed, disconnect the jumper cables in the reverse order of connection.

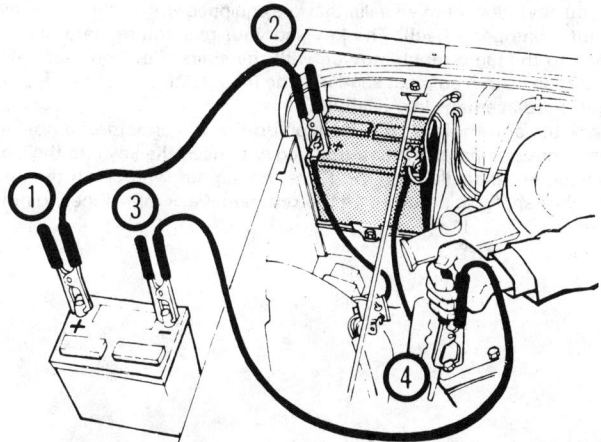

Make the booster battery cable connections in the numerical order shown (note that the negative cable of the booster battery is NOT attached to the negative terminal of the dead battery)

Jacking and towing

Jacking

Warning: *The jack supplied with this vehicle should only be used for raising the vehicle when changing a tire or placing jackstands under the frame. Never work under the vehicle or start the engine while this jack is being used as the only means of support.*

The vehicle should be on level ground. Place the shift lever in Park, if you have an automatic transaxle, or First gear if you have a manual transaxle. Block the wheel diagonally opposite the wheel being changed. Set the parking brake. **Warning:** *When one front wheel is lifted off the ground, neither the automatic nor the manual transaxle will prevent the vehicle from moving and possibly slipping off the jack, even if they have been placed in gear as described above. To prevent inadvertent movement of the vehicle while changing a tire, always set the parking brake and block the wheel diagonally opposite the wheel being changed.*

Remove the spare tire and jack from stowage. Remove the wheel cover (if so equipped) with the tapered end of the lug nut wrench by inserting and twisting the handle and then prying against the inner wheel cover flange. Loosen, but do not remove, the lug nuts (one-half turn is sufficient). **Caution:** *If you're removing the front wheel, don't loosen the front wheel hub nut.*

Place the scissors-type jack under the side of the vehicle and adjust the jack height with the jack handle so it fits in the notch in the vertical rocker panel flange nearest the wheel to be changed. There is a front and rear jacking notch on each side of the vehicle **(see illustration)**. When lifting the vehicle by any other means, special care must be ex-

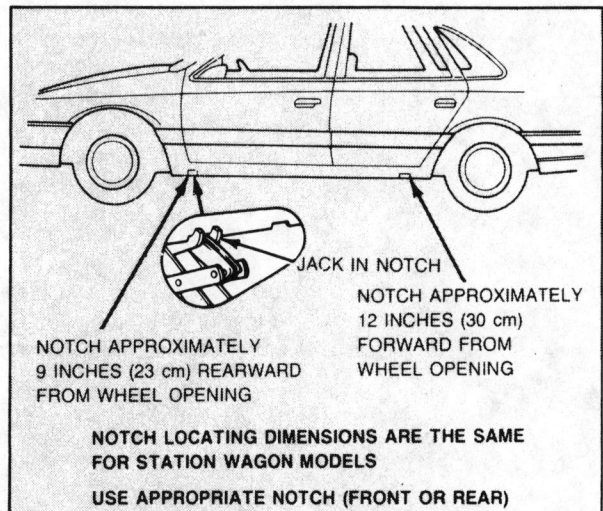

JACK IN NOTCH

NOTCH APPROXIMATELY 12 INCHES (30 cm) FORWARD FROM WHEEL OPENING

NOTCH APPROXIMATELY 9 INCHES (23 cm) REARWARD FROM WHEEL OPENING

NOTCH LOCATING DIMENSIONS ARE THE SAME FOR STATION WAGON MODELS

USE APPROPRIATE NOTCH (FRONT OR REAR)

The jack must be engaged in the notch in the rocker panel flange nearest the wheel to be changed — there is a front and rear jacking notch on each side of the vehicle

ercised to avoid damage to the fuel tank, filler neck, exhaust system or underbody. **Caution:** *Do not raise the vehicle with a bumper jack. The bumpers could be damaged. Also, jack slippage may occur, causing personal injury.*

Turn the jack handle clockwise until the wheel clears the ground. Remove the lug nuts and the wheel. Mark the location of the anti-theft lug nut on the wheel before removing it. Pull the wheel off and immediately replace it with the spare.

Replace the lug nuts with the beveled edges facing in. Tighten them snugly and carefully. Don't attempt to tighten them completely until the vehicle is lowered or it could slip off the jack.

Turn the jack handle counterclockwise to lower the vehicle. Remove the jack and tighten the lug nuts in a crisscross pattern.

Align the wheel cover with the valve stem extension matching the hole in the cover. Install the cover and be sure that it's snapped in place all the way around.

Stow the tire, jack and wrench. Unblock the wheels.

Anti-theft wheel lug nuts

If you have aluminum wheels, they are equipped with anti-theft wheel lug nuts (one per wheel). The key and your registration card are attached to the lug wrench stowed with the spare tire. Don't lose the registration card. You must send it to the manufacturer, not the dealer, to get a replacement key if yours is lost.

Mark the anti-theft lug nut location on the wheel before removing it. To remove or install the anti-theft lug nut, insert the key into the slot in the lug nut **(see illustration)**. Place the lug nut wrench on the key and, while applying pressure on the key, remove or install the lug nut.

Towing

If equipped with an automatic transaxle, the vehicle may be towed on all four wheels at speeds less than 35 mph for distances up to 50 miles. Vehicles equipped with a manual transaxle are not limited in distance.

Towing equipment specifically designed for this purpose should be used and should be attached to the main structural members of the vehicle and not the bumper or brackets.

Safety is a major consideration when towing and all applicable state and local laws must be obeyed. A safety chain system must be used for all towing.

While towing, the parking brake should be released and the transaxle should be in Neutral. The steering must be unlocked (ignition switch in the Off position). Remember that power brakes will not work with the engine off.

To remove or install the anti-theft lug nut, insert the key into the slot in the lug nut, then place the lug wrench on the key and remove or install the lug nut

Automotive chemicals and lubricants

A number of automotive chemicals and lubricants are available for use during vehicle maintenance and repair. They include a wide variety of products ranging from cleaning solvents and degreasers to lubricants and protective sprays for rubber, plastic and vinyl.

Cleaners

Carburetor cleaner and choke cleaner is a strong solvent for gum, varnish and carbon. Most carburetor cleaners leave a dry-type lubricant film which will not harden or gum up. Because of this film it is not recommended for use on electrical components.

Brake system cleaner is used to remove grease and brake fluid from the brake system where clean surfaces are absolutely necessary. It leaves no residue and often eliminates brake squeal caused by contaminants.

Electrical cleaner removes oxidation, corrosion and carbon deposits from electrical contacts, restoring full current flow. It can also be used to clean spark plugs, carburetor jets, voltage regulators and other parts where an oil-free surface is desired.

Demoisturants remove water and moisture from electrical components such as alternators, voltage regulators, electrical connectors and fuse blocks. It is non-conductive, non-corrosive and non-flammable.

Degreasers are heavy-duty solvents used to remove grease from the outside of the engine and from chassis components. They can be sprayed or brushed on, and, depending on the type, are rinsed off either with water or solvent.

Lubricants

Motor oil is the lubricant formulated for use in engines. It normally contains a wide variety of additives to prevent corrosion and reduce foaming and wear. Motor oil comes in various weights (viscosity ratings) from 5 to 80. The recommended weight of the oil depends on the season, temperature and the demands on the engine. Light oil is used in cold climates and under light load conditions. Heavy oil is used in hot climates and where high loads are encountered. Multi-viscosity oils are designed to have characteristics of both light and heavy oils and are available in a number of weights from 5W-20 to 20W-50.

Gear oil is designed to be used in differentials, manual transaxles and other areas where high-temperature lubrication is required.

Chassis and wheel bearing grease is a heavy grease used where increased loads and friction are encountered, such as for wheel bearings, balljoints, tie rod ends and universal joints.

High temperature wheel bearing grease is designed to withstand the extreme temperatures encountered by wheel bearings in disc brake equipped vehicles. It usually contains molybdenun disulfide (moly), which is a dry-type lubricant.

White grease is a heavy grease for metal to metal applications where water is a problem. White grease stays soft under both low and high temperatures (usually from −100°F to +190°F), and will not wash off or dilute in the presence of water.

Assembly lube is a special extreme pressure lubricant, usually containing moly, used to lubricate high-load parts such as main and rod bearings and cam lobes for initial start-up of a new engine. The assembly lube lubricates the parts without being squeezed out or washed away until the engine oiling system begins to function.

Silicone lubricants are used to protect rubber, plastic, vinyl and nylon parts.

Graphite lubricants are used where oils cannot be used due to contamination problems, such as in locks. The dry graphite will lubricate metal parts while remaining uncontaminated by dirt, water, oil or acids. It is electrically conductive and will not foul electrical contacts in locks such as the ignition switch.

Moly penetrants loosen and lubricate frozen, rusted and corroded fasteners and prevent future rusting or freezing.

Heat-sink grease is a special electrically non-conductive grease that is used for mounting HEI ignition modules where it is essential that heat be transferred away from the module.

Sealants

RTV sealant is one of the most widely used gasket compounds. Made from silicone, RTV is air curing, it seals, bonds, waterproofs, fills surface irregularities, remains flexible, doesn't shrink, is relatively easy to remove, and is used as a supplementary sealer with almost all low and medium temperature gaskets.

Anaerobic sealant is much like RTV in that it can be used either to seal gaskets or to form gaskets by itself. It remains flexible, is solvent resistant and fills surface imperfections. The difference between an anaerobic sealant and an RTV-type sealant is in the curing. RTV cures when exposed to air, while an anaerobic sealant cures only in the absence of air. This means that an anaerobic sealant cures only after the assembly of parts, sealing them together.

Thread and pipe sealant is used for sealing hydraulic and pneumatic fittings and vacuum lines. It is usually made from a teflon compound, and comes in a spray, a paint-on liquid and as a wrap-around tape.

Chemicals

Anti-seize compound prevents seizing, galling, cold welding, rust and corrosion in fasteners. High temperature anti-seize, usually made with copper and graphite lubricants, is used for exhaust system and manifold bolts.

Anaerobic locking compounds are used to keep fasteners from vibrating or working loose, and cure only after installation, in the absence of air. Medium strength locking compound is used for small nuts, bolts and screws that you expect to be removing later. High strength locking compound is for large nuts, bolts and studs which you don't intend to be removing on a regular basis.

Oil additives range from viscosity index improvers to chemical treatments that claim to reduce internal engine friction. It should be noted that most oil manufacturers caution against using additives with their oils.

Gas additives perform several functions, depending on their chemical makeup. They usually contain solvents that help dissolve gum and varnish that build up on carburetor and intake parts. They also serve to break down carbon deposits that form on the inside surfaces of the combustion chambers. Some additives contain upper cylinder lubricants for valves and piston rings, and others chemicals to remove condensation from the gas tank.

Miscellaneous

Brake fluid is specially formulated hydraulic fluid that can withstand the heat and pressure encountered in brake systems. Care must be taken that this fluid does not come in contact with painted surfaces or plastics. An opened container should always be resealed to prevent contamination by water or dirt.

Weatherstrip adhesive is used to bond weatherstripping around doors, windows and trunk lids. It is sometimes used to attach trim pieces.

Undercoating is a petroleum-based tar-like substance that is designed to protect metal surfaces on the underside of the vehicle from corrosion. It also acts as a sound-deadening agent by insulating the bottom of the vehicle.

Waxes and polishes are used to help protect painted and plated surfaces from the weather. Different types of paint may require the use of different types of wax and polish. Some polishes utilize a chemical or abrasive cleaner to help remove the top layer of oxidized (dull) paint on older vehicles. In recent years many non-wax polishes that contain a wide variety of chemicals such as polymers and silicones have been introduced. These non-wax polishes are usually easier to apply and last longer than conventional waxes and polishes.

Safety first!

Regardless of how enthusiastic you may be about getting on with the job at hand, take the time to ensure that your safety is not jeopardized. A moment's lack of attention can result in an accident, as can failure to observe certain simple safety precautions. The possibility of an accident will always exist, and the following points should not be considered a comprehensive list of all dangers. Rather, they are intended to make you aware of the risks and to encourage a safety conscious approach to all work you carry out on your vehicle.

Essential DOs and DON'Ts

DON'T rely on a jack when working under the vehicle. Always use approved jackstands to support the weight of the vehicle and place them under the recommended lift or support points.

DON'T attempt to loosen extremely tight fasteners (i.e. wheel lug nuts) while the vehicle is on a jack — it may fall.

DON'T start the engine without first making sure that the transmission is in Neutral (or Park where applicable) and the parking brake is set.

DON'T remove the radiator cap from a hot cooling system — let it cool or cover it with a cloth and release the pressure gradually.

DON'T attempt to drain the engine oil until you are sure it has cooled to the point that it will not burn you.

DON'T touch any part of the engine or exhaust system until it has cooled sufficiently to avoid burns.

DON'T siphon toxic liquids such as gasoline, antifreeze and brake fluid by mouth, or allow them to remain on your skin.

DON'T inhale brake lining dust — it is potentially hazardous (see *Asbestos* below)

DON'T allow spilled oil or grease to remain on the floor — wipe it up before someone slips on it.

DON'T use loose fitting wrenches or other tools which may slip and cause injury.

DON'T push on wrenches when loosening or tightening nuts or bolts. Always try to pull the wrench toward you. If the situation calls for pushing the wrench away, push with an open hand to avoid scraped knuckles if the wrench should slip.

DON'T attempt to lift a heavy component alone — get someone to help you.

DON'T rush or take unsafe shortcuts to finish a job.

DON'T allow children or animals in or around the vehicle while you are working on it.

DO wear eye protection when using power tools such as a drill, sander, bench grinder, etc. and when working under a vehicle.

DO keep loose clothing and long hair well out of the way of moving parts.

DO make sure that any hoist used has a safe working load rating adequate for the job.

DO get someone to check on you periodically when working alone on a vehicle.

DO carry out work in a logical sequence and make sure that everything is correctly assembled and tightened.

DO keep chemicals and fluids tightly capped and out of the reach of children and pets.

DO remember that your vehicle's safety affects that of yourself and others. If in doubt on any point, get professional advice.

Asbestos

Certain friction, insulating, sealing, and other products — such as brake linings, brake bands, clutch linings, torque converters, gaskets, etc. — contain asbestos. *Extreme care must be taken to avoid inhalation of dust from such products since it is hazardous to health*. If in doubt, assume that they *do* contain asbestos.

Fire

Remember at all times that gasoline is highly flammable. Never smoke or have any kind of open flame around when working on a vehicle. But the risk does not end there. A spark caused by an electrical short circuit, by two metal surfaces contacting each other, or even by static electricity built up in your body under certain conditions, can ignite gasoline vapors, which in a confined space are highly explosive. Do not, under any circumstances, use gasoline for cleaning parts. Use an approved safety solvent.

Always disconnect the battery ground (–) cable *at the battery* before working on any part of the fuel system or electrical system. Never risk spilling fuel on a hot engine or exhaust component.

It is strongly recommended that a fire extinguisher suitable for use on fuel and electrical fires be kept handy in the garage or workshop at all times. Never try to extinguish a fuel or electrical fire with water.

Fumes

Certain fumes are highly toxic and can quickly cause unconsciousness and even death if inhaled to any extent. Gasoline vapor falls into this category, as do the vapors from some cleaning solvents. Any draining or pouring of such volatile fluids should be done in a well ventilated area.

When using cleaning fluids and solvents, read the instructions on the container carefully. Never use materials from unmarked containers.

Never run the engine in an enclosed space, such as a garage. Exhaust fumes contain carbon monoxide, which is extremely poisonous. If you need to run the engine, always do so in the open air, or at least have the rear of the vehicle outside the work area.

If you are fortunate enough to have the use of an inspection pit, never drain or pour gasoline and never run the engine while the vehicle is over the pit. The fumes, being heavier than air, will concentrate in the pit with possibly lethal results.

The battery

Never create a spark or allow a bare light bulb near the battery. The battery normally gives off a certain amount of hydrogen gas, which is highly explosive.

Always disconnect the battery ground (–) cable *at the battery* before working on the fuel or electrical systems.

If possible, loosen the filler caps or cover when charging the battery from an external source. Do not charge at an excessive rate or the battery may burst.

Take care when adding water and when carrying a battery. The electrolyte, even when diluted, is very corrosive and should not be allowed to contact clothing or skin.

Always wear eye protection when cleaning the battery to prevent the caustic deposits from entering your eyes.

Household current

When using an electric power tool, inspection light, etc., which operates on household current, always make sure that the tool is correctly connected to its plug and that, where necessary, it is properly grounded. Do not use such items in damp conditions and, again, do not create a spark or apply excessive heat in the vicinity of fuel or fuel vapor.

Secondary ignition system voltage

A severe electric shock can result from touching certain parts of the ignition system (such as the spark plug wires) when the engine is running or being cranked, particularly if components are damp or the insulation is defective. In the case of an electronic ignition system, the secondary system voltage is much higher and could prove fatal.

Conversion factors

Length (distance)

Inches (in)	X	25.4	= Millimetres (mm)	X	0.0394 = Inches (in)
Feet (ft)	X	0.305	= Metres (m)	X	3.281 = Feet (ft)
Miles	X	1.609	= Kilometres (km)	X	0.621 = Miles

Volume (capacity)

Cubic inches (cu in; in³)	X	16.387	= Cubic centimetres (cc; cm³)	X	0.061 = Cubic inches (cu in; in³)
Imperial pints (Imp pt)	X	0.568	= Litres (l)	X	1.76 = Imperial pints (Imp pt)
Imperial quarts (Imp qt)	X	1.137	= Litres (l)	X	0.88 = Imperial quarts (Imp qt)
Imperial quarts (Imp qt)	X	1.201	= US quarts (US qt)	X	0.833 = Imperial quarts (Imp qt)
US quarts (US qt)	X	0.946	= Litres (l)	X	1.057 = US quarts (US qt)
Imperial gallons (Imp gal)	X	4.546	= Litres (l)	X	0.22 = Imperial gallons (Imp gal)
Imperial gallons (Imp gal)	X	1.201	= US gallons (US gal)	X	0.833 = Imperial gallons (Imp gal)
US gallons (US gal)	X	3.785	= Litres (l)	X	0.264 = US gallons (US gal)

Mass (weight)

Ounces (oz)	X	28.35	= Grams (g)	X	0.035 = Ounces (oz)
Pounds (lb)	X	0.454	= Kilograms (kg)	X	2.205 = Pounds (lb)

Force

Ounces-force (ozf; oz)	X	0.278	= Newtons (N)	X	3.6 = Ounces-force (ozf; oz)
Pounds-force (lbf; lb)	X	4.448	= Newtons (N)	X	0.225 = Pounds-force (lbf; lb)
Newtons (N)	X	0.1	= Kilograms-force (kgf; kg)	X	9.81 = Newtons (N)

Pressure

Pounds-force per square inch (psi; lbf/in²; lb/in²)	X	0.070	= Kilograms-force per square centimetre (kgf/cm²; kg/cm²)	X	14.223 = Pounds-force per square inch (psi; lbf/in²; lb/in²)
Pounds-force per square inch (psi; lbf/in²; lb/in²)	X	0.068	= Atmospheres (atm)	X	14.696 = Pounds-force per square inch (psi; lbf/in²; lb/in²)
Pounds-force per square inch (psi; lbf/in²; lb/in²)	X	0.069	= Bars	X	14.5 = Pounds-force per square inch (psi; lbf/in²; lb/in²)
Pounds-force per square inch (psi; lbf/in²; lb/in²)	X	6.895	= Kilopascals (kPa)	X	0.145 = Pounds-force per square inch (psi; lbf/in²; lb/in²)
Kilopascals (kPa)	X	0.01	= Kilograms-force per square centimetre (kgf/cm²; kg/cm²)	X	98.1 = Kilopascals (kPa)

Torque (moment of force)

Pounds-force inches (lbf in; lb in)	X	1.152	= Kilograms-force centimetre (kgf cm; kg cm)	X	0.868 = Pounds-force inches (lbf in; lb in)
Pounds-force inches (lbf in; lb in)	X	0.113	= Newton metres (Nm)	X	8.85 = Pounds-force inches (lbf in; lb in)
Pounds-force inches (lbf in; lb in)	X	0.083	= Pounds-force feet (lbf ft; lb ft)	X	12 = Pounds-force inches (lbf in; lb in)
Pounds-force feet (lbf ft; lb ft)	X	0.138	= Kilograms-force metres (kgf m; kg m)	X	7.233 = Pounds-force feet (lbf ft; lb ft)
Pounds-force feet (lbf ft; lb ft)	X	1.356	= Newton metres (Nm)	X	0.738 = Pounds-force feet (lbf ft; lb ft)
Newton metres (Nm)	X	0.102	= Kilograms-force metres (kgf m; kg m)	X	9.804 = Newton metres (Nm)

Power

Horsepower (hp)	X	745.7	= Watts (W)	X	0.0013 = Horsepower (hp)

Velocity (speed)

Miles per hour (miles/hr; mph)	X	1.609	= Kilometres per hour (km/hr; kph)	X	0.621 = Miles per hour (miles/hr; mph)

Fuel consumption*

Miles per gallon, Imperial (mpg)	X	0.354	= Kilometres per litre (km/l)	X	2.825 = Miles per gallon, Imperial (mpg)
Miles per gallon, US (mpg)	X	0.425	= Kilometres per litre (km/l)	X	2.352 = Miles per gallon, US (mpg)

Temperature

Degrees Fahrenheit = (°C x 1.8) + 32   Degrees Celsius (Degrees Centigrade; °C) = (°F - 32) x 0.56

*It is common practice to convert from miles per gallon (mpg) to litres/100 kilometres (l/100km),
where mpg (Imperial) x l/100 km = 282 and mpg (US) x l/100 km = 235*

Troubleshooting

Contents

This section provides an easy reference guide to the more common problems which may occur during the operation of your vehicle. These problems and possible causes are grouped under various components or systems; i.e. Engine, Cooling System, etc., and also refer to the Chapter and/or Section which deals with the problem.

Remember that successful troubleshooting is not a mysterious *black art* practiced only by professional mechanics. It's simply the result of a bit of knowledge combined with an intelligent, systematic approach to the problem. Always work by a process of elimination, starting with the simplest solution and working through to the most complex — and never overlook the obvious. Anyone can forget to fill the gas tank or leave the lights on overnight, so don't assume that you are above such oversights.

Finally, always get clear in your mind why a problem has occurred and take steps to ensure that it doesn't happen again. If the electrical system fails because of a poor connection, check all other connections in the system to make sure that they don't fail as well. If a particular fuse continues to blow, find out why — don't just go on replacing fuses. Remember, failure of a small component can often be indicative of potential failure or incorrect functioning of a more important component or system.

Engine

1 Engine will not rotate when attempting to start

1   Battery terminal connections loose or corroded. Check the cable terminals at the battery. Tighten the cable or remove corrosion as necessary.
2   Battery discharged or faulty. If the cable connections are clean and tight on the battery posts, turn the key to the On position and switch on the headlights and/or windshield wipers. If they fail to function, the battery is discharged.
3   Automatic transaxle not completely engaged in Park or Neutral or clutch pedal not completely depressed.
4   Broken, loose or disconnected wiring in the starting circuit. Inspect all wiring and connectors at the battery, starter solenoid and ignition switch.
5   Starter motor pinion jammed in flywheel ring gear. If manual transaxle, place transaxle in gear and rock the vehicle to manually turn the engine. Remove starter and inspect pinion and flywheel at earliest convenience (Chapter 5).
6   Starter solenoid faulty (Chapter 5).
7   Starter motor faulty (Chapter 5).
8   Ignition switch faulty (Chapter 12).

2 Engine rotates but will not start

1   Fuel tank empty.
2   Fault in the fuel injection system (Chapters 4 and 5).
3   Battery discharged (engine rotates slowly). Check the operation of electrical components as described in the previous Section.
4   Battery terminal connections loose or corroded (see previous Section).
5   Fuel injector or fuel pump faulty (Chapter 4).
6   Excessive moisture on, or damage to, ignition components (Chapter 5).
7   Worn, faulty or incorrectly gapped spark plugs (Chapter 1).
8   Broken, loose or disconnected wiring in the starting circuit (see previous Section).
9   Distributor loose, causing ignition timing to change. Turn the distributor as necessary to start the engine, then set the ignition timing as soon as possible (Chapter 1).
10   Broken, loose or disconnected wires at the ignition coil or faulty coil (Chapter 5).

3 Starter motor operates without rotating engine

1   Starter pinion sticking. Remove the starter (Chapter 5) and inspect.
2   Starter pinion or flywheel teeth worn or broken. Remove the flywheel/driveplate access cover from the oil pan and inspect.

4 Engine hard to start when cold

1   Battery discharged or low. Check as described in Section 1.
2   Fault in the fuel injection system (Chapters 4 and 5).
3   Fuel injection system in need of overhaul (Chapter 4).
4   Distributor rotor carbon tracked and/or damaged (Chapters 1 and 5).

5 Engine hard to start when hot

1   Air filter clogged (Chapter 1).
2   Fault in the fuel injection system (Chapters 4 and 5).
3   Fuel not reaching the fuel injection system (see Section 2).

6 Starter motor noisy or excessively rough in engagement

1   Pinion or flywheel gear teeth worn or broken. Remove the cover at the rear of the engine (if so equipped) and inspect.
2   Starter motor mounting bolts loose or missing.

7 Engine starts but stops immediately

1   Loose or faulty electrical connections at distributor, coil or alternator.
2   Fault in the fuel injection system (Chapters 4 and 5).
3   Insufficient fuel reaching the fuel injector. Check the fuel pressure (Chapter 5) or have the fuel injection pressure checked by your dealer or a properly equipped shop.
4   Vacuum leak at the gasket surfaces of the intake manifold, fuel charging assembly or throttle body. Make sure that all mounting bolts/nuts are tightened securely and that all vacuum hoses connected to the fuel injection assembly and manifold are positioned properly and in good condition.

8 Engine lopes while idling or idles erratically

1   Vacuum leakage. Check the mounting bolts/nuts at the fuel injection unit and intake manifold for tightness. Make sure that all vacuum hoses are connected and in good condition. Use a stethoscope or a length of fuel hose held against your ear to listen for vacuum leaks while the engine is running. A hissing sound will be heard. A soapy water solution will also detect leaks. Check the fuel injector and intake manifold gasket surfaces.
2   Fault in the fuel injection system (Chapters 4 and 5).
3   Leaking EGR valve or plugged PCV valve (see Chapters 1 and 6).
4   Air filter clogged (Chapter 1).
5   Fuel pump not delivering sufficient fuel to the fuel injector (see Chapter 4).
6   Fuel injection system out of adjustment (Chapter 4).
7   Leaking head gasket. If this is suspected, take the vehicle to a repair shop or dealer where the engine can be pressure checked.
8   Timing chain or sprockets worn (Chapter 2).
9   Camshaft lobes worn (Chapter 2).

9 Engine misses at idle speed

1   Spark plugs worn or not gapped properly (Chapter 1).
2   Fault in the fuel injection system (Chapters 4 and 5).
3   Faulty spark plug wires (Chapter 1).

10 Engine misses throughout driving speed range

1   Fuel filter clogged and/or impurities in the fuel system (Chapter 1).
2   Faulty or incorrectly gapped spark plugs (Chapter 1).
3   Fault in the fuel injection system (Chapters 4 and 5).

4   Incorrect ignition timing (Chapter 5).
5   Check for cracked distributor cap, disconnected distributor wires and damaged distributor components (Chapter 1).
6   Leaking spark plug wires (Chapter 1).
7   Faulty emissions system components (Chapter 6).
8   Low or uneven cylinder compression pressures. Remove the spark plugs and test the compression with a gauge (Chapter 2).
9   Weak or faulty ignition system (Chapter 5).
10 Vacuum leaks at the fuel injection unit, intake manifold or vacuum hoses (see Section 8).

11 Engine stalls

1   Idle speed incorrect. Refer to the VECI label and Chapter 4, then take the vehicle to a dealer (idle speed is not adjustable).
2   Fuel filter clogged and/or water and impurities in the fuel system (Chapter 1).
3   Distributor components damp or damaged (Chapter 5).
4   Fault in the fuel injection system or sensors (Chapters 4 and 5).
5   Faulty emissions system components (Chapter 6).
6   Faulty or incorrectly gapped spark plugs (Chapter 1). Also check the spark plug wires (Chapter 1).
7   Vacuum leak at the fuel injection unit, intake manifold or vacuum hoses. Check as described in Section 8.

12 Engine lacks power

1   Incorrect ignition timing (Chapter 5).
2   Fault in the fuel injection system (Chapters 4 and 5).
3   Excessive play in the distributor shaft. At the same time, check for a damaged rotor, faulty distributor cap, wires, etc. (Chapters 1 and 5).
4   Faulty or incorrectly gapped spark plugs (Chapter 1).
5   Fuel injection system not adjusted properly or excessively worn (Chapter 4).
6   Faulty coil (Chapter 5).
7   Brakes binding (Chapter 1).
8   Automatic transaxle fluid level incorrect (Chapter 1).
9   Clutch slipping (Chapter 8).
10 Fuel filter clogged and/or impurities in the fuel system (Chapter 1).
11 Emissions control system not functioning properly (Chapter 6).
12 Use of substandard fuel. Fill the tank with the proper octane fuel.
13 Low or uneven cylinder compression pressures. Test with a compression tester, which will detect leaking valves and/or a blown head gasket (Chapter 2).

13 Engine backfires

1   Emissions system not functioning properly (Chapter 6).
2   Fault in the fuel injection system (Chapters 4 and 5).
3   Ignition timing incorrect (Chapter 5).
4   Faulty secondary ignition system (cracked spark plug insulator, faulty plug wires, distributor cap and/or rotor) (Chapters 1 and 5).
5   Fuel injection unit in need of adjustment or worn excessively (Chapter 4).
6   Vacuum leak at the fuel injection unit, intake manifold or vacuum hoses. Check as described in Section 8.
7   Valves sticking (Chapter 2).

14 Pinging or knocking engine sounds during acceleration or uphill

1   Incorrect grade of fuel. Fill the tank with fuel of the proper octane rating.
2   Fault in the fuel injection system (Chapters 4 and 5).
3   Ignition timing incorrect (Chapter 5).
4   Fuel injection unit in need of adjustment (Chapter 4).
5   Improper spark plugs. Check the plug type against the VECI label located in the engine compartment. Also check the plugs and wires

for damage (Chapter 1).
6   Worn or damaged distributor components (Chapter 5).
7   Faulty emissions system (Chapter 6).
8   Vacuum leak. Check as described in Section 9.

15 Engine diesels (continues to run) after switching off

1   Idle speed too high. Refer to Ignition timing section in Chapter 5; take vehicle to a dealer.
2   Fault in the fuel injection system (Chapters 4 and 5).
3   Ignition timing incorrectly adjusted (Chapter 5).
4   Excessive engine operating temperature. Probable causes of this are a malfunctioning thermostat, clogged radiator, faulty water pump (Chapter 3).

Engine electrical system

16 Battery will not hold a charge

1   Alternator drivebelt defective or not adjusted properly (Chapter 1).
2   Electrolyte level low or battery discharged (Chapter 1).
3   Battery terminals loose or corroded (Chapter 1).
4   Alternator not charging properly (Chapter 5).
5   Loose, broken or faulty wiring in the charging circuit (Chapter 5).
6   Short in the vehicle wiring causing a continual drain on battery (refer to Chapter 12 and the Wiring Diagrams).
7   Battery defective internally.

17 Ignition light fails to go out

1   Fault in the alternator or charging circuit (Chapter 5).
2   Alternator drivebelt defective or not properly adjusted (Chapter 1).

18 Ignition light fails to come on when key is turned on

1   Instrument cluster warning light bulb defective (Chapter 12).
2   Alternator faulty (Chapter 5).
3   Fault in the instrument cluster printed circuit, dashboard wiring or bulb holder (Chapter 12).

Fuel system

19 Excessive fuel consumption

1   Dirty or clogged air filter element (Chapter 1).
2   Incorrectly set ignition timing (Chapter 5).
3   Emissions system not functioning properly (Chapter 6).
4   Fuel injection system internal parts excessively worn or damaged (Chapter 4).
5   Low tire pressure or incorrect tire size (Chapter 1).

20 Fuel leakage and/or fuel odor

1   Leak in a fuel feed or vent line (Chapter 4).
2   Tank overfilled. Fill only to automatic shut-off.
3   Evaporative emissions system filter clogged (Chapter 6).
4   Vapor leaks from system lines (Chapter 4).
5   Fuel injection internal parts excessively worn or out of adjustment (Chapter 4).

Cooling system

21   Overheating

1   Insufficient coolant in the system (Chapter 1).
2   Water pump drivebelt defective or not adjusted properly (Chapter 1).
3   Radiator core blocked or radiator grille dirty and restricted (Chapter 3).
4   Thermostat faulty (Chapter 3).
5   Fan blades broken or cracked (Chapter 3).
6   Radiator cap not maintaining proper pressure. Have the cap pressure tested by gas station or repair shop.
7   Ignition timing incorrect (Chapter 5).

22   Overcooling

Thermostat faulty (Chapter 3).

23   External coolant leakage

1   Deteriorated or damaged hoses or loose clamps. Replace hoses and/or tighten the clamps at the hose connections (Chapter 1).
2   Water pump seals defective. If this is the case, water will drip from the weep hole in the water pump body (Chapter 3).
3   Leakage from radiator core or header tank. This will require the radiator to be professionally repaired (see Chapter 3 for removal procedures).
4   Engine drain plug leaking (Chapter 1) or water jacket core plugs leaking (see Chapter 2).

24   Internal coolant leakage

Note: Internal coolant leaks can usually be detected by examining the oil. Check the dipstick and inside of the rocker arm cover for water deposits and an oil consistency like that of a milkshake.
1   Leaking cylinder head gasket. Have the cooling system pressure tested.
2   Cracked cylinder bore or cylinder head. Dismantle the engine and inspect (Chapter 2).

25   Coolant loss

1   Too much coolant in the system (Chapter 1).
2   Coolant boiling away due to overheating (see Section 15).
3   External or internal leakage (see Sections 23 and 24).
Note: Head gasket leaks that result in mysterious coolant loss from 1986 through 1988 Taurus' and 1987 and 1988 Sables may be the problem. If the vehicle has a four-cylinder engine, installation of a newly-designed head gasket should cure it — have your dealer service department refer to Technical Service Bulletin (TSB) 88-8-8. If the vehicle has a V6 engine, a new head gasket and head bolts may be required — have your dealer service department refer to TSB 88-8-7.
4   Faulty radiator cap. Have the cap pressure tested.

26   Poor coolant circulation

1   Inoperative water pump. A quick test is to pinch the top radiator hose closed with your hand while the engine is idling, then let it loose. You should feel the surge of coolant if the pump is working properly (Chapter 1).
2   Restriction in the cooling system. Drain, flush and refill the system (Chapter 1). If necessary, remove the radiator (Chapter 3) and have it reverse flushed.
3   Water pump drivebelt defective or not adjusted properly (Chapter 1).
4   Thermostat sticking (Chapter 3).

Clutch

27   Fails to release (pedal pressed to the floor — shift lever does not move freely in and out of Reverse)

1   Worn cable (Chapter 8).
2   Clutch plate warped or damaged (Chapter 8).
3   Worn or dry clutch release shaft bushing (Chapter 8).

28   Clutch slips (engine speed increases with no increase in vehicle speed)

1   Linkage out of adjustment (Chapter 8).
2   Clutch plate oil soaked or lining worn. Remove clutch (Chapter 8) and inspect.
3   Clutch plate not seated. It may take 30 or 40 normal starts for a new one to seat.

29   Grabbing (chattering) as clutch is engaged

1   Oil on clutch plate lining. Remove (Chapter 8) and inspect. Correct any leakage source.
2   Worn or loose engine or transaxle mounts. These units move slightly when the clutch is released. Inspect the mounts and bolts (Chapter 2).
3   Worn splines on clutch plate hub. Remove the clutch components (Chapter 8) and inspect.
4   Warped pressure plate or flywheel. Remove the clutch components and inspect.

30   Squeal or rumble with clutch fully disengaged (pedal depressed)

1   Worn, defective or broken release bearing (Chapter 8).
2   Worn or broken pressure plate springs (or diaphragm fingers) (Chapter 8).

31   Clutch pedal stays on floor when disengaged

Linkage or release bearing binding. Inspect the linkage or remove the clutch components as necessary.

Manual transaxle

32   Noisy in Neutral with engine running

1   Input shaft bearing worn.
2   Damaged main drive gear bearing.
3   Worn countershaft bearings.
4   Worn or damaged countershaft end play shims.

33   Noisy in all gears

1   Any of the above causes, and/or:
2   Insufficient lubricant (see the checking procedures in Chapter 1).

34   Noisy in one particular gear

1   Worn, damaged or chipped gear teeth for that particular gear.
2   Worn or damaged synchronizer for that particular gear.

35   Slips out of high gear

1   Transaxle loose on clutch housing (Chapter 7).
2   Shift rods interfering with the engine mounts or clutch lever (Chapter 7).
3   Shift rods not working freely (Chapter 7).

4   Dirt between the transaxle case and engine or misalignment of the transaxle (Chapter 7).
5   Worn or improperly adjusted linkage (Chapter 7).

36   Difficulty in engaging gears

1   Clutch not releasing completely (see clutch adjustment in Chapter 8).
2   Loose, damaged or out-of-adjustment shift linkage. Make a thorough inspection, replacing parts as necessary (Chapter 7).

37   Oil leakage

1   Excessive amount of lubricant in the transaxle (see Chapter 1 for correct checking procedures). Drain lubricant as required.
2   Driveaxle oil seal (Chapter 8) or speedometer oil seal in need of replacement (Chapter 7).

Automatic transaxle

Note: *Due to the complexity of the automatic transaxle, it's difficult for the home mechanic to properly diagnose and service this component. For problems other than the following, the vehicle should be taken to a dealer or reputable mechanic.*

38   General shift mechanism problems

1   Chapter 7 deals with checking and adjusting the shift linkage on automatic transaxles. Common problems which may be attributed to poorly adjusted linkage are:
   Engine starting in gears other than Park or Neutral.
   Indicator on shifter pointing to a gear other than the one actually being used.
   Vehicle moves when in Park.
2   Refer to Chapter 7 to adjust the linkage.

39   Transaxle will not downshift with accelerator pedal pressed to the floor

Chapter 7 deals with adjusting the throttle cable to enable the transaxle to downshift properly.

40   Transaxle slips, shifts rough, is noisy or has no drive in forward or reverse gears

1   There are many probable causes for the above problems, but the home mechanic should be concerned with only one possibility — fluid level.
2   Before taking the vehicle to a repair shop, check the level and condition of the fluid as described in Chapter 1. Correct fluid level as necessary or change the fluid and filter if needed. If the problem persists, have a professional diagnose the probable cause.

41   Fluid leakage

1   Automatic transaxle fluid is a deep red color. Fluid leaks should not be confused with engine oil, which can easily be blown by air flow to the transaxle.
2   To pinpoint a leak, first remove all built-up dirt and grime from around the transaxle. Degreasing agents and/or steam cleaning will achieve this. With the underside clean, drive the vehicle at low speeds so air flow will not blow the leak far from its source. Raise the vehicle and determine where the leak is coming from. Common areas of leakage are:

a) Pan: Tighten the mounting bolts and/or replace the pan gasket as necessary (see Chapter 7).
b) Filler pipe: Replace the rubber seal where the pipe enters the transaxle case.
c) Transaxle oil lines: Tighten the connectors where the lines enter the transaxle case and/or replace the lines.
d) Vent pipe: Transaxle overfilled and/or water in fluid (see checking procedures, Chapter 1).
e) Speedometer connector: Replace the O-ring where the speedometer cable enters the transaxle case (Chapter 7).

Driveaxles

42   Clicking noise in turns

Worn or damaged outer joint. Check for cut or damaged seals. Repair as necessary (Chapter 8).

43   Knock or clunk when accelerating after coasting

Worn or damaged inner joint. Check for cut or damaged seals. Repair as necessary (Chapter 8)

44   Shudder or vibration during acceleration

1   Excessive joint angle. Have checked and correct as necessary (Chapter 8).
2   Worn or damaged CV joints. Repair or replace as necessary (Chapter 8).
3   Sticking CV joint assembly. Correct or replace as necessary (Chapter 8).

Rear axle

45   Noise

1   Road noise. No corrective procedures available.
2   Tire noise. Inspect tires and check tire pressures (Chapter 1).
3   Rear wheel bearings loose, worn or damaged (Chapter 10).

Brakes

Note: *Before assuming that a brake problem exists, make sure that the tires are in good condition and inflated properly (see Chapter 1), that the front end alignment is correct and that the vehicle is not loaded with weight in an unequal manner.*

46   Vehicle pulls to one side during braking

1   Defective, damaged or oil contaminated disc brake pads on one side. Inspect as described in Chapter 9.
2   Excessive wear of brake pad material or disc on one side. Inspect and correct as necessary.
3   Loose or disconnected front suspension components. Inspect and tighten all bolts to the specified torque (Chapter 10).
4   Defective caliper assembly. Remove the caliper and inspect for a stuck piston or other damage (Chapter 9).

47   Noise (high-pitched squeal with the brakes applied)

Disc brake pads worn out. The noise comes from the wear sensor rubbing against the disc (does not apply to all vehicles) or the actual pad backing plate itself if the material is completely worn away. Replace the pads with new ones immediately (Chapter 9). If the pad material has worn completely away, the brake rotors should be inspected for damage as described in Chapter 9.

48 Excessive brake pedal travel

1   Partial brake system failure. Inspect the entire system (Chapter 9) and correct as required.
2   Insufficient fluid in the master cylinder. Check (Chapter 1), add fluid and bleed the system if necessary (Chapter 9).
3   Rear brakes not adjusting properly. Make a series of starts and stops while the vehicle is in Reverse. If this does not correct the situation, remove the drums and inspect the self-adjusters (Chapter 9).

49 Brake pedal feels spongy when depressed

1   Air in the hydraulic lines. Bleed the brake system (Chapter 9).
2   Faulty flexible hoses. Inspect all system hoses and lines. Replace parts as necessary.
3   Master cylinder mounting bolts/nuts loose.
4   Master cylinder defective (Chapter 9).

50 Excessive effort required to stop vehicle

1   Power brake booster not operating properly (Chapter 9).
2   Excessively worn linings or pads. Inspect and replace if necessary (Chapter 9).
3   One or more caliper pistons or wheel cylinders seized or sticking. Inspect and rebuild as required (Chapter 9).
4   Brake linings or pads contaminated with oil or grease. Inspect and replace as required (Chapter 9).
5   New pads or shoes installed and not yet seated. It will take a while for the new material to seat against the drum (or rotor).

51 Pedal travels to the floor with little resistance

Little or no fluid in the master cylinder reservoir caused by leaking wheel cylinder(s), leaking caliper piston(s), loose, damaged or disconnected brake lines. Inspect the entire system and correct as necessary.

52 Brake pedal pulsates during brake application

1   Caliper improperly installed. Remove and inspect (Chapter 9).
2   Rotor defective. Remove the rotor (Chapter 9) and check for excessive lateral runout and parallelism. Have the rotor resurfaced or replace it with a new one.

Suspension and steering systems

53 Vehicle pulls to one side

1   Tire pressures uneven (Chapter 1).
2   Defective tire (Chapter 1).
3   Excessive wear in suspension or steering components (Chapter 10).
4   Front end in need of alignment.
5   Front brakes dragging. Inspect the brakes as described in Chapter 9.

54 Shimmy, shake or vibration

1   Tire or wheel out-of-balance or out-of-round. Have professionally balanced.

2   Loose, worn or out-of-adjustment wheel bearings (Chapter 10).
3   Shock absorbers and/or suspension components worn or damaged (Chapter 10).

55 Excessive pitching and/or rolling around corners or during braking

1   Defective shock absorbers. Replace as a set (Chapter 10).
2   Broken or weak springs and/or suspension components. Inspect as described in Chapter 10.

56 Excessively stiff steering

1   Lack of fluid in power steering fluid reservoir (Chapter 1).
2   Incorrect tire pressures (Chapter 1).
3   Front end out of alignment.

57 Excessive play in steering

1   Excessive wear in suspension or steering components (Chapter 10).
2   Steering gearbox damaged (Chapter 10).

58 Lack of power assistance

1   Steering pump drivebelt faulty or not adjusted properly (Chapter 1).
2   Fluid level low (Chapter 1).
3   Hoses or lines restricted. Inspect and replace parts as necessary.
4   Air in power steering system. Bleed the system (Chapter 10).

59 Excessive tire wear (not specific to one area)

1   Incorrect tire pressures (Chapter 1).
2   Tires out-of-balance. Have professionally balanced.
3   Wheels damaged. Inspect and replace as necessary.
4   Suspension or steering components excessively worn (Chapter 10).

60 Excessive tire wear on outside edge

1   Inflation pressures incorrect (Chapter 1).
2   Excessive speed in turns.
3   Front end alignment incorrect (excessive toe-in). Have professionally aligned.
4   Suspension arm bent or twisted (Chapter 10).

61 Excessive tire wear on inside edge

1   Inflation pressures incorrect (Chapter 1).
2   Front end alignment incorrect. Have professionally aligned.
3   Loose or damaged steering components (Chapter 10).

62 Tire tread worn in one place

1   Tires out-of-balance.
2   Damaged or buckled wheel. Inspect and replace if necessary.
3   Defective tire (Chapter 1).

Chapter 1   Tune-up and routine maintenance

Contents

Specifications

Recommended lubricants and fluids

Engine oil
  Type . . . .   API grade SF, SF/CC or SF/CD
  Viscosity . . . .   See accompanying chart
  Capacity
    Four-cylinder engine . . . .   5.0 qts
    3.0L V6 engine . . . .   4.0 qts
    3.8L V6 engine . . . .   5.0 qts

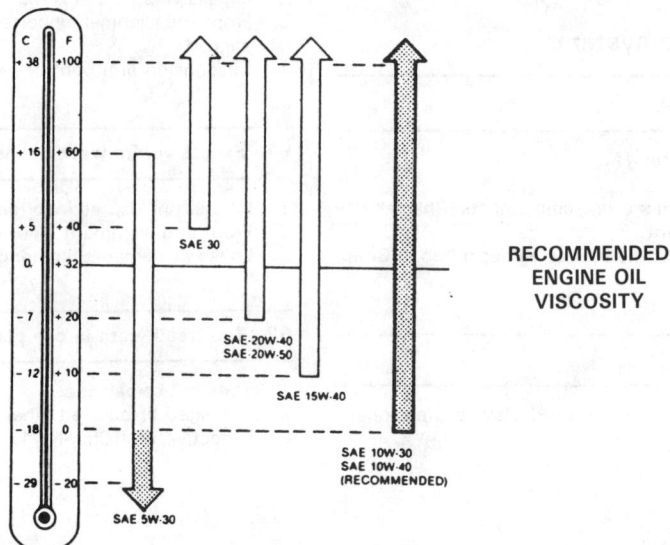

RECOMMENDED ENGINE OIL VISCOSITY

SAE 30

SAE 20W-40
SAE 20W-50

SAE 15W-40

SAE 10W-30
SAE 10W-40
(RECOMMENDED)

SAE 5W-30

Brake fluid type	DOT 3 heavy duty brake fluid
Power steering fluid type	Motorcraft **Type F** automatic transmission fluid (part no. XT-1-QF)
Automatic transaxle fluid	
Type	
1986 and 1987	Motorcraft **Type H** automatic transmission fluid (part no. ESP-M2C166-H)
1988 on	Motorcraft **MERCON** automatic transmission fluid (part no. XT-2-QDX)
Capacity	
ATX/FLC three-speed	8.3 qts
AXOD four-speed	12.9 qts
Manual transaxle lubricant	
Type	
1986 and 1987	Motorcraft **Type F** or **DEXRON II** ATF
1988 on	Motorcraft **MERCON** ATF (part no. XT-2-QDX)
Capacity (approximate)	6.2 qts
Coolant type	Ethylene glycol-based antifreeze and water
Cooling system capacity (approximate)	
Four-cylinder engine	8.3 qts
3.0L V6 engine	11.8 qts
3.8L V6 engine	12.1 qts
Rear wheel bearing grease	NLGI no. 2 grease (part no. C1AZ-19590-B)

General

Drivebelt tension (with tool no. T63L-8620-A)	
Power steering/air conditioning	
New belt	150 to 190 lbs
Used belt	140 to 160 lbs
Alternator	
New belt	120 to 160 lbs
Used belt	80 to 100 lbs
Radiator cap pressure	
Standard	16 psi
Lower limit (must hold pressure)	13 psi
Upper limit (must relieve pressure)	18 psi
Idle speed	Refer to *Vehicle Emission Control Information label*

Brakes

Front disc brake pad thickness (minimum)	1/8 in
Rear drum brake shoe lining thickness (minimum)	1/16 in

Ignition system

Recommended spark plugs	Refer to *Vehicle Emission Control Information label*
Spark plug gap	Refer to *Vehicle Emission Control Information label*

Torque specifications

	Ft-lbs
Wheel lug nuts	80 to 105
Spark plugs	6 to 10
Oil pan drain plug	25 to 35
Automatic transaxle pan bolts	10 to 15

1 Introduction to routine maintenance

Refer to illustrations 1.2a, 1.2b, 1.2c, 1.2d and 1.2e

Warning: *The electric cooling fan on these models can activate at any time, even when the ignition is in the Off position. Disconnect the fan motor or negative battery cable when working in the vicinity of the fan.*

This Chapter is designed to help the home mechanic maintain the Ford Taurus/Mercury Sable with the goals of maximum performance, economy, safety and reliability in mind.

On the following pages is a master maintenance schedule, followed by procedures dealing specifically with each item on the schedule. Visual checks, adjustments, component replacement and other helpful items are included. Refer to the accompanying illustrations of the engine compartment and the underside of the vehicle for the locations of various components.

Servicing your vehicle in accordance with the mileage/time maintenance schedule and the step-by-step procedures will result in a planned maintenance program that should produce a long and reliable service life. Keep in mind that it is a comprehensive plan, so maintaining some items but not others at the specified intervals will not produce the same results.

As you service your vehicle, you will discover that many of the procedures can — and should — be grouped together because of the nature of the particular procedure you're performing or because of the close proximity of two otherwise unrelated omponents to one another.

For example, if the vehicle is raised for chassis lubrication, you should inspect the exhaust, suspension, steering and fuel systems while you're under the vehicle. When you're rotating the tires, it makes good sense to check the brakes since the wheels are already removed. Finally, let's suppose you have to borrow or rent a torque wrench. Even if you only need it to tighten the spark plugs, you might as well check the torque of as many critical fasteners as time allows.

The first step in this maintenance program is to prepare yourself before the actual work begins. Read through all the procedures you're planning to do, then gather up all the parts and tools needed. If it looks as if you might run into problems during a particular job, seek advice from a mechanic or an experienced do-it-yourselfer.

1.2a 3.0L V6 engine compartment

1 Brake fluid reservoir
2 Air cleaner
3 Battery
4 Spark plug wires
5 VECI label
6 Engine oil filler cap
7 Drivebelt routing diagram
8 Engine oil dipstick
9 Power steering fluid dipstick
10 Radiator cap
11 Alternator
12 Coolant reservoir
13 Windshield washer fluid
     reservoir
14 Distributor cap

BRAKE MASTER CYLINDER RESERVOIR

AUTOMATIC TRANSAXLE DIPSTICK
CHECK WITH ENGINE RUNNING AND
TRANSAXLE IN "PARK"

FLUID LEVEL AT
OPERATING TEMPERATURE
150° TO 170° F
(66° TO 77° C)

DO NOT
DRIVE
MARK

AIR FILTER
REPLACE ELEMENT
AT RECOMMENDED
INTERVAL

BATTERY

ENGINE OIL DRAIN PLUG
DRAIN AND REFILL WITH
SPECIFIED OIL AT
RECOMMENDED INTERVAL

DO NOT ADD
OIL BEYOND
"FULL"

FULL

ENGINE OIL
LEVEL DIPSTICK

MAINTAIN OIL IN
SAFE RANGE

ADD 1 QUART

ENGINE OIL
FILL CAP

POWER STEERING PUMP DIPSTICK
FLUID SHOULD BE IN THE FULL
COLD OR FULL HOT RANGE
DEPENDING UPON TEMPERATURE

RADIATOR CAP

OIL FILTER
COAT GASKET WITH ENGINE
OIL. REPLACE AT RECOMMENDED
INTERVAL

COOLANT
RECOVERY SYSTEM
RESERVOIR

WINDSHIELD
WASHER
RESERVOIR

PCV VALVE
REPLACE AT RECOMMENDED
INTERVAL

FUEL INJECTED V6

3.8

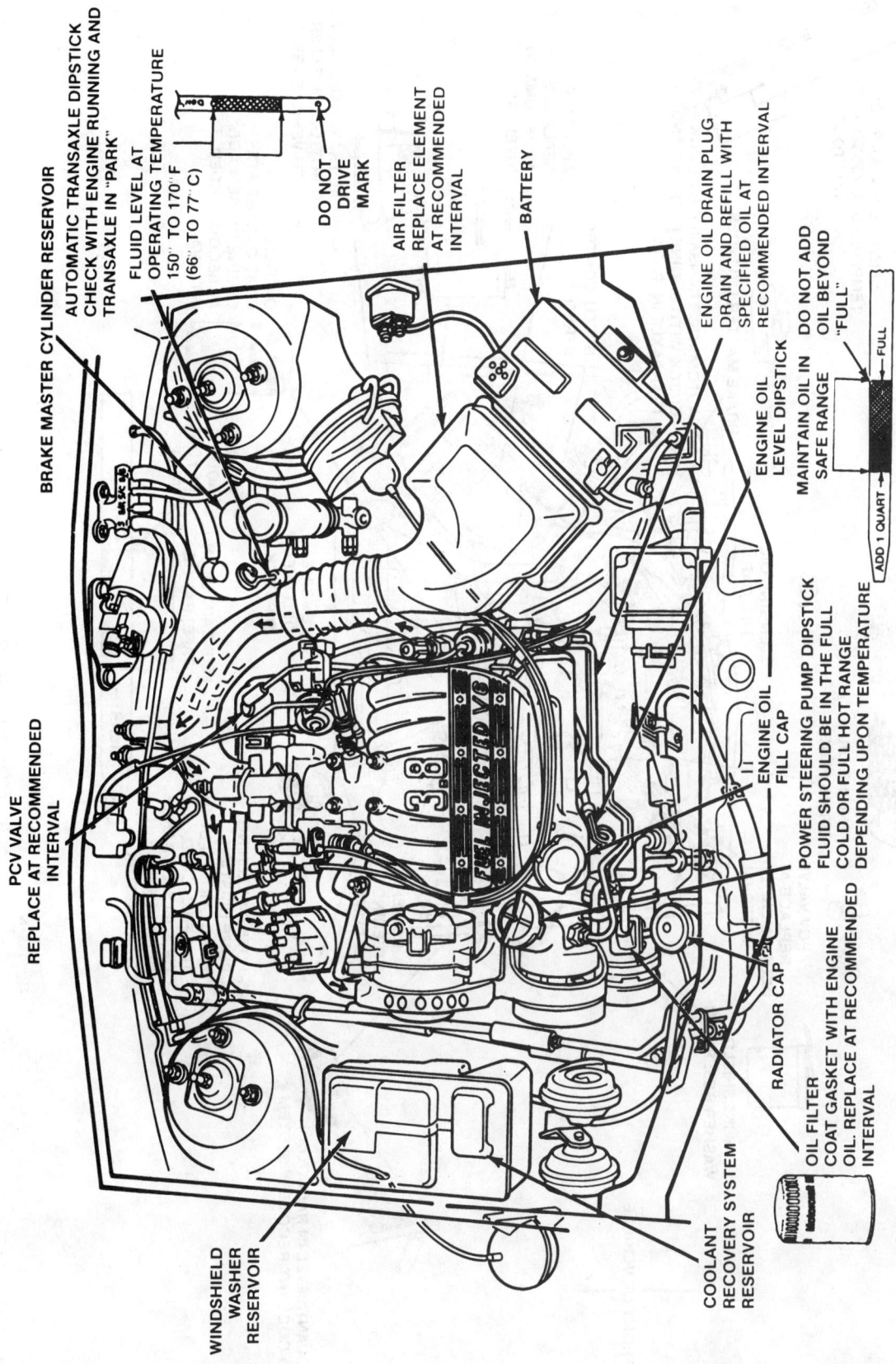

1.2b 3.8L V6 engine compartment

FLUID LEVEL AT
OPERATING TEMPERATURE
150° TO 170° F (66° TO 77°C)

FLUID LEVEL AT ROOM
TEMPERATURE 70° TO 95°F
(21° TO 35°C)

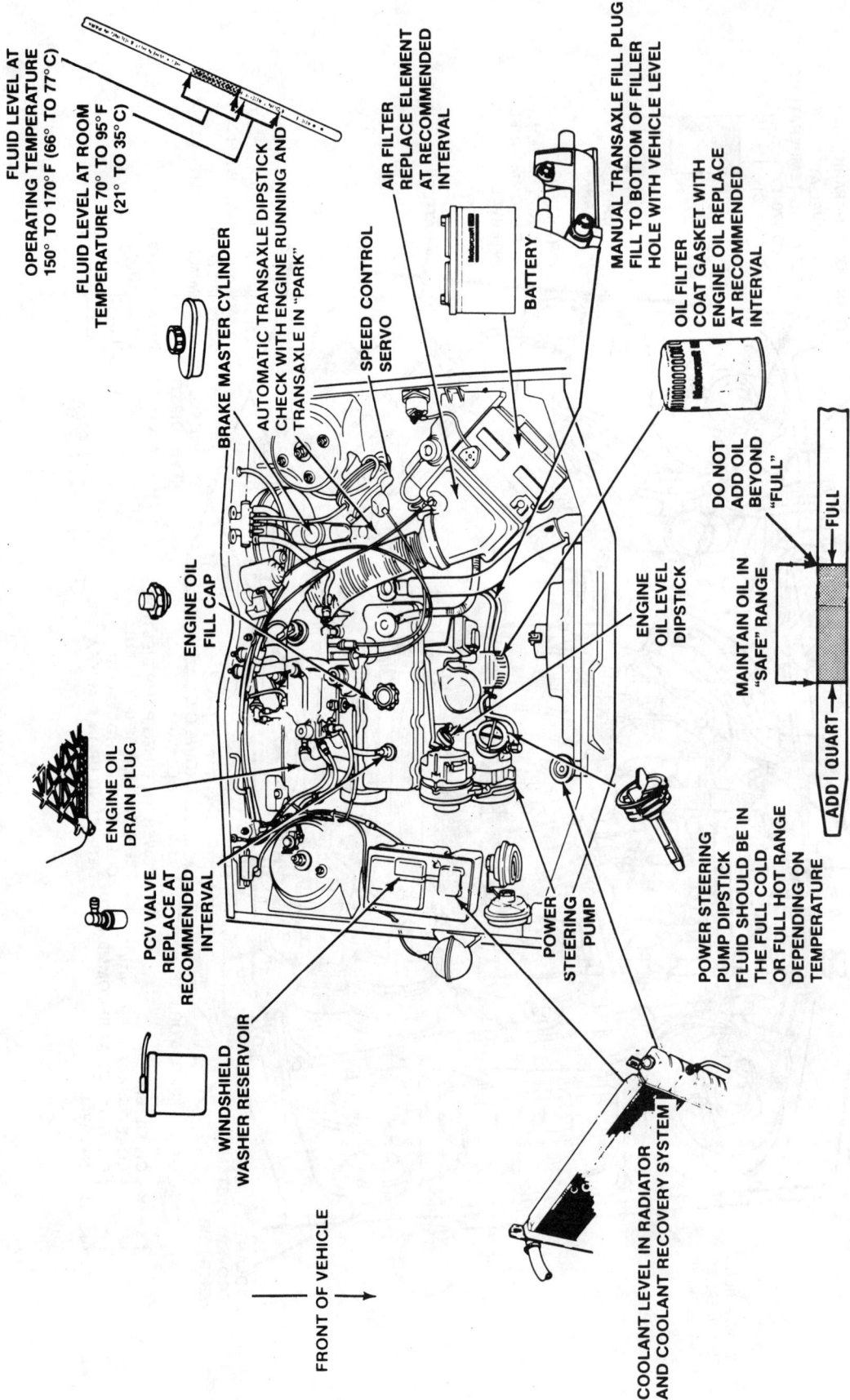

BRAKE MASTER CYLINDER

AUTOMATIC TRANSAXLE DIPSTICK
CHECK WITH ENGINE RUNNING AND
TRANSAXLE IN "PARK"

SPEED CONTROL
SERVO

AIR FILTER
REPLACE ELEMENT
AT RECOMMENDED
INTERVAL

BATTERY

MANUAL TRANSAXLE FILL PLUG
FILL TO BOTTOM OF FILLER
HOLE WITH VEHICLE LEVEL

OIL FILTER
COAT GASKET WITH
ENGINE OIL REPLACE
AT RECOMMENDED
INTERVAL

ENGINE OIL
FILL CAP

ENGINE OIL DRAIN PLUG

PCV VALVE
REPLACE AT
RECOMMENDED
INTERVAL

WINDSHIELD
WASHER RESERVOIR

FRONT OF VEHICLE

COOLANT LEVEL IN RADIATOR
AND COOLANT RECOVERY SYSTEM

POWER STEERING
PUMP DIPSTICK
FLUID SHOULD BE IN
THE FULL COLD
OR FULL HOT RANGE
DEPENDING ON
TEMPERATURE

POWER
STEERING
PUMP

ENGINE
OIL LEVEL
DIPSTICK

MAINTAIN OIL IN
"SAFE" RANGE

DO NOT
ADD OIL
BEYOND
"FULL"

FULL

ADD I QUART

1.2c   Four-cylinder engine compartment

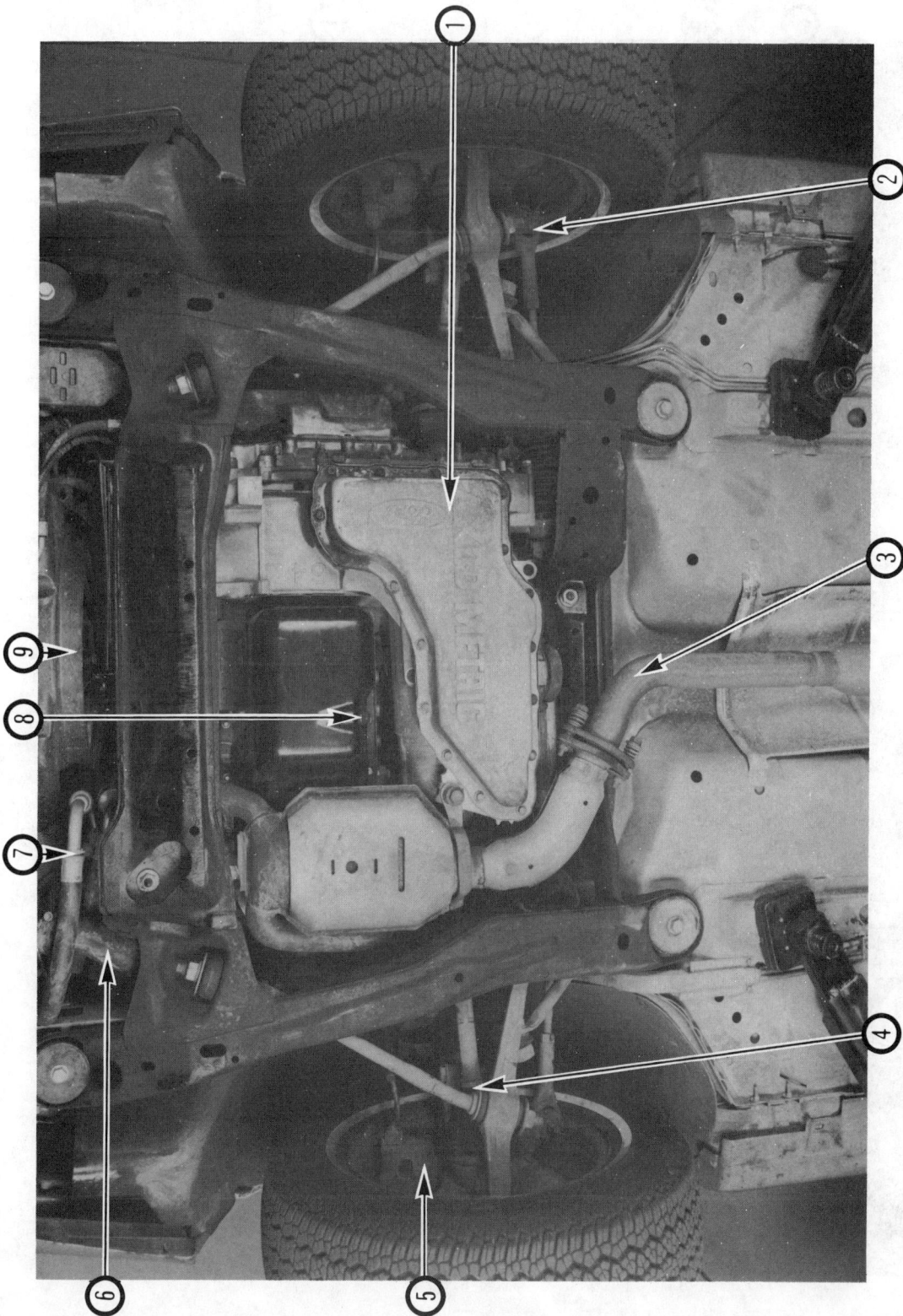

1.2d Typical engine compartment underside components

1 Automatic transaxle	7 Transaxle cooler
2 Steering tie-rod end	8 Oil drain plug
3 Exhaust pipe	9 Radiator
4 Driveaxle boot	
5 Disc brake caliper	
6 Lower radiator hose	

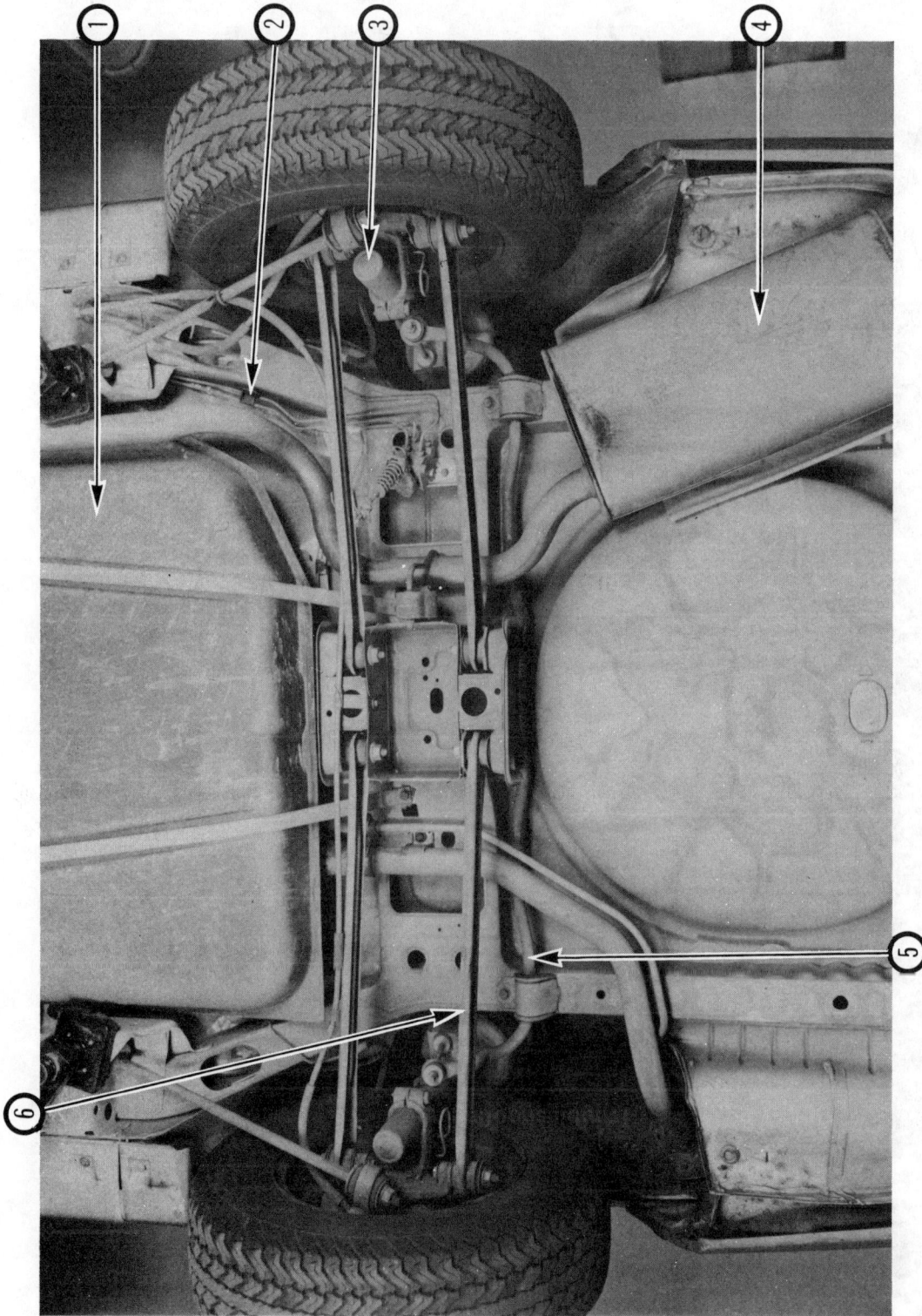

1.2e Typical vehicle rear underside components

1 Fuel tank
2 Brake line
3 Rear shock strut
4 Muffler
5 Rear sway bar
6 Rear suspension arm

2 Ford Taurus/Mercury Sable Maintenance schedule

The following maintenance intervals are based on the assumption that the vehicle owner will be doing the maintenance or service work, as opposed to having a dealer service department do the work. Although the time/mileage intervals are loosely based on factory recommendations, most have been shortened to ensure, for example, that such items as lubricants and fluids are checked/changed at intervals that promote maximum engine/driveline service life. Also, subject to the preference of the individual owner interested in keeping his or her vehicle in peak condition at all times, and with the vehicle's ultimate resale in mind, many of the maintenance procedures may be performed more often than recommended in the following schedule. We encourage such owner initiative.

When the vehicle is new it should be serviced intially by a factory authorized dealer service department to protect the factory warranty. In many cases the initial maintenance check is one at no cost to the owner.

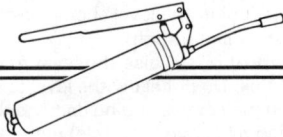

Every 250 miles or weekly, whichever comes first

Check the engine oil level (Section 4)
Check the engine coolant level (Section 4)
Check the windshield washer fluid level (Section 4)
Check the brake fluid level (Section 4)
Check the tires and tire pressures (Section 5)

Every 3000 miles or 3 months, whichever comes first

All items listed above plus . . .
Check the power steering fluid level (Section 6)
Check the automatic transaxle fluid level (Section 7)
Change the engine oil and oil filter (Section 8)

Every 6000 miles or 6 months, whichever comes first

All items listed above plus . . .
Adjust the clutch pedal (Section 9)
Inspect/replace the underhood hoses (Section 10)
Check/adjust the drivebelts (Section 11)
Check/service the battery (Section 12)

Every 12,000 miles or 12 months, whichever comes first

All items listed above plus . . .
Inspect/replace the windshield wiper
blades (Section 13)
Replace the air filter (Section 14)
Check the PCV valve and crankcase ventilation
filter (Section 15)
Check the fuel system (Section 16)
Replace the fuel filter (Section 17)
Inspect the cooling system (Section 18)
Inspect the exhaust system (Section 19)
Rotate the tires (Section 20)
Inspect the steering and suspension
components (Section 21)
Inspect the brake system (Section 22)
Lubricate the parking brake cable (Section 22)
Lubricate the automatic transaxle control
linkage (Section 23)
Check/replenish the manual transaxle
lubricant (Section 24)

Every 30,000 miles or 30 months, whichever comes first

Check and repack the rear wheel
bearings (Section 25)
Replace the spark plugs (Section 26)
Check/replace the spark plug wires, distributor cap
and rotor (Section 27)
Service the cooling system (drain, flush and
refill) (Section 28)
Change the automatic transaxle fluid and
filter (Section 29)

3   Tune-up sequence

The term *tune-up* is used in this manual to represent a combination of individual operations rather than one specific procedure.

If, from the time the vehicle is new, the routine maintenance schedule is followed closely and frequent checks are made of fluid levels and high wear items, as suggested throughout this manual, the engine will be kept in relatively good running condition and the need for additional work will be minimized.

More likely than not, however, there will be times when the engine is running poorly. This is even more likely if a used vehicle, which has not received regular and frequent maintenance checks, is purchased. In such cases, an engine tune-up will be needed outside of the regular routine maintenance intervals.

The first step in any tune-up or diagnostic procedure to help correct a poor running engine is a cylinder compression check. A compression check (see Chapter 2 Part C) will help determine the condition of internal engine components and should be used as a guide for tune-up and repair procedures. If, for instance, a compression check indicates serious internal engine wear, a conventional tune-up will not improve the performance of the engine and would be a waste of time and money. Because of its importance, the compression check should be done by someone with the right equipment and the knowledge to use it properly.

The following procedures are those most often needed to bring a generally poor running engine back into a proper state of tune.

Minor tune-up

Clean, inspect and test the battery (Section 12)
Check all engine related fluids (Section 4)
Check and adjust the drivebelts (Section 11)
Replace the spark plugs (Section 26)
Inspect the distributor cap and rotor (Section 27)
Inspect the spark plug and coil wires (Section 27)
Check and adjust the idle speed (Chapter 4)
Check the PCV valve (Section 15)
Check the air filter (Section 14)
Check the cooling system (Section 18)
Check all underhood hoses (Section 10)

Major tune-up

All items listed under Minor tune-up, plus . . .
Check the EGR system (Chapter 6)
Check the ignition system (Chapter 5)
Check the charging system (Chapter 5)
Check the fuel system (Chapter 4)
Replace the air and crankcase ventilator filters (Sections 14 and 15)
Replace the distributor cap and rotor (Section 27)
Replace the spark plug wires (Section 27)

4   Fluid level checks

Warning: *The electric cooling fan on these models can activate at any time, even when the ignition is in the Off position. Disconnect the fan motor or negative battery cable when working in the vicinity of the fan.*

Refer to illustrations 4.2, 4.4, 4.6, 4.8 and 4.15

1   Fluids are an essential part of the lubrication, cooling, brake and windshield washer systems. Because the fluids gradually become depleted and/or contaminated during normal operation of the vehicle, they must be periodically replenished. See *Recommended lubricants, fluids and capacities* at the beginning of this Chapter before adding fluid to any of the following components. **Note:** *The vehicle must be on level ground when fluid levels are checked.*

Engine oil

2   The oil level is checked with a dipstick, which is located on the front of the engine, near the alternator **(see illustration)**. The dipstick extends through a metal tube down into the oil pan.

3   The oil level should be checked before the vehicle has been driven, or about 15 minutes after the engine has been shut off. If the oil is checked immediately after driving the vehicle, some of the oil will re-

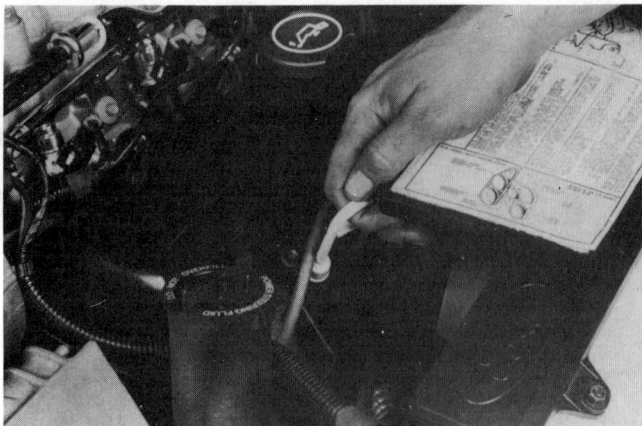

4.2   The engine oil dipstick is located on the front (radiator) side of the engine (V6 engine shown)

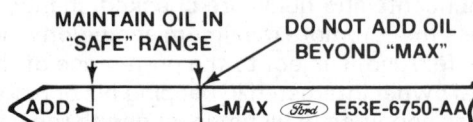

4.4   The oil level should be in the safe area — if it's below the ADD line, add enough oil to bring the level into the safe area (DO NOT add more oil if the level is at the MAX line)

main in the upper part of the engine, resulting in an inaccurate reading on the dipstick.

4   Pull the dipstick from the tube and wipe all the oil from the end with a clean rag or paper towel. Insert the clean dipstick all the way back into the tube and pull it out again. Note the oil at the end of the dipstick. At its highest point, the level should be above the ADD mark, in the SAFE range **(see illustration)**.

5   It takes one quart of oil to raise the level from the ADD mark to the circle on the dipstick. Do not allow the level to drop below the ADD mark or oil starvation may cause engine damage. Conversely, overfilling the engine (adding oil above the circle) may cause oil fouled spark plugs, oil leaks or oil seal failures.

6   To add oil, remove the filler cap located on the left end of the rocker arm cover **(see illustration)**. After adding oil, wait a few minutes to allow the level to stabilize, then pull out the dipstick and check the level again. Add more oil if required. Install the filler cap and tighten it by hand only.

4.6   The twist-off oil filler cap is located on the rocker arm cover

4.8 The engine coolant and windshield washer reservoirs are contained in the same housing but are separate — be sure to add only the correct fluids — the caps are clearly marked

4.15 The brake fluid level should be kept between the MIN and MAX marks on the translucent plastic reservoir — unscrew the cap to add fluid

7   Checking the oil level is an important preventive maintenance step. A consistently low oil level indicates oil leakage through damaged seals, defective gaskets or past worn rings or valve guides. If the oil looks milky in color or has water droplets in it, the cylinder head gasket may be blown or the head or block may be cracked. The engine should be checked immediately. The condition of the oil should also be checked. Whenever you check the oil level, slide your thumb and index finger up the dipstick before wiping off the oil. If you see small dirt or metal particles clinging to the dipstick, the oil should be changed (Section 8).

Engine coolant

Warning: *Do not allow antifreeze to come in contact with your skin or painted surfaces of the vehicle. Flush contaminated areas immediately with plenty of water. Do not store new coolant or leave old coolant lying around where it's accessible to children or pets — they are attracted by its sweet taste. Ingestion of even a small amount of coolant can be fatal! Wipe up garage floor and drip pan coolant spills immediately. Keep antifreeze containers covered and repair leaks in your cooling system immediately.*

8   All vehicles covered by this manual are equipped with a pressurized coolant recovery system. A white plastic coolant reservoir located in the right front corner of the engine compartment is connected by a hose to the radiator filler neck. The coolant and windshield washer reservoirs are contained in the same housing, so always be sure to add only the correct fluids to each; the filler caps are clearly marked **(see illustration)**. If the engine overheats, coolant escapes through a valve in the radiator cap and travels through the hose into the reservoir. As the engine cools, the coolant is automatically drawn back into the cooling system to maintain the correct level.

9   The coolant level in the reservoir should be checked regularly. **Warning:** *Do not remove the radiator cap to check the coolant level when the engine is warm.* The level in the reservoir varies with the temperature of the engine. When the engine is cold, the coolant level should be at or slightly above the ADD mark on the reservoir. Once the engine has warmed up, the level should be at or near the FULL HOT mark. If it isn't, allow the engine to cool, then remove the cap from the reservoir and add a 50/50 mixture of ethylene glycol based antifreeze and water.

10   Drive the vehicle and recheck the coolant level. Do not use rust inhibitors or additives. If only a small amount of coolant is required to bring the system up to the proper level, water can be used. However, repeated additions of water will dilute the antifreeze and water solution. In order to maintain the proper ratio of antifreeze and water, always top up the coolant level with the correct mixture. An empty plastic milk jug or bleach bottle makes an excellent container for mixing coolant.

11   If the coolant level drops consistently, there may be a leak in the system. Inspect the radiator, hoses, filler cap, drain plugs and water

pump (see Section 18). If no leaks are noted, have the radiator cap pressure tested by a service station.

12   If you have to remove the radiator cap, wait until the engine has cooled completely, then wrap a thick cloth around the cap and turn it to the first stop. If coolant or steam escapes, let the engine cool down longer, then remove the cap.

13   Check the condition of the coolant as well. It should be relatively clear. If it is brown or rust colored, the system should be drained, flushed and refilled. Even if the coolant appears to be normal, the corrosion inhibitors wear out, so it must be replaced at the specified intervals.

Brake fluid

14   The brake fluid level is checked by looking through the plastic reservoir mounted on the master cylinder. The master cylinder is mounted on the front of the power booster unit in the left rear corner of the engine compartment.

15   The fluid level should be between the MAX and MIN lines on the side of the reservoir **(see illustration)**.

16   If the fluid level is low, wipe the top of the reservoir and the cap with a clean rag to prevent contamination of the system as the cap is unscrewed.

17   Add only the specified brake fluid to the reservoir (refer to *Recommended lubricants and fluids* at the front of this Chapter or to your owner's manual). Mixing different types of brake fluid can damage the system. Fill the reservoir to the MAX line. **Warning:** *Brake fluid can harm your eyes and damage painted surfaces, so use extreme caution when handling or pouring it. Do not use brake fluid that has been standing open or is more than one year old. Brake fluid absorbs moisture from the air. Excess moisture can cause a dangerous loss of braking effectiveness.*

18   While the reservoir cap is off, check the master cylinder reservoir for contamination. If rust deposits, dirt particles or water droplets are present, the system should be drained and refilled by a dealer service department or repair shop.

19   After filling the reservoir to the proper level, make sure the cap is seated to prevent fluid leakage and/or contamination.

20   The fluid level in the master cylinder will drop slightly as the brake shoes or pads at each wheel wear down during normal operation. If the brake fluid level drops consistently, check the entire system for leaks immediately. Examine all brake lines, hoses and connections, along with the calipers, wheel cylinders and master cylinder (see Section 22).

21   When checking the fluid level, if you discover one or both reservoirs empty or nearly empty, the brake system should be bled Chapter 9).

Windshield washer fluid

22   The windshield washer system fluid reservoir is the rear tank of the combination engine coolant/windshield washer assembly mounted

on the right side of the engine compartment. Be sure to add the correct fluids to each of the reservoirs (see illustration 4.8).
23 In milder climates, plain water can be used in the reservoir, but it should be kept no more than 2/3 full to allow for expansion if the water freezes. In colder climates, use windshield washer system antifreeze, available at any auto parts store, to lower the freezing point of the fluid. Mix the antifreeze with water in accordance with the manufacturer's directions on the container. **Caution:** *Do not use cooling system antifreeze — it will damage the vehicle's paint.*

---

5   Tire and tire pressure checks

Refer to illustrations 5.2, 5.3, 5.4a, 5.4b and 5.8

1   Periodic inspection of the tires may spare you the inconvenience of being stranded with a flat tire. It can also provide you with vital information regarding possible problems in the steering and suspension systems before major damage occurs.
2   The original tires on this vehicle are equipped with 1/2-inch side bands that will appear when tread depth reaches 1/16-inch, but they don't appear until the tires are worn out. Tread wear can be monitored with a simple, inexpensive device known as a tread depth indicator (see illustration).
3   Note any abnormal tread wear (see illustration). Tread pattern irregularities such as cupping, flat spots and more wear on one side than the other are indications of front end alignment and/or balance problems. If any of these conditions are noted, take the vehicle to a tire shop or service station to correct the problem.
4   Look closely for cuts, punctures and embedded nails or tacks. Sometimes a tire will hold air pressure for a short time or leak down very slowly after a nail has embedded itself in the tread. If a slow leak persists, check the valve stem core to make sure it is tight (see illustration). Examine the tread for an object that may have embedded itself in the tire or for a ''plug'' that may have begun to leak (radial tire punctures are repaired with a plug that is installed in the puncture). If a puncture is suspected, it can be easily verified by spraying a solution of soapy water onto the puncture area (see illustration). The soapy solu-

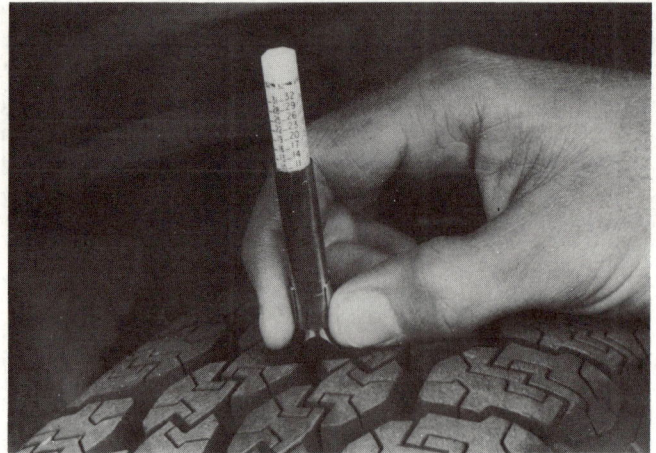

5.2   A tire tread depth indicator should be used to monitor tire wear — they are available at auto parts stores and service stations, and cost very little

tion will bubble if there is a leak. Unless the puncture is unusually large, a tire shop or service station can normally repair the tire.
5   Carefully inspect the inner sidewall of each tire for evidence of brake fluid leakage. If you see any, inspect the brakes immediately.
6   Correct air pressure adds miles to the lifespan of the tires, improves mileage and enhances overall ride quality. Tire pressure cannot be accurately estimated by looking at a tire, especially if it's a radial. A tire pressure gauge is essential. Keep an accurate gauge in the glovebox. The pressure gauges attached to the nozzles of air hoses at gas stations are often inaccurate.
7   Always check tire pressure when the tires are cold. Cold, in this case, means the vehicle has not been driven over a mile in the three hours preceding a tire pressure check. A pressure rise of four to eight

Condition	Probable cause	Corrective action	Condition	Probable cause	Corrective action
Shoulder wear	• Underinflation (both sides wear) • Incorrect wheel camber (one side wear) • Hard cornering • Lack of rotation	• Measure and adjust pressure. • Repair or replace axle and suspension parts. • Reduce speed. • Rotate tires.	Feathered edge Toe wear	• Incorrect toe	• Adjust toe-in.
Center wear	• Overinflation • Lack of rotation	• Measure and adjust pressure. • Rotate tires.	Uneven wear	• Incorrect camber or caster • Malfunctioning suspension • Unbalanced wheel • Out-of-round brake drum • Lack of rotation	• Repair or replace axle and suspension parts. • Repair or replace suspension parts. • Balance or replace. • Turn or replace. • Rotate tires.

5.3   This chart will help you determine the condition of your tires, the probable cause(s) of abnormal wear and the corrective action necessary

5.4a If a tire loses air on a steady basis, check the valve core first to make sure it's snug (special inexpensive wrenches are commonly available at auto parts stores)

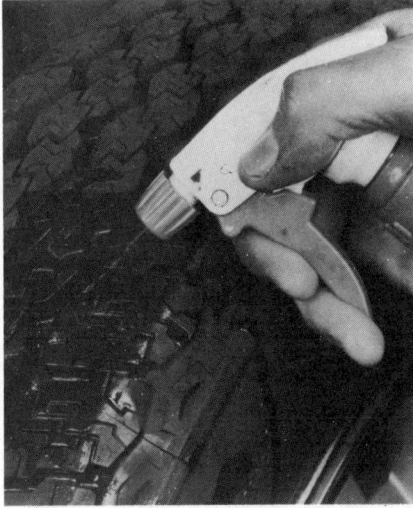

5.4b If the valve core is tight, raise the corner of the vehicle with the low tire and spray a soapy water solution onto the tread as the tire is turned slowly — slow leaks will cause small bubbles to appear

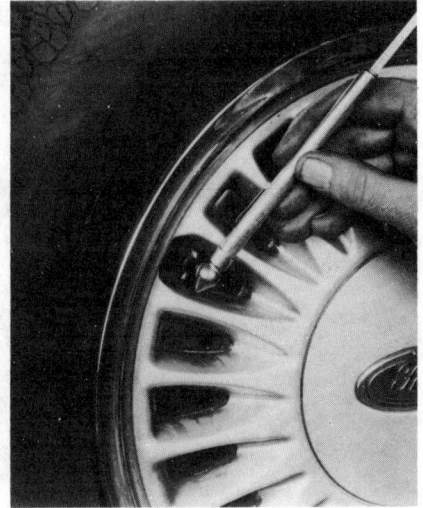

5.8 To extend the life of the tires, check the air pressure at least once a week with an accurate gauge (don't forget the spare!)

pounds is not uncommon once the tires are warm.

8 Unscrew the valve cap protruding from the wheel or hubcap and push the gauge firmly onto the valve stem (see illustration). Note the reading on the gauge and compare the figure to the recommended tire pressure shown on the tire placard on the driver's side door. Be sure to reinstall the valve cap to keep dirt and moisture out of the valve stem mechanism. Check all four tires and, if necessary, add enough air to bring them up to the recommended pressure.

9 Don't forget to keep the spare tire inflated to the specified pressure (refer to your owner's manual or the tire sidewall). Note that the pressure recommended for the compact spare is higher than for the tires on the vehicle.

6 Power steering fluid level check

Refer to illustrations 6.2 and 6.5

Warning: *The electric cooling fan on these models can activate at any time, even when the ignition is in the Off position. Disconnect the fan motor or negative battery cable when working in the vicinity of the fan.*

1 Check the power steering fluid level periodically to avoid steering system problems, such as damage to the pump. **Caution:** *DO NOT hold the steering wheel against either stop (extreme left or right turn) for more than five seconds. If you do, the power steering pump could be damaged.*

2 The power steering pump, located at the right front corner of the engine, is equipped with a twist-off cap with an integral fluid level dipstick (see illustration).

3 Park the vehicle on level ground and apply the parking brake.

4 Run the engine until it has reached normal operating temperature. With the engine at idle, turn the steering wheel back and forth several times to get any air out of the steering system. Shut the engine off, remove the cap by turning it counterclockwise, wipe the dipstick clean and reinstall the cap.

5 Remove the cap again and note the fluid level. It must be between the two lines designating the FULL HOT range (see illustration) (be sure to use the proper temperature range on the dipstick when checking the fluid level — the FULL COLD lines on the reverse side of the dipstick are only usable when the engine is cold).

6 Add small amounts of fluid until the level is correct. **Caution:** *Do not overfill the pump. If too much fluid is added, remove the excess with a clean syringe or suction pump.*

7 Check the power steering hoses and connections for leaks and wear (see Section 10).

8 Check the condition and tension of the power steering pump drivebelt (see Section 11).

6.2 The power steering fluid filler cap/dipstick is located at the front of the engine

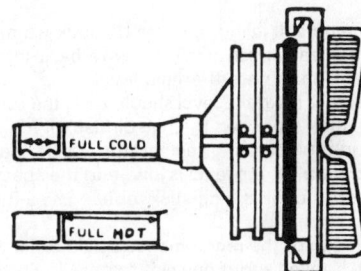

6.5 Once the engine is properly warmed up and the wheel has been turned back and forth a few times to rid the system of bubbles, pull the dipstick out and wipe it off, reinsert it and verify that the fluid level is in the FULL HOT range (be sure to use the proper range, one side is for checking the fluid cold) — if it isn't, add enough fluid to bring the level between the two lines

7.4 The automatic transaxle dipstick is located in a long tube at the rear of the engine compartment

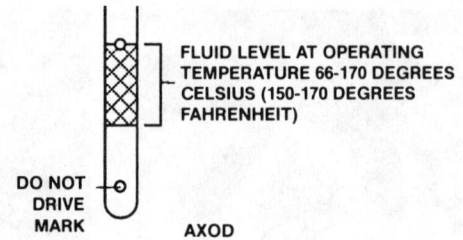

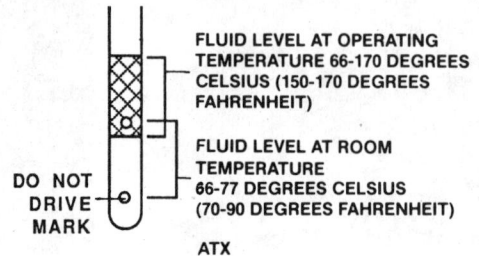

7.6 If the automatic transmission fluid is cold, the level should be between the two circles; if it's at operating temperature, the level should be between the two lines

7 Automatic transaxle fluid level check

Refer to illustrations 7.4 and 7.6

Warning: *The electric cooling fan on these models can activate at any time, even when the ignition is in the Off position. Disconnect the fan motor or negative battery cable when working in the vicinity of the fan.*

1   The automatic transaxle fluid level should be carefully maintained. Low fluid level can lead to slipping or loss of drive, while overfilling can cause foaming and loss of fluid. Either condition can cause transaxle damage.

2   Since transmission fluid expands as it heats up, the fluid level should only be checked when the transaxle is warm (at normal operating temperature). If the vehicle has just been driven over 20 miles (32 km), the transaxle can be considered warm. **Caution:** *If the vehicle has just been driven for a long time at high speed or in city traffic in hot weather, or if it has been pulling a trailer, an accurate fluid level reading cannot be obtained. Allow the transaxle to cool down for about 30 minutes.* You can also check the transaxle fluid level when the transaxle is cold. If the vehicle has not been driven for over five hours and the fluid is about room temperature (70 to 95°F), the transaxle is cold. However, the fluid level is normally checked with the transaxle warm to ensure accurate results.

3   Immediately after driving the vehicle, park it on a level surface, set the parking brake and start the engine. While the engine is idling, depress the brake pedal and move the selector lever through all the gear ranges, beginning and ending in Park.

4   Locate the automatic transaxle dipstick tube at the left rear corner of the engine compartment, behind the air cleaner housing **(see illustration)**.

5   With the engine still idling, pull the dipstick from the tube, wipe it off with a clean rag, push it all the way back into the tube and withdraw it again, then note the fluid level.

6   If the transaxle is cold, the level should be in the room temperature range on the dipstick (between the two circles); if it's warm, the fluid level should be in the operating temperature range (between the two lines) **(see illustration)**. If the level is low, add the specified automatic transmission fluid through the dipstick tube — use a funnel to prevent spills.

7   Add just enough of the recommended fluid to fill the transaxle to the proper level. It takes about one pint to raise the level from the low mark to the high mark when the fluid is hot, so add the fluid a little at a time and keep checking the level until it's correct.

8   The condition of the fluid should also be checked along with the level. If the fluid is black or a dark reddish-brown color, or if it smells burned, it should be changed (see Section 29). If you are in doubt about its condition, purchase some new fluid and compare the two for color and smell.

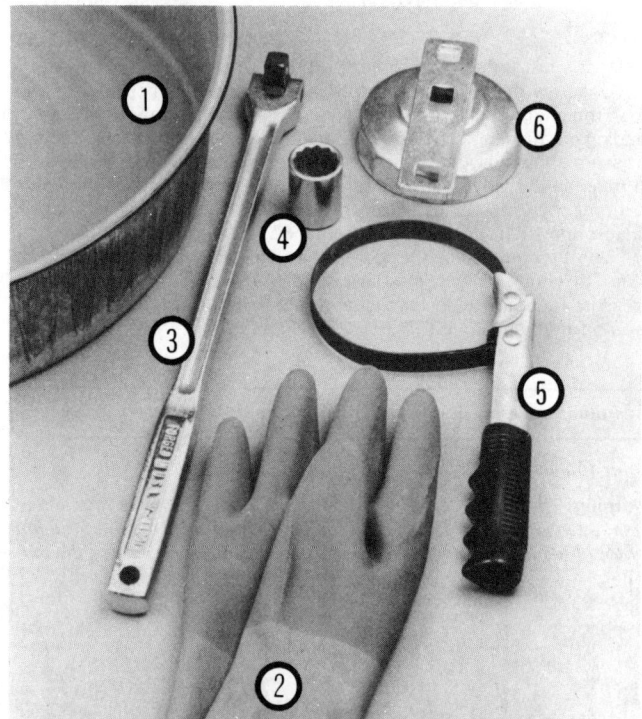

8.2   These tools are required when changing the engine oil and filter

1   **Drain pan** — *It should be fairly shallow in depth but wide, in order to prevent spills*
2   **Rubber gloves** — *When removing the drain plug and filter it is inevitable that you will get oil on your hands (the gloves will prevent burns)*
3   **Breaker bar** — *Sometimes the oil drain plug is pretty tight and a long breaker bar is needed to loosen it*
4   **Socket** — *To be used with the breaker bar or a ratchet (must be the correct size to fit the drain plug)*
5   **Filter wrench** — *This is a metal band-type wrench, which requires clearance around the filter to be effective*
6   **Filter wrench** — *This type fits on the bottom of the filter and can be turned with a ratchet or breaker bar (different size wrenches are available for different types of filters)*

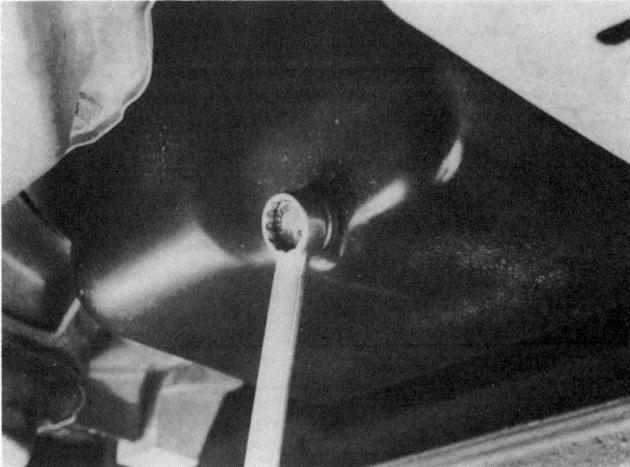

8.7 Use a box end wrench or six-point socket to remove the oil drain plug without rounding it off

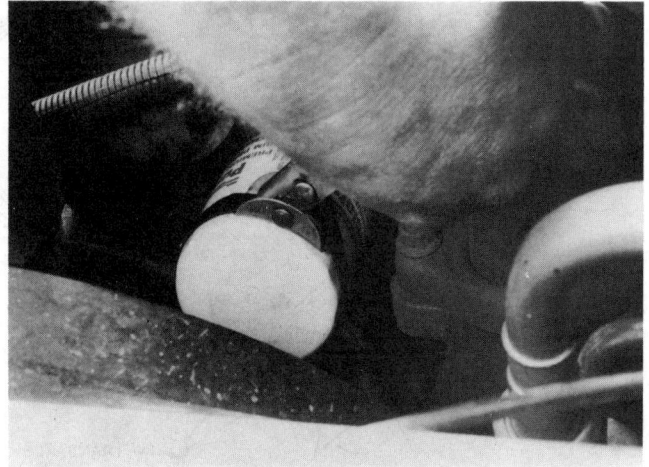

8.12 The oil filter is usually on very tight and will require a special wrench for removal — DO NOT use the wrench to tighten the new filter

8 Engine oil and filter change

Refer to illustrations 8.2, 8.7, 8.12 and 8.16

Warning: *The electric cooling fan on these models can activate at any time, even when the ignition is in the Off position. Disconnect the fan motor or negative battery cable when working in the vicinity of the fan.*

1 Frequent oil changes are the most important preventive maintenance procedures that can be done by the home mechanic. As engine oil ages, in becomes diluted and contaminated, which leads to premature engine wear.

2 Make sure that you have all the necessary tools before you begin this procedure **(see illustration)**. You should also have plenty of rags or newspapers handy for mopping up oil spills.

3 Access to the oil drain plug and filter will be improved if the vehicle can be lifted on a hoist, driven onto ramps or supported by jackstands. **Warning:** *Do not work under a vehicle supported only by a bumper, hydraulic or scissors-type jack — always use jackstands!*

4 If you haven't changed the oil on this vehicle before, get under it and locate the oil drain plug and the oil filter. The exhaust components will be warm as you work, so note how they are routed to avoid touching them when you are under the vehicle.

5 Start the engine and allow it to reach normal operating temperature — oil and sludge will flow out more easily when warm. If new oil, a filter or tools are needed, use the vehicle to go get them and warm up the engine/oil at the same time. Park on a level surface and shut off the engine when it's warmed up. Remove the oil filler cap from the rocker arm cover.

6 Raise the vehicle and support it on jackstands. Make sure it is safely supported!

7 Being careful not to touch the hot exhaust components, position a drain pan under the plug in the bottom of the engine **(see illustration)**, then remove the plug. It's a good idea to wear an old glove while unscrewing the plug the final few turns to avoid being scalded by hot oil.

8 It may be necessary to move the drain pan slightly as oil flow slows to a trickle. Inspect the old oil for the presence of metal particles.

9 After all the oil has drained, wipe off the drain plug with a clean rag. Any small metal particles clinging to the plug would immediately contaminate the new oil.

10 Clean the area around the drain plug opening, reinstall the plug and tighten it securely, being careful not to strip the threads.

11 Move the drain pan into position under the oil filter, located on the front (radiator side) of the engine.

12 Loosen the oil filter by turning it counterclockwise with a filter wrench **(see illustration)**. Any standard filter wrench will work.

13 Sometimes the oil filter is screwed on so tightly that it cannot be loosened. If it is, punch a metal bar or long screwdriver directly through it, as close to the engine as possible, and use it as a T-bar to turn the filter. Be prepared for oil to spurt out of the canister as it is punctured.

8.16 Lubricate the gasket with clean oil before installing the filter on the engine

14 Once the filter is loose, use your hands to unscrew it from the block. Just as the filter is detached from the block, immediately tilt the open end up to prevent the oil inside the filter from spilling out. **Warning:** *The engine exhaust manifold may still be hot, so be careful.*

15 Using a clean rag, wipe off the mounting surface on the block. Also, make sure that none of the old gasket remains stuck to the mounting surface. It can be removed with a scraper if necessary.

16 Compare the old filter with the new one to make sure they are the same type. Smear some engine oil on the rubber gasket of the new filter and screw it into place **(see illustration)**. Overtightening the filter will damage the gasket, so don't use a filter wrench. Most filter manufacturers recommend tightening the filter by hand only. Normally they should be tightened 3/4-turn after the gasket contacts the block, but be sure to follow the directions on the filter or container.

17 Remove all tools and materials from under the vehicle, being careful not to spill the oil in the drain pan, then lower the vehicle.

18 Add new oil to the engine through the oil filler cap in the rocker arm cover. Use a funnel to prevent oil from spilling onto the top of the engine. Pour four quarts of fresh oil into the engine. Wait a few minutes to allow the oil to drain into the pan, then check the level on the dipstick (see Section 4 if necessary). If the oil level is in the SAFE range, install the filler cap.

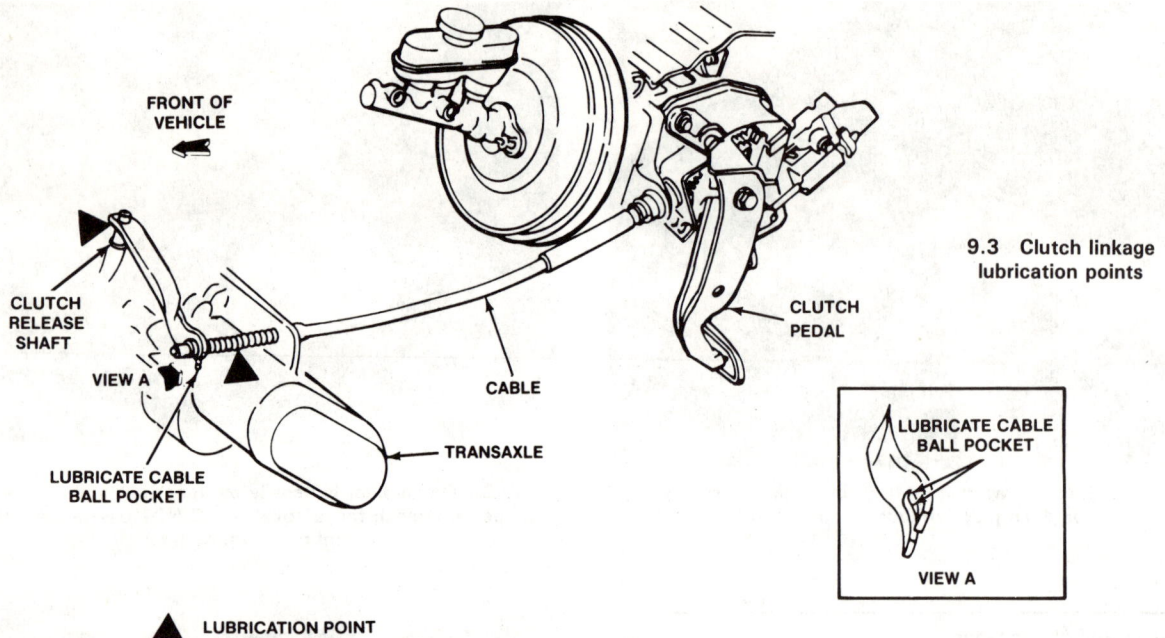

9.3 Clutch linkage lubrication points

FRONT OF VEHICLE

CLUTCH RELEASE SHAFT

VIEW A

LUBRICATE CABLE BALL POCKET

CABLE

TRANSAXLE

CLUTCH PEDAL

LUBRICATE CABLE BALL POCKET

VIEW A

▲ LUBRICATION POINT

19 Start the engine and run it for about a minute. While the engine is running, look under the vehicle and check for leaks at the oil pan drain plug and around the oil filter. If either one is leaking, stop the engine and tighten the plug or filter slightly.

20 Wait a few minutes, then recheck the level on the dipstick. Add oil as necessary to bring the level into the SAFE range.

21 During the first few trips after an oil change, make it a point to check frequently for leaks and proper oil level.

22 The old oil drained from the engine cannot be reused in its present state and should be discarded. Oil reclamation centers, auto repair shops and gas stations will normally accept the oil, which can be recycled. After the oil has cooled, it can be drained into a container (plastic jugs, bottles, milk cartons, etc.) for transport to a disposal site.

9 Clutch pedal adjustment

Refer to illustration 9.3

1 All vehicles covered in this manual are equipped with a cable-operated clutch actuating mechanism which incorporates a self-adjusting device.

2 At the specified intervals, pull up on the clutch pedal and then push down until you hear a click, indicating that the adjuster has operated.

3 It is a good idea to lubricate the clutch linkage at the time of adjustment **(see illustration)**.

10 Underhood hose check and replacement

Warning: *The electric cooling fan on these models can activate at any time, even when the ignition is in the Off position. Disconnect the fan motor or negative battery cable when working in the vicinity of the fan. Replacement of air conditioning hoses must be left to a dealer service department or air conditioning shop that has the equipment to depressurize the system safely. Never remove air conditioning components or hoses until the system has been depressurized.*

General

1 High temperatures under the hood can cause the deterioration of the rubber and plastic hoses used for engine, accessory and emission systems operation. Periodic inspection should be made for cracks, loose clamps, material hardening and leaks.

2 Information specific to the cooling system hoses can be found in Section 18.

3 Most (but not all) hoses are secured to the fittings with clamps. Where clamps are used, check to be sure they haven't lost their tension, allowing the hose to leak. If clamps aren't used, make sure the hose has not expanded and/or hardened where it slips over the fitting, allowing it to leak.

PCV system hose

4 To reduce hydrocarbon emissions, crankcase blow-by gas is vented through the PCV valve in the rocker arm cover to the intake manifold via a rubber hose. The blow-by gases mix with incoming air in the intake manifold before being burned in the combustion chambers.

5 Check the PCV hose for cracks, leaks and other damage. Disconnect it from the rocker arm cover and the intake manifold and check the inside for obstructions. If it's clogged, clean it out with solvent.

Vacuum hoses

6 It is quite common for vacuum hoses, especially those in the emissions system, to be color coded or identified by colored stripes molded into each hose. Various systems require hoses with different wall thicknesses, collapse resistance and temperature resistance. When replacing hoses, be sure the new ones are made of the same material.

7 Often the only effective way to check a hose is to remove it completely from the vehicle. If more than one hose is removed, be sure to label the hoses and fittings to ensure correct installation.

8 When checking vacuum hoses, be sure to include any plastic T-fittings in the check. Inspect the fittings for cracks and the hose where it fits over each fitting for distortion, which could cause leakage.

9 A small piece of vacuum hose (1/4-inch inside diameter) can be used as a stethoscope to detect vacuum leaks. Hold one end of the hose to your ear and probe around vacuum hoses and fittings, listening for the "hissing" sound characteristic of a vacuum leak. **Warning:** *When probing with the vacuum hose stethoscope, be careful not to allow your body or the hose to come into contact with moving engine components such as drivebelts, the cooling fan, etc.*

Fuel hose

Warning: *There are certain precautions which must be taken when inspecting or servicing fuel system components. Work in a well ventilated area and do not allow open flames (cigarettes, appliance pilot lights, etc.) or bare light bulbs near the work area. Mop up any spills immediately and do not store fuel-soaked rags where they could ignite.*

10 The fuel lines are usually under a small amount of pressure, so if any fuel lines are to be disconnected be prepared to catch spilled fuel. **Warning:** *If your vehicle is equipped with fuel injection you must relieve the fuel system pressure before servicing the fuel lines. Refer to Chapter 4 for the fuel system pressure relief procedure.*

11 Check all rubber fuel lines for deterioration and chafing. Check especially for cracks in areas where the hose bends and just before fittings, such as where a hose attaches to the fuel pump, fuel filter and fuel injection unit.

12 High quality fuel line, usually identified by the word *Fluroelastomer* printed on the hose, should be used for fuel line replacement. Never, under any circumstances, use unreinforced vacuum line, clear plastic tubing or water hose for fuel lines.

13 Spring-type clamps are commonly used on fuel lines. These clamps often lose their tension over a period of time, and can be ''sprung'' during the removal process. As a result, it is recommended that all spring-type clamps be replaced with screw clamps whenever a hose is replaced.

Metal lines

14 Sections of metal line are often used for fuel line between the fuel pump and fuel injection unit. Check carefully to be sure the line has not been bent and crimped and that cracks have not started in the line, particularly where bends occur.

15 If a section of metal fuel line must be replaced, use seamless steel tubing only, since copper and aluminum tubing do not have the strength necessary to withstand vibration caused by the engine.

16 Check the metal brake lines where they enter the master cylinder and brake proportioning unit (if used) for cracks in the lines and loose fittings. Any sign of brake fluid leakage calls for an immediate thorough inspection of the brake system.

11 Drivebelt check, adjustment and replacement

Warning: *The electric cooling fan on these models can activate at any time, even when the ignition is in the Off position. Disconnect the fan motor or negative battery cable when working in the vicinity of the fan.*

1 The accessory drivebelts, also referred to as V-belts or simply fan belts, are located at the right end of the engine. The condition and tension of the drivebelts are critical to the operation of the engine and accessories. Excessive tension causes bearing wear, while insufficient tension produces slippage, noise, component vibration and belt failure. Because of their composition and the high stresses to which they are subjected, drivebelts stretch and deteriorate as they get older. As a result, they must be periodically checked and adjusted.

Check

Refer to illustrations 11.2, 11.3, 11.4 and 11.5

2 The number and type of belts used on a particular vehicle depends on the accessories installed **(see illustration)**. Only the 3.0L V6 engine

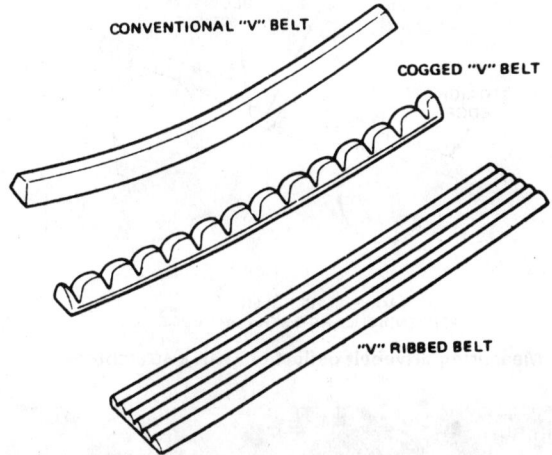

11.2 Different types of drivebelts are used to power the various accessories mounted on the engine

drivebelts require adjustment, as the four-cylinder and 3.8L V6 engines are equipped with automatic drivebelt tensioners.

3 With the engine off, open the hood and locate the drivebelts at the right end of the engine. With a flashlight, check each belt for separation of the rubber plies from each side of the core, a severed core, separation of the ribs from the rubber, cracks, torn or worn ribs and cracks in the inner ridges of the ribs. Also check for fraying and glazing, which give belts a shiny appearance **(see illustration)**. Both sides of each belt should be inspected, which means you'll have to twist them to check the undersides. Use your fingers to feel a belt where you can't see it. If any of the above conditions are evident, replace the belt as described below.

4 To check the tension of each belt in accordance with factory recommendations, install a drivebelt tension gauge (special tool no. T63L-8620-A) **(see illustration)**. Measure the tension in accordance with the tension gauge instructions and compare your measurement to the specified drivebelt tension for either a used or new belt. **Note:** *A ''new'' belt is defined as any belt which has not been run; a ''used'' belt is one that has been run for more than ten minutes.*

5 The special gauge is the most accurate way to check belt tension. However, if you don't have a gauge, and cannot borrow one, the following ''rule-of-thumb'' method is recommended as an alternative. Lay a straightedge across the longest free span (the distance between two pulleys) of the belt. Push down firmly on the belt at a point half way between the pulleys and see how much the belt moves (deflects).

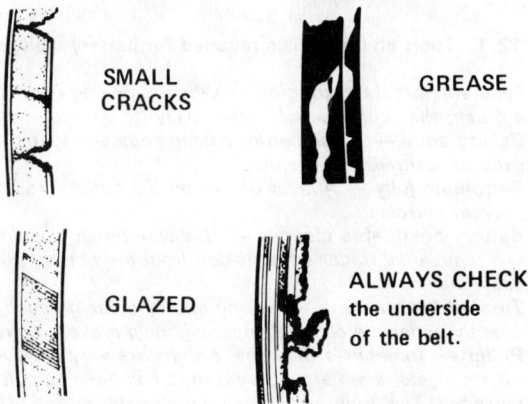

11.3 Here are some of the common problems associated with drivebelts (check the belts very carefully to prevent an untimely breakdown)

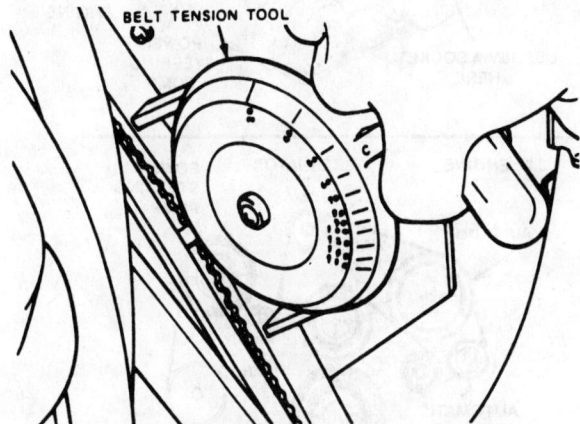

11.4 A drivebelt tension gauge is recommended for checking the belts on 3.0L V6 engines

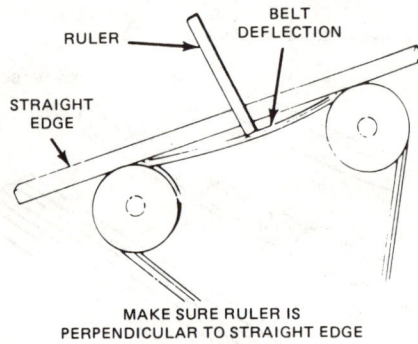

11.5 Measuring drivebelt deflection with a straightedge and ruler

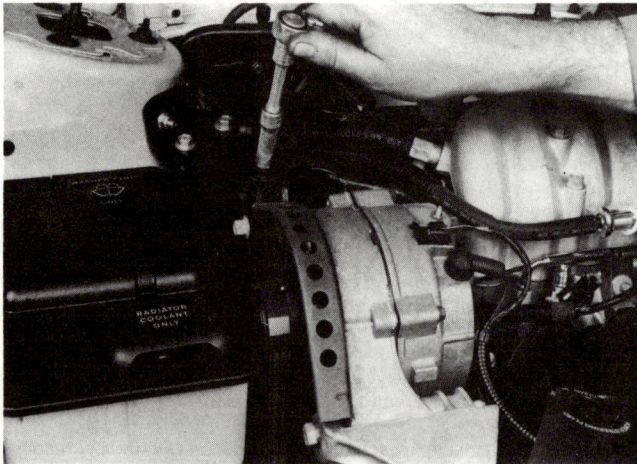

11.6a 3.0L V6 engine drivebelt adjustment details

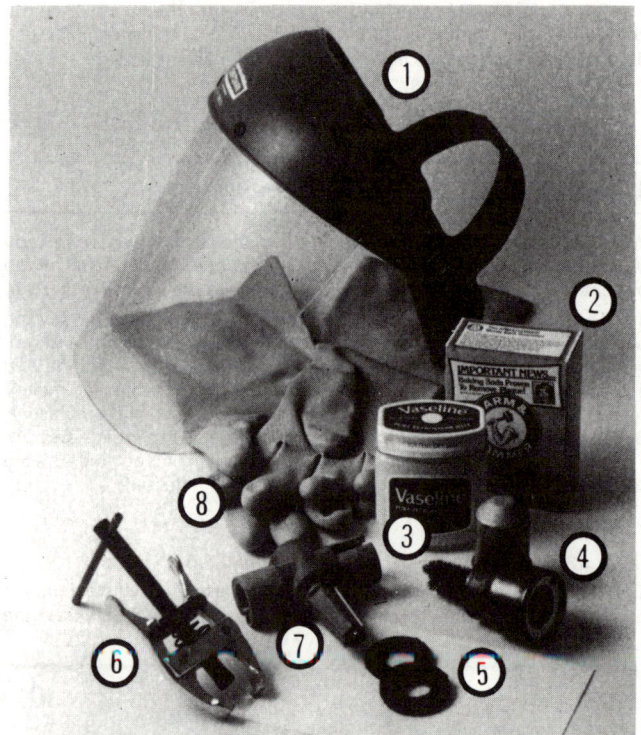

11.6b After loosening the locknut, a socket with an extension can be used to turn the adjusting bolt

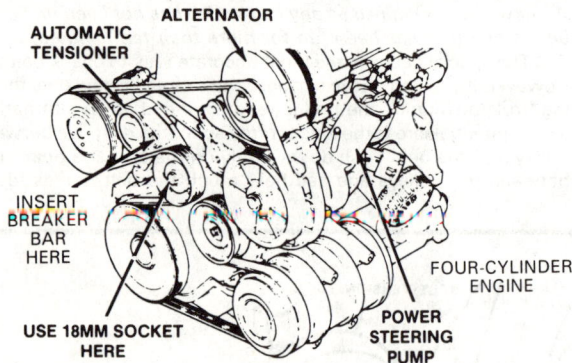

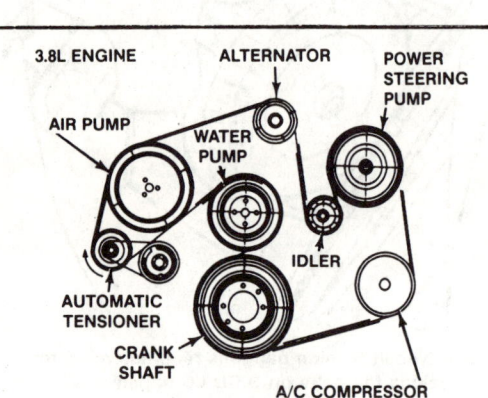

11.8 Drivebelt adjustment details for tensioner-equipped engines

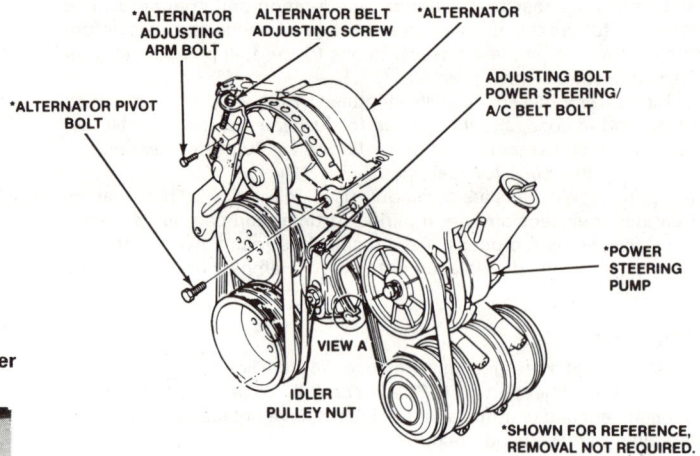

12.1 Tools and materials required for battery maintenance

1 **Face shield/safety goggles** — When removing corrosion with a brush, the acidic particles can easily fly up into your eyes
2 **Baking soda** — A solution of baking soda and water can be used to neutralize corrosion
3 **Petroleum jelly** — A layer of this on the battery posts will help prevent corrosion
4 **Battery post/cable cleaner** — This wire brush cleaning tool will remove all traces of corrosion from the battery posts and cable clamps
5 **Treated felt washers** — Placing one of these on each post, directly under the cable clamps, will help prevent corrosion
6 **Puller** — Sometimes the cable clamps are very difficult to pull off the posts, even after the nut/bolt has been completely loosened. This tool pulls the clamp straight up and off the post without damage
7 **Battery post/cable cleaner** — Here is another cleaning tool which is a slightly different version of number 4 above, but it does the same thing
8 **Rubber gloves** — Another safety item to consider when servicing the battery; remember that's acid inside the battery!

Measure the deflection with a ruler (see illustration). The belt should deflect 1/8 to 1/4-inch if the distance from pulley center-to-pulley center is less than 12 inches; it should deflect from 1/8 to 3/8-inch if the distance from pulley center-to-pulley center is over 12-inches.

Adjustment

Refer to illustrations 11.6a, 11.6b and 11.8

6   If the alternator drivebelt must be adjusted, first loosen the pivot bolt, then loosen the adjustment bolt that secures the alternator to the slotted bracket (see illustration). Turn the adjusting screw to adjust the drivebelt tension and retighten the pivot and adjustment bolts (see illustration). Recheck the belt tension using one of the above methods. Repeat this Step until the alternator drivebelt tension is correct.

7   If the power steering/air conditioner compressor drivebelt must be adjusted, locate the idler pulley on the right front corner of the block. Loosen the idler pulley bracket bolts slightly (see illustration 11.6a) and turn the adjuster bolt (clockwise to tighten the belt and counter-clockwise to loosen it). Be sure to tighten the bracket bolts after the belt is tensioned. Check the belt tension as described earlier in this Section.

8   If the vehicle is equipped with an air pump, loosen the pivot and adjustment bolts, then move the pump up or down as required to change the belt tension. The air pump has a cast-in lug designed to accept an open end wrench, which can be used as a lever to tension the belt (see illustration). Be sure to tighten the bolts when the belt tension is correct.

Replacement

9   To replace a belt, follow the above procedures for drivebelt adjustment, but slip the belt off the pulleys and remove it. On tensioner equipped models, use a ratchet or breaker bar to lift the tensioner and remove the drivebelt. Since belts tend to wear out more or less at the same time, it is a good idea to replace all of them at the same time. Mark each belt and the corresponding pulley grooves so the replacement belts can be installed properly.

10   Take the old belts with you when purchasing new ones in order to make a direct comparison for length, width and design.

11   When replacing a V-ribbed drivebelt (the wide one used to drive the power steering pump and A/C compressor), make sure that it fits properly into the pulley grooves — it must be completely engaged.

12   Adjust the belts as described earlier in this Section.

12 Battery check and maintenance

Refer to illustrations 12.1, 12.8a, 12.8b, 12.8c and 12.8d

Warning: *Certain precautions must be followed when checking and servicing the battery. Hydrogen gas, which is highly flammable, is always present in the battery cells, so keep lighted tobacco and all other open flames and sparks away from the battery. The electrolyte inside the battery is actually dilute sulfuric acid, which will cause injury if splashed on your skin or in your eyes. It will also ruin clothes and painted surfaces. When removing the battery cables, always detach the negative cable first and hook it up last!*

1   Battery maintenance is an important procedure which will help ensure that you are not stranded because of a dead battery. Several tools are required for this procedure (see illustration).

2   Before servicing the battery, always turn the engine and all accessories off and disconnect the cable from the negative terminal of the battery.

3   A sealed (sometimes called maintenance-free) battery is standard equipment on the Ford Taurus/Mercury Sable. The cell caps cannot be removed, no electrolyte checks are required and water cannot be added to the cells. However, if an aftermarket battery has been installed and it is a type that requires regular maintenance, the following procedure can be used.

4   Check the electrolyte level in each of the battery cells. It must be above the plates. There's usually a split-ring indicator in each cell to indicate the correct level. If the level is low, add distilled water only, then install the cell caps. Caution: *Overfilling the cells may cause electrolyte to spill over during periods of heavy charging, causing corrosion and damage to nearby components.*

5   If the positive terminal and cable clamp on your vehicle's battery is equipped with a rubber protector, make sure that it's not torn or damaged. It should completely cover the terminal.

6   The external condition of the battery should be checked periodically. Look for damage such as a cracked case.

7   Check the tightness of the battery cable clamps to ensure good electrical connections and inspect the entire length of each cable, looking for cracked or abraded insulation and frayed conductors.

8   If corrosion (visible as white, fluffy deposits) is evident, remove the cables from the terminals, clean them with a battery brush and reinstall them (see illustrations). Corrosion can be kept to a minimum

12.8a Battery terminal corrosion usually appears as light, fluffy powder

12.8b Removing a cable from the battery post with a wrench — sometimes special battery pliers are required for this procedure if corrosion has caused deterioration of the nut hex (always remove the ground cable first and hook it up last!)

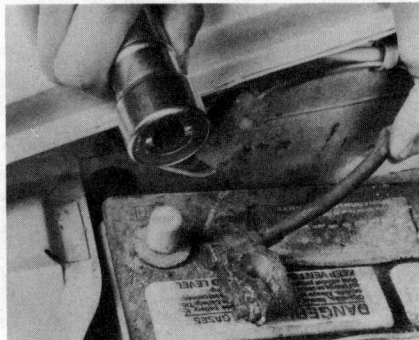

12.8c Regardless of the type of tool used to clean the battery post, a clean, shiny surface should be the result

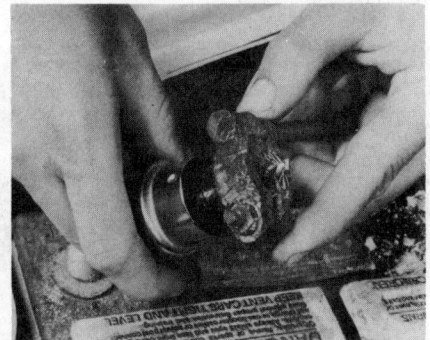

12.8d When cleaning the cable clamps, all corrosion must be removed (the inside of the clamp is tapered to match the taper on the post, so don't remove too much material)

by installing specially treated washers available at auto parts stores or by applying a layer of petroleum jelly or grease to the terminals and cable clamps after they are assembled.

9   Make sure that the battery carrier is in good condition and that the hold-down clamp bolt is tight. If the battery is removed (see Chapter 5 for the removal and installation procedure), make sure that no parts remain in the bottom of the carrier when it's reinstalled. When reinstalling the hold-down clamp, don't overtighten the bolt.

10 Corrosion on the carrier, battery case and surrounding areas can be removed with a solution of water and baking soda. Apply the mixture with a small brush, let it work, then rinse it off with plenty of clean water.

11 Any metal parts of the vehicle damaged by corrosion should be coated with a zinc-based primer, then painted.

12 Additional information on the battery, charging and jump starting can be found in Chapter 5 and at the front of this manual.

13 Windshield wiper blade check and replacement

1   Road film can build up on the wiper blades and affect their efficiency, so they should be washed regularly with a mild detergent solution.

Check

2   The windshield wiper and blade assembly should be inspected periodically. Even if you do not use your wipers, the sun and elements will dry out the rubber portions, causing them to crack and break apart. If inspection reveals hardened or cracked rubber, replace the wiper blades. If inspection reveals nothing unusual, wet the windshield, turn the wipers on, allow them to cycle several times, then shut them off. An uneven wiper pattern across the glass or streaks over clean glass indicate that the blades should be replaced.

3   The operation of the wiper mechanism can loosen the fasteners, so they should be checked and tightened, as necessary, at the same time the wiper blades are checked (see Chapter 12 for further information regarding the wiper mechanism).

Blade assembly replacement

Refer to illustration 13.4

Note: *The blade assembly has a rectangular hole located directly above the wiper arm mounting pin with no apparent provision for release. The hole serves for removal, since the release is internal.*

4   Cycle the wiper assembly to a position on the windshield where removal of the blade assembly can be performed without difficulty. Turn the ignition key off at the desired position. With the blade assembly resting on the windshield, insert a small standard screwdriver into the rectangular hole on top of the blade and push down on the coil spring inside the hole. While pressing down with the screwdriver, pull the wiper blade from the wiper arm pin **(see illustration)**.

5   To install the blade assembly, push it onto the pin until it snaps into place. Be sure that the blade assembly is securely attached to the wiper arm.

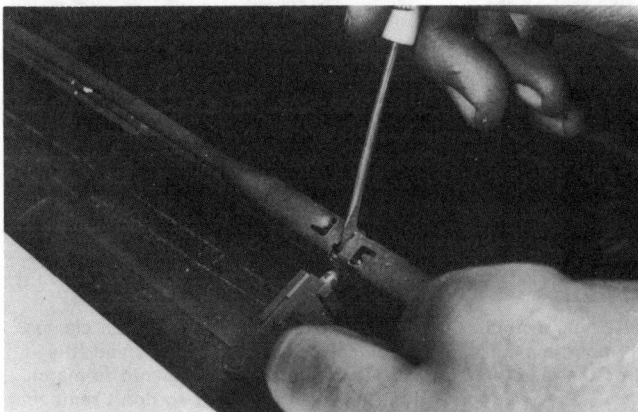

13.6 Pry up on the end of the wiper assembly frame with a coin or screwdriver to disengage the wiper blade element

Blade element replacement

Refer to illustration 13.6

6   At one end of the rubber blade element, insert a standard screwdriver between the blade and the metal backing strip **(see illustration)**. Press down and in, then twist the screwdriver clockwise to release the element from the retaining tab.

7   Slide the blade element out of the remaining tabs until the element is completely detached from the frame.

8   To install the element, slide the metal backing strip into four of the retaining tabs, then twist the backing strip into the fifth (end) tab.

9   Make sure that all the tabs are locked onto the metal backing strip before installing the blade on the wiper arm.

14 Air filter replacement

Refer to illustrations 14.1, 14.2 and 14.3

Warning: *The electric cooling fan on these models can activate at any time, even when the ignition is in the Off position. Disconnect the fan motor or negative battery cable when working in the vicinity of the fan.*

Note: *The air filter element cannot be cleaned. If inspection reveals that the element is dirty, install a new one.*

1   Disconnect the crankcase ventilation hose from the air cleaner housing cover **(see illustration)**.

13.4 Press down with a screwdriver blade, as shown, to release the wiper blade assembly from the arm

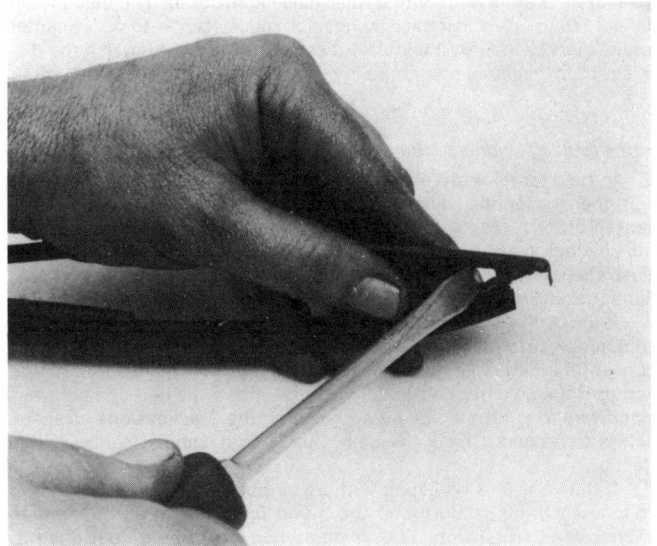

14.1 Pull the crankcase ventilation hose (arrow) off the fitting on the air cleaner housing

14.2 Reach behind the housing to release the two retaining clips (arrows)

14.3 Note the direction the filter creases face during removal so the new one will be installed in the same direction

2   Release the two air cleaner housing cover clips and lift the cover off **(see illustration)**.
3   Remove the filter element. Note that the creases in the paper element are facing down **(see illustration)**. The new element must be installed the same way or it won't fit.
4   Check the inner sealing surface of the cover for evidence of leakage past the air cleaner element. Place a light on the inside (clean side) of the filter and look through the filter at the light. If the light cannot be seen or if there are holes in the element, no matter how small, replace it with a new one.
5   Clean the inner sealing surface between the air cleaner housing and cover.
6   Before installing the new air filter element, check it for deformed seals and holes in the paper. If the element is marked *TOP* be sure the marked side faces up. The paper creases must face down.
7   Position the cover on the housing and make sure it is seated all the way around, then install the cover clips.
8   Reconnect the duct and tighten the hose clamp securely.

15 PCV valve and crankcase ventilation filter check

Warning: *The electric cooling fan on these models can activate at any time, even when the ignition is in the Off position. Disconnect the fan motor or negative battery cable when working in the vicinity of the fan.*
Note: *To maintain efficient operation of the PCV system, clean the hoses and check the PCV valve and crankcase ventilation filter at the intervals recommended in the maintenance schedule. For additional information on the PCV system, refer to Chapter 6.*

PCV valve
Refer to illustration 15.2

1   Locate the PCV valve on the rocker arm cover.
2   To check the valve, first pull it out of the rocker arm cover **(see illustration)** and shake it — if it rattles, reinstall it in the cover.
3   Start the engine and allow it to idle, then disconnect the PCV hose from the air cleaner housing and feel for vacuum at the hose. If vacuum is felt, the PCV valve/system is working properly.
4   If no vacuum is felt, the oil filler cap, hoses or rocker arm cover gasket may be leaking or the PCV valve may be bad. Check for vacuum leaks at the valve, filler cap, filter assembly (if used) and all hoses.
5   Pull straight up on the valve to remove it. Check the rubber grommet in the rocker arm cover for cracks and distortion. If it's damaged, replace it.
6   If the valve is clogged with deposits, remove and check the PCV system filter. On some vehicles, the filter is integral with the oil filler cap — if your vehicle is equipped with an integral type PCV filter, a plastic hose is connected between the cap and the air cleaner housing. On other vehicles, the filter assembly is in a separate housing. Again, check the rubber grommet between the PCV filter and the rocker arm

cover for cracks and distortion. Replace it if it's damaged.
7   If the valve is clogged, the hoses are also probably plugged. Remove the hose between the valve and the intake manifold and the hose between the filter and the air cleaner housing and clean them with solvent.
8   After cleaning the hoses, inspect them for damage, wear and deterioration. Make sure the hoses fit snugly on the fittings.
9   If necessary, install a new PCV valve. **Note:** *The elbow is not part of the PCV valve. A new valve will not include the elbow. The original must be transferred to the new valve. If a new elbow is purchased, it may be necessary to soak it in warm water for up to an hour to slip it onto the new valve. Do not attempt to force the elbow onto the valve or it will break.*
10   Install the clean PCV system hoses. Make sure that the PCV valve and hoses are secure.

Crankcase ventilation filter
Refer to illustration 15.12

11   The crankcase ventilation system screens the oily fumes from the crankcase before they are drawn into the air cleaner and burned in the engine. Some models are equipped with a crankcase ventilation filter system consisting of a filter located in the rocker arm cover and connected by a hose or hoses to the air cleaner housing. Other models are equipped with only a hose between the rocker arm cover and the air cleaner. The filter and hose should be checked and cleaned if necessary at the specified intervals.

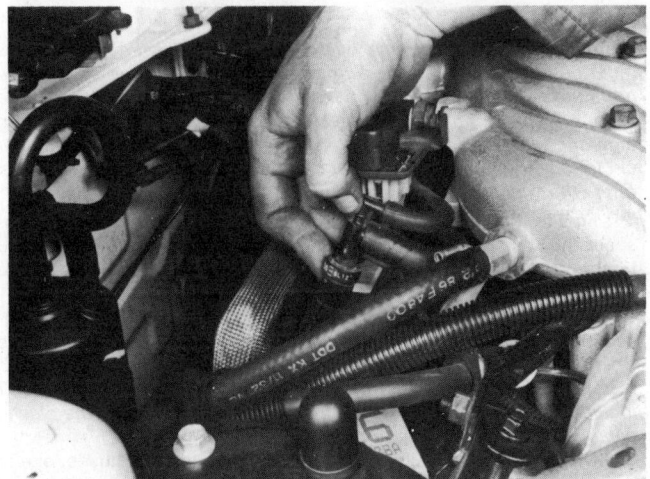

15.2 Pull the PCV valve out and shake it — a rattling sound indicates it is not clogged

12 Remove the filter (if equipped) and hose from the engine (see illustration).

13 Wash the filter in mineral spirits or solvent and inspect it for a buildup of oily residue. If the filter is clogged, replace it with a new one.

14 Soak the hose in mineral spirits or solvent and clean it by passing a long brush or cloth attached to a long wire through it.

15 Allow the filter and hose to air dry, then reinstall them on the engine.

16   Fuel system check

Warning: *Certain precautions should be observed when inspecting or servicing the fuel system components. Work in a well ventilated area and do not allow open flames (cigarettes, appliance pilot lights, etc.) near the work area. Mop up spills immediately. Do not store fuel soaked rags where they could ignite. It is a good idea to keep a dry chemical (Class B) fire extinguisher near the work area any time the fuel system is being serviced.*

1   If you smell gasoline while driving or after the vehicle has been sitting in the sun, inspect the fuel system immediately.

2   Remove the gas filler cap and inspect if for damage and corrosion. The gasket should have an unbroken sealing imprint. If the gasket is damaged or corroded, install a new cap.

3   Inspect the fuel feed and return lines for cracks. Make sure that the connections between the fuel lines and fuel injection system and between the fuel lines and the in-line fuel filter are tight. **Warning:** *You must relieve fuel system pressure before servicing fuel system components. The fuel system pressure relief procedure is outlined in Chapter 4.*

4   Since some components of the fuel system — the fuel tank and part of the fuel feed and return lines, for example — are underneath the vehicle, they can be inspected more easily with the vehicle raised on a hoist. If a hoist is unavailable, raise the vehicle and support it on jackstands.

5   With the vehicle raised and safely supported, inspect the gas tank and filler neck for punctures, cracks and other damage. The connection between the filler neck and the tank is particularly critical. Sometimes a rubber filler neck will leak because of loose clamps or deteriorated rubber. Inspect all fuel tank mounting brackets and straps to be sure that the tank is securely attached to the vehicle. **Warning:** *Do not, under any circumstances, try to repair a fuel tank (except rubber components). A welding torch or any open flame can easily cause fuel vapors inside the tank to explode.*

6   Carefully check all rubber hoses and metal lines leading away from the fuel tank. Check for loose connections, deteriorated hoses, crimped lines and other damage. Repair or replace damaged sections as necessary (Chapter 4).

17   Fuel filter replacement

Refer to illustration 17.2

Warning: *Gasoline is extremely flammable, so extra safety precautions must be observed when working on any part of the fuel system. Do not smoke and do not allow open flames or bare light bulbs near the vehicle. Also, do not perform fuel system maintenance procedures in a garage where a natural gas type appliance, such as a water heater or clothes dryer, with a pilot light is present. Before removing the fuel filter, the fuel system pressure must be relieved. See Chapter 4.*

1   Locate the fuel filter on the right frame rail, near the fuel tank. Inspect the hose fittings at both ends of the filter to see if they're clean. If more than a light coating of dust is present, clean the fittings before proceeding.

2   Removal of the hairpin clip from each fitting is a two-stage procedure. First spread the two clip legs apart about 1/8-inch to disengage them, then push in on them. Pull on the other end of the clip to detach it from the fitting (see illustration). **Caution:** *If the new filter doesn't include new clips, don't use any tools or you may damage the plastic clips, which will have to be reused.*

3   Once both hairpin clips are released, grasp the fuel hoses, one at a time, and pull them straight off the filter.

4   After the hoses have been detached, check the clips for damage and distortion. If they were damaged in any way during removal, new

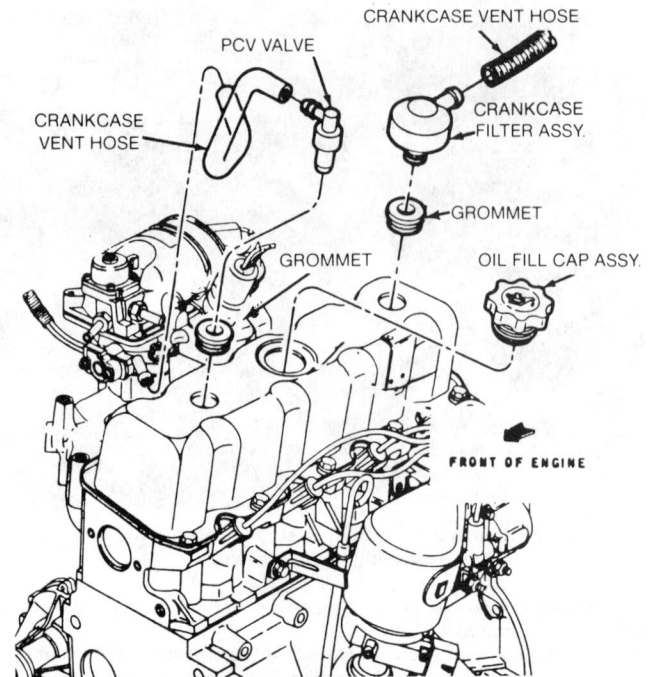

15.12 Some models have a crankcase ventilation hose (and on some models, a filter) assembly such as this one which should be cleaned with solvent when the PCV valve is checked

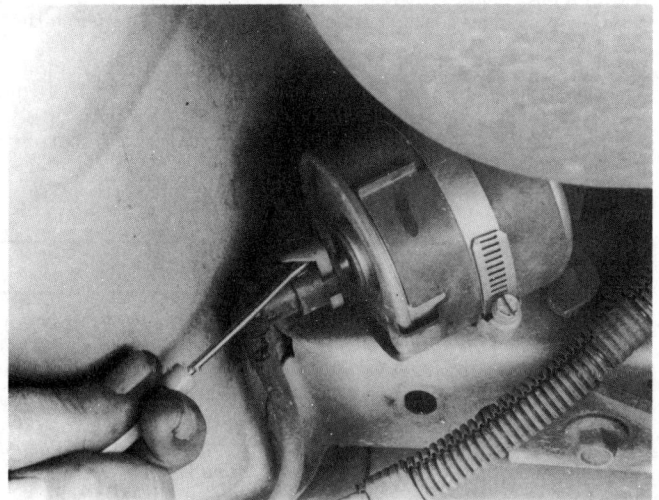

17.2 A small screwdriver can be used to disconnect the fuel lines, but be careful not to damage the clips if they are to be reused (most filters come with replacement clips)

ones must be used when the hoses are reattached to the new filter (if new clips are packaged with the filter, be sure to use them in place of the originals).

5   Note which way the arrow on the filter is pointing — the new filter must be installed the same way. Loosen the clamp screw and detach the filter from the bracket.

6   Install the new filter in the bracket with the arrow pointing in the right direction. Tighten the clamp screw securely.

7   Carefully push each hose onto the filter until it's seated against the collar on the fitting, then install the hairpin clips. The triangular shaped side of each clip must point away from the filter. Make sure the clips are securely attached to the hose fittings. — if they come off, the hoses could back off the filter and a fire could result!

8   Start the engine and check for fuel leaks.

ALWAYS CHECK hose for chafed or burned areas that may cause an untimely and costly failure.

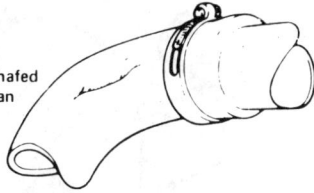

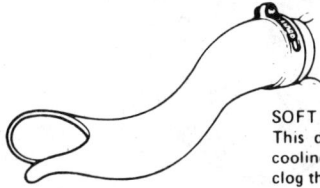

SOFT hose indicates inside deterioration. This deterioration can contaminate the cooling system and cause particles to clog the radiator.

HARDENED hose can fail at any time. Tightening hose clamps will not seal the connection or stop leaks.

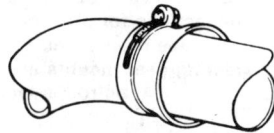

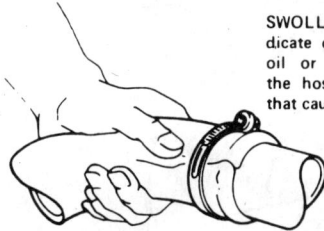

SWOLLEN hose or oil soaked ends indicate danger and possible failure from oil or grease contamination. Squeeze the hose to locate cracks and breaks that cause leaks.

18.4 Hoses, like drivebelts, have a habit of failing at the worst possible time — to prevent the inconvenience of a blown radiator or heater hose, inspect them carefully, as shown here

18 Cooling system check

Refer to illustration 18.4

Warning: *The electric cooling fan on these models can activate at any time, even when the ignition is in the Off position. Disconnect the fan motor or negative battery cable when working in the vicinity of the fan.*

1 Many major engine failures can be attributed to a faulty cooling system. If the vehicle is equipped with an automatic transaxle, the cooling system also plays an important role in prolonging transaxle life because it cools the transmission fluid.
2 The engine should be cold for the cooling system check, so perform the following procedure before the vehicle is driven for the day or after it has been shut off for at least three hours.
3 Remove the radiator cap and clean it thoroughly, inside and out, with clean water. Also clean the filler neck on the radiator. The presence of rust or corrosion in the filler neck means the coolant should be changed (Section 28). The coolant inside the radiator should be relatively clean and transparent. If it's rust colored, drain the system and refill it with new coolant.
4 Carefully check the radiator hoses and the smaller diameter heater hoses **(see illustration)**. Inspect each coolant hose along its entire length, replacing any hose which is cracked, swollen or deteriorated. Cracks will show up better if the hose is squeezed. Pay close attention to hose clamps that secure the hoses to cooling system components. Hose clamps can pinch and puncture hoses, resulting in coolant leaks.
5 Make sure that all hose connections are tight. A leak in the cooling system will usually show up as white or rust colored deposits on the area adjoining the leak. If wire-type clamps are used on the hoses, it may be a good idea to replace them with screw-type clamps.
6 Clean the front of the radiator and air conditioning condenser with compressed air, if available, or a soft brush. Remove all bugs, leaves, etc. embedded in the radiator fins. Be extremely careful not to damage the cooling fins or cut your fingers on them.

7 If the coolant level has been dropping consistently and no leaks are detectable, have the radiator cap and cooling system pressure checked at a service station.

19 Exhaust system check

1 With the engine cold (at least three hours after the vehicle has been driven), check the complete exhaust system from the engine to the end of the tailpipe. Ideally, the inspection should be done with the vehicle on a hoist to permit unrestricted access. If a hoist is not available, raise the vehicle and support it securely on jackstands.
2 Check the exhaust pipes and connections for evidence of leaks, severe corrosion and damage. Make sure that all brackets and hangers are in good condition and tight.
3 At the same time, inspect the underside of the body for holes, corrosion, open seams, etc. which may allow exhaust gases to enter the passenger compartment. Seal all body openings with silicone or body putty.
4 Rattles and other noises can often be traced to the exhaust system, especially the mounts and hangers. Try to move the pipes, muffler and catalytic converter. If the components can come in contact with the body or suspension parts, secure the exhaust system with new mounts.
5 Check the running condition of the engine by inspecting inside the end of the tailpipe. The exhaust deposits here are an indication of engine state-of-tune. If the pipe is black and sooty or coated with white deposits, the engine is in need of a tune-up, including a thorough fuel system inspection and adjustment.

20 Tire rotation

Refer to illustration 20.2

1 The tires should be rotated at the specified intervals and whenever uneven wear is noticed. Since the vehicle will be raised and the tires removed anyway, check the brakes also (Section 22).
2 Radial tires must be rotated in a specific pattern **(see illustration)**.

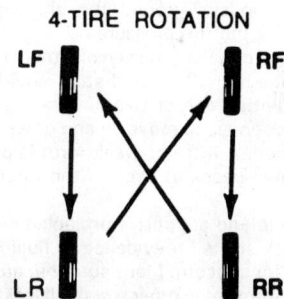

4-TIRE ROTATION

LF   RF

LR   RR

20.2 The recommended tire rotation pattern for radial tire equipped models

3 Refer to the information in *Jacking and towing* at the front of this manual for the proper procedure to follow when raising the vehicle and changing a tire. If the brakes are to be checked, do not apply the parking brake, as stated.
4 The vehicle must be raised on a hoist or supported on jackstands to get all four wheels off the ground. Make sure the vehicle is safely supported!
5 After the rotation procedure is finished, check and adjust the tire pressures as necessary and be sure to check the lug nut tightness.

21 Steering and suspension check

Note: *The steering linkage and suspension components should be checked periodically. Worn or damaged suspension and steering linkage components can result in excessive and abnormal tire wear, poor ride quality and vehicle handling and reduced fuel economy. For detailed illustrations of the steering and suspension components, refer to Chapter 10.*

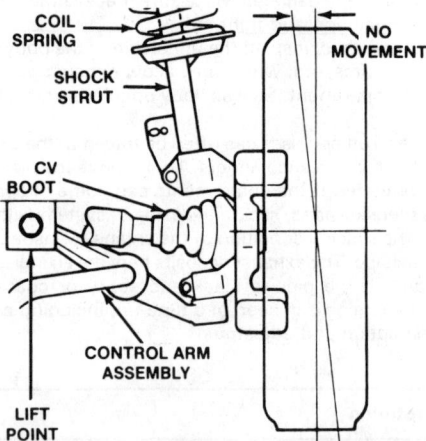

21.10   To check the suspension balljoints, try to move the lower edge of each front tire/wheel in and out while watching/feeling for movement at the top of the tire and balljoints

21.11   To check the steering gear mounts and tie-rod connections for play, grasp each front tire like this and try to move it back and forth — if play is noted, check the steering gear mounts and make sure they're tight; if either tie-rod is worn or bent, replace it

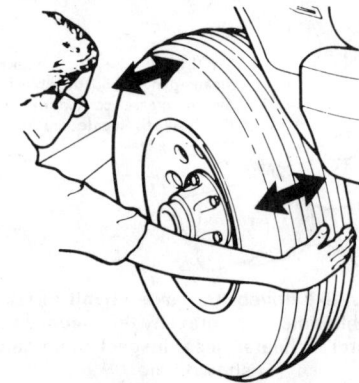

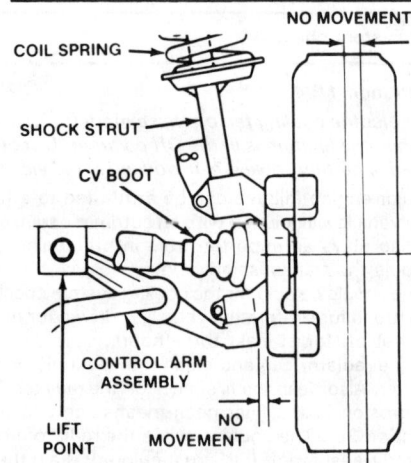

21.12   To check the wheel bearings, try to move the tire in and out — if any play is noted, or if the bearings feel rough or sound noisy when the tire is rotated, replace the wheel bearings

Strut check

1   Park the vehicle on level ground, turn the engine off and set the parking brake. Check the tire pressures.
2   Push down at one corner of the vehicle, then release it while noting the movement of the body. It should stop moving and come to rest in a level position within one or two bounces.
3   If the vehicle continues to move up and down or if it fails to return to its original position, a worn or weak strut is probably the reason.
4   Repeat the above check at each of the three remaining corners of the vehicle.
5   Raise the vehicle and support it on jackstands.
6   Check the shock struts for evidence of fluid leakage. A light film of fluid is no cause for concern. Make sure that any fluid noted is from the shocks and not from some other source. If leakage is noted, replace the struts as a set.
7   Check the struts to be sure that they are securely mounted and undamaged. Check the upper mounts for damage and wear. If damage or wear is noted, replace the struts as a set.
8   If struts must be replaced, refer to Chapter 10 for the procedure.

Steering and suspension check

Refer to illustrations 21.10 and 21.11

9   Visually inspect the steering system components for damage and distortion. Look for leaks and damaged seals, boots and fittings.
10   Wipe the lower end of the steering knuckle and control arm. Have an assistant grasp the lower edge of the tire and move the wheel in and out **(see illustration)** while you look for movement at the steering knuckle-to-control arm joint. If there is any movement, the suspension balljoint must be replaced.
11   Grasp each front tire at the front and rear edges, push in at the rear, pull out at the front and feel for play in the steering system components **(see illustration)**. If any free play is noted, check the steering gear mounts and the tie-rod balljoints for looseness. If the steering gear mounts are loose, tighten them. If the tie-rods are loose, the balljoints may be worn (check to make sure the nuts are tight). Additional steering and suspension system information and illustrations can be found in Chapter 10.

Front wheel bearing check

Refer to illustration 21.12

Note: *The front wheel bearings are a "cartridge" design and are permanently lubricated and sealed at the factory. They require no scheduled maintenance or adjustment. They can, however, be checked for excessive play. If the following check indicates that either of the front bearings is faulty, replace both bearings.*

12   Grasp each front tire at the front and rear edges, then push in and out on the wheel and feel for play **(see illustration)**. There should be

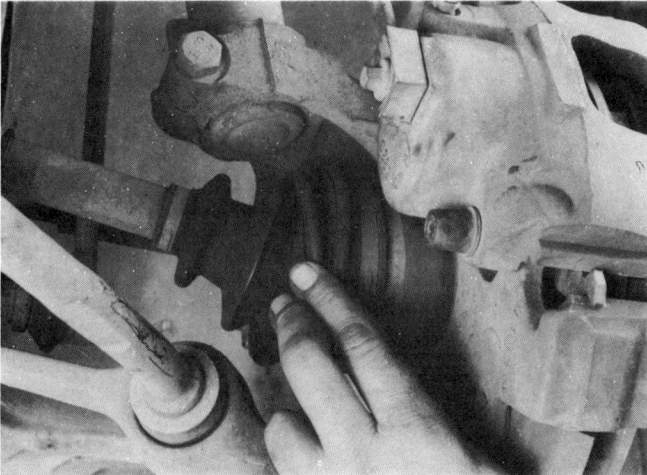

21.14 Flex the driveaxle boots by hand to check for cracks and leaking grease

22.11 The front disc brake pad material thickness can be checked through the caliper inspection hole

no noticeable movement. Turn the wheel and listen for noise from the bearings. If any of these conditions are noted, refer to Chapter 10 for the bearing replacement procedure.

Driveaxle Constant Velocity (CV) joint boot check
Refer to illustration 21.14

13 If the driveaxle rubber boots are damaged or deteriorated, serious and costly damage can occur to the CV joints.
14 It is very important that the boots be kept clean, so wipe them off before inspection. Check the four boots (two on each driveaxle) for cracks, tears, holes, deteriorated rubber and loose or missing clamps. Pushing on the boot surface can reveal cracks not ordinarilly visible **(see illustration)**.
15 If damage or deterioration is evident, check the CV joints for damage (Chapter 8) and replace the boot(s) with new ones.

22 Brake check

Note: *In addition to the specified intervals, the brake system should be inspected each time the wheels are removed or a malfunction is indicated. Because of the obvious safety considerations, the following brake system checks are some of the most important maintenance procedures you can perform on your vehicle.*

Symptoms of brake system problems

1 The disc brake pads have built-in wear indicators which should make a high pitched squealing or scraping noise when they are worn to the replacement point. When you hear this noise, replace the pads immediately or expensive damage to the rotors could result.
2 Any of the following symptoms could indicate a potential brake system defect. The vehicle pulls to one side when the brake pedal is depressed, the brakes make squealing or dragging noises when applied, brake pedal travel is excessive, the pedal pulsates and brake fluid leaks are noted (usually on the inner side of the tire or wheel). If any of these conditions are noted, inspect the brake system immediately.

Brake lines and hoses

Note: *Steel tubing is used throughout the brake system, with the exception of flexible, reinforced hoses at the front wheels and as connectors at the rear axle. Periodic inspection of these lines is very important.*

3 Park the vehicle on level ground and turn the engine off.
4 Remove the wheel covers. Loosen, but do not remove, the lug nuts on all four wheels.
5 Raise the vehicle and support it securely on jackstands.
6 Remove the wheels (see *Jacking and towing* at the front of this book, or refer to your owner's manual, if necessary).
7 Check all brake hoses and lines for cracks, chafing of the outer

cover, leaks, blisters and distortion. Check all threaded fittings for leaks and make sure the brake hose mounting bolts and clips are secure.
8 If leaks or damage are discovered, they must be fixed immediately. Refer to Chapter 9 for detailed information on brake system repair procedures.

Front disc brakes
Refer to illustration 22.11

9 If it hasn't already been done, raise the front of the vehicle and support it securely on jackstands. Apply the parking brake and remove the front wheels.
10 The disc brake calipers, which contain the pads, are now visible. Each caliper has an outer and an inner pad — all pads should be checked.
11 Note the pad thickness by looking through the inspection hole in the caliper **(see illustration)**. If the lining material is 1/8-inch thick or less, or if it is tapered from end to end, the pads should be replaced (see Chapter 9). Keep in mind that the lining material is riveted or bonded to a metal plate or shoe — the metal portion is not included in this measurement.
12 Check the condition of the brake disc. Look for score marks, deep scratches and overheated areas (they will appear blue or discolored). If damage or wear is noted, the disc can be removed and resurfaced by an automotive machine shop or replaced with a new one. Refer to Chapter 9 for more detailed inspection and repair procedures.

Rear drum brakes
Refer to illustrations 22.13 and 22.16

13 A check of the brake lining thickness can be made after prying out the rubber inspection hole cover **(see illustration)**. A complete brake inspection requires removal of the brake drums as described below.

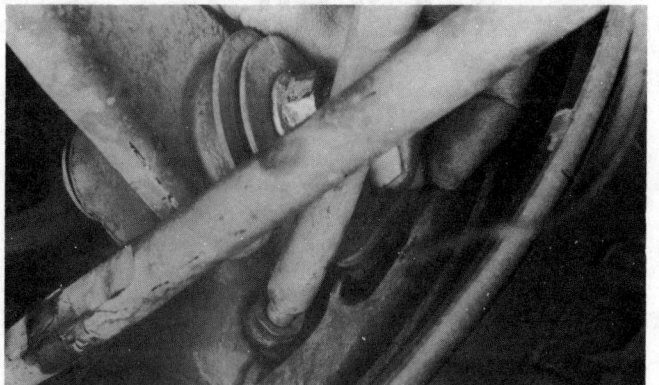

22.13 Pry out the rubber cover in the backing plate and use a flashlight to check the rear brake shoe lining thickness

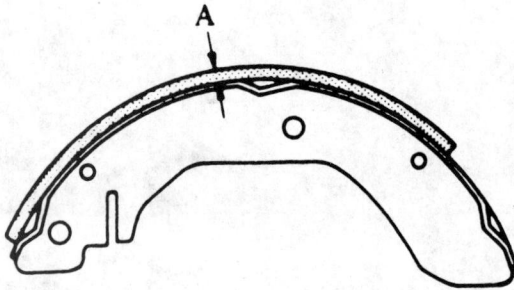

22.16   The rear brake shoe lining thickness (A) is measured from the outer surface of the lining to the metal shoe

14 Refer to Chapter 9 and remove the rear brake drums.
15 **Warning:** *Brake dust produced by lining wear and deposited on brake components contains asbestos, which is hazardous to your health. DO NOT blow it out with compressed air and DO NOT inhale it! DO NOT use gasoline or solvents to remove the dust. Brake system cleaner should be used to flush the dust into a drain pan. After the brake components are wiped clean with a damp rag, dispose of the contaminated rag(s) and solvent in a covered and labelled container. Try to use non-asbestos replacement parts whenever possible.*
16 Note the thickness of the lining material on the rear brake shoes (**see illustration**) and look for signs of contamination by brake fluid and grease. If the lining material is within 1/16-inch of the recessed rivets or metal shoes, replace the brake shoes with new ones. The shoes should also be replaced if they are cracked, glazed (shiny lining surfaces) or contaminated with brake fluid or grease. See Chapter 9 for the replacement procedure.
17 Check the shoe return and hold-down springs and the adjusting mechanism to make sure they are installed correctly and in good condition. Deteriorated or distorted springs, if not replaced, could allow the linings to drag and wear prematurely.
18 Check the wheel cylinders for leakage by carefully peeling back the rubber boots. If brake fluid is noted behind the boots, the wheel cylinders must be replaced (see Chapter 9).

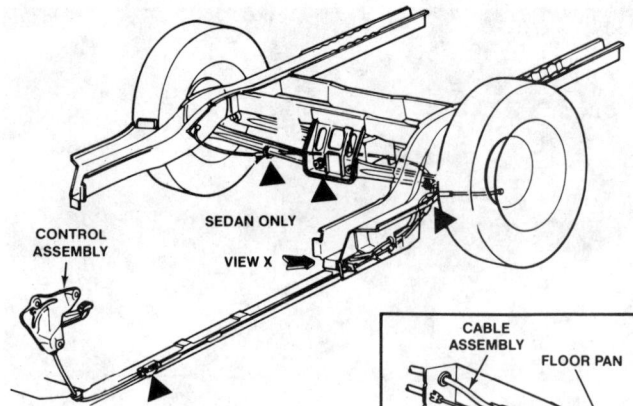

CONTROL ASSEMBLY
SEDAN ONLY
VIEW X

▲ LUBRICATON POINTS

*SHOWN FOR REFERENCE, REMOVAL NOT REQUIRED

CABLE ASSEMBLY
FLOOR PAN
CABLE ADJUSTER BRACKET
*NUT ADJUSTER
VIEW X

WAGON ONLY

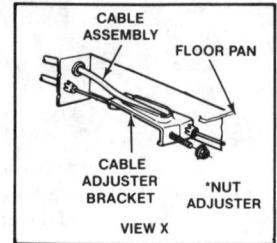

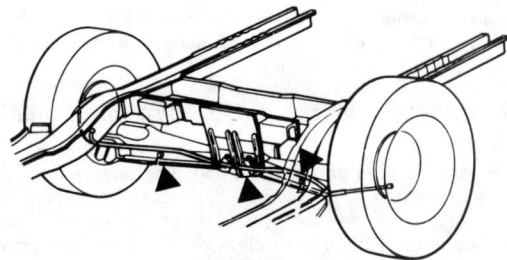

22.23   Lubricate the parking brake cable linkage, adjuster assembly, connectors and the areas of the parking brake cable that come in contact with the other parts of the vehicle, as shown

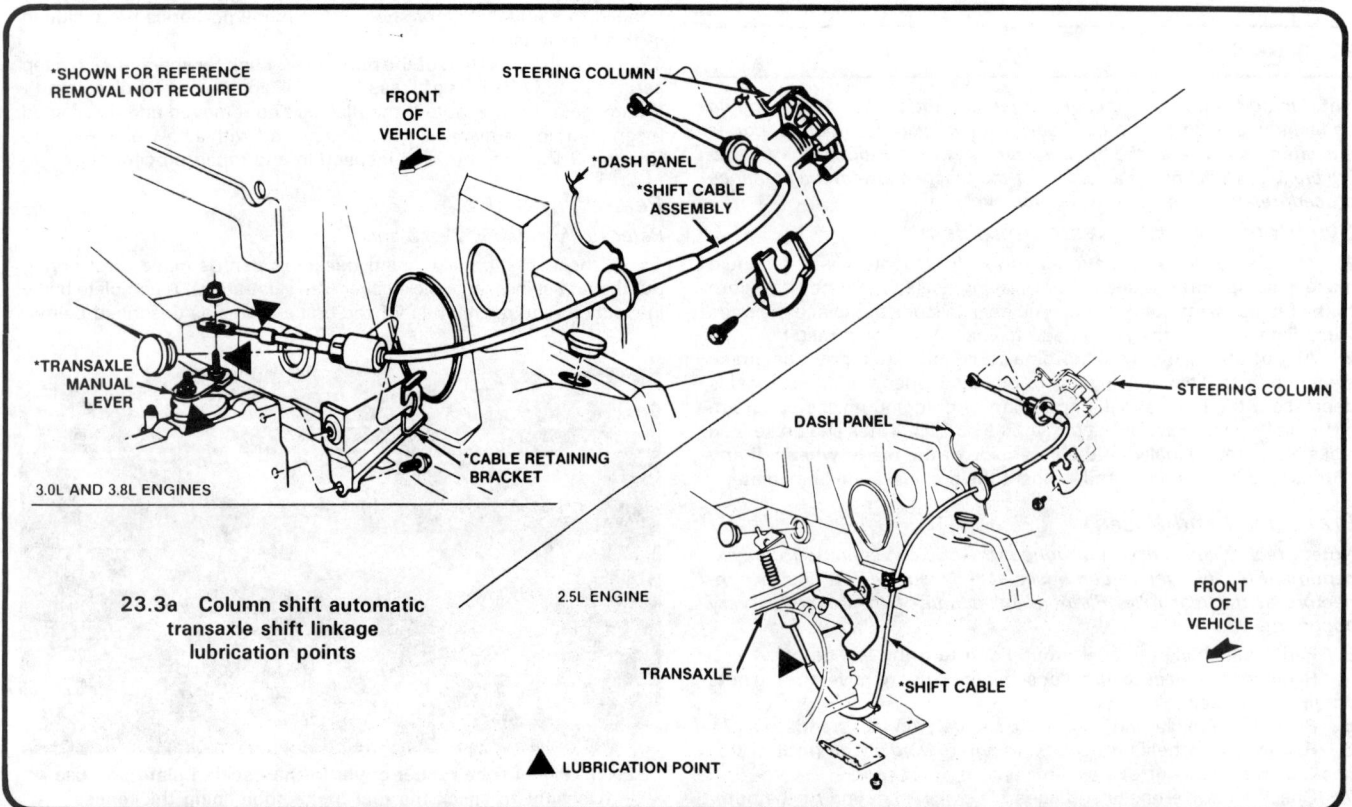

*SHOWN FOR REFERENCE REMOVAL NOT REQUIRED
FRONT OF VEHICLE
STEERING COLUMN
*DASH PANEL
*SHIFT CABLE ASSEMBLY
*TRANSAXLE MANUAL LEVER
*CABLE RETAINING BRACKET
3.0L AND 3.8L ENGINES

23.3a   Column shift automatic transaxle shift linkage lubrication points

2.5L ENGINE
STEERING COLUMN
DASH PANEL
FRONT OF VEHICLE
TRANSAXLE
*SHIFT CABLE

▲ LUBRICATION POINT

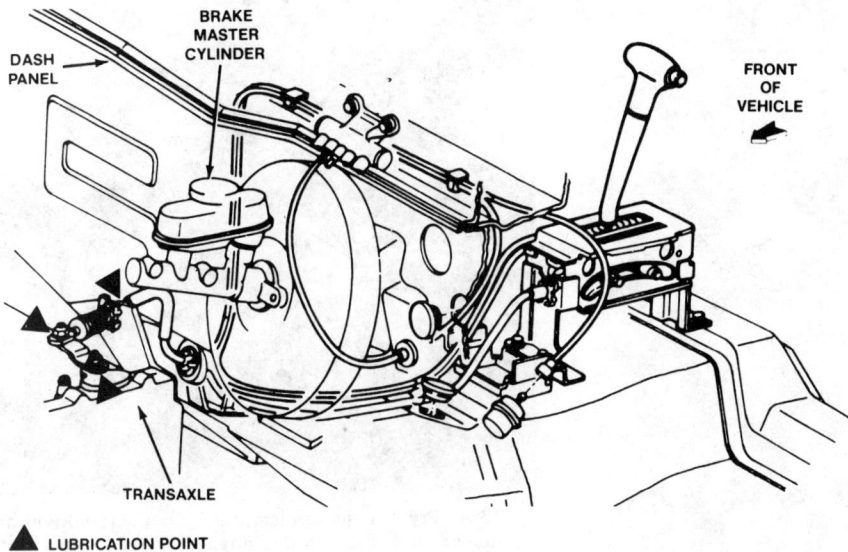

23.3b Floor shift automatic transaxle shift linkage lubrication points

▲ LUBRICATION POINT

19 Check the drums for cracks, score marks, deep scratches and hard spots, which will appear as small discolored areas. If imperfections cannot be removed with emery cloth, the drums must be resurfaced by an automotive machine shop (see Chapter 9 for more detailed information).
20 Refer to Chapter 9 and install the brake drums.
21 Install the wheels, but do not lower the vehicle yet.

Parking brake

Refer to illustration 22.23

Note: *The parking brake cable and linkage should be periodically checked and lubricated. This maintenance procedure helps prevent the parking brake cable adjuster or the linkage from binding and adversely affecting the operation or adjustment of the parking brake.*

Lubrication
22 Set the parking brake.
23 Apply multi-purpose grease to the parking brake linkage, adjuster assembly, connectors and the areas of the parking brake cable that come in contact with the other parts of the vehicle **(see illustration)**.
24 Release the parking brake and repeat the lubrication procedure.
25 Remove the jackstands and lower the vehicle.
26 Tighten the wheel lug nuts to the specified torque and install the wheel covers.

Check
27 The easiest, and perhaps most obvious, method of checking the parking brake is to park the vehicle on a steep hill with the parking brake set and the transaxle in Neutral. If the parking brake cannot prevent the vehicle from rolling, refer to Chapter 9 and adjust it.

23 Automatic transaxle control linkage lubrication

Refer to illustrations 23.3a and 23.3b
1 Open the hood and locate the shift cable running up the backside of the transaxle on the left side.
2 Clean the linkage and pivot points at the upper end of the cable.
3 Lubricate the shift linkage and pivot points with multi-purpose grease **(see illustrations)**.

24 Manual transaxle lubricant level check

Refer to illustration 24.1
Note: *The transaxle lubricant level and quality should not deteriorate under normal driving conditions. However, it is recommended that you check the level occasionally. The most convenient time would be when your vehicle is raised for another reason, such as an engine oil change.*

1 The transaxle has an inspection and filler plug which must be removed to check the lubricant level **(see illustration)**. If the vehicle is raised to gain access to the plug, be sure to support it safely on jackstands — do not crawl under a vehicle which is supported only by a jack!
2 Remove the plug from the transaxle and use your little finger to reach inside the housing and feel the lubricant level. It should be at or very near the bottom of the plug hole.
3 If it isn't, add the recommended lubricant through the plug hole with a syringe or squeeze bottle.
4 Install and tighten the plug securely and check for leaks after the first few miles of driving.

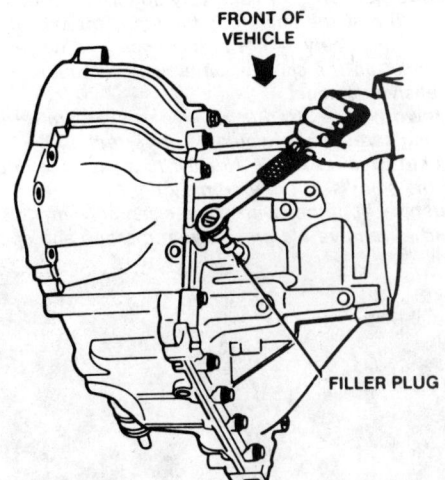

24.1 The manual transaxle filler plug is located on the side of the case — remove it with a socket and ratchet

25 Rear wheel bearing check and repack

Refer to illustrations 25.1, 25.3, 25.7, 25.9, 25.10a, 25.10b, 25.11a and 25.11b

Warning: *Dust created by the brake system contains asbestos, which is harmful to your health. Never blow it out with compressed air and don't inhale any of it. Do not, under any circumstances, use petroleum-based solvents to clean brake parts. Use brake cleaner or denatured alcohol only.*

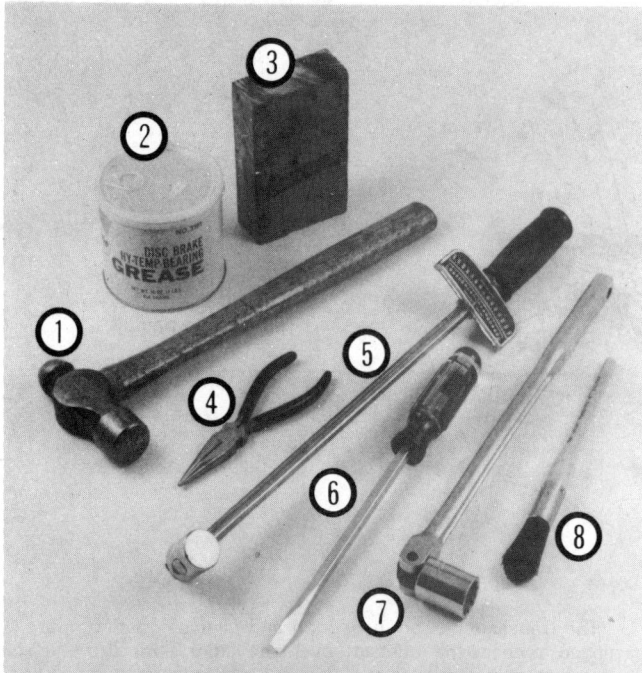

25.1 **Tools and materials needed for rear wheel bearing maintenance**

1 **Hammer** — *A common hammer will do just fine*
2 **Grease** — *High-temperature grease which is formulated specially for wheel bearings should be used*
3 **Wood block** — *If you have a scrap piece of 2x4, it can be used to drive the new seal into the hub*
4 **Needle-nose pliers** — *Used to straighten and remove the cotter pin in the spindle*
5 **Torque wrench** — *This is very important in this procedure; if the bearing is too tight, the wheel won't turn freely — if it is too loose, the wheel will 'wobble' on the spindle. Either way, it could mean extensive damage*
6 **Screwdriver** — *Used to remove the seal from the hub (a long screwdriver would be preferred)*
7 **Socket/breaker bar** — *Needed to loosen the nut on the spindle if it is extremely tight*
8 **Brush** — *Together with some clean solvent, this will be used to remove old grease from the hub and spindle*

25.3 **Pry out the grease seal with a screwdriver or special hooked tool, such as this one, available at auto parts stores**

1   Several tools and related materials are required for the following procedure (**see illustration**). Be sure to have them on hand before beginning. Remove the rear brake drum/hub assembly (Chapter 9).
2   Check the bearings for proper lubrication and signs that the grease has been contaminated by dirt or water (it will have a gritty feel or a milky-white appearance).
3   Use a screwdriver or seal removal tool to pry the grease seal out of the hub (discard the seal) (**see illustration**).
4   Clean the bearings with solvent and dry them with compressed air.
5   Check the bearings for wear, pitting and scoring of the rollers and cage. Light discoloration of the bearing surfaces is normal, but if the surfaces are badly worn or damaged, replace the bearings with new ones.
6   Clean the hub with solvent and remove the old grease from the hub cavity.
7   Inspect the bearing races for wear, signs of overheating, pitting and corrosion. If the races are worn or damaged, drive them out with a hammer and punch (**see illustration**).
8   Drive the new races in with a section of pipe and a hammer, but be very careful not to damage them or get them cocked in the bore.
9   Pack the bearings with high-temperature, multi-purpose EP grease prior to installation. Work generous amounts of grease in from the back of the cage so the grease is forced up through the rollers (**see illustration**).

25.7 **The bearing races can be driven out with a hammer and punch (work carefully and don't damage the hub)**

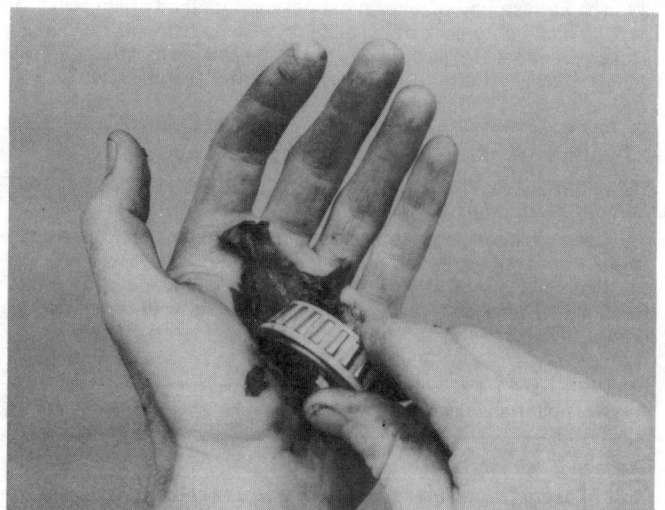

25.9 **Pack the wheel bearing by working the grease into the rollers from the back side**

25.10a Put a small amount of grease into the hub cavity . . .

25.10b . . . and on the spindle

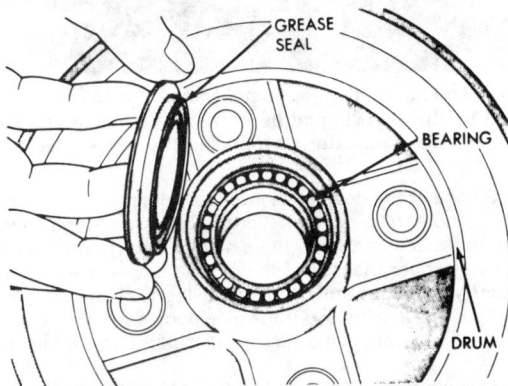

25.11a Make sure the bearing is in place in the hub . . .

25.11b . . . then tap the seal into place with a hammer and block of wood

10 Add a small amount of grease to the hub cavity and to the center of the spindle (see illustrations).
11 Lubricate the outer edge of the new grease seal, insert the bearing and press the seal into position with the lip facing in (see illustration). Make sure the seal is seated completely in the hub by tapping it evenly into place using a hammer and block of wood (see illustration). Apply grease to the seal cavity and lip and the polished sections of the spindle.
12 Install the hub and drum assembly as described in Chapter 9.

26 Spark plug replacement

Refer to illustrations 26.2, 26.5a, 26.5b, 26.6 and 26.10
Warning: *The electric cooling fan on these models can activate at any time, even when the ignition is in the Off position. Disconnect the fan motor or negative battery cable when working in the vicinity of the fan.*

1 The spark plugs are located on the front (radiator) side of the engine on four-cylinder models and on both sides on V6 models.
2 In most cases, the tools necessary for spark plug replacement include a spark plug socket which fits onto a ratchet (spark plug sockets are padded inside to prevent damage to the porcelain insulators on the new plugs), various extensions and a gap gauge to check and adjust the gaps on the new plugs (see illustration). A special plug wire removal tool is available for separating the wire boots from the spark plugs, but it isn't absolutely necessary. A torque wrench should be used to tighten the new plugs.
3 The best approach when replacing the spark plugs is to purchase the new ones in advance, adjust them to the proper gap and replace the plugs one at a time. When buying the new spark plugs, be sure to obtain the correct plug type for your particular engine. This infor-

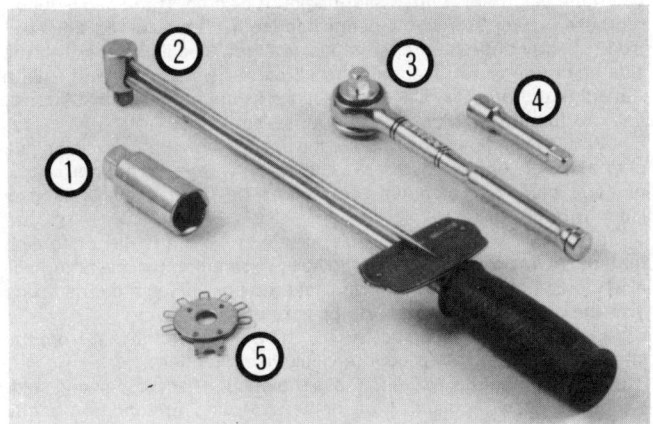

26.2 Tools required for changing spark plugs

1 **Spark plug socket** — *This will have special padding inside to protect the spark plug porcelain insulator*
2 **Torque wrench** — *Although not mandatory, use of this tool is the best way to ensure that the plugs are tightened properly*
3 **Ratchet** — *Standard hand tool to fit the plug socket*
4 **Extension** — *Depending on model and accessories, you may need special extensions and universal joints to reach one or more of the plugs*
5 **Spark plug gap gauge** — *This gauge for checking the gap comes in a variety of styles. Make sure the gap for your engine is included*

26.5a   Spark plug manufacturers recommend using a wire-type gauge when checking the gap — if the wire does not slide between the electrodes with a slight drag, adjustment is required

26.5b   To change the gap, bend the *side* electrode only, as indicated by the arrows, and be very careful not to crack or chip the porcelain insulator surrounding the center electrode

mation can be found on the *Emission Control Information label* located under the hood and in the factory owner's manual. If differences exist between the plug specified on the emissions label and in the owner's manual, assume that the emissions label is correct.

4   Allow the engine to cool completely before attempting to remove any of the plugs. While you are waiting for the engine to cool, check the new plugs for defects and adjust the gaps.

5   The gap is checked by inserting the proper thickness gauge between the electrodes at the tip of the plug (see illustration). The gap between the electrodes should be the same as the one specified on the *Emissions Control Information label*. The wire should just slide between the electrodes with a slight amount of drag. If the gap is incorrect, use the adjuster on the gauge body to bend the curved side electrode slightly until the proper gap is obtained (see illustration). If the side electrode is not exactly over the center electrode, bend it with the adjuster until it is. Check for cracks in the porcelain insulator (if any are found, the plug should not be used).

6   With the engine cool, remove the spark plug wire from one spark plug. Pull only on the boot at the end of the wire — do not pull on the wire. A plug wire removal tool should be used if available (see illustration).

7   If compressed air is available, use it to blow any dirt or foreign material away from the spark plug hole. A common bicycle pump will also work. The idea here is to eliminate the possibility of debris falling into the cylinder as the spark plug is removed.

8   Place the spark plug socket over the plug and remove it from the engine by turning it in a counterclockwise direction.

9   Compare the spark plug to those shown in the accompanying color photos to get an indication of the general running condition of the engine.

10   Thread one of the new plugs into the hole until you can no longer turn it with your fingers, then tighten it with a torque wrench (if available) or the ratchet. It might be a good idea to slip a short length of rubber hose over the end of the plug to use as a tool to thread it into place (see illustration). The hose will grip the plug well enough to turn it, but will start to slip if the plug begins to cross-thread in the hole — this will prevent damaged threads and the accompanying repair costs.

11   Before pushing the spark plug wire onto the end of the plug, inspect it following the procedures outlined in Section 27.

12   Attach the plug wire to the new spark plug, again using a twisting motion on the boot until it is seated on the spark plug.

13   Repeat the procedure for the remaining spark plugs, replacing them one at a time to prevent mixing up the spark plug wires.

27   Spark plug wire, distributor cap and rotor check and replacement

Warning: *The electric cooling fan on these models can activate at any time, even when the ignition is in the Off position. Disconnect the fan motor or negative battery cable when working in the vicinity of the fan.*

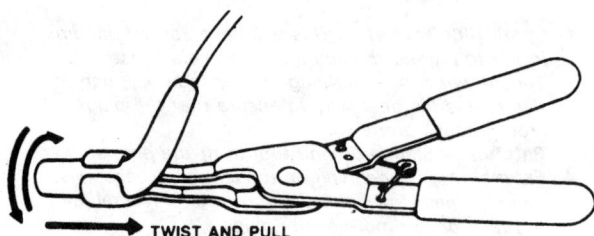

26.6   When removing the spark plug wires, pull only on the boot and use a twisting/pulling motion

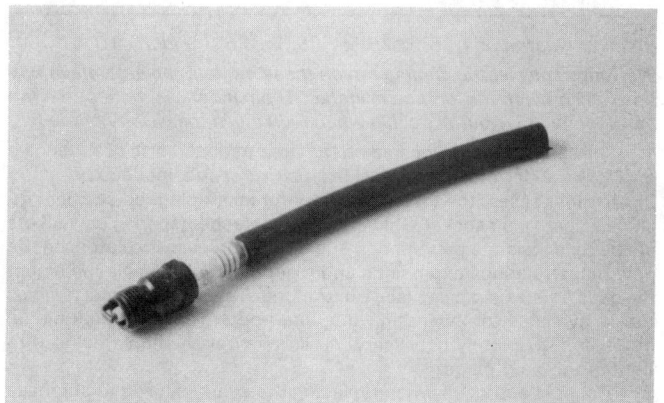

26.10   A length of 3/16-inch ID rubber hose will save time and prevent damaged threads when installing the spark plugs

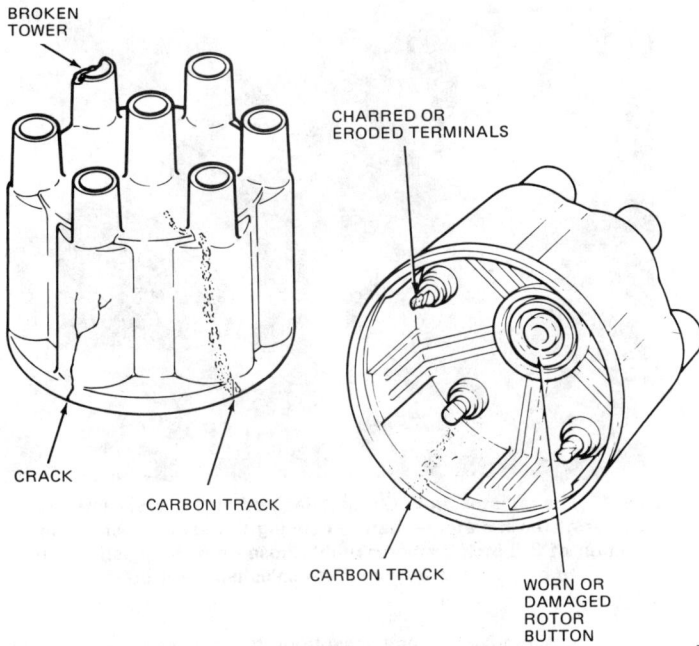

27.11 Shown here are some of the common defects to look for when inspecting the distributor cap (if in doubt about its condition, install a new one)

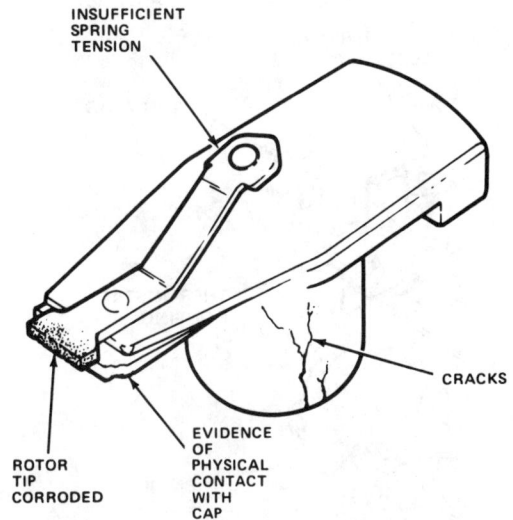

27.12 The ignition rotor should be checked for wear and corrosion as indicated here (if in doubt about its condition, replace it with a new one)

Spark plug wires

Note: *Every time a spark plug wire is detached from a spark plug, the distributor cap or the coil, silicone dielectric compound (a white grease available at auto parts stores) must be applied to the inside of each boot before reconnection. Use a small standard screwdriver to coat the entire inside surface of each boot with a thin layer of the compound.*

1 The spark plug wires should be checked and, if necessary, replaced at the same time new spark plugs are installed.

2 The easiest way to identify bad wires is to make a visual check while the engine is running. In a dark, well-ventilated garage, start the engine and look at each plug wire. Be careful not to come into contact with any moving engine parts. If there is a break in the wire, you will see arcing or a small spark at the damaged area. If arcing is noticed, make a note to obtain new wires.

3 The spark plug wires should be inspected one at a time, beginning with the spark plug for the number one cylinder (the one nearest the right end of the engine), to prevent confusion. Clearly label each original plug wire with a piece of tape marked with the correct number. The plug wires must be reinstalled in the correct order to ensure proper engine operation. See Chapter 2 for illustrations of the cylinder locations and the corresponding plug wire terminals on the cap.

4 Disconnect the plug wire from the first spark plug. A removal tool can be used (see illustration 26.6), or you can grab the wire boot, twist it slightly and pull the wire free. *Do not pull on the wire itself, only on the rubber boot.*

5 Push the wire and boot back onto the end of the spark plug. It should fit snugly. If it doesn't, detach the wire and boot once more and use a pair of pliers to carefully crimp the metal connector inside the wire boot until it does.

6 Using a clean rag, wipe the entire length of the wire to remove built-up dirt and grease.

7 Once the wire is clean, check for burns, cracks and other damage. Do not bend the wire sharply or you might break the conductor.

8 Disconnect the wire from the distributor. Again, pull only on the rubber boot. Check for corrosion and a tight fit. Replace the wire in the distributor.

9 Inspect each of the remaining spark plug wires, making sure that each one is securely fastened at the distributor and spark plug when the check is complete.

10 If new spark plug wires are required, purchase a set for your specific engine model. Pre-cut wire sets with the boots already installed are available. Remove and replace the wires one at a time to avoid mix-ups in the firing order.

Distributor cap and rotor

Refer to illustrations 27.11, 27.12 and 27.13

Note: *It is common practice to install a new distributor cap and rotor each time new spark plug wires are installed. If you're planning to install new wires, install a new cap and rotor also. But if you are planning to reuse the existing wires, be sure to inspect the cap and rotor to make sure that they are in good condition.*

11 Remove the mounting screws and detach the cap from the distributor. Check it for cracks, carbon tracks and worn, burned or loose terminals (see illustration)

12 Check the rotor for cracks and carbon tracks. Make sure the center terminal spring tension is adequate and look for corrosion and wear on the rotor tip (see illustration).

13 Replace the cap and rotor if damage or defects are found. Note that the rotor is held on the shaft by two screws and is indexed so it can only be installed one way. Before installing the cap, apply silicone dielectric compound to the rotor tip (see illustration) (see Note at beginning of this Section).

14 When installing a new cap, remove the wires from the old cap one at a time and attach them to the new cap in the exact same location — do not simultaneously remove all the wires from the old cap or firing order mix-ups may occur.

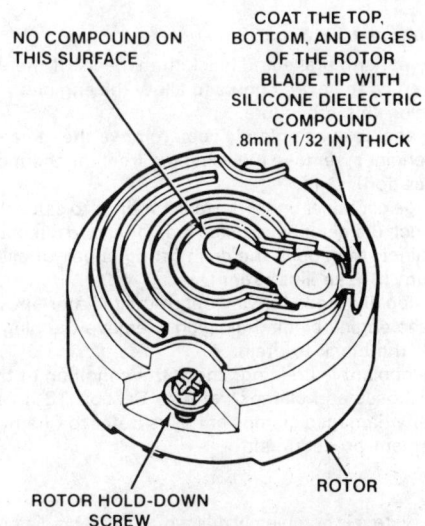

27.13 Apply silicone dielectric compound (grease) to the rotor, as shown, before installing the distributor cap

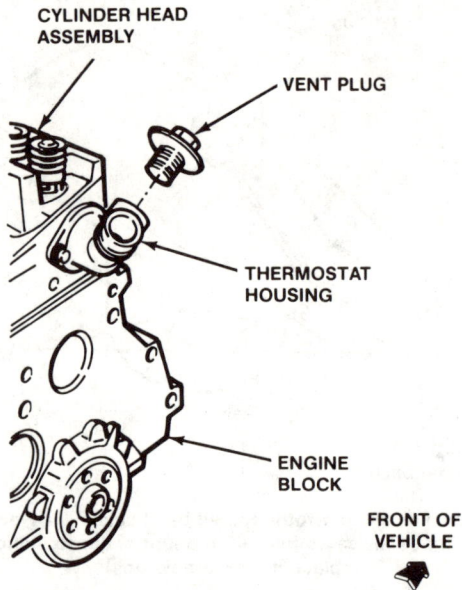

28.3   Four-cylinder engine vent plug details — the plug must be removed during servicing to bleed air out of the system

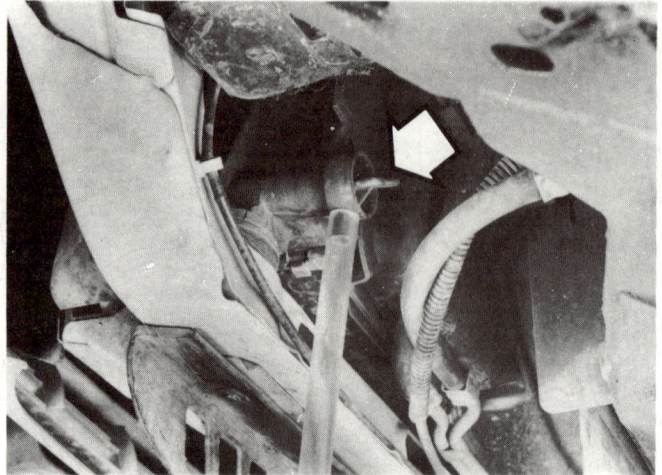

28.4   The radiator drain fitting is located at the lower left front corner of the radiator — before opening the valve, push a short section of 3/8-inch diameter rubber hose onto the plastic fitting to prevent the coolant from splashing as it drains

28   Cooling system servicing (draining, flushing and refilling)

Warning: *The electric cooling fan on these models can activate at any time, even when the ignition is in the Off position. Disconnect the fan motor or negative battery cable when working in the vicinity of the fan. Antifreeze is a corrosive and poisonous solution, so be careful not to spill any of the coolant mixture on the vehicle's paint or your skin. If this happens, rinse immediately with plenty of clean water. Consult local authorities regarding proper disposal procedures for antifreeze before draining the cooling system. In many areas, reclamation centers have been established to collect used oil and coolant mixtures.*

1   Periodically, the cooling system should be drained, flushed and refilled to replenish the antifreeze mixture and prevent formation of rust and corrosion, which can impair the performance of the cooling system and cause engine damage. When the cooling system is serviced, all hoses and the radiator cap should be checked and replaced if necessary.

Draining

Refer to illustrations 28.3 and 28.4

2   Apply the parking brake and block the wheels. If the vehicle has just been driven, wait several hours to allow the engine to cool down before beginning this procedure.

3   Once the engine is completely cool, remove the radiator cap. On four-cylinder engines, remove the vent plug from the thermostat housing **(see illustration)**.

4   Move a large container under the radiator drain to catch the coolant. Attach a 3/8-inch diameter hose to the drain fitting to direct the coolant into the container, then open the drain fitting (a pair of pliers may be required to turn it) **(see illustration)**.

5   After the coolant stops flowing out of the radiator, move the container under the engine block drain plug. Remove the plug and allow the coolant in the block to drain.

6   While the coolant is draining, check the condition of the radiator hoses, heater hoses and clamps (refer to Section 18 if necessary).

7   Replace any damaged clamps or hoses (refer to Chapter 3 for detailed replacement procedures).

Flushing

8   Once the system is completely drained, flush the radiator with fresh water from a garden hose until water runs clear at the drain. The flushing action of the water will remove sediments from the radiator

but will not remove rust and scale from the engine and cooling tube surfaces.

9   These deposits can be removed by the chemical action of a cleaner such as Ford *Cooling System Fast Flush*. Follow the procedure outlined in the manufacturer's instructions. If the radiator is severely corroded, damaged or leaking, it should be removed (Chapter 3) and taken to a radiator repair shop.

10   Remove the overflow hose from the coolant recovery reservoir. Drain the reservoir and flush it with clean water, then reconnect the hose.

Refilling

11   Close and tighten the radiator drain. Install and tighten the block drain plug. On four-cylinder engines, install the vent plug.

12   Place the heater temperature control in the maximum heat position.

13   Slowly add new coolant (a 50/50 mixture of water and antifreeze) to the radiator until it is full. Add coolant to the reservoir up to the lower mark.

14   Leave the radiator cap off and run the engine in a well-ventilated area until the thermostat opens (coolant will begin flowing through the radiator and the upper radiator hose will become hot).

15   Turn the engine off and let it cool. Add more coolant mixture to bring the level back up to the lip on the radiator filler neck.

16   Squeeze the upper radiator hose to expel air, then add more coolant mixture if necessary. Replace the radiator cap.

17   Start the engine, allow it to reach normal operating temperature and check for leaks.

29   Automatic transaxle fluid and filter change

Refer to illustrations 29.5, 29.8a, 29.8b, 29.9a, 29.9b and 29.11

Note: *Periodic fluid and filter changes are not specified by the factory as normal maintenance items. However, if the vehicle is driven continuously or under severe conditions, fluid and filter changes should be done at regular intervals.*

1   Before beginning work, purchase the specified transmission fluid (see *Recommended lubricants and fluids* in Chapter 1) and a new filter. The filter will come with a new pan gasket and O-ring.

2   The fluid should be drained immediately after the vehicle has been driven. More sediment and contaminants will be removed with the fluid if it's hot. **Caution:** *Fluid temperature can exceed 350° in a hot transaxle, so wear gloves when draining the fluid.*

3   After the vehicle has been driven to warm up the fluid, raise it and support it on jackstands.

4   Position a drain pan under the transaxle. Be careful not to touch any of the hot exhaust components.

5   Remove all of the pan bolts except for the two at the rear corners

CARBON DEPOSITS

Symptoms: Dry sooty deposits indicate a rich mixture or weak ignition. Causes misfiring, hard starting and hesitation.

Recommendation: Check for a clogged air cleaner, high float level, sticky choke and worn ignition points. Use a spark plug with a longer core nose for greater anti-fouling protection.

OIL DEPOSITS

Symptoms: Oily coating caused by poor oil control. Oil is leaking past worn valve guides or piston rings into the combustion chamber. Causes hard starting, misfiring and hesition.

Recommendation: Correct the mechanical condition with necessary repairs and install new plugs.

TOO HOT

Symptoms: Blistered, white insulator, eroded electrode and absence of deposits. Results in shortened plug life.

Recommendation: Check for the correct plug heat range, over-advanced ignition timing, lean fuel mixture, intake manifold vacuum leaks and sticking valves. Check the coolant level and make sure the radiator is not clogged.

PREIGNITION

Symptoms: Melted electrodes. Insulators are white, but may be dirty due to misfiring or flying debris in the combustion chamber. Can lead to engine damage.

Recommendation: Check for the correct plug heat range, over-advanced ignition timing, lean fuel mixture, clogged cooling system and lack of lubrication.

HIGH SPEED GLAZING

Symptoms: Insulator has yellowish, glazed appearance. Indicates that combustion chamber temperatures have risen suddenly during hard acceleration. Normal deposits melt to form a conductive coating. Causes misfiring at high speeds.

Recommendation: Install new plugs. Consider using a colder plug if driving habits warrant.

GAP BRIDGING

Symptoms: Combustion deposits lodge between the electrodes. Heavy deposits accumulate and bridge the electrode gap. The plug ceases to fire, resulting in a dead cylinder.

Recommendation: Locate the faulty plug and remove the deposits from between the electrodes.

NORMAL

Symptoms: Brown to grayish-tan color and slight electrode wear. Correct heat range for engine and operating conditions.

Recommendation: When new spark plugs are installed, replace with plugs of the same heat range.

ASH DEPOSITS

Symptoms: Light brown deposits encrusted on the side or center electrodes or both. Derived from oil and/or fuel additives. Excessive amounts may mask the spark, causing misfiring and hesitation during acceleration.

Recommendation: If excessive deposits accumulate over a short time or low mileage, install new valve guide seals to prevent seepage of oil into the combustion chambers. Also try changing gasoline brands.

WORN

Symptoms: Rounded electrodes with a small amount of deposits on the firing end. Normal color. Causes hard starting in damp or cold weather and poor fuel economy.

Recommendation: Replace with new plugs of the same heat range.

DETONATION

Symptoms: Insulators may be cracked or chipped. Improper gap setting techniques can also result in a fractured insulator tip. Can lead to piston damage.

Recommendation: Make sure the fuel anti-knock values meet engine requirements. Use care when setting the gaps on new plugs. Avoid lugging the engine.

SPLASHED DEPOSITS

Symptoms: After long periods of misfiring, deposits can loosen when normal combustion temperature is restored by an overdue tune-up. At high speeds, deposits flake off the piston and are thrown against the hot insulator, causing misfiring.

Recommendation: Replace the plugs with new ones or clean and reinstall the originals.

MECHANICAL DAMAGE

Symptoms: May be caused by a foreign object in the combustion chamber or the piston striking an incorrect reach (too long) plug. Causes a dead cylinder and could result in piston damage.

Recommendation: Remove the foreign object from the engine and/or install the correct reach plug.

29.5   Remove all but two of the rear pan bolts, then carefully pry the pan loose from the transaxle case — be careful, too much force could damage the flange and cause leaks

(see illustration). Unscrew the two remaining bolts several turns, but leave them in place to support the pan.

6   Carefully separate the pan from the transaxle case and allow the fluid to drain out. Try not to splash fluid as the gasket seal is broken and the pan is detached. Once the fluid has drained, remove the two bolts and detach the pan.

7   Scrape all traces of the old gasket from the pan and the transaxle case, then clean the pan with solvent and dry it with compressed air — DO NOT use a rag to wipe out the pan (lint from the rag could contaminate the transaxle).

8   Remove the filter bolts or clip and detach the filter (see illustrations). Discard the filter and the O-ring.

9   Attach the new O-ring(s) or clip to the new filter (see illustrations), then bolt the filter to the transaxle.

10   Position the new gasket on the pan, then hold the pan against the transaxle case and install the bolts or clip.

11   Tighten the pan bolts to the specified torque in a criss-cross pattern (see illustration). Work up to the final torque in three steps. Caution: Don't overtighten the bolts or the pan flange could be distorted and leaks could result.

12   Refill the transaxle with fluid (see Section 7 if necessary).

13   Lower the vehicle, drive it for several miles, then recheck the fluid level and look for leaks at the transaxle pan.

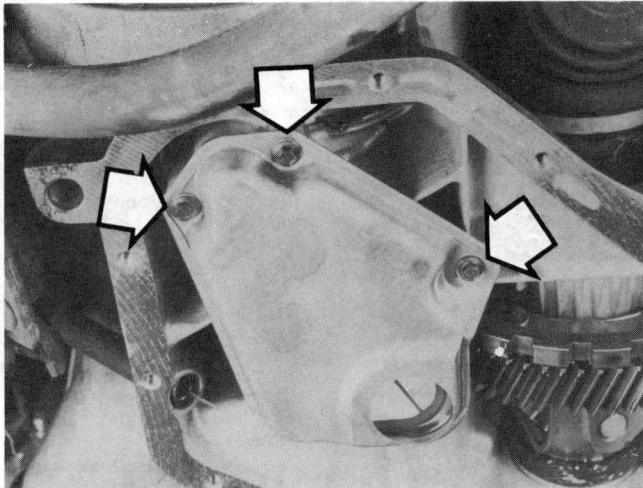

29.8a   On some transaxles, the filter is held in place by bolts (arrows), . . .

29.8b   . . . while others have a clip (arrow) which is pulled down to release the filter

29.9   Some transaxles have an O-ring which fits in a recess in the filter housing, . . .

29.9b   . . . while others have two O-rings which fit on the filter tube

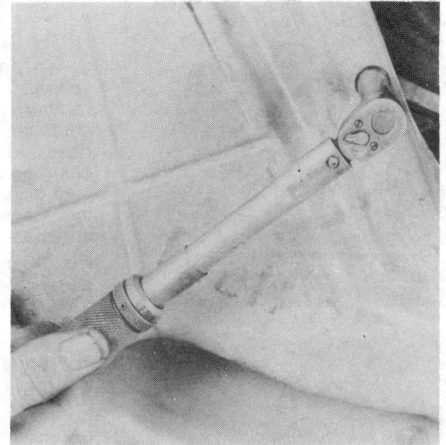

29.11   Tighten the transaxle pan bolts with a torque wrench — follow a criss-cross pattern and work up to the final torque in three steps to avoid warping the pan flange

Chapter 2 Part A   Four-cylinder engine

Contents

Specifications

General
Cylinder numbers (drivebelt end-to-transaxle end)   1-2-3-4
Firing order   1-3-4-2

Camshaft lobe lift
Intake . . . .   0.249 in
Exhaust . . . .   0.239 in
Allowable lift loss. . . . .   0.005 in

Torque specifications   **Ft-lbs**
Intake manifold bolts . . . .   15 to 23
Exhaust manifold bolts
  Step 1 . . . .   5 to 7
  Step 2 . . . .   20 to 30
Rocker arm bolts
  Step 1 . . . .   4 to 7
  Step 2 . . . .   20 to 26
Rocker arm cover bolts. . . . .   6 to 8
Cylinder head bolts
  Step 1 . . . .   52 to 59
  Step 2 . . . .   70 to 76

Torque specifications (continued)

Oil pan-to-engine bolts . . . .   15 to 23
Oil pump bolts . . . .   15 to 23
Oil pan-to-transaxle bolts . . . .   30 to 39
Damper upper bracket bolts . . . .   40 to 55
Damper lower bracket bolts . . . .   21 to 30
Front engine mount bolts . . . .   40 to 55
Front engine mount nuts . . . .   55 to 75
Rear engine mount-to-block upper bolt . . . .   40 to 55
Rear engine mount-to-block lower bolt . . . .   70 to 96
Rear engine mount-to-block stud . . . .   70 to 96
Rear engine mount through-bolt . . . .   40 to 55
Rear engine mount lower stud nut . . . .   50 to 75

1 General information

This Part of Chapter 2 is devoted to in-vehicle repair procedures for the four-cylinder engine. All information concerning engine removal and installation, repairs which require engine removal and engine block and cylinder head overhaul can be found in Part C of this Chapter.

The following repair procedures are based on the assumption that the engine is installed in the vehicle. If the engine has been removed from the vehicle and mounted on a stand, many of the steps outlined in this Part of Chapter 2 will not apply.

The specifications included in this Part of Chapter 2 apply only to the procedures contained in this Part. Part C of Chapter 2 contains the specifications necessary for cylinder head and engine block rebuilding.

2 Repair operations possible with the engine in the vehicle

Many major repair operations can be accomplished without removing the engine from the vehicle.

Clean the engine compartment and the exterior of the engine with some type of pressure washer before any work is done. A clean engine will make the job easier and will help keep dirt out of the internal areas of the engine.

Depending on the components involved, it may be a good idea to remove the hood to improve access to the engine as repairs are performed (refer to Chapter 11 if necessary).

If vacuum, exhaust, oil or coolant leaks develop, indicating a need for gasket or seal replacement, the repairs can generally be made with the engine in the vehicle. The intake and exhaust manifold gaskets, oil pan gasket and cylinder head gasket are all accessible with the engine in place.

Exterior engine components such as the intake and exhaust manifolds, the oil pan (and the oil pump), the water pump, the starter motor, the alternator, the distributor and the fuel injection system can be removed for repair with the engine in place.

Since the cylinder head can be removed without pulling the engine, valve component servicing can also be accomplished with the engine in the vehicle.

In extreme cases caused by a lack of necessary equipment, repair or replacement of piston rings, pistons, connecting rods and rod bearings is possible with the engine in the vehicle. However, this practice is not recommended because of the cleaning and preparation work that must be done to the components involved.

3 Rocker arm cover — removal and installation

Removal

1   Remove the oil filler cap and set it aside.
2   Disconnect the PCV valve and breather hose assembly from the rocker arm cover.
3   Detach the throttle linkage cable from the top of the rocker arm cover.
4   Disconnect the cruise control cable, if equipped, from the top of the rocker arm cover.
5   Remove the mounting bolts and detach the cover from the engine.

6   Clean the cylinder head and rocker arm cover mating surfaces. Use lacquer thinner or acetone to remove all traces of oil.

Installation

7   Before installing the rocker arm cover, refer to Section 10 and make sure the cylinder head bolts are tight.
8   Lay the new gasket in place, then lower the cover onto the head (if the neoprene rubber gasket is undamaged, it can be reused). Make sure the holes are lined up, then install the bolts finger tight. **Note:** *No sealant is required when installing the rocker arm cover. However, In order to prevent the gasket from sticking to the head and cover the next time removal is required, a very thin layer of RTV sealant can be applied to both sides of the gasket.*
9   Tighten the bolts to the specified torque in a criss-cross pattern.
10   The rest of installation is the reverse of removal.

4 Rocker arms and pushrods — removal, inspection and installation

Refer to illustrations 4.4, 4.5a, 4.5b, 4.5c and 4.11

Removal

1   Remove the rocker arm cover (Section 3).
2   Beginning at the front (drivebelt end) of the cylinder head, loosen and remove the rocker arm mounting bolts.
3   Remove the rocker arms, fulcrums and pushrods and store them with their respective mounting bolts. Store each set of valve components separately in a marked plastic bag to ensure that they are reinstalled in their original locations.
4   Remove the pushrods and store them separately to make sure they don't get mixed up during installation **(see illustration)**.

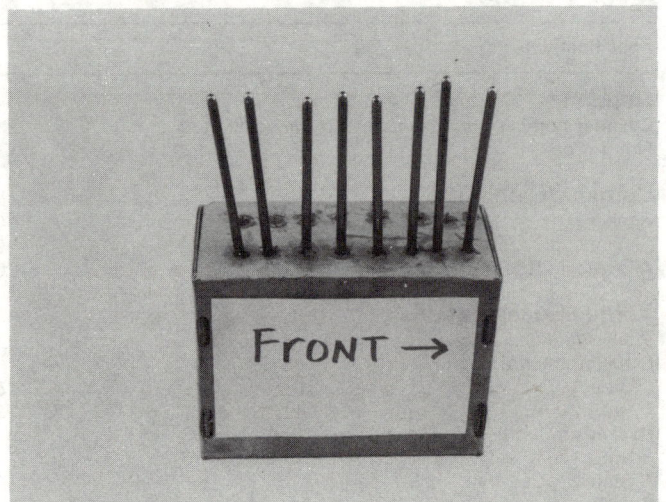

4.4 A perforated cardboard box can be used to store the pushrods to ensure that they are reinstalled in their original locations — note the label indicating the front of the engine

Chapter 2 Part A Four-cylinder engines

Inspection

5   Check each rocker arm for wear, cracks and other damage, especially where the pushrods and valve stems contact the rocker arm faces **(see illustration)**. Check the fulcrum seat in each rocker arm and the fulcrum faces **(see illustrations)**. Look for galling, stress cracks and unusual wear patterns. If the rocker arms are worn or damaged, replace them with new ones and install new fulcrums as well.
6   Make sure the oil hole at the pushrod end of each rocker arm is open.
7   Inspect the pushrods for cracks and excessive wear at the ends. Roll each pushrod across a piece of plate glass to see if it's bent (if it wobbles, it's bent).

Installation

8   Lubricate the lower end of each pushrod with clean engine oil or moly-base grease and install it in its original location. Make sure each pushrod seats completely in the lifter socket.
9   Bring the number one piston to top dead center on the compression stroke (Section 5).
10 Apply moly-base grease to the ends of the valve stems and the upper ends of the pushrods before placing the rocker arms in position.
11 Set both number one cylinder rocker arms **(see illustration)**, the number two cylinder intake rocker arm and the number three cylinder exhaust rocker arm in place, then install the fulcrums and the bolts. Apply moly-base grease to the fulcrums to prevent damage to the mating surfaces before engine oil pressure builds up. Tighten the bolts to the specified torque.
12 Turn the crankshaft 180° in the normal direction of rotation until the number four piston is at TDC on the compression stroke. The distributor rotor should be pointing in the direction of terminal number four on the cap (if the cap is removed, the rotor should be pointing toward the engine block).
13 Install the remaining rocker arms and fulcrums and tighten the bolts to the specified torque.
14 Install the rocker arm cover (Section 3).
15 Start the engine, listen for unusual valvetrain noises and check for oil leaks at the rocker arm cover joint.

---

5   Top Dead Center (TDC) for number 1 piston — locating

Refer to illustrations 5.5, 5.6 and 5.7

1   Top Dead Center (TDC) is the highest point in the cylinder that each piston reaches as it travels up-and-down when the crankshaft turns. Each piston reaches TDC on the compression stroke and again on the exhaust stroke, but TDC generally refers to piston position on the compression stroke. The timing marks on the flywheel (vehicles with a manual transaxle) or the driveplate (vehicles with an automatic transaxle) are referenced to the number one piston at TDC on the compression stroke.
2   Positioning the piston(s) at TDC is an essential part of many procedures such as rocker arm removal, timing chain and sprocket replacement and distributor removal.
3   Before beginning this procedure, be sure to disconnect the coil wire from the distributor cap and ground it to prevent damage to the coil (see Chapter 5).

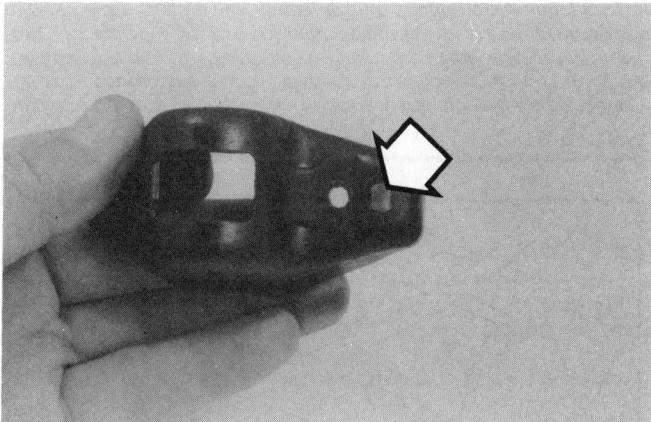
4.5a   Check the rocker arm surfaces that contact the valve stem and pushrod (arrow) . . .

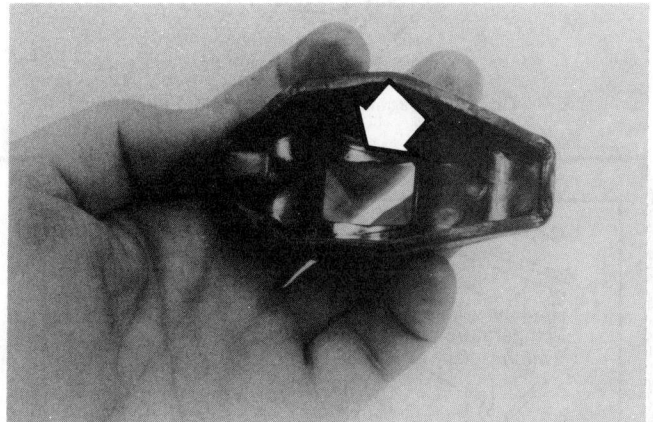
4.5b   . . . the fulcrum seats in the rocker arms . . .

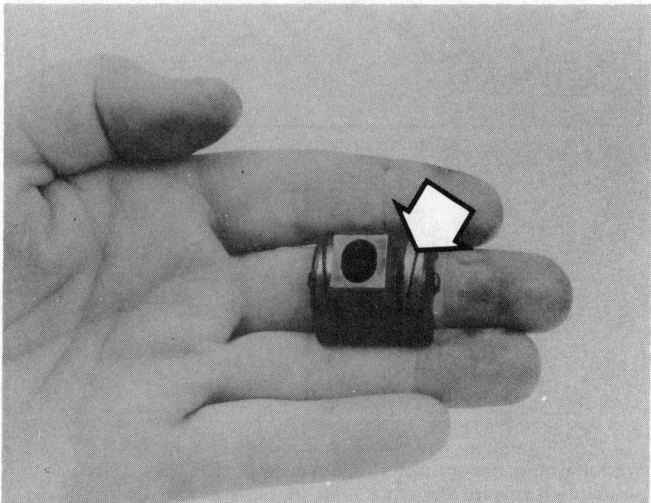
4.5c   . . . and the fulcrums themselves for wear and galling

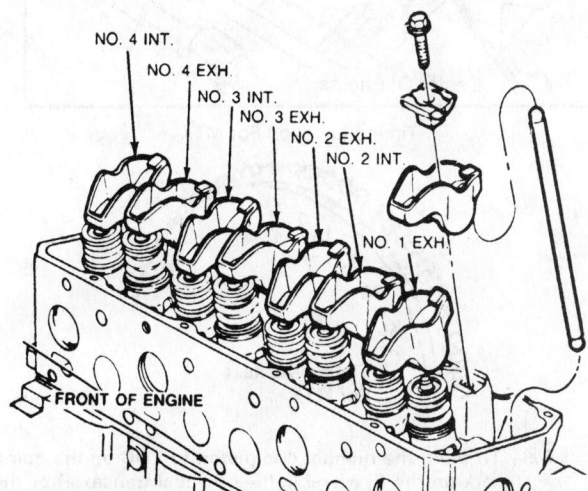
4.11   Rocker arms and related components — exploded view

4   In order to bring any piston to TDC, the crankshaft must be turned using one of the methods outlined below. When looking at the front of the engine (on the passenger side of the vehicle), normal crankshaft rotation is *clockwise*. **Warning:** *Before beginning this procedure, be sure to place the transaxle in Neutral.*

   a) The preferred method is to turn the crankshaft with a large socket and breaker bar attached to the pulley bolt threaded into the front of the crankshaft.
   b) A remote starter switch, which may save some time, can also be used. Attach the switch leads to the small ignition switch terminal and the positive (red) battery cable terminal on the starter solenoid (mounted near the battery). Once the piston is close to TDC, use a socket and breaker bar as described above.
   c) If an assistant is available to turn the ignition switch to the Start position in short bursts, you can get the piston close to TDC without a remote starter switch. Use a socket and breaker bar as described in Paragraph a) to complete the procedure.

5   Note the postion of the terminal for the number one spark plug wire on the distributor cap (it's marked with a 1) **(see illustration)**. Use a scribe or chalk to make a mark on the distributor directly under the terminal. Remove the screws, detach the cap from the distributor and set it aside.

6   Turn the crankshaft (see Paragraph 4 above) until the triangular notch on the flywheel/driveplate is aligned with the stationary pointer in the bellhousing inspection window **(see illustration)**. **Note:** *Although the 5° BTDC mark on the flywheel (manual transaxle) and the triangular notch (5° BTDC mark) on the driveplate (automatic transaxle) are really intended for initial engine timing, they're close enough for any procedure which requires that the number one piston be set at TDC.*

7   Look at the distributor rotor — it should be pointing directly at the mark you made on the distributor body **(see illustration)**. If the rotor is pointing at the terminal for the number four spark plug (toward the engine), the number one piston is at TDC on the exhaust stroke.

8   To get the piston to TDC on the compression stroke, turn the crankshaft one complete revolution (360°) clockwise. The rotor should now be pointing at the mark on the distributor. When the rotor is pointing at the number one spark plug wire terminal in the distributor cap and the timing marks are aligned, the number one piston is at TDC on the compression stroke.

9   After the number one piston has been positioned at TDC on the compression stroke, TDC for any of the remaining cylinders can be located by turning the crankshaft 180° at a time and following the firing order (1-3-4-2).

---

6   Valve springs, retainers and seals — replacement

Refer to illustrations 6.8a, 6.8b, 6.9, 6.14 and 6.16

Note: *Broken valve springs and defective valve stem seals can be replaced without removing the cylinder head. Two special tools and a compressed air source are normally required to perform this operation, so read through this Section carefully and rent or buy the tools before beginning the job. If compressed air is not available, a length of nylon*

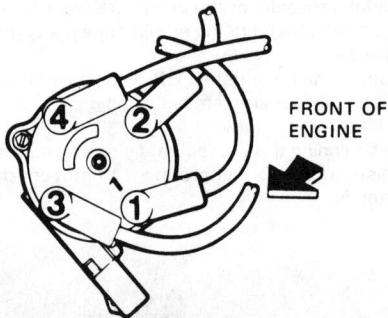

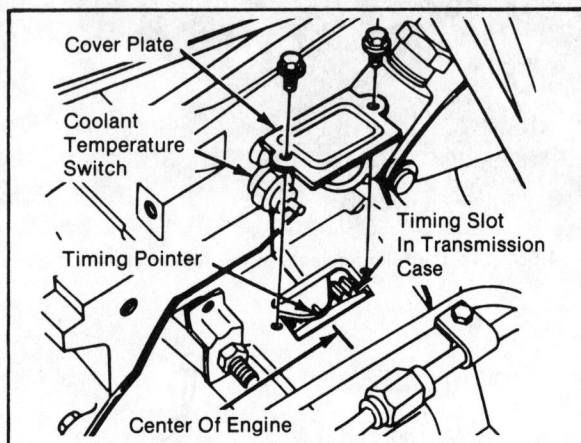

5.5   Distributor spark plug wire terminal locations

Timing Location For MTX

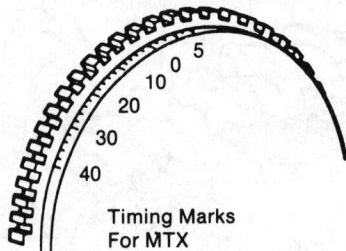

Timing Marks For MTX

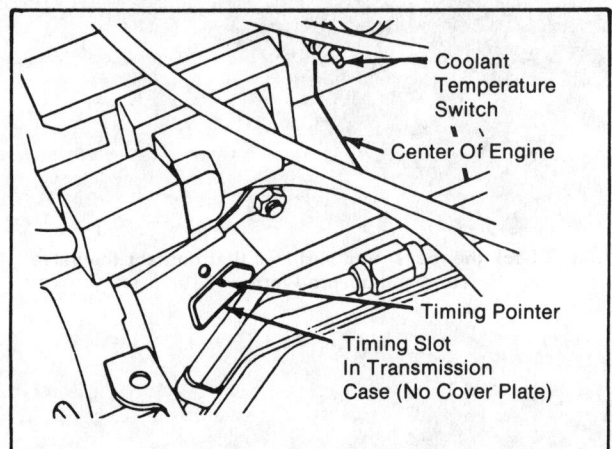

Timing Location For ATX

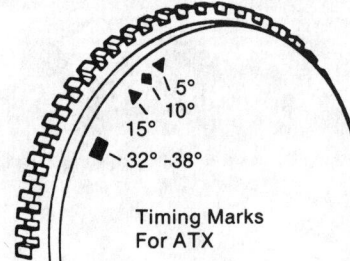

Timing Marks For ATX

5.6   To bring the number one piston to TDC on the compression stroke, turn the crankshaft clockwise until the 5° BTDC mark on the flywheel (left — manual transaxle) or the triangle pointing toward the crankshaft (right — automatic transaxle) is aligned with the stationary pointer in the inspection window, . . .

5.7 . . . then see if the rotor is pointing at the mark on the distributor body (the mark corresponds to the location of the number one spark plug wire terminal in the distributor cap)

6.8a Once the spring is depressed . . .

6.8b . . . the keepers can be removed with a small magnet or a pair of needle-nose pliers or forceps

6.9 It doesn't really matter how you remove the old valve stem seals, since they will be discarded, but be sure that you don't scratch, nick or otherwise damage the valve stems

rope can be used to keep the valves from falling into the cylinder during this procedure.

1   Remove the rocker arm cover from the cylinder head (see Section 3).
2   Remove the spark plug from the cylinder with the defective valve component. If all of the valve stem seals are being replaced, remove all of the spark plugs.
3   Turn the crankshaft until the piston in the affected cylinder is at top dead center on the compression stroke (refer to Section 5 for instructions). If you're replacing all of the valve stem seals, begin with cylinder number one and work on the valves for one cylinder at a time. Move from cylinder-to-cylinder following the firing order sequence (1-3-4-2).
4   Thread an adapter into the spark plug hole and connect an air hose from a compressed air source to it. Most auto parts stores can supply the air hose adapter. **Note:** *Many cylinder compression gauges utilize a screw-in fitting that may work with your air hose quick-disconnect fitting.*
5   Remove the rocker arm mounting bolt, the rocker arm/fulcrum and the pushrod for the valve with the defective part. If all of the valve stem seals are being replaced, all of the rocker arms and pushrods should be removed (refer to Section 4).
6   Apply compressed air to the cylinder. The valves should be held in place by the air pressure. If the valve faces or seats are in poor condition, leaks may prevent the air pressure from retaining the valves — refer to the alternative procedure below.
7   If you don't have access to compressed air, an alternative method can be used. Position the piston at a point just before TDC on the compression stroke, then feed a long piece of nylon rope through the spark plug hole until it fills the combustion chamber. Be sure to leave the end of the rope hanging out of the engine so it can be removed easily. Use a large breaker bar and socket to turn the crankshaft in the normal direction of rotation until *slight* resistance is felt.
8   Stuff shop rags into the cylinder head oil return holes to prevent parts from falling into the engine, then use a valve spring compressor to compress the spring/damper assembly. Remove the keepers with a small pair of needle-nose pliers, a magnet or a forceps **(see illustrations)**. **Note:** *A couple of different types of tools are available for compressing the valve springs with the head in place. One type grips the lower spring coils and presses on the retainer as the knob is turned, while the other type, shown here, utilizes the rocker arm mounting bolt for leverage. Both types work very well, although the lever type is usually less expensive.*
9   Remove the spring retainer and valve spring/damper assembly and set them aside. Using a pair of pliers, remove the valve stem seal **(see illustration)** and discard it. **Note:** *If air pressure fails to hold the valve in the closed position during this operation, the valve face or seat is probably damaged. If so, the cylinder head will have to be removed for additional repair operations.*

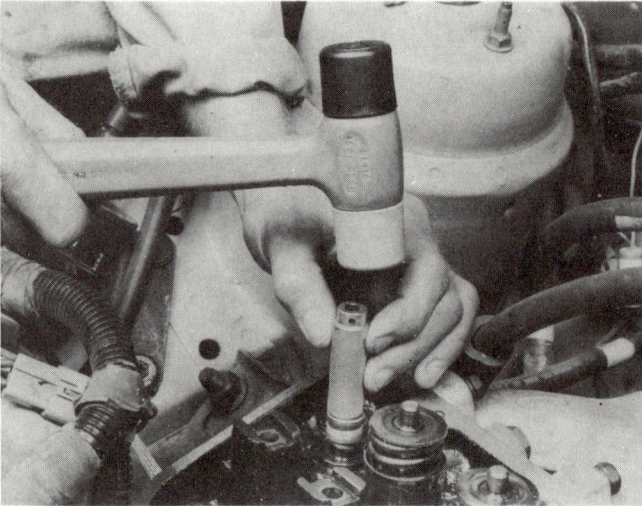

6.14   A deep socket and hammer can be used to seat the
new seals on the valve guides

6.16   Keepers don't always want to stay in place so apply
a small dab of grease to each one before installation — it
will hold them in place on the valve stem as the spring
is released

10 Wrap a rubber band or tape around the top of the valve stem so
the valve won't fall into the combustion chamber, then release the air
pressure. **Note:** *If a rope was used instead of air pressure, turn the
crankshaft slightly in the direction opposite normal rotation.*
11 Inspect the valve stem for damage. Rotate the valve in the guide
and check the end for eccentric movement, which would indicate that
the valve is bent.
12 Move the valve up-and-down in the guide and make sure it doesn't
bind. If the valve stem binds, the valve is bent or the guide is damaged.
In either case, the head will have to be removed for repair.
13 Reapply air pressure to the cylinder to retain the valve in the closed
position, then remove the tape or rubber band from the valve stem.
If a rope was used instead of air pressure, rotate the crankshaft in the
normal direction of rotation until slight resistance is felt.
14 Lubricate the valve stem with engine oil and install a new valve
stem seal. Use a 5/8-inch deep socket and a hammer to seat the seal
squarely on the valve guide **(see illustration)**. Note that intake seals
have a wide band near the base and a ring near the top, while exhaust
seals have two rings.
15 Place the valve spring/damper assembly in position, then install
the retainer.
16 Compress the valve spring assembly and carefully install the
keepers in the grooves in the valve stem. Apply a small dab of grease
to the inside of each keeper to hold it in place if necessary **(see
illustration)**.
17 Remove the pressure from the spring tool and make sure the
keepers are seated.
18 Disconnect the air hose and remove the adapter from the spark
plug hole. If a rope was used in place of air pressure, pull it out of the
cylinder.
19 Refer to Section 4 and install the rocker arm and pushrod.
20 If you are replacing all of the seals, repeat the procedure for each
valve assembly. Remember, the piston for each cylinder must be positioned at TDC before removing the valve keepers.
21 Install the spark plug(s) and hook up the wire(s).
22 Install the rocker arm cover (Section 3).
23 Start and run the engine, then check for oil leaks and unusual
sounds coming from the rocker arm cover area.

7   Camshaft lobe lift — measurement

Refer to illustration 7.4
1   In order to determine the extent of cam lobe wear, the lobe lift
should be checked prior to camshaft removal. Since the camshaft cannot be removed with the engine in the vehicle, removal and installation
is covered in Part C.
2   Remove the rocker arm cover(s) (Section 3).

3   Position the number one piston at TDC on the compression stroke
(see Section 4).
4   Beginning with the valves for the number one cylinder, mount a
dial indicator on the engine and position the plunger against the top
surface of the first rocker arm. The plunger should be directly above
and in line with the pushrod **(see illustration)**.
5   Zero the dial indicator, then very slowly turn the crankshaft in the
normal direction of rotation until the indicator needle stops and begins
to move in the opposite direction. The point at which it stops indicates
maximum cam lobe lift.
6   Record this figure for future reference, then reposition the piston
at TDC on the compression stroke.
7   Move the dial indicator to the other number one cylinder rocker
arm and repeat the check. Be sure to record the results for each valve.
8   Repeat the same check for the remaining valves. Since each piston
must be at TDC on the compression stroke for this procedure, work
from cylinder-to-cylinder following the firing order.
9   After the check is complete, compare the results to the Specifications. If camshaft lobe lift is less than specified, cam lobe wear has
occurred and a new camshaft should be installed (refer to Chapter 2C).

8   Intake manifold — removal and installation

Refer to illustrations 8.4, 8.5, 8.6, 8.7 and 8.11
Removal
1   Refer to Chapter 4 and relieve the fuel system pressure.

7.4   To measure cam lobe lift, secure a dial indicator to
the head next to each valve (one at a time) — position the
dial indicator plunger tip against the rocker arm, directly
above the pushrod

8.4   Remove the throttle cable/cruise control bracket bolts
(arrows) and set the cable/bracket assembly aside

8.5   Label and detach the vacuum hoses shown here (arrows)

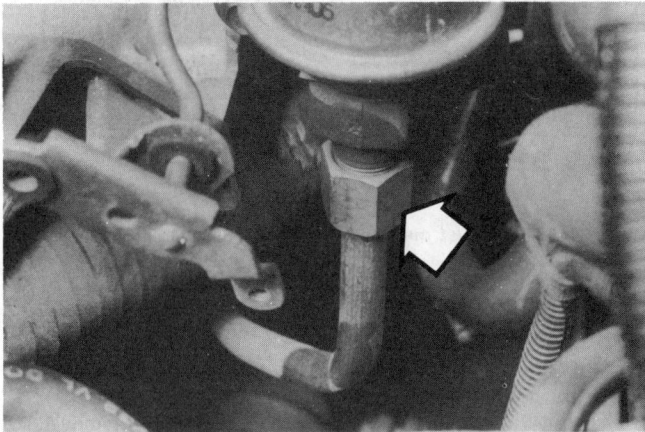

8.6   Disconnect the pipe from the EGR valve by
unscrewing the threaded fitting (arrow)

8.7   Detach the coolant tube fitting (arrow) from the back
of the intake manifold

2   Disconnect the cable from the negative terminal of the battery.
3   Drain the cooling system (refer to Chapter 1) and detach all coolant hoses from the manifold.
4   Remove the CFI fuel charging assembly (Chapter 4), then remove the throttle cable bracket (see illustration).
5   Label and detach the remaining wires, the power brake vacuum hose, the cruise control vacuum hose, the EGR valve vacuum hose, the PCV hose and any other vacuum hoses (see illustration) attached to the throttle body or the intake manifold.
6   Disconnect the pipe from the EGR valve (see illustration).
7   Disconnect the oxygen sensor wire and detach the coolant inlet tube fitting from the intake manifold (see illustration).
8   Remove the bolts and separate the manifold from the head. Caution: Do not pry between the gasket mating surfaces.

Installation

Note: The mating surfaces of the cylinder head and manifold must be perfectly clean when the manifold is installed. Gasket removal solvents in aerosol cans are available at most auto parts stores and may be helpful when removing old gasket material that is stuck to the head and manifold (since the manifold is made of aluminum, aggressive scraping can cause damage). Be sure to follow the directions printed on the container.

9   Use a gasket scraper to remove all traces of sealant and old gasket material, then clean the mating surfaces with lacquer thinner or acetone. If there is old sealant or oil on the mating surfaces when the manifold is installed, vacuum leaks may develop.

10   Use a tap of the correct size to chase the threads in the bolt holes, then use compressed air (if available) to remove the debris from the holes. Warning: Wear safety glasses or a face shield to protect your eyes when using compressed air!
11   Apply a thin, uniform layer of RTV sealant to the manifold mating surfaces and to the cylinder head side of the gasket. Slip one bolt into place at each end of the manifold, hang the new gasket over the bolts, then position the manifold on the head and thread the bolts into place. Install the remaining bolts, then tighten them to the specified torque in the recommended sequence (see illustration). Work up to the final torque in three steps.
12   The rest of installaton is the reverse of removal.

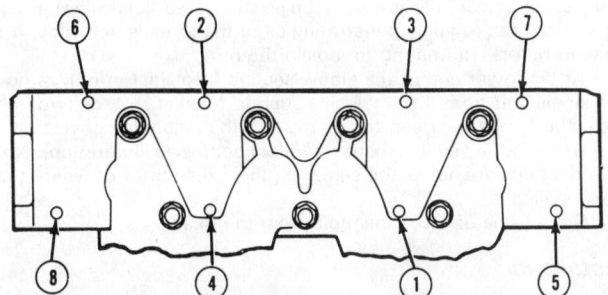

8.11   Intake manifold bolt TIGHTENING sequence

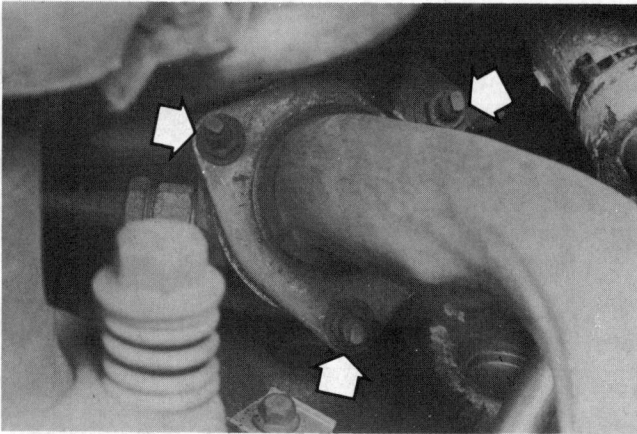

9.6 To remove the exhaust pipe between the manifold and the catalytic converter, remove the three flange nuts at the manifold (arrows) . . .

9.7 . . . and the two bolt and spring assemblies attaching the pipe to the catalytic converter — the bracket bolt must be removed as well

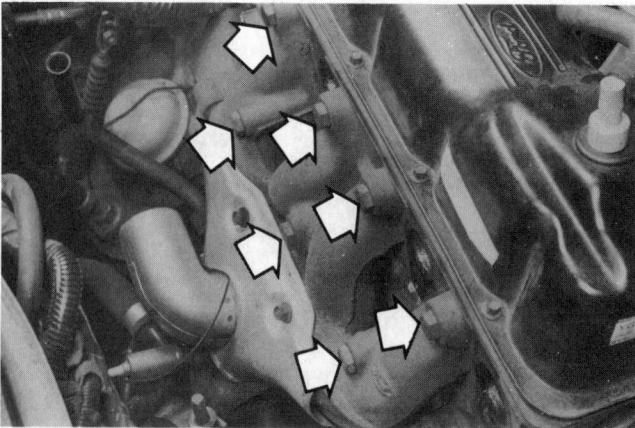

9.8 The exhaust manifold is attached to the head with seven bolts (four short ones and three long ones)

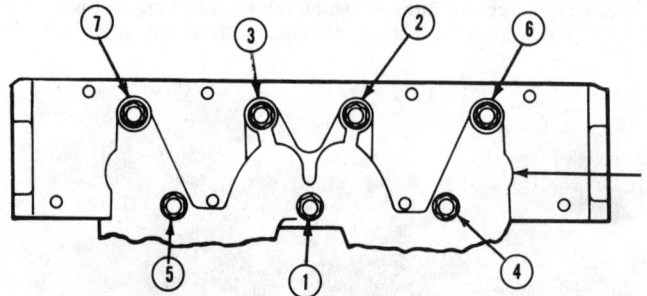

9.12 Exhaust manifold bolt TIGHTENING sequence

traces of carbon deposits.

11 Hold the manifold in place and install the bolts.

12 When tightening the bolts, follow the recommended sequence **(see illustration)** and be sure to use a torque wrench. Tighten the bolts in two steps until the specified torque is reached.

13 The remaining installation steps are the reverse of removal.

9 Exhaust manifold — removal and installation

Refer to illustrations 9.6, 9.7, 9.8 and 9.12

Removal

1 Disconnect the negative battery cable from the battery.

2 Remove the intake manifold (refer to the previous Section).

3 Disconnect the oxygen sensor wire connector and detach the Thermactor check valve hose at the tube assembly. Remove the bracket-to-EGR valve nuts (see Chapter 6).

4 Loosen the clamp and detach the heated air intake duct from the manifold shield.

5 Raise the vehicle and support it on jackstands.

6 Locate the elbow shaped section of exhaust pipe between the exhaust manifold and the catalytic converter. Remove the nuts from the three exhaust manifold-to-exhaust pipe studs **(see illustration)**. It may be a good idea to apply penetrating oil to the threads and allow it to soak in before attempting to loosen the nuts.

7 At the lower end of the elbow section **(see illustration)**, remove the single bolt from the small pipe support bracket and the two bolts from the flange between the elbow and the catalytic converter.

8 Remove the seven exhaust manifold bolts **(see illustration)**. Note that the bolts are not all the same length — keep track of where they are installed.

9 Detach the exhaust manifold from the head.

Installation

10 The manifold and cylinder head mating surfaces must be clean before the manifold is reinstalled. Use a gasket scraper to remove all

10 Cylinder head — removal and installation

Refer to illustrations 10.8, 10.9, 10.12 and 10.18

Removal

1 Remove the intake manifold (Section 8).

2 Remove the exhaust manifold (Section 9).

3 Refer to Section 3 and remove the rocker arm cover.

4 Drain the cooling system (Chapter 1). Detach the radiator hose from the thermostat housing on the left end of the engine. Disconnect the coolant temperature sensor wire, remove the nut that secures the ground wire to the thermostat housing and unplug the wire from the electric cooling fan temperature switch (located in the head directly below the thermostat housing) (see Chapter 3).

5 Remove the ignition coil bracket-to-head bolt, loosen the bracket-to-block bolt and pivot the bracket forward (refer to Chapter 5 if necessary).

6 Remove the distributor cap and wires (see Chapter 3).

7 Remove the drivebelt (see Chapter 1).

8 Remove the engine oil dipstick tube bracket bolt **(see illustration)**.

9 Remove the ground strap and bracket bolts from the front end (drivebelt end) of the cylinder head **(see illustration)**.

10 Remove the rocker arms and pushrods (Section 4).

11 Loosen the head bolts in 1/4-turn increments until they can be removed by hand. Work from bolt-to-bolt in a pattern that's the reverse of the tightening sequence shown in illustration 10.18. Note that the rear bolts are longer than the front ones — they must be installed in their original locations.

10.8 Remove the dipstick tube bracket bolt (arrow) from the radiator side . . .

10.9 . . . and the ground strap and bracket bolts (arrows) from the front (drivebelt end) of the cylinder head

10.12 If you must pry the cylinder head loose from the block, do it at the front of the head like this, using the right engine mount as a fulcrum — if you attempt to pry the head loose from the block anywhere else, you will damage it!

12 Separate the head from the block. If it's stuck, carefully pry up on the front end of the head, using the motor mount as a fulcrum (**see illustration**). **Caution:** *DO NOT attempt to pry the head free anywhere else or damage may occur.*

Installation

13 The mating surfaces of the cylinder head and block must be perfectly clean when the head is installed. Use a gasket scraper to remove all traces of carbon and old gasket material, then clean the mating surfaces with lacquer thinner or acetone. If there is oil on the mating surfaces when the head is installed, the gasket may not seal correctly and leaks could develop. When working on the block, stuff the cylinders with clean shop rags to keep out debris. Use a vacuum cleaner to remove any debris that falls into the cylinders.

14 Check the block and head mating surfaces for nicks, deep scratches and other damage. If damage is slight, it can be removed with a file; if it's excessive, machining may be the only alternative.

15 Use a tap of the correct size to chase the threads in the head bolt holes. Mount each bolt in a vise and run a die down the threads to remove corrosion and restore the threads. Dirt, corrosion, sealant and damaged threads will affect torque readings.

16 Since there are no cylinder head alignment dowels, make sure the gasket is properly aligned after setting the head in place. Use Permatex High Tack or a similar adhesive to ensure that the head gasket doesn't move while the head is being lowered onto the block.

17 After applying a few dabs of Permatex to the side of the new gasket that faces the block, set it in place.

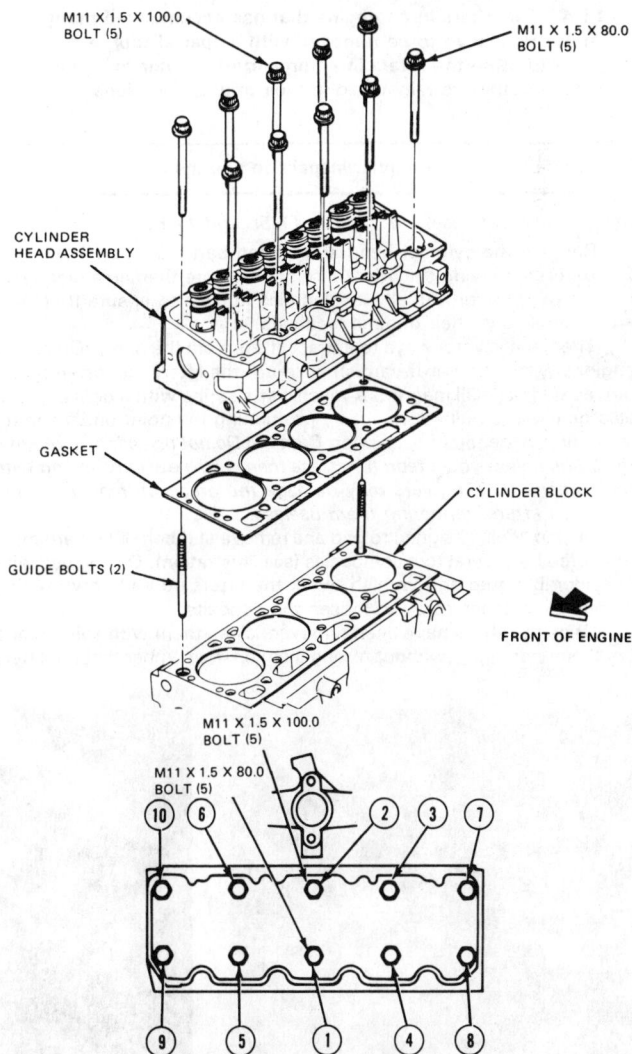
10.18 Cylinder head bolt TIGHTENING sequence — note that the bolts at the front of the head are shorter than the bolts at the rear

18 Lower the cylinder head onto the block. Install the cylinder head bolts in their original locations and tighten them finger tight. Following the recommended sequence (**see illustration**), tighten the bolts in two steps to the specified torque.

19 The remaining installation steps are the reverse of removal.

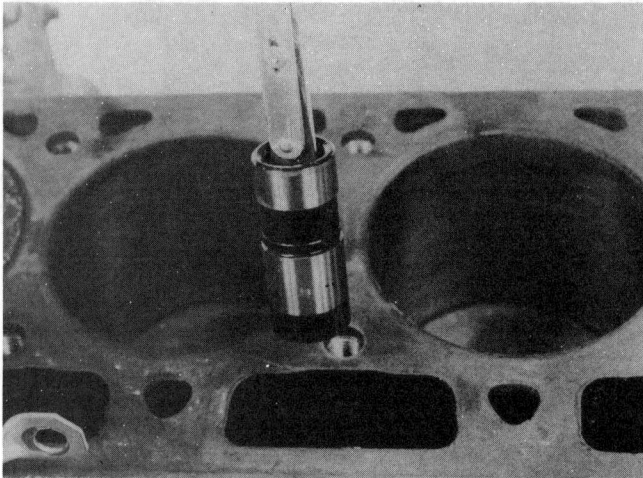

11.4   The lifters in an engine that has accumulated many miles may have to be removed with a special tool — be sure to store the lifters in an organized manner to make sure they're reinstalled in their original locations

11   Valve lifters — removal, inspection and installation

Refer to illustrations 11.4, 11.6a, 11.6b and 11.6c

1   Remove the cylinder head and related parts (Section 10).
2   Before removing the lifters, arrange to store them in a clearly labelled box or in individually labeled plastic bags to ensure that they are reinstalled in their original locations.
3   There are several ways to extract lifters from the bores. On newer engines without a lot of varnish build-up, the lifters can often be removed with a small magnet. A machinist's scribe with a bent end can also be used to pull lifters out by positioning the point under the retainer ring in the top of each lifter. **Caution:** *Do not use pliers to remove the lifters unless you intend to replace them with new ones (along with the camshaft). The pliers may damage the precision machined and hardened lifters, rendering them useless.*
4   Special tools designed to grip and remove stubborn lifters are manufactured by several tool companies **(see illustration)**. On engines with considerable gum and varnish, work the lifters up and down, using carburetor cleaner spray to loosen the deposits.
5   Once the lifters have been removed, clean them with solvent and dry them thoroughly without mixing them up. Remember that the lifters

must be reinstalled in their original bores in the block.
6   Check each lifter wall, pushrod seat and foot for scuffing, score marks and uneven wear. Each lifter foot (the surface that rides on the cam lobe) must be slightly convex, although this can be difficult to determine by eye. If the base of the lifter is concave **(see illustrations)**, the lifters and camshaft must be replaced. If the lifter walls are damaged or worn, inspect the lifter bores in the engine block as well. If the pushrod seats **(see illustration)** are worn, check the pushrod ends.
7   If new lifters are being installed, a new camshaft must also be installed. If a new camshaft is installed, then use new lifters as well. Never install used lifters unless the original camshaft is used and the lifters can be installed in their original locations.
8   Coat each lifter foot with assembly lube or moly-based grease before reinstalling in the block.

12   Oil pan — removal and installation

Refer to illustrations 12.5, 12.10a, 12.10b, 12.11 and 12.16
Note: *The following procedure is based on the assumption that the engine is in place in the vehicle. If it has been removed, merely unbolt the oil pan and detach it from the block.*

Removal

1   Disconnect the cable from the negative terminal of the battery.
2   Raise the vehicle and place it securely on jackstands.
3   Drain the oil (refer to Chapter 1 if necessary).
4   Drain the coolant (refer to Chapter 1 if necessary).
5   If your vehicle is equipped with a manual transaxle, remove the roll restrictor **(see illustration)**.
6   Remove the starter motor (refer to Chapter 5).
7   Remove the elbow-shaped exhaust pipe section between the exhaust manifold and the catalytic converter (refer to Chapter 4).
8   Detach the coolant tube which is fastened to the lower radiator hose, the water pump and the tabs on the oil pan (refer to Chapter 4).
Warning: *To avoid the possibility of splashing coolant into your eyes, don't stand or lie directly under the junction between the coolant tube and the lower radiator hose. When the coolant tube is detached from the lower radiator hose, residual coolant may spill out.*
9   If the vehicle is equipped with air conditioning and/or power steering, remove the compressor/steering pump drivebelt, detach the compressor from the bracket and detach the bracket from the block (refer to Chapter 3). Push the air conditioning low pressure line off to the side. Tie it out of the way if necessary. **Warning:** *Do not disconnect the refrigerant fittings.*
10   Remove the oil pan bolts **(see illustrations)**. Note that two of the bolts, located in the recess for the access cover, are larger than the others.

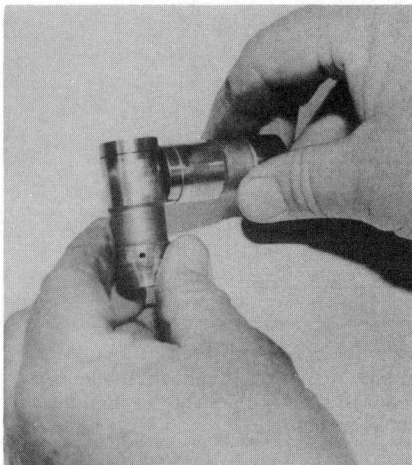

11.6a   The foot of each lifter should be slightly convex — the side of another lifter can be used as a straightedge to check it; if it appears flat, it's worn and must not be reused

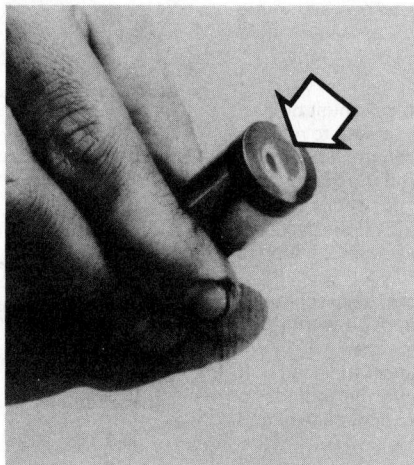

11.6b   If the bottom (foot) of any lifter is worn concave, scratched or galled, replace the entire set with new lifters

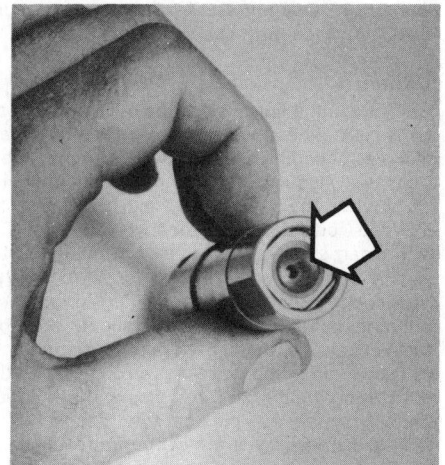

11.6c   Check the pushrod seat (arrow) in the top of each lifter for excessive wear

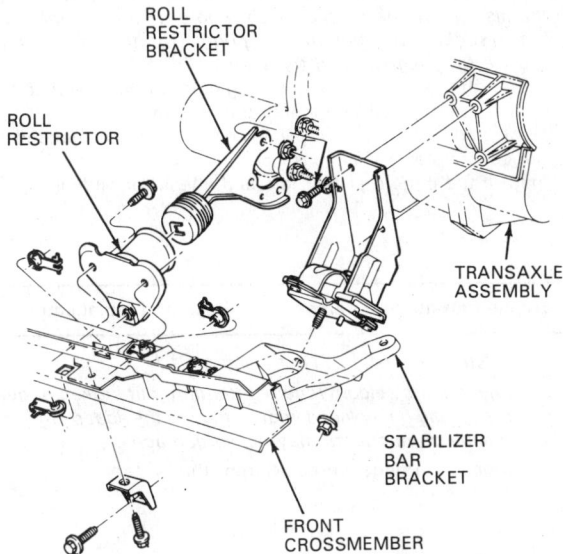

12.5 To remove the roll restrictor (used on vehicles with a manual transaxle), remove the bolts and U-nuts that attach it to the front crossmember, remove the nuts attaching the bracket to the starter motor-to-transaxle mounting studs and pull the restrictor and bracket out as an assembly

11 Because of the sealant used, the oil pan may be difficult to remove. Do not attempt to pry it loose from the block. Use a large rubber hammer to dislodge it, then remove it from the engine (see illustration).

Installation

12 Use a gasket scraper to remove all traces of old gasket material and sealant from the pan and block. Wipe the sealing surfaces with a cloth saturated with lacquer thinner or acetone.
13 Make sure the holes in the block are clean (use a tap to remove any sealant or corrosion from the threads).
14 It's also a good idea to remove and clean the oil pump pick-up tube and screen assembly. After cleaning both parts, install them (see the next Section).
15 Apply a thin layer of GE Pressure-Sensitive Adhesive to the gasket mating surfaces on the engine and to the block side of the new oil pan gasket. **Warning:** *Use the adhesive only in a well-ventilated area.*
16 After the adhesive has become tacky, apply a 1/8-inch bead of RTV sealant to the joints between the front cover and block and between the rear seal retainer and block (four places) (see illustration).

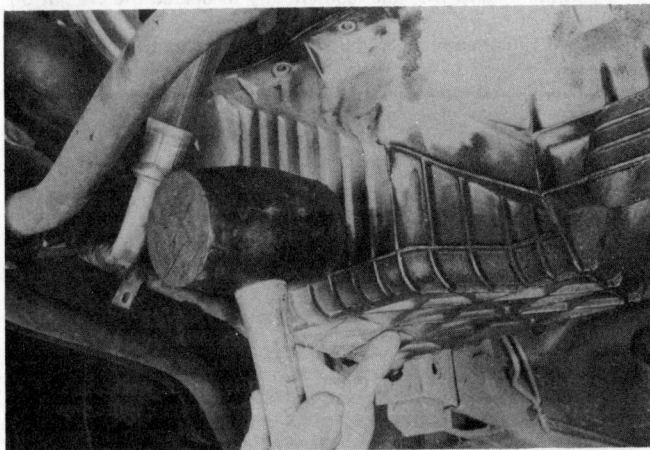

12.11   To break the oil pan loose, carefully tap it with a large rubber hammer — don't attempt to pry the pan loose or you'll damage the sealing flanges on the pan and/or the mating surfaces of the block and oil leaks will result

12.10a The oil pan is held in place with several small bolts along the flanges (arrows — some bolts not visible) . . .

12.10b . . . and two large bolts (arrows) on either side of the flywheel/driveplate access plate

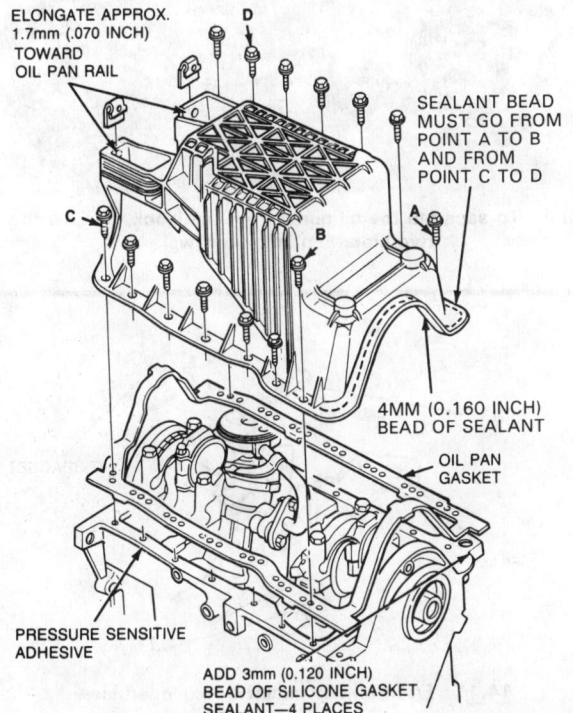

12.16 Oil pan gasket sealant application details

17 Immediately position the gasket against the block and press it into place to flatten the beads of RTV sealant applied in Step 16.

18 Apply a 5/32-inch bead of RTV sealant to the mating surfaces in the cutout areas at the ends of the pan. The beads should run from corner bolt hole-to-corner bolt hole.

19 Install the oil pan within two minutes after forming the beads of RTV.

20 Install the oil pan flange bolts and tighten them enough to compress the sealant until the oil pan holes are aligned with the two tapped holes in the transaxle, but loose enough to allow the pan to move relative to the block.

21 Install the two oil pan-to-transaxle bolts and tighten them to the specified torque to align the oil pan with the transaxle, then loosen the bolts 1/2-turn.

22 Tighten all oil pan flange bolts to the specified torque.

23 Tighten the two oil pan-to-transaxle bolts to the specified torque.

24 The remainder of installation is the reverse of removal.

13 Oil pump — removal and installation

Refer to illustration 13.2

Removal

1 Remove the oil pan as described in Section 12.

2 Remove the oil pump mounting bolts and detach the oil pump and intermediate driveshaft **(see illustration)**.

Installation

3 Prime the oil pump by filling the inlet port with engine oil. Rotate the pump shaft until oil flows from the outlet port.

4 Insert the intermediate driveshaft into the oil pump. Install the pump and driveshaft as an assembly. **Caution:** *Don't attempt to force the*

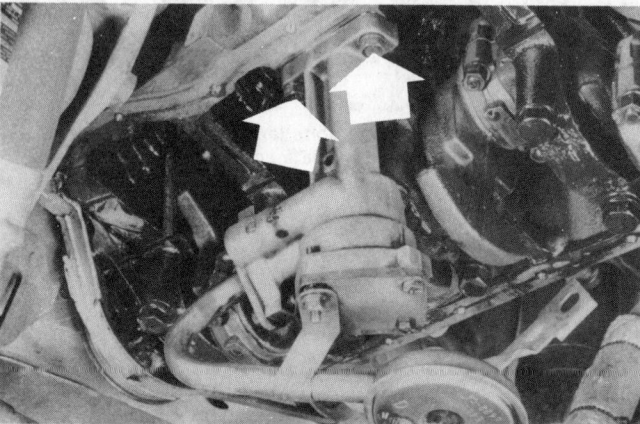

13.2 To separate the oil pump from the block, remove the two mounting bolts (arrows)

pump into position if it won't seat. The driveshaft may not be aligned with the distributor shaft. To align the end of the driveshaft with the distributor socket, remove the oil pump, rotate the intermediate driveshaft a few degrees and try again.

5 Tighten the two oil pump mounting bolts to the specified torque.

6 Refer to Section 12 and install the oil pan.

7 Fill the crankcase to the proper level with the recommended engine oil (refer to Chapter 1 if necessary).

8 Operate the engine at fast idle and check for oil leaks.

14 Engine mounts and dampers — check and replacement

Refer to illustrations 14.11, 14.12 and 14.17

Note: *Engine mounts seldom require attention, but broken or deteriorated mounts should be replaced immediately or the added strain placed on the driveline components may cause damage.*

1 Disconnect the negative cable from the battery.

Check

Warning: *Do not place any part of your body under the engine when it is supported only by a jack. Jack failure could result in severe injury or death!*

2 During the check, the engine must be raised slightly to remove the weight from the mounts.

3 Raise the vehicle and support it securely on jackstands, then position the jack under the engine oil pan. Place a large block of wood between the jack head and the oil pan, then carefully raise the engine just enough to take the weight off the mounts.

4 Check the mounts to see if the rubber is cracked, hardened or separated from the metal plates. Sometimes the rubber will split right down the center.

5 Check for relative movement between the mount plates and the engine, transaxle or frame/body (use a large screwdriver or pry bar to attempt to move the mounts). If movement is noted, lower the engine and tighten the mount fasteners. Rubber preservative should be applied to the mounts to slow deterioration.

Engine mount replacement

6 Remove the lower damper bolt from the right side of the engine.

7 Raise the vehicle and support it securely on jackstands (if not already done).

8 Position a jack under the oil pan. Use a block of wood between the oil pan and jack to distribute the weight.

9 Remove the nuts attaching the engine mounts to the subframe.

10 Raise the engine with the jack enough to unload the weight on the mounts.

11 On A/C equipped models, detach the front mount from the com-

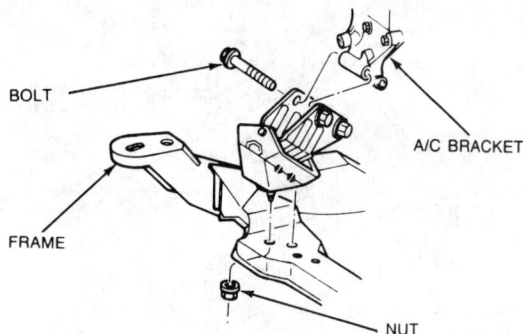

14.11 Front engine mount — exploded view

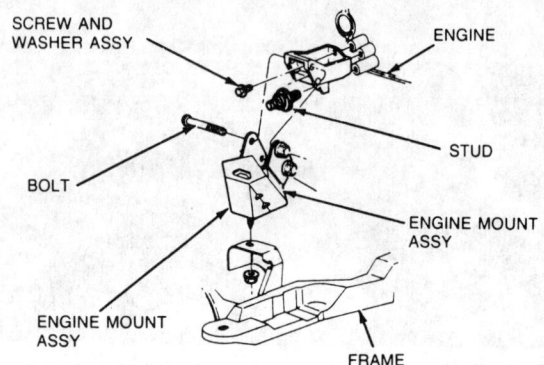

14.12 Rear engine mount — exploded view

pressor bracket. Remove the two through-bolts and remove the mount from the vehicle **(see illustration)**.

12 Attach the new mount to the engine bracket with two through-bolts **(see illustration)**.

13 Lower the engine into place.

14 Reinstall the engine mount-to-frame nuts.

15 Tighten the fasteners to the specified torque.

Damper replacement

Note: *Whenever self-locking fasteners are removed, replace them with new self-locking fasteners.*

16 Dampers should be replaced whenever they are leaking, bent, or otherwise damaged.

17 Remove the bolt attaching the lower end of the damper to the engine bracket **(see illustration)**.

18 Remove the bolts attaching the upper damper bracket to the shock tower bracket.

19 Remove the engine damper.

20 Separate the damper from the mounting bracket by removing the top nut cover and nut. Reinstall in the reverse order.

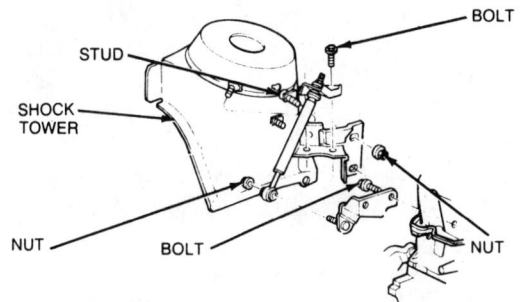

14.17   Engine damper components — exploded view

21 Position the damper lower sleeve to line up with the engine bracket notch. Secure it with a new bolt.

22 Position the engine damper with the upper bracket on the shock tower bracket, securing it with new bolts.

23 Tighten the fasteners to the specified torque.

Chapter 2 Part B   V6 engines

Contents

Specifications

General

Cylinder numbers (drivebelt end-to-transaxle — see illustration 11.9)	
Rear bank	1-2-3
Front bank	4-5-6
Firing order	1-4-2-5-3-6
Compression	See Chapter 2 Part C
Timing chain deflection.	6 degrees (see text)
Collapsed tappet gap (nominal)	0.088 to 0.0189 in

Torque specifications

All engines

	Ft-lbs
Damper right side bracket-to-shock tower nuts	21 to 30
Right damper-to-shock tower bracket bolts	40 to 55
Right damper-to-alternator bracket bolt	21 to 30
Damper left side bracket-to-frame nuts	21 to 30
Left damper-to-bracket bolts	21 to 30
Left damper-to-insulator bolt	21 to 30

3.0L V6 engine only   Ft-lbs (unless otherwise indicated)

Camshaft sprocket-to-camshaft bolt	40 to 51
Crankshaft pulley-to-damper bolt.	20 to 28
Vibration damper-to-crankshaft bolt	141 to 169
Cylinder head bolts	
Step 1	48 to 54
Step 2	63 to 80
Exhaust manifold bolts/studs	15 to 22
Intake manifold-to-cylinder head bolts	
Step 1	11
Step 2	18
Step 3	24
Oil inlet tube-to-main bearing cap nut	30 to 40
Oil inlet tube-to-block bolt	15 to 22
Oil pan-to-block bolt	80 to 106 in-lbs
Oil filter adapter-to-timing chain cover bolt	18 to 22
Oil pump-to-bearing cap bolt.	30 to 40
Rocker arm fulcrum-to-cylinder head bolts	
Step 1	5 to 11
Step 2	20 to 28
Rocker arm cover-to-cylinder head bolt/stud	80 to 106 in-lbs
Timing chain cover-to-block bolts	
6 mm	6 to 8
8 mm	15 to 22
Engine mount through bolt	40 to 55
Engine mount-to-frame nut	55 to 75

3.8L V6 engine only

Camshaft sprocket-to-camshaft bolt	15 to 22
Crankshaft pulley-to-damper bolt.	20 to 28
Vibration damper-to-crankshaft bolt	93 to 121
Cylinder head bolts	
Step 1	37
Step 2	45
Step 3	52
Step 4	59
Exhaust manifold bolts/studs	15 to 22
Intake manifold-to-cylinder head bolts	
Step 1	7
Step 2	15
Step 3	24
Oil inlet tube-to-main bearing cap nut	30 to 40
Oil inlet tube-to-block bolt	15 to 22
Oil pan-to-block bolt	80 to 106 in-lbs
Oil filter adapter-to-timing chain cover bolt	18 to 22
Rocker arm cover-to-cylinder head bolt/stud	80 to 106 in-lbs
Rocker arm fulcrum-to-cylinder head bolts	
Step 1	5 to 11
Step 2	18 to 26
Timing chain cover-to-block bolt	15 to 22
Front engine mount-to-A/C bracket nut	40 to 55
Front engine mount-to-frame nut	55 to 75
Rear engine mount-to-transaxle bracket nut	70 to 90
Rear engine mount-to-frame nut	55 to 75

1 General information

This Part of Chapter 2 is devoted to in-vehicle repair procedures for the V6 engines. All information concerning engine removal and installation, repairs which require engine removal and engine block and cylinder head overhaul can be found in Part C of this Chapter.

The following repair procedures are based on the assumption that the engine is installed in the vehicle. If the engine has been removed from the vehicle and mounted on a stand, many of the steps outlined in this Part of Chapter 2 will not apply.

The specifications included in this Part of Chapter 2 apply only to the procedures contained in this Part. Part C of Chapter 2 contains the specifications necessary for cylinder head and engine block rebuilding.

2 Repair operations possible with the engine in the vehicle

Refer to illustrations 2.5a, 2.5b and 2.5c

Many major repair operations can be accomplished without removing the engine from the vehicle.

Clean the engine compartment and the exterior of the engine with some type of pressure washer before any work is done. A clean engine will make the job easier and will help keep dirt out of the internal areas of the engine.

Depending on the components involved, it may be a good idea to remove the hood to improve access to the engine as repairs are performed (refer to Chapter 11 if necessary).

If vacuum, exhaust, oil or coolant leaks develop, indicating a need for gasket or seal replacement, the repairs can generally be made with

2.5a   Drivebelt end view of 3.0L V6 engine

2.5b   Front view of 3.0L V6 engine

2.5c   Rear view of 3.0L V6 engine

the engine in the vehicle. The intake and exhaust manifold gaskets, oil pan gasket and cylinder head gaskets are all accessible with the engine in place.

Exterior engine components such as the intake and exhaust manifolds, the oil pan (and the oil pump), the water pump, the starter motor, the alternator, the distributor and the fuel injection system components can be removed for repair with the engine in place (see illustrations).

Since the cylinder heads can be removed without pulling the engine, valve component servicing can also be accomplished with the engine in the vehicle.

In extreme cases caused by a lack of necessary equipment, repair or replacement of piston rings, pistons, connecting rods and rod bearings is possible with the engine in the vehicle. However, this practice is not recommended because of the cleaning and preparation work that must be done to the components involved.

3   Rocker arm covers — removal and installation

Refer to illustrations 3.3a and 3.3b

1   Disconnect the negative cable from the battery.

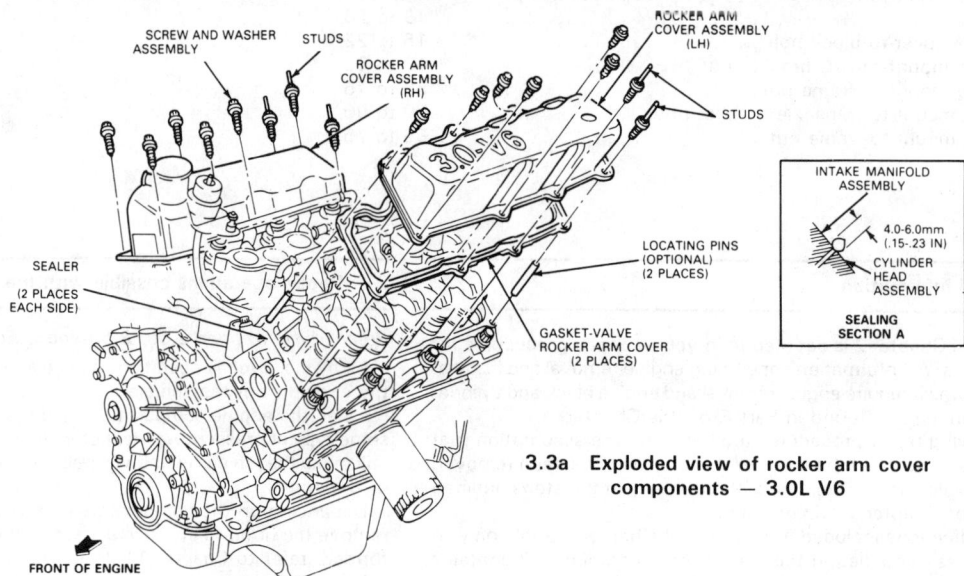

SCREW AND WASHER ASSEMBLY

STUDS

ROCKER ARM COVER ASSEMBLY (RH)

ROCKER ARM COVER ASSEMBLY (LH)

STUDS

SEALER
(2 PLACES EACH SIDE)

LOCATING PINS (OPTIONAL) (2 PLACES)

GASKET-VALVE ROCKER ARM COVER (2 PLACES)

INTAKE MANIFOLD ASSEMBLY

4.0-6.0mm (.15-.23 IN)

CYLINDER HEAD ASSEMBLY

SEALING SECTION A

FRONT OF ENGINE

3.3a   Exploded view of rocker arm cover components — 3.0L V6

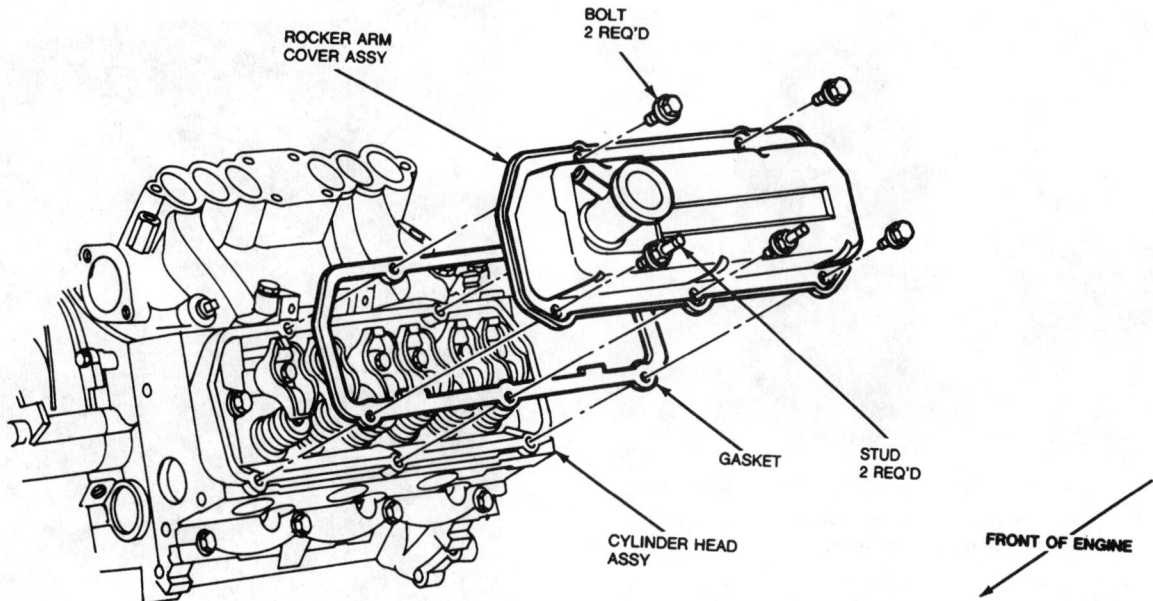

ROCKER ARM
COVER ASSY

BOLT
2 REQ'D

GASKET

STUD
2 REQ'D

CYLINDER HEAD
ASSY

FRONT OF ENGINE

3.3b Exploded view of rocker arm cover components — 3.8L V6

2   Disconnect the ignition wires from the spark plugs on the side(s) you are disassembling. If they are not numbered, tag them for reassembly.
3   Note the location of the wire routing clips and studs (see illustrations) and pull the clips off the studs.
4   If the front cover is being removed, take off the oil filler cap and on 3.0L models, disconnect the breather hose.
5   If the rear cover is being removed, remove the PCV valve (Chapter 6) and, on 3.8L models, position the air cleaner aside. On 3.0L models, remove the EGR tube from the exhaust manifold for access. If you are removing the rocker cover as part of another service procedure, remove the upper intake manifold (plenum) as described in Chapter 4.
6   Remove the rocker cover attaching bolts.
7   Carefully remove the cover. If the cover is stuck, tap it with a soft-face hammer to break it loose.
8   Remove all traces of gasket material from the head and cover. Clean off any oil or dirt with acetone or lacquer thinner and a cloth.
9   Lightly oil all bolt threads prior to installation.
10   On 3.0L models, apply a bead of RTV sealer at the cylinder head to intake manifold rail step (two places per rail).

11   Position a new gasket and install the rocker cover.
12   Tighten the bolts to the specified torque, working around the cover in several steps.
13   Reinstall the parts removed for access. Be sure to add coolant if it was drained.

4   Rocker arms and pushrods — removal, inspection, installation and adjustment

Removal, inspection and installation
Refer to illustrations 4.2, 4.3 and 4.5

1   Remove the rocker arm cover(s) (Section 3).
2   Loosen the rocker arm fulcrum bolt until you can pivot the rocker arm to one side and pull the pushrod out of the valve lifter (see illustration).
3   If you are removing more than one pushrod, store them in a holder made from a cardboard box (see illustration) so they can be returned to their original locations.
4   If you are going to remove all of the rocker arms, mark them so

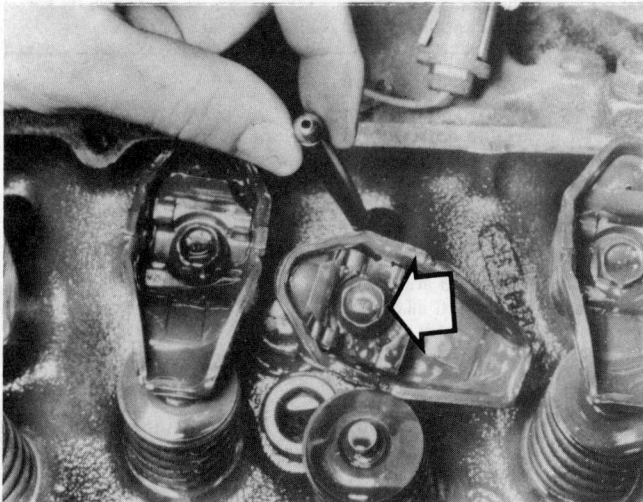

4.2 Loosen the nut or bolt (arrow) and pivot the rocker arm to the side to remove the pushrod

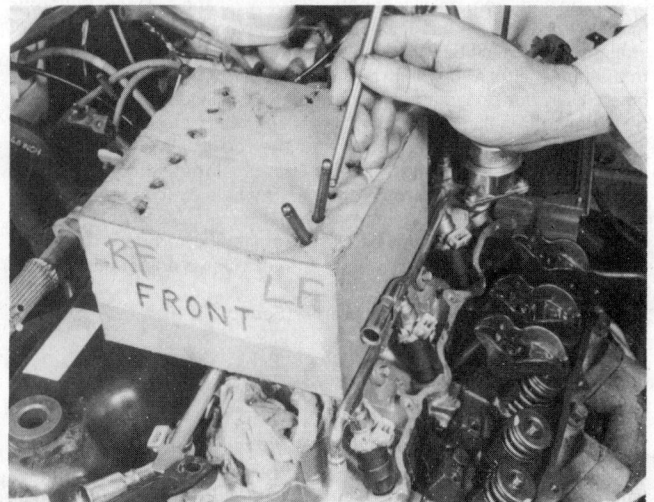

4.3 A perforated cardboard box can be used to store the pushrods to ensure installation in their original locations

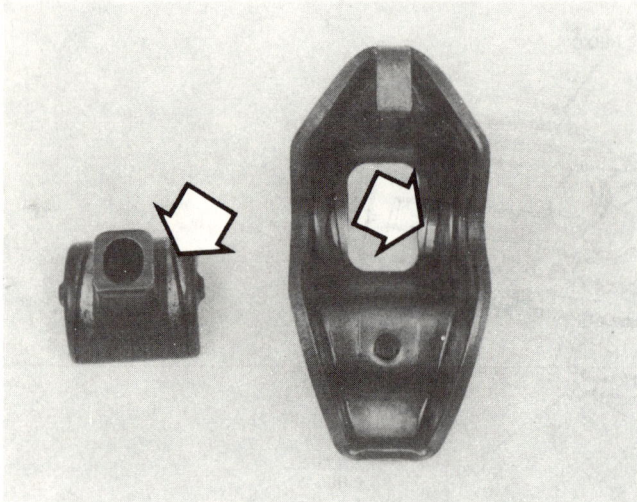

4.5   Check the rocker arm and fulcrum for wear and
galling (arrows)

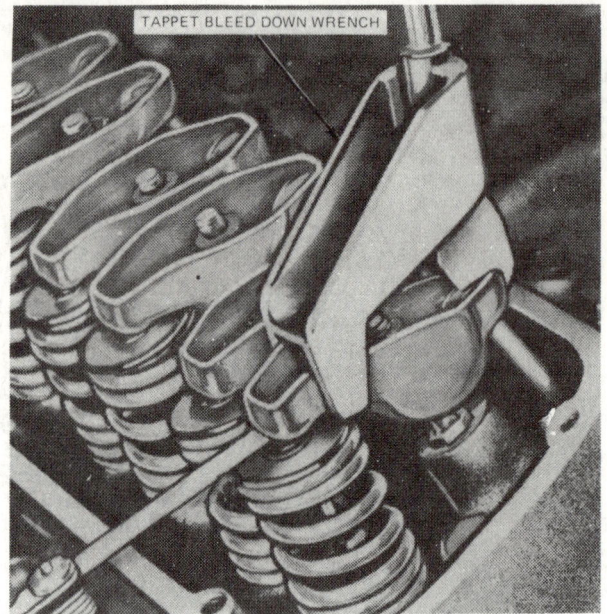

4.11   Checking valve clearance with a lifter bleed down
tool and feeler gauge

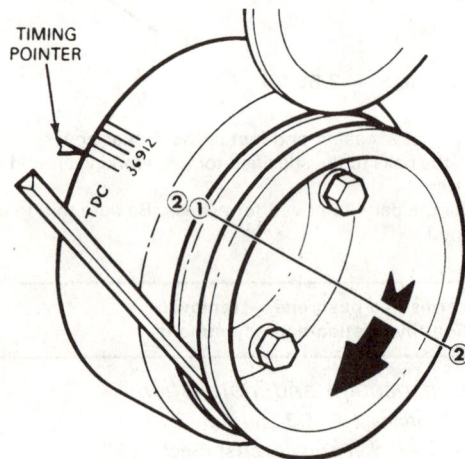

POSITION 1 —
NO. 1 AT TDC, AT
END OF COMPRESSION
STROKE

POSITION 2 —
ROTATE CRANKSHAFT 360°
(ONE REVOLUTION) CLOCKWISE,
FROM POSITION 1

4.12   Positioning the crankshaft for valve clearance check

they can be returned to their original locations — don't mix them up!
5   Clean and examine all components for wear and damage. Pushrods may be rolled over a flat surface such as a piece of glass to check for straightness. Check the fulcrums and rockers for galling and wear. Wear frequently occurs at the points where the pushrods contact the rockers (see illustration). Replace any parts showing evidence of wear.
6   Prior to installation, apply moly-base grease or engine assembly lube to the fulcrums and the ends of the rocker arms.
7   Check to be sure that the valve lifter is all the way down before installing the pushrod. Turn the crankshaft with a wrench until the lifter is down, if needed.
8   Tighten the rocker arm bolt to the specified torque.
9   If any parts have been replaced, check valve adjustment as described below.
10   Reinstall the rocker arm cover(s) (Section 3).

Adjustment
Refer to illustrations 4.11 and 4.12
Note: *adjustment is normally only needed when parts have been replaced or valves and/or seats have been ground a considerable amount.*

11   Using Ford lifter bleed-down tool T70P-6513-A or equivalent (see illustration), press on the rocker arm until the lifter leaks down. Check the clearance between the valve stem and rocker arm with a feeler gauge. Compare it to the specifications and write it down. Repeat this

procedure for each valve in the order shown below. **Note:** *The arrangement of intake (I) and exhaust valves (E), starting at the front (drivebelt) end, is as follows:*
Left side (front)
    3.0L — I-E-I-E-I-E
    3.8L — E-I-E-I-E-I
Right side (rear)
    3.0L — E-I-E-I-E-I
    3.8L — I-E-I-E-I-E
12   Set the number 1 piston at Top Dead Center (TDC) on the compression stroke (Section 11). This is position 1 (see illustration).
13   Check the following valves:
    Intake — 1, 3 and 6
    Exhaust — 1, 2 and 4
14   Rotate the crankshaft to position 2 and check the following valves:
    Intake — 2, 4 and 5
    Exhaust — 3, 5 and 6
If the clearances are within specification, install the rocker arm covers.
15   If there is not enough clearance, use a shorter pushrod; too much clearance, use a longer one (available from your dealer).

5   Valve springs, retainers and seals — replacement

Refer to illustrations 5.8, 5.9, 5.14 and 5.15
Note: *Broken valve springs and defective valve stem seals can be replaced without removing the cylinder head. Two special tools and a compressed air source are normally required to perform this operation, so read through this Section carefully and rent or buy the tools before beginning the job. If compressed air is not available, a length of nylon rope can be used to keep the valves from falling into the cylinder during this procedure.*

1   Refer to Section 3 and remove the rocker arm cover from the affected cylinder head. If all of the valve stem seals are being replaced, remove both rocker arm covers.
2   Remove the spark plug from the cylinder which has the defective component. If all of the valve stem seals are being replaced, all of the spark plugs should be removed.
3   Turn the crankshaft until the piston in the affected cylinder is at top dead center on the compression stroke (refer to Section 11 for instructions). If you are replacing all of the valve stem seals, begin with cylinder number one and work on the valves for one cylinder at a time. Move from cylinder-to-cylinder following the firing order sequence (1-4-2-5-3-6).

5.8 Compress the spring and remove the keepers with a
magnet or needle-nose pliers

5.9 Once the valve spring assembly is removed, the seal
can be pulled off the valve guide boss

4 Thread an adapter into the spark plug hole and connect an air hose
from a compressed air source to it. Most auto parts stores can supply
the air hose adapter. **Note:** *Many cylinder compression gauges utilize
a screw-in fitting that may work with your air hose quick-disconnect
fitting.*
5 Remove the bolt, fulcrum and rocker arm for the valve with the
defective part and pull out the pushrod. If all of the valve stem seals
are being replaced, all of the rocker arms and pushrods should be removed (refer to Section 4).
6 Apply compressed air to the cylinder. The valves should be held
in place by the air pressure. If the valve faces or seats are in poor condition, leaks may prevent the air pressure from retaining the valves —
refer to the alternative procedure below.
7 If you do not have access to compressed air, an alternative method
can be used. Position the piston at a point just before TDC on the compression stroke, then feed a long piece of nylon rope through the spark
plug hole until it fills the combustion chamber. Be sure to leave the
end of the rope hanging out of the engine so it can be removed easily.
Use a large breaker bar and socket to rotate the crankshaft in the normal
direction of rotation until slight resistance is felt.
8 Stuff shop rags into the cylinder head holes above and below the
valves to prevent parts and tools from falling into the engine, then use
a valve spring compressor to compress the spring/damper assembly.
Remove the keepers with small needle-nose pliers or a magnet **(see
illustration). Note:** *A couple of different types of tools are available
for compressing the valve springs with the head in place. One type
grips the lower spring coils and presses on the retainer as the knob
is turned, while the other type, shown here, utilizes the rocker arm
bolt for leverage. Both types work very well, although the lever type
is usually less expensive.*
9 Remove the spring retainer shield and valve spring assembly, then
remove the valve stem umbrella-type guide seal **(see illustration). Note:**
*If air pressure fails to hold the valve in the closed position during this
operation, the valve face or seat is probably damaged. If so, the cylinder
head will have to be removed for additional repair operations.*
10 Wrap a rubber band or tape around the top of the valve stem so
the valve will not fall into the combustion chamber, then release the
air pressure. **Note:** *If a rope was used instead of air pressure, turn the
crankshaft slightly in the direction opposite normal rotation.*
11 Inspect the valve stem for damage. Rotate the valve in the guide
and check the end for eccentric movement, which would indicate that
the valve is bent.
12 Move the valve up-and-down in the guide and make sure it doesn't
bind. If the valve stem binds, either the valve is bent or the guide is
damaged. In either case, the head will have to be removed for repair.
13 Reapply air pressure to the cylinder to retain the valve in the closed
position, then remove the tape or rubber band from the valve stem.
If a rope was used instead of air pressure, rotate the crankshaft in the
normal direction of rotation until slight resistance is felt.
14 Lubricate the valve stem with engine oil and install a new umbrella-
type guide seal **(see illustration).** 3.0L intake seals have a silver band
while the exhaust seals have a red band.

5.14 Carefully seat the valve seal using a deep socket
and hammer

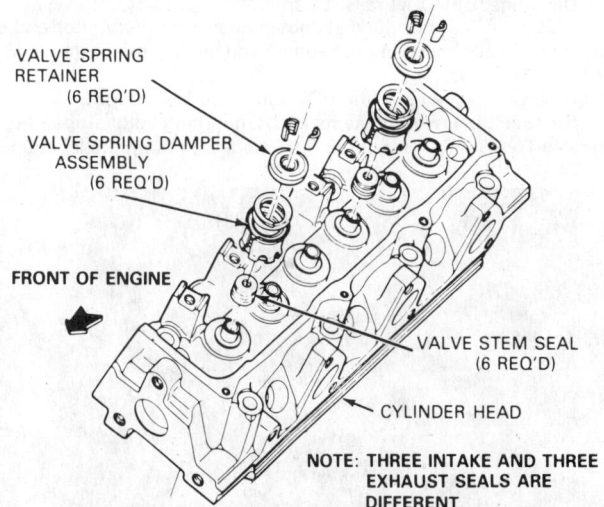

VALVE SPRING
RETAINER
(6 REQ'D)

VALVE SPRING DAMPER
ASSEMBLY
(6 REQ'D)

FRONT OF ENGINE

VALVE STEM SEAL
(6 REQ'D)

CYLINDER HEAD

NOTE: THREE INTAKE AND THREE
EXHAUST SEALS ARE
DIFFERENT

5.15 Exploded view of valve spring components
(3.0L shown, 3.8L similar)

15 Install the spring assembly and spring seat (where applicable) in
position over the valve **(see illustration).**
16 Install the valve spring retainer. Compress the valve spring
assembly.
17 Position the keepers in the grooves. Apply a small dab of grease
to the inside of each keeper to hold it in place if necessary **(see illustra-**

CRANKCASE VENTILATION
TUBE ASSY
NOTE:
FOR PROPER INSTALLATION,
TUBE MUST BE FULLY
ENGAGED INTO TUBE ON OIL
FILLER ADAPTER PART
OF LH ROCKER ARM COVER ASSY

CONNECTOR HOSE

NUT AND WASHER

LOWER INTAKE
MANIFOLD STUD

FRONT OF ENGINE

TUBE (PART OF
ROCKER ARM COVER ASSY)

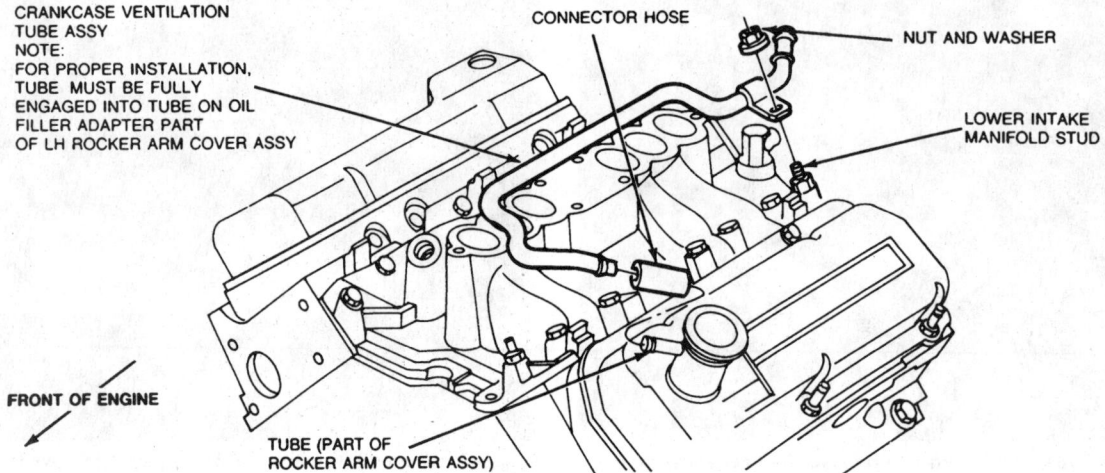

6.5   Remove the PCV tube bracket nut and lift the tube out (3.8L)

tion 6.16 in **Chapter 2 Part A**). Remove the pressure from the spring tool and make sure the keepers are seated.

18 Disconnect the air hose and remove the adapter from the spark plug hole. If a rope was used in place of air pressure, pull it out of the cylinder.

19 Refer to Section 4 and install the rocker arm(s) and pushrod(s).

20 Install the spark plug(s) and hook up the wire(s).

21 Refer to Section 3 and install the rocker arm cover(s).

22 Start and run the engine, then check for oil leaks and unusual sounds coming from the rocker arm cover area.

6   Intake manifold — removal and installation

Refer to illustrations 6.5, 6.8, 6.10, 6.11a, 6.11b, 6.13a and 6.13b

1   Remove the upper intake manifold and throttle body (Chapter 4).

2   Disconnect the coolant hoses from the intake manifold.

3   Disconnect the fuel rails (Chapter 4).

4   3.0L only — if not done already, remove the distributor and coil with bracket as described in Chapter 5 and remove the pushrods (Section 4).

5   3.8L only — remove the PCV tube **(see illustration)**.

6   Remove the lower intake manifold mounting bolts/studs (this requires a Torx T-50 driver bit on 3.0L models), noting the locations of

the studs for reinstallation.

7   Remove the intake manifold. It may be necessary to pry on the end of the manifold with a screwdriver to break the RTV seal. Use care to avoid damaging machined surfaces.

8   Clean away all traces of old gasket material **(see illustration)**. Remove oil and dirt with a cloth and solvent, such as acetone or lacquer thinner.

9   Lightly oil all bolts and studs prior to assembly.

10 Apply a 1/8-inch bead of RTV sealer (Ford D6AZ-19562 or equivalent) at each corner where the head joins the engine block **(see illustration)**.

11 Position the new gaskets on the engine with adhesive (Ford D7AZ-19B508-A or equivalent). Be sure the locating pins/tabs fit properly **(see illustrations)**. **Note:** *Assembly must be completed within several minutes. Don't allow the RTV sealer to dry.*

12 Carefully set the lower manifold into place. Be sure the gaskets don't shift out of place. Install the bolts and studs in their original locations.

13 Tighten the bolts/studs in numerical sequence **(see illustrations)**, reaching the specified torque in several stages.

14 Reinstall all parts removed for access in the reverse order of removal.

15 Refill the cooling system and run the engine. Check the ignition timing (if the distributor was removed).

16 Check for fuel, vacuum and coolant leaks.

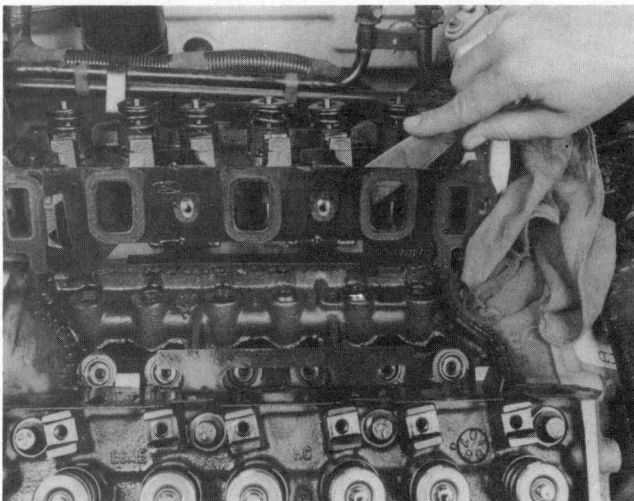

6.8   Use a scraper to remove the intake manifold gaskets

6.10   Put extra sealer in the four corners before installing the new gaskets

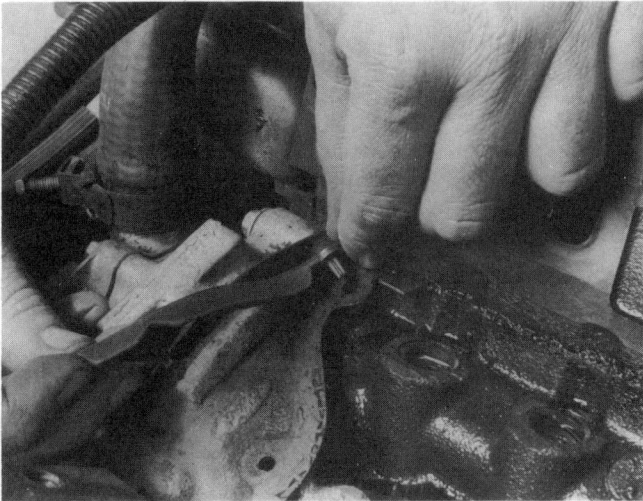

6.11a The end seals have locating pins which must be pressed into place

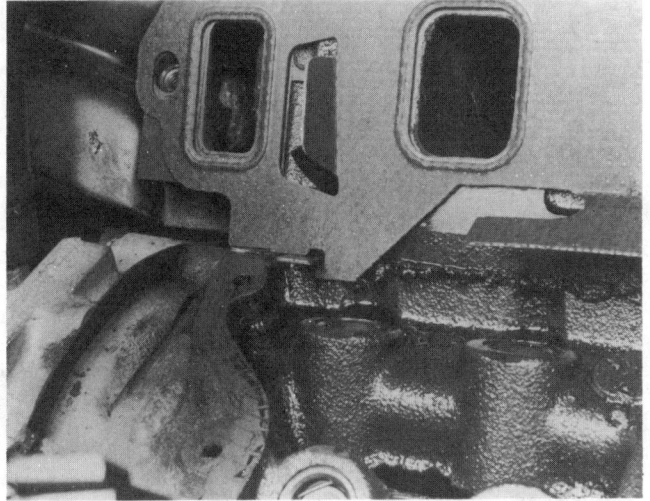

6.11b Be sure the locking tabs on the gaskets are engaged

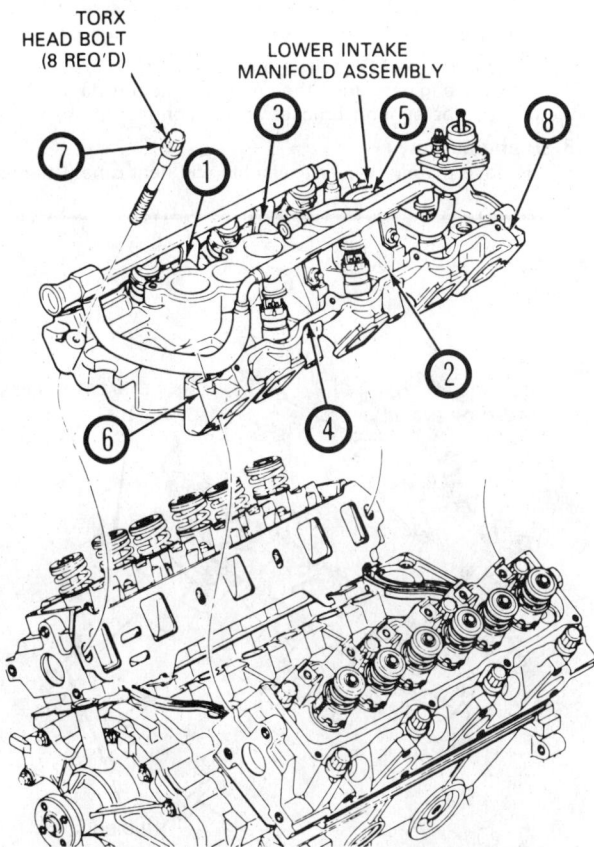

6.13a 3.0L manifold bolt tightening sequence

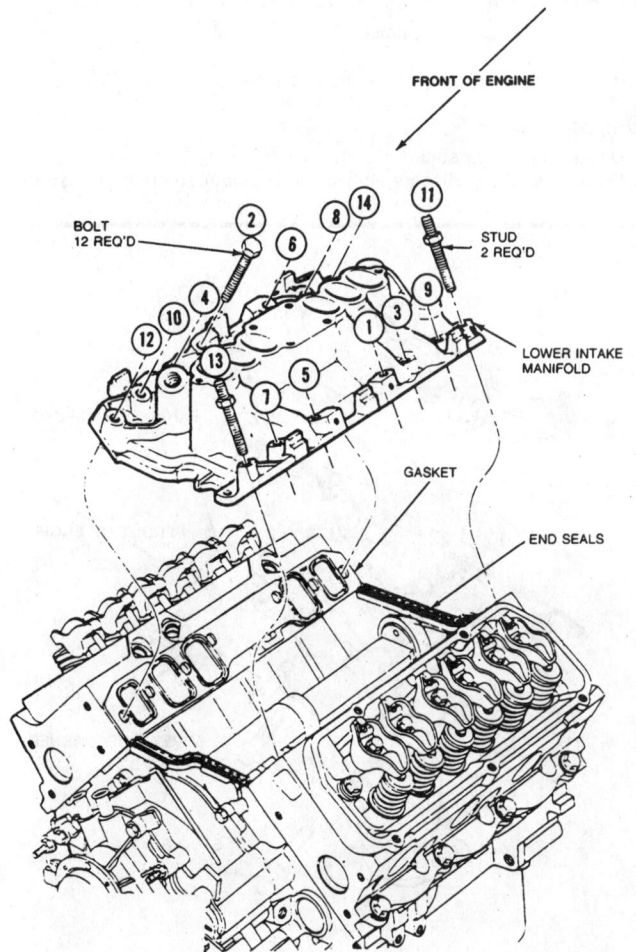

6.13b 3.8L manifold bolt tightening sequence

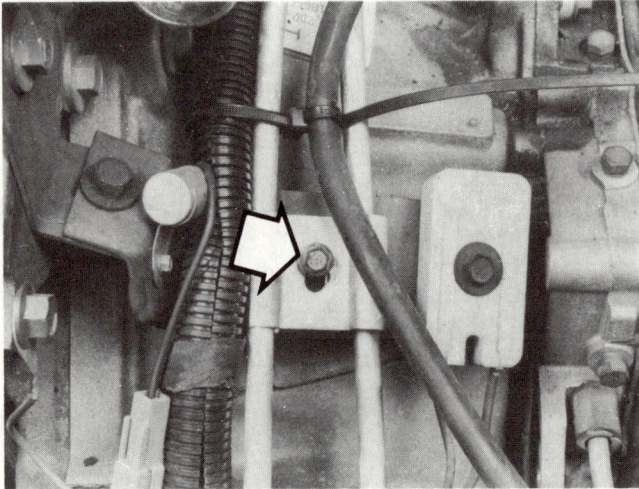

7.4   Unbolt the cooling line bracket (arrow) to allow the line to move (3.0L)

7.5   Slip the front manifold around the dipstick and power steering line

7   Exhaust manifolds — removal and installation

Refer to illustrations 7.4, 7.5, 7.17a, 7.17b, 7.17c and 7.17d

1   Disconnect the exhaust pipe(s) from the manifold(s) being removed (Chapter 4).
2   Remove the spark plugs from the side(s) being removed (Chapter 1).

Front manifold

3   Unbolt the oil dipstick tube bracket.
4   On 3.0L engines, disconnect the upper power steering (pressure) hose from the pump (Chapter 10) and remove the cooling line support bracket **(see illustration)**.
5   Unbolt and remove the exhaust manifold from the vehicle **(see illustration)**.

Rear manifold

6   Disconnect the EGR tube from the manifold (Chapter 6).
7   On 3.0L engines, drain the cooling system (Chapter 1), remove the heater tube support bracket and disconnect the heater hoses.

3.8L engine only

8   Remove the air cleaner assembly and heat tube (Chapter 6).

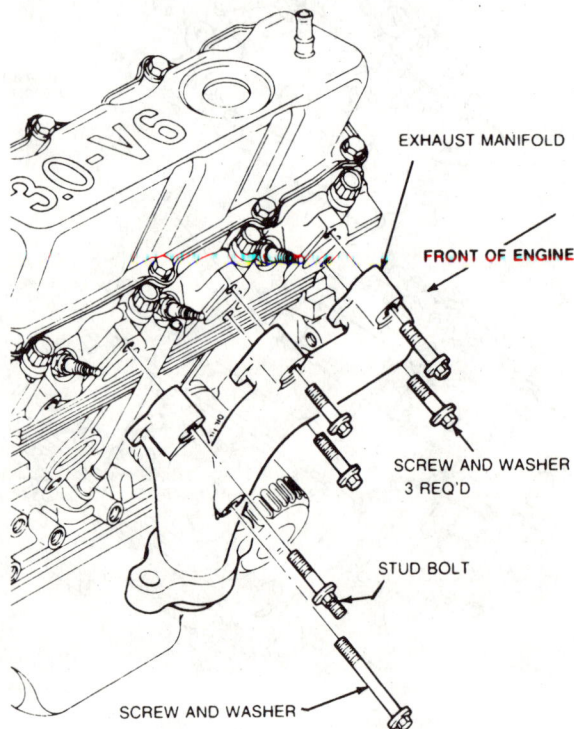

7.17a   Front exhaust manifold components (3.0L) — exploded view

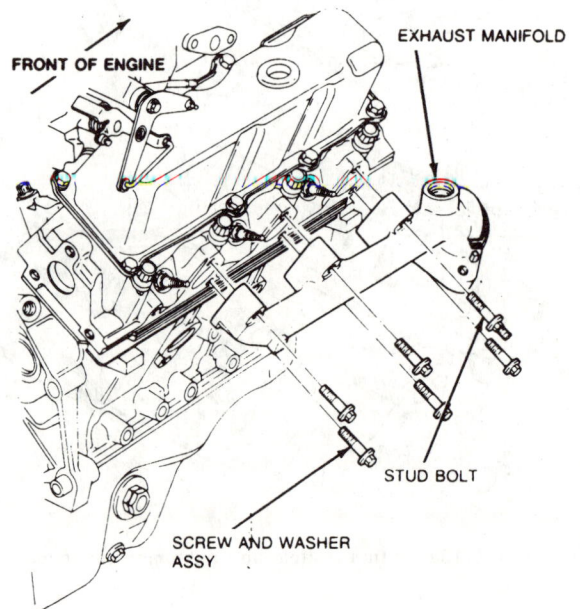

7.17b   Rear exhaust manifold components (3.0L) — exploded view

7.17c Front exhaust manifold components (3.8L) — exploded view

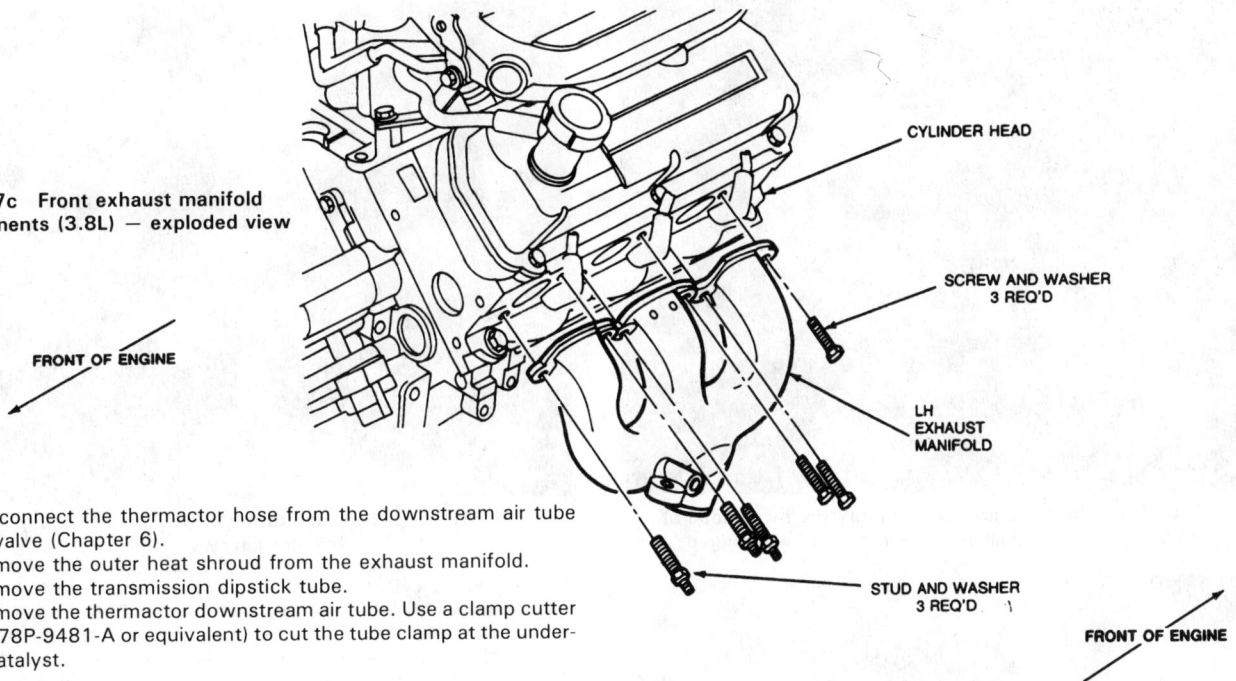

FRONT OF ENGINE

CYLINDER HEAD

SCREW AND WASHER
3 REQ'D

LH EXHAUST MANIFOLD

STUD AND WASHER
3 REQ'D

FRONT OF ENGINE

9   Disconnect the thermactor hose from the downstream air tube check valve (Chapter 6).
10 Remove the outer heat shroud from the exhaust manifold.
11 Remove the transmission dipstick tube.
12 Remove the thermactor downstream air tube. Use a clamp cutter (Ford T78P-9481-A or equivalent) to cut the tube clamp at the underbody catalyst.

All engines
13 Unbolt and remove the exhaust manifold from the vehicle.

Installation

14 Clean all gasket surfaces thoroughly and inspect the manifold(s) for cracks and damage. Check the fasteners and bolt holes for stripped or damaged threads.
15 Lightly oil all bolts prior to installation.
16 Position the manifold in place on the cylinder head. On 3.8L engines, use a gasket. Install a pilot bolt (left side — lower front bolt on number 5 cylinder, right side — lower rear bolt on number 2 cylinder). **Note:** *Slight warpage of the exhaust manifold may cause a misalignment between the bolt holes in the head and manifold. Elongate the holes in the manifold as necessary to correct the misalignment. Do not elongate the pilot hole.*
17 Install the remaining bolts and studs in their correct locations **(see illustrations)** and tighten them to the specified torque.
18 Reinstall the remaining parts in the reverse order of removal.
19 Add coolant if needed, run the engine and check for exhaust leaks.

8   Cylinder heads — removal and installation

Refer to illustrations 8.21a, 8.21b, 8.25, 8.27a and 8.27b
1   Drain the cooling system (Chapter 1).
2   Disconnect the negative cable from the battery.
3   Remove the air cleaner assembly.
4   Remove the drivebelt(s) (Chapter 1).

3.0L — front head
5   Remove the main drivebelt idler assembly (Chapter 3).
6   If so equipped, remove the power steering pump mounting nuts, leaving the hoses connected.
7   Remove the coil bracket (Chapter 5) and ground wire.

3.0L — rear head
8   Remove the alternator adjusting/engine shock bracket.
9   Remove the ground strap at the engine lifting eye and unbolt the throttle cable support bracket from the opposite end of the head.

3.8L front head
10 Remove the alternator and bracket (Chapter 5).
11 If so equipped, remove the power steering pump, leaving the hoses connected.
12 If equipped with air conditioning, unbolt the A/C compressor from

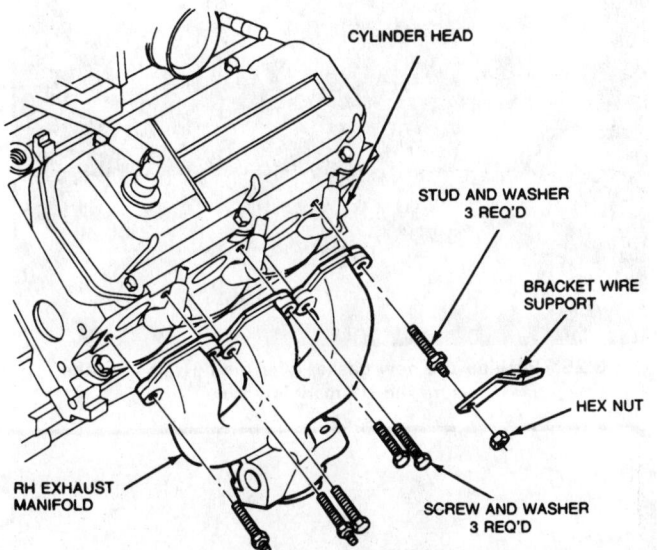

CYLINDER HEAD

STUD AND WASHER
3 REQ'D

BRACKET WIRE SUPPORT

HEX NUT

RH EXHAUST MANIFOLD

SCREW AND WASHER
3 REQ'D

7.17d Rear exhaust manifold components (3.8L) — exploded view

the mounting bracket, leaving the hoses connected. Set the compressor aside. **Warning:** *Don't disconnect refrigerant hoses unless the system has been discharged by a professional.*

3.8L — rear head
13 Disconnect the thermactor tube support bracket from the rear of the cylinder head.
14 Remove the drivebelt idler assembly.
15 Remove the thermactor pump (Chapter 6).

All engines
16 Remove the intake manifold (Section 6).
17 Remove the exhaust manifold(s) (Section 7).
18 Remove the rocker arm cover(s) (Section 3).
19 Loosen the rocker arm fulcrum bolts enough to allow the rocker arms to be lifted off the pushrods and rotate them to one side.
20 Remove the pushrods (Section 4). Store them so they can be reinstalled in the same location.

8.21a   Once the bolts are removed, pry the head loose at
a point where the gasket surfaces won't be damaged

8.21b   Slip the studs through the power steering
bracket (arrows)

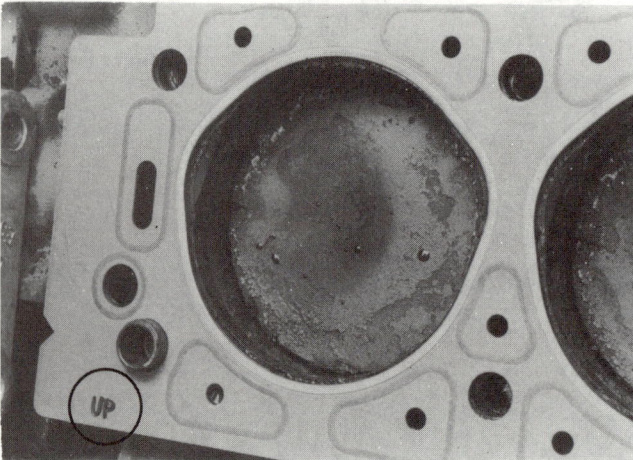

8.25   Position the new gasket over the dowels — make
sure the UP mark is visible

21 Remove the cylinder head bolts and lift the head(s) off the engine
(see illustration). When removing the front head from a 3.0L engine,
lift the head clear of the locating dowels and pull it toward the transaxle, so the power steering pump studs slip out of the bracket (see
illustration). Place the pump aside in such a way that the fluid won't
leak out.
22 Thoroughly remove all traces of gasket material with a gasket
scraper and clean all parts with solvent. Use a rag and acetone or lacquer thinner to remove any traces of oil. See Chapter 2 Part C for
cylinder head inspection procedures.
23 Use a tap of the correct size to chase the threads in the head bolt
holes. On 3.0L engines, run a rethreading die along the threads of the
head bolts. 3.8L engines require new bolts. Lightly oil the threads of
the bolts except as noted below.
24 Recheck all head bolt holes and cylinder bores for any traces of
coolant, oil or other foreign matter. Remove as needed.
25 Position the new gasket over the dowel pins on the block. The top
of the gasket should be stamped TOP or THIS SIDE UP to ensure correct
installation (see illustration). Don't use sealer on the gaskets. Note:
3.8L engines require new bolts every time the head is installed. Apply
a thin coat of sealant (Ford D8AZ-19554-A or equivalent) to the threads
of the short cylinder head bolts (nearest to the exhaust manifold).

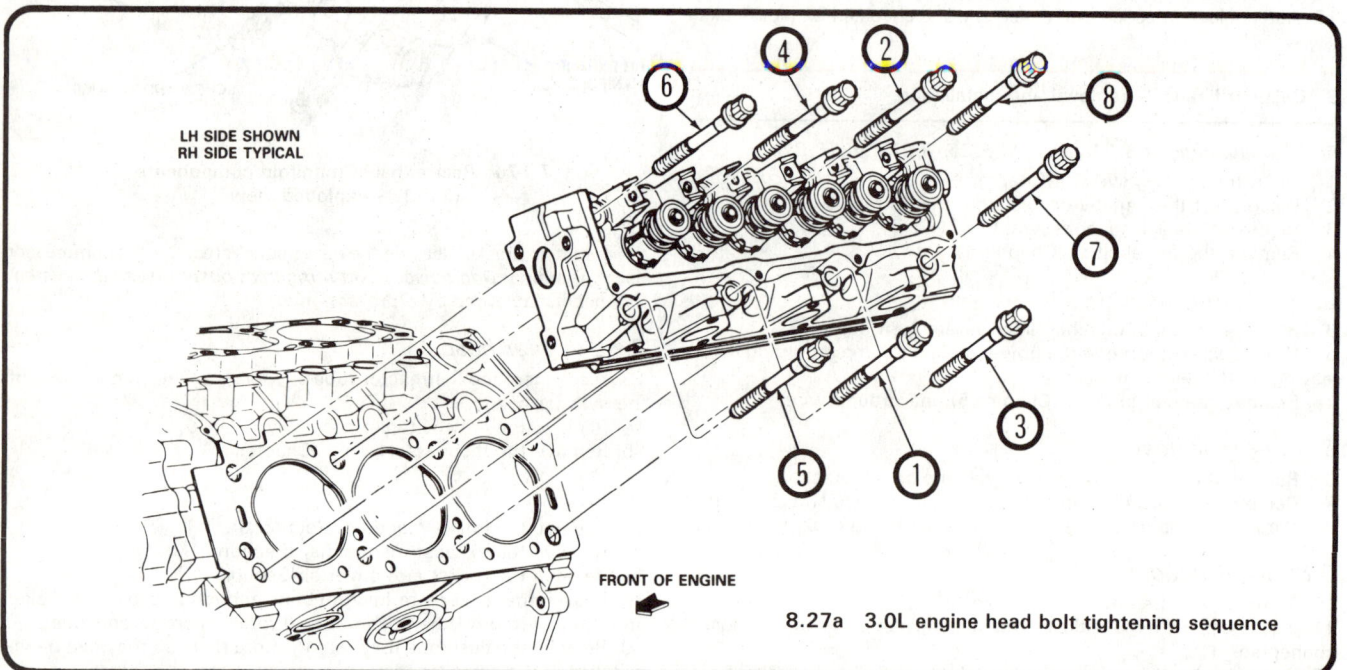

LH SIDE SHOWN
RH SIDE TYPICAL

FRONT OF ENGINE

8.27a   3.0L engine head bolt tightening sequence

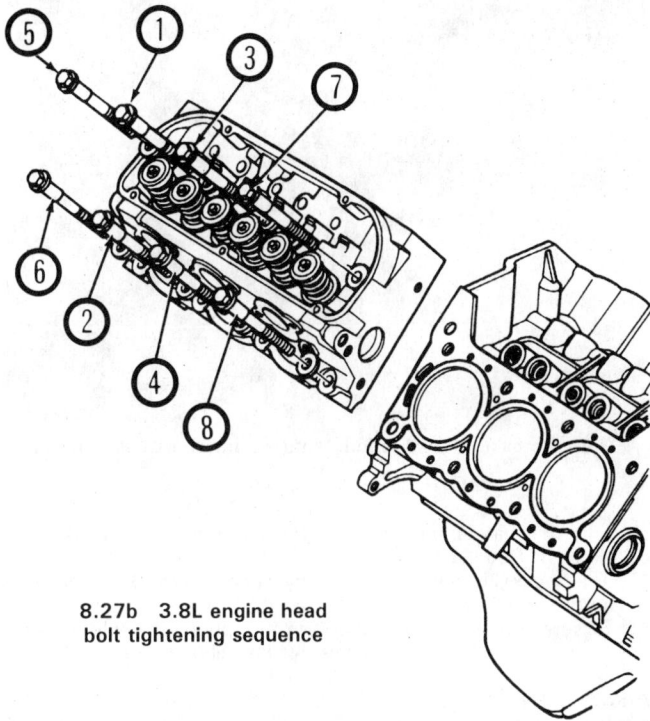

8.27b 3.8L engine head
bolt tightening sequence

26 Install the head bolts finger tight.
27 Following the sequence shown **(see illustrations)**, tighten the head bolts in several stages to the specified torque.
28 On 3.8L engines only, loosen the head bolts two or three turns and retighten them in the same sequence as before to the same torque specification. **Note:** *When cylinder head bolts have been tightened using the above procedure, it is not necessary to retighten bolts after extended engine operation. However, bolts may be rechecked for tightness if desired.*
29 Reinstall the parts removed in the reverse order of removal. Lubricate the rocker arm components with oil conditioner (Ford D9AZ-19579-C or equivalent) or high viscosity engine oil.
30 Install the pushrods in their original locations. For each valve, rotate the crankshaft until the valve lifter is at its lowest position. Install the rocker arms, fulcrums and bolts. Tighten to the specified torque. Repeat until all are done.
31 Refill the cooling system, change the oil and filter (Chapter 1) and run the engine. Check the ignition timing and inspect for any leaks.
32 If a component has been replaced or the valves ground, check valve clearance as described in Section 4.

9 Crankshaft front oil seal — replacement

Refer to illustrations 9.3, 9.4, 9.5, 9.8 and 9.9

1 Disconnect the negative cable from the battery and remove the drivebelt(s) (Chapter 1).
2 Raise the front of the vehicle and support it securely on jackstands. Remove the right front wheel. Remove the plastic inner fender liner (Chapter 11).
3 Mark the vibration damper and pulley so the pulley can be reinstalled in the same relative position. Remove the four bolts attaching the lower pulley to the vibration damper **(see illustration)** and remove the pulley.
4 Remove the vibration damper with a puller (Ford T58P-6316-D and T82L-6316-B or equivalent). **Caution:** *Don't use a gear puller as it will damage the damper. Use a puller with bolts that thread into the hub* **(see illustration)**.
5 Carefully pry out the old seal with a screwdriver or seal puller **(see illustration)**.
6 Clean and inspect the seal bore and crankshaft surfaces for

9.3 Once the fender liner has been removed, the crankshaft pulley is accessible

9.4 Remove the vibration damper with a puller while keeping the crankshaft from turning with a screwdriver

9.5 Carefully pry the seal out of the bore — DO NOT nick or scratch the crankshaft

damage, nicks, burrs or other roughness which may cause a new seal to fail. Correct as necessary.
7 Lubricate the new seal lip with moly-base grease and the outside edge of the seal with engine oil and install it with the special tools (Ford T82L-6316-A T70P-6B070-A) or equivalents.

9.8   The seal can be installed with a large socket and hammer

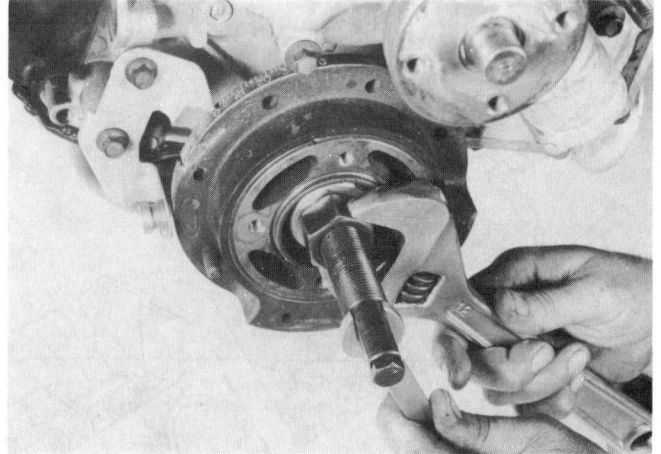

9.9   Installing the vibration damper with an installation tool

8   If special tools are unavailable, carefully tap the seal into place using a large socket and a hammer **(see illustration)**.

9   Apply RTV sealer to the keyway in the damper and position the damper on the crankshaft. Be sure the keyway is aligned with the crankshaft key. Install the damper using an installation tool (Ford T82L-6316-A) or equivalent **(see illustration)**. If unavailable, start the damper on with a soft-faced hammer and finish installation using the damper retaining bolt. Tighten the bolt to the specified torque.

10   Reinstall the remaining parts in the reverse order of removal.

11   Run the engine and check for oil leaks.

10   Timing chain cover — removal and installation

Refer to illustrations 10.14, 10.16a, 10.16b and 10.18

Note: *The 3.8L engine has the oil pump mounted in the timing chain cover.*

Removal

1   Disconnect the negative cable from the battery.

2   Drain the cooling system and remove the drivebelt(s) (Chapter 1).

3   Remove the right front wheel and inner fender liner (Chapter 11).

4   Remove the idler pulley and bracket assembly (Chapter 3).

5   Remove the water pump (Chapter 3).

3.8L engine only

6   Disconnect the upper radiator hose from the thermostat housing.

7   Remove the oil pan (Section 14).

8   Remove the distributor (Chapter 5).

All engines

9   On vehicles so equipped, unbolt the power steering pump and set it aside without disconnecting the hoses.

10   On A/C equipped models, unbolt the front compressor support bracket without removing the compressor. **Warning:** *The air conditioning system is under high pressure. Don't loosen any fittings, as sudden discharge could cause severe injury.*

11   Remove the vibration damper (Section 9).

12   Remove the timing chain cover bolts.

13   Tap the cover loose with a soft face hammer and remove it from the engine. **Caution:** *Do not use excessive force or you may crack the cover. If the cover is difficult to remove, recheck for remaining bolts. On 3.8L engines, the Allen head bolt under the oil filter housing is easy to miss.*

14   Thoroughly clean and inspect all parts and remove all traces of gasket material **(see illustration)**. Remove oil film with a solvent such as lacquer thinner or acetone.

3.8L engine only

15   To remove the intermediate shaft from the front cover, remove the clip from the shaft and slide the shaft out of the cover.

16   To install the shaft, make a mark one inch from the end **(see illustration)**. Insert the shaft until it seats in the oil pump and snap the

clip onto the shaft so the top of the clip is just below the mark made on the shaft **(see illustration)**.

17   The oil pump is mounted in the timing chain cover. See Section 15 for further information.

18   Be sure the camshaft thrust button and spring assembly are properly seated in the end of the camshaft **(see illustration)**.

Installation

19   Position the cover in place using contact adhesive (Ford D7AZ-19B508-A or equivalent) with a new gasket. Apply pipe sealer (Ford D6AZ-19558-A or equivalent) to the threads of the bolts.

20   Tighten the bolts to the specified torque.

21   Reinstall the remaining parts in the reverse order of removal.

22   Add oil and coolant as needed, run the engine and check for leaks.

11   Top Dead Center (TDC) for number 1 piston — locating

Refer to illustrations 11.6 and 11.9

1   Top Dead Center (TDC) is the highest point in the cylinder that each piston reaches as it travels up-and-down when the crankshaft turns. Each piston reaches TDC on the compression stroke and again on the exhaust stroke, but TDC generally refers to piston position on the compression stroke. The timing marks are referenced to the number one piston at TDC on the compression stroke.

2   Positioning the piston(s) at TDC is an essential part of many procedures such as in-vehicle valve train service, timing chain and sprocket replacement and distributor removal.

3   In order to bring any piston to TDC, the crankshaft must be turned

10.14   Scrape away all gasket material, then clean the mating surfaces with lacquer thinner or acetone

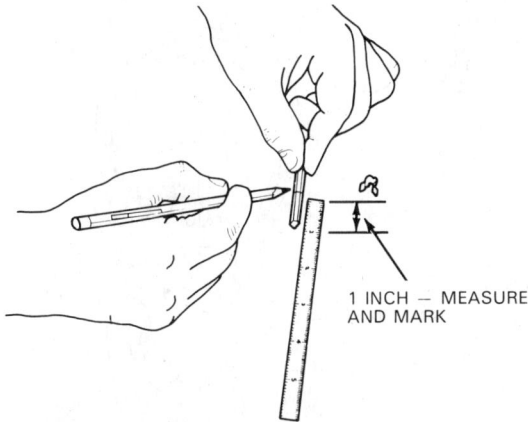

10.16a Intermediate shaft reference mark location

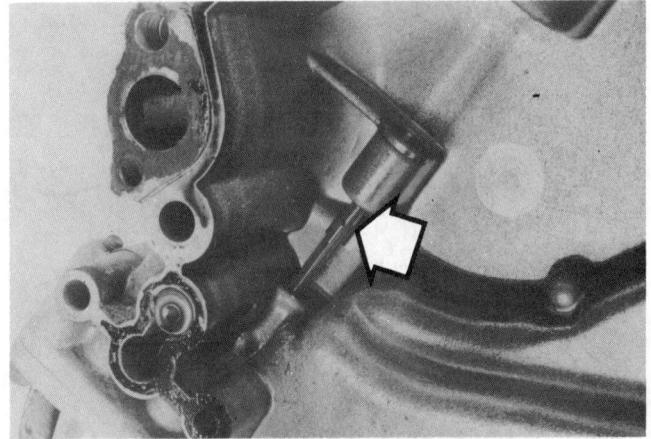

1 INCH — MEASURE AND MARK

10.16b Intermediate shaft clip location (arrow) inside the timing chain cover

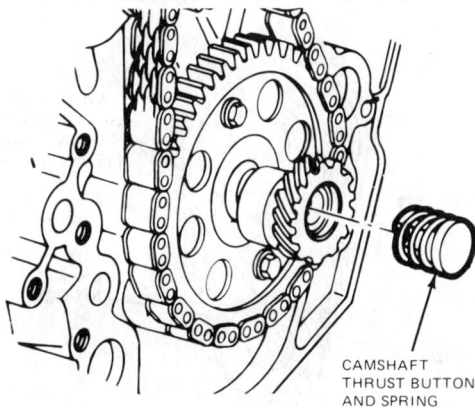

CAMSHAFT THRUST BUTTON AND SPRING

10.18 Camshaft thrust button and spring (3.8L engine)

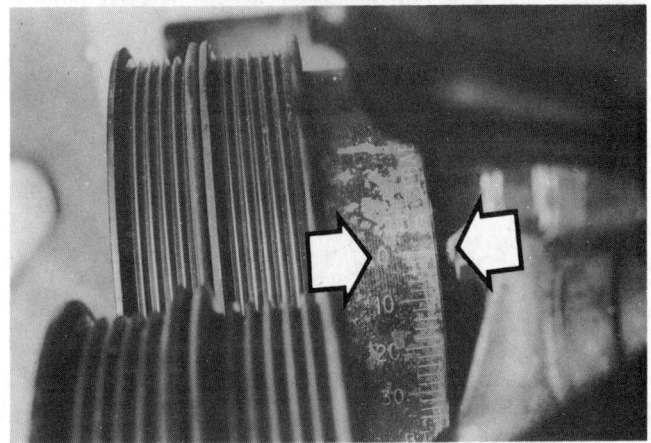

11.6 Align the 0 mark on the vibration damper with the stationary pointer on the timing cover (arrows) — the drivebelts have been removed for clarity

using one of the methods outlined below. When looking at the front of the engine, normal crankshaft rotation is clockwise. **Warning:** *Before beginning this procedure, be sure to place the transmission in Neutral and disable the ignition system by removing the coil wire from the distributor cap and grounding it.*

a) The preferred method is to turn the crankshaft with a large socket and breaker bar attached to the large bolt that's threaded into the front of the crankshaft.

b) A remote starter switch, which may save some time, can also be used. Attach the switch leads to the S (switch) and B (battery) terminals on the starter solenoid. Once the piston is close to TDC, use a socket and breaker bar as described in the previous paragraph.

c) If an assistant is available to turn the ignition switch to the Start position in short bursts, you can get the piston close to TDC without a remote starter switch. Use a socket and breaker bar as described in Paragraph a) to complete the procedure.

4   Locate the number one spark plug wire terminal in the distributor cap, then mark the distributor base directly under the terminal or make a mark on the engine directly opposite the terminal.
5   Remove the distributor cap as described in Chapter 1.
6   Turn the crankshaft (see Paragraph 3 above) until the ignition timing mark for TDC (usually a zero or a T) is aligned with the pointer **(see illustration)**.
7   The rotor should now be pointing directly at the mark you made earlier. If it is 180° off, the piston is at TDC on the exhaust stroke.
8   If the cylinder was on the exhaust stroke, turn the crankshaft one complete turn (360°) clockwise. The rotor should now be pointing at the mark. When the rotor is pointing at the number one spark plug wire terminal in the distributor cap (which is indicated by the mark on the distributor base or engine) and the ignition timing marks are aligned, the number one piston is at TDC on the compression stroke.
9   After the number one piston has been positioned at TDC on the compression stroke, TDC for any of the remaining cylinders can be located by turning the crankshaft and following the firing order **(see illustration)**.

CYLINDER NUMBERING AND DISTRIBUTOR LOCATION

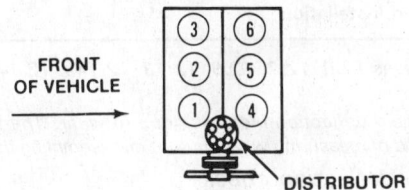

FRONT OF VEHICLE

```
3   6
2   5
1   4
```

DISTRIBUTOR

FIRING ORDER AND ROTATION

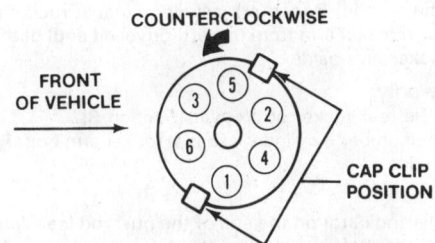

COUNTERCLOCKWISE

FRONT OF VEHICLE

```
  3   5
6       2
  1   4
```

CAP CLIP POSITION

FIRING ORDER — 1-4-2-5-3-6

11.9 Cylinder numbers and firing order

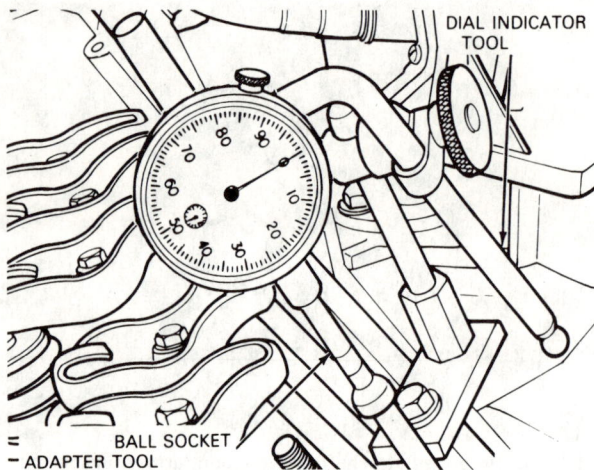

12.6   Mount a dial indicator on the pushrod to check valve
lifter movement

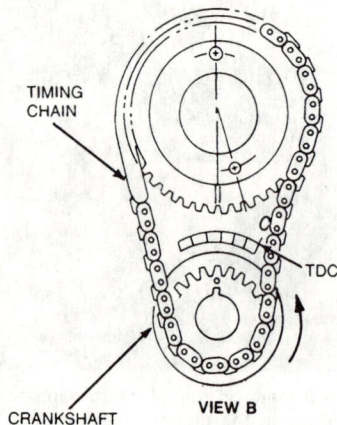

12.7   Turn the crankshaft clockwise until the number 1
piston is at TDC on the compression stroke

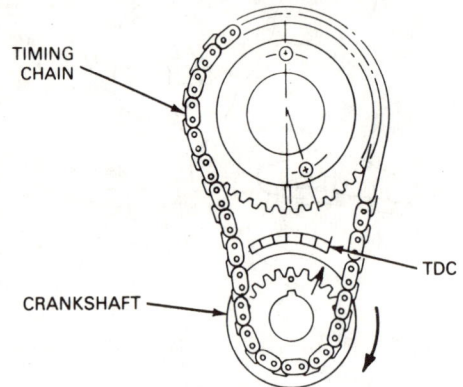

12.9   Turn the crankshaft counterclockwise until
movement occurs at the pushrod and dial indicator

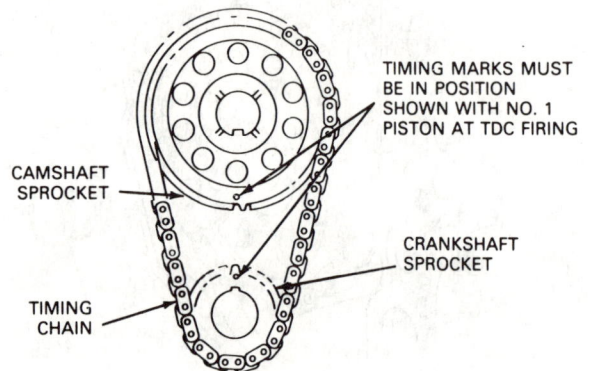

12.13   Aligning the timing marks

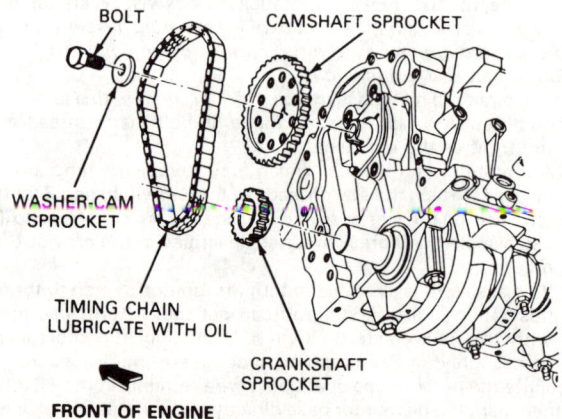

FRONT OF ENGINE

12.14a   Exploded view of timing chain components (3.0L engine)

---

12   Timing chain and sprockets — check, removal and installation

Refer to illustrations 12.6, 12.7, 12.9, 12.13, 12.14a, 12.14b, 12.18
and 12.21

Note: *Timing chain deflection increases due to wear. The following
check is a method of measuring wear without disassembling the engine.*

Timing chain deflection check

3.0L engine only
1   Disconnect the negative cable from the battery.
2   Remove the front rocker arm cover (Section 3).
3   Loosen the number 5 (center) cylinder exhaust rocker arm bolt.
This is the fourth rocker arm from the left (drivebelt end) of the engine.
Rotate the rocker arm aside.

3.8L engine only
4   Remove the rear rocker arm cover (Section 3).
5   Loosen the number 3 cylinder exhaust rocker arm bolt. Rotate the
rocker arm aside.

All engines
6   Install a dial indicator on the end of the pushrod **(see illustration)**.
7   Turn the crankshaft clockwise until TDC is reached (Section 11).
This will take up the slack on the right side of the chain **(see illustration)**.
8   Zero the dial indicator.
9   Slowly turn the crankshaft counterclockwise until the first movement is seen on the dial indicator **(see illustration)**. Stop and observe

the timing marks to determine the number of degrees from TDC.
10 If the reading exceeds 6 degrees, replace the timing chain and
sprockets.

Removal

11 Position the number 1 piston at Top Dead Center (Section 11).
12 Remove the timing chain cover (Section 10). Do not turn the crankshaft during damper removal.
13 Check that the upper and lower timing chain sprocket marks are
aligned **(see illustration)**. If they are not, install the vibration damper
bolt and use it to turn the crankshaft clockwise until the two marks
are adjacent to each other.
14 Remove the camshaft sprocket retaining bolt **(see illustration)** and
(3.8L models only) distributor gear **(see illustration)**.

CRANKSHAFT

KEY

FRONT OF ENGINE

SPACER

NOTE:
MUST BE INSTALLED
PRIOR TO KEY

TIMING CHAIN

KEY

CRANKSHAFT
SPROCKET

CAMSHAFT

CAMSHAFT
SPROCKET

BALANCE SHAFT
AND DRIVE GEAR

NOTE:
THOROUGHLY COAT ALL
GEAR TEETH WITH
ESE-M2C39-F OIL
PRIOR TO INSTALLATION

BOLT

WASHER

DISTRIBUTOR DRIVE
GEAR

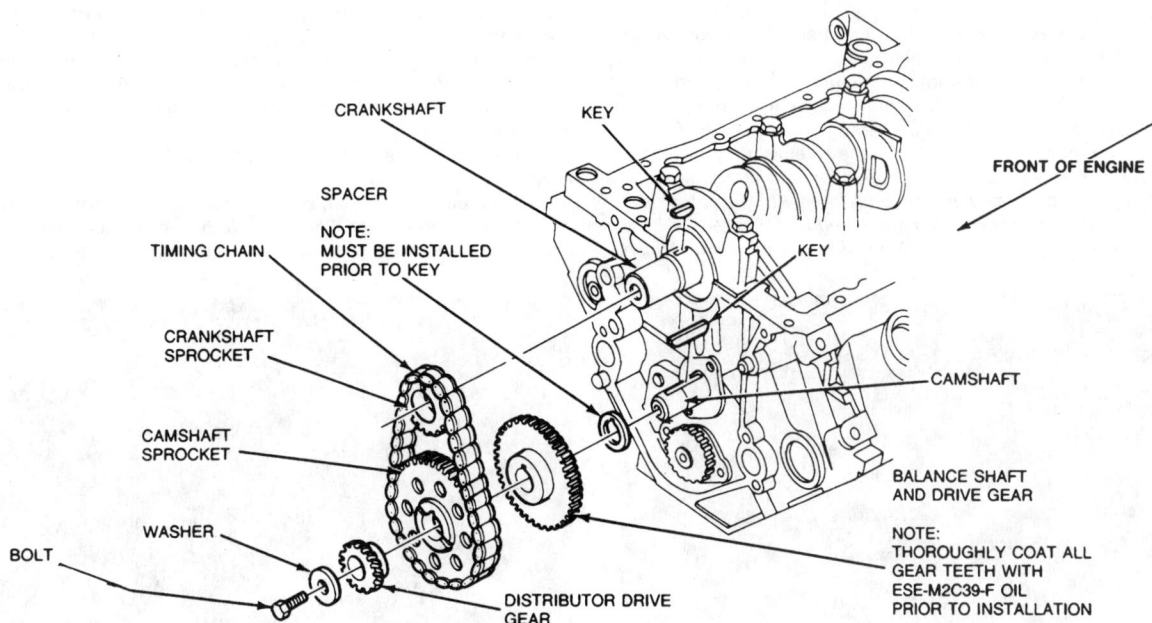

12.14b Exploded view of timing chain components (3.8L engine — the engine is upside down in this view)

15 Pull the camshaft sprocket away from the engine and move it down slightly to release the chain from the crankshaft sprocket.
16 If the crankshaft sprocket won't come off by hand, carefully pry it off with two screwdrivers.
17 3.8L engines are equipped with a balance shaft. It is not necessary to remove the balance shaft gear for chain replacement. If camshaft access is desired, note the location of the balance shaft timing marks and reinstall the gears the same way.

Installation

18 Reinstall the crankshaft sprocket (**see illustration**), making sure the keyway and timing mark are at the top (12 o'clock position).
19 If the sprocket is difficult to install, slip a length of pipe over the crankshaft and tap the sprocket into place with a small hammer. Make sure the key does not slip out of place.
20 Place the chain around the camshaft sprocket with the timing mark facing down (6 o'clock position). Slip the chain over the crankshaft sprocket and position the camshaft sprocket on the camshaft.
21 At this point, the timing marks should be adjacent (camshaft

sprocket mark at 6 o'clock and crankshaft sprocket mark at 12 o'clock) (**see illustration**). **Caution:** *Severe engine damage could result from improper timing.*
22 Install the distributor gear (3.8L engines only) and tighten the camshaft sprocket bolt to the specified torque.
23 Reinstall the remaining parts in the reverse order of removal. Be sure the thrust spring and button (3.8L engine) are properly seated and lubricated.
24 Add coolant and oil as needed, run the engine and check for leaks.

---

13 Valve lifters — removal, inspection and installation

Refer to illustrations 13.3a, 13.3b, 13.4a, 13.4b, 13.6a, 13.6b and 13.6c

1 Remove the intake manifold (Section 6).
2 Remove the rocker arms and pushrods (Section 4).
3 There are several ways to extract the lifters from the bores. Special

12.18 The crankshaft sprocket should have the keyway at the top (12 o'clock)

12.21 The timing marks (arrows) should be directly across from each other

tools designed to grip and remove lifters (Ford T70L-6500-A or equivalent) are manufactured by several tool companies and are widely
available (see illustration), but may not be needed in every case. On
newer engines without a lot of varnish buildup, the lifters can often
be removed with a small magnet (see illustration) or even with your
fingers. A machinist's scribe with a bent end can be used to pull the
lifters out by positioning the point under the retainer ring in the top
of each lifter. Caution: *Do not use pliers to remove the lifters unless
you intend to replace them with new ones (along with the camshaft).
The pliers may damage the precision machined and hardened lifters,
rendering them useless. On engines with considerable gum and varnish,*
*work the lifters up and down, using carburetor cleaner spray to loosen
the deposits.*
4   Before removing the lifters, arrange to store them in a clearly labelled box to ensure that they are reinstalled in their original locations.
Remove the lifters and store them where they will not get dirty (see
illustrations).
5   Clean the lifters with solvent and dry them thoroughly while still
keeping them in order.
6   Check each lifter wall, pushrod seat and foot for scuffing, score
marks and uneven wear. Each lifter foot (the surface that rides on the
cam lobe) must be slightly convex, although this can be difficult to

13.3a   Stuck lifters can be removed with a special tool

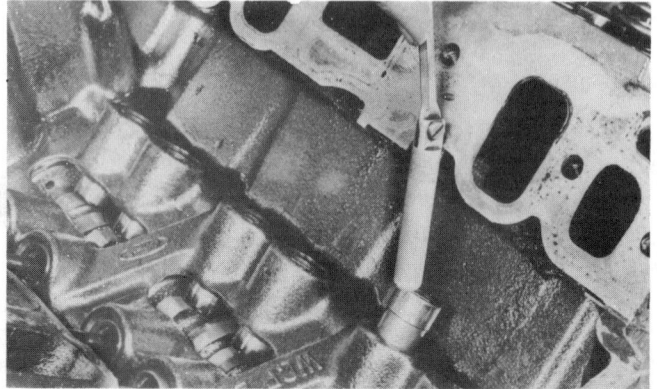

13.3b   You may be able to remove the lifters with a magnet

13.4a   Be sure to store the lifters in an organized manner
to make sure they are reinstalled in their original locations

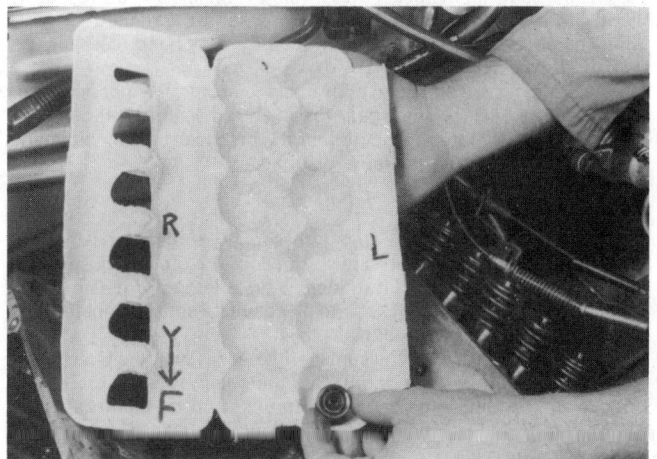

13.4b   Old egg cartons work well for lifter storage

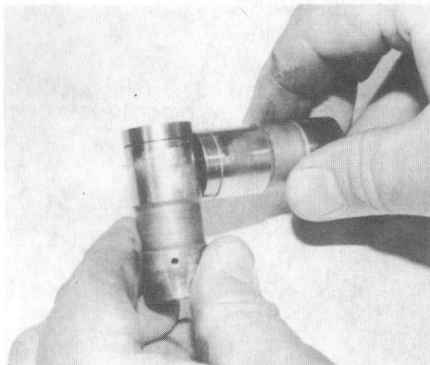

13.6a   The foot of each lifter should be
slightly convex — the side of another
lifter can be used as a straightedge to
check it; if it appears flat, it is worn
and must not be reused

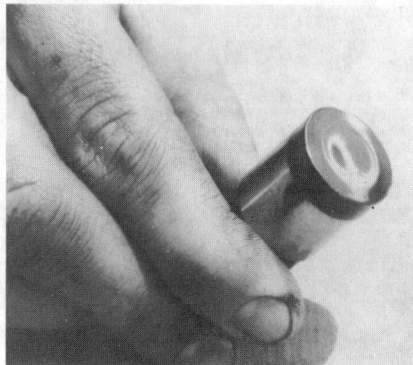

13.6b   If the bottom of any lifter is
worn concave, scratched or galled,
replace the entire set with new lifters

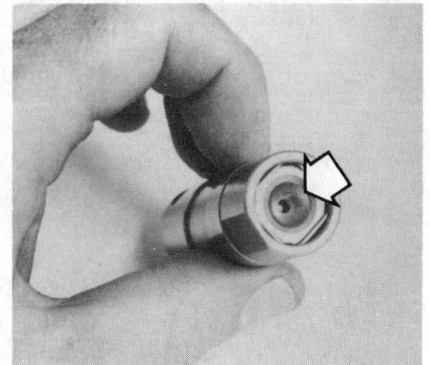

13.6c   Check the pushrod seat (arrow)
in the top of each lifter for wear

determine by eye. If the base of the lifter is concave (see illustrations), the lifters and camshaft must be replaced. If the lifter walls are damaged or worn (which is not very likely), inspect the lifter bores in the engine block as well. If the pushrod seats (see illustration) are worn, check the pushrod ends.

7   If new lifters are being installed, a new camshaft must also be installed. If a new camshaft is installed, then use new lifters as well. Never install used lifters unless the original camshaft is used and the lifters can be installed in their original locations.

14   Oil pan — removal and installation

Refer to illustrations 14.9, 14.10 and 14.11

1   Disconnect the negative cable from the battery.
2   Remove the oil dipstick.
3   Drain the oil and remove the oil filter (Chapter 1).
4   If equipped with a low oil level sensor, remove the retainer clip from the oil pan sensor and unplug the wire harness from the sensor.
5   Remove the catalytic converter and pipe assembly (Chapter 4).
6   Remove the starter motor (Chapter 5).
7   Remove the lower bellhousing (driveplate) cover, if equipped.
8   Unbolt the oil pan and remove it from the vehicle. If the pan is difficult to break loose, tap on it with a rubber mallet.
9   Remove all traces of gasket material from the mating surfaces (see illustration) and clean the oil pan with solvent.

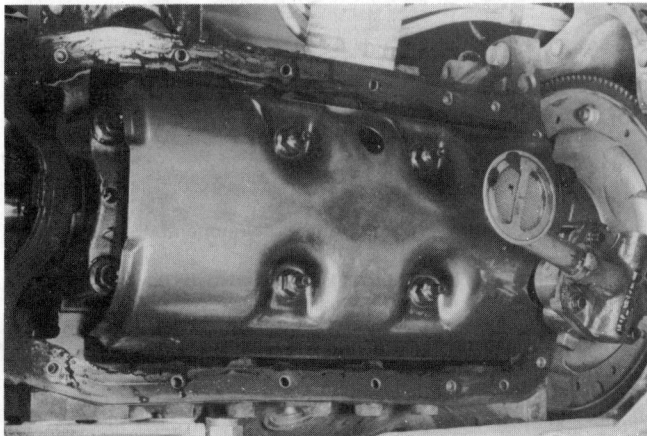

10   Install a new gasket on the oil pan (see illustration) using contact adhesive (Ford D7AZ-19B508-A or equivalent).
11   Apply a 1/5-inch bead of RTV sealer (Ford D6AZ-19562-A or equivalent) to the junctions of the block and rear main bearing cap and also the timing chain cover for a total of four places (see illustration). Install the end seals, if applicable. Note: *Follow gasket manufacturers instructions. Don't allow the sealer to dry before installing the pan.*
12   Position the oil pan on the engine block and install the bolts, tighten-

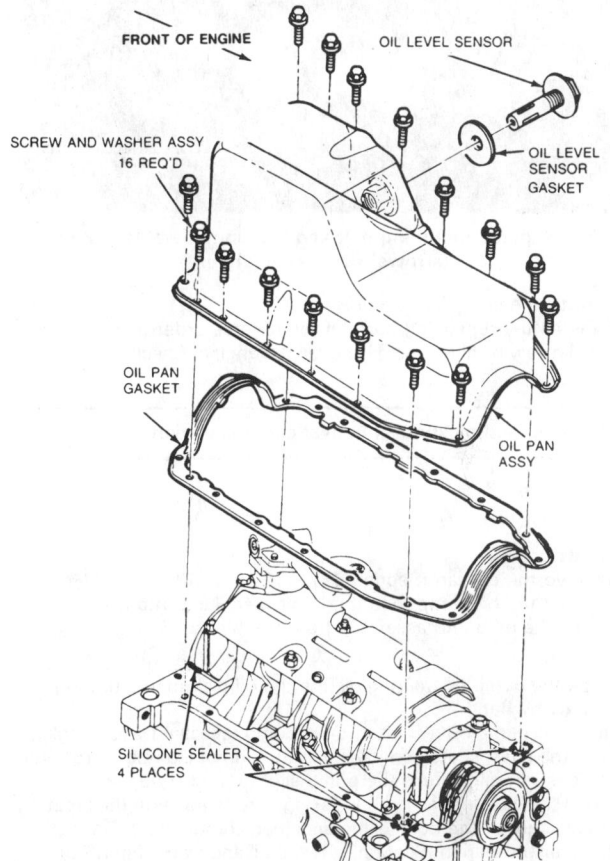

14.10   Exploded view of 3.0L engine oil pan components

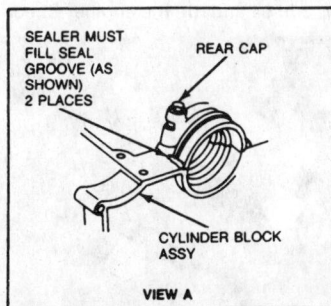

14.9   The one piece oil pan gasket on the 3.0L engine may be peeled off easily

14.11   Apply sealer to the junctions of the rear bearing cap-to-block and timing chain cover-to-block (3.8L engine shown)

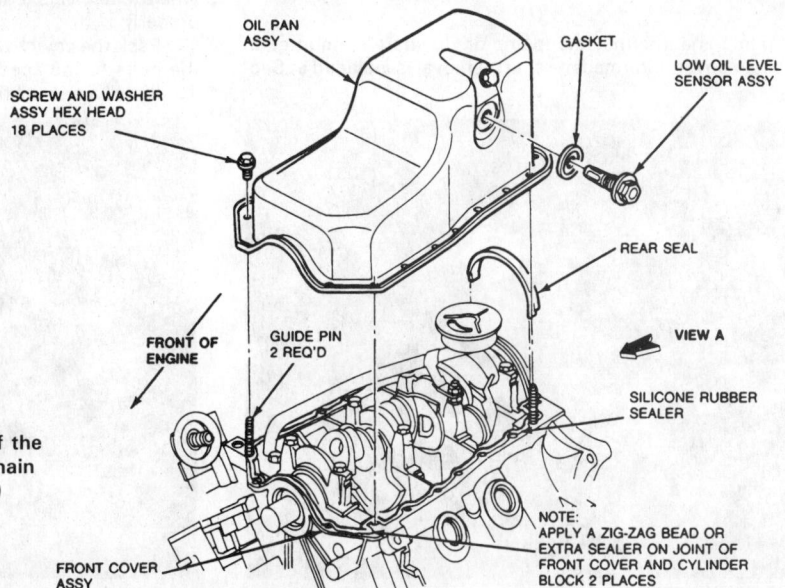

15.2   Oil pump mounting bolt and locating dowel locations (arrows) (3.0L engine)

ing them to the specified torque.

13 Reinstall the remaining parts in the reverse order of removal.

14 Install a new oil filter, add oil and run the engine. Check for oil leaks.

15   Oil pump and pickup — removal and installation

3.0L engine

Refer to illustrations 15.2 and 15.5

Removal

1   Remove the oil pan (Section 14).

2   Remove the oil pump mounting bolt **(see illustration)**.

3   Lower the oil pump assembly from the block.

Installation

4   Prime the pump by pouring oil into the oil pickup and turning the pump shaft by hand.

5   Fit the oil pump driveshaft into the pump **(see illustration)**, taking care that the shaft seats completely in the pump. Do not try to force it. If it does not align, turn the pump slightly and try again.

6   Install the oil pump assembly, taking care to position the locating dowel and tighten the bolt to the specified torque.

7   Reinstall the oil pan (Section 14), add oil and a new filter. Run the engine and check for leaks.

3.8L engine

Refer to illustrations 15.10a and 15.10b

Removal

8   The oil pump and intermediate (pump drive) shaft is mounted in the timing chain cover. Intermediate shaft removal is included in Section 10.

15.10a   3.8L engine oil pickup mounting nut

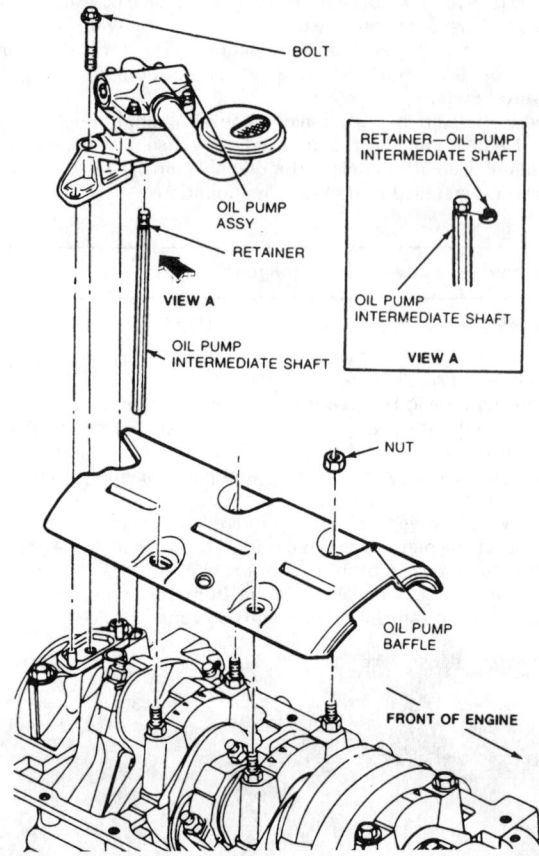

15.5   Exploded view of oil pump components (3.0L engine)

9   Remove the oil filter (Chapter 1) and remove the cover bolts. Clean and inspect the oil pump cavity. If the oil pump gear pocket in the timing chain cover is damaged or worn, replace the cover.

10 The oil pump pickup is mounted within the oil pan. For access, remove the oil pan (Section 14). Remove the pickup tube nut and the two mounting bolts **(see illustrations)**. Lower the pickup from the engine.

Installation

11 Install the pump gears in the housing so they are seated flush with the cover surface. If the gears don't seat fully, check the drive gear where it connects to the intermediate shaft. It probably wasn't engaged properly.

12 Pack the cavity with petroleum jelly and install the cover. Tighten the bolts to the specified torque.

13 Install a new oil filter, add oil and run the engine. Check for leaks.

15.10b   3.8L engine oil pickup mounting bolts

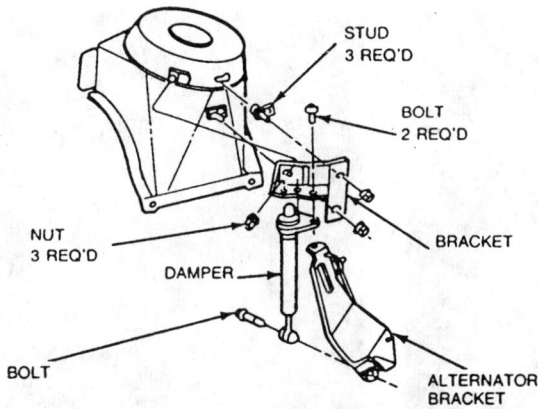

16.7 Right side damper mounting details

16 Engine mounts and dampers — check and replacement

Refer to illustrations 16.7, 16.14, 16.25a, 16.25b, 16.25c, 16.27a, 16.27b, 16.34 and 16.47

Warning: *Do not place any part of your body under the engine when it is supported only by a jack. Jack failure could result in severe injury or death!*

Note: *Transaxle mount replacement is covered in Chapter 7.*

Check

1 The engine mounts may be inspected with the engine in the vehicle.
2 Disconnect the negative cable at the battery.
3 Raise the vehicle and support it securely on jackstands.
4 Position a jack under the engine oil pan, using a block of wood to protect the pan.
5 Raise the engine slightly to take the weight off the engine mounts. Inspect the mounts for cracks and separation. Sometimes the rubber will split right down the center. Replace as needed.
6 The dampers should be replaced whenever they are found to be leaking, bent, or otherwise damaged. **Note:** *Whenever self-locking fasteners are removed, replace them with new self-locking fasteners.*

Damper replacement

Right side — 3.0L engine

7 Remove the bolt attaching the lower end of the damper to the engine bracket **(see illustration)**.
8 Remove the bolts attaching the upper damper bracket to the shock tower bracket.
9 Remove the engine damper.
10 Position the damper lower sleeve to line up with the engine bracket notch. Secure it with a new bolt.

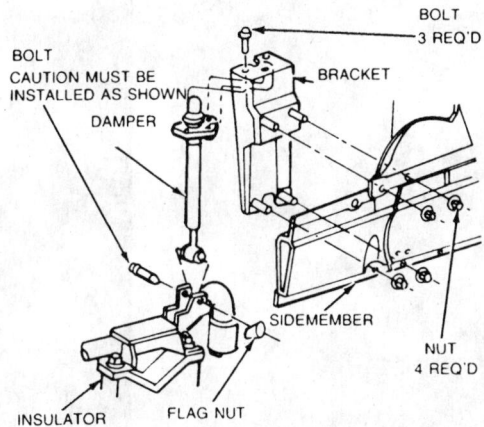

16.14 Left side damper mounting details

11 Position the engine damper with the upper bracket to the shock tower bracket, securing it with new bolts.
12 Tighten the fasteners to the specified torque.

Left side — 3.0L engine

13 Remove speed control servo and bracket, on vehicles so equipped.
14 Remove the bolt and flag nut attaching the lower end of the damper to the transmission mount bracket **(see illustration)**.
15 Remove the bolts attaching the upper damper bracket to the side rail bracket.
16 Remove the damper from the vehicle.
17 Install the lower end of the damper into the engine mount attaching bracket, being careful to align the groove in the damper sleeve with the notch in the bracket.
18 Insert the bolt through the bracket and damper. Hand start the new flag nut. **Note:** *Bolt must be inserted with the head toward the engine.*
19 Pull the damper into position against the side rail mounting bracket. Secure it with three new bolts.
20 Tighten the fasteners to the specified torque.
21 Reinstall the speed control servo, if equipped.

Engine mount replacement

3.0L engine — front and rear

22 Remove the lower damper bolt from the right side of the engine **(see illustration 16.7)**.
23 Raise the vehicle and support it securely on jackstands.
24 Position a jack under the oil pan. Use a block of wood between the oil pan and jack to distribute the weight.
25 Remove the nuts attaching the engine mounts to the subframe **(see illustrations)**.

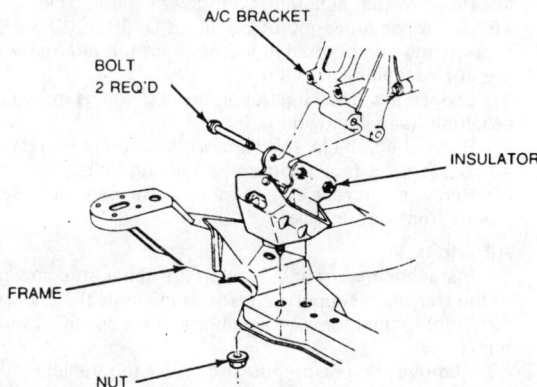

RH FRONT, NO. 2

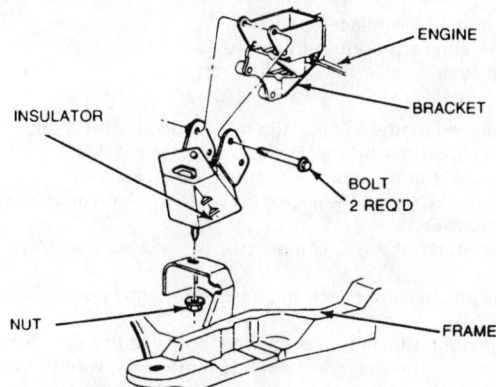

RH REAR, NO. 3

16.25a 3.0L engine mounts — exploded view

16.25b   The 3.0L front mount attaching nut is hidden in the subframe

16.25c   3.0L rear engine mount attaching nut (arrow)

16.27a   The 3.0L front engine mount through bolts are accessible through the right front fenderwell

16.27b   3.0L rear engine mount through-bolts

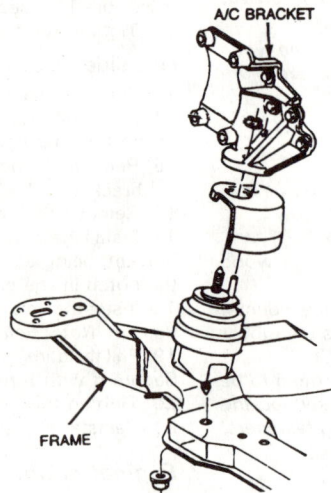
16.34   3.8L front engine mount — exploded view

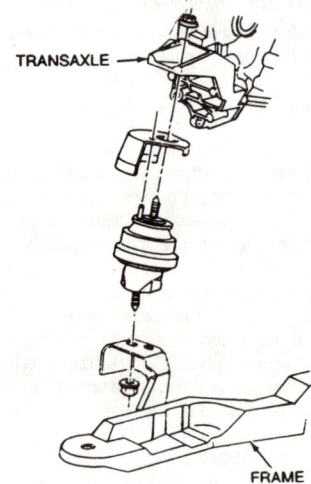
16.47   3.8L rear engine mount — exploded view

26 Raise the engine with the jack enough to remove the weight from the mounts.
27 Remove the through bolts (see illustrations) and remove the mount(s) from the vehicle.
28 Attach the new mount(s) to the engine bracket(s) with two through bolts.
29 Lower the engine into place.
30 Reinstall the engine mount-to-frame nuts.
31 Tighten the fasteners to the specified torque.

3.8L engine — front
32 On A/C equipped models, unbolt the A/C compressor (Chapter 3) without disconnecting the refrigerant lines and set it aside.
33 Raise the vehicle and support it securely on jackstands.
34 Remove the nut attaching the engine mount to the A/C compressor bracket (see illustration).
35 Temporarily attach the A/C compressor to its bracket with two lower bolts.
36 Support the engine with a jack and a block of wood under the oil pan.
37 Remove the nuts attaching the engine mounts to the subframe.
38 Raise the engine with the jack enough to remove the weight from the mounts.
39 Remove the mount from the vehicle.
40 Remove the heat shield from the mount.
41 Installation is the reverse of removal. Tighten the fasteners to the specified torque.

3.8L engine — rear
42 Raise the vehicle and support it securely on jackstands.
43 Remove the nuts attaching the engine mounts to the subframe.
44 Remove the front and rear exhaust attaching bolts at the manifold and flex coupling. Remove the catalytic converter (Chapter 6).
45 Remove the jackstands and lower the vehicle.
46 Use an engine support bar (Ford D79P-6000-B or equivalent) to support the engine. Install a J-hook on the alternator bracket. Raise the engine about one-inch.
47 Loosen the attaching nut on the rear engine mount and heat shield assembly (see illustration).
48 Raise the vehicle and support it securely on jackstands.
49 Loosen the four subframe attaching bolts.
50 Remove the rear engine mount attaching nut. Remove the rear mount from the vehicle.

All engines
51 Install the mount and position the upper stud and anti-rotation pin to the transaxle support bracket. Hand start the lower attaching nut.
52 Tighten the four subframe bolts to the specified torque (see Chapter 7).
53 Remove the jackstands and lower the vehicle.
54 Tighten the top attaching nut on the rear mount.
55 Lower the engine and remove the support bar.
56 Raise the vehicle and support it securely on jackstands.
57 Reinstall the catalytic converter.
58 Tighten the engine mount attaching nuts to the specified torque.

Chapter 2 Part C
General engine overhaul procedures

Contents

Specifications

Four-cylinder engine

General

Cylinder compression pressure	101 psi minimum (see text)
Oil pressure (hot at 2000 rpm)	55 to 70 psi

Cylinder head and valves

Warpage limit	0.003 inch in any 6 inches; 0.006 in overall
Minimum valve margin	1/32 in
Intake valve	
seat angle	45°
stem diameter	
standard	0.3415 to 0.3422 in
0.015 oversize	0.3566 to 0.3572 in
0.030 oversize	0.3716 to 0.3722 in
valve stem-to-guide clearance	
recommended	0.018 in
service limit	0.0010 to 0.0027 in
Exhaust valve	
seat angle	45°
stem diameter	
standard	0.3411 to 0.3418 in
0.015 oversize	0.3561 to 0.3568 in
0.030 oversize	0.3711 to 0.3718 in
valve stem-to-guide clearance	
recommended	0.023 in
service limit	0.0015 to 0.0032 in
Valve spring pressure	
valve closed	70.0 to 78.0 lbs at 1.50 in
valve open	174.5 to 190.5 lbs at 1.10 in
Valve spring free length (approximate)	1.76 in
Valve spring installed height	1.49 in
Valve lifter	
diameter (standard)	0.8740 to 0.8744 in
lifter-to-bore clearance	0.0007 to 0.0027 in

Four-cylinder engine (continued)
Crankshaft and connecting rods
Connecting rod journal
    diameter . . . . 2.1232 to 2.1240 in
    bearing oil clearance
        desired . . . . 0.0008 to 0.0015 in
        allowable . . . . 0.0008 to 0.0024 in
Connecting rod side clearance (end play)
    standard . . . . 0.0035 to 0.0105 in
    service limit . . . . 0.014 in
Main bearing journal
    diameter . . . . 2.2489 2.2490 in
    bearing oil clearance
        desired . . . . 0.0008 to 0.0015 in
        allowable . . . . 0.0008 to 0.0024 in
Crankshaft end play
    standard . . . . 0.004 to 0.008 in
    service limit . . . . 0.012 in

Pistons and rings
Piston diameter
    coded red . . . . 3.6783 to 3.6789 in
    coded blue . . . . 3.6795 to 3.6801 in
    coded yellow . . . . 3.6807 to 3.6811 in
Piston-to-bore clearance limit (select fit) . . . . 0.0036 to 0.0056 in
Piston ring end gap
    compression rings . . . . 0.008 to 0.016 in
    oil ring (steel rail) . . . . 0.015 to 0.055 in

Camshaft
Lobe lift
    intake . . . . 0.249 in
    exhaust . . . . 0.239 in
Allowable lobe lift loss . . . . 0.005 in
End play . . . . 0.009 in maximum
Timing chain deflection . . . . 1/2 in maximum
Theoretical valve lift at zero lash
    intake . . . . 0.392 in
    exhaust . . . . 0.377 in
Bearing inside diameter (all) . . . . 2.010 to 2.009 in
Bearing oil clearance
    standard . . . . 0.001 to 0.003 in
    service limit . . . . 0.006 in

Torque specifications
	Ft-lbs
Camshaft thrust plate bolts	6 to 9
Camshaft tensioner bolts	6 to 9
Camshaft sprocket bolt	41 to 56
Connecting rod cap nuts	21 to 26
Crankshaft pulley bolt	140 to 170
Crankshaft rear oil seal retainer bolts	6 to 9
Flywheel/driveplate bolts	54 to 64
Main bearing cap bolts	51 to 66
Timing chain cover bolts	6 to 9

3.0L V6 engine

General
Cylinder compression pressure . . . . 101 psi minimum (see text)
Oil pressure (hot at 2000 rpm) . . . . 40 to 60 psi

Cylinder head and valves
Warpage limit . . . . 0.003 inch in any 6 inches (0.006 overall)
Minimum valve margin . . . . 1/32 in
Intake valve
    seat angle . . . . 45°
    stem diameter
        standard . . . . 0.3134 to 0.3126 in
        0.015 oversize . . . . 0.3283 to 0.3276 in
        0.030 oversize . . . . 0.3433 to 0.3425 in
    stem-to-guide clearance . . . . 0.0010 to 0.0028 in

Exhaust valve
    seat angle . . . .   45°
    stem diameter
        standard . . . .   0.3129 to 0.3121 in
        0.015 oversize . . . .   0.3279 to 0.3271 in
        0.030 oversize . . . .   0.3428 to 0.3420 in
    stem-to-guide clearance . . . .   0.0015 to 0.0033 in
Valve spring pressure (not including dampener)
    valve open . . . .   162 to 180 lbs at 1.16 in
    valve closed . . . .   59 to 65 lbs at 1.58 in
Valve spring free length (approximate) . . . .   1.84 in
Valve lifter
    diameter (standard) . . . .   0.8740 to 0.8745 in
    lifter-to-bore clearance . . . .   0.0007 to 0.0027 in

Crankshaft and connecting rods
Connecting rod journal
    diameter . . . .   2.1253 to 2.1261 in
    out-of-round limit . . . .   0.0003 in
    taper limit . . . .   0.0006 in
    bearing oil clearance
        desired . . . .   0.0010 to 0.0014 in
        allowable . . . .   0.0008 to 0.0027 in
Connecting rod side clearance (end play)
    standard . . . .   0.006 to 0.014 in
    service limit . . . .   0.014 in
Main bearing journal
    diameter . . . .   2.5190 to 2.5198 in
    out-of-round limit . . . .   0.0003 in
    taper limit . . . .   0.0006 in
    runout limit . . . .   0.002 in
    bearing oil clearance
        desired . . . .   0.0001 to 0.0014 in
        allowable . . . .   0.0005 to 0.0023 in
    crankshaft end play
        standard . . . .   0.004 to 0.008 in
        service limit . . . .   0.012 in maximum

Pistons and rings
Piston-to-bore clearance limits
    standard . . . .   0.0014 to 0.0022 in
    service limit . . . .   0.0032 in
Piston ring end gap
    compression rings . . . .   0.010 to 0.020 in
    oil ring . . . .   0.010 to 0.049 in
Side clearance
    compression rings . . . .   0.0016 to 0.0037 in
    oil rings . . . .   Snug fit

Camshaft
Lobe lift
    intake . . . .   0.260 in
    exhaust . . . .   0.260 in
Allowable lobe lift loss . . . .   0.005 in
Theoretical valve lift at zero lash
    intake . . . .   0.419 in
    exhaust . . . .   0.419 in
End play *
    standard . . . .   0.003 to 0.007 in
    service limit . . . .   0.005 in
* Note: *End play adjustment is not required on models equipped with a thrust spring*
Journal-to-bearing clearance . . . .   0.001 to 0.003 in
Journal diameter (all) . . . .   2.0074 to 2.0084 in
Cam bearing inside diameter . . . .   2.0094 to 2.0104 in
Runout limit . . . .   0.005 in (runout of no. 2 or no. 3 relative to no. 1 and no. 4)
Out-of-round limit . . . .   0.004 in
Bearing bore inside diameter
    No. 1 . . . .   2.1531 to 2.1541 in
    No. 2 . . . .   2.1334 to 2.1344 in
    No. 3 . . . .   2.1334 to 2.1344 in
    No. 4 . . . .   2.1531 to 2.1541 in
Bearing oil clearance
    standard . . . .   0.001 0.003 in
    service limit . . . .   0.006 in

3.0L V6 engine (continued)

Torque specifications   Ft-lbs
Camshaft sprocket-to-camshaft bolt .... 40 to 51
Camshaft thrust plate bolts .... 6 to 8
Connecting rod cap nuts
   1986 and 1987
      step 1 .... 20 to 28
      step 2 .... Back off 2 turns
      step 3 .... 20 to 25
   1988 on .... 23 to 29
Driveplate bolts .... 54 to 64
Main bearing cap bolts .... 65 to 81
Timing chain cover bolts .... 15 to 22

3.8L V6 engine

General
Cylinder compression pressure .... 101 psi minimum (see text)
Oil pressure (hot at 2500 rpm) .... 40 to 60 psi

Cylinder head and valves
Warpage limit..................................... 0.007 in
Minimum valve margin .... 1/32 in
Intake valve
   seat angle .... 44.5°
   stem diameter................................... 0.3423 to 0.3415 in
   valve stem-to-guide clearance .... 0.001 to 0.0028 in
Exhaust valve
   seat angle .... 44.5°
   stem diameter................................... 0.3418 to 0.3410 in
   valve stem-to-guide clearance .... 0.0015 to 0.0033 in
Valve spring pressure (not including dampener)
   valve open .... 190 lbs at 1.28 in
   valve closed .... 73 lbs at 1.70 in
Valve lifter
   diameter (standard) .... 0.8740 to 0.8745 in
   lifter-to-bore clearance........................ 0.0007 to 0.0027 in

Crankshaft and connecting rods
Connecting rod journal
   diameter .... 2.3103 to 2.3111 in
   bearing oil clearance
      desired .... 0.001 to 0.0014 in
      allowable .... 0.00086 to 0.0027 in
Connecting rod side clearance (end play)
   standard .... 0.0047 to 0.0114 in
   service limit .... 0.014 in maximum
Main bearing journal
   diameter .... 2.5190 to 2.5198 in
   bearing oil clearance
      desired .... 0.001 to 0.0014 in
      allowable .... 0.0005 to 0.0023 in
Crankshaft end play (at thrust bearing) .... 0.004 to 0.008 in

Pistons and rings
Piston-to-bore clearance limit .... 0.0014 to 0.0032 in
Piston ring end gap
   compression rings .... 0.01 to 0.02 in
   oil ring .... 0.015 to 0.0583 in

Camshaft
Bearing journal diameter (all) .... 2.0515 to 2.0505 in
Bearing oil clearance (all) .... 0.001 to 0.003 in

Torque specifications   Ft-lbs
Main bearing cap bolts .... 65 to 81
Connecting rod cap nuts .... 31 to 36
Camshaft sprocket-to-camshaft bolt .... 15 to 22
Camshaft thrust plate bolts......................... 6 to 10
Driveplate-to-crankshaft bolts .... 54 to 64

1 General information

Included in this portion of Chapter 2 are the general overhaul procedures for the cylinder head(s) and internal engine components.

The information ranges from advice concerning preparation for an overhaul and the purchase of replacement parts to detailed, step-by-step procedures covering removal and installation of internal engine components and the inspection of parts.

The following Sections have been written based on the assumption that the engine has been removed from the vehicle. For information concerning in-vehicle engine repair, as well as removal and installation of the external components necessary for the overhaul, see Part A or B of this Chapter and Section 7 of this Part.

The Specifications included here in Part C are only those necessary for the inspection and overhaul procedures which follow. Refer to Parts A and B for additional Specifications.

2 Cylinder compression check

Refer to illustrations 2.4 and 2.5

1   A compression check will tell you what mechanical condition the upper end (pistons, rings, valves, head gasket) of your engine is in. Specifically, it can tell you if the compression is low due to leakage caused by worn piston rings, defective valves and seats or a blown head gasket. **Note:** *The engine must be at normal operating temperature, the oil must be at the proper level and the battery must be fully charged during this check.*

2   Begin by cleaning the area around the spark plugs before you remove them (compressed air should be used, if available, otherwise a small brush or even a bicycle tire pump will work). The idea is to prevent dirt from getting into the cylinders as the compression check is done. Remove all of the spark plugs from the engine. Be careful not to burn yourself.

3   Detach the coil wire from the center terminal of the distributor cap and ground it on the engine block. Use a jumper wire with alligator clips at each end to ensure a good ground.

4   With the compression gauge in the number one spark plug hole (see illustration), depress the accelerator pedal all the way to the floor to open the throttle valve. Crank the engine over at least four compression strokes while watching the gauge. The compression should build up quickly in a healthy engine. Low compression on the first stroke, followed by gradually increasing pressure on successive strokes, indicates worn piston rings. A low compression reading on the first stroke, which does not build up during successive strokes, indicates

2.4 Use a compression gauge with a fitting that threads into the spark plug hole (position the gauge so it can be seen through the windshield as you open the throttle by depressing the accelerator and use the ignition key to crank the engine over)

Maximum PSI	Minimum PSI	Maximum PSI	Minimum PSI
134	101	164	123
136	102	166	124
138	104	168	126
140	105	170	127
142	107	172	129
144	108	174	131
146	110	176	132
148	111	178	133
150	113	180	135
152	114	182	136
154	115	184	138
156	117	186	140
158	118	188	141
160	120	190	142
162	121	192	144

2.5 Cylinder compression pressure chart

leaking valves or a blown head gasket (a cracked head could also be the cause). Record the highest gauge reading obtained.

5   Repeat the procedure for the remaining cylinders and compare the results to the Specifications and chart (see illustration). The difference between the highest and lowest readings should not exceed those shown on the chart.

6   Add some engine oil (about three squirts from a plunger-type oil can) to each cylinder, through the spark plug hole, and repeat the test.

7   If the compression increases after the oil is added, the piston rings are definitely worn. If the compression does not increase significantly, the leakage is occurring at the valves or head gasket. Leakage past the valves may be caused by burned valve seats and/or faulty, warped, cracked or bent valves.

8   If two adjacent cylinders have equally low compression, there is a strong possibility that the head gasket between them is blown. The appearance of coolant in the combustion chambers or the crankcase would verify this condition.

9   If the compression is unusually high, the combustion chambers are probably coated with carbon deposits. If that's the case, the cylinder head should be removed and decarbonized.

10 If compression is way down or varies greatly between cylinders, it would be a good idea to have a leak-down test performed by an automotive repair shop. This test will pinpoint exactly where the leakage is occurring and how severe it is.

3 Engine overhaul — general information

Refer to illustration 3.4

It's not always easy to determine when, or if, an engine should be completely overhauled, as a number of factors must be considered.

High mileage is not necessarily an indication that an overhaul is needed, while low mileage doesn't preclude the need for an overhaul. Frequency of servicing is probably the most important consideration. An engine that's had regular and frequent oil and filter changes, as well as other required maintenance, will most likely give many thousands of miles of reliable service. Conversely, a neglected engine may require an overhaul very early in its life.

Excessive oil consumption is an indication that piston rings, valve seals and/or valve guides are in need of attention. Make sure that oil leaks aren't responsible before deciding that the rings and/or guides are bad. Have a cylinder compression or leakdown test performed by an experienced tune-up mechanic to determine the extent of the work required.

If the engine is making obvious knocking or rumbling noises, the connecting rod and/or main bearings may be at fault. Check the oil pressure with a gauge installed in place of the oil pressure sending unit **(see illustration)** and compare it to the Specifications. If it's extremely low, the bearings and/or oil pump are probably worn out.

Loss of power, rough running, excessive valve train noise and high oil or fuel consumption rates may also point to the need for an overhaul, especially if they're all present at the same time. If a complete tune-up doesn't remedy the situation, major mechanical work is the only solution.

An engine overhaul involves restoring the internal parts to the specifications of a new engine. During an overhaul, the piston rings are replaced and the cylinder walls are reconditioned (rebored and/or honed). If a rebore is done, new pistons are required. The main bearings, connecting rod bearings and camshaft bearings are generally replaced with new ones and, if necessary, the crankshaft may be reground to restore the journals. Generally, the valves are serviced as well, since they're usually in less-than-perfect condition at this point. While the engine is being overhauled, other components, such as the distributor, starter and alternator, can be rebuilt as well. The end result should be a like new engine that will give many trouble free miles. **Note:** *Critical cooling system components such as the hoses, drivebelts, thermostat and water pump MUST be replaced with new parts when an engine is overhauled. The radiator should be checked carefully to ensure that it isn't clogged or leaking; if in doubt, have it rodded out, recored or replace it with a new one. Also, we don't recommend overhauling the oil pump (except 3.8L) — install a new one when an engine is rebuilt.*

Before beginning the engine overhaul, read through the entire procedure to familiarize yourself with the scope and requirements of the job. Overhauling an engine isn't difficult, but it is time consuming. Plan on the vehicle being tied up for a minimum of two weeks, especially if parts must be taken to an automotive machine shop for repair or reconditioning. Check on availability of parts and make sure that any necessary special tools and equipment are obtained in advance. Most work can be done with typical hand tools, although a number of precision measuring tools are required for inspecting parts to determine if they must be replaced. Often an automotive machine shop will handle the inspection of parts and offer advice concerning reconditioning and replacement. **Note:** *Always wait until the engine has been completely disassembled and all components, especially the engine block, have been inspected before deciding what service and repair operations must be performed by an automotive machine shop.* Since the block's condition will be the major factor to consider when determining whether to overhaul the original engine or buy a rebuilt one, never purchase parts or have machine work done on other components until the block has been thoroughly inspected. As a general rule, time is the primary cost of an overhaul, so it doesn't pay to install worn or substandard parts.

As a final note, to ensure maximum life and minimum trouble from a rebuilt engine, everything must be assembled with care in a spotlessly clean environment.

4 Engine rebuilding alternatives

The do-it-yourselfer is faced with a number of options when performing an engine overhaul. The decision to replace the engine block, piston/connecting rod assemblies and crankshaft depends on a number of factors, with the number one consideration being the condition of the block. Other considerations are cost, access to machine shop facilities, parts availability, time required to complete the project and the extent of prior mechanical experience on the part of the do-it-yourselfer.

Some of the rebuilding alternatives include:

Individual parts — If the inspection procedures reveal that the engine block and most engine components are in reusable condition, purchasing individual parts may be the most economical alternative. The block, crankshaft and piston/connecting rod assemblies should all be inspected carefully. Even if the block shows little wear, the cylinder bores should be surface honed.

Crankshaft kit — This rebuild package consists of a reground crankshaft and a matched set of pistons and connecting rods. The pistons will already be installed on the connecting rods. Piston rings and the necessary bearings will be included in the kit. These kits are commonly available for standard cylinder bores, as well as for engine blocks which have been bored to a regular oversize.

3.4 An oil pressure gauge can be installed in the hole where the oil pressure sending unit is normally located

Short block — A short block consists of an engine block with a crankshaft and piston/connecting rod assemblies already installed. All new bearings are incorporated and all clearances will be correct. The existing camshaft, valve train components, cylinder head(s) and external parts can be bolted to the short block with little or no machine shop work necessary.

Long block — A long block consists of a short block plus an oil pump, oil pan, cylinder head(s), rocker arm cover(s), camshaft and valve train components, timing sprockets and chain or gears and timing cover. All components are installed with new bearings, seals and gaskets incorporated throughout. The installation of manifolds and external parts is all that's necessary.

Give careful thought to which alternative is best for you and discuss the situation with local automotive machine shops, auto parts dealers and experienced rebuilders before ordering or purchasing replacement parts.

5 Engine removal — methods and precautions

If you've decided that an engine must be removed for overhaul or major repair work, several preliminary steps should be taken.

Locating a suitable place to work is extremely important. Adequate work space, along with storage space for the vehicle, will be needed. If a shop or garage isn't available, at the very least a flat, level, clean work surface made of concrete or asphalt is required.

Cleaning the engine compartment and engine before beginning the removal procedure will help keep tools clean and organized.

An engine hoist or A-frame will also be necessary. Make sure the equipment is rated in excess of the combined weight of the engine and accessories. Safety is of primary importance, considering the potential hazards involved in lifting the engine out of the vehicle.

If the engine is being removed by a novice, a helper should be available. Advice and aid from someone more experienced would also be helpful. There are many instances when one person cannot simultaneously perform all of the operations required when lifting the engine out of the vehicle.

Plan the operation ahead of time. Arrange for or obtain all of the tools and equipment you'll need prior to beginning the job. Some of the equipment necessary to perform engine removal and installation safely and with relative ease are (in addition to an engine hoist) a heavy duty floor jack, complete sets of wrenches and sockets as described in the front of this manual, wooden blocks and plenty of rags and cleaning solvent for mopping up spilled oil, coolant and gasoline. If the hoist must be rented, make sure that you arrange for it in advance and perform beforehand all of the operations possible without it. This will save you money and time.

Plan for the vehicle to be out of use for quite a while. A machine shop will be required to perform some of the work which the do-it-

6.12   To disconnect the wires, insert a small screwdriver behind the tabs (arrows) and pull the connectors apart

6.15   Tie the compressor aside and cap off all the disconnected refrigerant fittings

yourselfer can't accomplish without special equipment. These shops often have a busy schedule, so it would be a good idea to consult them before removing the engine in order to accurately estimate the amount of time required to rebuild or repair components that may need work.

Always be extremely careful when removing and installing the engine. Serious injury can result from careless actions. Plan ahead, take your time and a job of this nature, although major, can be accomplished successfully.

6   Engine — removal and installation

Refer to illustrations 6.12, 6.15, 6.21, 6.24, 6.27 and 6.28
Warning: *Do not place any part of your body below the engine when it is supported by a hoist or other lifting device. Hoist failure could result in severe injury or death! Sudden discharge of the air conditioning system may freeze flesh, causing frostbite or loss of eyesight. Have a dealer service department or gas station discharge the system prior to disconnecting any A/C components.*

6.21   Carefully separate the converter from the driveplate

Removal

1   On A/C equipped vehicles, check the clearance around the air conditioning compressor to determine if sufficient clearance exists to unbolt the compressor from the brackets and set it aside without disconnecting the hoses. If insufficient clearance exists to remove the engine with the compressor set aside, have the system discharged by a dealer service department or a service station.
2   Disconnect the negative cable from the battery.
3   Place fender covers over the fenders and cowl and remove the hood (Chapter 11).
4   Remove the air cleaner and duct assembly (Chapter 4).
5   Remove the front wheels (Chapter 1).
6   Drain the cooling system and engine oil and remove the oil filter (Chapter 1).
7   Label the vacuum lines, coolant and emissions hoses, wiring connectors, ground straps and fuel lines to ensure correct reinstallation. Pieces of masking tape with numbers written on them work well.
8   Disconnect all coolant hoses running between the engine and the vehicle.
9   Remove the cooling fan, shroud and radiator (Chapter 3).
10   Remove the drivebelts (Chapter 1) and, on four-cylinder engines, remove the water pump pulley. Remove the belt tensioner on the 3.8L engines.
11   Relieve fuel system pressure and disconnect the fuel lines connecting the engine to the chassis (Chapter 4). Plug or cap all open fittings.
12   Carefully disconnect the vacuum lines, emissions hoses, fuel lines, ground straps and electrical connectors **(see illustration)** which connect the engine to the vehicle. Refer to Chapters 4, 5 and 6 as needed.

13   Disconnect the throttle cable (and TV linkage and speed control cable, when equipped) from the throttle body (Chapter 4) and check behind the engine for any speedometer cable brackets attached to the engine.
14   On power steering equipped vehicles, unbolt the power steering pump (Chapter 10).
15   On A/C equipped vehicles, unbolt the compressor (Chapter 3) and set it aside if clearance exists **(see illustration)**. If clearance is insufficient, disconnect the refrigerant hoses only after system discharge (see Step 1). **Warning:** *Wear eye protection as a precaution while disconnecting hoses in case of residual pressure.*
16   On 3.8L engines, refer to Chapter 6 and remove the thermactor pump. Remove the water pump (Chapter 3) and crankshaft pulley.
17   Remove the starter motor (Chapter 5).
18   Unbolt the exhaust system from the engine (Chapter 4).
19   Remove the engine damper(s) (see Chapter 2 Part A or B).
20   On automatic transaxle models, remove the converter housing inspection cover. On four-cylinder models with the ATX transaxle, remove the timing window cover at the transaxle and rotate the crankshaft until the driveplate timing marker is aligned with the timing pointer. Mark the crankshaft pulley at the 12 o'clock position (TDC) (see Chapter 2 Part A). Rotate the crankshaft pulley mark to the 6 o'clock (BDC) position.
21   Refer to Chapter 7 and remove the torque converter-to-driveplate nuts. **Note:** *Models with an ATX transaxle must have the driveplate timing marker aligned with the BDC mark for proper engine removal and installation.* Push the converter back slightly toward the transaxle **(see illustration)**.

6.24 Typical engine mount through bolts

6.27 Secure the engine lifting sling with a bolt and large washer

22 Detach the cooler lines from the transaxle cooler (Chapter 7).
23 Remove the transaxle-to-engine block bolts.
24 Remove the through bolts from the engine mounts **(see illustration)**.
25 Recheck to be sure nothing is still connecting the engine to the vehicle. On four-cylinder models with a manual transaxle, remove the engine damper brace.
26 Lower the vehicle and then support the transaxle with a floor jack. Place a block of wood between them to prevent damage.
27 Attach an engine lifting sling to the lifting brackets on the engine. If either bracket is missing, attach the chain with a longer bolt and washer **(see illustration)**. Position a hoist and connect the sling to it. Take up the slack until there is slight tension on the hoist. If the chain presses against the distributor cap, remove the cap.
28 Raise the engine slightly above the mounts. Remove any remaining bolts attaching the transaxle to the rear engine mount and carefully separate the engine from the transaxle. Slowly raise the engine out of the engine compartment **(see illustration)**. Avoid snagging or bending anything as you lift the engine out.
29 Place the engine on a strong workbench or remove the flywheel/driveplate and mount it on an engine stand.

Installation

30 On manual transaxle models, use a clutch alignment tool to install the pressure plate (Chapter 7).
31 Carefully lower the engine into the engine compartment, ensuring that the engine mounts line up.
32 On automatic transaxle models, guide the torque converter pilot into the crankshaft, following the procedure outlined in Chapter 7.
33 With manual transaxle models, guide the input shaft into the crankshaft pilot bearing until it slips in all the way (bellhousing flush with engine block).
34 Install the transaxle-to-engine bolts and tighten them securely.
Caution: *Do not use the bolts to force the transmission and engine into alignment! To do so may damage major components.*
35 Reinstall the remaining components and fasteners in the reverse order of removal.
36 Refill coolant, oil, power steering and transmission fluids as needed.
37 Run the engine and check for proper operation and leaks.

---

7 Engine overhaul — disassembly sequence

1 It's much easier to disassemble and work on the engine if it's mounted on a portable engine stand. A stand can often be rented quite cheaply from an equipment rental yard. Before the engine is mounted on a stand, the flywheel/driveplate should be removed from the engine.
2 If a stand isn't available, it's possible to disassemble the engine with it blocked up on a sturdy workbench or on the floor. Be extra careful not to tip or drop the engine when working without a stand.
3 If you're going to obtain a rebuilt engine, all external components

6.28 As the engine is lifted out, check carefully for wires and hoses that weren't disconnected

must come off first, to be transferred to the replacement engine, just as they will if you're doing a complete engine overhaul yourself. These include:

Alternator and brackets
Emissions control components
Distributor, spark plug wires and spark plugs
Thermostat and housing cover
Water pump
EFI components
Intake/exhaust manifolds
Oil filter
Engine mounts
Clutch and flywheel/driveplate

Note: *When removing the external components from the engine, pay close attention to details that may be helpful or important during installation. Note the installed position of gaskets, seals, spacers, pins, brackets, washers, bolts and other small items.*

4 If you're obtaining a short block, which consists of the engine block, crankshaft, pistons and connecting rods all assembled, then the cylinder head(s), oil pan and oil pump will have to be removed as well. See *Engine rebuilding alternatives* for additional information regarding the different possibilities to be considered.
5 If you're planning a complete overhaul, the engine must be disassembled and the internal components removed in the following order:

Rocker arm cover(s)
Intake and exhaust manifolds

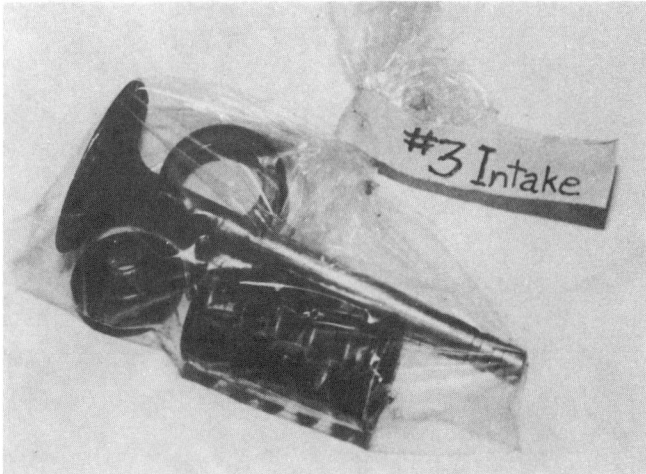

8.2 A small plastic bag, with an appropriate label, can be used to store the valve train components so they can be kept together and reinstalled in the correct guide

8.3b If the valve won't pull through the guide, deburr the edge of the stem end and the area around the top of the keeper groove with a file

Rocker arms and pushrods
Valve lifters
Cylinder head(s)
Timing cover
Timing chain and sprockets
Camshaft
Oil pan
Oil pump
Piston/connecting rod assemblies
Crankshaft and main bearings

6 Before beginning the disassembly and overhaul procedures, make sure the following items are available:
Common hand tools
Small cardboard boxes or plastic bags for storing parts
Gasket scraper
Ridge reamer
Vibration damper puller
Micrometers
Telescoping gauges
Dial indicator set
Valve spring compressor
Cylinder surfacing hone

8.3a Use a valve spring compressor to compress the spring, then remove the keepers from the valve stem

Piston ring groove cleaning tool
Electric drill motor
Tap and die set
Wire brushes
Oil gallery brushes
Cleaning solvent

8 Cylinder head — disassembly

Refer to illustrations 8.2, 8.3a and 8.3b

Note: *New and rebuilt cylinder heads are commonly available for most engines at dealerships and auto parts stores. Due to the fact that some specialized tools are necessary for the disassembly and inspection procedures, and replacement parts may not be readily available, it may be more practical and economical for the home mechanic to purchase replacement head(s) rather than taking the time to disassemble, inspect and recondition the original(s).*

1 Cylinder head disassembly involves removal of the intake and exhaust valves and related components. If they're still in place, remove the rocker arm bolts, fulcrums and rocker arms from the cylinder head studs. Label the parts or store them separately so they can be reinstalled in their original locations.
2 Before the valves are removed, arrange to label and store them, along with their related components, so they can be kept separate and reinstalled in the same valve guides they are removed from (**see illustration**).
3 Compress the springs on the first valve with a spring compressor and remove the keepers (**see illustration**). Carefully release the valve spring compressor and remove the retainer, the shield, the springs and the spring seat. Remove the umbrella-type seal from the guide, then pull the valve out of the head. If the valve binds in the guide (won't pull through), push it back into the head and deburr the area around the keeper groove with a fine file or whetstone (**see illustration**).
4 Repeat the procedure for the remaining valves. Remember to keep all the parts for each valve together so they can be reinstalled in the same locations.
5 Once the valves and related components have been removed and stored in an organized manner, the head should be thoroughly cleaned and inspected. If a complete engine overhaul is being done, finish the engine disassembly procedures before beginning the cylinder head cleaning and inspection process.

9 Cylinder head — cleaning and inspection

Refer to illustrations 9.12, 9.14, 9.15, 9.16, 9.17 and 9.18

1 Thorough cleaning of the cylinder head(s) and related valve train components, followed by a detailed inspection, will enable you to

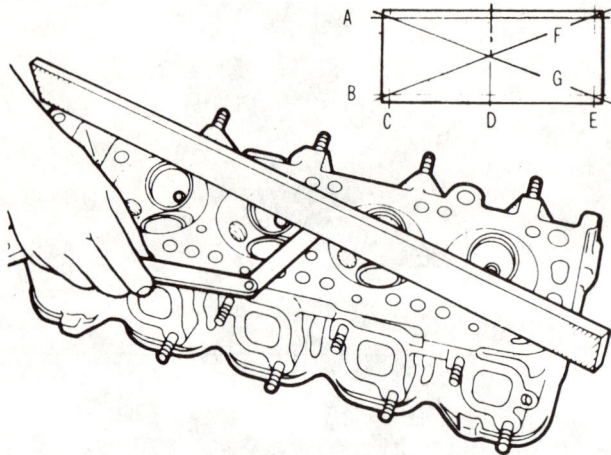

9.12   Check the cylinder head gasket surface for warpage
by trying to slip a feeler gauge under the straightedge
(see the Specifications for the maximum warpage allowed
and use a feeler gauge of that thickness)

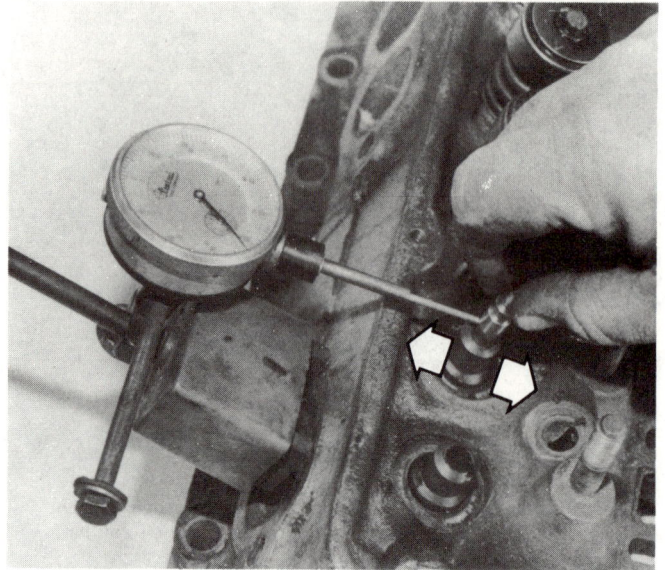

9.14   A dial indicator can be used to determine the valve
stem-to-guide clearance (move the valve stem as
indicated by the arrows)

decide how much valve service work must be done during the engine overhaul.

Cleaning

2   Scrape all traces of old gasket material and sealing compound off the head gasket, intake manifold and exhaust manifold sealing surfaces. Be very careful not to gouge the cylinder head. Special gasket removal solvents that soften gaskets and make removal much easier are available at auto parts stores.
3   Remove all built up scale from the coolant passages.
4   Run a stiff wire brush through the various holes to remove deposits that may have formed in them.
5   Run an appropriate size tap into each of the threaded holes to remove corrosion and thread sealant that may be present. If compressed air is available, use it to clear the holes of debris produced by this operation.
6   Clean the rocker arm pivot bolt threads with an appropriate sized tap, if needed.
7   Clean the cylinder head with solvent and dry it thoroughly. Compressed air will speed the drying process and ensure that all holes and recessed areas are clean. **Note:** *Decarbonizing chemicals are available and may prove very useful when cleaning cylinder heads and valve train components. They are very caustic and should be used with caution. Be sure to follow the instructions on the container.*
8   Clean the rocker arms, fulcrums, bolts and pushrods with solvent and dry them thoroughly (don't mix them up during the cleaning process). Compressed air will speed the drying process and can be used to clean out the oil passages.
9   Clean all the valve springs, shields, keepers and retainers with solvent and dry them thoroughly. Do the components from one valve at a time to avoid mixing up the parts.
10   Scrape off any heavy deposits that may have formed on the valves, then use a motorized wire brush to remove deposits from the valve heads and stems. Again, make sure the valves don't get mixed up.

Inspection

Cylinder head

11   Inspect the head very carefully for cracks, evidence of coolant leakage and other damage. If cracks are found, a new cylinder head should be obtained.
12   Using a straightedge and feeler gauge, check the head gasket mating surface for warpage **(see illustration)**. If the warpage exceeds the specified limit, it can be resurfaced at an automotive machine shop.
13   Examine the valve seats in each of the combustion chambers. If they're pitted, cracked or burned, the head will require valve service that is beyond the scope of the home mechanic.
14   Check the valve stem-to-guide clearance by measuring the lateral movement of the valve stem with a dial indicator attached securely to the head **(see illustration)**. The valve must be in the guide and ap-

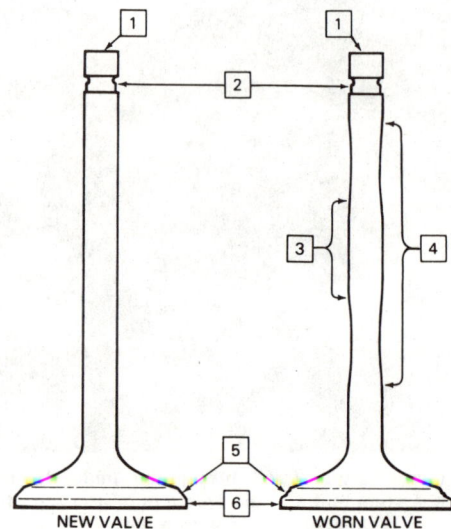

9.15   Check for valve wear at the points shown here

1   Valve tip   4   Stem (most worn area)
2   Keeper groove   5   Valve face
3   Stem (least worn area)   6   Margin

proximately 1/16-inch off the seat. The total valve stem movement indicated by the gauge needle must be divided by two to obtain the actual clearance. After this is done, if there's still some doubt regarding the condition of the valve guides they should be checked by an automotive machine shop (the cost should be minimal).

Valves

15   Carefully inspect each valve face for uneven wear, deformation, cracks, pits and burned areas **(see illustration)**. Check the valve stem for scuffing and galling and the neck for cracks. Rotate the valve and check for any obvious indication that it's bent. Look for pits and excessive wear on the end of the stem. The presence of any of these conditions indicates the need for valve service by an automotive machine shop.
16   Measure the margin width on each valve **(see illustration)**. Any valve with a margin narrower than 1/32-inch will have to be replaced with a new one.

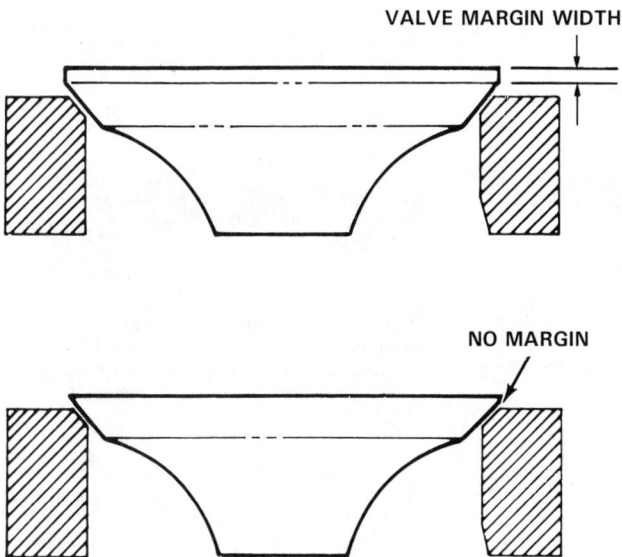

9.16 The margin width on each valve must be as specified (if no margin exists, the valve cannnot be reused)

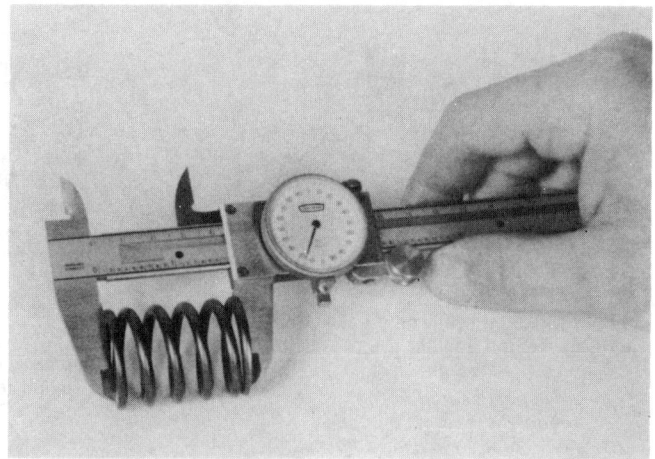

9.17 Measure the free length of each valve spring with a dial or vernier caliper

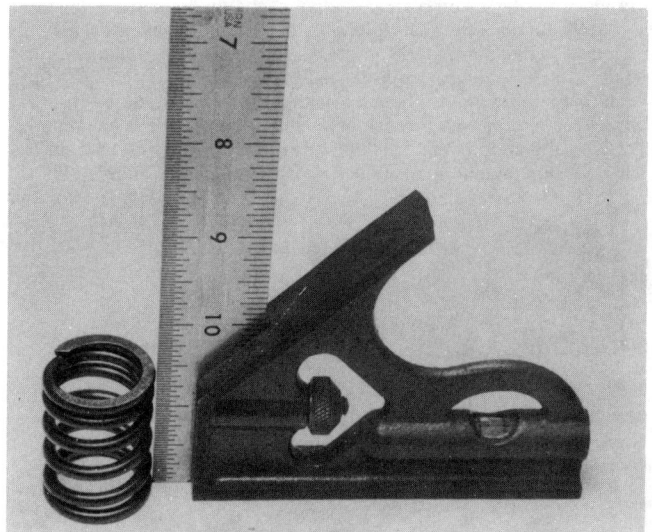

9.18 Check each valve spring for squareness

Valve components

17 Check each valve spring for wear (on the ends) and pits. Measure the free length and compare it to the Specifications (see illustration). Any springs that are shorter than specified have sagged and should not be reused. The tension of all springs should be checked with a special fixture before deciding that they're suitable for use in a rebuilt engine (take the springs to an automotive machine shop for this check).

18 Stand each spring on a flat surface and check it for squareness (see illustration). If any of the springs are distorted or sagged, replace all of them with new parts.

19 Check the spring retainers and keepers for obvious wear and cracks. Any questionable parts should be replaced with new ones, as extensive damage will occur if they fail during engine operation.

Rocker arm components

20 Check the rocker arm faces (the areas that contact the pushrod ends and valve stems) for pits, wear, galling, score marks and rough spots. Check the rocker arm pivot contact areas and fulcrums as well. Look for cracks in each rocker arm and bolt.

21 Inspect the pushrod ends for scuffing and excessive wear. Roll each pushrod on a flat surface, like a piece of plate glass, to determine if it's bent.

22 Check the rocker arm studs in the cylinder heads for damaged threads and secure installation.

23 Any damaged or excessively worn parts must be replaced with new ones.

24 If the inspection process indicates that the valve components are in generally poor condition and worn beyond the limits specified, which is usually the case in an engine that's being overhauled, reassemble the valves in the cylinder head and refer to Section 10 for valve servicing recommendations.

25 If the inspection turns up no excessively worn parts, and if the valve faces and seats are in good condition, the valve train components can be reinstalled in the cylinder head without major servicing. Refer to the appropriate Section for the cylinder head reassembly procedure.

10 Valves — servicing

1 Because of the complex nature of the job and the special tools and equipment needed, servicing of the valves, the valve seats and the valve guides, commonly known as a valve job, is best left to a professional.

2 The home mechanic can remove and disassemble each head, do the initial cleaning and inspection, then reassemble and deliver it to a dealer service department or an automotive machine shop for the actual valve servicing.

3 The dealer service department, or automotive machine shop, will remove the valves and springs, recondition or replace the valves and valve seats, recondition the valve guides, check and replace the valve springs, spring retainers or rotators and keepers (as necessary), replace the valve seals with new ones, reassemble the valve components and make sure the installed spring height is correct. The cylinder head gasket surface will also be resurfaced if it's warped.

4 After the valve job has been performed by a professional, the head will be in like new condition. When the head is returned, be sure to clean it again before installation on the engine to remove any metal particles and abrasive grit that may still be present from the valve service or head resurfacing operations. Use compressed air, if available, to blow out all the oil holes and passages.

11 Cylinder head — reassembly

Refer to illustrations 11.3, 11.5, 11.6 and 11.8

1 Regardless of whether or not a head was sent to an automotive repair shop for valve servicing, make sure it's clean before beginning reassembly.

2 If a head was sent out for valve servicing, the valves and related components will already be in place. Begin the reassembly procedure with Step 8.

3 Install new seals on each of the intake valve guides. Using a hammer and a deep socket or seal installation tool, gently tap each seal

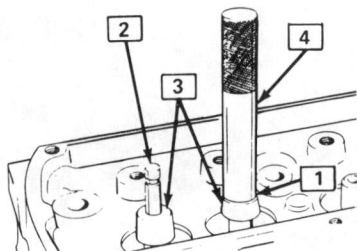

11.3   Make sure the new valve stem seals are seated against the tops of the valve guides

1 Valve seal seated in tool
2 Deburr the end of the valve stem before installing the seal
3 Seal
4 Valve seal installation tool

11.5   Typical valve spring, shield and retainer

11.6   Apply a small dab of grease to each keeper as shown here before installation — it will hold them in place on the valve stem as the spring is released

into place until it's completely seated on the guide **(see illustration)**. Don't twist or cock the seals during installation or they won't seal properly on the valve stems. The umbrella-type seals are installed over the valves after the valves are in place.

4   Beginning at one end of the head, lubricate and install the first valve. Apply moly-base grease or clean engine oil to the valve stem.

5   Drop the spring seat or shim(s) over the valve guide and set the valve springs, shield and retainer in place **(see illustration)**.

6   Compress the springs with a valve spring compressor. Position the

11.8   Be sure to check the valve spring installed height (the distance from the top of the seat/shims to the bottom of the retainer)

keepers in the groove, then slowly release the compressor and make sure the keepers seat properly. Apply a small dab of grease to each keeper to hold it in place if necessary **(see illustration)**.

7   Repeat the procedure for the remaining valves. Be sure to return the components to their original locations — don't mix them up!

8   Check the installed valve spring height with a ruler graduated in 1/32-inch increments or a dial caliper. If the head was sent out for service work, the installed height should be correct (but don't automatically assume that it is). The measurement is taken from the top of each spring seat or shim(s) to the bottom of the retainer **(see illustration)**. If the height is greater than specified, shims can be added under the springs to correct it. **Caution:** *Don't, under any circumstances, shim the springs to the point where the installed height is less than specified.*

9   Apply moly-base grease to the rocker arm faces and the fulcrums, then install the rocker arms and fulcrums on the cylinder head. Thread the bolts in three or four turns only (when the heads are installed on a V6 engine, the bolts will be tightened following a specific procedure).

12   Flywheel/driveplate — removal and installation

Refer to illustrations 12.2, 12.3 and 12.7

1   Remove the engine (Section 5). Remove the clutch and pressure plate.

2   Paint match marks on the crankshaft and flywheel/driveplate **(see illustration)**.

3   Remove the flywheel/driveplate **(see illustration)**.

4   Clean and inspect the flywheel/driveplate for cracks and/or damaged ring gear teeth. Replace if needed.

5   3.0L V6 engine replacement driveplates are balanced at the factory and require no further balancing. If the driveplate on a 3.8L engine

12.2   Make match marks (arrows) for reassembly

12.3   Keep the crankshaft from turning with a screwdriver inserted through a hole in the driveplate

12.7 Be sure to reinstall the lockplate

13.1a To keep the crankshaft from turning, thread a couple of flywheel or driveplate bolts into the crankshaft and have an assistant wedge a large screwdriver between them . . .

is to be replaced, check if the original driveplate has balance pins or rivets installed. If so, new balance rivets (E2DZ-6A32-A or equivalent) must be installed on the new driveplate in the same position as on the original driveplate.

6   Coat the threads of the mounting bolts with Ford sealant with Teflon (D8AZ-19554-A or equivalent).

7   Position the flywheel/driveplate on the crankshaft so the match marks align. Install the lock plate (see illustration), when equipped, and then the bolts. Note that the bolt holes may be staggered so the driveplate can only go on one way. Tighten the bolts in a diagonal pattern, working up to the specified torque in several steps.

8   On manual transmission models, reinstall the clutch disc and pressure plate (Chapter 7).

9   Reinstall the engine (Section 5).

13 Crankshaft oil seals — replacement

Front seal — four-cylinder engine

Refer to illustrations 13.1a, 13.1b, 13.2, 13.3 and 13.4

Note: *This procedure requires engine removal. For front seal replacement on V6 models, see Chapter 2B.*

1   With the engine out of the vehicle and the crankshaft immobilized (see illustration), remove the pulley mounting bolt with a breaker bar (see illustration).

2   Draw the pulley off the crankshaft with a puller (see illustration).

3   Using a large screwdriver, carefully pry the oil seal out of the cover (see illustration).

13.1b . . . while you loosen the crankshaft pulley bolt with a breaker bar and socket

13.2 The pulley on some engines may slide off the crankshaft easily, while on others a puller may be needed

13.3 Carefully pry out the front cover seal with a screwdriver (be careful not to nick or gouge the seal bore walls)

13.4   Clean the bore, then apply grease or oil to the outer edge of the new seal and drive it squarely into the opening with a large socket and hammer — DO NOT damage the seal in the process!

13.8   The quick and dirty way to replace the rear crankshaft oil seal is to pry out the old one with a screwdriver, lubricate the crankshaft journal and the lip of the new seal with moly-base grease and push the new seal into place — the trouble is, the seal lip is pretty stiff and can be easily damaged during installation if you're not careful

4   Clean the bore in the cover and coat the outer edge of the new seal with engine oil or multi-purpose grease. Using a socket with an outside diameter slightly smaller than the outside diameter of the seal, carefully drive the new seal into place with a hammer (see illustration). If a socket isn't available, a short section of large diameter pipe will work. Check the seal after installation to be sure that the spring didn't pop out of place.
5   Apply moly-base grease to the seal contact surface of the pulley hub, then slide the pulley onto the crankshaft. The keyway in the pulley hub must be aligned with the Woodruff key in the crankshaft nose.
6   Install the bolt and tighten it to the specified torque.

Rear seal — four-cylinder engine
Refer to illustrations 13.8, 13.11, 13.12, 13.14, 13.15a and 13.15b
7   The engine must be removed from the vehicle for this procedure and the transaxle and flywheel/driveplate must be separated from the engine.
8   The seal can be replaced without dropping the oil pan or removing

the seal retainer. However, this method is not recommended because the lip of the seal is quite stiff and it's possible to cock the seal in the retainer bore or damage it during installation. If you want to take the chance, pry out the old seal with a screwdriver (see illustration). Apply moly-base grease to the crankshaft seal journal and the lip of the new seal and carefully push the new seal into place. The lip is stiff so carefully work it onto the seal journal of the crankshaft with a smooth object like the end of an extension (see illustration 13.14) as you tap the seal into place. Don't rush it or you may damage the seal.
9   The following method is recommended but requires removal of the oil pan (refer to Chapter 2A) and the seal retainer.
10   After the oil pan has been removed, remove the bolts, detach the seal retainer and peel off all the old gasket material.
11   Position the seal and retainer assembly on a couple of wood blocks on a workbench and drive the old seal out with a punch (see illustration).
12   Drive the new seal into the retainer with a block of wood (see illustration) or a section of pipe slightly smaller in diameter than the outside diameter of the seal.

13.11   After removing the retainer assembly from the block, support it on a couple of wood blocks and drive out the old seal with a hammer and punch

13.12   Drive the new seal into the retainer with a block of wood or a section of pipe, if you have one large enough — make sure that you don't cock the seal in the retainer bore

13.14   Because the seal lip is quite stiff, it won't slide over the end of the crankshaft very easily — if you lubricate the journal and the seal lip with moly-base grease and carefully work the seal over the journal with a smooth, blunt object, you'll get it on without damaging it

13.15a   Since it might be damaged during installation of the retainer assembly, leave the gasket off until the seal lip has been worked onto the crankshaft, then drop it into place and position it with a couple of retainer bolts

13 Lubricate the crankshaft seal journal and the lip of the new seal with moly-base grease.

14 Slowly and carefully push the seal onto the crankshaft. The seal lip is stiff, so work it onto the crankshaft with a smooth object such as the end of an extension (see illustration) as you push the retainer against the block.

15 Slide the new gasket into place between the retainer and the block (see illustration), then install and tighten all the retainer bolts to the specified torque. The bottom sealing flange of the retainer must not extend below the bottom sealing flange (oil pan rail) of the block (see illustration).

16 The remaining steps are the reverse of removal.

Rear seal — V6 engines

Refer to illustrations 13.18, 13.20, 13.22 and 13.23

17 Remove the driveplate (and rear cover plate, if so equipped) (Section 12). **Caution:** *Be careful to avoid scratching or damaging the seal surfaces, which could ruin the crankshaft or block.*

18 Using a sharp awl, punch one hole into the seal between the lip and the engine block (see illustration).

19 Screw in the threaded end of Ford tool T77L-9533-B or equivalent. Use the tool to remove the seal.

20 If the special tool is unavailable, you may be able to pry the seal out with a screwdriver (see illustration).

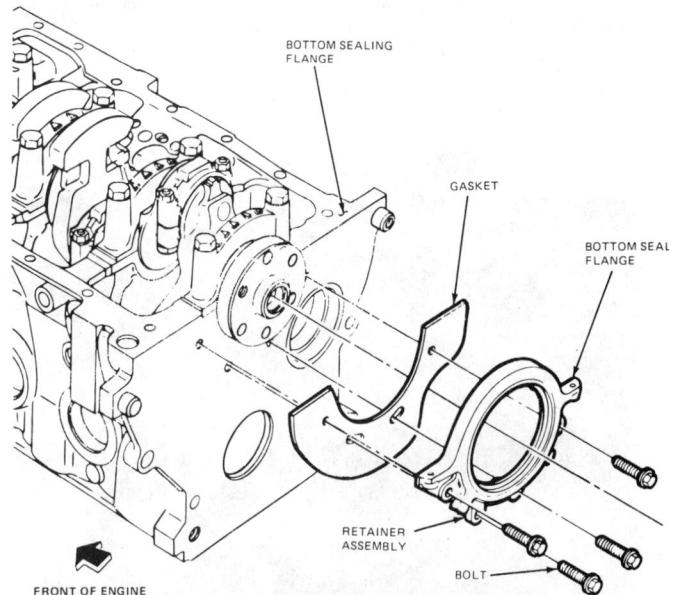

13.15b   The oil seal retainer bottom sealing flange must be even with the sealing flange on the block (there are no dowel pins to locate the retainer)

13.18   Do not damage the crankshaft when punching a hole in the seal

13.20   You may be able to gently pry the seal out, but don't scratch the sealing surfaces

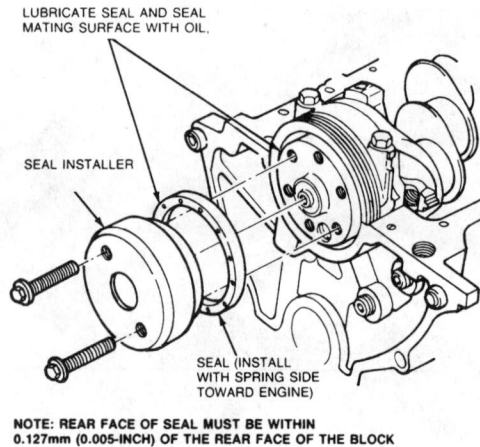

13.22   A special Ford tool is used to install the seal

13.23   Tap around the seal, slowly working it into position flush with the block surface

21 Thoroughly clean the seal bore and crankshaft sealing surface and lubricate the new seal with engine oil.
22 Place the new seal on Ford installer tool T82L-6701-A **(see illustration)** or equivalent. Position the tool and seal on the crankshaft. Alternate bolt tightening to properly seat the seal (driveplate bolts may be used if needed).
23 If the special tool is not available, carefully work the seal lip over the end of the crankshaft and tap the seal in with a hammer and blunt drift until it's seated in the bore **(see illustration)**. **Note:** *The rear face of this seal must be within 0.005-inch of the rear face of the block.*
24 Reinstall the driveplate (Section 12).
25 Reinstall the engine (Section 5).

14   Front cover, timing chain and sprockets — removal, inspection and installation (four-cylinder engine only)

Removal
Refer to illustrations 14.4a, 14.4b, 14.5, 14.6, 14.11 and 14.12

1   The engine must be removed from the vehicle for this procedure (Section 5).
2   Remove the oil pan (refer to Chapter 2A).
3   Remove the crankshaft pulley (refer to Section 13).
4   Remove the front cover mounting bolts **(see illustration)**. Pry the cover away from the block with a large screwdriver or pry bar **(see illustration)**. **Caution:** *Pry only at the point shown or damage to the cover gasket mating surface may result and oil leaks could develop.*
5   Remove the timing chain damper assembly from the cover **(see illustration)** and inspect it for wear. If it's excessively worn, replace it.
6   Remove the bolts and detach the timing chain tensioner **(see illustration)**. Check the tensioner slipper (the surface on which the chain rides). If grooves more than 0.060-inch deep are present, replace the tensioner.

14.4a   Remove all six front cover bolts . . .

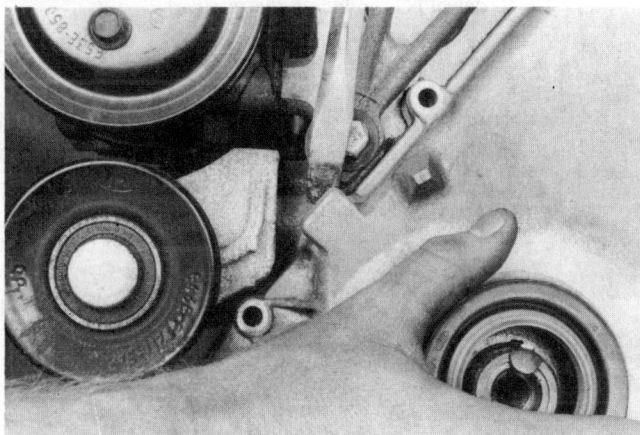

14.4b   . . . then wedge a screwdriver between the right engine mount bracket bolt and the lug on the cover and gently pry the cover off (it's made of aluminum, so be very careful not to damage it)

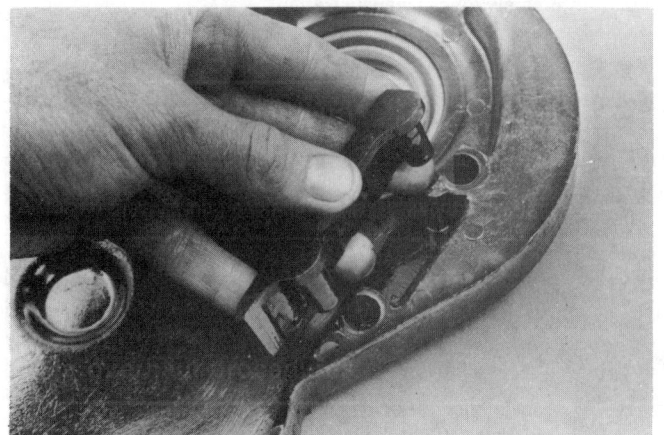

14.5   Remove and inspect the timing chain damper assembly — if it is heavily worn, replace it

14.6 To detach the timing chain tensioner, remove the two mounting bolts (arrows)

14.11 Turn the crankshaft until the timing marks (arrows) on the sprockets are aligned opposite each other

14.12 Remove the camshaft sprocket, crankshaft sprocket and timing chain as an assembly — the chain doesn't have enough sideplay to allow for sprocket removal one at a time

7 Turn the crankshaft in a counterclockwise direction (viewed from the front of the engine) to take up the slack on the *left* side of the chain.

8 Make a reference mark on the block at the approximate mid-point of the left chain run, then measure from the point to the chain and record the distance.

9 Turn the crankshaft in the other direction to take up the slack on the *right* side of the chain. Force the left side of the chain out with your finger and take a second measurement from the reference mark on the block.

10 Subtract the first measurement from the second measurement to obtain the chain deflection. Compare it to the Specifications. If chain deflection is excessive, replace the chain and both sprockets with new ones.

11 Turn the crankshaft until the timing marks on the sprockets are aligned (**see illustration**). The marks are small dimples drilled near the outer edges.

12 Remove the camshaft sprocket mounting bolt and washer. If the

crankshaft turns, install a couple of flywheel bolts in the rear end of the crankshaft and wedge a screwdriver between them. Slide both sprockets and the timing chain forward (**see illustration**) and remove them as an assembly.

Installation

Refer to illustrations 14.14, 14.20a and 14.20b

Timing chain and sprockets

13 Use a gasket scraper to remove all traces of old gasket material and sealant from the cover and engine block, then clean the mating surfaces with a cloth saturated with lacquer thinner or acetone. Clean the chain and sprockets with solvent.

14 Make sure the dowel pin in the camshaft and the Woodruff key in the crankshaft are in place, then slide both sprockets and the timing chain onto the shafts with the timing marks aligned (**see illustration**).

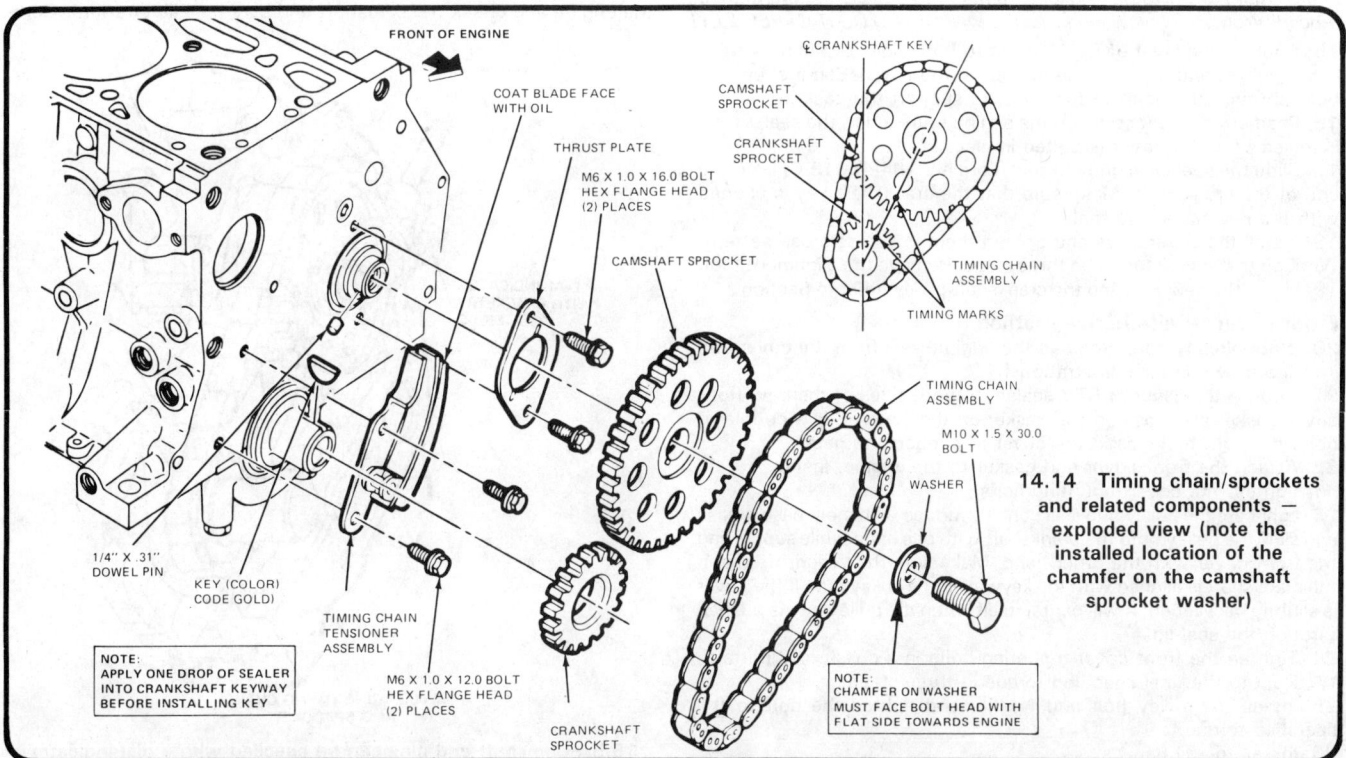

14.14 Timing chain/sprockets and related components — exploded view (note the installed location of the chamfer on the camshaft sprocket washer)

14.20a   While supporting the cover near the seal bore, drive out the old seal from the inside with a hammer and punch

14.20b   Clean the bore, then apply a small amount of grease or oil to the outer edge of the new seal and drive it squarely into the opening with a large socket and a hammer — DO NOT damage the seal in the process!

Each sprocket has a slot that must be aligned with the pin in the camshaft or the key in the crankshaft. Install the camshaft bolt and washer and tighten the bolt to the specified torque. **Note:** *The washer on the camshaft sprocket bolt must be installed with the chamfer OUT, facing the bolt head (which means that the flat side of the washer must be next to the sprocket).* Install the tensioner and tighten the bolts to the specified torque. Lubricate the timing chain, sprockets and tensioner with engine oil. Position the chain damper assembly in the front cover.

Front cover — factory method

Note: *The following method for front cover installation, which is recommended by the factory, requires that the new crankshaft oil seal be installed in the cover after the cover is installed on the engine. That's because the seal lip actually seals against the pulley hub rather than the crankshaft, which makes it difficult to align the cover precisely without the pulley in place on the crankshaft. However, the factory procedure also requires a special front cover alignment tool that slides onto the nose of the crankshaft. If you don't have access to the tool and/or don't want to purchase it from a Ford dealer, the alternative procedure outlined below works just as well, IF YOU DO IT CAREFULLY!*

15 Apply a thin layer of RTV sealant to both sides of the new front cover gasket and position the gasket on the cover. Slip a couple of bolts through the holes in the cover to support the gasket.
16 Position the front cover on the engine (remember, the seal will be installed *after* the cover is bolted in place).
17 Slide the special alignment tool (Ford no. T84P-6019-C) onto the end of the crankshaft. Make sure that the crankshaft key is aligned with the keyway in the tool.
18 Install the cover bolts and tighten them in a criss-cross pattern. Work up to the final torque in three steps. Remove the alignment tool.
19 Install the new seal and the crankshaft pulley (refer to Section 11).

Front cover — alternative method

20 If not already done, remove the original seal from the cover and install a new one **(see illustrations)**.
21 Apply a thin layer of RTV sealant to both sides of the new front cover gasket and position the gasket on the cover. Slip a couple of bolts through the holes in the cover to support the gasket.
22 Attach the front cover and gasket to the engine. Install, but do not tighten, the cover mounting bolts.
23 Lubricate the pulley hub seal contact surface with moly-base grease and slide the pulley onto the crankshaft with one hand while supporting the front cover with the other hand. Make sure the Woodruff key in the crankshaft is aligned with the keyway in the pulley hub. If the cover is slightly misaligned, it will center itself when the pulley hub is pushed through the seal lip.
24 Tighten the front cover mounting bolts in a criss-cross pattern. Work up to the final specified torque in three steps.
25 Install the pulley bolt and washer and tighten the bolt to the specified torque.
26 Install the oil pan.

---

15   Camshaft, balance shaft and bearings — removal, inspection and installation

---

Refer to illustrations 15.5, 15.7, 15.10, 15.12 and 15.14

1 To help determine if the camshaft is worn, the lobe lift can be checked with the engine in place in the vehicle (Chapter 2A). If the camshaft lobe lift is less than specified, cam lobe wear has occurred and a new camshaft and lifters should be installed.
2 The camshaft cannot be removed with the engine in the vehicle. If camshaft (or balance shaft) replacement is required, the engine must be removed before proceeding (Section 5).
3 Once the engine has been lifted from the vehicle and secured on a work stand, remove the timing chain and sprockets (Section 14 or Chapter 2 Part B, depending on which engine you have).
4 Remove and store the valve lifters (Chapter 2A or 2B).
5 On four-cylinder and 3.0L V6 engines, mount a dial indicator on the engine and check the camshaft end play **(see illustration)**. Com-

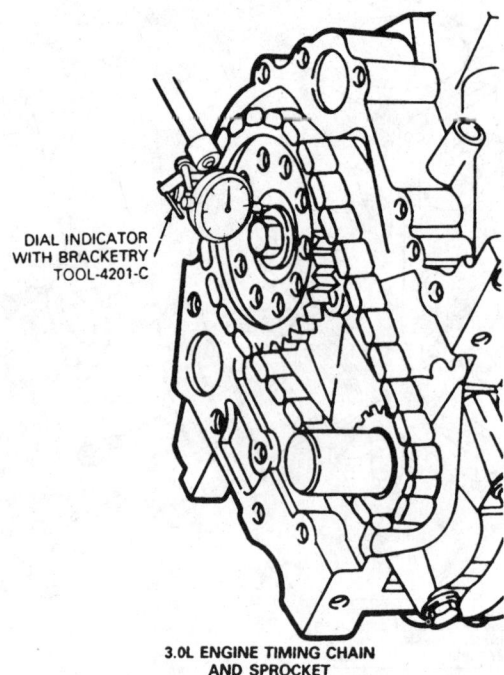

DIAL INDICATOR
WITH BRACKETRY
TOOL-4201-C

**3.0L ENGINE TIMING CHAIN
AND SPROCKET**

15.5   Camshaft end play can be checked with a dial indicator

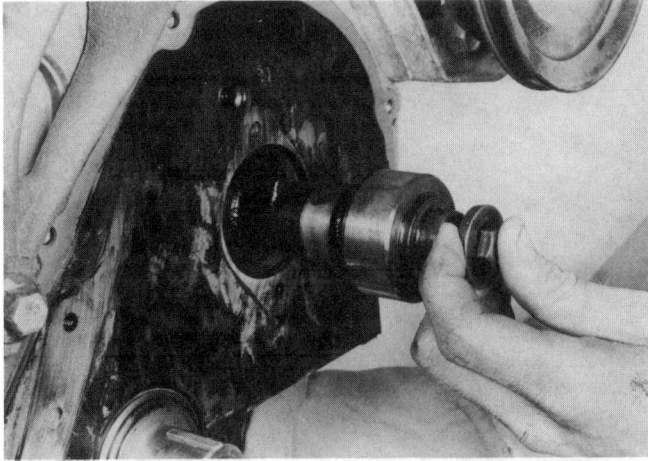

15.7 After removing the thrust plate, thread a bolt into the end of the camshaft to use as a handle during removal and installation

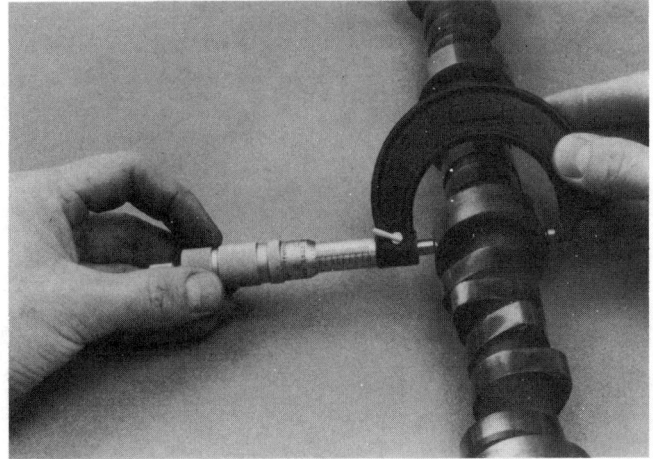

15.10 The camshaft bearing journal diameters are checked to pinpoint excessive wear and out-of-round conditions

pare it to the Specifications. If it is excessive, a new thrust plate should be installed. 3.8L V6 engines have a thrust spring and don't require adjustment.

6 Remove the camshaft and/or balance shaft thrust plate retaining bolts and detach the plate from the block.

7 To remove the camshaft, thread a long bolt into the end of the camshaft to use as a handle **(see illustration)**. The threads are metric, so be sure to use a bolt of the proper diameter and thread pitch.

8 To remove the balance shaft (3.8L V6 only), remove the thrust plate and carefully guide the shaft out of the block.

9 After the camshaft (or balance shaft) has been removed from the engine, cleaned with solvent and dried, inspect the bearing journals for uneven wear, pitting and evidence of seizure. If the journals are damaged, the bearing inserts in the block are probably damaged also.

10 If they appear to be in good condition, measure the bearing journals with a micrometer **(see illustration)** to determine their size and whether or not they're out-of-round. The inside diameter of each bearing can be measured with a telescoping gauge and micrometer. Subtract each journal diameter from the corresponding bearing inside diameter to obtain the bearing oil clearance. Compare the clearance for each bearing to the Specifications. If it is excessive for any of the bearings, have new bearings installed by an automotive machine shop.

11 Check the camshaft lobes for heat discoloration, score marks, chipped areas, pitting and uneven wear. If the lobes are in good condition and the lobe lift measurements are within the specified limits, the camshaft can be reinstalled (assuming that the bearing journals are in acceptable condition).

12 Camshaft lobe lift can be checked with the camshaft installed in the engine (Chapter 2A or 2B) or after it has been removed. The following procedure will pinpoint lobe wear after the camshaft has been removed and can be used to verify the lobe lift measurements done with the engine in the vehicle. Measure the major (A) and minor (B) diameters of each lobe with a vernier caliper or a micrometer and record the results **(see illustration)**. The difference between the two is the lobe lift. If the measured lift for any lobe is less than specified, replace the camshaft.

13 Camshaft and/or balance shaft bearing replacement requires special tools and expertise that place it outside the realm of the home mechanic. Take the block to an automotive machine shop to ensure that the job is done correctly.

14 Lubricate the camshaft lobes and journals and/or balance shaft journals with moly-base grease or engine assembly lube **(see illustration)**.

15 Slide the camshaft or balance shaft into the engine. Support the shaft near the block and be careful not to scrape or nick the bearings.

16 Apply moly-base grease to the rear of the thrust plate, then install it on the block and tighten the mounting bolts to the specified torque.

17 Install the timing chain, sprockets, timing chain tensioner, front cover, oil seal and crankshaft hub/pulley (refer to Chapter 2B or Sections 12 and 13 as needed).

18 Install the oil pan (Chapter 2A or 2B).

19 Lubricate the valve lifters with clean engine oil and install them

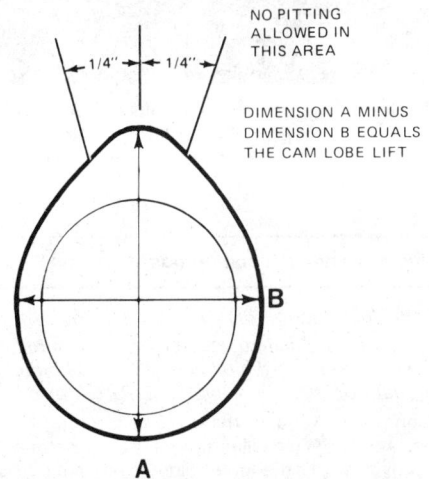

15.12 To verify camshaft lobe lift, measure the major (A) and minor (B) diameters of each lobe with a micrometer or vernier caliper — subtract the minor diameter from the major diameter to arrive at the lobe lift

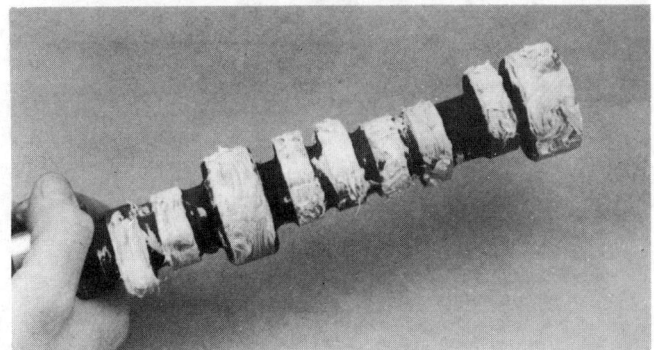

15.14 Be sure to apply moly-base grease or engine assembly lube to the cam lobes and bearing journals before installing the camshaft

in the block. If the original lifters are being reinstalled, be sure to return them to their original locations.

20 On four-cylinder engines, install the cylinder head (Chapter 2A).

21 The remaining installation steps are the reverse of removal.

22 Before starting the engine, add the correct amounts of the recommended oil and coolant and install a new oil filter (Chapter 1).

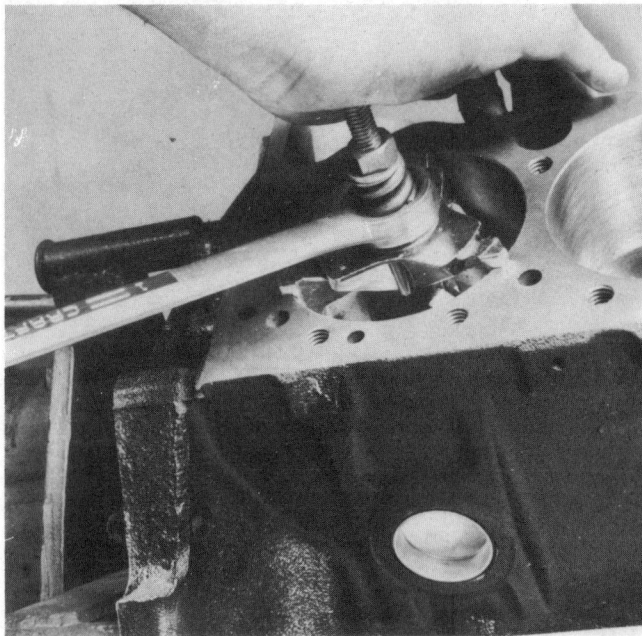

16.1   A ridge reamer is required to remove the ridge from the top of each cylinder — do this before removing the pistons!

16.3   Check the connecting rod side clearance with a feeler gauge as shown

16   Pistons and connecting rods — removal

Refer to illustrations 16.1, 16.3 and 16.5

Note: *Prior to removing the piston/connecting rod assemblies, remove the cylinder head(s), the oil pan and the oil pump by referring to the appropriate Sections in Chapter 2, Part A or B.*

1   Completely remove the ridge at the top of each cylinder with a ridge reaming tool (**see illustration**). Follow the manufacturer's instructions provided with the tool. Failure to remove the ridge before attempting to remove the piston/connecting rod assemblies may result in piston breakage.
2   After the cylinder ridges have been removed, turn the engine upside-down so the crankshaft is facing up.
3   Before the connecting rods are removed, check the end play with feeler gauges. Slide them between the first connecting rod and the crankshaft throw until the play is removed (**see illustration**). The end play is equal to the thickness of the feeler gauge(s). If the end play exceeds the service limit, new connecting rods will be required. If new rods (or a new crankshaft) are installed, the end play may fall under the specified minimum (if it does, the rods will have to be machined to restore it — consult an automotive machine shop for advice if necessary). Repeat the procedure for the remaining connecting rods.
4   Check the connecting rods and caps for identification marks. If they aren't plainly marked, use a small center punch to make the appropriate number of indentations on each rod and cap (1 — 4 or 6, depending on the engine type and cylinder they're associated with).
5   Loosen each of the connecting rod cap nuts 1/2-turn at a time until they can be removed by hand. Remove the number one connecting rod cap and bearing insert. Don't drop the bearing insert out of the cap. Slip a short length of plastic or rubber hose over each connecting rod cap bolt to protect the crankshaft journal and cylinder wall as the piston is removed (**see illustration**). Push the connecting rod/piston assembly out through the top of the engine. Use a wooden hammer handle to push on the upper bearing insert in the connecting rod. If resistance is felt, double-check to make sure that all of the ridge was removed from the cylinder.
6   Repeat the procedure for the remaining cylinders. After removal, reassemble the connecting rod caps and bearing inserts in their respective connecting rods and install the cap nuts finger tight. Leaving the old bearing inserts in place until reassembly will help prevent the connecting rod bearing surfaces from being accidentally nicked or gouged.

16.5   To prevent damage to the crankshaft journals and cylinder walls, slip sections of hose over the rod bolts before removing the pistons

17   Crankshaft — removal

Refer to illustrations 17.1, 17.3, 17.4a, 17.4b and 17.4c

Note: *The crankshaft can be removed only after the engine has been removed from the vehicle. It's assumed that the flywheel or driveplate, vibration damper/crankshaft pulley hub, timing chain (V6 engines only), oil pan, oil pump and piston/connecting rod assemblies have already been removed. If you are working on a four-cylinder engine, the seal housing must be unbolted and separated from the block before proceeding with crankshaft removal.*

1   Before the crankshaft is removed, check the end play. Mount a dial indicator with the stem in line with the crankshaft and just touching one of the crank throws (**see illustration**).

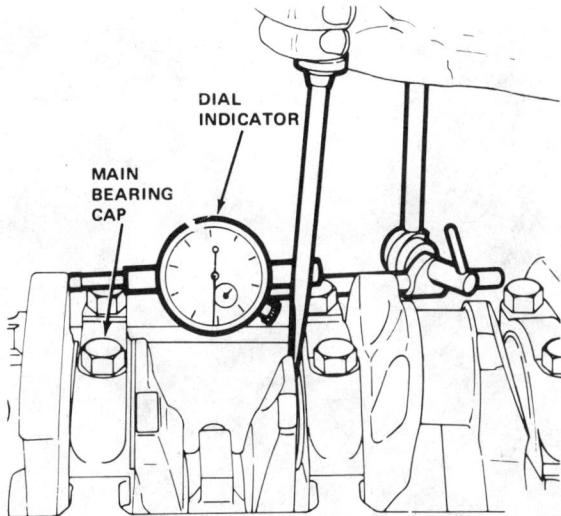

17.1 Checking crankshaft end play with a dial indicator

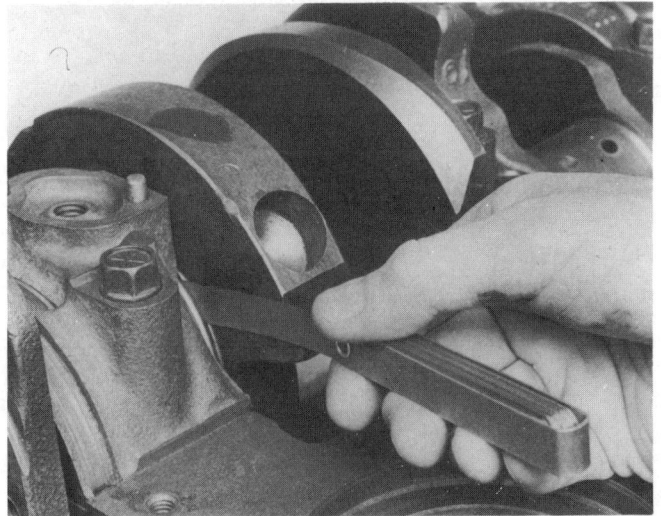

17.3 Checking crankshaft end play with a feeler gauge

17.4a Use a center punch or number stamping dies to mark the main bearing caps to ensure that they are reinstalled in their original locations on the block (make the punch marks near one of the bolt heads)

17.4b Mark the caps in order from the front of the engine to the rear (one mark for the front cap, two for the second one and so on) — the rear cap doesn't have to be marked since it cannot be installed in any other location

2   Push the crankshaft all the way to the rear and zero the dial indicator. Next, pry the crankshaft to the front as far as possible and check the reading on the dial indicator. The distance that it moves is the end play. If it's greater than specified, check the crankshaft thrust surfaces for wear. If no wear is evident, new main bearings should correct the end play.

3   If a dial indicator isn't available, feeler gauges can be used. Gently pry or push the crankshaft all the way to the front of the engine. Slip feeler gauges between the crankshaft and the front face of the thrust main bearing to determine the clearance (see illustration).

4   Check the main bearing caps to see if they're marked to indicate their locations. They should be numbered consecutively from the front of the engine to the rear. If they aren't, mark them with number stamping dies or a center punch (see illustrations). Main bearing caps generally have a cast-in arrow, which points to the front of the engine (see illustration). Loosen each of the main bearing cap bolts 1/4-turn at a time each, until they can be removed by hand.

5   Gently tap the caps with a soft-face hammer, then separate them from the engine block. If necessary, use the bolts as levers to remove the caps. Try not to drop the bearing inserts if they come out with the caps.

6   Carefully lift the crankshaft out of the engine. It's a good idea to

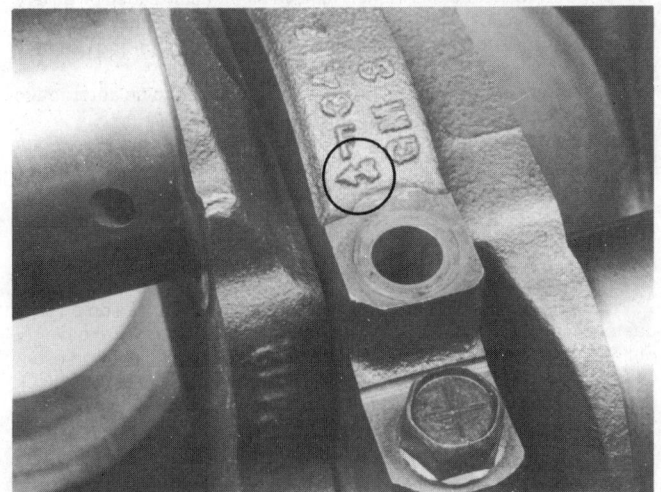

17.4c The arrow on the main bearing cap indicates the front of the engine

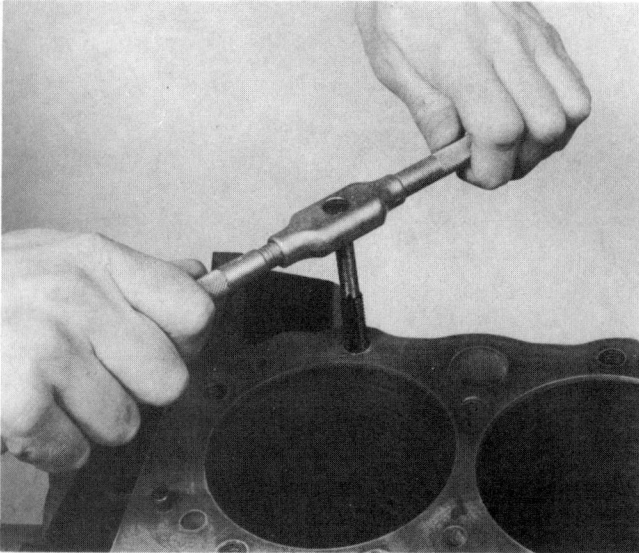

18.8 All bolt holes in the block — particularly the main bearing cap and head bolt holes — should be cleaned and restored with a tap (be sure to remove debris from the holes after this is done)

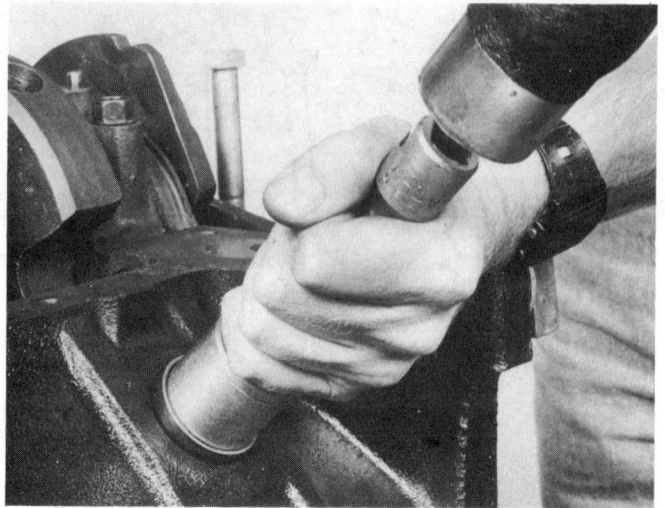

18.10 A large socket on an extension can be used to drive the new core plugs into the bores

have an assistant available, since the crankshaft is quite heavy. With the bearing inserts in place in the engine block and main bearing caps, return the caps to their respective locations on the engine block and tighten the bolts finger tight.

18 Engine block — cleaning

Refer to illustrations 18.8 and 18.10

Note: *The core plugs (also known as freeze or soft plugs) may be difficult or impossible to retrieve if they're driven into the block coolant passages.*

1   Drill a small hole in the center of each core plug and pull them out with an auto body type dent puller.
2   Using a gasket scraper, remove all traces of gasket material from the engine block. Be very careful not to nick or gouge the gasket sealing surfaces.
3   Remove the main bearing caps and separate the bearing inserts from the caps and the engine block. Tag the bearings, indicating which cylinder they were removed from and whether they were in the cap or the block, then set them aside.
4   Using a breaker bar or ratchet, remove all of the threaded oil gallery plugs from the block. The plugs are usually very tight — they may have to be drilled out and the holes retapped. Discard the plugs and use new ones when the engine is reassembled.
5   If the engine is extremely dirty it should be taken to an automotive machine shop to be steam cleaned or hot tanked.
6   After the block is returned, clean all oil holes and oil galleries one more time. Brushes specifically designed for this purpose are available at most auto parts stores. Flush the passages with warm water until the water runs clear, dry the block thoroughly and wipe all machined surfaces with a light, rust preventative oil. If you have access to compressed air, use it to speed the drying process and to blow out all the oil holes and galleries.
7   If the block isn't extremely dirty or sludged up, you can do an adequate cleaning job with hot soapy water and a stiff brush. Take plenty of time and do a thorough job. Regardless of the cleaning method used, be sure to clean all oil holes and galleries very thoroughly, dry the block completely and coat all machined surfaces with light oil.
8   The threaded holes in the block must be clean to ensure accurate torque readings during reassembly. Run the proper size tap into each of the holes to remove any rust, corrosion, thread sealant or sludge and to restore any damaged threads **(see illustration)**. If possible, use compressed air to clear the holes of debris produced by this operation. Now is a good time to clean the threads on the head bolts and the main

bearing cap bolts as well.
9   Reinstall the main bearing caps and tighten the bolts finger tight.
10   After coating the sealing surfaces of the new core plugs with RTV sealant, install them in the engine block **(see illustration)**. Make sure they're driven in straight and seated properly or leakage could result. Special tools are available for this purpose, but equally good results can be obtained using a large socket, with an outside diameter that will just slip into the core plug, a 1/2-inch drive extension and a hammer.
11   Apply non-hardening sealant (such as Permatex number 2 or Teflon tape) to the new oil gallery plugs and thread them into the holes in the block. Make sure they're tightened securely.
12   If the engine isn't going to be reassembled right away, cover it with a large plastic trash bag to keep it clean.

19 Engine block — inspection

Refer to illustrations 19.4a, 19.4b and 19.4c

1   Before the block is inspected, it should be cleaned as described in Section 18. Double-check to make sure the ridge at the top of each cylinder has been completely removed.
2   Visually check the block for cracks, rust and corrosion. Look for stripped threads in the threaded holes. It's also a good idea to have the block checked for hidden cracks by an automotive machine shop that has the special equipment to do this type of work. If defects are found, have the block repaired, if possible, or replaced.
3   Check the cylinder bores for scuffing and scoring.
4   Measure the diameter of each cylinder at the top (just under the ridge area), center and bottom of the cylinder bore, parallel to the crankshaft axis **(see illustrations)**. Next, measure each cylinder's diameter at the same three locations *across* the crankshaft axis. Compare the results to the Specifications. If the cylinder walls are badly scuffed or scored, or if they're out-of-round or tapered beyond the limits given in the Specifications, have the engine block rebored and honed at an automotive machine shop. If a rebore is done, oversize pistons and rings will be required.
5   If the cylinders are in reasonably good condition and not worn to the outside of the limits, and if the piston-to-cylinder clearances can be maintained properly, then they don't have to be rebored. Honing is all that's necessary (Section 20).

20 Cylinder honing

Refer to illustrations 20.3a and 20.3b

1   Prior to engine reassembly, the cylinder bores must be honed so the new piston rings will seat correctly and provide the best possible combustion chamber seal. **Note:** *If you don't have the tools or don't*

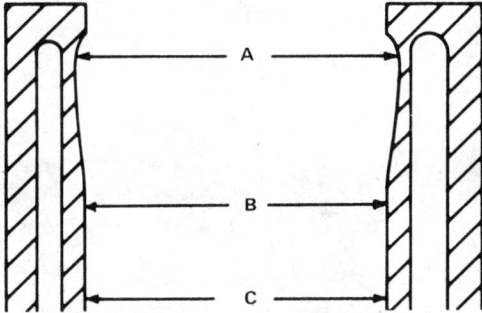

19.4a Measure the diameter of each cylinder just under the wear ridge (A), at the center (B) and at the bottom (C)

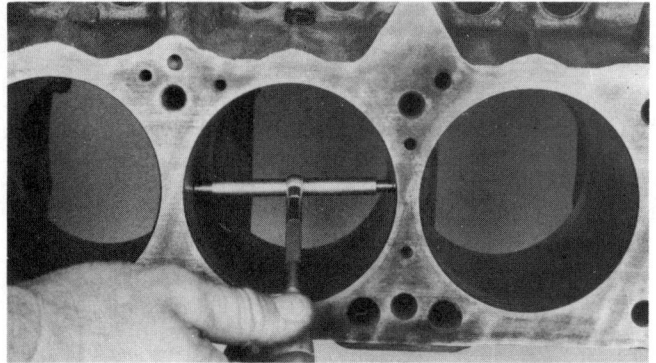

19.4b The ability to "feel" when the telescoping gauge is at the correct point will be developed over time, so work slowly and repeat the check until you are satisfied that the bore measurement is accurate

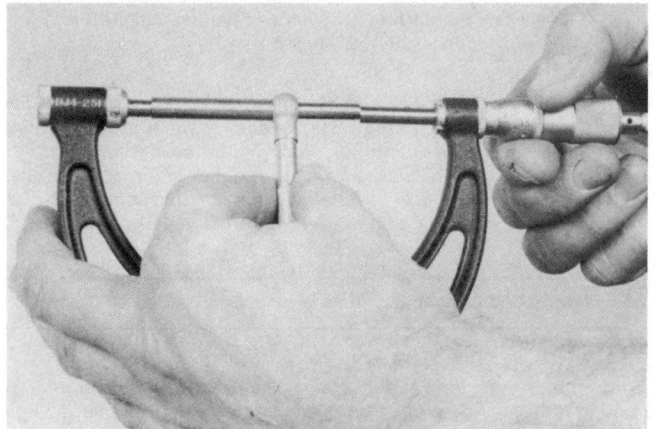

19.4c The gauge is then measured with a micrometer to determine the bore size

want to tackle the honing operation, most automotive machine shops will do it for a reasonable fee.

2   Before honing the cylinders, install the main bearing caps and tighten the bolts to the specified torque.

3   Two types of cylinder hones are commonly available — the flex hone or "bottle brush" type and the more traditional surfacing hone with spring-loaded stones. Both will do the job, but for the less experienced mechanic the "bottle brush" hone will probably be easier to use. You'll also need plenty of light oil or honing oil, some rags and an electric drill motor. Proceed as follows:

a)   Mount the hone in the drill motor, compress the stones and slip it into the first cylinder **(see illustration)**. Be sure to wear safety goggles or a face shield!

b)   Lubricate the cylinder with plenty of oil, turn on the drill and move the hone up-and-down in the cylinder at a pace that will produce a fine crosshatch pattern on the cylinder walls. Ideally, the crosshatch lines should intersect at approximately a 60° angle **(see illustration)**. Be sure to use plenty of lubricant and don't take off any more material than is absolutely necessary to produce the desired finish. **Note:** *Piston ring manufacturers may specify a smaller crosshatch angle than the traditional 60° — read and follow any instructions included with the new rings.*

c)   Don't withdraw the hone from the cylinder while it's running. Instead, shut off the drill and continue moving the hone up-and-down in the cylinder until it comes to a complete stop, then compress the stones and withdraw the hone. If you're using a "bottle brush" type hone, stop the drill motor, then turn the chuck in the normal direction of rotation while withdrawing the hone from the cylinder.

d)   Wipe the oil out of the cylinder and repeat the procedure for the remaining cylinders.

4   After the honing job is complete, chamfer the top edges of the cylinder bores with a small file so the rings won't catch when the pistons are installed. **Be very careful not to nick the cylinder walls with the end of the file.**

5   The entire engine block must be washed again very thoroughly with warm, soapy water to remove all traces of the abrasive grit produced during the honing operation. **Note:** *The bores can be considered clean when a white cloth — dampened with clean engine oil — used*

20.3a A "bottle brush" hone will produce better results if you have never done cylinder honing before

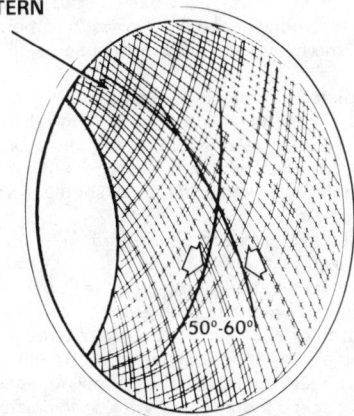

CROSSHATCH PATTERN

50°-60°

20.3b The cylinder hone should leave a smooth, crosshatch pattern with the lines intersecting at approximately a 60-degree angle

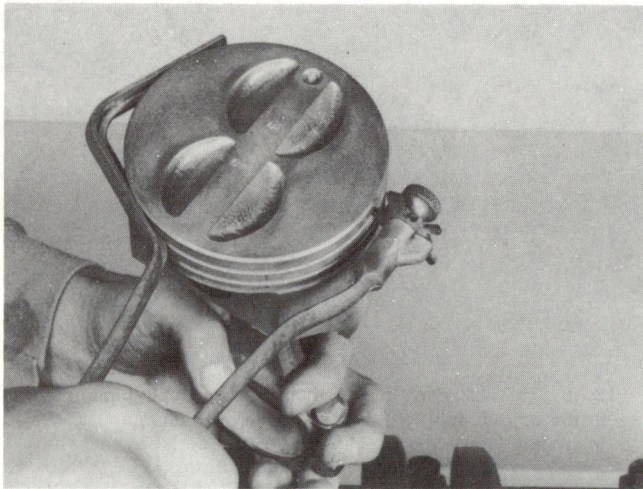

21.4a   The piston ring grooves can be cleaned with a special tool, as shown here, . . .

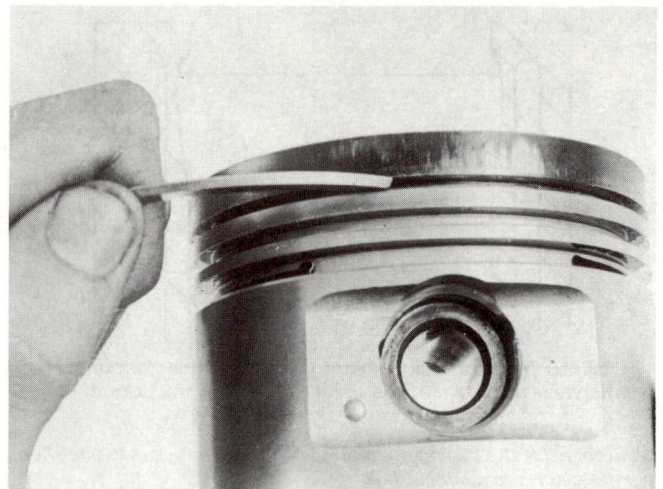

21.4b   . . . or a section of a broken ring

to wipe them out doesn't pick up any more honing residue, which will show up as gray areas on the cloth. Be sure to run a brush through all oil holes and galleries and flush them with running water.
6   After rinsing, dry the block and apply a coat of light rust preventive oil to all machined surfaces. Wrap the block in a plastic trash bag to keep it clean and set it aside until reassembly.

21   Pistons and connecting rods — inspection

Refer to illustrations 21.4a, 21.4b, 21.10 and 21.11

1   Before the inspection process can be carried out, the piston/connecting rod assemblies must be cleaned and the original piston rings removed from the pistons. **Note:** *Always use new piston rings when the engine is reassembled.*
2   Using a piston ring installation tool, carefully remove the rings from the pistons. Be careful not to nick or gouge the pistons in the process.
3   Scrape all traces of carbon from the top of the piston. A handheld wire brush or a piece of fine emery cloth can be used once the majority of the deposits have been scraped away. Do not, under any circumstances, use a wire brush mounted in a drill motor to remove deposits from the pistons. The piston material is soft and will be eroded away by the wire brush.
4   Use a piston ring groove cleaning tool to remove carbon deposits from the ring grooves. If a tool isn't available, a piece broken off the old ring will do the job. Be very careful to remove only the carbon deposits — don't remove any metal and do not nick or scratch the sides of the ring grooves (**see illustrations**).
5   Once the deposits have been removed, clean the piston/rod assemblies with solvent and dry them with compressed air (if available). Make sure the oil return holes in the back sides of the ring grooves are clear.
6   If the pistons and cylinder walls aren't damaged or worn excessively, and if the engine block is not rebored, new pistons won't be necessary. Normal piston wear appears as even vertical wear on the piston thrust surfaces and slight looseness of the top ring in its groove. New piston rings, on the other hand, should always be used when an engine is rebuilt.
7   Carefully inspect each piston for cracks around the skirt, at the pin bosses and at the ring lands.
8   Look for scoring and scuffing on the thrust faces of the skirt, holes in the piston crown and burned areas at the edge of the crown. If the skirt is scored or scuffed, the engine may have been suffering from overheating and/or abnormal combustion, which caused excessively high operating temperatures. The cooling and lubrication systems should be checked thoroughly. A hole in the piston crown is an indication that abnormal combustion (preignition) was occurring. Burned areas at the edge of the piston crown are usually evidence of spark knock (detonation). If any of the above problems exist, the causes must be corrected or the damage will occur again.

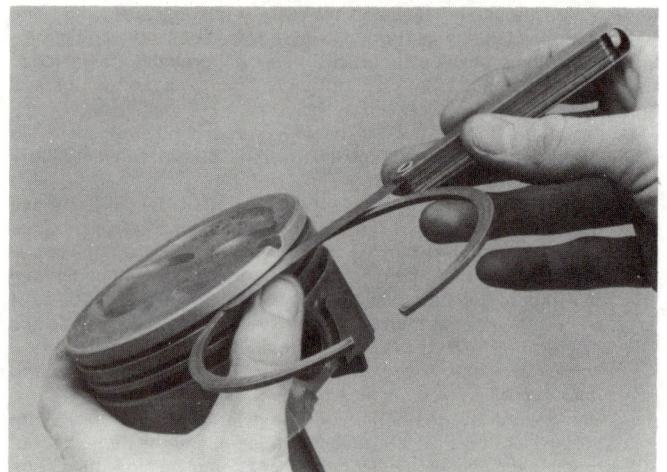

21.10   Check the ring side clearance with a feeler gauge at several points around the groove

9   Corrosion of the piston, in the form of small pits, indicates that coolant is leaking into the combustion chamber and/or the crankcase. Again, the cause must be corrected or the problem may persist in the rebuilt engine.
10   Measure the piston ring side clearance by laying a new piston ring in each ring groove and slipping a feeler gauge in beside it (**see illustration**). Check the clearance at three or four locations around each groove. Be sure to use the correct ring for each groove; they are different. If the side clearance is greater than specified, new pistons will have to be used.
11   Check the piston-to-bore clearance by measuring the bore (see Section 19) and the piston diameter. Make sure the pistons and bores are correctly matched. Measure the piston across the skirt, at a 90° angle to and in line with the piston pin (**see illustration**). Subtract the piston diameter from the bore diameter to obtain the clearance. If it's greater than specified, the block will have to be rebored and new pistons and rings installed.
12   Check the piston-to-rod clearance by twisting the piston and rod in opposite directions. Any noticeable play indicates excessive wear, which must be corrected. The piston/connecting rod assemblies should be taken to an automotive machine shop to have the pistons and rods rebored and new pins installed.
13   If the pistons must be removed from the connecting rods for any reason, they should be taken to an automotive machine shop. While they are there have the connecting rods checked for bend and twist, since automotive machine shops have special equipment for this purpose. **Note:** *Unless new pistons and/or connecting rods must be installed, do not disassemble the pistons and connecting rods.*

21.11 Measure the piston diameter at a 90° angle to the piston pin and in line with it

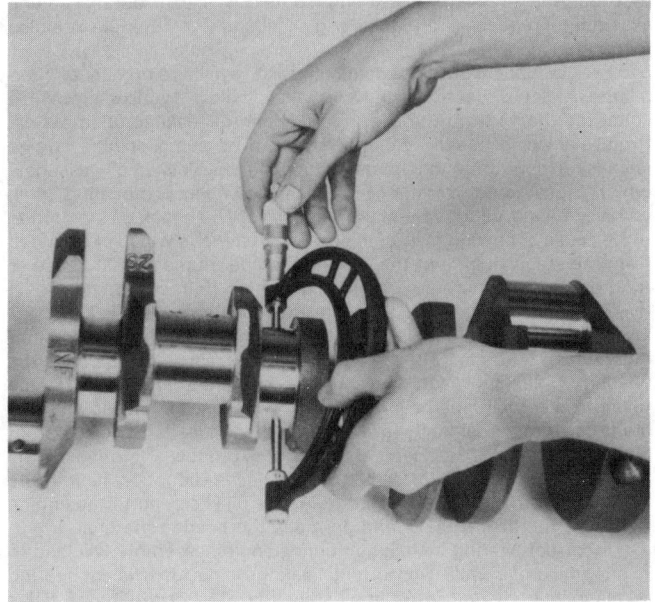

22.2 Measure the diameter of each crankshaft journal at several points to detect taper and out-of-round conditions

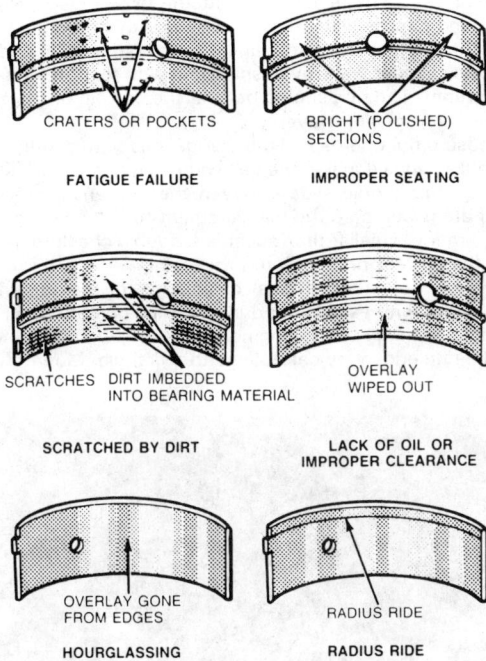

23.1 Bearing failure diagnosis

14 Check the connecting rods for cracks and other damage. Temporarily remove the rod caps, lift out the old bearing inserts, wipe the rod and cap bearing surfaces clean and inspect them for nicks, gouges and scratches. After checking the rods, replace the old bearings, slip the caps into place and tighten the nuts finger tight.

22 Crankshaft — inspection

Refer to illustration 22.2

1 Clean the crankshaft with solvent and dry it with compressed air (if available). Be sure to clean the oil holes with a stiff brush and flush them with solvent. Check the main and connecting rod bearing journals

for uneven wear, scoring, pits and cracks. Check the rest of the crankshaft for cracks and other damage.
2 Using a micrometer, measure the diameter of the main and connecting rod journals and compare the results to the Specifications (**see illustration**). By measuring the diameter at a number of points around each journal's circumference, you'll be able to determine whether or not the journal is out-of-round. Take the measurement at each end of the journal, near the crank throws, to determine if the journal is tapered.
3 If the crankshaft journals are damaged, tapered, out-of-round or worn beyond the limits given in the Specifications, have the crankshaft reground by an automotive machine shop. Be sure to use the correct size bearing inserts if the crankshaft is reconditioned. **Note:** *3.8L V6 engine crankshaft journal refinishing is limited to 0.010 inch undersize. Further main journal refinishing may result in fatigue failure of the crankshaft.*
4 Refer to Section 23 and examine the main and rod bearing inserts.

23 Main and connecting rod bearings — inspection

Refer to illustration 23.1

1 Even though the main and connecting rod bearings should be replaced with new ones during the engine overhaul, the old bearings should be retained for close examination, as they may reveal valuable information about the condition of the engine (**see illustration**).
2 Bearing failure occurs because of lack of lubrication, the presence of dirt or other foreign particles, overloading the engine and corrosion. Regardless of the cause of bearing failure, it must be corrected before the engine is reassembled to prevent it from happening again.
3 When examining the bearings, remove them from the engine block, the main bearing caps, the connecting rods and the rod caps and lay them out on a clean surface in the same general position as their location in the engine. This will enable you to match any bearing problems with the corresponding crankshaft journal.
4 Dirt and other foreign particles get into the engine in a variety of ways. It may be left in the engine during assembly, or it may pass through filters or the PCV system. It may get into the oil, and from there into the bearings. Metal chips from machining operations and normal engine wear are often present. Abrasives are sometimes left in engine components after reconditioning, especially when parts are not thoroughly cleaned using the proper cleaning methods. Whatever the source, these foreign objects often end up embedded in the soft bearing material and are easily recognized. Large particles will not embed in the bearing and will score or gouge the bearing and journal. The best prevention for this cause of bearing failure is to clean all parts

thoroughly and keep everything spotlessly clean during engine assembly. Frequent and regular engine oil and filter changes are also recommended.

5   Lack of lubrication (or lubrication breakdown) has a number of inter-related causes. Excessive heat (which thins the oil), overloading (which squeezes the oil from the bearing face) and oil leakage or throw off (from excessive bearing clearances, worn oil pump or high engine speeds) all contribute to lubrication breakdown. Blocked oil passages, which usually are the result of misaligned oil holes in a bearing shell, will also oil starve a bearing and destroy it. When lack of lubrication is the cause of bearing failure, the bearing material is wiped or extruded from the steel backing of the bearing. Temperatures may increase to the point where the steel backing turns blue from overheating.

6   Driving habits can have a definite effect on bearing life. Full throttle, low speed operation (lugging the engine) puts very high loads on bearings, which tends to squeeze out the oil film. These loads cause the bearings to flex, which produces fine cracks in the bearing face (fatigue failure). Eventually the bearing material will loosen in pieces and tear away from the steel backing. Short trip driving leads to corrosion of bearings because insufficient engine heat is produced to drive off the condensed water and corrosive gases. These products collect in the engine oil, forming acid and sludge. As the oil is carried to the engine bearings, the acid attacks and corrodes the bearing material.

7   Incorrect bearing installation during engine assembly will lead to bearing failure as well. Tight fitting bearings leave insufficient bearing oil clearance and will result in oil starvation. Dirt or foreign particles trapped behind a bearing insert result in high spots on the bearing which lead to failure.

24   Engine overhaul — reassembly sequence

1   Before beginning engine reassembly, make sure you have all the necessary new parts, gaskets and seals as well as the following items on hand:

Common hand tools
A 1/2-inch drive torque wrench
Piston ring installation tool
Piston ring compressor
Short lengths of rubber or plastic hose
  to fit over connecting rod bolts
Plastigage
Feeler gauges
A fine-tooth file
New engine oil

Engine assembly lube or moly-base grease
RTV-type gasket sealant
Anaerobic-type gasket sealant
Thread locking compound

2   In order to save time and avoid problems, engine reassembly must be done in the following general order:

New camshaft bearings (and balance shaft bearings
  on 3.8L V6 engines) (must be done by automotive machine shop)
Piston rings
Crankshaft and main bearings
Piston/connecting rod assemblies
Camshaft and lifters
Timing chain and sprockets
Cylinder head(s), pushrods and rocker arms
Timing cover
Oil pump
Oil pan
Intake and exhaust manifolds
Rocker arm cover(s)
Flywheel/driveplate

25   Piston rings — installation

Refer to illustrations 25.3, 25.4, 25.5, 25.9a, 25.9b and 25.12

1   Before installing the new piston rings, the ring end gaps must be checked. It's assumed that the piston ring side clearance has been checked and verified correct (Section 21).

2   Lay out the piston/connecting rod assemblies and the new ring sets so the ring sets will be matched with the same piston and cylinder during the end gap measurement and engine assembly.

3   Insert the top (number one) ring into the first cylinder and square it up with the cylinder walls by pushing it in with the top of the piston **(see illustration)**. The ring should be near the bottom of the cylinder, at the lower limit of ring travel.

4   To measure the end gap, slip feeler gauges between the ends of the ring until a gauge equal to the gap width is found **(see illustration)**. The feeler gauge should slide between the ring ends with a slight amount of drag. Compare the measurement to the Specifications. If the gap is larger or smaller than specified, double-check to make sure you have the correct rings before proceeding.

5   If the gap is too small, it must be enlarged or the ring ends may come in contact with each other during engine operation, which can cause serious damage to the engine. The end gap can be increased by filing the ring ends very carefully with a fine file. Mount the file in

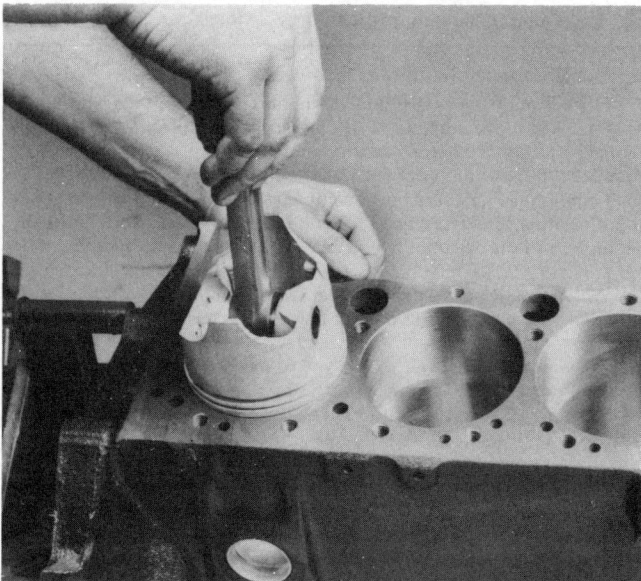

25.3   When checking piston ring end gap, the ring must be square in the cylinder bore (this is done by pushing the ring down with the top of a piston as shown)

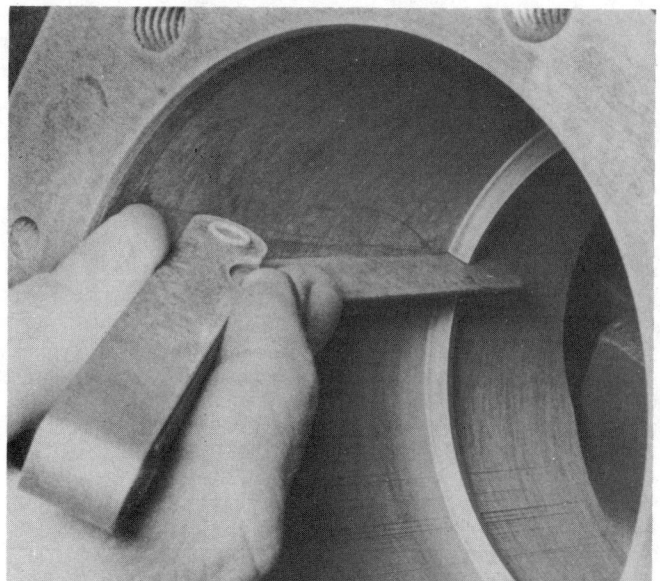

25.4   With the ring square in the cylinder, measure the end gap with a feeler gauge

a vise equipped with soft jaws, slip the ring over the file with the ends contacting the file face and slowly move the ring to remove material from the ends. When performing this operation, file only from the outside in (see illustration).

6 Excess end gap isn't critical unless it's greater than 0.040-inch. Again, double-check to make sure you have the correct rings for your engine.

7 Repeat the procedure for each ring that will be installed in the first cylinder and for each ring in the remaining cylinders. Remember to keep rings, pistons and cylinders matched up.

8 Once the ring end gaps have been checked/corrected, the rings can be installed on the pistons.

9 The oil control ring (lowest one on the piston) is installed first. It's composed of three separate components. Slip the spacer/expander into the groove (see illustration). If an anti-rotation tang is used, make sure it's inserted into the drilled hole in the ring groove. Next, install the lower side rail. Don't use a piston ring installation tool on the oil ring side rails, as they may be damaged. Instead, place one end of the side rail into the groove between the spacer/expander and the ring land, hold it firmly in place and slide a finger around the piston while pushing the rail into the groove (see illustration). Next, install the upper side rail in the same manner.

10 After the three oil ring components have been installed, check to make sure that both the upper and lower side rails can be turned

smoothly in the ring groove.

11 The number two (middle) ring is installed next. It's stamped with a mark which must face up, toward the top of the piston. **Note:** *Always follow the instructions printed on the ring package or box — different manufacturers may require different approaches. Do not mix up the top and middle rings, as they have different cross sections.*

12 Use a piston ring installation tool and make sure the identification mark is facing the top of the piston, then slip the ring into the middle groove on the piston (see illustration). Don't expand the ring any more than is necessary to slide it over the piston.

13 Install the number one (top) ring in the same manner. Make sure the mark is facing up. Be careful not to confuse the number one and number two rings.

14 Repeat the procedure for the remaining pistons and rings.

26 Crankshaft — installation and main bearing oil clearance check

Refer to illustrations 26.10, 26.14, 26.18a, 26.18b and 26.18c

1 Crankshaft installation is the first step in engine reassembly. It's assumed at this point that the engine block and crankshaft have been

25.5 If the end gap is too small, clamp a file in a vise and file the ring ends (from the outside in only) to enlarge the gap slightly

25.9a Installing the spacer/expander in the oil control ring groove

25.9b DO NOT use a piston ring installation tool when installing the oil ring side rails

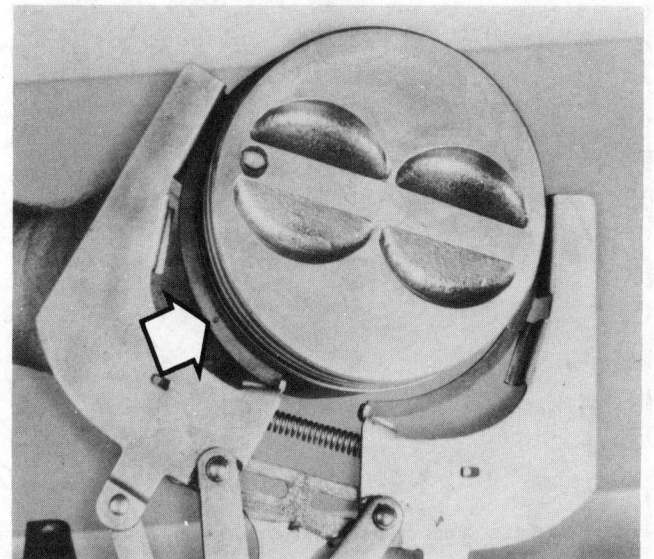
25.12 Installing the compression rings with a ring expander — the mark (arrow) must face up

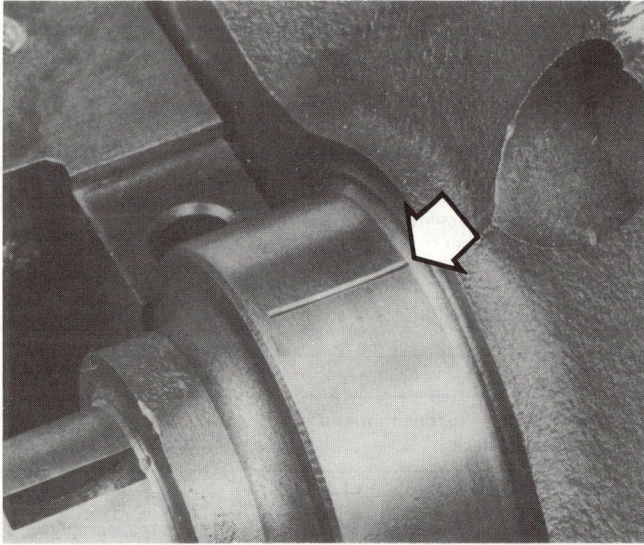

26.10   Lay the Plastigage strips (arrow) on the main bearing journals, parallel to the crankshaft centerline

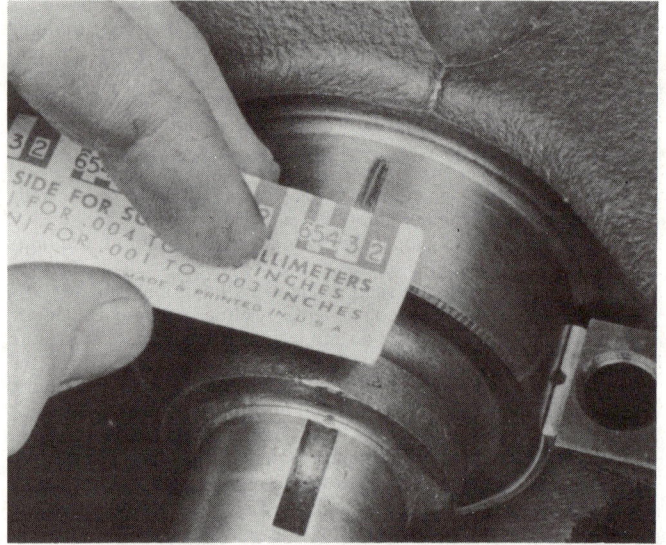

26.14   Compare the width of the crushed Plastigage to the scale on the container to determine the main bearing oil clearance (always take the measurement at the widest point of the Plastigage); be sure to use the correct scale — standard and metric scales are included

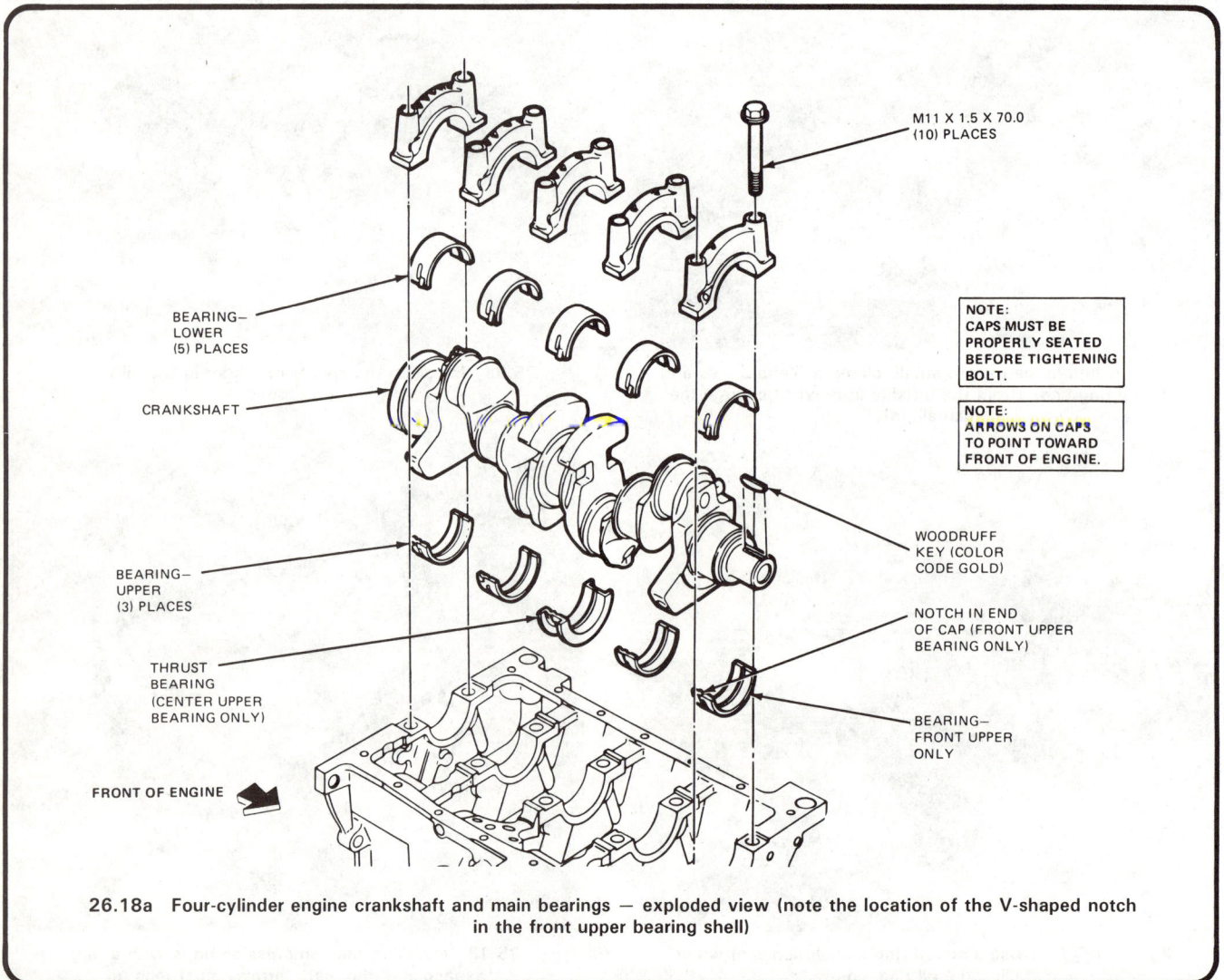

M11 X 1.5 X 70.0
(10) PLACES

BEARING—
LOWER
(5) PLACES

CRANKSHAFT

BEARING—
UPPER
(3) PLACES

THRUST
BEARING
(CENTER UPPER
BEARING ONLY)

FRONT OF ENGINE

NOTE:
CAPS MUST BE
PROPERLY SEATED
BEFORE TIGHTENING
BOLT.

NOTE:
ARROWS ON CAPS
TO POINT TOWARD
FRONT OF ENGINE.

WOODRUFF
KEY (COLOR
CODE GOLD)

NOTCH IN END
OF CAP (FRONT UPPER
BEARING ONLY)

BEARING—
FRONT UPPER
ONLY

26.18a   Four-cylinder engine crankshaft and main bearings — exploded view (note the location of the V-shaped notch in the front upper bearing shell)

cleaned, inspected and repaired or reconditioned.

2 Position the engine with the bottom facing up.

3 Remove the main bearing cap bolts and lift out the caps. Lay them out in the proper order to ensure correct installation.

4 If they're still in place, remove the old bearing inserts from the block and the main bearing caps. Wipe the main bearing surfaces of the block and caps with a clean, lint free cloth. They must be kept spotlessly clean.

5 Clean the back sides of the new main bearing inserts and lay one bearing half in each main bearing saddle in the block. Lay the other bearing half from each bearing set in the corresponding main bearing cap. Make sure the tab on the bearing insert fits into the recess in the block or cap. Also, the oil holes in the block must line up with the oil holes in the bearing insert. Do not hammer the bearing into place and do not nick or gouge the bearing faces. No lubrication should be used at this time.

6 The flanged thrust bearing must be installed in the third cap and saddle.

7 Clean the faces of the bearings in the block and the crankshaft main bearing journals with a clean, lint free cloth. Check or clean the oil holes in the crankshaft, as any dirt here can go only one way — straight through the new bearings.

8 Once you're certain the crankshaft is clean, carefully lay it in position in the main bearings.

9 Before the crankshaft can be permanently installed, the main bearing oil clearance must be checked.

10 Trim several pieces of the appropriate size of Plastigage (they must be slightly shorter than the width of the main bearings) and place one piece on each crankshaft main bearing journal, parallel with the journal axis (see illustration).

11 Clean the faces of the bearings in the caps and install the caps in their respective positions (don't mix them up) with the arrows pointing toward the front of the engine. Don't disturb the Plastigage.

12 Starting with the center main and working out toward the ends, tighten the main bearing cap bolts, in three steps, to the specified torque. Don't rotate the crankshaft at any time during this operation.

13 Remove the bolts and carefully lift off the main bearing caps. Keep them in order. Don't disturb the Plastigage or rotate the crankshaft. If any of the main bearing caps are difficult to remove, tap them gently from side-to-side with a soft-face hammer to loosen them.

14 Compare the width of the crushed Plastigage on each journal to the scale printed on the Plastigage container to obtain the main bearing oil clearance (see illustration). Check the Specifications to make sure it's correct.

15 If the clearance is not as specified, the bearing inserts may be the wrong size (which means different ones will be required). Before deciding that different inserts are needed, make sure that no dirt or oil was between the bearing inserts and the caps or block when the clearance was measured. If the Plastigage was wider at one end than the other, the journal may be tapered (refer to Section 18).

16 Carefully scrape all traces of the Plastigage material off the main bearing journals and/or the bearing faces. Don't nick or scratch the bearing faces.

17 Carefully lift the crankshaft out of the engine. Clean the bearing faces in the block, then apply a thin, uniform layer of clean moly-base grease or engine assembly lube to each of the bearing surfaces. Be sure to coat the thrust faces as well as the journal face of the thrust bearing.

18 Make sure the crankshaft journals are clean, then lay the crankshaft back in place in the block. Clean the faces of the bearings in the caps, then apply lubricant to them. Install the caps in their respective positions with the arrows pointing toward the front of the engine. Note that on V6 engines the rear cap must have a special sealant (Ford D6AZ-19562-A or equivalent) applied in a 1/8 inch bead to the rear main bearing cap-to-cylinder block parting line. Install the bolts (see illustrations).

19 Tighten all except the third cap bolts (the one with the thrust bear-

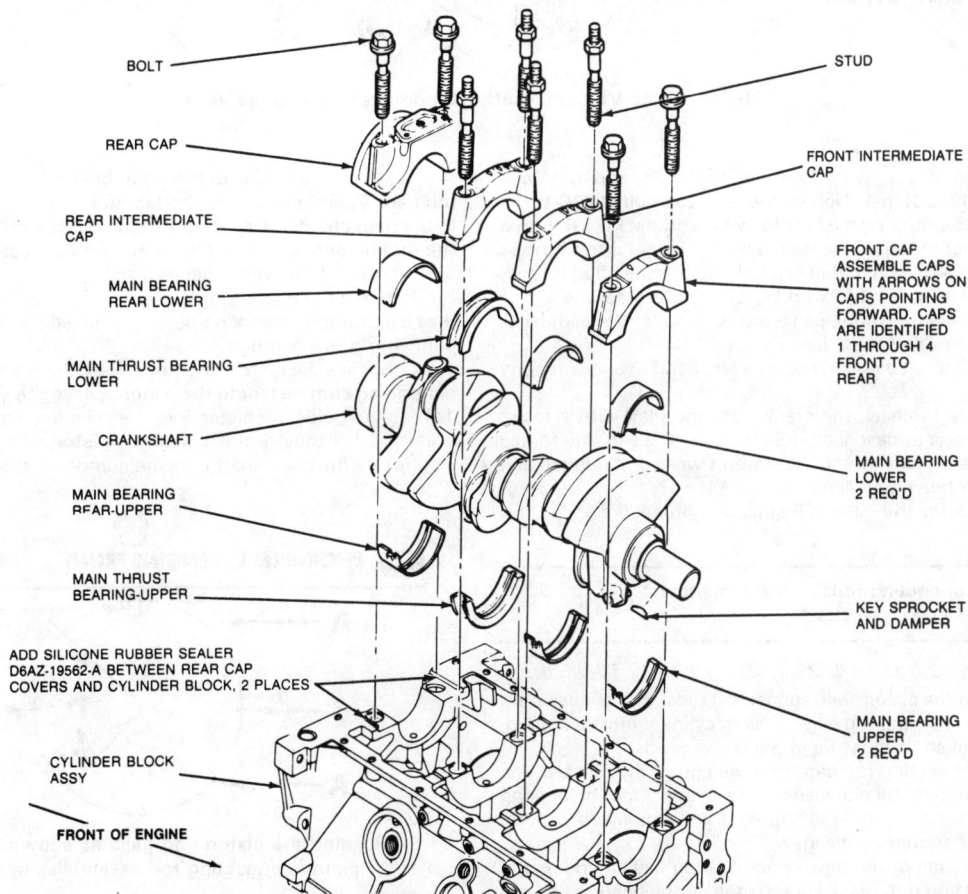

26.18b 3.0L V6 crankshaft components — exploded view

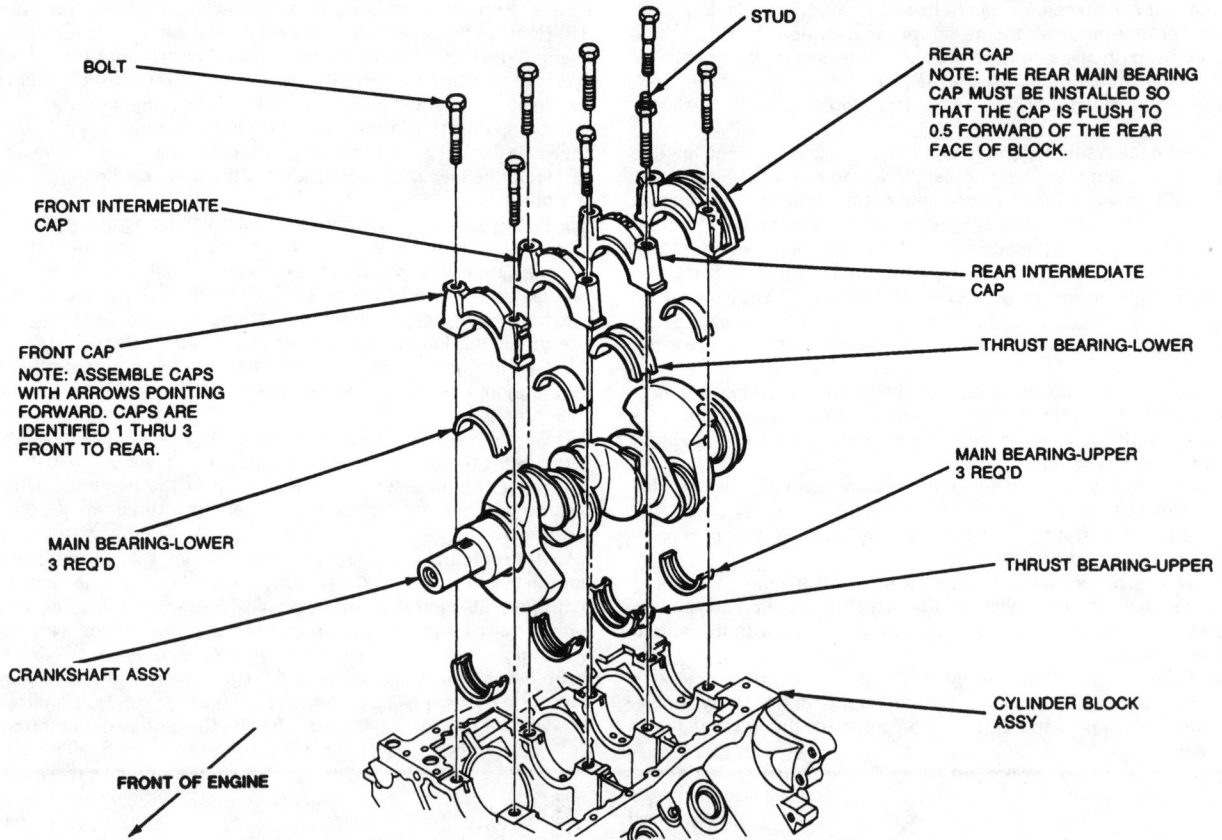

26.18c   3.8L V6 crankshaft components — exploded view

ing) to the specified torque (work from the center out and approach the final torque in three steps). Tighten the third cap bolts to 10-to-12 ft-lbs. Tap the ends of the crankshaft forward and backward with a lead or brass hammer to line up the main bearing and crankshaft thrust surfaces. Retighten all main bearing cap bolts to the specified torque, starting with the third main and working out toward the ends.

20 On manual transmission equipped models, install a new pilot bearing in the end of the crankshaft (see Chapter 8).

21 Rotate the crankshaft a number of times by hand to check for any obvious binding.

22 The final step is to check the crankshaft end play with a feeler gauge or a dial indicator as described in Section 17. The end play should be correct if the crankshaft thrust faces aren't worn or damaged and new bearings have been installed.

23 See Section 13 for the oil seal installation procedure.

---

27   Pistons and connecting rods — installation and rod bearing oil clearance check

Refer to illustrations 27.5, 27.8, 27.9, 27.11 and 27.13

1   Before installing the pistons and connecting rods, the cylinder walls must be perfectly clean, the top edge of each cylinder must be chamfered, and the crankshaft must be in place.

2   Remove the connecting rod cap from the end of the number one connecting rod. Remove the old bearing inserts and wipe the bearing surfaces of the connecting rod and cap with a clean, lint free cloth. They must be kept spotlessly clean.

3   Clean the back side of the new upper bearing half, then lay it in place in the connecting rod. Make sure the tab on the bearing fits into the recess in the rod. Don't hammer the bearing insert into place and be very careful not to nick or gouge the bearing face. Don't lubricate the bearing at this time.

4   Clean the back side of the other bearing insert and install it in the rod cap. Again, make sure the tab on the bearing fits into the recess in the cap, and don't apply any lubricant. It's critically important that the mating surfaces of the bearing and connecting rod are perfectly clean and oil free when they're assembled.

5   Position the piston ring gaps at 120° intervals around the piston **(see illustration)**, then slip a section of plastic or rubber hose over each connecting rod cap bolt.

6   Lubricate the piston and rings with clean engine oil and attach a piston ring compressor to the piston. Leave the skirt protruding about 1/4-inch to guide the piston into the cylinder. The rings must be compressed until they're flush with the piston.

7   Rotate the crankshaft until the number one connecting rod journal

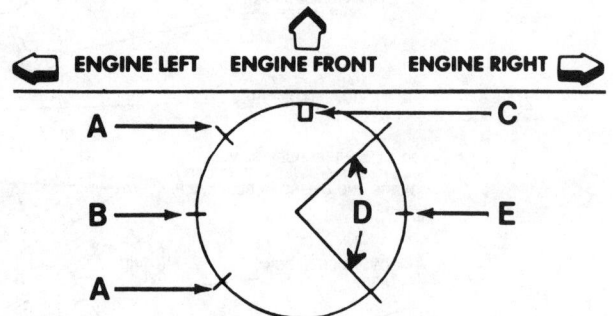

27.5   Position the piston ring gaps as shown before installing the piston/connecting rod assemblies in the engine

A *Oil ring rail gaps*
B *2nd compression ring gap*
C *Notch or arrow in piston*
D *Oil ring spacer gap (tang in hole or slot with arc)*
E *Top compression ring gap*

27.8 The notch or arrow in each piston must face the FRONT of the engine as the pistons are installed

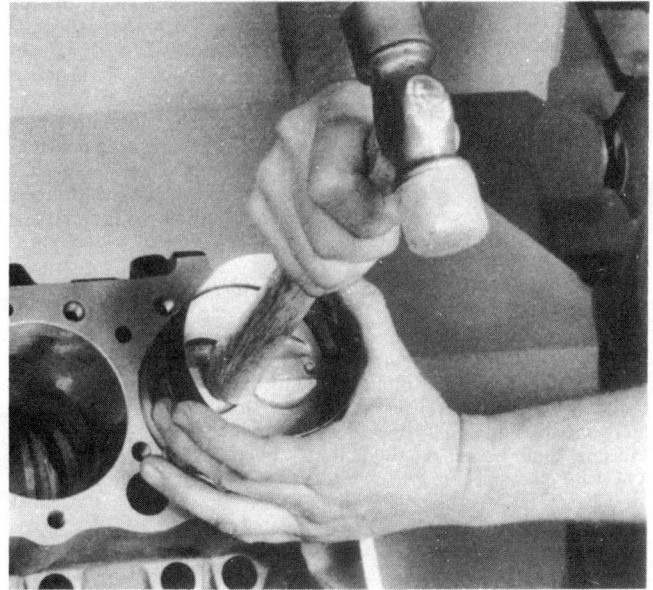

27.9 The piston can be driven (gently) into the cylinder bore with the end of a wooden hammer handle

is at BDC (bottom dead center) and apply a coat of engine oil to the cylinder walls.

8   With the notch or arrow on top of the piston (see illustration) facing the front of the engine, gently insert the piston/connecting rod assembly into the number one cylinder bore and rest the bottom edge of the ring compressor on the engine block. Tap the top edge of the ring compressor to make sure it's contacting the block around its entire circumference.

9   Carefully tap on the top of the piston with the end of a wooden hammer handle (see illustration) while guiding the end of the connecting rod into place on the crankshaft journal. The piston rings may try to pop out of the ring compressor just before entering the cylinder bore, so keep some downward pressure on the ring compressor. Work slowly, and if any resistance is felt as the piston enters the cylinder, stop immediately. Find out what's hanging up and fix it before proceeding. Do not, for any reason, force the piston into the cylinder, as you might break a ring and/or the piston.

10   Once the piston/connecting rod assembly is installed, the connecting rod bearing oil clearance must be checked before the rod cap is permanently bolted in place.

11   Cut a piece of the appropriate size Plastigage slightly shorter than the width of the connecting rod bearing and lay it in place on the number one connecting rod journal, parallel with the journal axis (see illustration).

12   Clean the connecting rod cap bearing face, remove the protective hoses from the connecting rod bolts and install the rod cap. Make sure the mating mark on the cap is on the same side as the mark on the connecting rod. Install the nuts and tighten them to the specified torque, working up to it in three steps. **Note:** *Use a thin-wall socket to avoid erroneous torque readings that can result if the socket is wedged between the rod cap and nut.* Do not rotate the crankshaft at any time during this operation.

13   Remove the rod cap, being very careful not to disturb the Plastigage. Compare the width of the crushed Plastigage to the scale printed on the Plastigage container to obtain the oil clearance (see illustration). Compare it to the Specifications to make sure the clearance is correct. If the clearance is not as specified, the bearing inserts may be the wrong size (which means different ones will be required). Before deciding that different inserts are needed, make sure that no dirt or oil was between the bearing inserts and the connecting rod or cap when the clearance was measured. Also, recheck the journal diameter. If the Plastigage was wider at one end than the other, the journal may be tapered (refer to Section 22).

27.11 Lay the Plastigage strips on each rod bearing journal, parallel to the crankshaft centerline

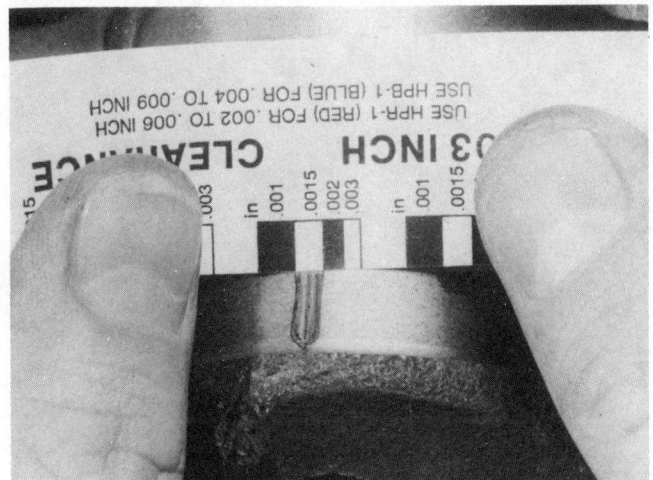

27.13 Measuring the width of the crushed Plastigage to determine the rod bearing oil clearance (be sure to use the correct scale — standard and metric scales are included)

14 Carefully scrape all traces of the Plastigage material off the rod journal and/or bearing face. Be very careful not to scratch the bearing — use your fingernail or a piece of hardwood. Make sure the bearing faces are perfectly clean, then apply a uniform layer of clean moly-base grease or engine assembly lube to both of them. You'll have to push the piston into the cylinder to expose the face of the bearing insert in the connecting rod — be sure to slip the protective hoses over the rod bolts first.

15 Slide the connecting rod back into place on the journal, remove the protective hoses from the rod cap bolts, install the rod cap and tighten the nuts to the specified torque. Again, work up to the torque in three steps.

16 Repeat the entire procedure for the remaining piston/connecting rod assemblies. Keep the back sides of the bearing inserts and the inside of the connecting rod and cap perfectly clean when assembling them. Make sure you have the correct piston for the cylinder and that the notch on the piston faces to the front of the engine when the piston is installed. Remember, use plenty of oil to lubricate the piston before installing the ring compressor. Also, when installing the rod caps for the final time, be sure to lubricate the bearing faces adequately.

17 After all the piston/connecting rod assemblies have been properly installed, rotate the crankshaft a number of times by hand to check for any obvious binding.

18 As a final step, the connecting rod end play must be checked. Refer to Section 16 for this procedure. Compare the measured end play to the Specifications to make sure it's correct. If it was correct before disassembly and the original crankshaft and rods were reinstalled, it should still be right. If new rods or a new crankshaft were installed, the end play may be too small. If so, the rods will have to be removed and taken to an automotive machine shop for resizing.

28 Initial start-up and break-in after overhaul

1 Once the engine has been installed in the vehicle, double-check the engine oil and coolant levels.

2 With the spark plugs out of the engine and the ignition system disabled (see Section 2), crank the engine until oil pressure registers on the gauge or light.

3 Install the spark plugs, hook up the plug wires and restore the ignition system functions (Section 2).

4 Start the engine. It may take a few moments for the gasoline to reach the injectors, but the engine should start without a great deal of effort.

5 After the engine starts, it should be allowed to warm up to normal operating temperature. While the engine is warming up, make a thorough check for oil and coolant leaks.

6 Shut the engine off and recheck the engine oil and coolant levels.

7 Drive the vehicle to an area with minimum traffic, accelerate at full throttle from 30 to 50 mph, then allow the vehicle to slow to 30 mph with the throttle closed. Repeat the procedure 10 or 12 times. This will load the piston rings and cause them to seat properly against the cylinder walls. Check again for oil and coolant leaks.

8 Drive the vehicle gently for the first 500 miles (no sustained high speeds) and keep a constant check on the oil level. It is not unusual for an engine to use oil during the break-in period.

9 At approximately 500 to 600 miles, change the oil and filter.

10 For the next few hundred miles, drive the vehicle normally. Do not pamper it or abuse it.

11 After 2000 miles, change the oil and filter again and consider the engine fully broken in.

Chapter 3 Cooling, heating and air conditioning systems

Contents

Specifications

General
Drivebelt tension . . . . See Chapter 1

Torque specifications
Water outlet bolts

  Four-cylinder engine . . . . 12 to 18
  V6 engines . . . . 6 to 9
Water pump mounting bolts
  Four-cylinder engine . . . . 15 to 22
  V6 engines
    Small bolts . . . . 6 to 8
    Large bolts . . . . 15 to 22

Ft-lbs

1 General information

Engine cooling system

The Taurus and Sable are equipped with a pressurized engine cooling system that's thermostatically controlled by a coolant temperature switch in the thermostat housing. A conventional water pump, mounted on the front of the block and driven by the crankshaft through a drivebelt, moves coolant through the engine. The coolant flows around each cylinder and toward the rear of the engine. Cast-in passages direct coolant around the intake and exhaust ports, the spark plug areas and the exhaust valve guides.

The thermostat is located in a housing at the rear (driver's side) of

the head on all three engines. During warm-up, the closed thermostat prevents coolant from circulating through the radiator. As the engine nears normal operating temperature, the thermostat opens and allows coolant to travel through the radiator, where it's cooled before returning to the engine.

The radiator is a cross-flow type with vacuum brazed aluminum fins and tubes. The end tanks are made of nylon. Radiator and fan shroud mounting brackets are an integral part of the tank's design. Because of its construction, the radiator cannot be serviced by the home mechanic. If it's damaged, it must be taken to a radiator shop.

The electric cooling fan system consists of a two-speed fan on all engines equipped with an automatic transaxle or a one-speed fan on all four-cylinder engines with a manual transaxle, and an electric motor attached to a fan shroud located behind the radiator.

Heating system

The heating system consists of a blower fan and heater core located inside the dashboard, the heater hoses connecting the heater core to the engine cooling system and the heater/air conditioning control assembly on the dashboard.

Hot engine coolant is circulated through the heater core at all times. When the heater is activated, a flap door opens to expose the heater box to the passenger compartment. A fan switch on the control panel activates the blower motor, which forces air through the core, heating the air.

Air conditioning system

The air conditioning system consists of a condenser mounted in front of the radiator, an evaporator mounted inside the heater/air conditioner duct inside the dashboard, a compressor mounted on the engine, a firewall mounted accumulator (filter-drier), containing a high-pressure relief valve, and the plumbing connecting all the components.

The heater blower fan forces the warmer air of the passenger compartment through the evaporator core (sort of a radiator-in-reverse), transferring the heat from the air to the refrigerant. The liquid refrigerant boils off into low pressure vapor, taking the heat with it when it leaves the evaporator.

2 Antifreeze — general information

Warning: *Do not allow antifreeze to contact your skin or painted surfaces of the vehicle. Flush contacted areas immediately with plenty of water. Don't store new coolant or leave old coolant lying around where it's easily accessible to children and pets — they are attracted by its sweet taste. Ingestion of even a small amount can be fatal. Wipe up garage floor and drip pan coolant spills immediately. Keep antifreeze containers covered and repair leaks in your cooling system as soon as they are discovered.*

The cooling system should be filled with a water/ethylene glycol based antifreeze solution which will prevent freezing down to at least –20 °F. It also provides protection against corrosion and increases the coolant boiling point.

The cooling system should be drained, flushed and refilled at least every other year (see Chapter 1). The use of antifreeze solutions for periods longer than two years could result in damage from the formation of rust and scale in the system.

Before adding coolant to the system, check all hose connections and fittings — antifreeze can leak through very minute openings.

The ideal mixture of antifreeze to water which you should use depends on the relative weather conditions. The mixture should contain at least 50 percent antifreeze, but never more than 70 percent antifreeze.

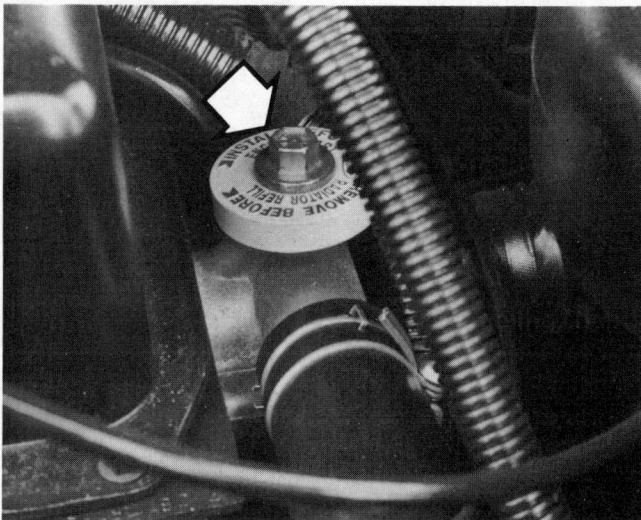

3.4 On the four cylinder engine, the vent plug (arrow) must be removed before you refill the radiator and installed before the engine is started

3 Thermostat — replacement

Refer to illustrations 3.4, 3.6a, 3.6b, 3.6c, 3.7a, 3.7b and 3.9

Removal

1 Disconnect the cable from the negative terminal of the battery.
2 Position a drain pan below the radiator.
3 Remove the radiator cap, attach a section of rubber hose to the drain tube and open the fitting. Drain the radiator until the coolant level is below the water outlet connection housing. Close the fitting.
4 If you're working on a four-cylinder engine, remove the vent plug from the water outlet connection housing **(see illustration)**.
5 Loosen the hose clamp and disconnect the upper radiator hose from the water outlet connection housing.
6 Remove the mounting bolts **(see illustrations)** and detach the water outlet connection housing. **Note:** *If the housing is difficult to remove, tap it gently with a soft-face hammer or a piece of wood. Don't try to pry the housing loose, or damage to the gasket sealing surfaces may occur and leaks may develop.*
7 If the thermostat is still in the V6 engine water outlet housing, rotate it counterclockwise to remove it **(see illustration)**. If it's stuck to the intake manifold (V6 engine) or the cylinder head (four-cylinder engine), carefully pry it out with a small screwdriver **(see illustration)**.

Installation

8 Remove all gasket material and old sealant from the mating surfaces of the housing and cylinder head, then clean them with a cloth saturated with lacquer thinner or acetone.
9 To install the thermostat in the four-cylinder engine, align the tab on the thermostat with the notch in the water outlet connection housing and press the thermostat in to seat against the gasket. To install the V6 engine thermostat, make sure the ball check valve is at the top, then push the thermostat into the water outlet housing and turn it clockwise to lock it in place **(see illustration)**.

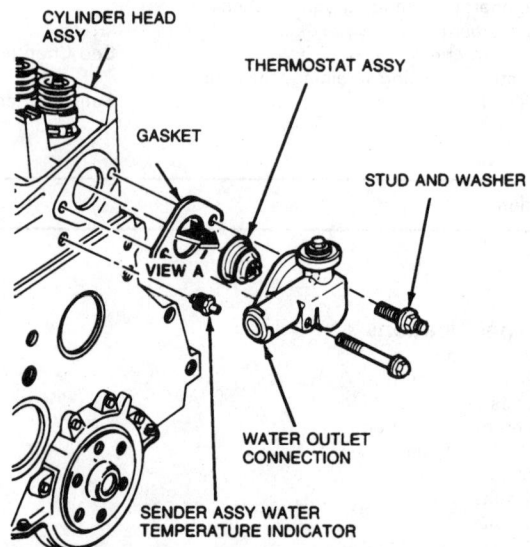

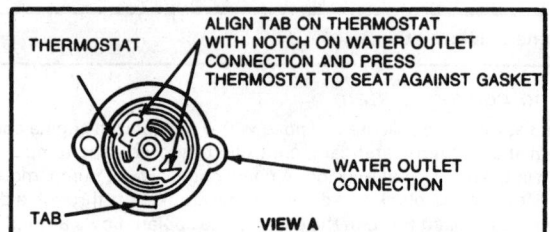

3.6a An exploded view of the water outlet connection assembly on the four-cylinder engine

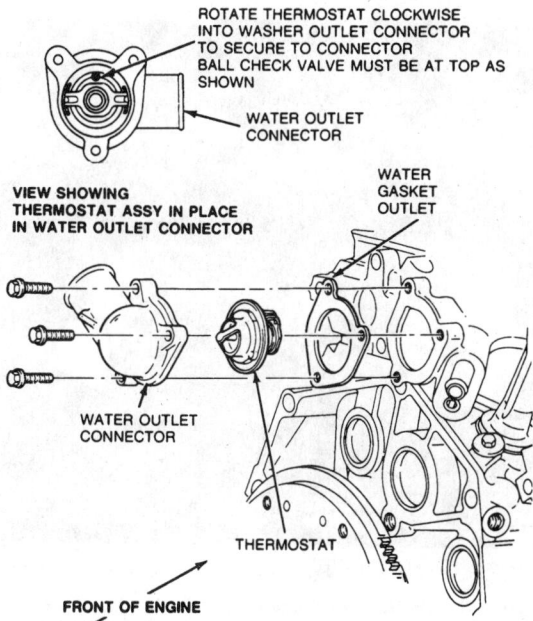

3.6b An exploded view of the water outlet connection assembly on the 3.0L V6 engine

10 Apply a thin layer of RTV sealant to both sides of the new gasket, then position it on the housing and use the bolts to hold it in place.

11 Place the water outlet connection housing and gasket in position on the cylinder head or manifold and thread the bolts into the holes. Tighten the bolts to the specified torque.

12 The remainder of installation is the reverse of removal. Be sure to check carefully for leaks as the engine warms up to normal operating temperature.

4 Electric cooling fan — description, check and component replacement

Refer to illustrations 4.5, 4.13 and 4.14

Warning: *To avoid possible injury or damage, DO NOT operate the engine with the hood open until the fan has been examined for cracks or damage. Never attempt to repair a fan with damaged blades — replace it.*

Description

1 The electric cooling fan is wired so that it operates only when the ignition switch is in the Run position. It cannot operate after the ignition switch is turned to the Off position. **Warning:** *Unplug the cooling fan prior to performing any underhood service, since the fan could cycle if the ignition switch is left in the On position, even though the engine is not running.*

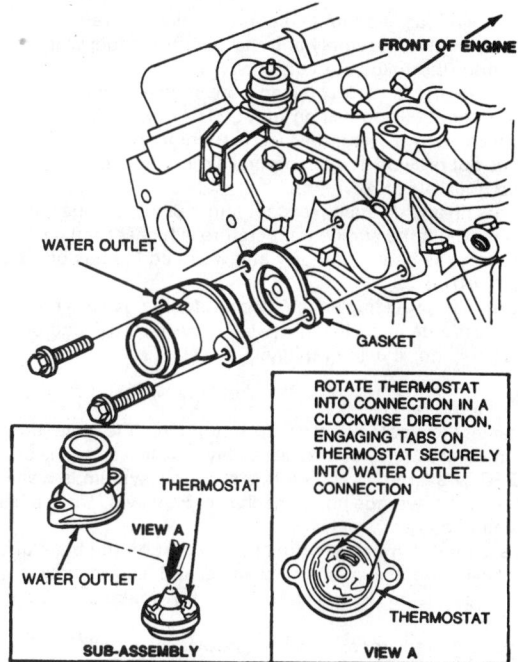

3.7b To remove the thermostat from the intake manifold of a V6 engine (as shown, or the cylinder head of a four-cylinder engine), gently pry it loose with a small screwdriver

3.6c An exploded view of the water outlet connection assembly on the 3.8L V6 engine

3.7a To remove the thermostat from the V6 engine water outlet connection housing, turn it counterclockwise (place a shop rag over the frame to prevent cutting your fingers)

3.9 When installing the thermostat in the V6 engine water outlet connection housing, make sure the ball check valve (arrow) is at the top — push the thermostat in, then turn it clockwise to lock it in place

2   The cooling fan is controlled during vehicle operation by the integrated relay control assembly and the EEC-IV module which energize the fan under the following conditions:

  a) Turns on the fan at low speed if the engine temperature is higher than normal (it comes on on at 215°F, goes off at 210°F). It also comes on when the A/C is running and the vehicle speed does not provide enough natural airflow (it comes on at 43 mph and goes off at 48 mph).

  b) Turns on at high speed (except four-cylinder engine with manual transaxle) if the engine temperature is higher than desirable and the fan has been operating at low speed (comes on at 230°F, goes off at 224°F).

  c) Turns off (providing engine coolant temperature is not too high) if throttle demand is high (wide open throttle) and/or the A/C clutch is not cycling rapidly.

Check

3   Because the electric cooling fan motor circuit is under the control of the ''integrated relay control assembly,'' which in turn is controlled by the EEC-IV system, a complete test of this system is well beyond the scope of the average home mechanic. However, there are several things you can check.

4   Locate the fan motor electrical connector on the back of the fan motor. Unplug it and inspect the terminal and plug to make sure they are free of corrosion. Plug in the connector. Make sure it's plugged in securely.

5   Remove the radiator sight shield (the plastic protector with the VECI label on it) and make sure that the 24-wire plug of the integrated relay control module **(see illustration)** is securely attached (it's held on with a small bolt, which should be snug).

6   Examine the wires between the integrated relay control module and the fan to make sure that they're in good condition. If they're frayed or broken, repair them.

7   Using a continuity tester, check the continuity between the terminals of the engine coolant temperature switch. Warm up the engine and allow the coolant temperature to exceed its normal operating range. When the coolant gets hot, the resistance between the coolant temperature switch terminals should drop to virtually zero and the circuit to the fan motor should be energized.

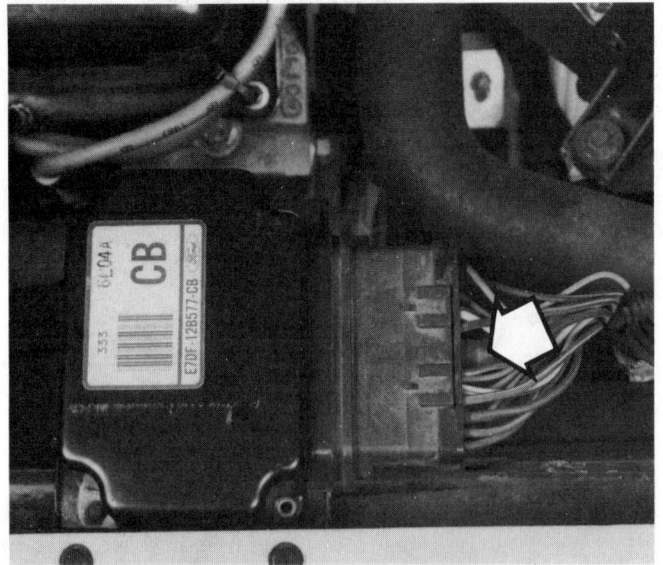

4.5 When the fan fails to come on like it should, one of the first things to check is the integrated relay control assembly's 24-wire electrical connector (arrow) which, if loose, can cause an open in the circuit between the fan motor, the coolant temperature switch and the computer

  a) If the resistance across the temperature switch terminals doesn't drop when the coolant heats up, the switch is bad. Replace it.

  b) If the resistance across the temperature switch terminals does drop (thereby closing the circuit to the fan motor), the temperature switch is okay and the fan should come on.

8   If the fan motor still doesn't come on, the motor itself may be faulty. Unplug the motor electrical connector and attach a pair of fused jumper wires between the fan motor terminals and the battery terminals. If the fan motor still doesn't work, replace it.

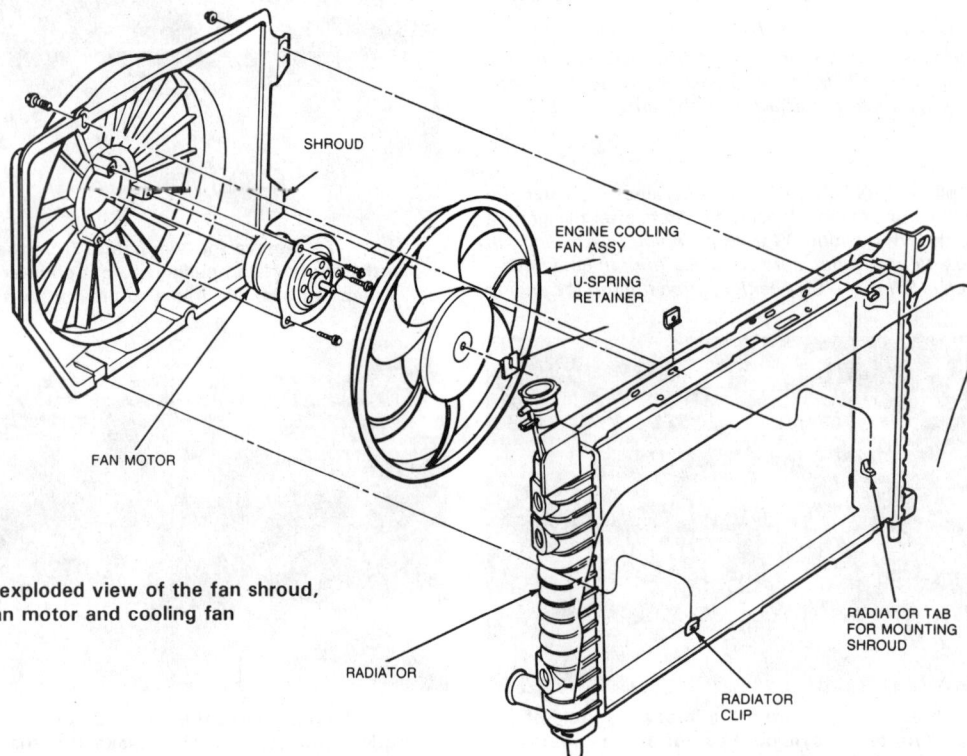

4.13 An exploded view of the fan shroud, fan motor and cooling fan

SHROUD

ENGINE COOLING FAN ASSY

U-SPRING RETAINER

FAN MOTOR

RADIATOR

RADIATOR CLIP

RADIATOR TAB FOR MOUNTING SHROUD

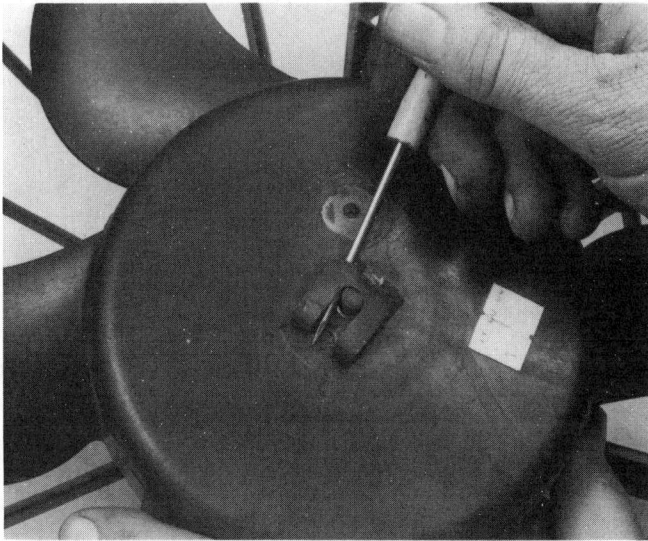

4.14 Use a small screwdriver to pry off the retaining clip which secures the cooling fan to the motor shaft

9 If the fan does come on when energized by the battery, two further possibilities exist:
   a) There is an open in the circuit somewhere between the temperature switch, the computer, the control relay and the motor, in which case you can often troubleshoot the problem with a test light or continuity tester.
   b) If the circuits check out, there is a problem with either the integrated relay control assembly or with the computer itself. Take the vehicle to a dealer service department and have the system diagnosed and repaired.

Component replacement

10 Detach the cable from the negative terminal of the battery.
11 If you haven't already done so, remove the screws and detach the radiator sight shield. Locate the integrated relay control assembly located on top of the radiator support. Remove the retaining bolt and unplug the electrical connector **(see illustration 4.5)**, then remove the control assembly.
12 If you haven't already done so, unplug the fan motor electrical connector.
13 To detach the fan/shroud assembly from the radiator, remove the nut from the upper left corner and the bolt from the upper right corner of the shroud **(see illustration)**, then lift the fan/shroud assembly off its mounting tabs on the radiator. **Note:** *It may be necessary to tilt the assembly slightly to clear assorted engine plumbing when lifting it out.*
14 Place the fan/shroud assembly on a workbench with the fan facing up. Using a small screwdriver, pry the fan retainer off the motor shaft **(see illustration)** and remove the fan.
15 Remove the three fan motor mounting bolts and detach the motor from the shroud assembly.
16 Installation is the reverse of removal.

5 Radiator — removal and installation

Refer to illustrations 5.9a, 5.9b, 5.9c, 5.10, 5.11 and 5.12
1 Detach the cable from the negative terminal of the battery.
2 Drain the coolant from the radiator (see Chapter 1).
3 Remove the "sight shield" (the plastic protector attached to the upper crossmember).
4 Unscrew and remove the integral relay control assembly (see Section 4). It's not necessary to unplug it — just set it aside.
5 Loosen the hose clamp and detach the upper hose from the radiator.
6 Detach the overflow hose from the radiator filler neck.
7 Unplug the alternator wire harness assembly from the alternator and detach it from the shroud, then set it aside.

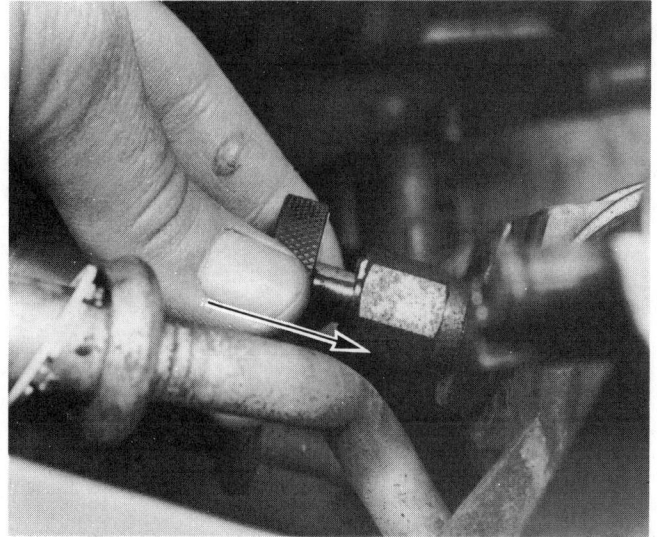

5.9a Some oil cooler line fittings must be detached with Cooler Line Disconnect Tool T82L-9500-AH, or equivalent — simply insert the tool as far as it will go into each fitting as shown . . .

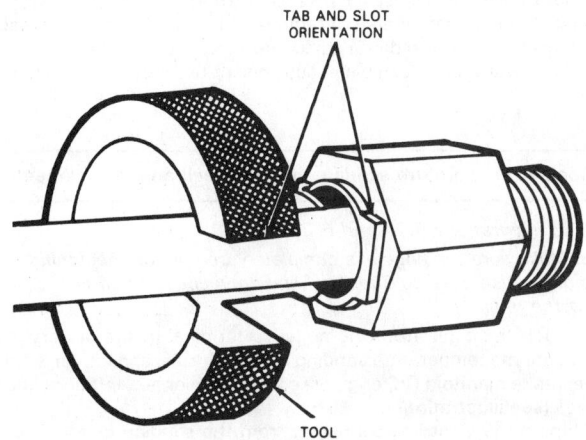

5.9b . . . with the slot on the knurled flange of the tool aligned with the tab on the edge of the fitting bore, . . .

5.9c . . . then pull on the line and separate it from the fitting

8 Remove the electric cooling fan and shroud assembly (see Section 4).
9 If your vehicle is equipped with an automatic transaxle, disconnect the upper and lower oil cooler line fittings. **Note:** *Some vehicles are equipped with special oil cooler line fittings which must be detached with cooler line disconnect tool T82L-9500-AH* **(see illustrations)**. Cap the fittings and the lines to prevent leakage.
10 Working underneath the vehicle, remove the two bracket bolts that

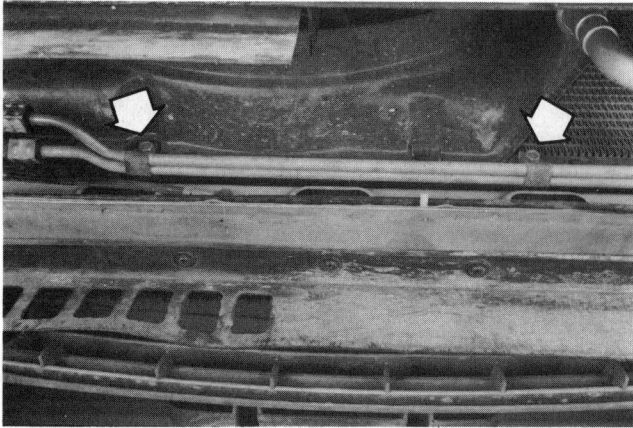

5.10   Before attempting to remove the radiator, be sure to remove the transaxle oil cooler bracket bolts (arrows) from the bottom of the radiator

5.11   Remove the two bolts (left one shown) attaching the upper edge of the radiator to the radiator support

attach the transaxle oil cooler lines to the bottom edge of the radiator **(see illustration)**.
11   Remove the two bolts attaching the top of the radiator to the radiator support **(see illustration)**. Lift the radiator from the vehicle.
12   Inspect the nylon tank radiator upper mounting bushings for damage. Replace if necessary **(see illustration)**.
13   Installation is the reverse of removal. Make sure the plastic pads on the bottom of the radiator tanks are resting on rubber pads.
14   When installation is complete, add coolant to the system (see Chapter 1).

6   Coolant temperature sending unit — check and replacement

Refer to illustrations 6.2a and 6.2b
Note: *Make sure the engine is completely cool before beginning this procedure. Also, refer to Chapter 1 and drain about 1 quart of coolant out of the radiator.*

1   Detach the cable from the negative terminal of the battery.
2   Locate the temperature sending unit on the left end (driver's side) of the intake manifold (V6 engines) or the cylinder head (four-cylinder engine) **(see illustrations)**.
3   Unplug the electrical connector from the sending unit.
4   Remove the sending unit (use a flank-drive, flare nut type wrench if available; otherwise, use a box wrench).
5   Wrap the threads of the new sending unit with teflon tape to prevent leaks.
6   Installation is the reverse of removal.

6.2a   The coolant temperature sending unit (arrow) is located at the left end (driver's side) of the intake manifold, next to the water outlet connection housing on a V6 (3.0L shown, 3.8L similar)

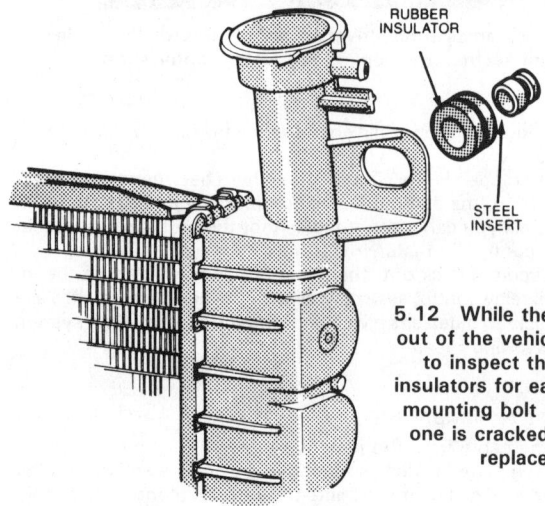

5.12   While the radiator is out of the vehicle, be sure to inspect the rubber insulators for each radiator mounting bolt — if either one is cracked or worn, replace it

7   Coolant reservoir — removal and installation

Refer to illustration 7.3
Note: *To prevent coolant and windshield washer fluid from spilling onto the vehicle, it's essential that you locate and install plugs for both the*

6.2b   On the four-cylinder engine, the coolant temperature sending unit (arrow) is located on the left end (driver's side) of the cylinder head

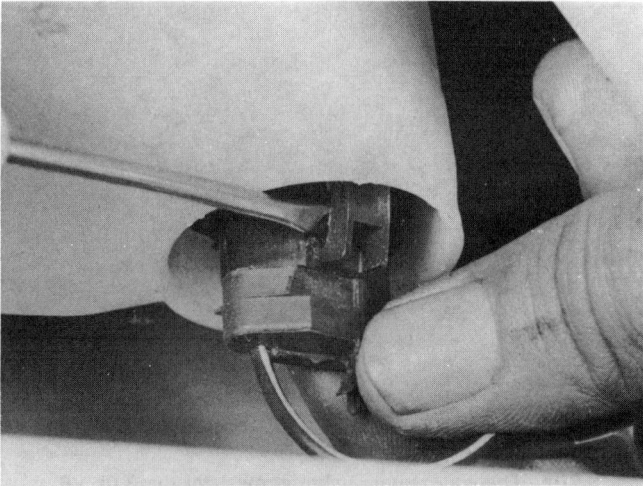

7.3 Before attempting to remove the coolant reservoir/ windshield washer fluid reservoir from the engine compartment, unplug the electrical connector

radiator overflow hose and and the windshield washer fluid hose while performing this procedure. A small pair of vise-grips should suffice for the overflow hose. A short section of clamped hose should do the trick for the washer fitting (look at the washer fluid hose and find an old piece of hose with the correct diameter).
1   Detach the cable from the negative terminal of the battery.
2   Remove the coolant/windshield washer fluid reservoir mounting bolt.
3   Raise the reservoir and unplug the windshield washer fluid pump electrical connector **(see illustration)**.
4   Detach the overflow hose from the radiator filler neck and clamp it to prevent the coolant in the reservoir from draining.
5   Detach the windshield washer fluid hose. **Note:** *If there is fluid in the windshield washer reservoir, it will run out when the hose is detached unless you immediately cap the fitting with a short section of clamped hose.*
6   Remove the reservoir.
7   Installation is the reverse of removal.

---

8   Water pump — check

Refer to illustration 8.3
1   A failure in the water pump can cause overheating and serious engine damage, because a defective pump will not circulate coolant through the engine.
2   There are two ways to check the operation of the water pump while it's in place on the engine. If either check indicates that the pump is defective, replace it with a new or rebuilt unit.
3   The water pump body has a ''weep'' hole in the under side **(see illustration)**. If the pump seal fails, small amounts of coolant will leak out of the hole. You'll need to get underneath the water pump to see the hole, so raise the vehicle and place it securely on jackstands. Use a flashlight to help determine if coolant is leaking from the pump.
4   If the water pump shaft bearing fails it will usually make a howling sound (don't confuse drivebelt slippage, which makes a squealing sound, with water pump bearing failure). Even before the bearing actually fails, shaft wear can be detected by grasping the pulley firmly and moving it up and down. If excessive play is noted, the shaft and/or bearing are worn and the pump should be replaced.

---

9   Water pump — removal and installation

Four-cylinder engine
Removal
1   Detach the cable from the negative terminal of the battery.
2   Drain the engine coolant (see Chapter 1).

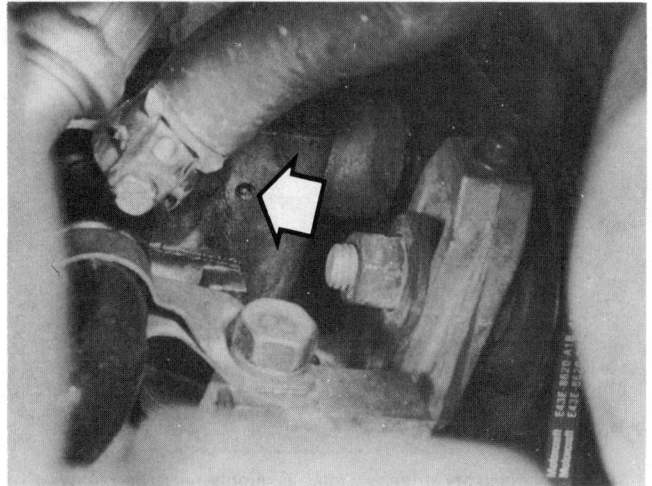

8.3 The ''weep hole'' on the underside of the water pump (arrow) will leak coolant if the pump seal fails (four-cylinder engine shown, V6 water pump weep holes similar)

3   Loosen the hose clamp and detach the water pump inlet tube from the water pump.
4   Loosen the water pump pulley bolts. **Note:** *Be sure the water pump pulley bolts are loosened before the drivebelt is loosened and removed.*
5   Loosen the belt tensioner and remove the drivebelt from the water pump pulley (see Chapter 1).
6   Remove the water pump pulley.
7   Loosen the hose clamp and detach the heater hose from the water pump.
8   Remove the three water pump bolts and detach the pump.

Installation
9   Make sure the mating surface of the engine block and the water pump are clean and free of gasket material.
10   Apply Perfect Seal Sealing Compound B5A-19554-A or equivalent to the water pump gasket, then position the water pump assembly and the new gasket on the block.
11   Install the three bolts and tighten them to the specified torque.
12   The remainder of installation is the reverse of removal.

V6 engines
Refer to illustrations 9.15, 9.18, 9.20a and 9.20b
Removal
13   Detach the cable from the negative terminal of the battery.
14   Drain the engine coolant (see Chapter 1).
15   Loosen the four water pump pulley bolts **(see illustration)**. **Note:**

9.15 Be sure to loosen the water pump pulley bolts before removing the drivebelt — note that there is insufficient clearance to actually remove the pulley, which must remain in place until the water pump assembly is removed from the engine compartment

9.18   The accessory drivebelt idler assembly must be removed to provide sufficient room to lift the water pump out — remove both nuts and the single bolt (arrows) to remove the idler

Be sure the water pump pulley bolts are loosened before the drivebelt is removed. But don't attempt to actually remove the pulley at this time — there is insufficient clearance between the nose of the pump shaft and the wheel housing. The pulley cannot be removed until the pump is removed from the engine.

16   Remove the drivebelt(s) (see Chapter 1).
17   Remove the alternator (see Chapter 5).
18   Remove the accessory drivebelt idler assembly bolts (**see illustration**).
19   Loosen the hose clamp and detach the heater hose from the water pump.
20   Remove the water pump bolts (**see illustrations**).
21   Remove the water pump from the timing chain cover.

Installation
22   Clean the mating surfaces of the water pump and the timing chain cover.
23   After coating the gasket with Contact Adhesive (D7AZ-19B508-A or the equivalent), place the new gasket in position on the water pump sealing surface.
24   With the pulley in place on the mounting studs of the water pump hub, position the water pump on the timing chain cover.
25   Coat the threads of the water pump bolts with Pipe Sealant (D8AZ-19558-A or the equivalent), install the bolts and tighten them to the specified torque.

9.20a   The water pump bolts (arrows) for the 3.0L V6 (two more bolts are hidden behind the idler assembly)

26   Install the water pump pulley bolts and snug them finger tight.
27   The remainder of installation is the reverse of removal.
28   Tighten the pulley-to-hub bolts securely after the drivebelts are installed.

---

10   Air conditioning and heating system — check and maintenance

---

Refer to illustrations 10.11, 10.15, 10.19 and 10.20

Air conditioning system
Warning: *The air conditioning system is under high pressure. Do not loosen any hose fittings or remove any components until after the system has been discharged by a dealer service department or an automotive air conditioning shop. And always wear eye protection when disconnecting air conditioning system fittings.*

1   The following maintenance checks should be performed on a regular basis to ensure that the air conditioner continues to operate at peak efficiency.
   a)   Inspect the condition of the compressor drivebelt. If it is worn or deteriorated, replace it (see Chapter 1).
   b)   Check the drivebelt tension and, if necessary, adjust it. (see Chapter 1).

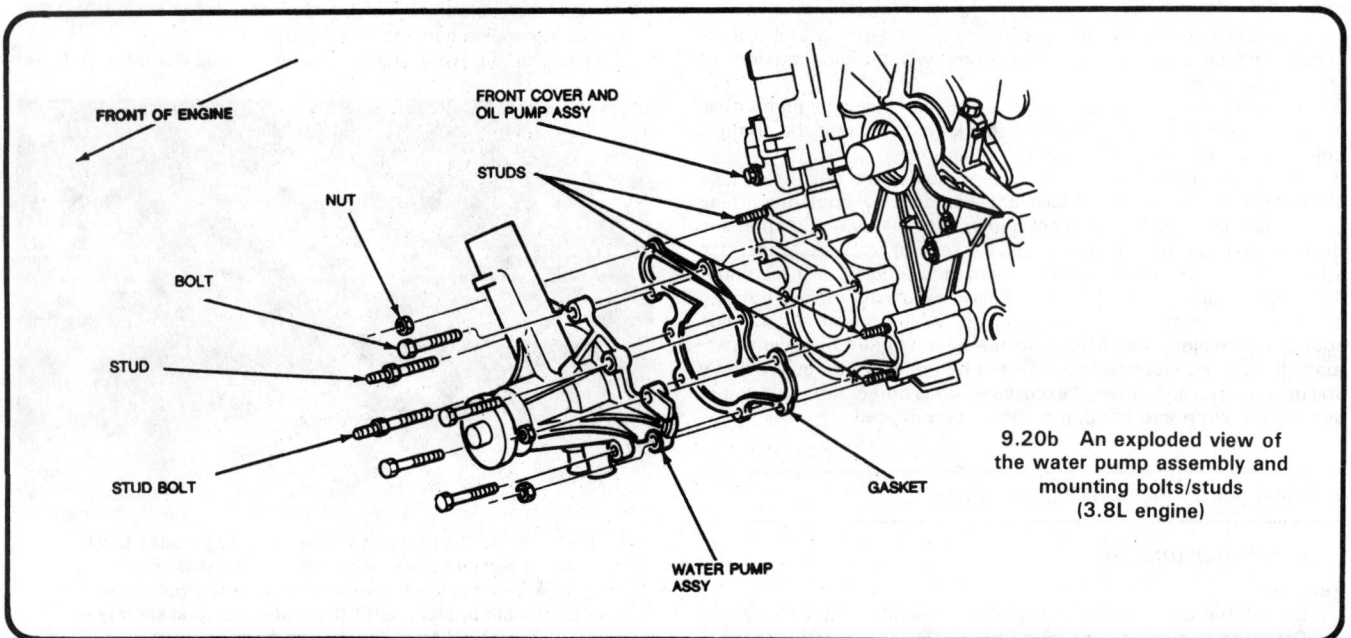

9.20b   An exploded view of the water pump assembly and mounting bolts/studs (3.8L engine)

c) Inspect the system hoses. Look for cracks, bubbles, hardening and deterioration. Inspect the hoses and all fittings for oil bubbles or seepage. If there is any evidence of wear, damage or leakage, replace the hose(s).

d) Inspect the condenser fins for leaves, bugs and any other foreign material that may have embedded itself in the fins. Use a ''fin comb'' or compressed air to remove debris from the condenser.

e) Make sure the system has the correct refrigerant charge.

2   It's a good idea to operate the system for about 10 minutes at least once a month. This is particularly important during the winter months because long term non-use can cause hardening, and subsequent failure, of the seals.

3   Because of the complexity of the air conditioning system and the special equipment necessary to service it, in depth troubleshooting and repairs are beyond the scope of this manual. However, simple checks and component replacement procedures are provided in this Chapter.

4   The most common cause of poor cooling is simply a low system refrigerant charge. If a noticeable drop in system cooling ability occurs, one of the following quick checks will help you determine whether the refrigerant level is low.

Receiver-drier/expansion valve type systems only

5   Warm up the engine to its normal operating temperature.

6   Place the air conditioning temperature selector at its coldest setting and put the blower at its highest setting. Open the doors (to make sure that the air conditioning system doesn't cycle off as soon as it cools the passenger compartment).

7   Inspect the sight glass, if equipped. If the refrigerant looks foamy, it's low. Charge the system (see below).

8   If there is no sight glass, feel the inlet and outlet pipes at the compressor. One side should be cold and one hot. If there is no perceptible difference between the two pipes, there is something wrong with the compressor or the system. It might be a low charge. Further testing of this type of system is beyond the scope of this manual. Take the vehicle to a dealer or automotive air conditioning shop.

Accumulator/orifice tube type systems only

9   Warm up the engine to its normal operating temperature.

10 Place the air conditioning temperature selector at its coldest setting and put the blower at its highest setting. Open the doors (to make sure that the air conditioning system doesn't cycle off as soon as it cools the passenger compartment).

11 With the compressor engaged — the clutch will make an audible click and the center of the clutch will rotate — feel the evaporator inlet pipe between the orifice and the accumulator with one hand while placing your other hand on the surface of the accumulator housing (see illustration).

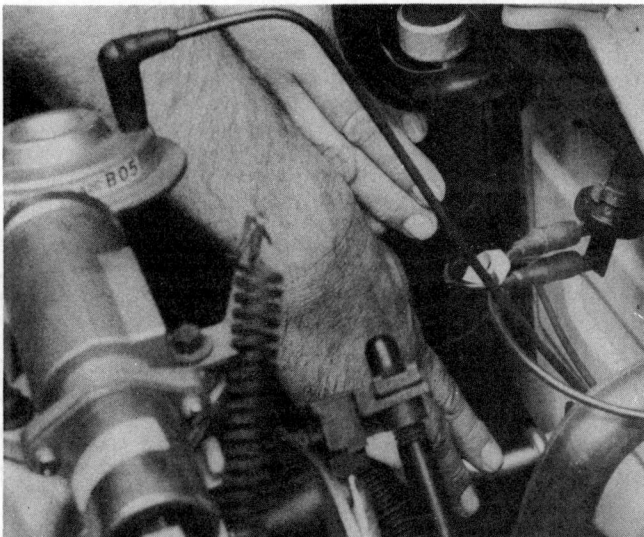

10.11 With the compressor running, place one hand on the accumulator and the other on the evaporator inlet pipe — if both feel about the same temperature, and a little cooler than the ambient air temperature, the freon level is okay; if the inlet pipe feels cooler than the accumulator, the freon charge is low

12 If both surfaces feel about the same temperature and if both feel a little cooler than the surrounding air, the refrigerant level is probably okay. Further inspection of the system is beyond the scope of this manual and should be left to a professional.

13 If the inlet pipe has frost accumulation or feels cooler than the accumulator surface, the refrigerant charge is low. Add refrigerant as described below.

Adding refrigerant (all systems)

14 Buy an automotive charging kit at an automotive parts store. A charging kit includes a 14-ounce can of refrigerant, a tap valve and a short section of hose which can be attached between the tap valve and the system low side service valve. Because one can of refrigerant may not be sufficient to bring the system charge up to its proper level, it's a good idea to buy a few additional cans. Make sure that one of the cans contains red refrigerant dye. If the system is leaking, the red dye will leak out with the refrigerant and help you pinpoint the location of the leak. Never add more than three cans.

15 Hook up the charging kit by following the manufacturer's instructions (see illustration). **Warning:** *DO NOT hook the charging kit hose to the high side of the system.*

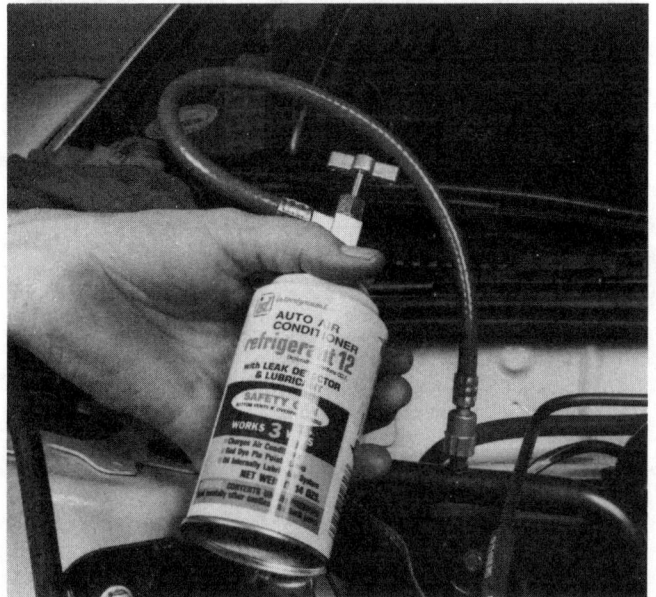

10.15 To add refrigerant to the air conditioning system, hook up a recharge kit following the manufacturer's instructions — add freon until both the accumulator and the evaporator inlet pipe feel about the same temperature (allow stabilization time between each addition), then add one more can

16 Warm up the engine and operate the system.

17 If the system in your vehicle is an accumulator type:

a) Add refrigerant to the low side of the system until both the accumulator surface and the evaporator inlet pipe feel about the same temperature. Allow stabilization time between each refrigerant addition.

b) Once the accumulator surface and the evaporator inlet pipe feel about the same temperature, add the contents remaining in the can.

18 If the system in your vehicle is a receiver-drier type, place a thermometer in the dashboard vent nearest the evaporator and add refrigerant until the indicated temperature is around 40 to 45°F.

Heating system

19 If the air coming out of the dashboard heater vents isn't hot, the problem could stem from any of the following causes:

a) The thermostat is stuck open, preventing the engine coolant from warming up enough to carry heat to the heater core. Replace the thermostat (see Section 3).

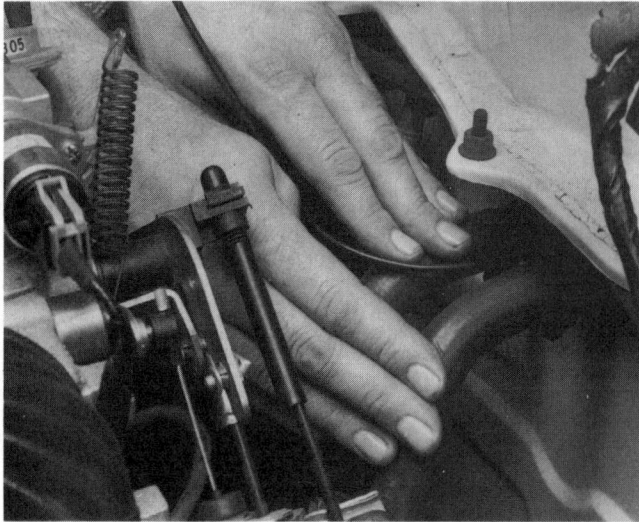

10.19   To determine whether there is an obstruction in the heater system, feel the two hoses at the firewall and compare their relative temperatures (with the engine warmed up and the heater turned on, both should be pretty hot — if they're both cool, there is a blockage in the inlet hose; if the inlet hose is hot and the outlet hose is cool, there's a blockage in the heater core itself)

10.20   Before checking the blower motor resistor or the blower motor, always check the blower switch by verifying with a test light or continuity tester that it passes current at each selector knob position

b)   A heater hose is blocked, preventing the flow of coolant through the heater core. Feel both heater hoses at the firewall **(see illustration)**. They should be hot. If one of them is cold, there is an obstruction in one of the hoses or in the heater core itself, or the valve itself is shut. Detach the hoses and either blow out the heater core with compressed air or back flush it with a water hose. If that fails to remove the obstruction, remove the two hoses and blow them out with compressed air.

c)   If the heater still fails to put out hot air, remove the heater core (see Section 13) and have it professionally back flushed. If flushing fails to remove the blockage from the heater core, the core must be replaced. Most radiator shops will not repair heater cores.

20   If the blower motor speed does not correspond to the setting selected on the blower switch, either the fuse is bad, the switch is bad, the blower motor resistor is burned out or the motor is bad.

a)   Before checking the blower motor or circuit, always check the fuse first.

b)   Check voltage at the blower motor.

c)   Pull the heating/air conditioning control assembly (see next Section) far enough from the dash to verify, with a test light, continuity tester or voltmeter, that current is reaching the blower switch on the control assembly **(see illustration)**. If the switch is not getting current, troubleshoot the circuit between the battery and the switch (see the wiring diagrams at the end of this manual).

d)   Locate the blower motor resistor behind the glove box (see Section 12). Check the resistor to make sure that it is getting current from the blower switch.

1)   If the resistor is not getting current, check the wire.

2)   If the wire is good, replace the switch (see Section 11).

e)   Using a test light, continuity tester or voltmeter, verify that the blower motor is getting current. If the blower motor is not getting current, replace the resistor (see Section 12).

21   If there isn't any air coming out of the vents, place your ear at the heating/air conditioning vent nearest the blower motor, and listen. Most motors are audible. Can you hear the motor running?

a)   If you can't (and have already verified that the blower switch and the blower motor resistor are good), the blower motor itself is probably bad. Replace it (see Section 12). **Note:** *You can determine the motor's condition by hooking up a fused jumper wire directly between the battery and the blower motor.*

b)   If you can hear the motor running, the vacuum operated doors may not be operating properly. If air comes out the defroster ducts when the engine is accelerated (lower intake vacuum), check the one-way vacuum valve (in the engine compartment, on the

firewall to the right of the two heater hoses) by sucking on it at both ends to make sure that it only allows intake manifold vacuum. Also check the vacuum lines on the back side of the heating and air conditioning control assembly to be sure that they're tightly attached. Further testing of the vacuum system for the doors is beyond the scope of this manual. Have the system diagnosed by a dealer service department.

22   If the carpet under the heater core is damp, or if antifreeze vapor or steam is coming through the vents, the heater core is leaking. Remove it (see Section 13) and install a new unit (most radiator shops will not repair a leaking heater core).

11   Heater and air conditioning control assembly — removal and installation

Heater only or manual A/C-heater systems

Control assembly

Refer to illustrations 11.3, 11.4, 11.5 and 11.6

Note: *The following procedure applies only to vehicles with a heater (but no A/C) and to vehicles with a manual heating/air conditioning system; if your vehicle is equipped with Electronic Automatic Temperature Control (EATC), see Step 16.*

1   Detach the cable from the negative terminal of the battery.

2   Remove the instrument panel finish applique (see Chapter 11).

3   Remove the four screws attaching the control assembly to the instrument panel **(see illustration)**.

11.3   To detach the heater/air conditioning control assembly from the dashboard, remove the four screws (arrows)

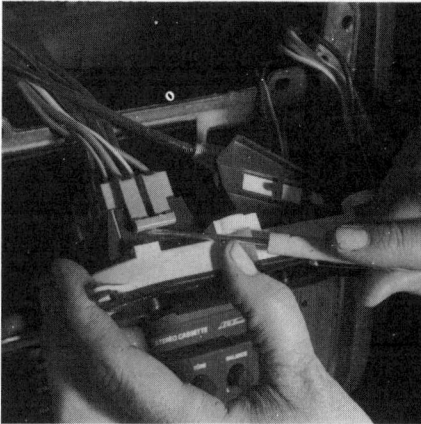

11.4 To unplug the electrical connectors from the heater/air conditioning control assembly, use a small screwdriver to spread the locking tangs

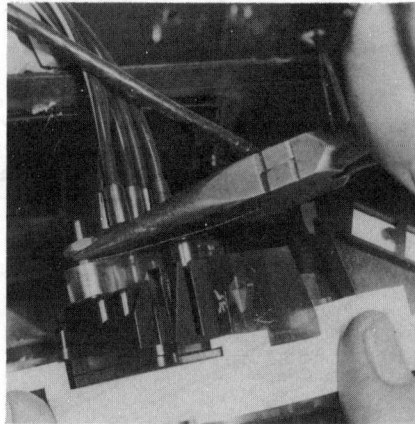

11.5 To detach the vacuum harness from the control assembly, use a pair of needle-nose pliers to remove the pushnuts, then pull the harness off the studs

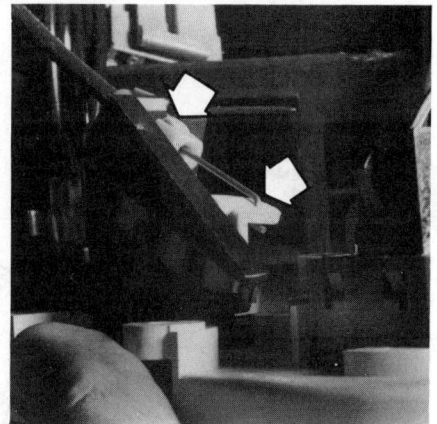

11.6 To detach the temperature control cable from the control assembly, pinch the tangs of the cable ferrule (arrow) together and release the cable from the retaining bracket, then unhook the end of the cable (arrow) from the lever arm

4   Pull the control assembly from the instrument panel opening and unplug the electrical connectors **(see illustration)**.
5   Remove the vacuum harness retaining nuts from their respective posts **(see illustration)** and detach the vacuum harness from the control assembly.
6   Disconnect the temperature control cable from the control assembly **(see illustration)**.
7   Installation is the reverse of removal. Be sure to use new pushnuts to connect the vacuum harness to the control assembly. **Caution:** *Push on the vacuum harness nuts. Do not attempt to screw them onto the post.*

Blower switch

8   Detach the cable from the negative terminal of the battery.
9   Remove the fan switch knob from the switch shaft by pulling it off the shaft.
10   Unscrew the control assembly from the dashboard (see above) and pull it out far enough to access the blower switch assembly.
11   Unplug the electrical connector(s) from the switch.
12   If your vehicle is not equipped with air conditioning, remove the screw from the underside of the control assembly which attaches the switch to the control assembly.
13   If your vehicle is equipped with air conditioning, remove the screw from the back side of the control assembly attaching the switch to the control assembly.

14   Remove the switch.
15   Installation is the reverse of removal.

Electronic Automatic Temperature Control (EATC) system

Note: *The functional test for the EATC system is beyond the scope of the average home mechanic. However, if you want to save the labor cost of replacing any of the following EATC components by doing it yourself once the problem has been diagnosed by an expert, the actual replacement procedures are relatively simple.*

Control assembly

Refer to illustration 11.19

16   Detach the cable from the negative terminal of the battery.
17   Pull out the lower left and right instrument panel snap-on finish panel inserts. Remove eight screws retaining the upper finish panel (see Chapter 11).
18   Pull the lower edge of the upper finish panel away from the instrument panel. It is best to grasp the finish panel from the lower left corner and pull the panel away by ''walking'' your hands around the panel in a clockwise direction.
19   Remove the four screws (they may have Torx heads, which require a special tool) retaining the control head **(see illustration)**. Pull the control head away from the instrument panel into a position which provides

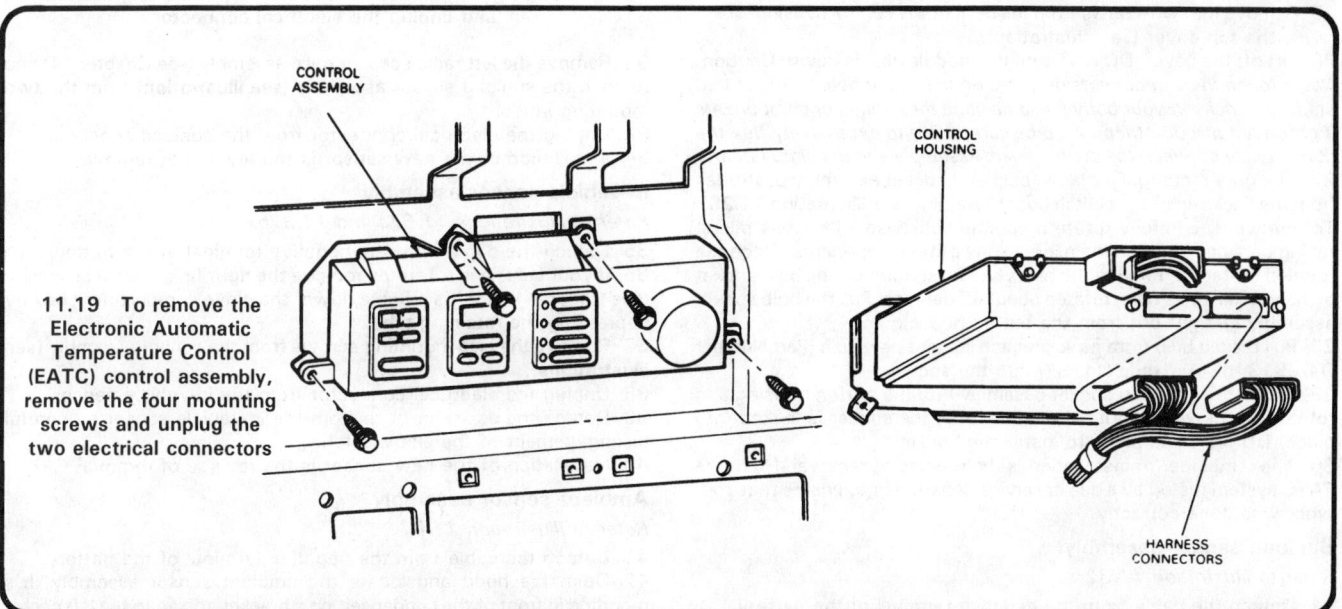

11.19 To remove the Electronic Automatic Temperature Control (EATC) control assembly, remove the four mounting screws and unplug the two electrical connectors

CONTROL ASSEMBLY

CONTROL HOUSING

HARNESS CONNECTORS

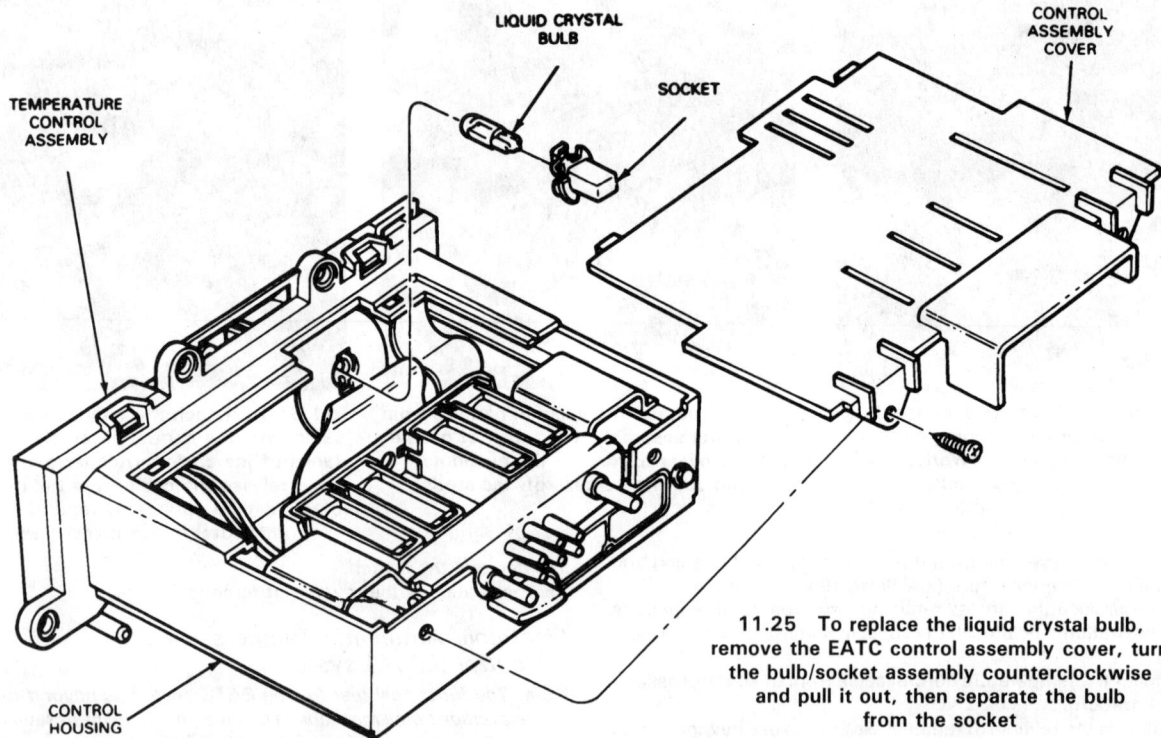

11.25   To replace the liquid crystal bulb, remove the EATC control assembly cover, turn the bulb/socket assembly counterclockwise and pull it out, then separate the bulb from the socket

access to the rear connectors.
20 Unplug the two electrical connectors from the control assembly.
21 Remove the two nuts which retain the vacuum harness. Pull the control assembly away from the instrument panel.
22 Installation is the reverse of removal.

Control assembly dial liquid crystal bulb

Refer to illustration 11.25

Note: *The following procedure is to be used for replacement of the liquid crystal light bulb. The procedure does not apply to the backlighting bulbs or the function indicator lamps (LEDs). If any of the function LEDs are inoperative, replace the control assembly.*

23 Remove the control assembly from the vehicle (see above).
24 Place the control assembly on a clean cardboard surface.
25 Remove the two screws from the back of the control housing which retain the top cover **(see illustration)**.
26 Lift off the cover. DO NOT turn the module upside down. **Caution:** *Never touch the components or traces on the circuit board. Any stored static electricity in your body could damage the circuits or components if grounded through them. Also be careful not to excessively flex the ribbon cable between the switch board assembly and the circuit board.*
27 The gray rectangular plastic bulb and socket assembly protrudes from the backside of the switch board assembly **(see illustration 11.25)**. To remove it, carefully rotate it counterclockwise with small pliers, taking care not to touch the pliers to any other components. Once the rotation is started, remove the pliers and finish rotating the bulb socket by hand until it has been rotated about 45 degrees. Pull the bulb socket assembly straight out from the button housing.
28 Pull the old bulb from its socket and install a new bulb (Part Number D4AZ-13466-A, Trade No. 37) into the socket.
29 Install the bulb and socket assembly into the button housing and rotate it clockwise about 45 degrees until the socket is locked into place. DO NOT use pliers to install the socket.
30 The remainder of installation is the reverse of removal. Have the EATC system tested by a dealer service department to ensure that your work was done correctly.

Sunload sensor assembly

Refer to illustration 11.32

31 Detach the cable from the negative terminal of the battery.

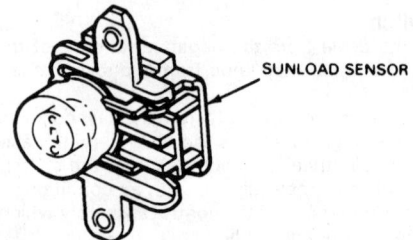

11.32   The EATC sunload sensor is hidden under the left dashboard speaker grille — to replace it, simply remove the grille (see Chapter 11), remove the two mounting screws and unplug the electrical connector

32 Remove the left radio speaker grille assembly (see Chapter 11) and remove the sunload sensor assembly **(see illustration)** from the two mounting studs.
33 Unplug the electrical connector from the sunload sensor.
34 Installation of the new sensor is the reverse of removal.

In-vehicle sensor assembly

Refer to illustrations 11.37a and 11.37b

35 Detach the cable from the negative terminal of the battery.
36 If your vehicle is a Taurus, remove the right finish panel assembly (see Chapter 11). If it's a Sable, lower the glove compartment box by depressing the retaining tabs.
37 Remove the two mounting screws from the sensor assembly **(see illustrations)**.
38 Unplug the electrical connector from the in-vehilce sensor.
39 Detach the aspirator hose from the in-vehicle sensor by careful disengagement of the elbow latch.
40 Installation of the new sensor is the reverse of removal.

Ambient sensor assembly

Refer to illustration 11.42

41 Detach the cable from the negative terminal of the battery.
42 Open the hood and locate the ambient sensor assembly. It's mounted in front of the condenser, on a bracket affixed to the left center

IN VEHICLE
SENSOR
(TAURUS ONLY)

INSTRUMENT
PANEL

LATCH
(ENGAGES LOCKING
RAMP ON SENSOR)

ELECTRICAL
CONNECTOR
(TO WIRING
ASSEMBLY

IN-VEHICLE
SENSOR AND BRACKET
ASSEMBLY

ASPIRATOR
HOSE

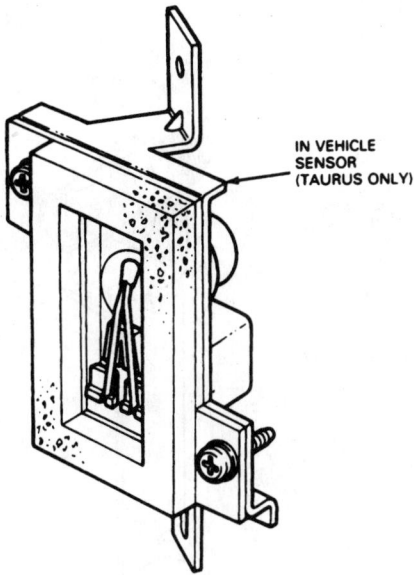

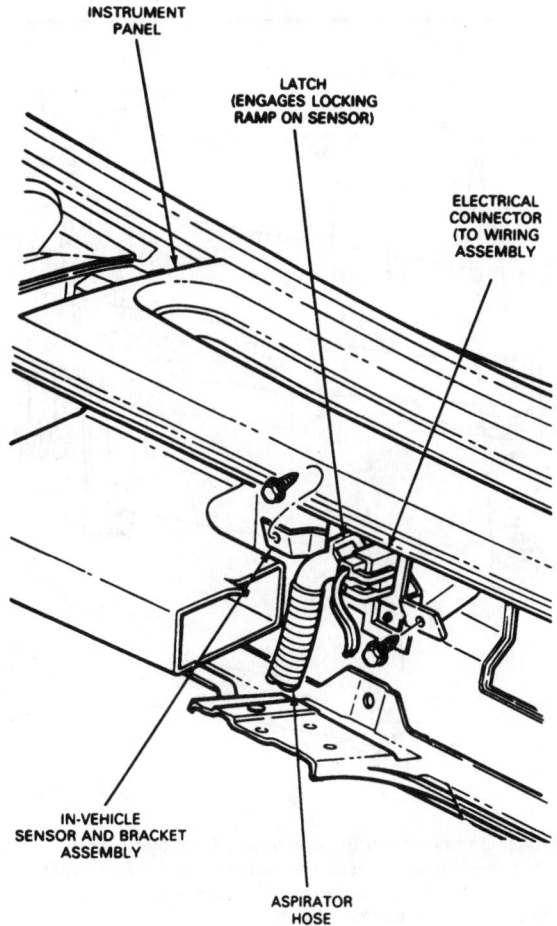

11.37a   On the Taurus, the EATC in-vehicle sensor is located behind the right finish panel (the radio opening panel) below the cluster opening finish panel — to replace it, simply remove the panel (see Chapter 11), remove the two mounting screws, pull it out, detach the aspirator hose and unplug the electrical connector

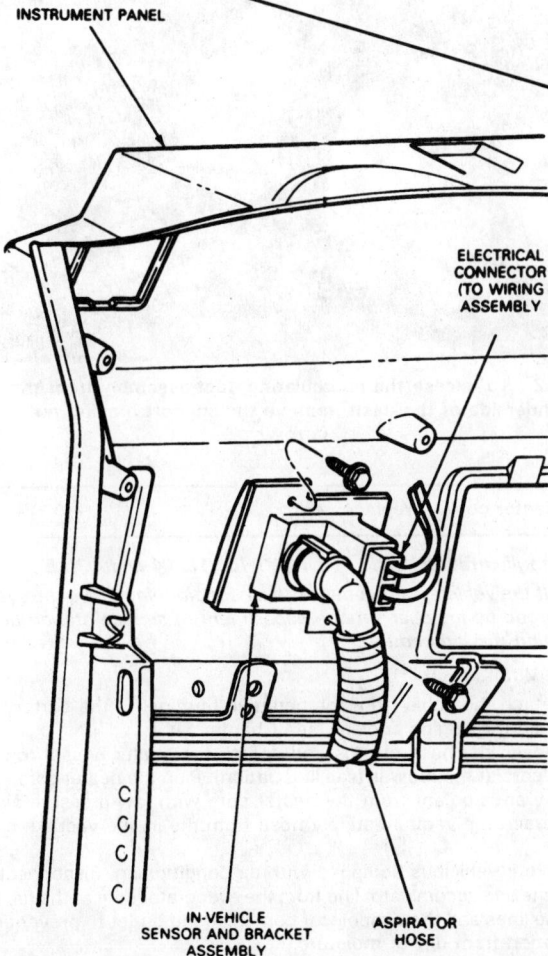

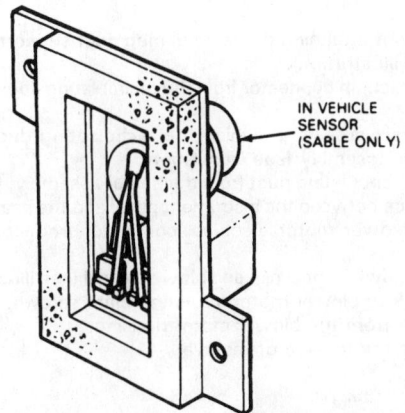

INSTRUMENT PANEL

ELECTRICAL
CONNECTOR
(TO WIRING
ASSEMBLY

IN-VEHICLE
SENSOR AND BRACKET
ASSEMBLY

ASPIRATOR
HOSE

IN VEHICLE
SENSOR
(SABLE ONLY)

11.37b   On the Sable, the EATC in-vehicle sensor is located behind the glove compartment — to replace it, drop the glove box, remove the two mounting screws, pull it out, detach the aspirator hose and unplug the electrical connector

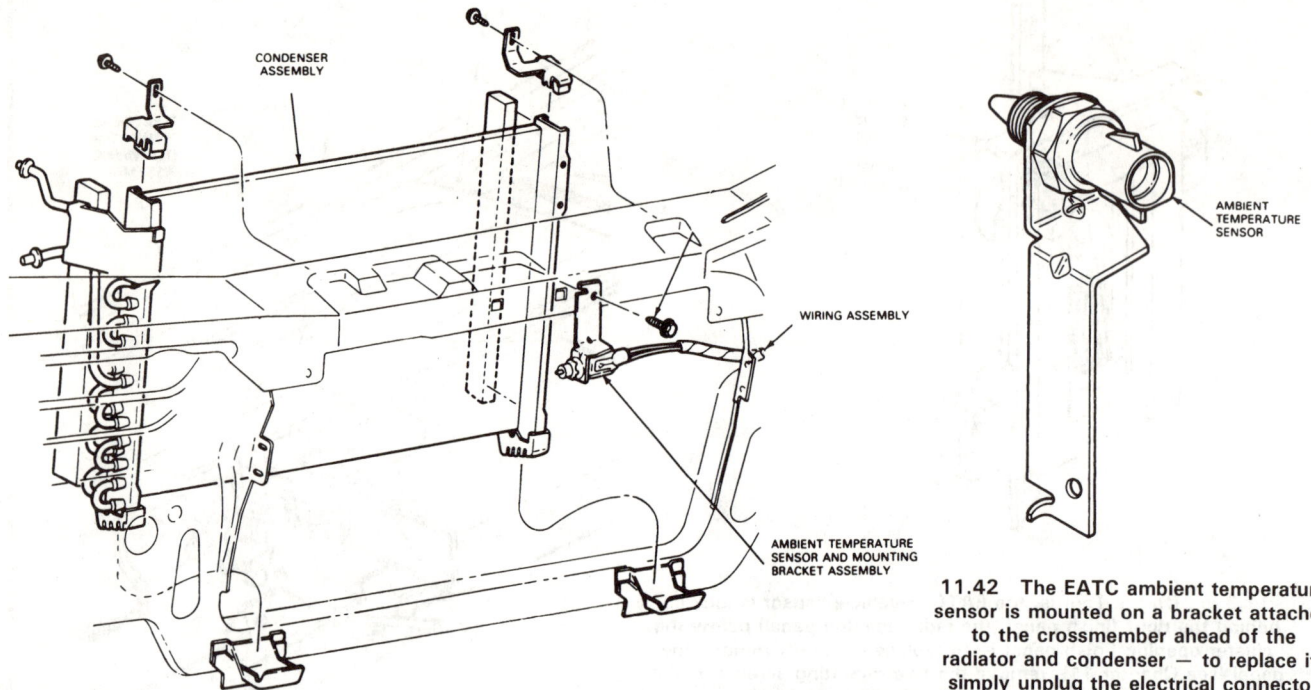

11.42   The EATC ambient temperature sensor is mounted on a bracket attached to the crossmember ahead of the radiator and condenser — to replace it, simply unplug the electrical connector and unscrew the sensor from the bracket

of the crossmember above the condenser **(see illustration)**.
43 Remove the ambient sensor mounting nut and remove the sensor.
44 Unplug the electrical connector from the sensor.
45 Installation is the reverse of removal.

---

12   Heater and air conditioning blower motor and resistor — replacement

Blower motor and wheel assembly
Refer to illustrations 12.2, 12.4 and 12.7

1   Open the glove compartment door, release the retainers and lower the door.
2   Remove the nut attaching the recirculating duct support bracket to the cowl **(see illustration)**.
3   Remove the vacuum connector from the recirculating door vacuum motor.
4   Remove the six screws attaching the recirculating duct to the heater/evaporator assembly **(see illustration)**.
5   Remove the recirculating duct from the heater assembly, lowering it through the space between the instrument panel and the heater case.
6   Unplug the blower motor electrical connector from the wiring harness.
7   Remove the blower wheel clip and blower wheel **(see illustration)**.
8   Remove the four blower motor mounting plate screws. Remove the blower motor from the blower motor housing.
9   Installation is the reverse of removal.

Blower motor resistor
Refer to illustration 12.11

10 Detach the cable from the negative terminal of the battery.
11 To access the blower motor resistor and thermal limiter assembly, open the glove compartment door, release the glove box retainers and let the glove box hang down. The blower motor resistor and thermal limiter assembly **(see illustration)** is installed on the heater case, to the left of the recirculating duct.
12 Unplug the electrical connector from the resistor assembly.
13 Remove the two resistor attaching screws and remove the resistor from the heater case.
14 Installation is the reverse of removal. **Caution:** *Do not apply sealer to the resistor assembly mounting surface.*

12.2   To release the recirculating duct assembly from the underside of the dash, remove the support bracket nut (arrow)

---

13   Heater core — replacement

Refer to illustrations 13.3, 13.7, 13.12, 13.14 and 13.15
Note: *If the vehicle is equipped with air conditioning, have the system discharged by a dealer service department or service station before beginning this procedure.*

Removal

1   Detach the cable from the negative terminal of the battery.
2   Drain the engine coolant (see Chapter 1).
3   Loosen the hose clamps and detach the heater hoses from the heater core at the firewall **(see illustration)**. Plug the heater core tubes or blow any coolant from the heater core with low-pressure air.
4   Detach the vacuum supply hose from the in-line vacuum check valve.
5   If your vehicle is equipped with air conditioning, disconnect the liquid line and accumulator line from the evaporator core at the firewall. Cap the lines and the evaporator core inlet and outlet to prevent contamination from dirt or moisture.
6   Remove the instrument panel (see Chapter 11).

BLOWER WHEEL

BLOWER MOTOR

OUTSIDE AIR INLET DUCT

RECIRC DUCT

RECIRC DOOR

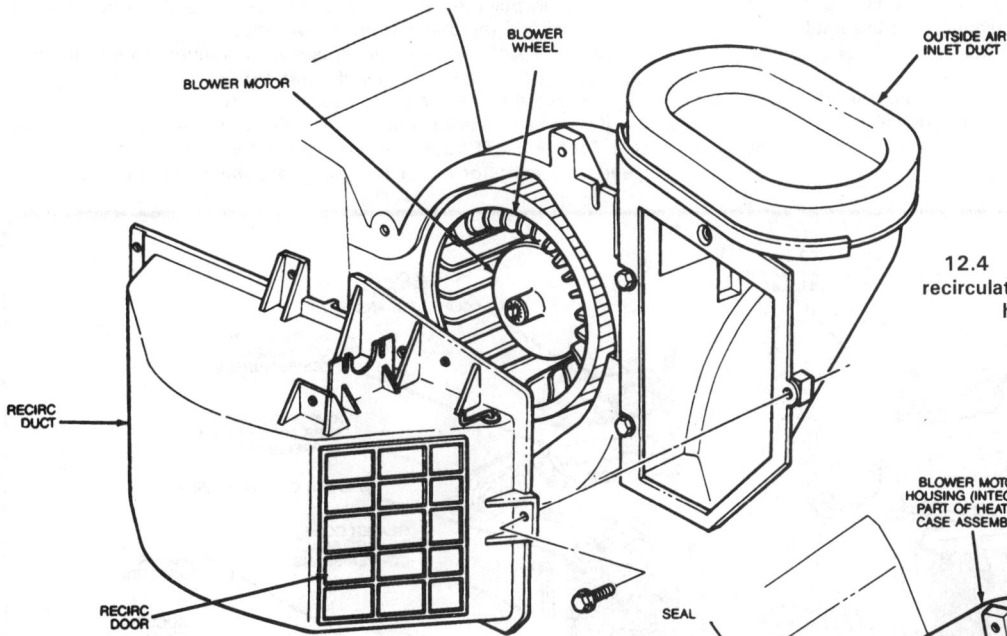

12.4 An exploded view of the recirculating duct and blower motor housing assemblies

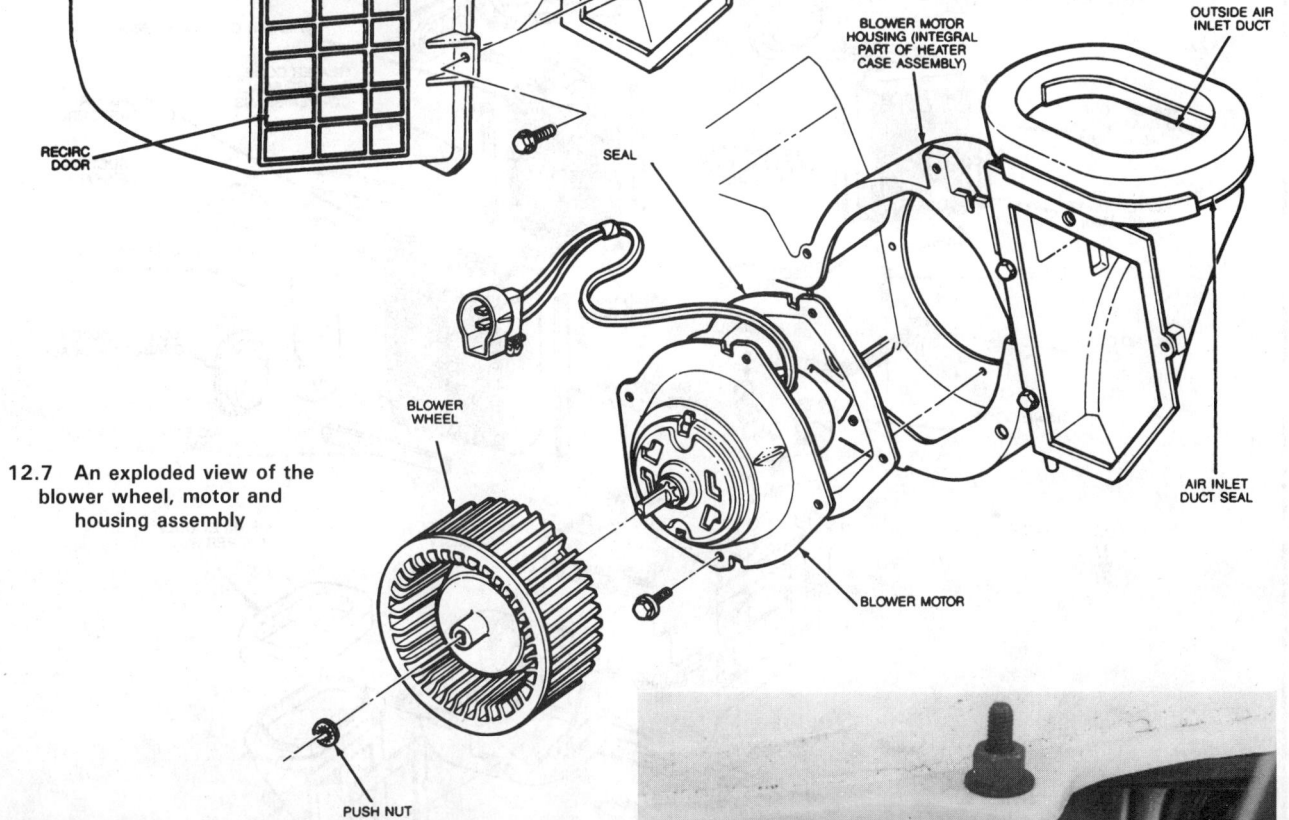

BLOWER MOTOR HOUSING (INTEGRAL PART OF HEATER CASE ASSEMBLY)

OUTSIDE AIR INLET DUCT

SEAL

AIR INLET DUCT SEAL

BLOWER WHEEL

BLOWER MOTOR

12.7 An exploded view of the blower wheel, motor and housing assembly

PUSH NUT

12.11 The blower motor resistor assembly is located on the left side of the recirculating duct assembly — to replace it, simply unplug the electrical connector and remove the mounting screws

13.3 Loosen the clamps, detach the heater hoses and plug both hoses as well as the heater core tubes to prevent coolant from leaking onto the vehicle

7   Remove the evaporator support bracket **(see illustration)** between the instrument panel and the recirculating duct assembly.
8   Remove the screws that attach the floor register to the bottom of the heater/evaporator case.
9   From the engine compartment side, remove the three nuts that attach the heater/evaporator case to the firewall.
10   Remove the two screws attaching the support brackets to the cowl top panel.

11   Carefully pull the heater/evaporator case assembly away from the dash panel and remove it from the vehicle.
12   Remove the in-line vacuum check valve/vacuum source line from the heater core tube seal **(see illustration)**.
13   Remove the seal from the heater core tubes.
14   If your vehicle is equipped with an Electronic Automatic Temperature Control (EATC) system, remove the three screws attaching the blend door actuator motor assembly **(see illustration)** to the heater/

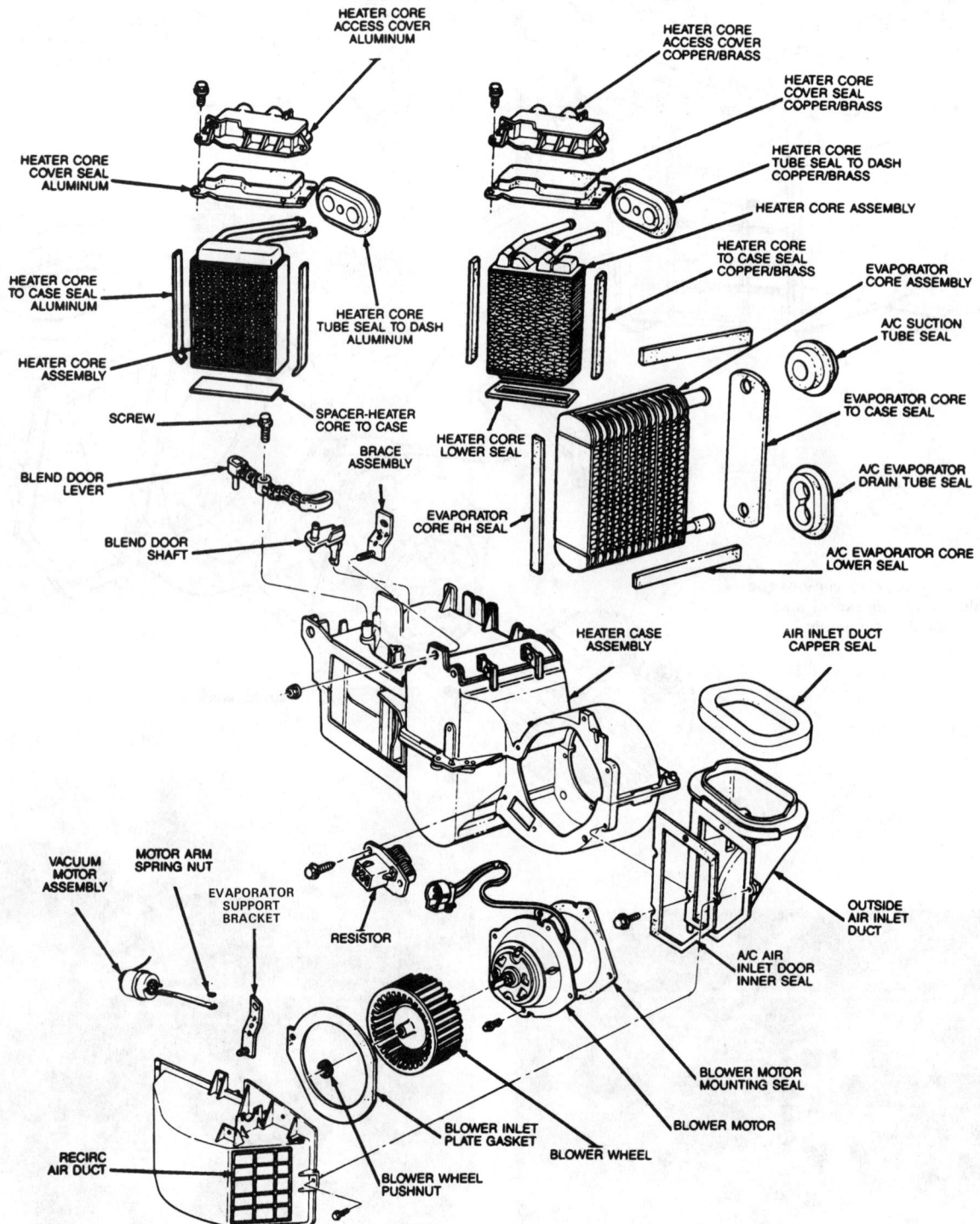

HEATER CORE ACCESS COVER ALUMINUM

HEATER CORE ACCESS COVER COPPER/BRASS

HEATER CORE COVER SEAL COPPER/BRASS

HEATER CORE COVER SEAL ALUMINUM

HEATER CORE TUBE SEAL TO DASH COPPER/BRASS

HEATER CORE ASSEMBLY

HEATER CORE TO CASE SEAL ALUMINUM

HEATER CORE TUBE SEAL TO DASH ALUMINUM

HEATER CORE ASSEMBLY

HEATER CORE TO CASE SEAL COPPER/BRASS

EVAPORATOR CORE ASSEMBLY

A/C SUCTION TUBE SEAL

EVAPORATOR CORE TO CASE SEAL

SCREW

SPACER-HEATER CORE TO CASE

HEATER CORE LOWER SEAL

BRACE ASSEMBLY

A/C EVAPORATOR DRAIN TUBE SEAL

BLEND DOOR LEVER

BLEND DOOR SHAFT

EVAPORATOR CORE RH SEAL

A/C EVAPORATOR CORE LOWER SEAL

HEATER CASE ASSEMBLY

AIR INLET DUCT CAPPER SEAL

VACUUM MOTOR ASSEMBLY

MOTOR ARM SPRING NUT

EVAPORATOR SUPPORT BRACKET

RESISTOR

OUTSIDE AIR INLET DUCT

A/C AIR INLET DOOR INNER SEAL

BLOWER MOTOR MOUNTING SEAL

BLOWER MOTOR

RECIRC AIR DUCT

BLOWER INLET PLATE GASKET

BLOWER WHEEL PUSHNUT

BLOWER WHEEL

13.7   The heater/evaporator support bracket must be disconnected before the heater/evaporator case assembly can be removed

HEATER CORE
ACCESS COVER

HEATER
CORE
TUBES

HEATER CORE
TUBE SEAL
(FOAM)

13.12 Be sure to remove the in-line
vacuum check valve/vacuum source
line from the heater core tube
seal — simply pull it through from
inside the vehicle

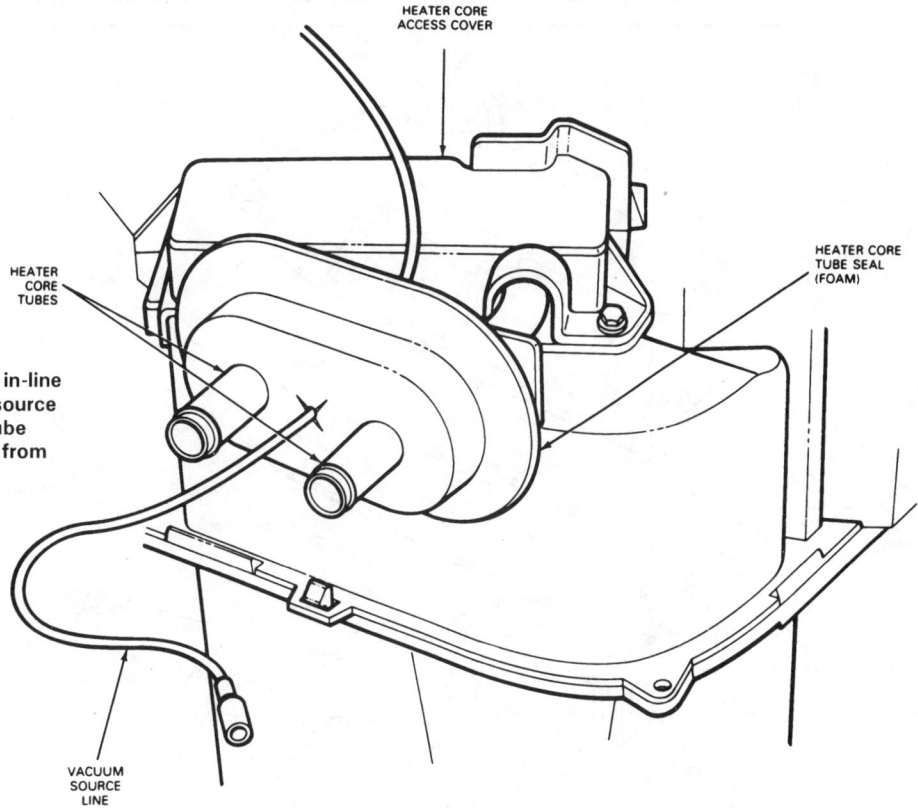

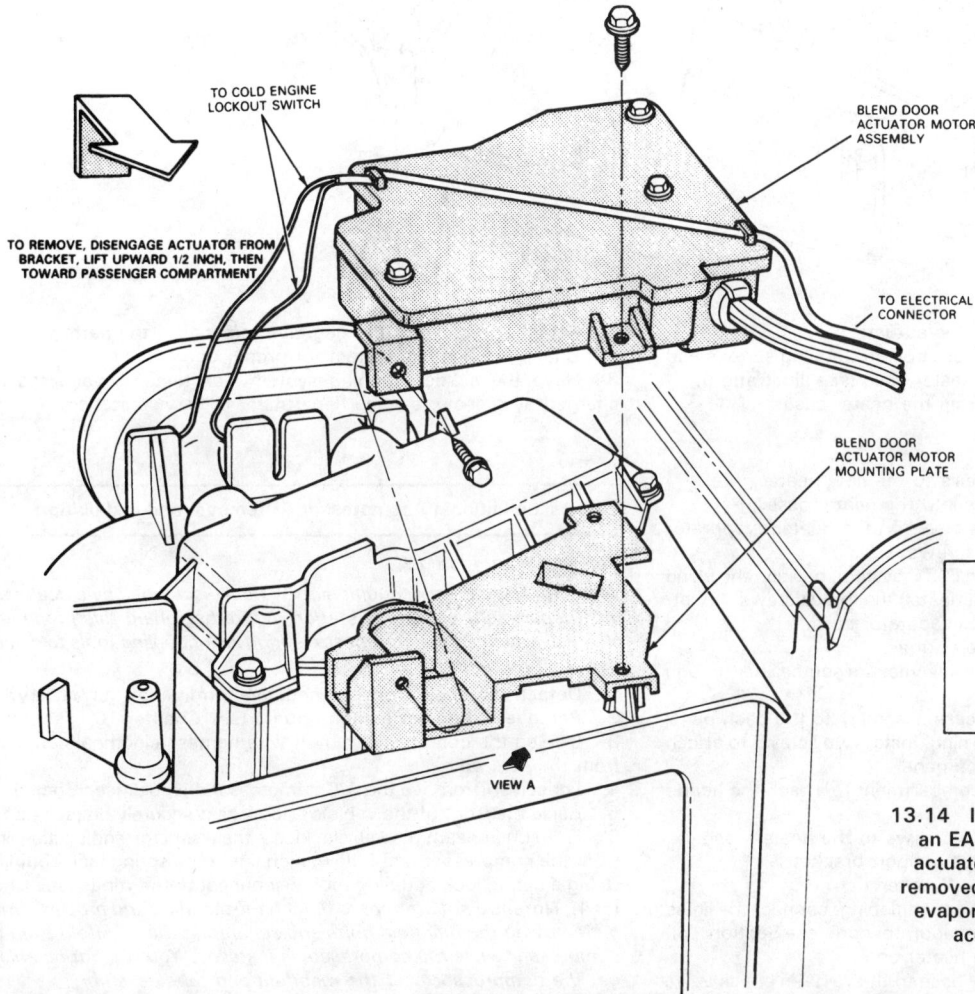

VACUUM
SOURCE
LINE

TO COLD ENGINE
LOCKOUT SWITCH

BLEND DOOR
ACTUATOR MOTOR
ASSEMBLY

TO REMOVE, DISENGAGE ACTUATOR FROM
BRACKET, LIFT UPWARD 1/2 INCH, THEN
TOWARD PASSENGER COMPARTMENT

TO ELECTRICAL
CONNECTOR

BLEND DOOR
ACTUATOR MOTOR
MOUNTING PLATE

VIEW A

VIEW A

13.14 If the vehicle is equipped with
an EATC system, the blend door
actuator motor assembly must be
removed from the top of the heater/
evaporator case assembly to gain
access to the heater core

HEATER CORE
ACCESS COVER

HEATER CORE
ACCESS COVER
AND CORE SEAL

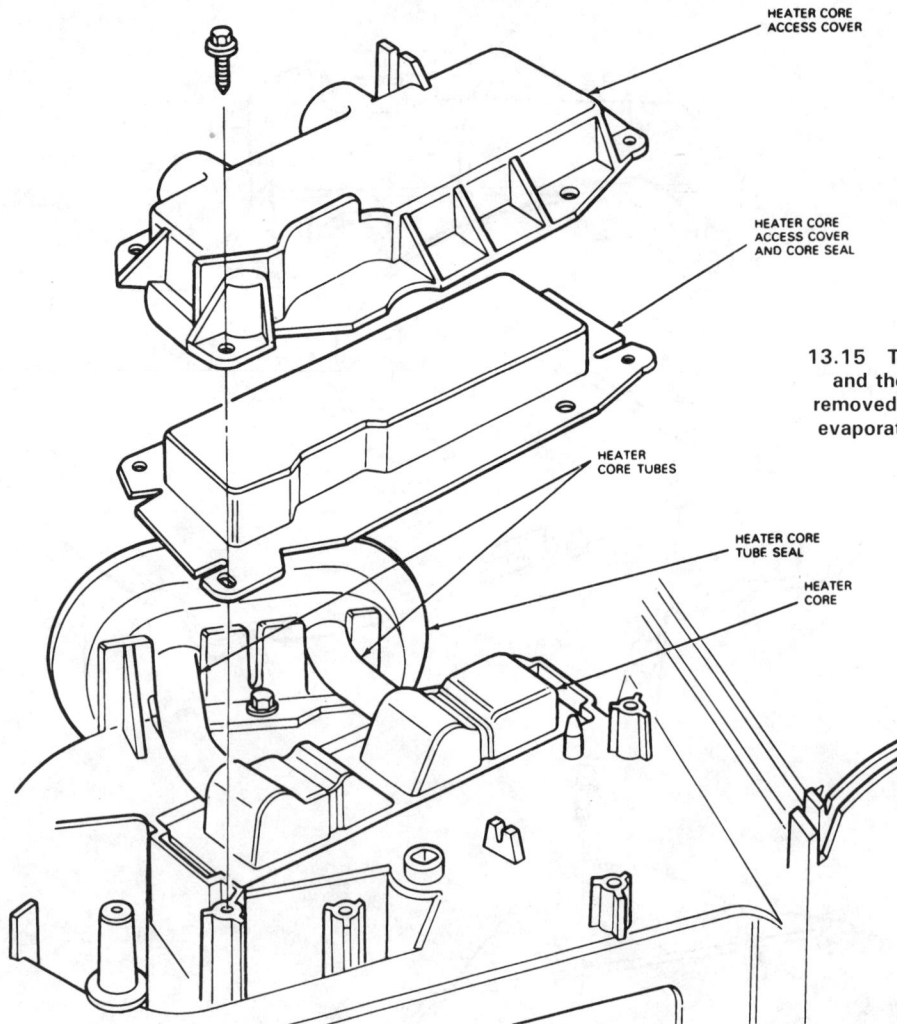

**13.15   The heater core access cover
and the cover/core seal must be
removed from the top of the heater/
evaporator case assembly to get at
the heater core**

HEATER
CORE TUBES

HEATER CORE
TUBE SEAL

HEATER
CORE

evaporator case assembly. Remove the actuator.
15 Remove the four heater core access cover attaching screws and remove the access cover from the heater case **(see illustration)**.
16 Lift the heater core and seals from the heater case.

Installation

17 Transfer the three foam core seals to the new heater core.
18 Install the heater core and seals into the heater case.
19 Position the heater case access cover on the heater/evaporator case and install the four attaching screws.
20 If your vehicle is equipped with an EATC system, position the blend door actuator to the blend door shaft. Install the three screws that attach the blend door actuator to the evaporator case.
21 Install the seal on the heater core tubes.
22 Install the in-line vacuum check valve/vacuum source line through the heater core tube seal.
23 Position the heater/evaporator case assembly to the dash panel and cowl top panel at the air inlet opening. Install two screws to attach the support brackets to the cowl top panel.
24 Install three nuts in the engine compartment to attach the heater case to the firewall.
25 Install the floor register and two screws to the heater case.
26 Install the heater/evaporator case support bracket.
27 Install the instrument panel (see Chapter 11).
28 If your vehicle is equipped with air conditioning, connect the liquid line and suction accumulator to the evaporator core (see Section 16).
29 Attach the heater hoses to the heater core.
30 Attach the black vacuum supply hose to the vacuum check valve in the engine compartment.
31 Add engine coolant (see Chapter 1).

32 Attach the cable to the negative terminal of the battery.
33 Check the heating system for proper operation.
34 Have the air conditioning system leak tested, evacuated and charged by a dealer service department or service station.

14   Air conditioning compressor — removal and installation

Refer to illustration 14.7
Warning: *Have the air conditioning system discharged by a dealer service department or service station before beginning this procedure. You will also need the correct size spring lock coupling tools to disconnect and reattach the lines.*

1   Detach the cable from the negative terminal of the battery.
2   Remove the power steering pump (see Chapter 10).
3   Unplug the compressor clutch wire harness electrical connector from the field coil.
4   Loosen and remove the A/C compressor drivebelt (see Chapter 1).
5   Raise the front of the vehicle and place it securely on jackstands.
6   From underneath the vehicle, locate the discharge and suction lines from the compressor and follow each line to its spring lock coupling. Using a spring lock coupling tool, disconnect both fittings (see Chapter 4). **Note:** *Do not attempt to detach the manifold and tube assembly by removing the manifold bolts and separating the manifold from the compressor while the compressor is installed. You will not be able to get the compressor past the manifold and tube assembly.*
7   Remove the four bolts **(see illustration)** that attach the compressor to its mounting bracket.

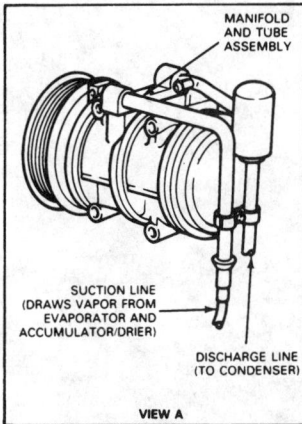

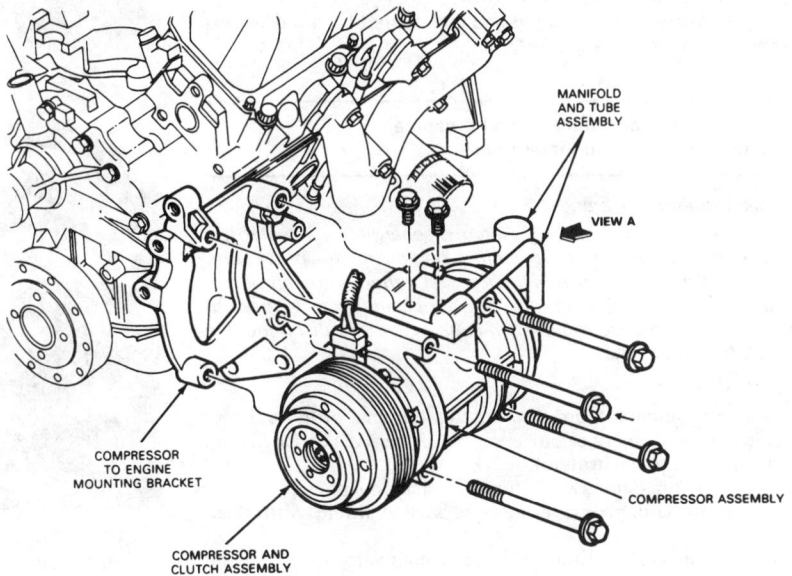

14.7 Compressor mounting details

8 From above, remove the compressor and manifold and tube assembly as a unit out the top (they must be removed out the top because the compressor will not clear the subframe crossmember).

9 On the bench, remove the manifold bolts and separate the manifold and tube assembly from the compressor.

10 If the compressor is to be replaced, remove the clutch and field coil assembly and install it on the new/rebuilt compressor.

11 Installation is the reverse of removal.

15   Air conditioning condenser — removal and installation

Refer to illustration 15.5

Warning: *Have the air conditioning system discharged by a dealer service department or service station before beginning this procedure.*

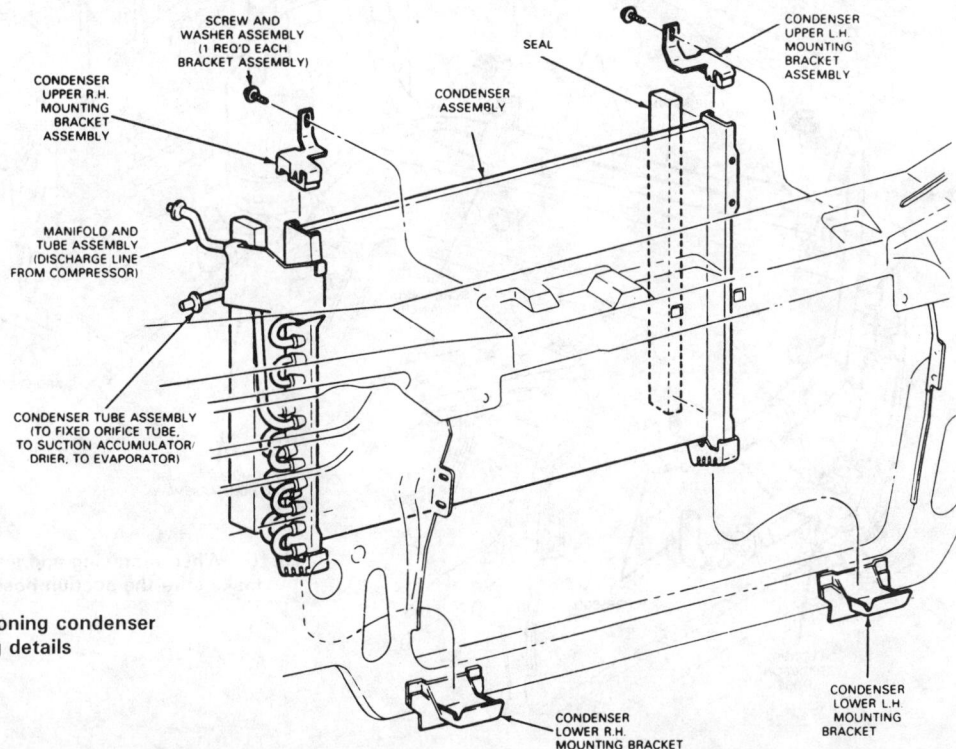

While you're at the dealer or repair shop, ask where you can obtain a 1/2-inch spring lock coupling tool. This tool is inexpensive but absolutely essential because the system lines cannot be disconnected or reattached without it.

1 Drain the cooling system (Chapter 1).

2 Remove the electric cooling fan and shroud assembly (see Section 4).

3 Remove the radiator (see Section 5).

4 Using a 1/2-inch spring lock coupling tool (see Chapter 4), disconnect the two refrigerant lines from the right side of the condenser.

5 Remove the bolts attaching the condenser to the radiator support **(see illustration)** and remove the condenser from the vehicle.

15.5 Air conditioning condenser mounting details

6   Installation is the reverse of removal.
7   The system must be recharged and leak tested by a dealer service department or service station.

16 Air conditioning accumulator and pressure switch — removal and installation

Refer to illustrations 16.2 and 16.10

Warning: *Have the air conditioning system discharged by a dealer service department or service station before beginning this procedure. While you're at the dealer or repair shop, ask where you can obtain a 1/2-inch spring lock coupling tool. This tool is inexpensive but absolutely essential because the system lines cannot be disconnected or reattached without it.*

Pressure switch

1   Disconnect the cable from the negative terminal of the battery.
2   Unplug the wire harness electrical connector from the clutch cycling pressure switch **(see illustration)**.
3   Unscrew the pressure switch from the accumulator.
4   Lubricate the O-ring on the pressure switch fitting with clean refrigerant oil.
5   Screw the pressure switch onto the accumulator nipple. If the threaded fitting is plastic, tighten the switch finger tight. If the threaded fitting is metal, tighten the switch with a wrench.
6   Reattach the wire harness to the switch.
7   Have the system recharged and the pressure switch checked for proper operation and refrigerant leakage by a dealer service department or an automotive air conditioning shop.

Accumulator

8   Disconnect the cable from the negative terminal of the battery.
9   Unplug the wire harness connector from the pressure switch on top of the accumulator **(see illustration 16.2)**.

16.2   To remove the accumulator pressure switch, unplug the electrical connector (arrow) and unscrew the switch

10   Using a spring lock coupling tool, disconnect the suction line at the spring lock coupling next to the compressor **(see illustration)**. Cap the hoses and the compressor to prevent contamination from dirt or moisture.
11   Using a spring lock coupling tool, disconnect the accumulator inlet tube at the evaporator. Cap the evaporator outlet and the accumulator inlet tube to prevent contamination from dirt or moisture.
12   Loosen the clamp screw and remove the accumulator.
13   Installation is the reverse of removal. Have the system recharged by a dealer service department or service station.

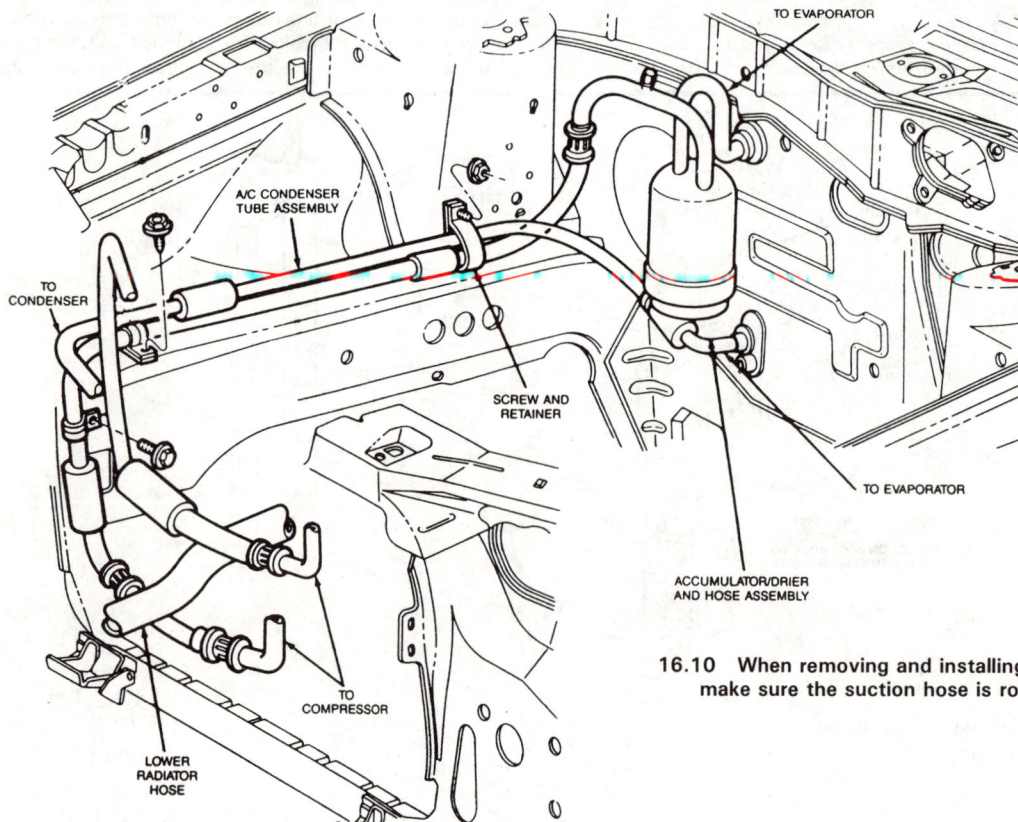

TO EVAPORATOR

A/C CONDENSER TUBE ASSEMBLY

TO CONDENSER

SCREW AND RETAINER

TO EVAPORATOR

ACCUMULATOR/DRIER AND HOSE ASSEMBLY

TO COMPRESSOR

LOWER RADIATOR HOSE

16.10   When removing and installing the accumulator, make sure the suction hose is routed correctly

Chapter 4   Fuel and exhaust systems

Contents

Specifications

Fuel pressure
Central Fuel Injection (CFI) . . . .   14.5 psi
Electronic Fuel Injection (EFI) . . . .   39 psi

Torque specifications   Ft-lbs

Four-cylinder engine
Throttle body-to-intake manifold . . . .   15 to 25

3.0L V6 engine
Throttle body-to-lower intake manifold . . . .   15 to 22

3.8L V6 engine
Upper intake manifold-to-lower intake manifold . . . .   19 to 28
Throttle body-to-upper intake manifold . . . .   15 to 22

---

1   General information

Fuel system

The fuel system consists of the fuel tank, the fuel pump, an air cleaner assembly, a fuel injection system and the various steel, plastic and/or nylon lines and fittings connecting everything together. The pump on fuel injected vehicles is electric and is mounted inside the fuel tank.

Exhaust system

All vehicles are equipped with either a single exhaust manifold (four-cylinder), or a pair of manifolds (V6), a catalytic converter, an exhaust pipe and a muffler. Any component of the exhaust system can be replaced. The "dual brick underbody" type converter used on the four-cylinder utilizes both a three-way catalyst and a conventional oxidation catalyst. The "under engine" catalyst used on the 3.0L V6 is a single three-way catalyst mounted under the oil pan. The 3.8L V6 engine has a trio of catalysts: a pair of small three-way catalysts immediately below each exhaust manifold and a larger conventional oxidation catalyst mounted in the exhaust pipe (refer to Chapter 6 for further details regarding the catalytic converter).

Replacement exhaust systems may differ from the production system on your vehicle in the number of basic pieces used. Factory installed exhaust systems have one-piece converters. The converter assembly is a bolt-on unit. A slip joint is used between the converter and muffler on four-cylinder underbody converter systems and the muffler is secured with a U-bolt. A slip joint is used between the resonator (3.0L V6) or converter (3.8L V6) and muffler and the muffler is secured with a U-bolt. All exhaust systems are usually serviced in four pieces. The rear section of the muffler inlet pipe (intermediate muffler inlet) is furnished separately from the muffler.

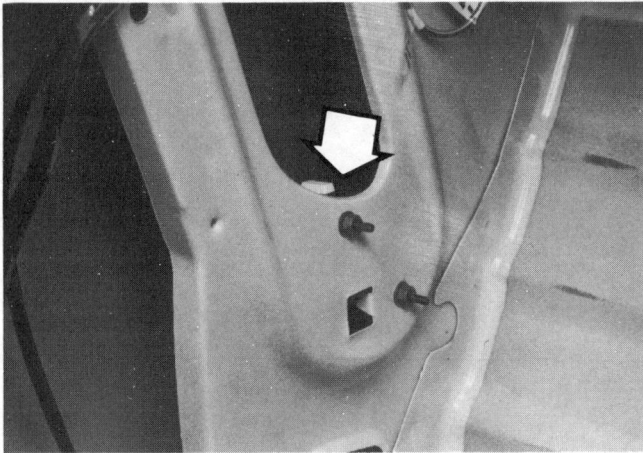

2.1a   On most sedans, the inertia switch is located on the left side of the trunk — to get at it, simply remove the two fasteners (one threaded and one pop type) and peel away the carpet

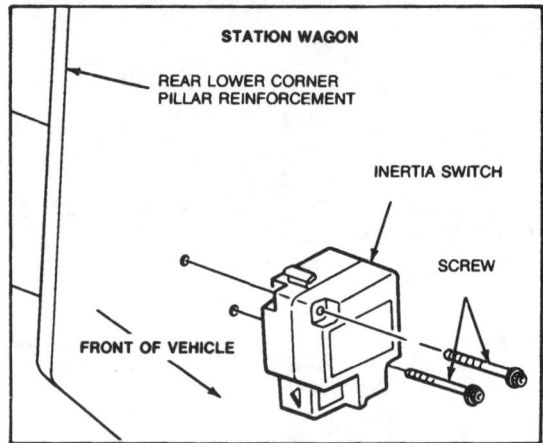

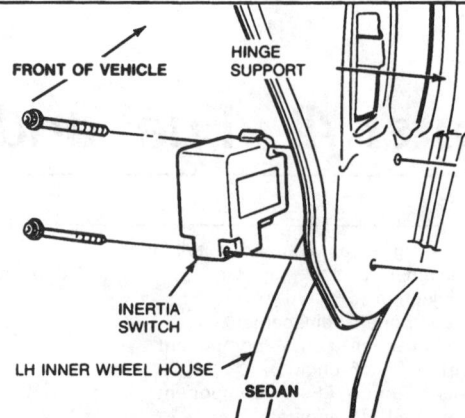

2   Fuel pressure relief procedure

Refer to illustrations 2.1a and 2.1b

All vehicles

1   The "inertia switch," which shuts off fuel to the engine in the event of a collision, affords a simple and convenient means by which fuel pressure can be relieved before servicing fuel injection components. If your vehicle is a sedan, open the trunk lid, peel back the carpet from the left side of the trunk and locate the inertia switch **(see illustrations)**. If the switch isn't there, open the driver's door and look for the switch on the door hinge support above the left inner wheel house. If your vehicle is a station wagon, you'll find the switch on the rear lower corner pillar reinforcement.
2   Locate the two nuts with the electrical wire running between them. Remove the two nuts and pull out the fuel system inertia switch.
3   There are two ways to open the fuel pump electrical circuit. Either unplug the inertia switch electrical connector or shake the switch itself vigorously (tapping it on the floor of the trunk will usually open the circuit).
4   Start the engine and allow it to run until it stops.
5   The fuel system pressure is now relieved. When finished working on the fuel system, simply plug the electrical connector back into the switch or, if you tapped the switch on the trunk to open the circuit, reset the inertia switch by depressing the square button.
6   Reinstall the inertia switch and tighten the two mounting nuts securely.

EFI vehicles only

7   If your are willing to purchase, or have access to, Ford's T80L-9974-B fuel pressure gauge (or equivalent) and T85L-9974-A adapter, the fuel pressure can be relieved through the Shrader valve on the fuel rail. **Warning:** *Never, however, attempt to relieve the fuel pressure through the Shrader valve without the gauge attached — fuel will spray out under the high pressure and could cause serious injury or a fire!*

3   Fuel lines and fittings — replacement

Warning: *The fuel system pressure must be relieved before disconnecting fuel lines and fittings (Section 2). Gasoline is extremely flammable, so extra precautions must be taken when working on any part of the fuel system. DO NOT smoke or allow open flames or bare light bulbs near the work area. Also, don't work in a garage where a natural gas appliance such as a water heater or clothes dryer is present.*

Push connect fittings — disassembly and reassembly

Refer to illustrations 3.5, 3.9, 3.10, 3.13 and 3.14
1   Ford uses two different push connect fitting designs. Fittings used with 3/8- and 5/16-inch diameter lines have a "hairpin" type clip; fit-

2.1b   On some sedans, the inertia switch is located on the hinge support behind the left inner wheel house — on the station wagon, it's located on the rear lower corner pillar reinforcement

tings used with 1/4-inch diameter lines have a "duck bill" type clip. The procedure used for releasing each type of fitting is different. The clips should be replaced whenever a connector is disassembled.
2   Disconnect all push connect fittings from fuel system components such as the fuel filter, the carburetor/fuel charging assembly, the fuel tank, etc. before removing the assembly.

3/8 and 5/16-inch fittings (hairpin clip)

3   Inspect the internal portion of the fitting for accumulations of dirt. If more than a light coating of dust is present, clean the fitting before disassembly.
4   Some adhesion between the seals in the fitting and the line will occur over a period of time. Twist the fitting on the line, then push and pull the fitting until it moves freely.
5   Remove the hairpin clip from the fitting by bending the shipping tab down until it clears the body **(see illustration)**. Then, using nothing but your hands, spread each leg about 1/8-inch to disengage the body and push the legs through the fitting. Finally, pull lightly on the triangular end of the clip and work it clear of the line and fitting. Remember, don't use any tools to perform this part of the procedure.

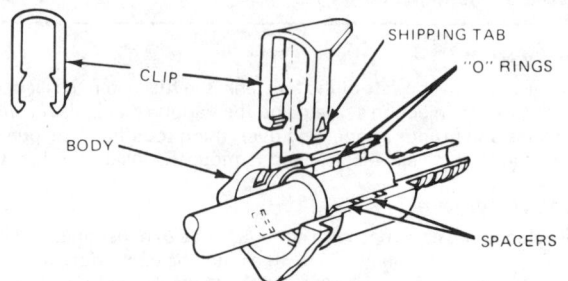

3.5   An exploded view of the hairpin clip type push connect fitting

PUSH UNTIL
CLICK IS HEARD

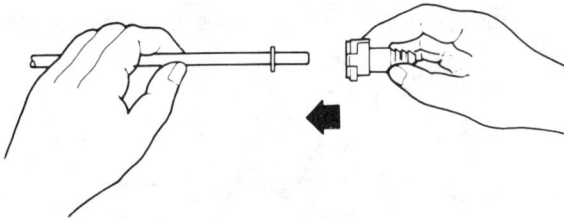

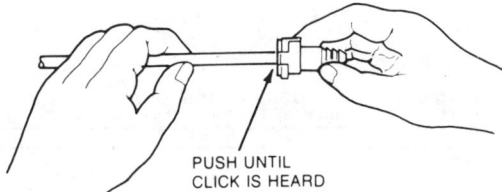

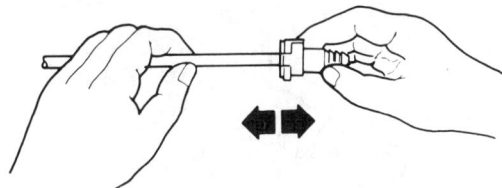

3.9 Connecting push connect fittings

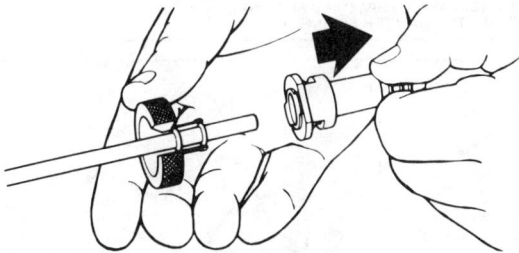

3.10 A push connect fitting with a duck bill clip

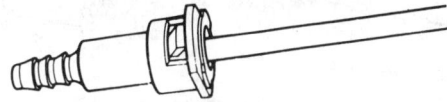

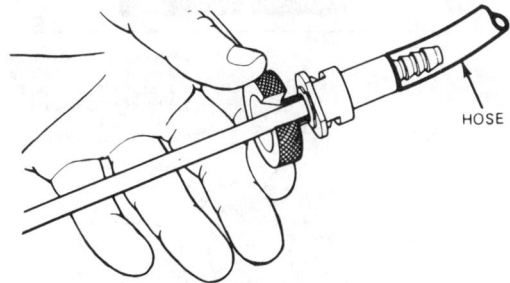

HOSE

3.13 Duck bill clip fitting removal using the special Ford disassembly tool

3.14 Pulling off the duck bill clip type push connect fitting

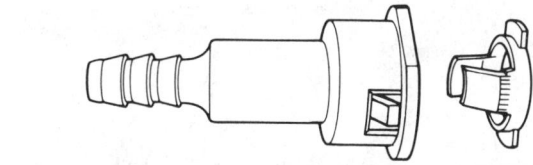

6 Grasp the fitting and hose and pull it straight off the line.
7 Do not reuse the original clip in the fitting. A new clip must be used.
8 Before reinstalling the fitting on the line, wipe the line end with a clean cloth. Inspect the inside of the fitting to ensure that it's free of dirt and/or obstructions.
9 To reinstall the fitting on the line, align them and push the fitting into place. When the fitting is engaged, a definite click will be heard. Pull on the fitting to ensure that it's completely engaged **(see illustration)**. To install the new clip, insert it into any two adjacent openings in the fitting with the triangular portion of the clip pointing *away* from the fitting opening. Using your index finger, push the clip in until the legs are locked on the outside of the fitting.

1/4-inch fittings (duck bill clip)
10 The duck bill clip type fitting consists of a body, spacers, O-rings and the retaining clip **(see illustration)**. The clip holds the fitting securely in place on the line. One of the two following methods must be used to disconnect this type of fitting.
11 Before attempting to disconnect the fitting, check the visible internal portion of the fitting for accumulations of dirt. If more than a light coating of dust is evident, clean the fitting before disassembly.
12 Some adhesion between the seals in the fitting and line will occur over a period of time. Twist the fitting on the line, then push and pull the fitting until it moves freely.
13 The *preferred method* used to disconnect the fitting requires a special tool. To disengage the line from the fitting, align the slot in the push connect disassembly tool (Ford Part No. T82L-9500-AH or equivalent tool) with either tab on the clip (90 degrees from the slots on the side of the fitting) and insert the tool **(see illustration)**. This disengages the duck bill from the line. **Note:** *Some fuel lines have a secondary bead which aligns with the outer surface of the clip. The*

bead can make tool insertion difficult. If necessary, use the alternative disassembly method described in Step 16.
14 Holding the tool and the line with one hand, pull the fitting off **(see illustration)**. **Note:** *Only moderate effort is necessary if the clip is properly disengaged. The use of anything other than your hands should not be required.*
15 After disassembly, inspect and clean the line sealing surface. Also inspect the inside of the fitting and the line for any internal parts that may have been dislodged from the fitting. Any loose internal parts should be immediately reinstalled (use the line to insert the parts).
16 The *alternative disassembly procedure* requires a pair of small Channelock pliers. The pliers must have a jaw width of 3/16-inch or less.
17 Align the jaws of the pliers with the openings in the side of the fitting and compress the portion of the retaining clip that engages the body. This disengages the retaining clip from the body (often one side of the clip will disengage before the other — both sides must be disengaged).
18 Pull the fitting off the line. **Note:** *Only moderate effort is required if the retaining clip has been properly disengaged. Do not use any tools for this procedure.*
19 Once the fitting is removed from the line end, check the fitting and line for any internal parts that may have been dislodged from the fitting. Any loose internal parts should be immediately reinstalled (use the line to insert the parts).
20 The retaining clip will remain on the line. Disengage the clip from the line bead to remove it. Do not reuse the retaining clip — install a new one!
21 Before reinstalling the fitting, wipe the line end with a clean cloth. Check the inside of the fitting to make sure that it's free of dirt and/or obstructions.
22 To reinstall the fitting, align it with the line and push it into place. When the fitting is engaged, a definite click will be heard. Pull on the fitting to ensure that it's fully engaged.
23 Install the new replacement clip by inserting one of the serrated edges on the duck bill portion into one of the openings. Push on the other side until the clip snaps into place.

Spring lock push connect fittings — disassembly and reassembly
Refer to illustrations 3.24, 3.28, 3.29, 3.30 and 3.37
24 The fuel supply and return lines used on some CFI and EFI engines utilize spring lock couplings instead of plastic push connect fittings

Connection and Disconnection Procedures

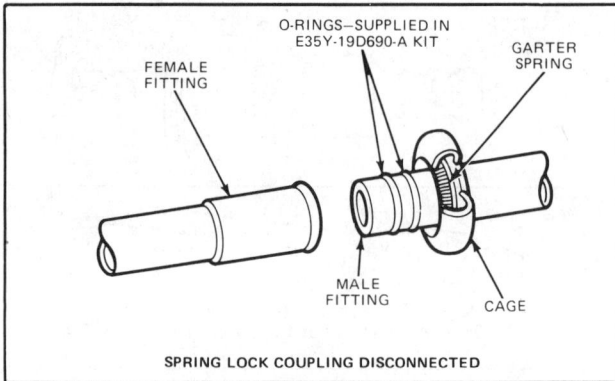

O-RINGS—SUPPLIED IN
E35Y-19D690-A KIT

GARTER
SPRING

FEMALE
FITTING

MALE
FITTING

CAGE

SPRING LOCK COUPLING DISCONNECTED

TO DISCONNECT COUPLING

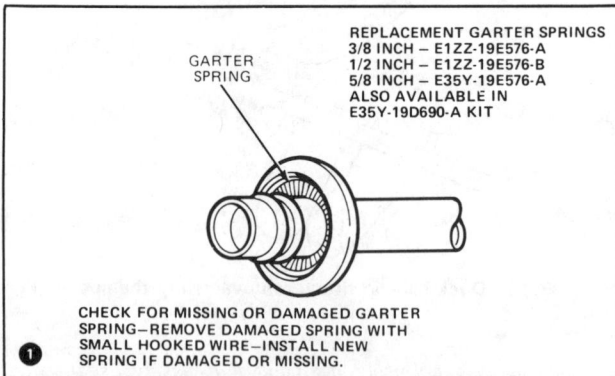

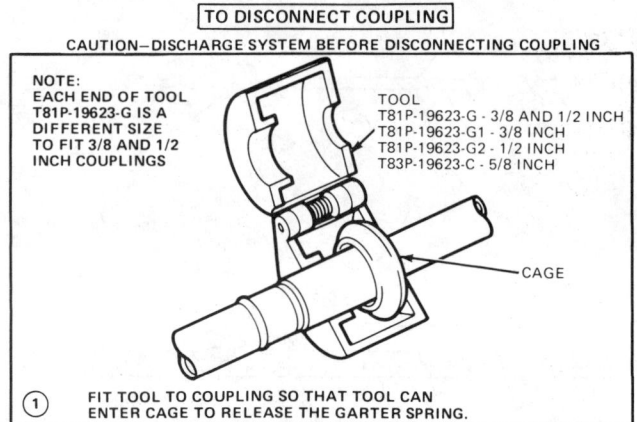

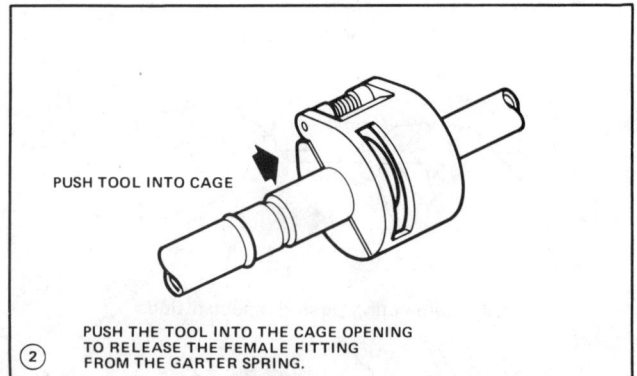

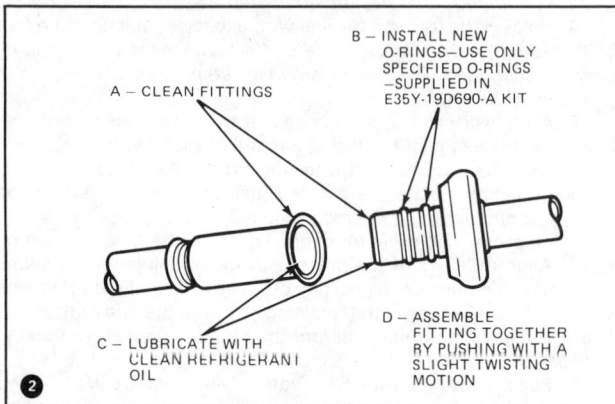

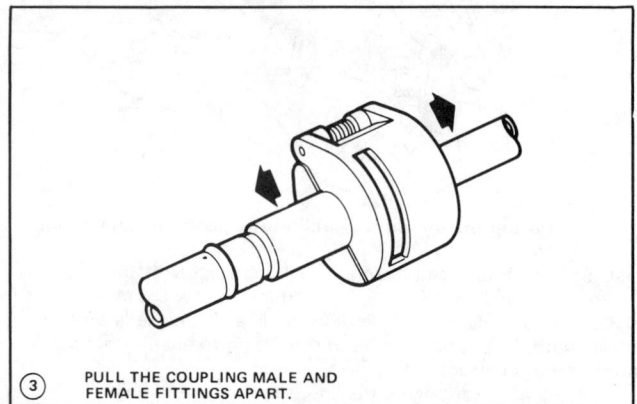

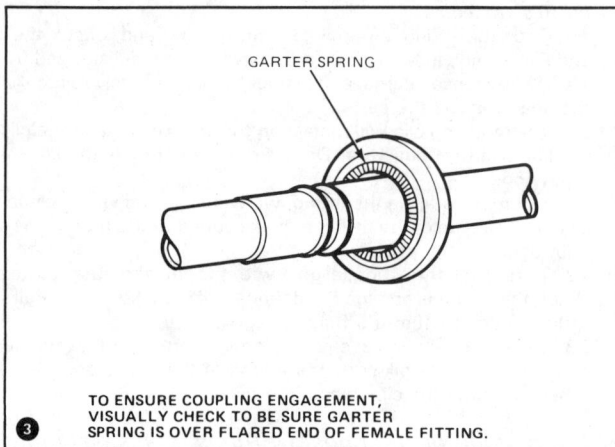

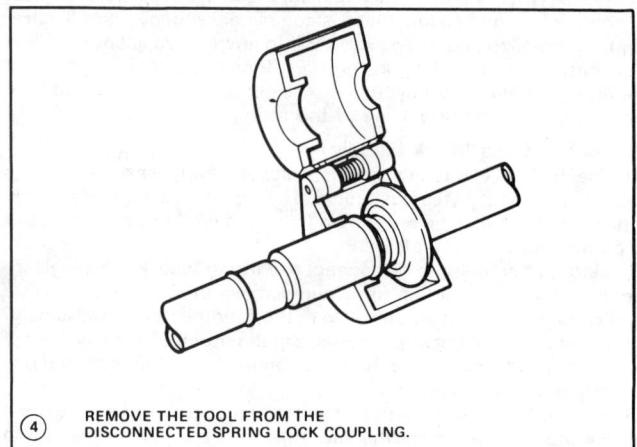

CAUTION—DISCHARGE SYSTEM BEFORE DISCONNECTING COUPLING

NOTE:
EACH END OF TOOL
T81P-19623-G IS A
DIFFERENT SIZE
TO FIT 3/8 AND 1/2
INCH COUPLINGS

TOOL
T81P-19623-G · 3/8 AND 1/2 INCH
T81P-19623-G1 · 3/8 INCH
T81P-19623-G2 · 1/2 INCH
T83P-19623-C · 5/8 INCH

CAGE

① FIT TOOL TO COUPLING SO THAT TOOL CAN
ENTER CAGE TO RELEASE THE GARTER SPRING.

TO CONNECT COUPLING

GARTER
SPRING

REPLACEMENT GARTER SPRINGS
3/8 INCH — E1ZZ-19E576-A
1/2 INCH — E1ZZ-19E576-B
5/8 INCH — E35Y-19E576-A
ALSO AVAILABLE IN
E35Y-19D690-A KIT

❶ CHECK FOR MISSING OR DAMAGED GARTER
SPRING—REMOVE DAMAGED SPRING WITH
SMALL HOOKED WIRE—INSTALL NEW
SPRING IF DAMAGED OR MISSING.

PUSH TOOL INTO CAGE

② PUSH THE TOOL INTO THE CAGE OPENING
TO RELEASE THE FEMALE FITTING
FROM THE GARTER SPRING.

A — CLEAN FITTINGS

B — INSTALL NEW
O-RINGS—USE ONLY
SPECIFIED O-RINGS
—SUPPLIED IN
E35Y-19D690-A KIT

C — LUBRICATE WITH
CLEAN REFRIGERANT
OIL

D — ASSEMBLE
FITTING TOGETHER
BY PUSHING WITH A
SLIGHT TWISTING
MOTION

❷

③ PULL THE COUPLING MALE AND
FEMALE FITTINGS APART.

GARTER SPRING

❸ TO ENSURE COUPLING ENGAGEMENT,
VISUALLY CHECK TO BE SURE GARTER
SPRING IS OVER FLARED END OF FEMALE FITTING.

④ REMOVE THE TOOL FROM THE
DISCONNECTED SPRING LOCK COUPLING.

3.24   When disconnecting and connecting spring lock coupling fittings, refer to this illustration for the proper garter
spring, O-ring and spring lock coupling tool part numbers

3.28 If the spring lock couplings are equipped with safety clips, pry them off with a small screwdriver

3.29 Open the spring-loaded halves of the spring lock coupling tool and place it in position around the coupling, then close it

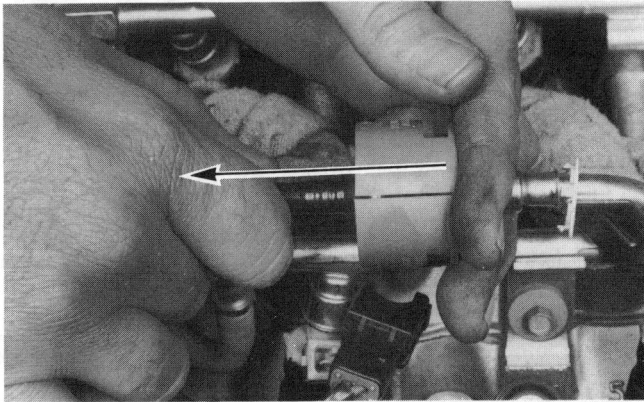

3.30 To disconnect the coupling, push the tool into the cage opening to release the female fitting from the garter spring, then pull the male and female fittings apart

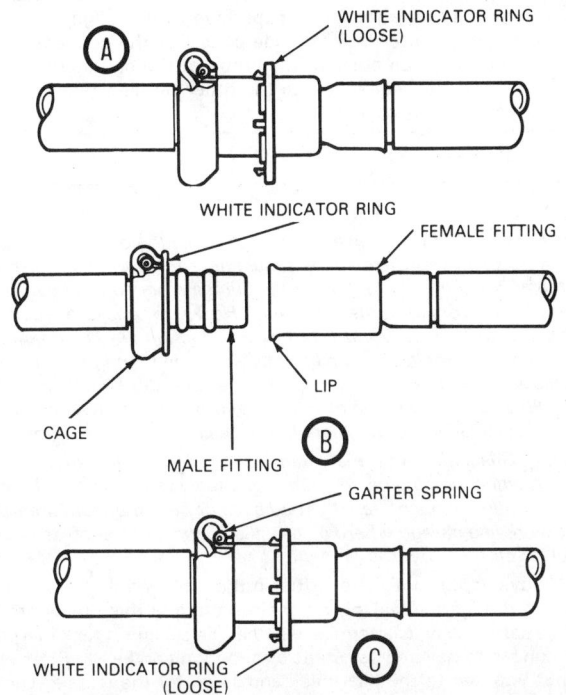

3.37 Spring lock coupling reconnection

a) *Before disassembly, locate the white indicator ring which may have slipped down the length of the fuel line.*
b) *After fittings have been separated, insert the white indicator ring into the cage on the male fitting.*
c) *At reassembly, the white indicator ring will pop free of the cage on the male fitting when the joint is fully made. This signifies that the garter spring inside the cage of the male fitting is properly seated over the lip of the female connector.*

at the engine fuel rail end. The male end of the spring lock coupling, which is girded by two O-rings, is inserted into a female flared end engine fitting. The coupling is secured by a garter spring which prevents disengagement by gripping the flared end of the female fitting **(see illustration)**.

25 The fuel feed and return line fittings are not the same diameter. To disconnect the 1/2-inch fuel feed line coupling, you will need to obtain a spring lock coupling tool D87L-9280-B or its equivalent; for the 3/8-inch return fitting, get tool D87L-9280-A or its equivalent (Ford dealers may not have these tools on hand, but they are readily available from manufacturers like Kent-Moore, Snap-on and Mac).

Disconnecting the coupling

26 Before detaching the spring lock coupling fittings, relieve the system fuel pressure (see Section 2).
27 Detach the cable from the negative terminal of the battery.
28 Pry the safety clip from each fitting with a small screwdriver **(see illustration)**.
29 Place the appropriately sized spring lock coupling disconnect tool in position **(see illustration)**.
30 Close the tool and push it into the open side of the cage to expand the garter spring and release the female fitting **(see illustration)**. **Note:** *The garter spring may not release if the tool is cocked while pushing it into the cage opening.*
31 Once the garter spring is expanded, pull the fittings apart.
32 Remove the tool.

Connecting the coupling

33 Make sure that the garter spring is in the cage of the male fitting. If it's missing, install a new spring by pushing it into the cage opening. If the garter spring is damaged, remove it from the cage with a small wire hook (do not use a screwdriver) and install a new spring (see illustration 3.24 for garter spring sizes).
34 Clean all dirt or foreign material from both pieces of the coupling.
Warning: *Use only the specified O-rings — they are made of a special*

material and the use of any other O-ring may allow the connection to leak intermittently during vehicle operation.
35 Lubricate the male fitting and O-rings and inside of the the female fitting with clean engine oil.
36 Install the plastic indicator ring into the cage opening if the indicator ring is to be used.
37 Fit the female fitting onto the male fitting and push them together until the garter spring snaps over the flared end of the female fitting. **Note:** *If the fitting is equipped with a plastic indicator ring, the ring will snap out of the cage opening when the coupling is connected to indicate engagement. If no indicator ring is used, make sure that the coupling is engaged by visual verification that the garter spring is over the flared end of the female fitting* **(see illustration)**.

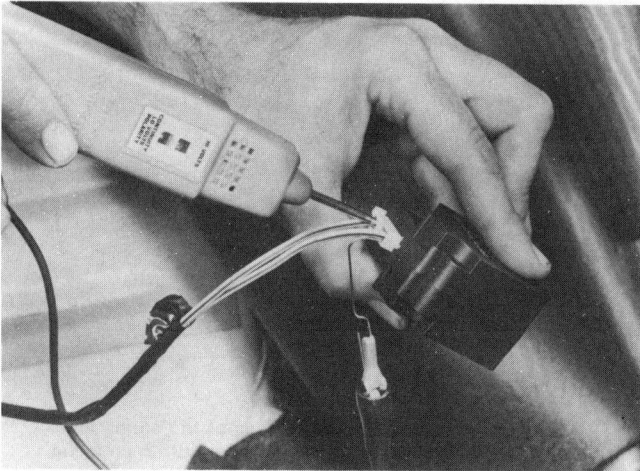

4.3 With the ignition switch off, check the inertia switch for continuity by attaching a paper clip to the alligator clip and poking it into the back side of one of the connector terminals, then pushing the probe of the continuity tester/test light into the other terminal

4 Fuel pump — check

Refer to illustrations 4.3 and 4.4

Note: *The electric fuel pump and circuit are an integral part of the EEC-IV system, so a complete diagnosis must determine whether the pump and the circuit are operating properly. Such a procedure is beyond the scope of the average home mechanic. However, a loss of fuel flow and/or pressure, usually indicated by a reduction in performance, is often a sign that the fuel pump has malfunctioned. Therefore, perform the following rudimentary check of the pump if the above symptoms occur. Further investigation of the fuel pump circuit, however, should be left to a qualified professional at a dealer service department.*

Warning: *Gasoline is extremely flammable, so extra precautions must be taken when working on any part of the fuel system. DO NOT smoke or allow open flames or bare light bulbs in or near the work area. And don't work in a garage where a natural gas appliance such as a water heater or clothes dryer is present.*

1   Always verify that there is fuel in the tank and that none of the lines and fittings are leaking fuel before starting this procedure.
2   The easiest way to determine whether the electric in-tank fuel pump is working is to have an assistant turn the ignition key to Start while you put your ear to the filler neck and listen for the telltale whirring sound that indicates the pump is operating. If the pump is silent, proceed to the next Step.
3   Locate the inertia switch (see Section 2) and, using a self-powered test light or continuity tester, make sure that it is allowing current to reach the pump **(see illustration)**. If the switch has opened the circuit, reset it.
4   Lower the fuel tank (see Section 5) and, again using a self-powered test light or continuity tester, check the continuity of the pump positive and ground terminals **(see illustration)**.

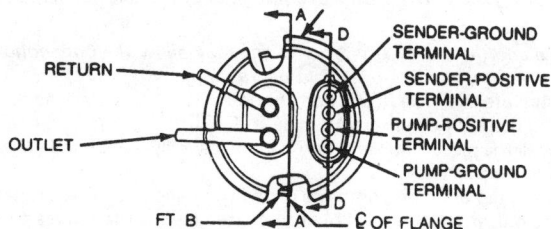

4.4 With the ignition switch off, check continuity between the pump positive and ground terminals — if continuity exists, determine whether the pump is operating by applying battery voltage to the pump positive terminal with a fused jumper cable

5   If there is no continuity, the pump is defective. Replace it (see Section 7).
6   If there is continuity, bypass the pump circuit and, using a fused jumper wire, apply battery voltage to the positive terminal of the pump. It should operate.
7   If the pump operates, there is an open in the circuit somewhere between the battery and the pump terminal. Troubleshoot and repair it (refer to the Wiring Diagrams at the end of this book).
8   If the pump doesn't operate, replace it (see Section 7).
9   Any further testing of the electric fuel pump, its relay or the circuit should be conducted by a dealer service department.

5 Fuel tank — removal and installation

Refer to illustrations 5.5, 5.8, 5.9a and 5.9b
Note: *Don't begin this procedure until the gauge indicates that the tank is empty or nearly empty. If the tank must be removed when it's full (for example, if the fuel pump malfunctions), siphon any remaining fuel from the tank prior to removal.*

Warning: *Gasoline is extremely flammable so extra precautions must be taken when working on any part of the fuel system. DO NOT smoke or allow open flames or bare light bulbs in or near the work area. Also, don't work in a garage if a natural gas appliance such as a water heater or clothes dryer is present.*

1   Relieve the fuel pressure (see Section 2).
2   Detach the cable from the negative terminal of the battery.
3   Raise the vehicle and support it securely on jackstands.
4   Unless the vehicle has been driven far enough to completely empty the tank, it's a good idea to siphon the residual fuel out before removing the tank from the vehicle. Siphon or pump the fuel out through the fuel filler pipe. A small diameter hose may be necessary because of the small trap door installed in the fuel filler pipe to prevent vapors from escaping during refueling. Fuel injected vehicles have reservoirs inside the tank to maintain fuel near the pump pick-up during vehicle cornering maneuvers and when the fuel level is low. The reservoirs could prevent siphon tubes or hoses from reaching the bottom of the fuel tank. This situation can be overcome by repositioning the siphon hose several times.
5   Loosen the hose clamps securing the fuel filler neck hose and the breather hose to the fuel tank **(see illustration)** and detach both hoses.

5.5 Before dropping the fuel tank, be sure to detach the fuel filler and breather hoses (arrows) — the right tank strap bolt is also visible in this photo (the left strap bolt, not shown, is on the other side of the spare tire well)

6   Place a transmission jack or floor jack under the tank and position a block of wood between the jack pad and the tank. Raise the jack until it's supporting the tank.
7   Remove the bolts from the rear ends of the fuel tank straps. The straps are hinged at the front end so you can swing them forward and down out of the way.
8   Gently lower the tank, slightly tilting it to the right and sliding it

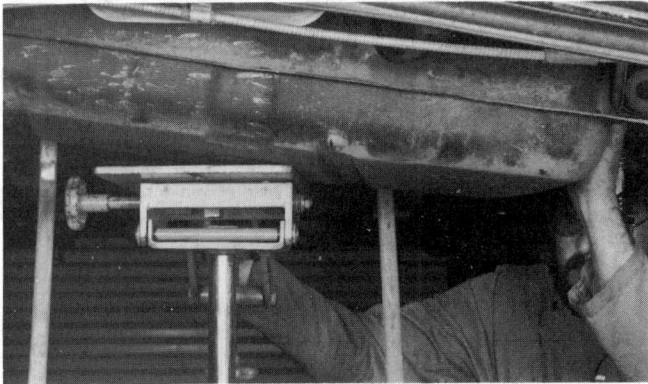

5.8 Drop the right side of the tank like this and slide the tank to the right a little when lowering it so the seam can clear the exhaust pipe

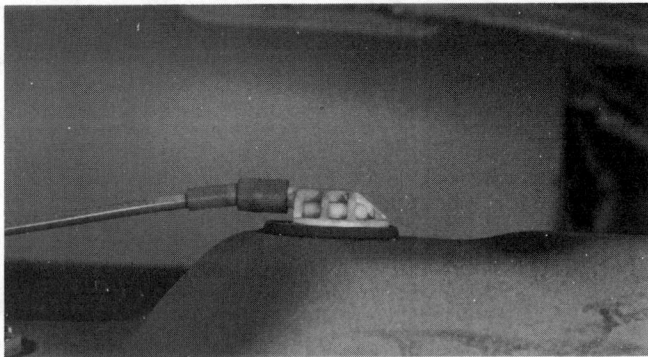

5.9b Detach the fuel vapor line, then remove the tank

toward the right to clear the exhaust pipe on the left **(see illustration)**. When the tank is low enough to allow access to the fuel lines, vapor hose and electrical connector, stop.

9   Unplug the electrical connector from the sending unit/fuel pump terminal **(see illustration)**, detach the fuel feed and return lines from the fuel tank (see Section 3), and detach the fuel vapor line from the vapor orifice **(see illustration)**. When all the connectors and fittings are disconnected, remove the tank from the vehicle.

10 If you're replacing the tank, or having it cleaned or repaired, refer to Section 7 and remove the sender unit (carburetor equipped vehicles) or fuel pump/sending unit (fuel injected vehicles). For information regarding tank cleaning and repair, refer to Section 6.

11 Refer to Section 7 and install the fuel pump/sending unit.

12 Installation is the reverse of removal.

---

6 Fuel tank cleaning and repair — general information

1   Repairs to the fuel tank or filler neck should be peformed by a professional with the proper training to carry out this critical and potentially dangerous work. Even after cleaning and flushing, explosive fumes can remain and could explode during repair of the tank.

2   If the fuel tank is removed from the vehicle, it should not be placed in an area where sparks or open flames could ignite the fumes coming out of the tank. Be especially careful inside garages where a natural gas appliance is located because the pilot light could cause an explosion.

---

7 Fuel pump — removal and installation

Refer to illustration 7.4

Warning: *Gasoline is extremely flammable, so extra precautions must be taken when working on any part of the fuel system. DO NOT smoke or allow open flames or bare light bulbs in or near the work area. Also,*

5.9a Once the tank is clear of the exhaust pipe and low enough to get at the sending unit/fuel pump electrical connector and fuel feed and return line fittings, disconnect them

don't work in a garage if a natural gas appliance such as a water heater or clothes dryer is present.

1   Relieve the fuel system pressure (see Section 2).

2   Remove the fuel tank (see Section 5).

3   Remove any dirt that has accumulated around the fuel pump attaching flange so that it won't fall into the tank when the fuel pump/sending unit is pulled out.

4   Using a **brass** punch, tap the lock ring counterclockwise until it's loose. Carefully pull the the fuel pump/sending unit assembly **(see illustration)** from the tank.

5   Remove the old lock ring gasket and discard it.

6   If you're planning to reinstall the original fuel pump/sending unit,

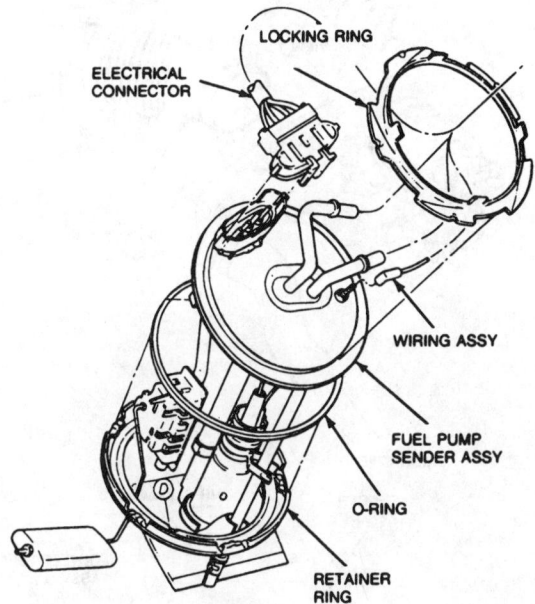

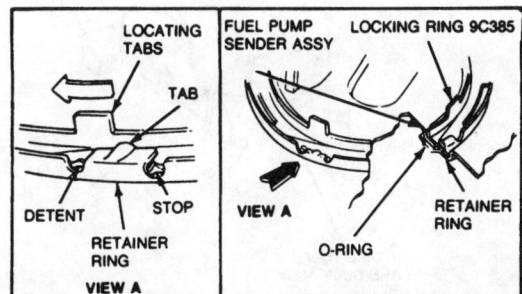

7.4 An exploded view of the sending unit/fuel pump assembly

remove the strainer, wash it in clean solvent, then push it back onto the metal pipe on the end of the pump. If you're installing a new pump/ sending unit, the assembly will include a new strainer.

7   Clean the fuel pump mounting flange and the tank mounting surface and seal ring groove.

8   Installation is the reverse of removal. Apply a thin coat of heavy grease to the new lock ring gasket to hold it in place during assembly.

8 Air cleaner housing — removal and installation

Refer to illustrations 8.1a, 8.1b and 8.1c

Removal

1   Loosen the air cleaner outlet tube clamp and disconnect the tube **(see illustrations)**.

2   Disconnect the vent hoses from the air cleaner cover.

3   Disconnect the hot air tube (four-cylinder engine only), the PCV inlet tube and the zip tube.

4   Disconnect the cold weather modulator vacuum hose at the temperature sensor (four-cylinder engine only).

5   Remove the air cleaner, retaining clips and air cleaner assembly.

6   Inspect the inside surfaces of the cover for traces of dirt leakage past the filter element. If dirt is evident, check the element seals for damage, verify that the right element is being used and make sure that the retaining clips are providing sufficient clamping force to keep the cover and housing together.

7   Remove the air cleaner element and clean the sealing surfaces on the tray and cover.

8   Install a new element (see Chapter 1) only after inspecting it for any damage — such as deformed seals or holes in the paper — that may have occurred during handling.

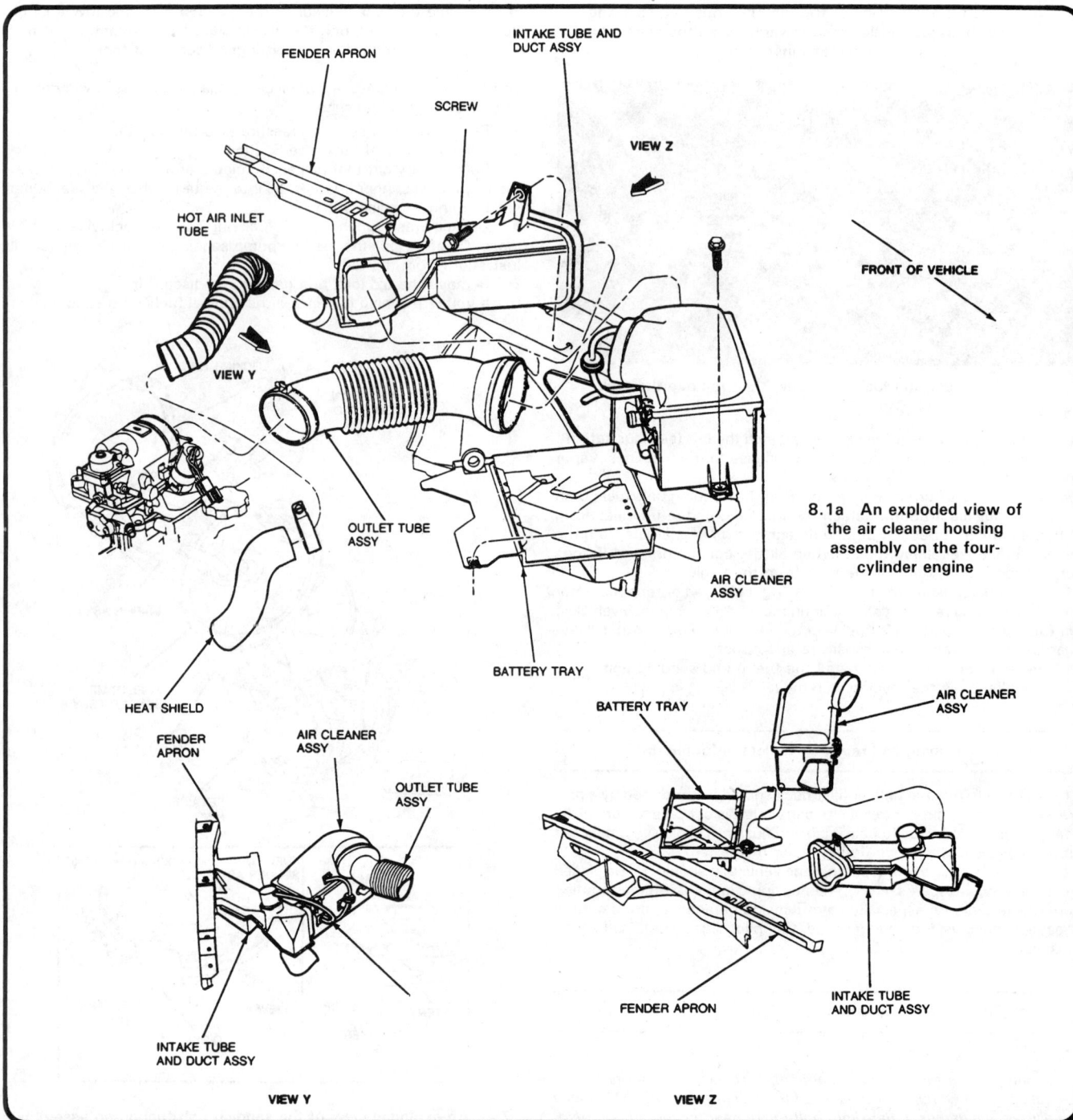

8.1a An exploded view of the air cleaner housing assembly on the four-cylinder engine

AIR CLEANER ASSY

BATTERY TRAY

INTAKE TUBE AND DUCT ASSY

FRONT OF VEHICLE

OUTLET TUBE ASSY

VIEW Z

FENDER APRON

VIEW Z

MANIFOLD ASSY

SCREW

BATTERY TRAY GROMMET

AIR CLEANER ASSY

INTAKE TUBE AND DUCT ASSY

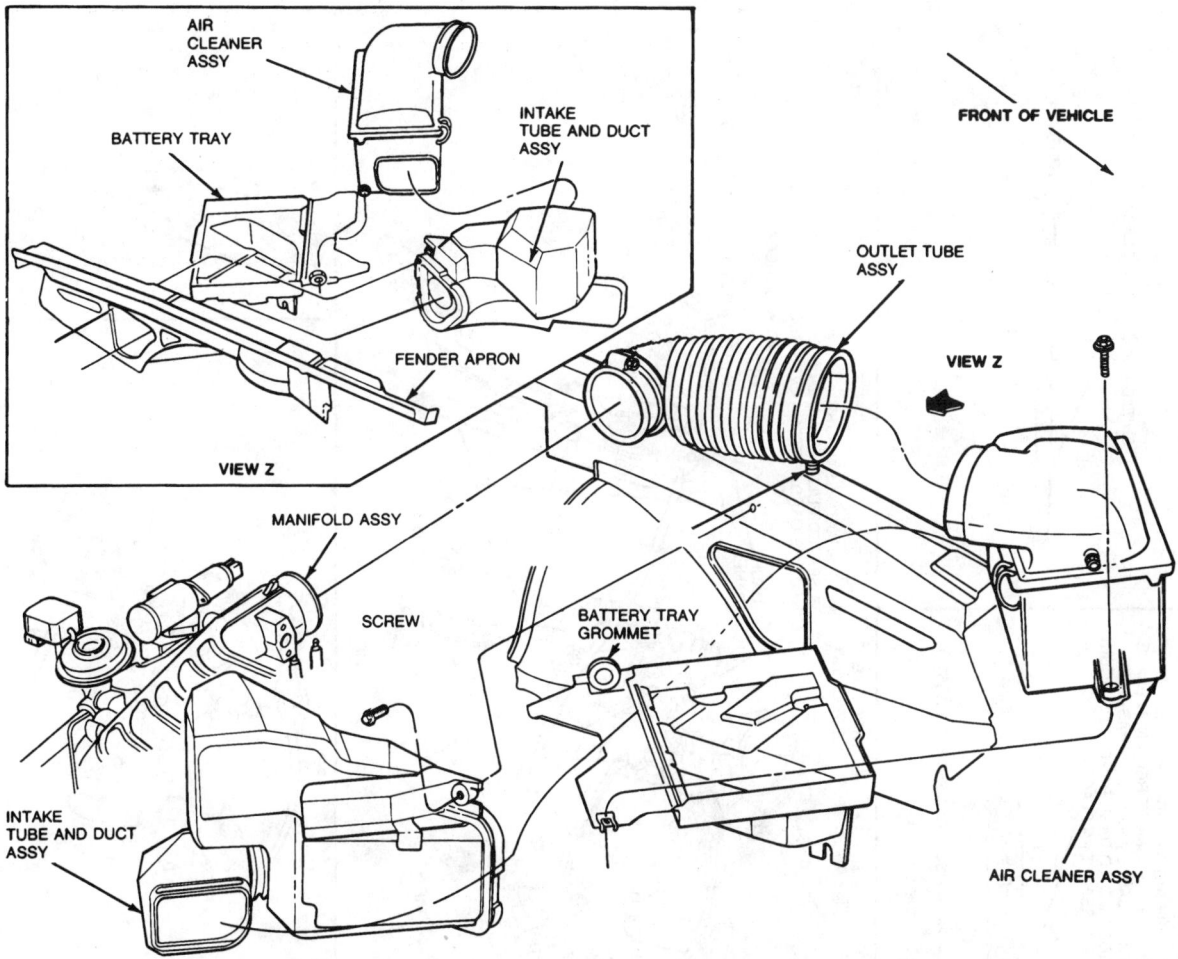

8.1b   An exploded view of the air cleaner housing assembly on the 3.0L V6 engine

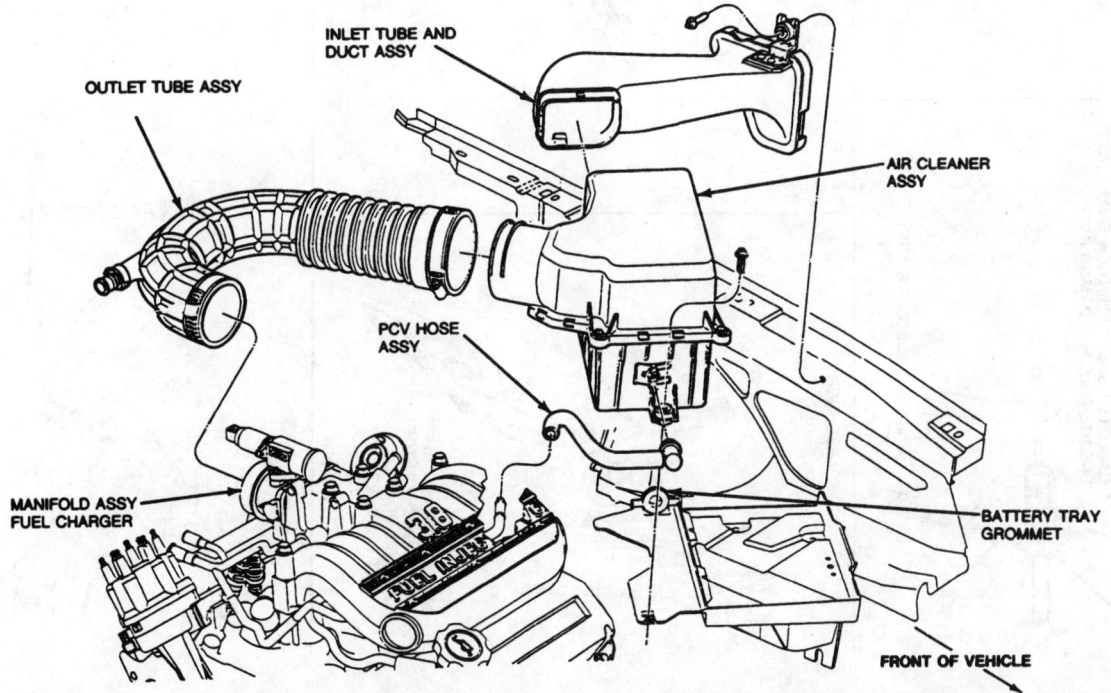

INLET TUBE AND DUCT ASSY

OUTLET TUBE ASSY

AIR CLEANER ASSY

PCV HOSE ASSY

MANIFOLD ASSY FUEL CHARGER

BATTERY TRAY GROMMET

FRONT OF VEHICLE

8.1c   An exploded view of the air cleaner housing assembly on the 3.8L V6 engine

154

SHIELD COLOR CODE BLACK

NOTE:
ACCELERATOR CABLE PROTECTIVE
COVER MUST REMAIN IN PLACE
UNTIL CABLE ASSY HAS BEEN
SECURED TO DASH PANEL AND SOUND
ABSORBER IS IN PLACE

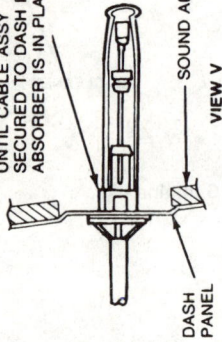

SOUND ABSORBER ASSY

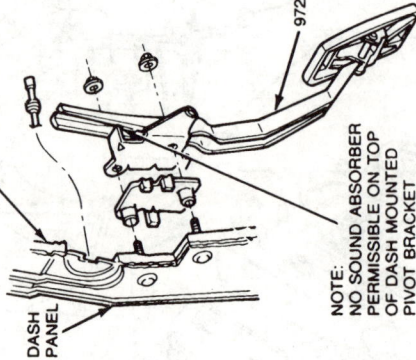

DASH PANEL

VIEW V

NOTE: SNAP CABLE HOUSING INTO DASH
PANEL BY ALIGNING LOCATOR ON CABLE
HOUSING WITH LOCATOR ON DASH PANEL.
CABLE HOUSING RETENTION SNAPS MUST
ENGAGE FULLY INTO DASH PANEL

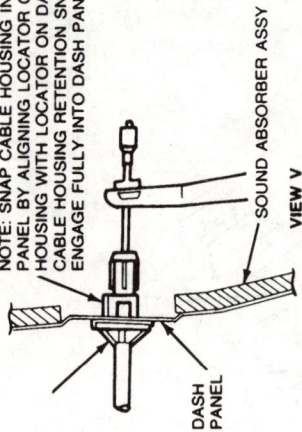

SOUND ABSORBER ASSY

DASH PANEL

VIEW V

SHAFT ASSY MUST
BE SEATED FULLY UPWARD
INTO THE CARBURETOR LEVER ASSY.

SOUND ABSORBER ASSY

SLIDING INNER MEMBER

DASH PANEL

VIEW V

VIEW W

VIEW X

7F332 ASSY

VIEW Z

THROTTLE LEVER ASSY

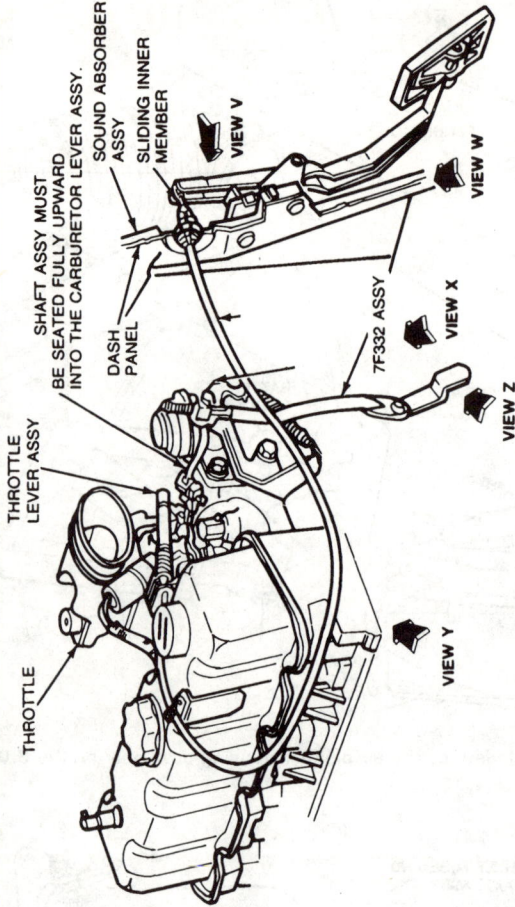

THROTTLE

VIEW Y

SOUND ABSORBER ASSY

DASH PANEL

9726 ASSY

NOTE:
NO SOUND ABSORBER
PERMISSIBLE ON TOP
OF DASH MOUNTED
PIVOT BRACKET

VIEW W

INTAKE MANIFOLD

VIEW X

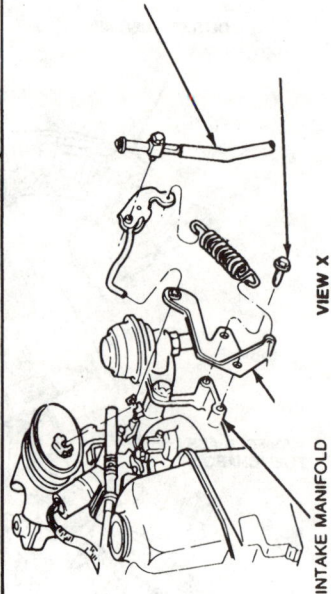

TRANSMISSION LEVER

VIEW Z

INTAKE MANIFOLD

VIEW Y

9.2 A typical throttle cable assembly (four-cylinder engine with automatic transaxle shown)

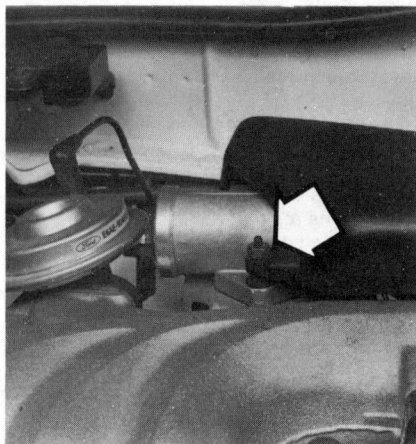

9.6a To remove the snow shield from the 3.0L V6, remove the nut (arrow) . . .

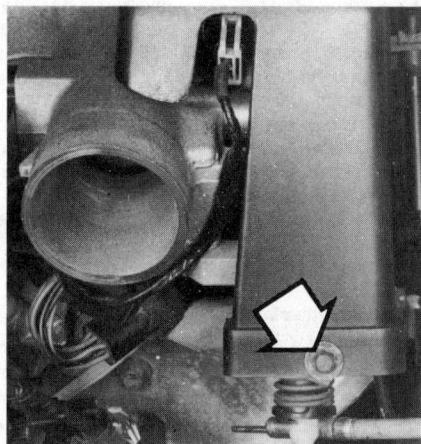

9.6b . . . and the bolt (arrow)

9.6c To remove the snow shield from the 3.8L V6, remove the two nuts (arrows)

Installation

9 Position the air cleaner assembly on the battery tray. Ensure that the mounting grommet is installed with the metal side up and the battery tray grommet is fully seated in the tray. Check the air cleaner cover hinge assembly. Tighten the retaining clips. **Note:** *The air cleaner assembly mounting tab must be engaged with the battery tray grommet.*

10 Install the screw through the rubber grommet (metal side up) into the J-clip in the battery tray.

11 If your vehicle is equipped with a four-cylinder engine, connect the cold weather modulator vacuum hose to the temperature sensor.

12 Connect the hot air inlet tube (four-cylinder engine only), PCV inlet tube, pulse air tube and zip tube.

13 Install the air cleaner outlet air tube. Tighten the clamp securely.

14 Connect the vent hoses to the air cleaner cover.

15 Start the engine and check for vacuum leaks around both ends of the the tube from the air cleaner to the throttle body. Service as required.

9   Throttle linkage components — removal and installation

Refer to illustrations 9.2, 9.6a, 9.6b, 9.6c, 9.7 and 9.8

Note: *The cable installation on your vehicle may differ somewhat from the illustrations shown here. If so, refer to the accompanying illustrations of other typical installations included within this Section.*

1 Detach the cable from the negative terminal of the battery, then remove the air cleaner outlet tube, if necessary (see Section 8).

2 Detach the cable snap-in nylon bushing from the accelerator pedal arm **(see illustration)**.

3 Detach the cable housing from the firewall by pinching the two tabs together and pushing them out from inside the passenger compartment.

4 Detach the cable from the retainer on the rocker arm cover.

5 Detach the cruise control cable from the accelerator cable, if so equipped.

6 Remove the snowshield, if equipped **(see illustrations)**.

7 Disconnect the cable at the throttle lever by inserting a screwdriver between the cable and the throttle lever and twisting the screwdriver **(see illustration)**.

8 Remove the screw attaching the cable housing to the engine mounting bracket **(see illustration)** and detach the cable from the bracket slot.

9 Installation is the reverse of removal.

10   Fuel injection system — general information

Central fuel injection

The Central Fuel Injection (CFI) system is a single point pulse time

9.7 To detach the throttle cable from the throttle lever arm, insert a small screwdriver between the cable end and the stud on the lever arm, then twist the screwdriver and the cable will pop loose (3.0L V6 engine shown, all others similar)

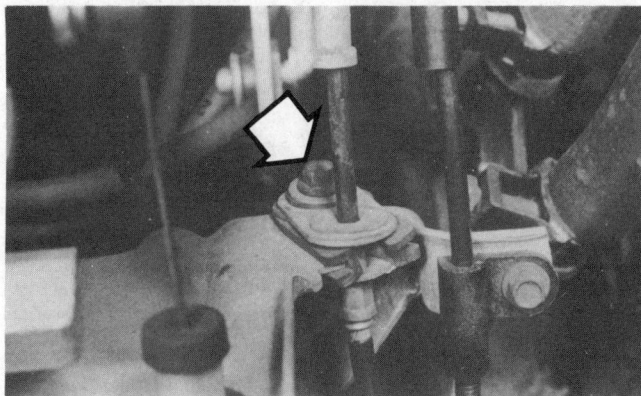

9.8 To detach the cable from the cable bracket, remove the retainer bolt (arrow) and slide the cable from its slot in the bracket (3.0L engine shown, 3.8L V6 similar)

modulated injection system. Fuel is metered into the air intake stream in accordance with engine demands by a single solenoid injection valve mounted in a throttle body on the intake manifold.

Fuel is supplied from the fuel tank by a low pressure, electric fuel pump mounted in the fuel tank. The fuel is filtered and sent to the fuel charging assembly injector fuel cavity and then to the regulator where the fuel delivery pressure is maintained at a nominal value of 14.5 psi. A single injector nozzle is mounted vertically above the throttle plates and connected in series with the fuel pressure regulator. Excess fuel supplied by the pump but not needed by the engine is returned to the fuel tank by a steel fuel return line.

The fuel charging assembly consists of five individual components which perform the fuel and air metering function. The throttle body assembly is attached to the conventional carburetor mounting pad on the intake manifold and houses the air control system, fuel injector nozzle, fuel pressure regulator, fuel pressure diagnostic valve, cold engine speed control and throttle position sensor.

Air flow to the engine is controlled by a single butterfly valve mounted in a two piece, die-cast aluminum housing called a throttle body. The butterfly valve is identical in configuration to the throttle plates of a conventional carburetor and is actuated by a similar pedal and linkage arrangement.

The fuel injector nozzle is mounted vertically above the throttle plate and is an electro-mechanical device which meters and atomizes the fuel delivered to the engine. The injector valve body consists of a solenoid actuated ball and seat valve assembly.

An electrical control signal from the EEC electronic processor activates the solenoid, causing the ball to move off the seat and allows fuel to flow. The injector flow orifice is fixed and the fuel supply is constant. Therefore, fuel flow to the engine is controlled by how long the solenoid is energized.

The pressure regulator is integral to the fuel charging main body near the rear of the air horn surface. The regulator is located so as to nullify the effects of the supply line pressure drops. Its design is such that it is not sensitive to back pressure in the return line to the tank.

A second function of the pressure regulator is to maintain fuel supply pressure upon fuel pump shutdown. The regulator functions as a downstream check valve and traps the fuel between itself and the fuel pump. The constant fuel pressure level after engine shutdown precludes fuel line vapor formation and allows for rapid restarts and stable idle operation immediately thereafter.

It regulates the fuel pressure to the injector nozzles at a constant nominal value of 14.5 psi.

The throttle actuator controls idle speed by modulating the throttle lever for the required air flow to maintain the desired engine rpm for any operating condition, from an idling cold engine to a warm engine at normal operating temperature. An idle tracking switch (ITS) determines when the throttle lever has contacted the actuator, signalling the need to control engine rpm. The DC motor extends or retracts a linear shaft through a gear reduction system. The motor direction is determined by the polarity of the applied voltage.

A throttle position sensor (non-adjustable) is mounted to the throttle shaft on the choke side of the fuel charging assembly and is used to supply a voltage output proportional to the change in the throttle position. The TP sensor is used by the computer (EEC) to determine the operation mode (closed throttle, part throttle and wide open throttle) for selection of the proper fuel mixture, spark and EGR at all engine speeds and loads.

Electronic Fuel Injection (EFI) system

The Electronic Fuel Injection (EFI) system used on the V6 engines is known as a multi-point, pulse time, speed density control design. On the 3.0L V6, fuel is metered into the intake air stream in accordance with engine demand through six injectors mounted on a tuned intake manifold. The injectors are energized in two groups of three injectors. Each group is activated once every other crankshaft revolution. On the 3.8L V6, fuel is metered into each intake port in a simultaneous triple-fire pattern: Injectors 1, 2 and 4 fire simultaneously, as do injectors 3, 5 and 6, to follow the engine firing order in accordance with engine demand through six injectors mounted on a tuned intake manifold.

On both systems, an on-board Electronic Engine Control (EEC-IV) computer accepts inputs from various engine sensors to compute the required fuel flow rate necessary to maintain a prescribed air/fuel ratio throughout the entire engine operational range. The computer then outputs a command to the fuel injectors to meter the approximate quantity of fuel.

The period of time that the injectors are energized (known as ''on time'' or ''pulse width'') is controlled by the EEC computer. Air entering the engine is sensed by speed, pressure and temperature sensors. The outputs of these sensors are processed by the EEC-IV computer. The computer determines the needed injector pulse width and outputs a command to the injector to meter the exact quantity of fuel.

The EEC-IV engine control system also determines and compensates for the age of the vehicle and its uniqueness and it even senses and

compensates for changes in altitude.

The fuel delivery systems for both designs are similar: An electric in-tank fuel pump forces pressurized fuel through a series of metal and plastic lines and an inline fuel filter/reservoir to the fuel charging manifold assembly.

The fuel charging manifold assembly incorporates electrically actuated fuel injectors directly above each intake port. When energized, the injectors spray a metered quantity of fuel into the intake air stream.

A constant fuel pressure drop is maintained across the injector nozzles by a pressure regulator. The regulator is connected in series with the fuel injectors and is positioned downstream from them. Excess fuel passes through the regulator and returns to the fuel tank through a fuel return line.

11 Fuel injection system — pressure check

Warning: *Gasoline is extremely flammable, so extra precautions must be taken when working on any part of the fuel system. DO NOT smoke or allow open flames or bare light bulbs in or near the work area. Also, don't work in a garage if a natural gas appliance such as a water heater or clothes dryer is present.*

Four-cylinder engine

Refer to illustration 11.1

1   The CFI fuel charging assembly is equipped with either hairpin clip type fittings (utilized on earlier systems) or spring lock coupling type fittings (used on later CFI systems). In either case, you will need to fabricate a special adapter setup for your standard fuel pressure gauge before you can attach it inline between the fuel feed line and the fuel charging assembly **(see illustration)**.

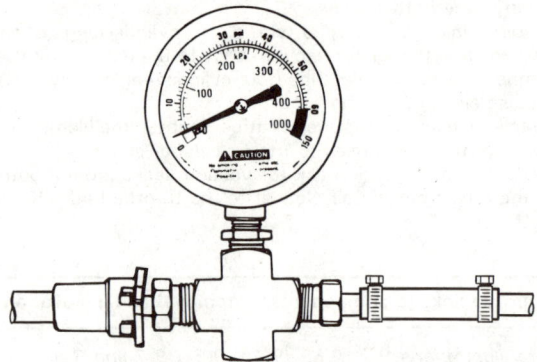

11.1 To adapt a standard fuel pressure gauge for use with a CFI assembly equipped with hairpin clip type fuel fittings, get a T-fitting that accepts the pressure gauge threaded fitting, two threaded male adapters — with male ends having an OD equal to the ID of the Ford hairpin clip type push connect fuel fitting (see Section 3) — then screw them into the T-fitting and assemble as shown here

2   Relieve the system fuel pressure (see Section 2).
3   Disconnect the fuel feed line hairpin clip type or spring lock type coupling and detach the fuel feed line (the bigger one) from the fuel charging assembly (see Section 3).
4   Install the fuel pressure gauge and adapter between the disconnected fuel line and the fuel charging assembly.
5   Reset the inertia switch (see Section 2).
6   Start the engine, check the fuel system pressure at idle and compare it to the specified fuel pressure. Accelerate the engine. The pressure should remain stable regardless of engine rpm.
7   If the indicated pressure is higher than specified, either the fuel pressure regulator is stuck closed (see Section 12) or there is an obstruction in the fuel return line.
8   If the indicated pressure is less than specified, either the fuel pump is malfunctioning (see Section 4), the injector is leaking (see Section 12), the fuel feed line is blocked or there is a leak somewhere in either the fuel feed or the fuel return line (see Section 3).
9   Relieve the system fuel pressure again, remove the gauge and reattach the line to the fuel charging assembly.
10   Reset the inertia switch, start the engine and check for leaks.

12.2 Before removing the fuel injector from the fuel charging assembly main body, unplug the electrical connector and set it aside, then remove the screw (arrow) and the retainer

V6 engines

11 With a Ford T80L-9974-B fuel pressure gauge (or equivalent) and adapter T85L-9974-A (or equivalent), the fuel pressure of all EFI equipped V6 engines can be measured easily and quickly. These models are equipped with Schrader valves, so it is not necessary to detach any fuel lines to read the fuel pressure.

12 The special Ford fuel pressure gauge/adapter assembly specified above is designed to *relieve* fuel pressure, as well as measure it, through the Schrader valve. If you have this gauge, you can use this method as an alternative to the fuel pressure relief procedure outlined in Section 2. **Warning:** *Never, however, attempt to relieve fuel pressure through the Schrader valve without this special setup.*

13 To attach the gauge, simply remove the valve cap, screw on the adapter and attach the gauge to the adapter.

14 Start the engine and allow it to reach a steady idle. Note the indicated fuel pressure reading and compare it to the specified pressure.

15 If the indicated fuel pressure is lower than specified, the problem is probably either a leaking fuel line, a malfunctioning fuel pump or a leaking injector.

16 If the indicated pressure is higher than specified, the cause could be a blocked fuel line or a stuck fuel pressure regulator. Refer to whichever of the following Sections that applies to the fuel injection system in your vehicle.

---

12 Central Fuel Injection (CFI) system — component replacement

---

Warning: *Gasoline is extremely flammable, so extra precautions must be taken when working on any part of the fuel system. DO NOT smoke or allow open flames or bare light bulbs in or near the work area. Also, don't work in a garage if a natural gas appliance such as a water heater or clothes dryer is present.*

Fuel injector

Refer to illustrations 12.2, 12.3a, 12.3b, 12.4, 12.5a and 12.5b

Note: *If you're replacing the fuel injector, it isn't necessary to remove the throttle body from the intake manifold. If, however, you need to replace the base gasket, the spacer gasket between the main body and the throttle body or the idle speed control (ISC) throttle actuator, the throttle body must be removed from the intake manifold. Other than the components specifically mentioned here, we do not recommend further disassembly of the fuel charging assembly.*

1 Detach the cable from the negative terminal of the battery.

2 Unplug the fuel injector wire harness connector and remove the screw and retainer **(see illustration)**.

3 Using a screwdriver, carefully pry the fuel injector out of the fuel charging assembly **(see illustrations)**.

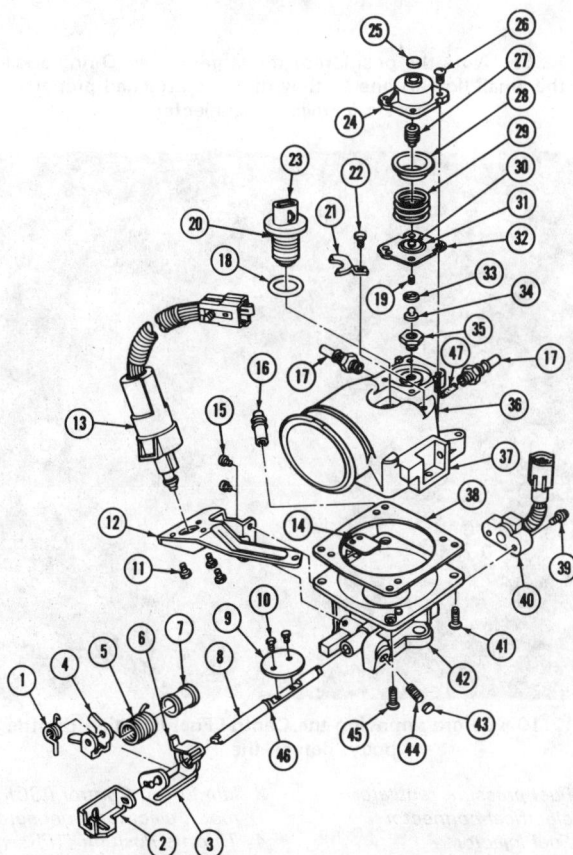

12.3a An exploded view of the CFI assembly

1 *Engine idle speed-up spring*	26 *Screw*
2 *Transmission linkage lever*	27 *Fuel pressure regulator*
3 *Throttle lever ball*	*adjusting screw*
4 *Idle speed-up control lever*	28 *Fuel pressure regulator cup*
5 *Throttle return spring*	29 *Fuel pressure regulator*
6 *Throttle lever*	*diaphragm spring*
7 *Throttle control*	30 *Fuel pressure regulator*
linkage bearing	*valve body*
8 *Air intake charge*	31 *Fuel pressure regulator*
throttle shaft	*diaphragm retainer*
9 *Air intake charge*	32 *Fuel pressure*
throttle plate	*regulator diaphragm*
10 *Screw*	33 *Fuel pressure regulator*
11 *Self-tapping screw*	*valve retainer*
12 *Engine throttle*	34 *Fuel pressure regulator*
positioner bracket	*valve assembly*
13 *ISC control assembly*	35 *Fuel pressure regulator*
14 *Engine air distribution plate*	*outlet tube*
15 *Screw*	36 *Fuel charging main*
16 *Emission inlet tube*	*body assembly*
17 *Fuel line quick-*	37 *Fuel charging main body*
connect fitting	38 *Fuel charging body gasket*
18 *O-ring*	39 *Screw*
19 *Fuel pressure regulator*	40 *Throttle position sensor*
valve spring	41 *Screw*
20 *O-ring*	42 *Throttle body*
21 *Fuel injector retainer*	43 *Expansion plug*
22 *Screw*	44 *Screw*
23 *Fuel injector*	45 *Screw*
24 *Fuel pressure regulator cover*	46 *Fuel charging shaft seal*
25 *Expansion plug*	47 *Fuel inlet screen*

12.3b   Carefully pry the injector out of the fuel charging assembly main body with a screwdriver

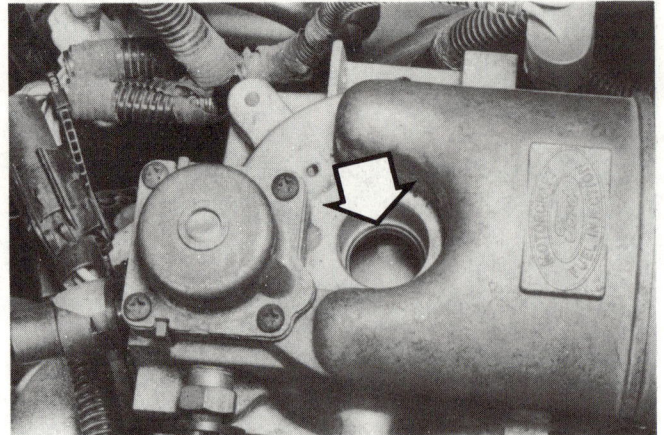

12.4   The small O-ring which seals the lower end of the injector (arrow) will often come off the injector during removal and stick to the walls of the injector bore — be sure to remove it

12.5a   If you're planning to reinstall the old injector, be sure to peel off the O-rings with a small screwdriver and discard them

12.5b   Note the position of the large (upper) O-ring and the small (lower) one — they must be attached properly before installing the injector

4   The injector has two O-rings — a large, upper O-ring and a small, lower one. The lower O-ring may stick to the wall of the fuel injector bore **(see illustration)**. Be sure to remove and discard it.

5   Whether you're replacing the injector or reinstalling the original, do not reuse the old O-rings. Carefully peel the O-rings off the old injector **(see illustration)**. Position the new O-rings as shown **(see illustration)** and lubricate them with clean engine oil.

6   Installation of the injector is the reverse of removal.

Base gasket

Refer to illustrations 12.10, 12.14a and 12.14b

7   Relieve the fuel system pressure (see Section 2).

8   Detach the cable from the negative terminal of the battery.

9   Remove the air intake duct (see Section 8).

10   Clearly label the wires and terminals on the throttle body, then unplug and set aside all wires **(see illustration)**.

11   Detach the PCV hose from the throttle body.

12   Detach the fuel pressure and return lines from the fuel charging assembly. (See Section 3 for a detailed description of fuel line fitting removal.)

13   Detach the throttle cable and (if equipped) cruise control cable assembly from the throttle rod (see Chapter 9).

14   If the vehicle is equipped with an automatic transaxle, remove the C-clip **(see illustration)** and detach the transmission downshift rod from the throttle shaft. Push down on the rod to detach it **(see illustration)**.

15   Remove the throttle body mounting nuts and detach the assembly and gasket from the intake manifold.

16   If the gasket was leaking, position a new gasket on the manifold, install the throttle body and tighten the mounting nuts to the specified torque.

17   The remainder of the installation procedure is the reverse of removal.

12.10   Before removing the Central Fuel Injection throttle body, detach the . . .

1   Fuel pressure regulator electrical connector
2   Fuel injector electrical connector
3   Idle Speed Control (ISC) motor electrical connector
4   Throttle Position (TP) sensor electrical connector
5   Fuel line fittings

12.14a If the vehicle is equipped with an automatic transaxle, pop the C-clip loose with a screwdriver, . . .

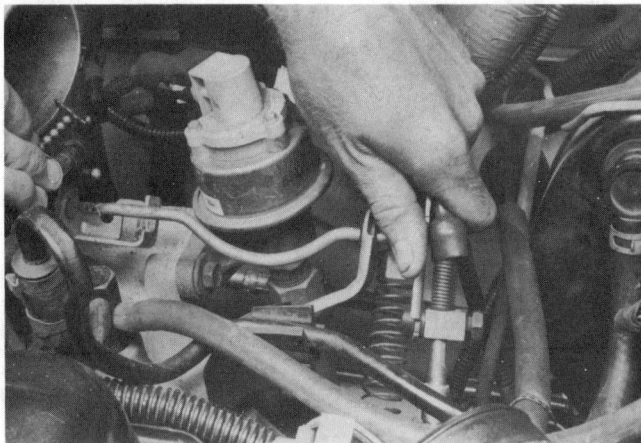

12.14b . . . then disengage the downshift rod from the throttle shaft linkage

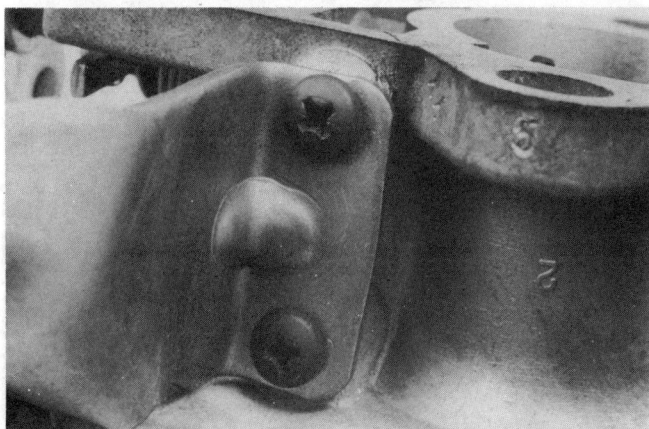

12.19a To remove the ISC motor bracket, lay the throttle body upside down on a workbench and remove these two screws, . . .

12.19b . . . followed by this one

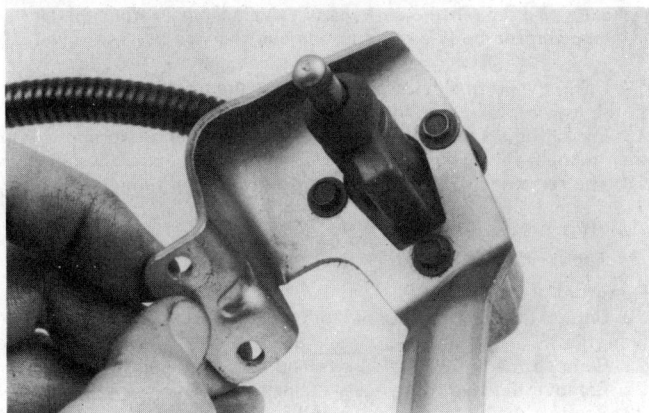

12.20 To detach the ISC motor from the bracket, remove the three mounting screws

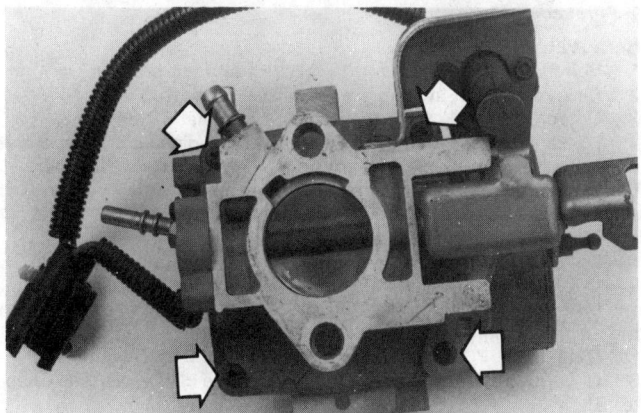

12.23 To separate the throttle body from the main body of the fuel charging assembly, remove the four screws (arrows)

Idle speed control (ISC) motor

Refer to illustrations 12.19a, 12.19b and 12.20

Note: *Handle the throttle body carefully when servicing it on the bench to avoid damage to the throttle plates.*

18 Remove the throttle body (see Steps 7 through 15).
19 Remove the three ISC bracket screws (**see illustrations**) and detach the ISC and bracket assembly from the throttle body.
20 Remove the three ISC mounting screws (**see illustration**) and separate the ISC from the mounting bracket.
21 Installation is the reverse of removal.

Fuel charging body gasket

Refer to illustration 12.23

22 Remove the throttle body and ISC (Steps 7 through 15 and Step 19).
23 Turn the fuel charging assembly over and remove the four screws attaching the throttle body to the fuel charging main body, then separate the two halves (**see illustration**).
24 Remove and discard the old gasket. If it's necessary to use a gasket scraper, don't damage the mating surface.
25 With the main body resting upside down on the bench, place the

13.11   To remove the air intake throttle body assembly, remove all six mounting bolts (arrows) — note that there are three different bolt lengths (two short, two medium and two long ones)

13.12   Lift the air intake throttle body assembly out of the vehicle very carefully to prevent damage to the TP sensor, air bypass valve, EGR valve, etc.

new gasket in position, attach the throttle body, install the four screws and tighten them evenly and securely.
26   Install the ISC and throttle body assembly.

13   Electronic Fuel Injection (EFI) — component replacement (3.0L V6 engine)

Note: *It isn't always necessary to disassemble the entire EFI system to replace most components. To determine what must be removed, carefully read the section which applies to the component(s) you wish to replace.*

Air intake/throttle body assembly
Refer to illustrations 13.11 and 13.12

Note: *If you are simply replacing the gasket between the air intake/ throttle body assembly and the intake manifold, it isn't necessary to remove the various components attached to the throttle body. Simply remove the entire assembly as a unit in accordance with the following procedure.*

Removal
1   Remove the fuel filler cap to relieve fuel tank pressure.
2   Relieve the fuel system pressure (see Section 2).
3   Detach the cable from the negative terminal of the battery.
4   Loosen the hose clamps and remove the engine air cleaner outlet tube between the air cleaner housing and the air throttle body.
5   Unplug the electrical connectors from the Throttle Position (TP) sensor, the air bypass valve, the Air Charge Temperature (ACT) sensor and the pressure feedback electronic EGR transducer.
6   Detach the throttle cable from the throttle linkage (see Section 9).
7   Clearly label, then detach, the main vacuum tree, pressure regulator and MAP sensor vacuum lines from the plenum vacuum tree and detach the single vacuum line from the EGR valve.
8   Detach the PCV hose from the PCV valve (see Chapter 1).
9   Unscrew and detach the EGR pipe from the EGR valve (see Chapter 6).
10   Remove the alternator support brace nut from the stud on the far right (passenger side) of the intake assembly, loosen the nut on the other end of the brace and remove the support brace (see Chapter 5).
11   Remove all six plenum bolts, including the stud on the far right mentioned in the Step above **(see illustration)**. Note that there are three lengths of bolts (two long, two medium and two short). The bolts must be reinstalled in the same holes.
12   Remove the air intake/throttle body assembly **(see illustration)**.
13   Remove and discard the old gasket.

Installation
14   Clean and inspect the mounting faces of the throttle body assembly and the lower intake manifold. Both surfaces must be clean and flat.
15   Clean and oil the manifold stud threads.
16   Install a new gasket.

13.20   To detach the air bypass valve assembly from the air intake throttle body assembly, remove the two bolts (arrows)

17   Using the guide pins as locators, install the throttle body assembly to the lower intake manifold.
18   Install the six bolts (two long, two medium and two short) into their respective holes and tighten them to the specified torque.
19   The remainder of installation is the reverse of removal.

Air bypass valve assembly
Refer to illustration 13.20

Removal
20   Unplug the electrical connector from the air bypass valve **(see illustration)**.
21   Remove the snow shield bolts and detach the snow shield.
22   Remove the two air bypass retaining screws.
23   Remove the air bypass valve and gasket. Discard the old gasket.

Installation
24   Make sure that both the throttle body and the air bypass valve gasket surfaces are clean.
25   Install the gasket on the throttle body surface and place the air bypass valve assembly in position. Install the mounting screws and tighten them securely.
26   The remainder of installation is the reverse of removal.

Throttle Position (TP) sensor
Refer to illustration 13.27

Removal
27   Unplug the throttle position sensor electrical connector **(see illustration)**.

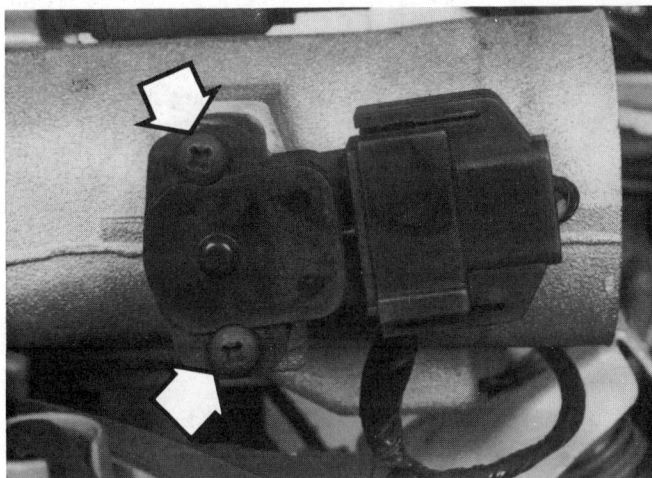

13.27 To remove the Throttle Position (TP) sensor, scribe an alignment mark on the sensor and the throttle body, uplug the wire harness connector, then remove both mounting screws (arrows)

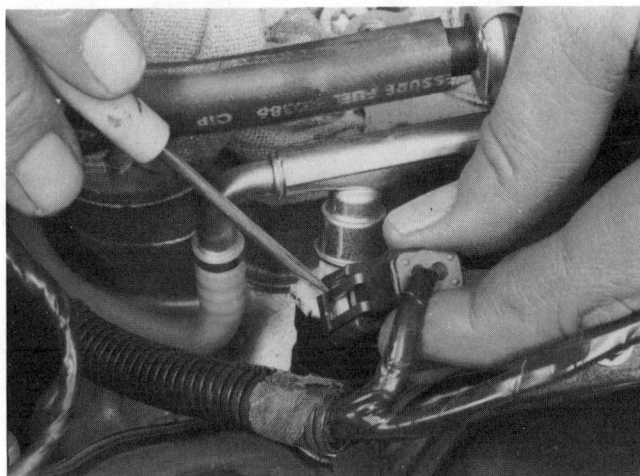

13.36 Use a small screwdriver to loosen the locking tangs on the fuel injector electrical connectors

13.38 To detach the fuel rail from the lower intake manifold, remove all four mounting bolts: two in the front (shown — arrows) and two in the back

13.39 Use a gentle lifting and rocking motion to disengage the fuel rail assembly and fuel injectors from the lower intake manifold (be very careful not to damage the hard rubber hose that connects the front and rear metal fuel rails on the distributor end of the engine — the clearance between the distributor base and the lower intake manifold is very tight)

28 Make scribe marks on the air throttle body and on the throttle position sensor to indicate the proper alignment during installation. **Note:** *The TP sensor is not adjustable, so these marks are very important.*
29 Remove the two throttle position sensor retaining screws.
30 Remove the throttle position sensor.

Installation

31 Ensure that the rotary tangs on the sensor are in proper alignment and that the red seal is inside the connector housing. Slide the rotary tangs into position over the throttle shaft blade, then rotate the TPS clockwise to the installed position. **Caution:** *Failure to install the TPS in this manner may result in excessive idle speeds.*
32 Align the scribe marks on the throttle body and throttle position sensor. Secure the sensor to the throttle body assembly with the two retaining screws and tighten them securely.
33 The remainder of installation is the reverse of removal.

Fuel rail

Refer to illustrations 13.36, 13.38 and 13.39

Removal
34 Remove the air intake throttle body (see above).
35 Detach the vacuum line from the fuel pressure regulator.
36 Using a small screwdriver, carefully unplug the electrical connectors from the fuel injectors (see illustration).
37 Using the special Ford spring lock coupling tool (3/8-inch for front

fitting and 1/2-inch for rear), or equivalent, disconnect the fuel line fittings, disconnect the fuel supply and fuel return lines (see Section 3).
38 Remove the four fuel injector manifold retaining bolts (see illustration).
39 Carefully disengage the fuel rail assembly from the fuel injectors by lifting and gently rocking the rail (see illustration).
40 If you are replacing injectors, O-rings or the fuel pressure regulator, see below.

Installation

41 Lubricate all lower O-rings with clean engine oil.
42 Carefully install the fuel rail assembly and injectors into the lower intake manifold, one side at a time. To ensure that the O-rings are seated, push down on the fuel rail.
43 While holding the fuel rail assembly in place, install the retaining bolts finger tight, one side at a time, then tighten them securely.
44 The remainder of installation is the reverse of removal.

Fuel injectors

Refer to illustrations 13.47 and 13.48

Removal
45 Remove the air intake throttle body (see above).
46 Remove the fuel rail assembly (see above).
47 Remove each injector by pulling on it while simultaneously rock-

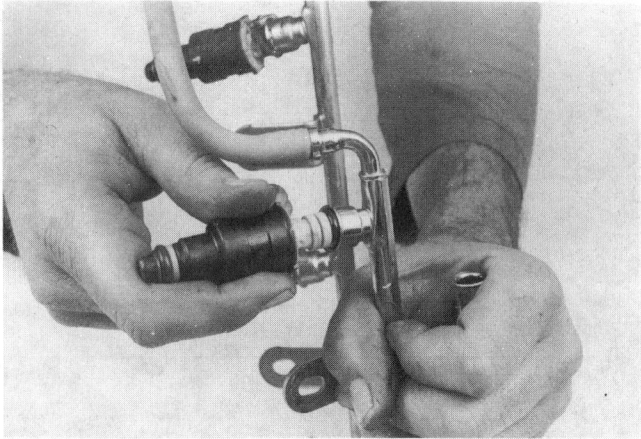

13.47   When pulling on an injector to remove it, use a gentle side-to-side rocking motion

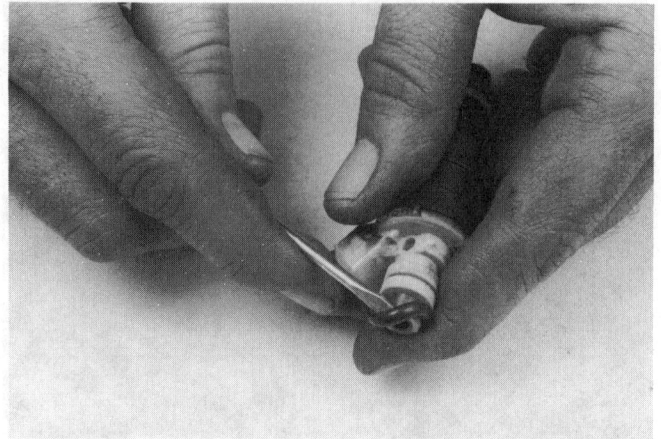

13.48   Use a small screwdriver to peel off the old O-rings from either end of the injectors — be extremely careful not to damage sealing areas or sensitive fuel metering orifices

13.54   Detach the vacuum line (arrow) before removing the fuel rail assembly or the pressure regulator

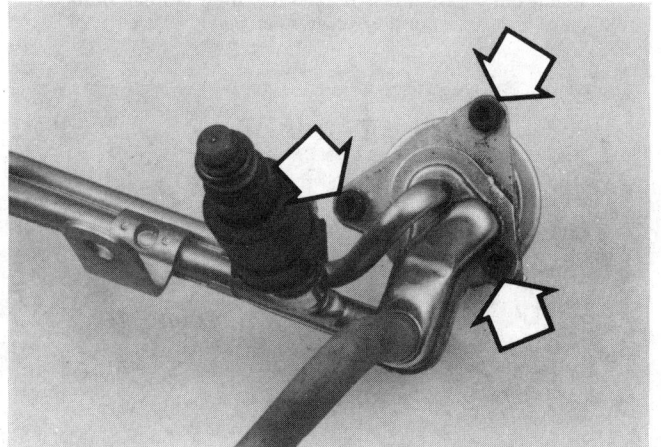

13.56   Remove the three Allen screws (arrows) to detach the fuel pressure regulator

ing it gently from side-to-side (see illustration).

48 Remove the old O-rings by carefully peeling them off with a small screwdriver (see illustration). **Caution:** *Handle the injectors and the fuel rail with extreme care to prevent damage to sealing areas and sensitive fuel metering orifices.*

49 Make sure that the injector caps are clean and free of contamination or damage.

Installation

50 Install each injector by using a light twisting, pushing motion.

51 The remainder of installation is the reverse of removal.

Fuel pressure regulator

Refer to illustrations 13.54 and 13.56

Removal

Note: *If you have the special tools, it is not absolutely necessary to remove the fuel rail assembly to remove the pressure regulator. If you don't have the tools, the fuel rail assembly must be removed.*

52 Remove the fuel tank filler cap to relieve pressure in the fuel tank.

53 Relieve the system fuel pressure (see Section 2).

54 Detach the vacuum line from the pressure regulator (see illustration).

55 If you have the right tools, remove the three Allen screws from the underside of the pressure regulator mounting plate.

56 If you do not have the tools to remove the three Allen screws from the pressure regulator mounting plate, remove the fuel rail assembly (see above), then remove the screws (see illustration).

57 Remove the pressure regulator assembly, gasket and O-ring. Discard the old gasket and O-ring.

Installation

58 Make sure that the gasket surfaces of the fuel pressure regulator and fuel rail assembly are clean. If scraping is necessary, be careful not to damage the fuel pressure regulator or fuel supply line gasket surfaces.

59 Lubricate the pressure regulator O-ring with clean engine oil.

60 Install the new O-ring and gasket on the regulator.

61 Install the fuel pressure regulator on the fuel rail assembly and tighten the three retaining screws securely.

---

14   Electronic Fuel Injection (EFI) — component replacement (3.8L V6 engine)

Upper intake manifold and throttle body

Refer to illustrations 14.3a, 14.3b and 14.7

Note: *If you are replacing the gasket between the upper and lower intake manifolds or servicing some component on the fuel rail assembly, follow this procedure. If you have to replace the gasket between the throttle body and the upper intake manifold, see the procedure after this one.*

Removal

1 Detach the cable from the negative terminal of the battery.

2 Remove the air cleaner housing outlet tube (see Section 8).

3 Unplug the electrical connectors from the air bypass valve, throttle position sensor and EGR position sensor (see illustrations).

4 Disconnect the throttle cable and the downshift cable from the throttle linkage (see Section 9).

EMISSION VACUUM
CONTROL CONNECTOR

EGR VALVE

THROTTLE BODY

FRONT OF ENGINE

FUEL PRESSURE
REGULATOR

PCV VALVE
6B890

CRANKCASE VENT
TUBE

FUEL INJECTOR

VIEW A

THROTTLE AIR
BYPASS VALVE

VIEW A

FUEL INJECTOR

FRONT OF ENGINE

DISTRIBUTOR
AND CAP ASSY

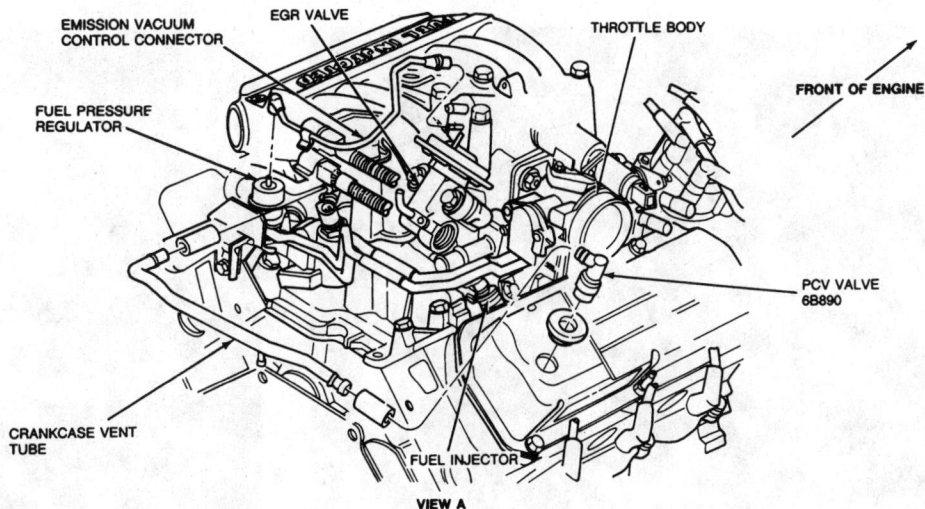

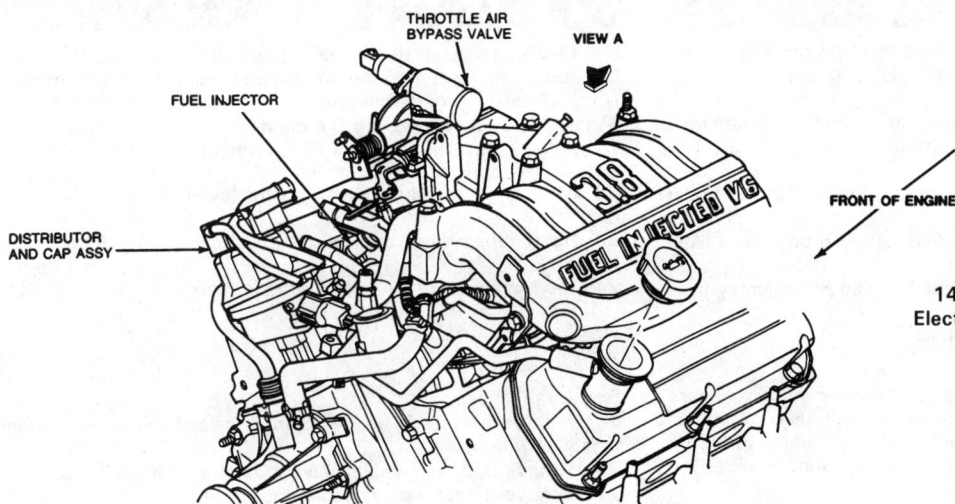

14.3a Basic components of the
Electronic Fuel Injection (EFI) system
used on the 3.8L V6

14.3b An exploded view of the EFI
assembly components on the
3.8L V6 engine

1 Shrader valve cap
2 Schrader valve
3 Fuel rail
4 Fuel pressure regulator
5 Fuel injector
6 Retainer
7 Thermostat
8 Gasket
9 Housing
10 Bolt
11 Throttle body
12 Gasket
13 Gasket
14 Air bypass valve
15 EGR valve assembly
16 Gasket
17 Bolt/stud
18 Upper intake manifold
19 Gasket
20 Lower intake manifold
21 Bolt
22 Fuel rail assembly

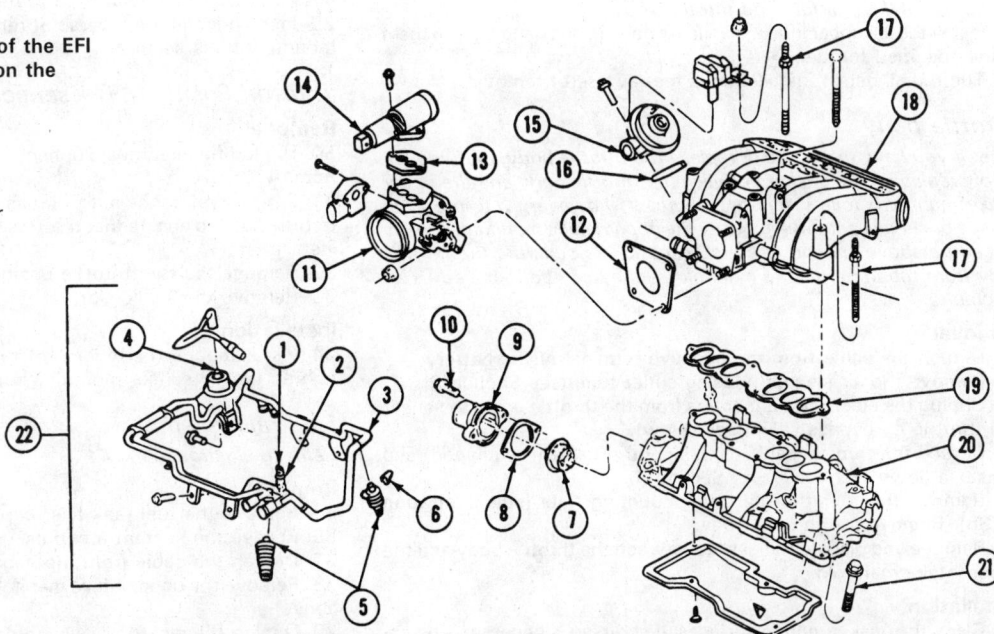

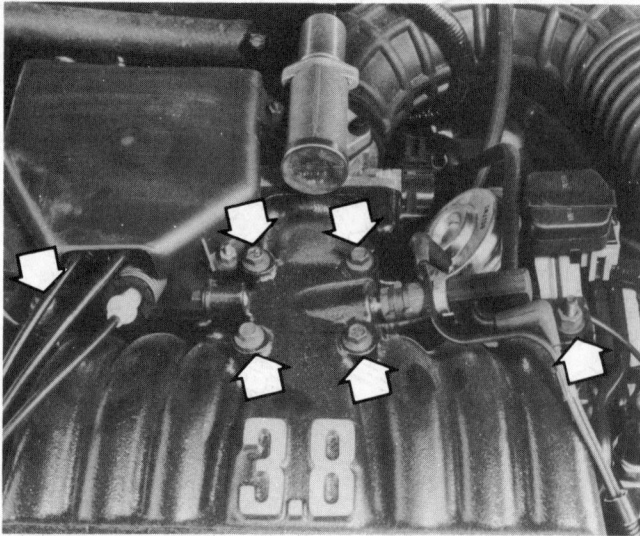

14.7   There are six bolts (arrows) that must be removed to detach the upper intake manifold assembly

5   Clearly label, then detach, the vacuum lines from the vacuum tree, the EGR valve and the fuel pressure regulator and the two canister purge lines from the fittings on the throttle body.
6   Detach the PCV hose from the fitting on the rear of the upper manifold.
7   Remove the six upper intake manifold retaining bolts (see illustration).
8   Remove the upper intake and throttle body as an assembly from the lower intake manifold.
9   Remove the old gasket and discard it.

Installation

10   Clean and inspect the gasket surfaces of the upper and lower intake manifolds. If it's necessary to scrape away any old gasket material, be extremely careful not to damage either gasket mating surface.
11   Position the new gasket on the lower intake mounting face. The use of alignment studs may be helpful.
12   Using the alignment studs to keep the gasket in position, place the upper intake manifold and throttle body assembly in position on the lower intake manifold. **Note:** *If the manifold is not equipped with alignment studs, make sure that the gasket remains in place when positioning the upper intake manfold and throttle body.*
13   Install the six upper intake manifold retaining bolts and tighten them to the specified torque.
14   The remainder of installation is the reverse of removal.

Throttle body

Note: *If you have to service or replace the throttle body, or if you are simply replacing the gasket between the throttle body and the upper intake manifold, follow this procedure. If, however, you intend to replace or service something below the upper intake manifold, see the procedure above instead (it's not necessary to separate the throttle body from the upper intake manifold — they can be removed as an assembly).*

Removal

15   Detach the cable from the negative terminal of the battery.
16   Remove the air cleaner housing outlet tube (see Section 9).
17   Unplug the electrical connectors from the throttle position sensor and throttle air bypass valve (see below).
18   Detach the throttle cable, cruise control cable (if equipped) and transaxle downshift cable (see Section 9).
19   Remove the four throttle body mounting nuts (see illustration 14.3b). Remove the throttle body.
20   Remove and discard the gasket between the throttle body and the upper intake manifold.

Installation

21   Clean the gasket mating surfaces. If scraping is necessary, be extremely careful not to damage either gasket surface or allow material to drop into the manifold.

14.25   To separate the air bypass valve from the throttle body, unplug the connector (A) and remove the mounting bolts (B — only one shown) — to detach the throttle position sensor, unplug the connector (C) and remove the retaining screws (D — only one shown)

22   Install the throttle body gasket on the four studs of the upper intake manifold.
23   Tighten the air intake throttle body attaching nuts to the specified torque.
24   The remainder of the installation is the reverse of removal.

Air bypass valve

Refer to illustration 14.25

Removal

25   Unplug the electrical connector from the air bypass valve assembly (see illustration).
26   Remove both air bypass valve mounting bolts.
27   Remove the air bypass valve and gasket.

Installation

28   Clean the gasket mating surfaces. **Note:** *If scraping is necessary, be extremely careful not to damage the air bypass valve or the throttle body gasket surfaces or drop material into the throttle body.*
29   Installation is the reverse of removal. Be sure to tighten the two mounting bolts securely.

Throttle Position (TP) sensor

Removal

30   Unplug the electrical connector from the TP sensor (see illustration 14.25).
31   Scribe a reference mark across the edge of the sensor and to the throttle body to ensure that the TP sensor is positioned correctly during installation.
32   Remove the two throttle position sensor retaining screws.
33   Remove the TP sensor.

Installation

34   Installation is the reverse of the removal procedure. Be sure to tighten the TP sensor mounting screws securely.

Fuel rail assembly

Refer to illustration 14.41

Removal

35   Remove the fuel tank filler cap and release fuel tank pressure.
36   Relieve the system fuel pressure (see Section 2).
37   Detach the cable from the negative terminal of the battery.
38   Remove the upper intake manifold and throttle body assembly (see above).
39   Unplug the electrical connectors from the fuel injectors.
40   Using Ford's special spring lock coupling remover tool (No. D87L-9280-A or B), or an equivalent tool, disconnect the crossover

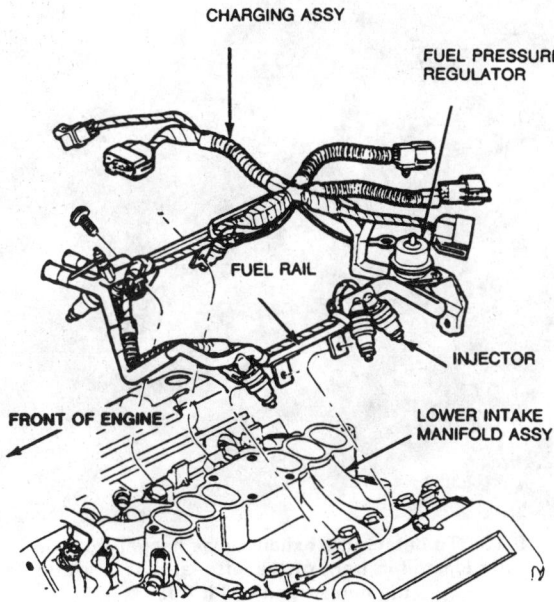

14.41 Fuel rail assembly mounting details

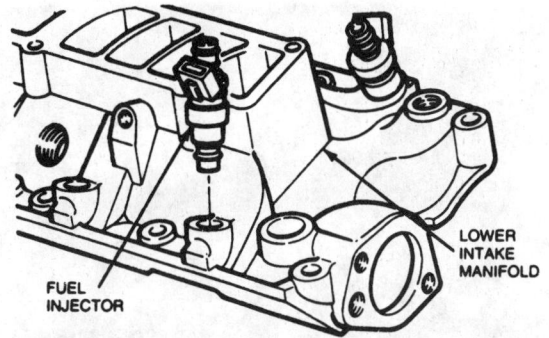

14.47 To detach an injector from the lower intake
manifold, pull on it while gently rocking it from side-to-side
at the same time

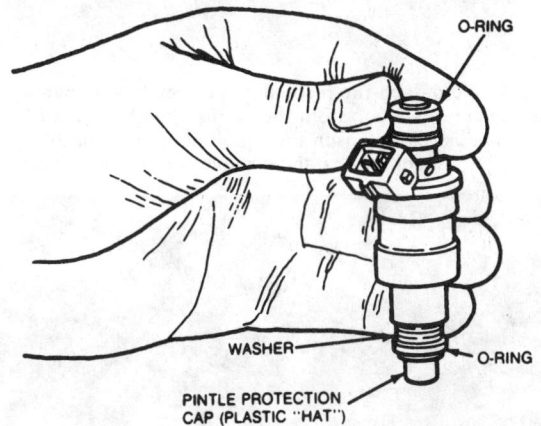

14.49 Besides replacing the two O-rings on the injectors,
always inspect the washer and the plastic "hat" that
protects the pintle — if either shows evidence of
deterioration, replace it

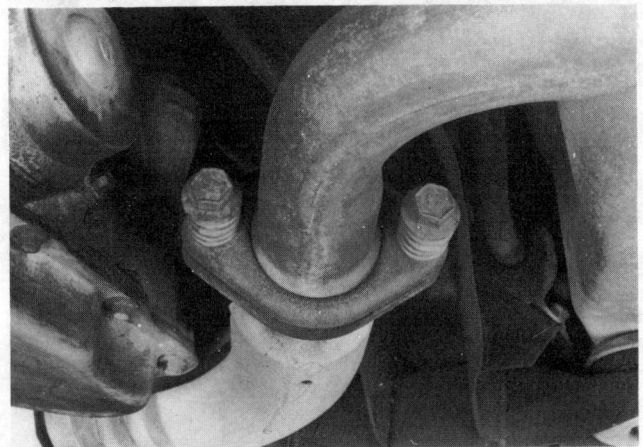

15.3 To detach the resonator (V6)/catalytic converter
(four-cylinder) section of the exhaust pipe from the exhaust
manifold connector pipe, remove the two flange bolts

fuel hose from the fuel rail assembly.

41 Remove the four (two per side) fuel rail assembly retaining bolts
(see illustration).

42 Carefully disengage the fuel rail from the fuel injectors and remove
it. Note: If it's easier, simply detach the fuel rail from the lower intake
manifold with the fuel injectors still attached, then detach the fuel injectors from the fuel rail (see below).

Installation

43 There are two ways to install the fuel rail:
  a) Install each of the injectors into the lower intake manifold first
      (see below), then place the fuel rail assembly over the injectors
      and push it onto them until it's firmly seated.
  b) Install the injectors into the fuel rail assembly first, place the fuel
      rail assembly and injectors in position on the lower intake manifold
      and carefully push and wiggle the injectors into their respective
      bores in the lower intake manifold.

44 Secure the fuel rail assembly to the lower intake manifold with the
four retaining bolts and tighten them securely.

45 The remainder of installation is the reverse of removal.

Fuel injectors

Refer to illustrations 14.47 and 14.49

Removal

46 Remove the fuel rail assembly (see above).

47 If you pulled the fuel rail off by itself, grasp each injector body and
pull up on it while gently rocking it from side-to-side (see illustration).
If you pulled off the fuel rail assembly with the injectors still attached,
carefully grasp each injector and detach it from the fuel rail by pulling
on it while simultaneously rocking it gently from side-to-side (see illustration 13.39).

48 After noting the positions of the O-rings on the injectors, remove
and discard them (see illustration 13.48).

49 Inspect the washer and the plastic "hat" covering the pintle on
the end of each injector (see illustration) for signs of deterioration.
Replace them if necessary. Note: If the hat is missing, look for it in
the intake manifold.

Installation

50 Lubricate the new O-rings with light grade oil (ESE-M2C39-F or
equivalent) and install them on the ends of each injector. Note: Do not
use silicone grease. It will clog the injectors.

51 Using a light twisting, pushing motion, install the injectors into
either the lower intake manifold or the fuel rail assembly (use whichever
method is easier for you).

52 Install the fuel rail assembly as outlined previously.

53 The remainder of installation is the reverse of removal.

15 Exhaust system components — replacement

Resonator pipe (V6 engine)/catalytic converter (four-cylinder engine)

Refer to illustrations 15.3 and 15.4

1 Detach the cable from the negative terminal of the battery.

2 Raise the vehicle and place it securely on jackstands.

15.4   To detach the resonator (V6)/catalytic converter
(four-cylinder) section from the muffler (rear) section of the
exhaust pipe, loosen the U-bolt nuts and pull the
resonator/catalytic converter loose

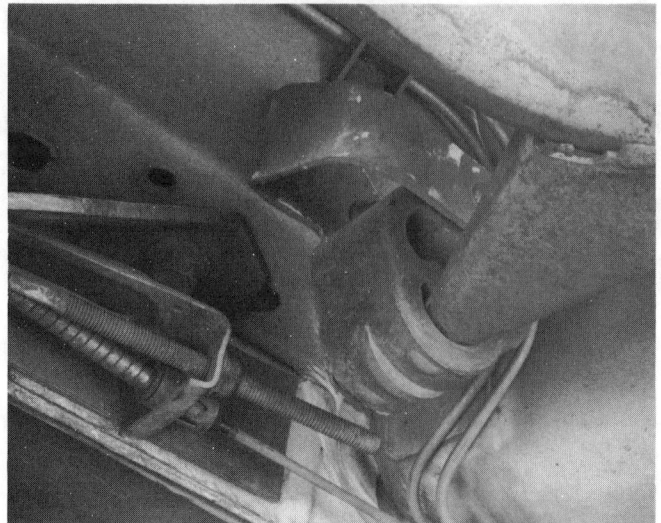

15.10   To detach the exhaust pipe hanger from the
insulator located in front of the left rear wheel, lift up on
the hanger and pull it free

15.11   To detach the exhaust pipe hanger from the
insulator located between the left rear control arms, pull
the hanger straight out

15.12   To detach the exhaust pipe hanger from the insulator
located above the muffler, pull the hanger straight out

3   Remove the two flange bolts just behind the transaxle (see illustration).
4   Loosen the U-bolt (see illustration) just behind the resonator (V6) or catalytic converter (four-cylinder).
5   Pull the resonator pipe/catalytic converter free of the exhaust pipe and remove it.
6   Installation is the reverse of removal.

Exhaust pipe/muffler
Refer to illustrations 15.10, 15.11 and 15.12
7   Detach the cable from the negative terminal of the battery.

8   Raise the vehicle and place it securely on jackstands.
9   Loosen the nuts on the U-bolt just behind the resonator (see illustration 15.4).
10   Detach the exhaust pipe hanger from the insulator on the left side of the vehicle, just in front of the left rear wheel (see illustration).
11   Detach the exhaust pipe hanger from the insulator located above and between the two left rear control arms (see illustration).
12   Detach the exhaust pipe hanger from the insulator located right above the muffler tip (see illustration).
13   Remove the exhaust pipe.
14   Installaton is the reverse of removal.

Chapter 5   Engine electrical systems

Contents

Specifications

Drivebelt deflection ....   See Chapter 1

Battery voltage
Engine off 12-volts
Engine running ....   14-to-15 volts

Ignition coil-to-distributor cap wire resistance ....   5000 ohms per foot

Ignition coil resistance
Primary resistance ....   0.3 to 1.0 ohms
Secondary resistance ....   8.0 to 11.5 K-ohms

1   General information

The engine electrical systems include all ignition, charging and starting components. Because of their engine-related functions, these components are considered separately from chassis electrical devices such as the lights, instruments, etc.

Be very careful when working on the engine electrical components. They are easily damaged if checked, connected or handled improperly. The alternator is driven by an engine drivebelt which could cause serious injury if your hands, hair or clothes become entangled in it with the engine running. Both the starter and alternator are connected directly to the battery and could arc or even cause a fire if mishandled, overloaded or shorted out.

Never leave the ignition switch on for long periods of time with the engine off. Don't disconnect the battery cables while the engine is running. Correct polarity must be maintained when connecting battery cables from another source, such as another vehicle, during jump starting. Always disconnect the negative cable first and hook it up last or the battery may be shorted by the tool being used to loosen the cable clamps.

Additional safety related information on the engine electrical systems can be found in *Safety first* near the front of this manual. It should be referred to before beginning any operation included in this Chapter.

2   Battery — removal and installation

Refer to illustration 2.2

1   Disconnect both cables from the battery terminals. **Caution:** *Always disconnect the negative cable first and hook it up last or the battery may be shorted by the tool being used to loosen the cable clamps.*

2.2   To remove the battery from the engine compartment, detach both battery cables and remove the hold down clamp (arrow) then carefully lift the battery out

2   Locate the battery hold-down clamp between the battery and the air cleaner housing (see illustration). Remove the bolt and the hold-down clamp.
3   Lift out the battery. Special straps that attach to the battery posts are available — lifting and moving the battery is much easier if you use one.
4   Installation is the reverse of removal.

3   Battery — emergency jump starting

Refer to the *Booster battery (jump) starting* procedure in the front part of this manual.

4   Battery cables — check and replacement

1   Periodically inspect the entire length of each battery cable for damage, cracked or burned insulation and corrosion. Poor battery cable connections can cause starting problems and decreased engine performance.
2   Check the cable-to-terminal connections at the ends of the cables for cracks, loose wire strands and corrosion. The presence of white, fluffy deposits under the insulation at the cable terminal connection is a sign that the cable is corroded and should be replaced. Check the terminals for distortion, missing mounting bolts and corrosion.
3   When replacing the cables, **always disconnect the negative cable first and hook it up last**, or the battery may be shorted by the tool used to loosen the cable clamps. Even if only the positive cable is being replaced, be sure to disconnect the negative cable from the battery first.
4   Disconnect and remove the cable. Make sure the replacement cable is the same length and diameter as the cable being replaced.
5   Clean the threads of the relay or ground connection with a wire brush to remove rust and corrosion. Apply a light coat of petroleum jelly to the threads to help prevent future corrosion.
6   Attach the cable to the relay or ground connection and tighten the mounting nut/bolt securely.
7   Before connecting the new cable to the battery, make sure that it reaches the battery post without having to be stretched.
8   Connect the positive cable first, followed by the negative cable.

5   Ignition system — general information

The Taurus/Sable ignition system is a solid state electronic design consisting of an ignition module, coil, distributor, the spark plug wires and the spark plugs. Mechanically, the system is similar to a breaker point system, except that the distributor cam and ignition points are replaced by an armature and magnetic pickup unit. The coil primary circuit is controlled by an amplifier module.

When the ignition is switched on, the ignition primary circuit is energized. When the distributor armature ''teeth'' or ''spokes'' approach the magnetic coil assembly, a voltage is induced which signals the amplifier to turn off the coil primary current. A timing circuit in the amplifier module turns the coil current back on after the coil field has collapsed.

When it's on, current flows from the battery through the ignition switch, the coil primary winding, the amplifier module and then to ground. When the current is interrupted, the magnetic field in the ignition coil collapses, inducing a high voltage in the coil secondary windings. The voltage is conducted to the distributor where the rotor directs it to the appropriate spark plug. This process is repeated continuously.

All vehicles are equipped with a gear driven distributor with a die cast base housing a ''Hall Effect'' vane switch stator assembly and a device for fixed octane adjustment.

All models use the Thick Film Integrated IV (TFI-IV) ignition module, which is housed in a molded thermoplastic box mounted on the base of the distributor. The TFI-IV module used on the four-cylinder engine includes a ''push start'' mode that allows push starting of the vehicle if necessary.

6   Ignition system — check

Refer to illustration 6.2
Warning: *Because of the very high secondary (spark plug) voltage generated by the ignition system, extreme care should be taken when this check is done.*

Calibrated ignition tester method

1   If the engine turns over but won't start, disconnect the spark plug lead from any spark plug and attach it to a calibrated ignition tester (available at most auto parts stores). Make sure the tester is designed for Ford ignition systems if a universal tester isn't available.
2   Connect the clip on the tester to a bolt or metal bracket on the engine (see illustration), crank the engine and watch the end of the tester to see if bright blue, well-defined sparks occur.

6.2   To use a calibrated ignition tester (available at most auto parts stores), simply disconnect a spark plug wire, attach the wire to the tester, clip the tester to a convenient ground (such as a rocker arm cover bolt or a ground wire attaching bolt) — if there is enough power to fire the plug, sparks will be clearly visible between the electrode tip and the tester body as the engine is turned over

3   If sparks occur, sufficient voltage is reaching the plug to fire it (repeat the check at the remaining plug wires to verify that the distributor cap and rotor are OK). However, the plugs themselves may be fouled, so remove and check them as described in Chapter 1 or install new ones.
4   If no sparks or intermittent sparks occur, remove the distributor cap and check the cap and rotor as described in Chapter 1. If moisture is present, use WD-40 (or a similar product) to dry out the cap and rotor, then reinstall the cap and repeat the spark test.
5   If there's still no spark, detach the secondary coil wire from the

distributor cap and hook it up to the tester (reattach the plug wire to the spark plug), then repeat the spark check.

6   If no sparks occur, check the primary (small) wire connections at the coil to make sure they're clean and tight. Refer to Section 7 and check the ignition coil supply voltage circuit. Make any necessary repairs, then repeat the check again.

7   If sparks now occur, the distributor cap, rotor, plug wire(s) or spark plug(s) (or all of them) may be defective.

8   If there's still no spark, the coil-to-cap wire may be bad (check the resistance with an ohmmeter and compare it to the Specifications). If a known good wire doesn't make any difference in the test results, the ignition coil, module or other internal components may be defective.

Alternative method

Note: *If you're unable to obtain a calibrated ignition tester, the following method will allow you to determine if the ignition system has spark, but it won't tell you if there's enough voltage produced to actually initiate combustion in the cylinders.*

9   Remove the wire from one of the spark plugs. Using an insulated tool, hold the wire about 1/4-inch from a good ground and have an assistant crank the engine.

10 If bright blue, well-defined sparks occur, sufficient voltage is reaching the plug to fire it. However, the plug(s) may be fouled, so remove and check them as described in Chapter 1 or install new ones.

11 If there's no spark, check the remaining wires in the same manner. A few sparks followed by no spark is the same condition as no spark at all.

12 If no sparks occur, remove the distributor cap and check the cap

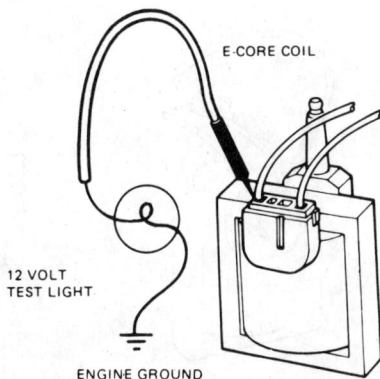

7.2   To check ignition coil primary circuit attach a 12-volt DC test light between the coil TACH terminal and a good engine ground

and rotor as described in Chapter 1. If moisture is present, use WD-40 (or a similar product) to dry out the cap and rotor, then reinstall the cap and repeat the spark test.

13 If there's still no spark, disconnect the secondary coil wire from the distributor cap, hold it about 1/4-inch from a good engine ground and crank the engine again.

14 If no sparks occur, check the primary (small) wire connections at the coil to make sure they're clean and tight. Refer to Section 7 and check the ignition coil supply voltage circuit. Make any necessary repairs, then repeat the check again.

15 If sparks now occur, the distributor cap, rotor, plug wire(s) or spark plug(s) (or all of them) may be defective.

16 If there's still no spark, the coil-to-cap wire may be bad (check the resistance with an ohmmeter and compare it to the Specifications). If a known good wire doesn't make any difference in the test results, the ignition coil, module or other internal components may be defective.

---

7   Ignition coil and circuits — check and coil replacement

Check

Refer to illustrations 7.2, 7.9, 7.12, 7.19, 7.29a, 7.29b, 7.38 7.46, 7.50a and 7.50b

Ignition coil primary circuit

1   Unplug the wiring harness connector from the ignition module. Inspect it for dirt, corrosion and damage, then plug it back in.

2   Attach a 12-volt DC test light between the coil TACH terminal and a good engine ground **(see illustration)**.

3   Crank the engine.

4   If the light flashes, or comes on but doesn't flash, go to Step 7.

5   If the light stays off or is very dim, go to Step 16.

6   Remove the test light.

Ignition coil primary resistance

7   Turn the ignition switch to Off.

8   Unplug the ignition coil wire harness connector. Inspect it for dirt, corrosion and damage.

9   Measure the resistance between the primary terminals of the ignition coil **(see illustration)**.

10 If the indicated resistance is within the specification limits, proceed to Step 12.

11 If the indicated resistance is less or more than specified, replace the ignition coil (Steps 49 through 52).

Ignition coil secondary resistance

12 Measure the resistance from the negative primary terminal to the secondary terminal of the ignition coil **(see illustration)**.

13 If the indicated resistance is within the specification, proceed to Step 25.

14 If the indicated resistance is less or more than the specified resistance, replace the ignition coil (Steps 49 through 52).

15 Reconnect the ignition coil wires.

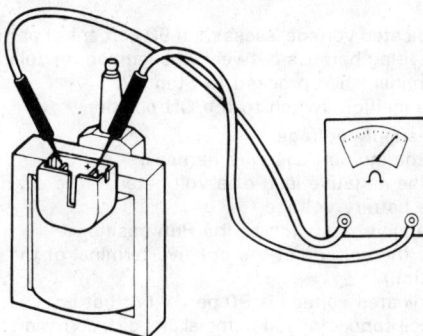

7.9   To measure the ignition coil primary resistance, touch the probes of an ohmmeter to the primary terminals

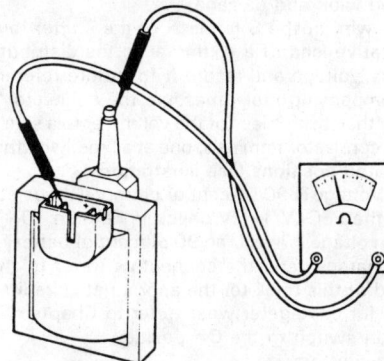

7.12   To measure ignition coil secondary resistance, touch the probes of an ohmmeter to the negative primary terminal and the secondary terminal of the coil

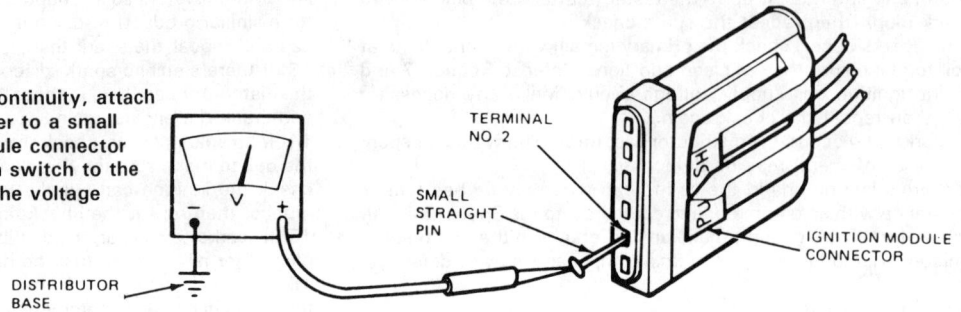

7.19 To check primary circuit continuity, attach the positve lead of a voltmeter to a small straight pin inserted into module connector terminal No. 2, turn the ignition switch to the Run position and measure the voltage

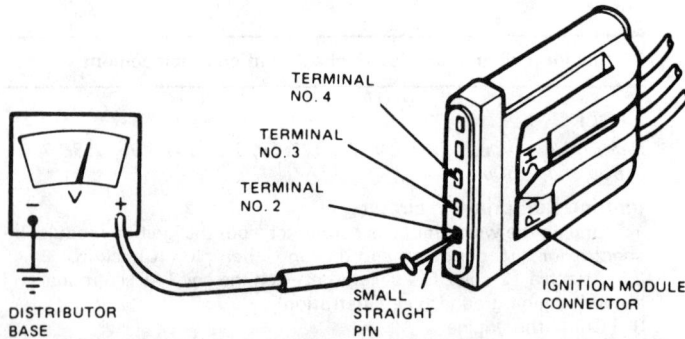

7.29a To check the wiring harness/module connector voltage, turn the ignition switch to each of the above positions . . .

CONNECTOR TERMINAL	WIRE/CIRCUIT	IGNITION SWITCH TEST POSITION
#2	TO IGNITION COIL (−) TERMINAL	RUN
#3	RUN CIRCUIT	RUN AND START
#4	START CIRCUIT	START

7.29b . . . while moving the voltmeter lead/straight pin to the wiring harness/module connector terminal indicated in the table for each test

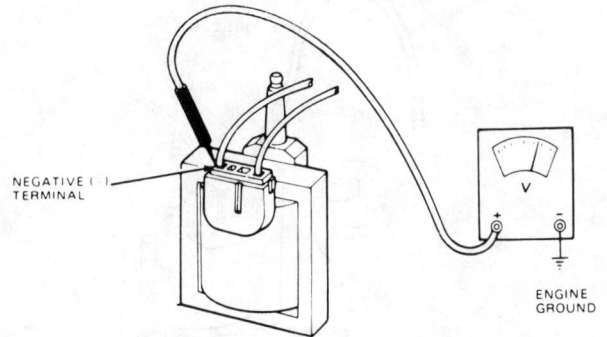

7.38 To measure ignition coil primary voltage, stick the voltmeter lead into the negative terminal

Primary circuit continuity

16 Unplug the wiring harness connector from the ignition module. Inspect it for dirt, corrosion and damage.
17 Attach the negative lead of a voltmeter to the distributor base.
18 Measure battery voltage and record it for future reference.
19 Attach the positive lead of the voltmeter to a small straight pin inserted into connector terminal 2 (see illustration). Caution: *Don't allow the straight pin to ground against anything.*
20 Turn the ignition switch to the Run position and measure the terminal 2 voltage.
21 If the measured voltage is 90 percent of battery voltage, proceed to the wiring harness check (Step 25).
22 If the measured voltage is less than 90 percent of battery voltage, proceed to Step 35.
23 Turn the ignition switch to the Off position.
24 Remove the straight pin.

Wiring harness

25 Unplug the wiring harness connector from the ignition module. Inspect it for dirt, corrosion and damage.
26 Disconnect the wire at the S terminal of the starter relay.
27 Attach the negative lead of a voltmeter to the distributor base.
28 Measure battery voltage and record it for future reference.
29 Using the accompanying table, measure the connector terminal voltage by attaching the positive lead of the voltmeter to a small straight pin inserted into the connector terminals, one at a time, with the ignition switch in the indicated positions (see illustrations).
30 If the indicated voltage is 90 percent of battery voltage at all three terminals, refer to the EEC-IV/TFI-IV check in Section 10.
31 If the indicated voltage is less than 90 percent of battery voltage, inspect the wiring harness and the connectors (refer to the wiring diagrams at the end of this book for the appropriate circuits). Check the ignition switch for damage or wear (refer to Chapter 12).
32 Turn the ignition switch to the Off position.
33 Remove the straight pin.
34 Reconnect the wire to the S terminal of the starter relay.

Ignition coil primary voltage

35 Attach the negative lead of a voltmeter to the distributor base.
36 Measure battery voltage and record it.
37 Turn the ignition switch to the Run position.

38 Measure the voltage at the negative terminal of the ignition coil (see illustration).
39 If the indicated voltage is 90 percent of battery voltage, inspect the wiring harness between the ignition module and the coil negative terminal.
40 If the indicated voltage is less than 90 percent of battery voltage, inspect the wiring harness between the ignition module and the coil negative terminal, then proceed to Step 42.
41 Turn the ignition switch to the Off position.

Ignition coil supply voltage

42 Unplug the ignition coil wire harness.
43 Attach the negative lead of a voltmeter to the distributor base.
44 Measure battery voltage.
45 Turn the ignition switch to the Run position.
46 Measure the voltage at the positive terminal of the ignition coil (see illustration).
47 If the indicated voltage is 90 percent of battery voltage, inspect the ignition coil connector and terminals for dirt, corrosion and damage. If both the connector and terminals are clean, replace the ignition coil (Steps 49 through 52).
48 If the indicated voltage is less than 90 percent of battery voltage, inspect and repair the circuit between the ignition coil and the ignition switch (refer to the wiring diagrams at the end of the book). Check the ignition switch for damage and wear (refer to Chapter 12).

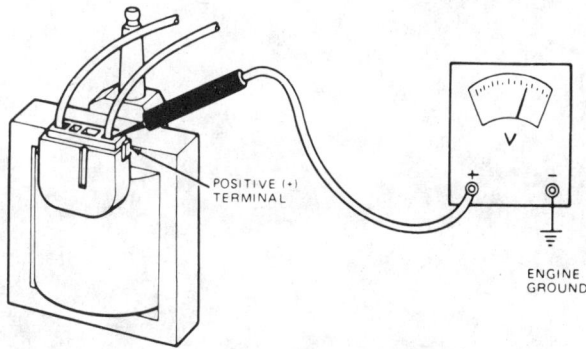

7.46 To measure ignition coil supply voltage, stick the voltmeter lead into the positive terminal

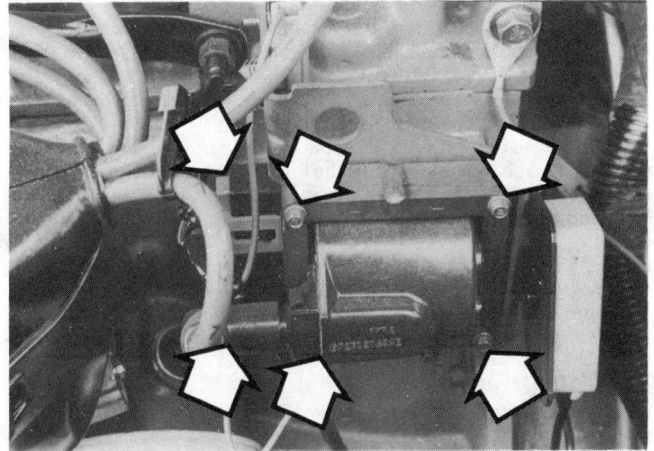

7.50a To remove the coil from the four-cylinder engine, unplug the secondary lead and the primary terminal connector, then remove the bracket bolts (arrows)

7.50b To remove the coil from a V6, unplug the secondary lead (arrow — obscured by the primary terminal connector in this photo) and the primary terminal connector (arrow — note the cover over the primary connector — be sure to push it back into position when the new coil is installed), then remove the bracket bolts (arrows)

8.2 Unplug the module electrical connector from the base of the distributor (V6 shown)

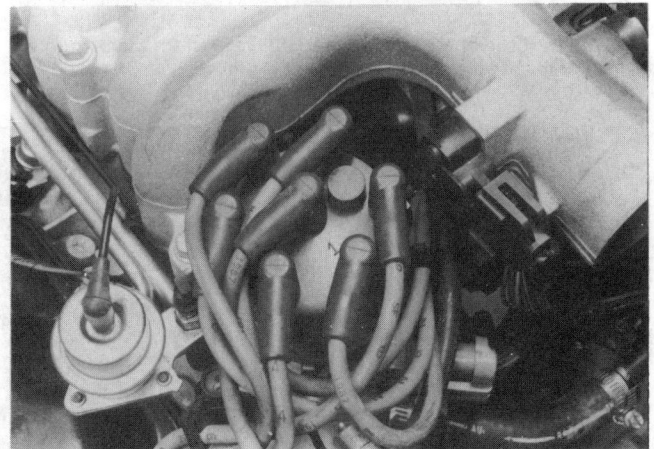

8.3 Look for the raised "1" on the top of the distributor cap next to the terminal for the number 1 spark plug wire — this is where the rotor should be pointing before you remove the distributor

Ignition coil replacement

49 Detach the cable from the negative terminal of the battery.
50 Unplug the coil secondary lead, then detach the primary terminal connector from the coil (see illustrations).
51 Remove the bracket bolts and detach the coil.
52 Installation is the reverse of removal.

8 Distributor — removal and installation

Refer to illustrations 8.2, 8.3, 8.7 and 8.8

Removal

1 Unplug the primary lead from the coil (see Section 7).
2 Unplug the module electrical connector (see illustration).
3 Note the raised "1" on the distributor cap (see illustration), which marks the terminal for the plug wire leading to the number 1 cylinder.
4 Remove the distributor cap (see Chapter 1).
5 If you have a remote starter:
  a) Remove the spark plug from the number 1 cylinder (see Chapter 1).
  b) Hook up the remote starter to the starter relay and the battery positive terminal in accordance with the manufacturer's instructions.
  c) Turn the engine over carefully by turning and releasing the igni-

tion key, or by quickly pushing and releasing the remote control starter switch button until the rotor is pointing toward the terminal for the number 1 cylinder.
  d) Detach the cable from the negative terminal of the battery.
  e) Proceed to Step 7.

6   If you don't have a remote starter:
   a) Detach the cable from the negative terminal of the battery.
   b) Locate the large bolt in the front of the crankshaft. Attach a rat-chet and socket to the bolt.
   c) Rotate the crankshaft until the rotor is pointing toward the number 1 plug wire terminal.
7   Make a mark on the edge of the distributor base directly below the rotor tip and in line with it (if the rotor has more than one tip, use the center one for reference) (see illustration). Also, mark the distributor base and the engine block to ensure that the distributor is installed correctly.
8   Remove the distributor hold down-bolt and clamp (see illustration), then pull the distributor straight up to remove it. Be careful not to disturb the intermediate driveshaft. Caution: *Do not turn the crankshaft while the distributor is removed, or the alignment marks will be useless.*

Installation

9   Insert the distributor into the engine in exactly the same relationship to the block that it was in when removed.
10   To mesh the helical gears on the camshaft and the distributor, it may be necessary to turn the rotor slightly. If the distributor doesn't seat completely, the hex shaped recess in the lower end of the distrib-utor shaft is not mating properly with the oil pump shaft. Recheck the alignment marks between the distributor base and the block to verify that the distributor is in the same position it was in before removal. Also check the rotor to see if it's aligned with the mark you made on the edge of the distributor base. Then, using a socket and ratchet on the crankshaft pulley bolt, turn the crankshaft in the normal direction of rotation (clockwise, viewed from the front). Because the gear on the distributor shaft is engaged with the gear on the camshaft, their relationship to one another will not change as long as the distributor is not lifted from the engine. Therefore, the rotor will turn but the oil pump shaft will not, because the two shafts are not yet engaged. When the hex shaped recess in the end of the distributor shaft and the oil pump shaft are aligned, the distributor will drop down over the pump shaft and the distributor housing will seat against the block.

Note: *If the crankshaft has been moved while the distributor is out, locate Top Dead Center (TDC) for the number one piston by removing the spark plug from the number 1 cylinder and, using a remote starter (or a socket and ratchet on the crankshaft pulley), rotate the crankshaft until the TDC mark on the crankshaft pulley (see Chapter 2) is aligned with the stationary pointer on the timing chain/belt cover. To verify that the number 1 piston is at TDC (and not beginning the intake stroke), place your thumb or finger tightly against the spark plug hole and try to prevent any air from escaping. If it is on TDC, the air pressure will force its way past your finger.*

11   With the base of the distributor seated against the block, turn the distributor to align the marks made on the distributor base and the block.

8.7   Mark the position of the rotor by painting or scribing an alignment mark on the edge of the distributor base directly under the tip of the rotor (arrow) to ensure proper reinstallation (V6 shown)

12   With the distributor marks aligned, the rotor should be pointing at the mark on the distributor housing.
13   Place the hold-down clamp in position and loosely install the bolt.
14   Install the distributor cap and tighten the cap screws securely.
15   Plug in the module electrical connector.
16   Reattach the spark plug wires to the plugs.
17   Connect the cable to the negative terminal of the battery.
18   Check the ignition timing (refer to Section 9) and tighten the distributor hold-down bolt securely.

9   Ignition timing — check and adjustment

Refer to illustrations 9.3a, 9.3b, 9.5 and 9.6

1   Apply the parking brake and block the wheels. Place the transmis-sion in Park (automatic) or Neutral (manual). Turn off all accessories (heater, air conditioner, etc.).
2   Start the engine and warm it up. Once it has reached operating temperature, turn it off.
3   Unplug the in-line spout connector located near the distributor (see illustrations).

8.8   After marking the position of the distributor in relation to the intake manifold (arrow), remove the hold-down bolt and clamp (V6 shown)

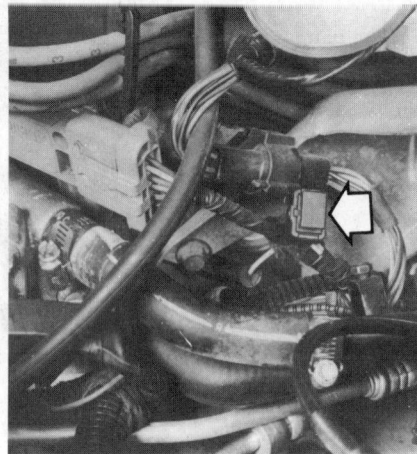

9.3a   The in-line spout connector (arrow) must be disconnected before the ignition timing is checked or adjusted — the connector in this photo is on a 3.0L V6 but is similar in appearance and proximity to the distributor on the other engines

9.3b   To disconnect the in-line spout connector, simply pull the plastic plug out of the housing (don't lose the plug — you will not be able to operate the vehicle if you misplace it)

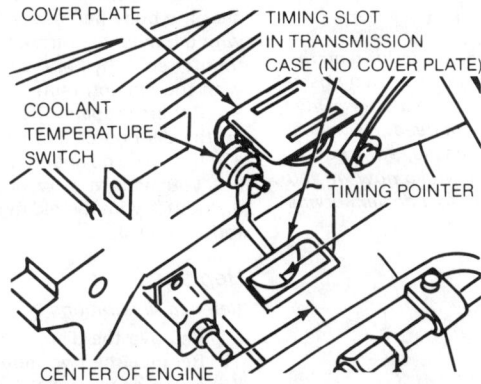

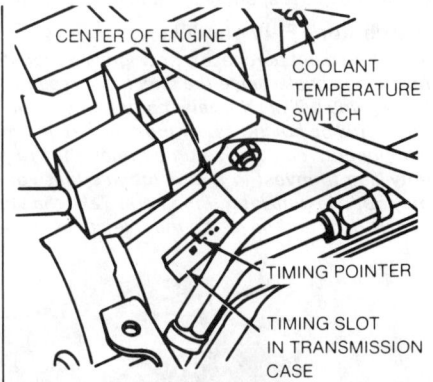

TIMING LOCATION FOR MTX — 2.5L

TIMING LOCATION FOR ATX — 2.5L

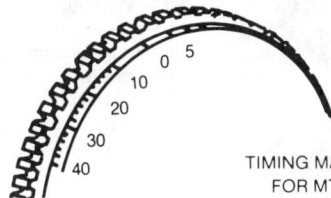

TIMING MARKS
FOR MTX

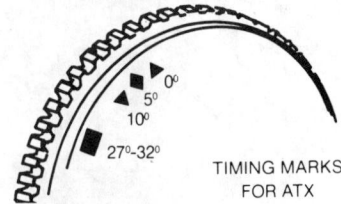

TIMING MARKS
FOR ATX

9.5 If your vehicle is equipped with a four-cylinder engine, the timing marks are located on the flywheel (manual) or driveplate (automatic), and the stationary timing marks are located on the edge of the slot — note that the manual transaxle equipped model has a cover plate over the timing slot that must be removed

4   Connect an inductive timing light and a tachometer in accordance with the manufacturer's instructions. **Caution:** *Make sure that the timing light and tach wires don't hang anywhere near the electric cooling fan or they may become entangled in the fan blades when it comes on.*
5   If your vehicle is equipped with a four-cylinder engine, locate the timing slot in the top of the bellhousing immediately below the thermostat housing in the left end of the cylinder head **(see illustration)**. If your vehicle is equipped with a manual transaxle, remove the screws and detach the cover plate.
6   If your vehicle is equipped with a V6 engine, locate the timing marks on the crankshaft vibration damper **(see illustration)**. **Note:** *You may have to clean the edge of the damper with a wire brush and solvent.*
7   Start the engine again.
8   If your vehicle is equipped with a four-cylinder engine, point the timing light through the slot at the flywheel (manual transaxle) or driveplate (automatic transaxle) and note whether the timing mark (the 10° mark on manual transaxle equipped vehicles or the triangle shaped mark on automatic transaxle equipped vehicles) is aligned with the timing pointer at the edge of the timing slot.
9   If your vehicle is equipped with a V6 engine, point the timing light at the timing marks on the vibration damper and note whether the 10° mark is aligned with the stationary pointer on the timing chain cover.
10 If the proper mark isn't aligned with the stationary pointer, loosen the distributor hold-down bolt. Turn the distributor clockwise (to retard timing) or counterclockwise (to advance timing) until the correct timing mark on the flywheel/driveplate is aligned with the stationary pointer. Tighten the distributor hold-down bolt securely when the timing is correct and recheck it to make sure it didn't change position when the bolt was tightened.
11 Turn off the engine.
12 Plug in the spout connector.
13 Restart the engine and check the idle speed. Because the engine is equipped with automatic idle speed control, idle rpm is not adjustable. If the idle rpm is not within the specified range (see the VECI label), take the vehicle to a dealer service department or repair shop. Adjustment requires specialized test equipment and procedures that are beyond the scope of the home mechanic.
14 Turn off the engine.
15 Remove the timing light and tachometer. **Note:** *The distributor used in all Taurus/Sable vehicles incorporates an octane adjustment feature. The adjustment is accomplished by replacing the standard zero degree rod located in the distributor with a three-degree or six-degree retard rod. However, changing the timing by using different octane rods without first having proper authorization is a violation of Federal emission laws.*

9.6 If your vehicle is equipped with a V6, the timing marks are located on the crankshaft vibration dampner and the stationary pointer if located on the front of the timing chain cover (accessory drivebelts removed for clarity)

10   Ignition module — check and replacement

Caution: *The ignition module is a delicate and relatively expensive electronic component. The following tests must be done with the right equipment by someone who knows how to use it properly. Failure to follow the step-by-step procedures could result in damage to the module and/or other electronic devices, including the EEC-IV microprocessor itself. Additionally, all devices under computer control are protected by a Federally mandated extended warranty. Check with your dealer before attempting to diagnose them yourself.*

Check
EEC-IV/TFI-IV
1   Unplug the wiring harness connector from the ignition module. Inspect it for dirt, corrosion and/or damage, then plug it back in.
2   Unplug the single wire connector located immediately above the ignition module connector (see Section 8).
3   Using a calibrated spark tester, check for spark (see Section 6).
4   If there is no spark, proceed to the distributor/TFI-IV module check (Step 7).
5   If there is spark, the problem lies either with the inferred mileage sensor (IMS) or within the EEC-IV electronic control module (ECM). Diagnosis of these items is beyond the scope of the home mechanic.

Take the vehicle to a dealer service department.

6   Remove the spark tester and reconnect the single wire connector.

Distributor/TFI-IV module

Note: *You must purchase a new ignition module before performing the following check. Since the check can result in only one of two possibilities (you will need a new module, or you won't), the odds are 50/50 that you'll be buying a new module that you may not need. Electronic components can't be returned once they're purchased, so if you're unwilling to invest in a new module that you may need now or you may not use until later, stop here. Take the vehicle to a dealer service department and have the module checked out.*

10.12   To detach the TFI-IV ignition module from the distributor base, remove the two screws (arrows) . . .

10.13   . . . then pull the module straight down to detach the spade terminals from the stator connector

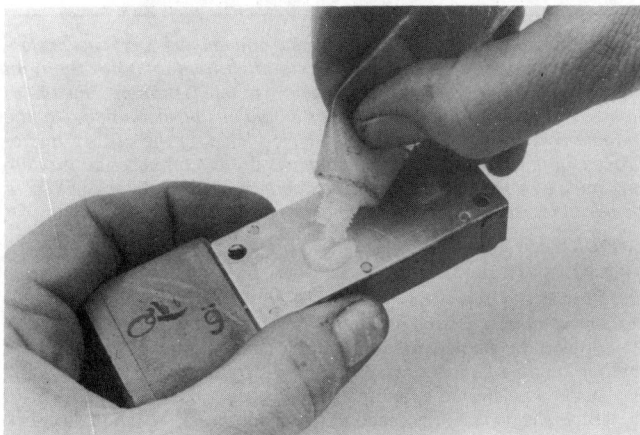

10.14   Be sure to wipe the back side of the module clean and apply a film of dielectric grease (essential for cool operation of the module) — DO NOT use any other type of grease

7   Remove the distributor (see Section 8).

8   Install a new module on the distributor (see Step 11 below). Connect the body harness to the TFI-IV. Make sure the unit is grounded with a jumper lead from the distributor to the engine. Rotate the distributor shaft by hand and check for spark at the secondary coil wire with the ignition tester (see Section 6).

9   If there is spark, the old module has failed. Leave the new module on the distributor and install the distributor (see Section 8).

10   If there is no spark, the sensor has failed. Your old module is okay but you need a new or rebuilt distributor. Install the new/rebuilt distributor with the old module (and put your new module on the shelf for another day!).

Replacement

Refer to illustrations 10.12, 10.13 and 10.14

11   Remove the distributor from the engine (refer to Section 8).

12   Remove the two module mounting screws with a 1/4-inch drive 7/32-inch deep socket **(see illustration)**.

13   Pull straight down on the module to disconnect the spade connectors from the stator connector **(see illustration)**.

14   Whether you are installing the old module or a new one, wipe the back side of the module clean with a soft, clean shop rag and apply a film of silicone dielectric grease to the back side of the module **(see illustration)**.

15   Installation is the reverse of removal. When plugging in the module, make sure that the three terminals are inserted all the way into the stator connector.

---

11   Distributor stator assembly — check and replacement

Check

1   The factory doesn't specify a check for the TFI-IV system stator (sensor). If the ignition module is good, but the system won't function normally, replace the stator.

Replacement

Refer to illustrations 11.9, 11.11, 11.12, 11.13, 11.14, 11.15, 11.19, 11.28a and 11.28b

2   Remove the distributor cap and position it out of the way with the wires attached.

3   Disconnect the TFI module from the wire harness.

4   Remove the distributor (refer to Section 8).

5   Remove the rotor (refer to Chapter 1 if necessary).

6   Although not absolutely necessary, it's a good idea to remove the ignition module (Section 10) to prevent possible damage to the module while the distributor is being disassembled.

7   Clamp the lower end of the distributor housing in a vise. Place shop rags in the vise jaws to prevent damage to the distributor and don't overtighten the vise.

8   Before removing the drive gear, note that the roll pin is slightly offset. When the distributor is reassembled, the roll pin cannot be reinstalled through the drive gear and distributor shaft holes unless the holes are perfectly lined up.

9   With an assistant holding the distributor steady in the vise, use a 5/32-inch diameter pin punch to hammer the roll pin out of the shaft **(see illustration)**.

10   Loosen the vise and reposition the distributor with the drive gear facing up.

11   Remove the drive gear with a small puller **(see illustration)**.

12   Before removing it from the distributor, check the shaft for burrs or built up residue, particularly around the drive gear roll pin hole **(see illustration)**. If burrs or residue are evident, polish the shaft with emery paper and wipe it clean to prevent damage to the lip seal and bushing in the distributor base.

13   After removing any burrs/residue, remove the shaft assembly by gently pulling on the plate. Note the relationship of the spacer washer to the distributor base before removing the washer **(see illustration)**.

14   Remove the octane rod retaining screw **(see illustration)**.

15   Lift the inner end of the rod off the stator retaining post **(see illustration)** and pull the octane rod from the distributor base. **Note:** *Don't lose the grommet installed in the octane rod hole. The grommet protects the electronic components of the distributor from moisture.*

16   Remove the two stator screws **(see illustration 11.15)**.

11.9 With the distributor shaft housing locked securely in a vise lined with several shop rags to prevent damage to the housing, drive out the roll pin with a 5/32-inch pin punch

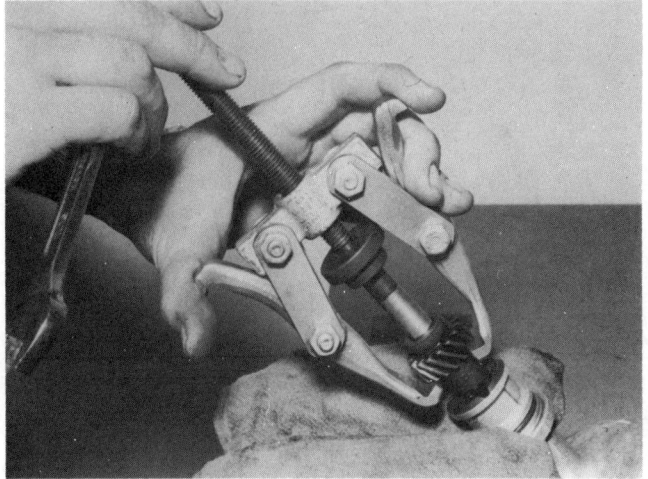

11.11 With the distributor shaft pointing up like this, use a small puller to separate the drive gear from the shaft

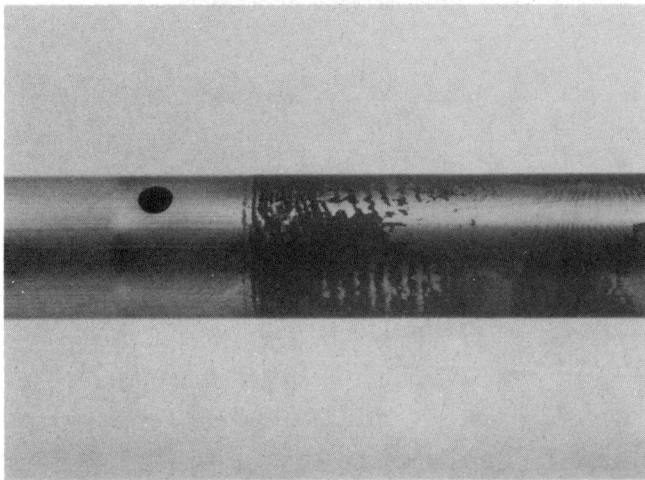

11.12 Inspect the distributor shaft for burrs and residue buildup in the vicinity of the hole for the drive gear roll pin (remove it with emery cloth to prevent damage to the distributor shaft bushing when removing and installing the shaft)

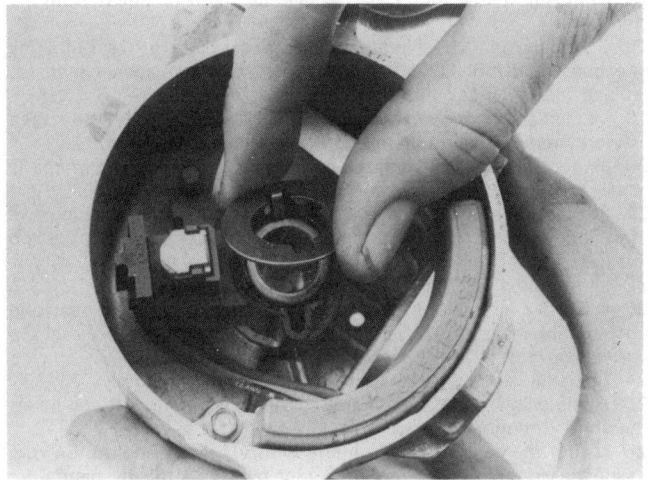

11.13 As soon as you remove the distributor shaft, note how the washer is installed before removing it (it could easily fall out and get lost)

11.14 To detach the octane rod from the distributor, remove the retaining screw (arrow) — note the condition of the small square rubber grommet that seals the octane rod hole when you pull the rod out (it seals the interior of the distributor to prevent moisture from damaging the electronics)

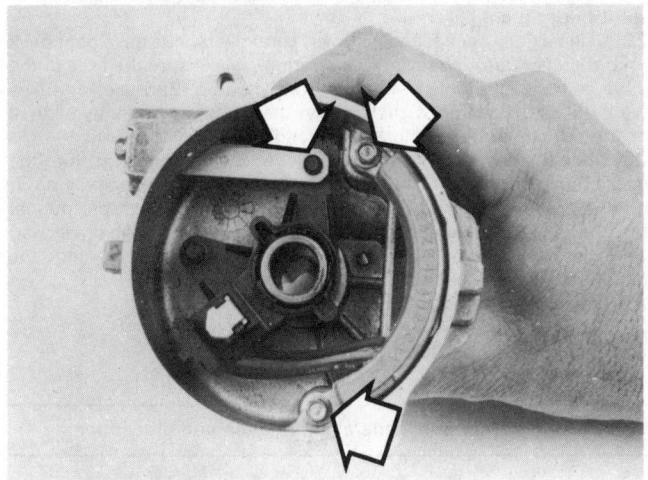

11.15 To remove the octane rod, lift the inner end of the rod off the stator assembly post (arrow) — to remove the stator assembly, remove both mounting screws (arrows) and lift the stator straight up off the posts

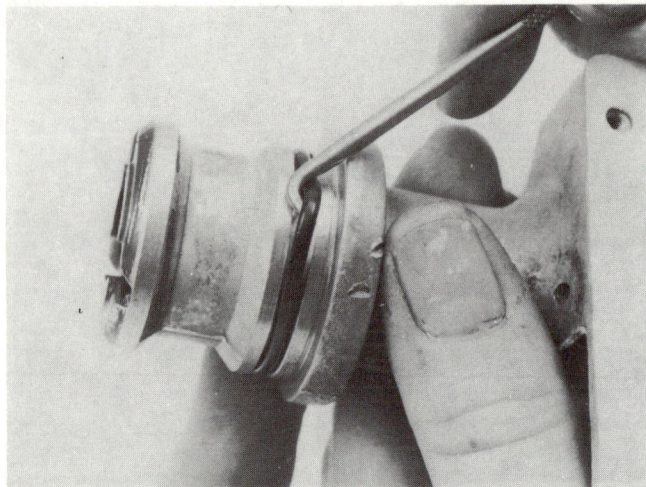

11.19   If the O-ring at the base of the distributor is worn
or damaged, replace it with a new one

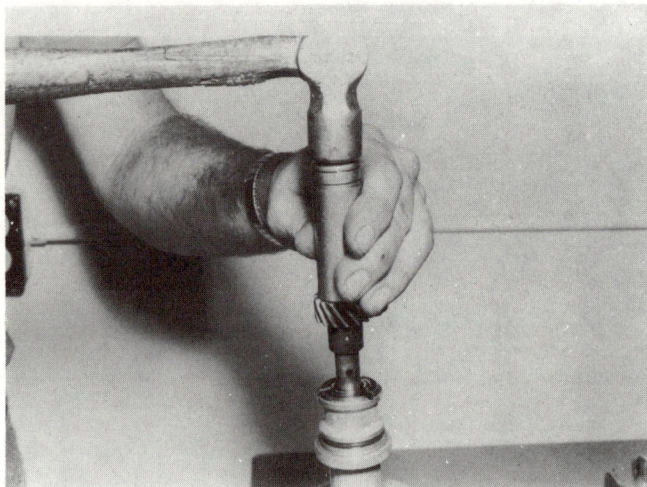

11.28a   After securing the distributor assembly upside
down in a vise, note the roll pin holes in the drive gear and
the shaft, then tap the drive gear onto the shaft with
a deep socket and hammer

17 Gently lift it straight up and remove the stator assembly from the distributor.
18 Check the shaft bushing in the distributor base for wear or signs of excessive heat buildup. If signs of wear and/or damage are evident, replace the complete distributor assembly.
19 Inspect the O-ring at the base of the distributor. If it's damaged or worn, remove it and install a new one (see illustration).
20 Inspect the base casting for cracks and wear. If any damage is evident, replace the distributor assembly.
21 Place the stator assembly in position over the shaft bushing and press it down onto the distributor base until it's completely seated on the posts.
22 Install the stator screws and tighten them securely.
23 Insert the octane rod through the hole in the distributor base and push the inner end of the rod onto the post. Note: *Make sure that the octane rod hole is proper sealed by the grommet.*
24 Reinstall the octane rod screw and tighten it securely.
25 Apply a light coat of engine oil to the distributor shaft and insert the shaft through the bushing.
26 Mount the distributor in the vise with the lower end up. Be sure to line the vise jaws with a few clean shop rags to protect the distributor base. Place a block of wood under the distributor shaft to support it and prevent it from falling out while the drive gear is being installed.
27 Using the paint marks you made on the drive gear and the distributor shaft housing, turn the shaft until the drive gear hole (and paint mark), the shaft hole and the the paint mark on the distributor shaft housing are aligned.
28 Using a deep socket and hammer, carefully tap the drive gear back onto the distributor shaft (see illustration). Make sure the hole in the drive gear and the hole in the shaft are lined up. Because the holes were drilled off center by the factory, they must be perfectly aligned or the roll pin cannot be installed (see illustration).
29 Once the drive gear is seated and the holes are lined up, turn the distributor sideways in the vise and, with an assistant steadying it, drive a new roll pin into the drive gear with a 5/32-inch pin punch. Make sure that neither end of the roll pin protrudes from the drive gear.
30 Check the distributor shaft for smooth rotation, then remove the distributor assembly from the vise.
31 Install the TFI-IV module (refer to Section 10).
32 Install the rotor (refer to Chapter 1 if necessary).
33 Install the distributor (refer to Section 8).

12 Charging system — general information and precautions

The charging system includes the alternator, either an internal or an external voltage regulator, a charge indicator or warning light, the battery, a fusible link and the wiring between all the components. The charging system supplies electrical power for the ignition system, the lights, the radio, etc. The alternator is driven by a drivebelt at the front (right end) of the engine.

11.28b   If the drive gear and shaft roll pin holes are
misaligned, the roll pin cannot be driven through the drive
gear and shaft holes — this drive gear must now be pulled
off the shaft and realigned

The purpose of the voltage regulator is to limit the alternator's voltage to a preset value. This prevents power surges, circuit overloads, etc., during peak voltage output. On EVR (external voltage regulator) systems, the regulator is mounted on the right fender apron of the vehicle. On IAR (integral alternator/regulator) systems, a solid state regulator is housed inside a plastic module mounted on the alternator itself.

The fusible link is a short length of insulated wire integral with the engine compartment wiring harness. The link is four wire gauges smaller in diameter than the circuit it protects. Production fusible links and their identification flags are identified by the flag color. Refer to Chapter 12 for detailed information regarding the identification colors of both production and service fusible links.

The charging system doesn't ordinarily require periodic maintenance. However, the drivebelt, battery and wires and connections should be inspected at the intervals outlined in Chapter 1.

Be very careful when making electrical circuit connections to a vehicle equipped with an alternator and note the following:

a) When reconnecting wires to the alternator from the battery, be sure to note the polarity.
b) Before using arc welding equipment to repair any part of the vehicle, disconnect the wires from the alternator and the battery terminals.

14.2a The electrical connectors on a typical IAR type alternator (four-cylinder engine shown)

14.2b The electrical connectors on a typical EVR type alternator (3.0L V6 shown)

c) Never start the engine with a battery charger connected.
d) Always disconnect both battery leads before using a battery charger.

13 Charging system — check

1   If a malfunction occurs in the charging circuit, do not immediately assume that the alternator is causing the problem. First check the following items:
  a) The battery cables where they connect to the battery. Make sure the connections are clean and tight.
  b) The battery electrolyte specific gravity. If it is low, charge the battery.
  c) Check the external alternator wiring and connections.
  d) Check the drivebelt condition and tension (see Chapter 1).
  e) Check the alternator mounting bolts for tightness.
  f) Run the engine and check the alternator for abnormal noise.
2   Using a voltmeter, check the battery voltage with the engine off. It should be approximately 12 volts.
3   Start the engine and check the battery voltage again. It should now be approximately 14 to 15 volts.
4   If the indicated voltage reading is less or more than the specified charging voltage, replace the voltage regulator. If replacing the regulator fails to restore the voltage to the specified range, the problem may be within the alternator.
5   Due to the special equipment necessary to test or service the alternator, is recommended that if a fault is suspected the vehicle be taken to a dealer or a shop with the proper equipment. Because of this the home mechanic should limit maintenance to checking connections and the inspection and replacement of the brushes.
6   The ammeter (ALT) gauge or alternator warning light on the instrument panel indicates charge or discharge — current passing into or out of the battery. With the electrical equipment switched on and the engine idling, the gauge needle may show a discharge condition. At fast idle or at normal driving speeds the needle should stay on the charge side of the gauge, with the charged state of the battery determining just how far over.
7   If the gauge does not show a change or the alternator light (if equipped) remains on, there is a problem in the system. Before inspecting the brushes or replacing the alternator, the battery condition, belt tension and electrical cable connections should be checked.

14 Alternator — removal and installation

Refer to illustrations 14.2a and 14.2b.
1   Detach the cable from the negative terminal of the battery.
2   Unplug the electrical connectors from the alternator (if the vehicle

is equipped with an IAR-type alternator) and the voltage regulator **(see illustrations)**.
3   Loosen the alternator adjustment and pivot bolts and detach the drivebelt (see Chapter 1).
4   Remove the adjustment and pivot bolts and separate the alternator from the engine.
5   Installation is the reverse of removal.
6   After the alternator is installed, adjust the drivebelt tension (see Chapter 1).

15 Alternator brushes (EVR-type alternator) — replacement

Refer to illustrations 15.1, 15.3a, 15.3b, 15.4, 15.6 and 15.11

1   **Note:** *Internal replacement parts for alternators may not be readily available in your area. Check into availability before proceeding. To determine the type and output of your alternator, always jot down the numbers located on the front housing* **(see illustration)** *and take them with you to the parts department.* Remove the alternator as described in Section 14.

15.1 Make sure that you write down the part number on the alternator before purchasing new brushes

15.3a   To separate the two end housings, remove all four through-bolts (arrows) — the waterproof cement (arrow right above the end cap for the rear rotor bearing) must also be removed

15.3b   Carefully pull apart the two end housings

2   Scribe a mark on both end housings and the stator to simplify reassembly.
3   Remove the through bolts, then remove the cement covering the access hole (see illustration) and separate the front housing and rotor from the rear housing and stator. Be careful that you do not separate the rear housing and stator (see illustration).
4   Use a soldering iron to unsolder and disengage the brush holder lead wire from the rectifier (see illustration).
5   Remove the two brush holder screws (see illustration 15.4) and lift the brush holder from the rear housing.
6   Insert a paper clip or a piece of stiff wire through the new brush holder (see illustration) to hold the new brushes in place.
7   Place the brush holder in position in the rear housing, making sure the wire protrudes through the hole in the rear end housing.
8   Install the brush holder screws through the new brush holder.
9   Press the brush holder lead onto the rectifier lead and solder them in place. Caution: The rectifier can be overheated and damaged if the soldering is not done quickly.
10   Place the rotor and front housing in position in the stator and rear housing. After aligning the scribe marks, install the through bolts.
11   Turn the fan and pulley to check for binding in the alternator. Withdraw the wire (see illustration) and seal the hole with waterproof cement. Caution: Do not use RTV-type sealer on the hole.

15.4   Before removing the brush holder mounting screws (arrows), unsolder the single lead wire (arrow) from the rectifier — work quickly so that you don't overheat the rectifier

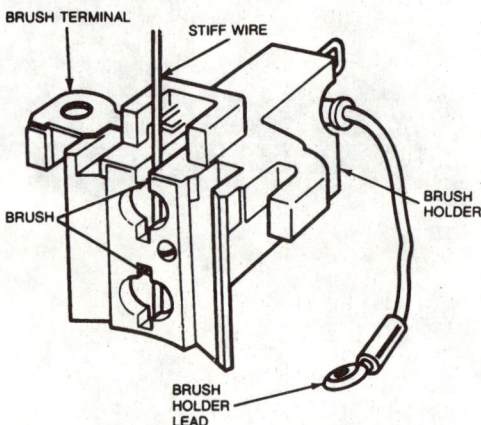

15.6   Insert a paper clip or a stiff piece of wire through the new brush holder to hold the brushes and springs in place while you install the brush/holder assembly and reassemble the alternator

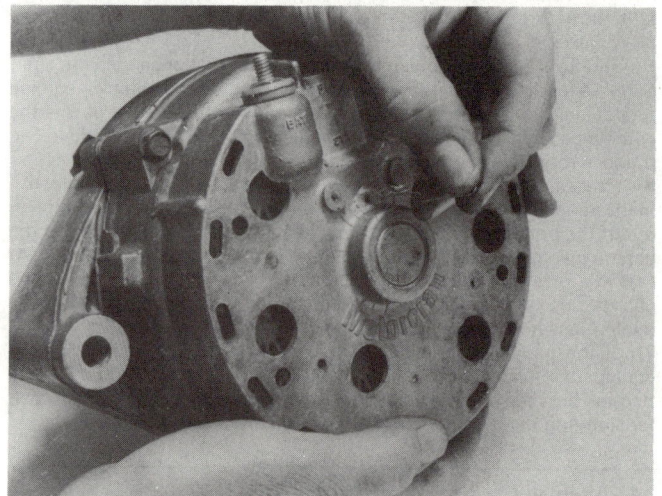

15.11   After the two end housings are reassembled and the through bolts are reinstalled, pull the wire retaining the brushes out through the hole in the rear housing and seal the hole with waterproof cement (do not use RTV-type sealer on the hole)

16.2 The external voltage regulator is located at the left front corner of the engine compartment (the battery has been removed in this photo for clarity) — to remove the regulator, simply unplug the wires and remove the two mounting bolts (arrows)

16 External Voltage Regulator (EVR) — replacement

Refer to illustration 16.2

1   Detach the cable from the negative terminal of the battery.
2   Locate the voltage regulator next to the battery (see illustration).
3   Although not absolutely necessary, it's easier to replace the regulator with the battery removed (see Section 2).
4   Unplug the electrical connector from the voltage regulator.
5   Remove the regulator mounting bolts.
6   Detach the regulator.
7   Installation is the reverse of removal.

17 Voltage regulator/alternator brushes (IAR-type alternator) — replacement

Refer to illustrations 17.3, 17.5 and 17.9

1   Remove the alternator (refer to Section 14).

17.3 To detach the voltage regulator/brush holder assembly, remove the four screws (arrows)

2   Set the alternator on a clean workbench.
3   Remove the four voltage regulator mounting screws (see illustration).
4   Detach the voltage regulator.
5   Detach the rubber plugs and remove the brush lead retaining screws and nuts to separate the brush leads from the holder (see illustration). Note that the screws have Torx heads and require a special screwdriver.
6   After noting the relationship of the brushes to the brush holder assembly, remove both brushes. Don't lose the springs.
7   If you're installing a new voltage regulator, insert the old brushes into the brush holder of the new regulator. If you're installing new brushes, insert them into the brush holder of the old regulator. Make sure the springs are properly compressed and the brushes are properly inserted into the recesses in the brush holder.
8   Install the brush lead retaining screws and nuts.
9   Insert a short section of wire, like a paper clip, through the hole in the voltage regulator (see illustration) to hold the brushes in the retracted position during regulator installation.
10 Carefully install the regulator. Make sure the brushes don't hang up on the rotor.
11 Install the voltage regulator screws and tighten them securely.
12 Remove the wire or paper clip.
13 Install the alternator (refer to Section 14).

17.5 To remove the brushes from the voltage regulator/brush holder assembly, detach the rubber plugs from the two brush lead wire screws and remove both screws (arrows)

17.9 Before installing the voltage regulator/brush holder assembly, insert a paper clip, as shown, to hold the brushes in place during installation — after installation, simply pull the paper clip out

18   Starting system — general information

The function of the starting system is to crank the engine to start it. The system is composed of the starter motor, starter relay, battery, switch and connecting wires.

Turning the ignition key to the Start position actuates the starter relay through the starter control circuit. The starter relay then connects the battery to the starter. The battery supplies the electrical energy to the starter motor, which does the actual work of cranking the engine.

Vehicles equipped with an automatic transaxle have a Neutral start switch in the starter control circuit, which prevents operation of the starter unless the shift lever is in Neutral or Park. The circuit on vehicles with a manual transaxle prevents operation of the starter motor unless the clutch pedal is depressed.

Never operate the starter motor for more than 30 seconds at a time without pausing to allow it to cool for at least two minutes. Excessive cranking can cause overheating, which can seriously damage the starter.

19   Starter motor and circuit — in-vehicle check

Note: *Before diagnosing starter problems, make sure the battery is fully charged.*

General check

1   If the starter motor doesn't turn at all when the switch is operated, make sure the shift lever is in Neutral or Park (automatic transaxle) or the clutch pedal is depressed (manual transaxle).
2   Make sure the battery is charged and that all cables at the battery and starter relay terminals are secure.
3   If the starter motor spins but the engine doesn't turn over, then the drive assembly in the starter motor is slipping and the starter motor must be replaced (see Section 20).
4   If, when the switch is actuated, the starter motor doesn't operate at all but the starter relay operates (clicks), then the problem lies with either the battery, the starter relay contacts or the starter motor connections.
5   If the starter relay doesn't click when the ignition switch is actuated, either the starter relay circuit is open or the relay itself is defective. Check the starter relay circuit (see the wiring diagrams at the end of this book) or replace the relay (see Section 21).
6   To check the starter relay circuit, remove the push-on connector from the relay wire (the red one with a blue stripe). Make sure that the connection is clean and secure and the relay bracket is grounded. If the connections are good, check the operation of the relay with a jumper wire. To do this, place the transaxle in Park (automatic) or Neutral (manual). Remove the push-on connector from the relay. Connect a jumper wire between the battery positive terminal and the exposed terminal on the relay. If the starter motor now operates, the starter relay is okay. The problem is in the ignition switch, Neutral start switch or in the starting circuit wiring (look for open or loose connections).
7   If the starter motor still doesn't operate, replace the starter relay (see Section 21).
8   If the starter motor cranks the engine at an abnormally slow speed, first make sure the battery is fully charged and all terminal connections are clean and tight. Also check the connections at the starter relay and battery ground. Eyelet terminals should not be easily rotated by hand. Also check for a short to ground. If the engine is partially seized, or has the wrong viscosity oil in it, it will crank slowly.

Starter cranking circuit test

Refer to illustration 19.12

Note: *To determine the location of excessive resistance in the starter circuit, perform the following simple series of tests.*

9   Disconnect the ignition coil wire from the distributor cap and ground it on the engine.
10   Connect a remote control starter switch from the battery terminal of the starter relay to the S terminal of the relay.
11   Connect a voltmeter positive lead to the starter motor terminal of the starter relay, then connect the negative lead to ground.
12   Make the test connections as shown **(see illustration)**. Refer to this illustration as you perform the following four tests.

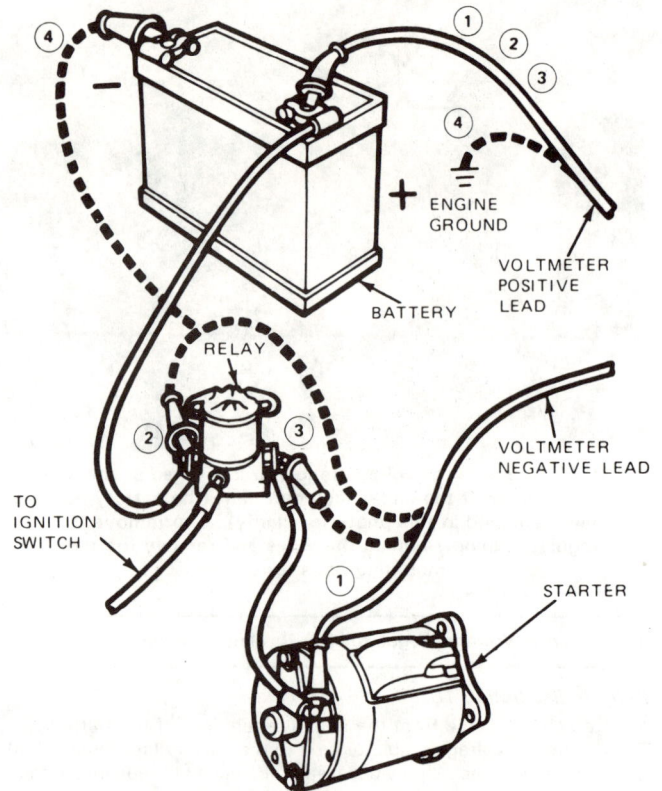

19.12   The four test lead connections for the starter cranking circuit test

13   Operate the ignition switch and take the voltmeter readings as soon as a steady figure is indicated. Don't allow the starter motor to turn for more than 30 seconds at a time.
14   The voltage drop in the circuit will be indicated by the voltmeter (put the voltmeter on the 0-to-2 volt range). The maximum allowable voltage drop should be:
   a)   0.5-volt with the voltmeter negative lead connected to the starter terminal and the positive lead connected to the battery positive terminal (Connection 1 in illustration 19.12).
   b)   0.1-volt with the voltmeter negative lead connected to the starter relay (battery side) and the positive lead connected to the positive terminal of the battery (Connection 2).
   c)   0.3-volt with the voltmeter negative lead connected to the starter relay (starter side) and the positive lead connected to the positive terminal of the battery (Connection 3).
   d)   0.3-volt with the voltmeter negative lead connected to the negative terminal of the battery and the positive lead connected to the engine ground (Connection 4).

20   Starter motor — removal and installation

Refer to illustrations 20.3 and 20.5

1   Detach the cable from the negative terminal of the battery.
2   Raise the vehicle and support it securely on jackstands.
3   Disconnect the large cable from the terminal on the starter motor **(see illustration)**.
4   Remove the two bolts attaching the rear support bracket **(see illustration 20.3)** and detach the bracket.
5   On four-cylinder engines, remove the three starter-to-bellhousing bolts. On V6 engines, remove the two starter-to-bellhousing bolts. Note that a ground cable is attached to the upper starter stud bolt **(see illustration)**.
6   Remove the starter. On vehicles equipped with an automatic trans-

20.3 To remove the starter motor from the engine, remove the bracket bolts and detach the starter cable (arrows) (3.0L V6 engine shown, others similar)

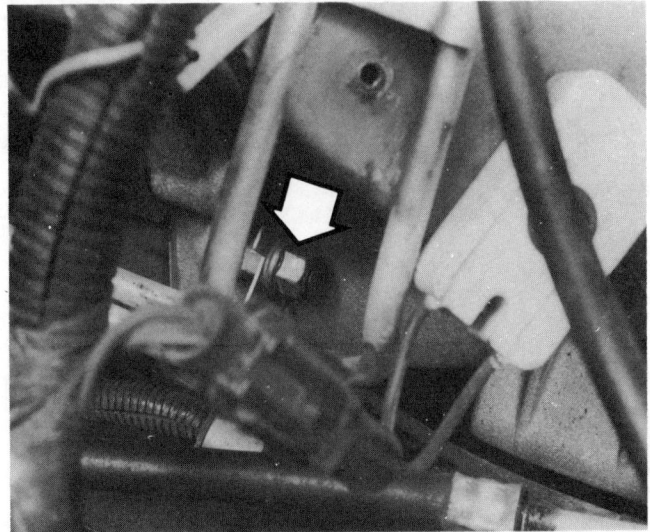

20.5 Note that the upper starter motor stud bolt is the attachment point for a ground cable (arrow) (3.0L V6 engine shown, others similar)

axle, the starter must be removed between the radiator and sub-frame. On vehicles with a manual transaxle, remove the starter between the sub-frame and the engine.

7   Installation is the reverse of removal.

21   Starter relay — removal and installation

Refer to illustration 21.2

1   Detach the cable from the negative terminal of the battery.
2   Label the wires and the terminals, then disconnect the Neutral safety switch wire (automatic transaxle only), the battery cable, the fusible link and the starter cable from the relay terminals **(see illustration)**.
3   Remove the mounting bolts and detach the relay.
4   Installation is the reverse of removal.

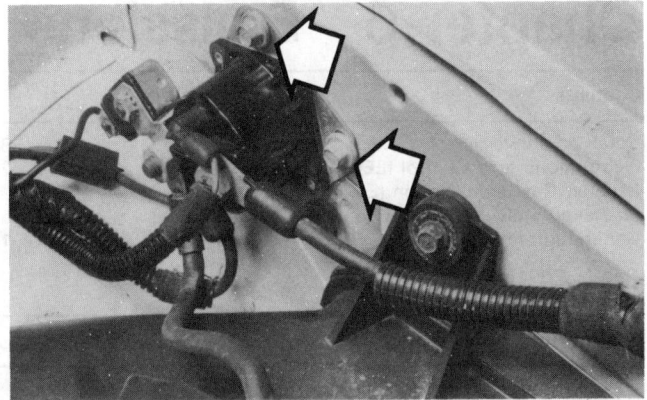

21.2 To replace the starter relay, clearly label and detach the wires, then remove the mounting bolts (arrows)

Chapter 6   Emissions control systems

Contents

1   General information

Refer to illustration 1.7

To prevent pollution of the atmosphere from incompletely burned and evaporating gases, and to maintain good driveability and fuel economy, a number of emission control systems are incorporated. They include the:

Electronic Engine Control (EEC-IV) system
Exhaust Gas Recirculation (EGR) system
Managed air thermactor system
Fuel evaporative emissions control system
Positive Crankcase Ventilation (PCV) system
Inlet air temperature control system (four-cylinder engine)
Catalytic converter

All of these systems are linked, directly or indirectly, to the EEC-IV system.

The Sections in this Chapter include general descriptions, checking procedures within the scope of the home mechanic and component replacement procedures (when possible) for each of the systems listed above.

Before assuming that an emissions control system is malfunctioning, check the fuel and ignition systems carefully. The diagnosis of some emission control devices requires specialized tools, equipment and training. If checking and servicing become too difficult or if a procedure is beyond your ability, consult a dealer service department.

This doesn't mean, however, that emission control systems are in general particularly difficult to maintain and repair. You can quickly and easily perform many checks and do most (if not all) of the regular maintenance at home with common tune-up and hand tools. **Note:** *The most frequent cause of emissions problems is simply a loose or broken vacuum hose or wire, so always check the hose and wiring connections first.*

Pay close attention to any special precautions outlined in this Chapter. It should be noted that the illustrations of the various systems may not exactly match the system installed on your vehicle because of changes made by the manufacturer during production or from year to year.

A Vehicle Emissions Control Information label is located in the engine compartment **(see illustration)**. This label contains important emissions specifications and adjustment information, as well as a vacuum hose schematic with emissions components identified. When servicing the engine or emissions systems, the VECI label in your particular vehicle should always be checked for up-to-date information.

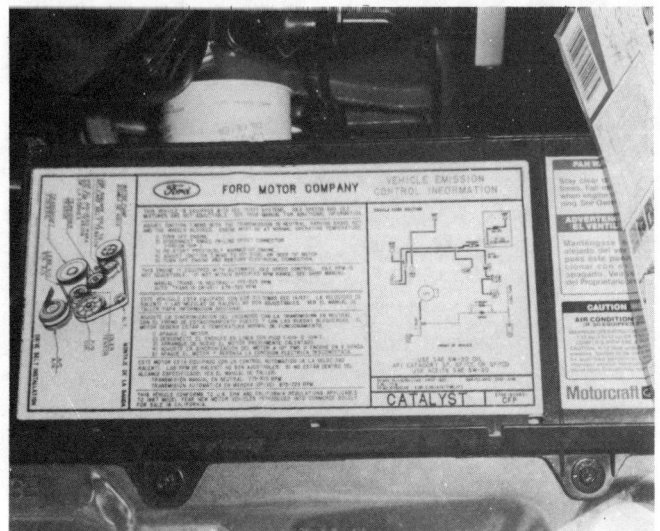

1.7   The Vehicle Emissions Control Information (VECI) label is located on the sight shield (the plastic eye protector attached to the upper radiator support)

2.3 V6 engines are equipped with a knock sensor located on the back side of the block — to replace a knock sensor, drain the engine coolant, unplug the electrical connector (already detached in this photo) and unscrew the sensor — be sure to wrap the threads with teflon tape to prevent coolant leaks when installing the new sensor

2.5 A typical Air Charge Temperature (ACT) sensor installed in the intake runner of a 3.0L V6 — to replace it, unplug the electrical connector and unscrew the sensor — be sure to wrap the threads with teflon tape to prevent air leaks when installing the new sensor

2.6 A typical EGR valve position (EVP) sensor (four-cylinder engine shown) — to replace it, simply unplug the electrical connector and remove the mounting screws

2.7 A typical Engine Coolant Temperature (ECT) sensor (3.0L V6 shown) — to replace it, drain the engine coolant to a level below that of the water outlet connection housing, unplug the electrical connector and unscrew the sensor — be sure to wrap the threads with teflon tape to prevent coolant leaks

2 Electronic Engine Control (EEC-IV) system

Refer to illustrations 2.3, 2.5, 2.6, 2.7, 2.8, 2.9, 2.11 and 2.14

General description

1   The Electronic Engine Control (EEC-IV) system consists of an on-board computer, known as the Electronic Control Assembly (ECA), and the information sensors, which monitor various functions of the engine and send data to the ECA. Based on the data and the information programmed into the computer's memory, the ECA generates output signals to control various engine functions.
2   The ECA, located inside the dashboard (behind the glove box, above the recirculating duct assembly), is the "brain" of the EEC-IV system. It receives data from a number of sensors and other electronic components (switches, relays, etc.). Based on the information it receives, the ECA generates output signals to control various relays, solenoids and other actuators (see below). The ECA is specifically calibrated to optimize the emissions, fuel economy and driveability of your vehicle. **Note:** *Because of a Federally-mandated extended warranty which covers the ECA, the information sensors and all components under its control, and because any damage to the ECA, the sensors and/or the control devices may void the warranty, it isn't a good idea to attempt diagnosis or replacement of the ECA at home. Take your vehicle to a dealer service department if the ECA or a system component malfunctions.*

it isn't a good idea to attempt diagnosis or replacement of the ECA at home. Take your vehicle to a dealer service department if the ECA or a system component malfunctions.

Information input sensors
3   Some engines are equipped with a knock sensor **(see illustration)** which signals the ECA when the engine "knocks," causing the ECA to alter ignition timing.
4   When battery voltage is applied to the air conditioner compressor clutch, a signal is sent to the ECA, which interprets the signal as an added load created by the compressor and increases engine idle speed accordingly to compensate.
5   The Air Charge Temperature sensor (ACT), threaded into a runner of the intake manifold **(see illustration)**, provides the ECA with fuel/air mixture temperature information. The ECA uses this information to correct fuel flow and control fuel flow during cold enrichment (cold starts).
6   The EGR Valve Position Sensor (EVP), located on the EGR valve **(see illustration)**, tells the ECA the position of the EGR valve.
7   The Engine Coolant Temperature (ECT) sensor, which is located near the water outlet connection **(see illustration)**, monitors engine coolant temperature. The ECT sends the ECA a constantly varying voltage signal which influences ECA control of the fuel mixture, ignition timing and EGR operation.
8   The Manifold Absolute Pressure (MAP) sensor, mounted on the firewall **(see illustration)**, measures the absolute pressure of the mixture in the intake manifold and sends a signal to the ECA that is proportional

2.8   A typical MAP sensor — to replace it, simply unplug the electrical connector and remove the two bracket bolts (one is hidden under the weatherstripping in this photo)

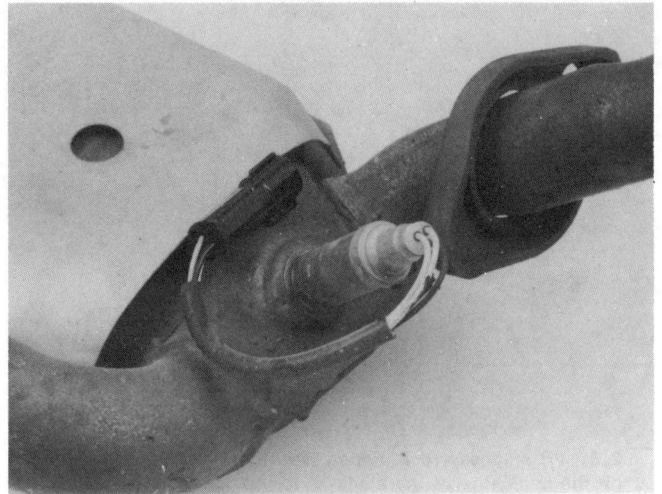

2.9   A typical exhaust gas oxygen (EGO) sensor installation (3.0L V6 engine catalytic converter pipe shown) — to replace it, unplug the electrical connector and unscrew the sensor — be sure to use anti-seize compound on the threads to prevent the sensor from welding itself to the pipe

2.11   A typical throttle position (TP) sensor (four-cylinder engine shown) — see Chapter 4 before attempting to perform any operations involving the TP sensor on your vehicle

2.14   A typical evaporative canister purge solenoid — to replace it, simply unplug the electrical connector, label the hoses and detach them

to absolute pressure.

9   The oxygen sensor (EGO), which is threaded into the exhaust manifold **(see illustration)**, constantly monitors the oxygen content of the exhaust gases. A voltage signal which varies in accordance with the difference between the oxygen content of the exhaust gases and the surrounding atmosphere is sent to the ECA. The ECA translates this exhaust gas oxygen content signal to fuel/air ratio, then alters it to the ideal ratio for current engine operating conditions.

10   The Profile Ignition Pick-up (PIP), integral with the distributor, informs the ECA of crankshaft position and speed. The PIP assembly consists of an armature with four windows and four metal tabs that rotate past a stator assembly (the Hall Effect switch).

11   The Throttle Position Sensor (TPS), which is mounted on the side of the throttle body **(see illustration)** and connected directly to the throttle shaft, senses throttle movement and position, then transmits an electrical signal to the ECA. This signal enables the ECA to determine when the throttle is closed, in its normal cruise condition or wide open.

12   The pressure feedback electronic (PFE) EGR transducer converts a varying exhaust pressure signal into a proportional analog voltage which is digitized by the EEC-IV processor. The EEC-IV processor uses the signal from the PFE transducer to compute the optimum EGR flow.

Output devices

13   The integrated relay control module, which is operated by the ECA, provides an output signal which controls operation of the A/C compressor clutch, the engine cooling fan and the fuel pump.

14   The Canister purge solenoid (CANP), located on the left fender well **(see illustration)**, switches manifold vacuum to operate the canister purge valve when a signal is received from the ECA. Vacuum opens the purge valve when the solenoid is energized.

15   The EGR control solenoid, located in the right rear corner of the engine compartment, switches manifold vacuum to operate the EGR valve on command from the ECA. Vacuum opens the EGR valve when the solenoid is energized.

16   The EGR shut-off solenoid is an electrically operated vacuum valve located between the manifold vacuum source and the EGR valve. A controlled vacuum bleed is located between the solenoid and the EGR valve. This vacuum bleed is a Backpressure Variable Transducer (BVT). These two devices operate the EGR valve for optimum performance. Solenoid switch vacuum is also supplied to the canister purge valve.

17   The EGR vent solenoid opens the EGR control solenoid vacuum line. When the vent solenoid is energized, the control solenoid opens the EGR valve.

18 The feedback control solenoid regulates the idle, off idle and main system fuel/air ratios in accordance with signals from the ECA.

19 On vehicles with a four-cylinder engine, the single, solenoid operated fuel injector is located in the throttle body. On vehicles with a V6 engine, the six injectors are located in the intake ports. The ECA controls the length of time each injector is open. The "open" time of the injector determines the amount of fuel delivered. For information regarding injector replacement, see Chapter 4.

20 The fuel pump relay is activated by the ECA when the ignition switch is in the On position. When the ignition switch is turned to the On position, the relay is activated to supply initial line pressure to the system. For information regarding fuel pump check and replacement, see Chapter 4.

21 The Idle Speed Control (ISC) motor (four-cylinder engine only) changes idle speed in accordance with signals from the ECA. For information regarding ISC replacement, see Chapter 4.

22 The TFI-IV ignition module, mounted on the side of the distributor base, triggers the ignition coil and determines dwell. The ECA uses a signal from the Profile Ignition Pick-Up to determine crankshaft position. Ignition timing is determined by the ECA, which then signals the module to fire the coil. For further information regarding the TFI-IV module, refer to the appropriate Section in Chapter 5.

23 The Wide Open Throttle (WOT) A/C cut-out circuit is energized by the ECA when a WOT condition is detected. During WOT, power to the A/C compressor clutch is disconnected until sometime after partial throttle operation resumes. For further information regarding the WOT A/C cut-out, refer to Chapter 4.

Checking

24 Because of the specialized test equipment needed to check the sensors and output devices, diagnosis of the components described above is well beyond the scope of the home mechanic. If engine driveability deteriorates, take the vehicle to a dealer service department to have the EEC-IV system checked.

Component replacement

Note: *Because of the Federally-mandated extended warranty which covers the ECA, the information sensors and the devices it controls, there's no point in replacing any of the following components yourself unless the warranty has expired. However, once the warranty has expired, you may wish to perform some of the following component replacement procedures yourself after having the problem diagnosed by a dealer service department or repair shop.*

Air Charge Temperature (ACT) sensor
25 Detach the cable from the negative terminal of the battery.
26 Locate the ACT sensor on the intake manifold **(see illustration 2.5)**.
27 Unplug the electrical connector from the sensor.
28 Remove the sensor with a wrench.
29 Wrap the threads of the new sensor with teflon tape to prevent air leaks.
30 Installation is the reverse of removal.

EGR Valve Position (EVP) sensor (four-cylinder engine)
31 Detach the cable from the negative terminal of the battery.
32 Locate the EVP sensor on the EGR valve **(see illustration 2.6)**.
33 Unplug the electrical connector from the sensor.
34 Remove the three mounting bolts and detach the sensor.
35 Installation is the reverse of removal.

Engine Coolant Temperature (ECT) sensor
36 Detach the cable from the negative terminal of the battery.
37 Locate the ECT sensor near the water outlet connection **(see illustration 2.7)**.
38 Unplug the electrical connector from the sensor.
39 Remove the sensor with a wrench.
40 Wrap the threads of the new sensor with teflon tape to prevent coolant leakage.
41 Installation is the reverse of removal.

Manifold Absolute Pressure (MAP) sensor
42 Detach the cable from the negative terminal of the battery.
43 Locate the MAP sensor on the firewall **(see illustration 2.8)**.
44 Unplug the electrical connector from the sensor.
45 Detach the vacuum line from the sensor.
46 Remove the two mounting bolts and detach the sensor.
47 Installation is the reverse of removal.

Exhaust Gas Oxygen (EGO) sensor
48 Detach the cable from the negative terminal of the battery.
49 Raise the vehicle and support it securely on jackstands. Locate the EGO sensor on the exhaust manifold (four-cylinder engine) or the catalytic converter pipe (V6 engine) **(see illustration 2.9)**.
50 Unplug the electrical connector from the sensor.
51 Remove the sensor with a wrench.
52 Coat the threads of the new sensor with anti-seize compound to prevent the threads from welding themselves to the manifold.
53 Installation is the reverse of removal.

Throttle Position Sensor (TPS) switch
54 Don't attempt to replace the TPS switch before studying the replacement procedure for the switch on your vehicle (see Chapter 4). Specialized calibration equipment is often necessary to adjust the switch once it's installed, making adjustment beyond the scope of the home mechanic.

Canister Purge Solenoid
55 Detach the cable from the negative terminal of the battery.
56 Locate the canister purge solenoid on the left side of the engine compartment, next to the left wheel well **(see illustration 2.14)**.
57 Unplug the electrical connector from the solenoid.
58 Label the vacuum hoses and ports, then detach the hoses.
59 Remove the solenoid.
60 Installation is the reverse of removal.

---

3 Exhaust Gas Recirculation (EGR) system

Refer to illustrations 3.17, 3.18a and 3.18b

General description

1 The EGR system is designed to reintroduce small amounts of exhaust gas into the combustion cycle, thus reducing the generation of nitrous oxide emissions. The amount of exhaust gas reintroduced and the timing of the cycle is controlled by various factors such as engine speed, altitude, manifold vacuum, exhaust system backpressure, coolant temperature and throttle angle. All EGR valves are vacuum actuated and the vacuum diagram for your particular vehicle is shown on the *Emissions Control Information label* in the engine compartment.

2 Two types of EGR valves are used on Taurus/Sable vehicles: the electronic (sonic) type, used on vehicles with a four-cylinder engine, and the Pressure Feedback Electronic (PFE) valve used on California 3.0L V6's and all 3.8L V6's.

Electronic EGR (sonic) valve (four-cylinder engine)
3 The electronic EGR valve controls EGR flow with an EGR valve position (EVP) sensor attached to the top of the valve. The valve is operated by a vacuum signal from the dual EGR solenoid valves or the electronic vacuum regulator which actuates the valve diaphragm. As supply vacuum overcomes the spring load, the diaphragm is actuated, lifting the pintle off the seat and allowing exhaust gas to recirculate. The amount of flow is proportional to the pintle position. The EVP sensor sends an electrical signal indicating its position to the ECA.

Pressure Feedback Electronic (PFE) EGR valve
4 The PFE valve is a conventional ported EGR valve with a back pressure sensing tube attached to it. The valve is used in conjunction with a pressure transducer which supplies pressure feedback to the EEC-IV processor. The EGR flow rate is proportional to the pressure drop across a remotely mounted, sharp-edged orifice.

5 Make sure that all vacuum hoses are correctly routed and securely attached. Replace cracked, crimped or broken hoses.

6 Make sure that there is no vacuum to the EGR valve at idle with the engine at normal operating temperature. **Note:** *The EVR solenoid on four-cylinder engines has a constant internal leak. You will notice a small vacuum signal (it should be less than 2 1/2 in-Hg at idle).*

7 Install a tachometer in accordance with the manufacturer's instructions.

8 If the vehicle is equipped with a V6 engine, unplug the Idle Air Bypass Valve electrical connector (see Chapter 4 if necessary).

9 Detach the vacuum supply hose from the EGR valve nipple. Plug the hose.

10 Place the transaxle in Neutral, start the engine, warm it up and allow it to idle. **Note:** *The engine's idle speed should not be altered. If the idle speed is high or low, have it adjusted by a dealer service*

3.17   Use a wrench to unscrew the threaded fitting attaching the EGR pipe to the EGR valve — it's a good idea to use anti-seize compound on the threads when installing the new valve to prevent the threads from welding to the valve (3.0L V6 engine shown)

3.18a   To detach the EGR valve from the throttle body/air intake of the 3.0L V6, remove the mounting bolts

3.18b   To detach the EGR valve from the intake manifold of the four-cylinder engine, remove the two mounting bolts

department before proceeding with this test.

11 Attach a hand vacuum pump to the EGR valve vacuum nipple and slowly apply five to ten inches of mercury vacuum.

12 If any of the following conditions occur when vacuum is applied to the EGR valve on a four-cylinder engine, replace the valve:
   a) The engine does not stall.
   b) The idle speed does not drop more than 100 rpm.
   c) The idle speed does not return to normal ($\pm$ 25 rpm) after the vacuum pump line is detached.

13 If either of the following conditions occurs when vacuum is applied to the EGR valve on V6 engines, replace the valve:
   a) If the engine stalls.
   b) If idle speed drops more than 100 rpm.
   c) If idle speed does not return to normal ($\pm$ 25 rpm) after the vacuum pump line is detached.

14 Unplug the vacuum pump and reattach the EGR vacuum supply line.

Component replacement

15 Detach the cable from the negative terminal of the battery.

16 On four-cylinder engines, unplug the electrical connector from the EGR valve position (EVP) sensor (see Section 2).

17 Using a wrench, unscrew the threaded fitting that attaches the EGR pipe to the EGR valve (see illustration).

18 Remove the EGR valve mounting bolts (see illustrations) and detach the valve and gasket from the intake manifold. Discard the old gasket.

19 If you are replacing the EGR valve but not the EVP sensor on a four-cylinder engine, remove the sensor from the old valve (see Section 2) and install it on the new valve.

20 Installation is otherwise the reverse of removal. Make sure that the gasket mating surfaces are clean and be sure to use a new EGR valve gasket. Note: *It's a good idea to use anti-seize compound on the threads of the EGR pipe to prevent them from welding to the EGR valve.*

4 Managed air thermactor system

Refer to illustrations 4.1, 4.3, 4.4 and 4.9

General description

1 The thermactor (air injection) exhaust emission control system (see illustration) reduces carbon monoxide and hydrocarbon content in the exhaust gases by injecting fresh air into the hot exhaust gases leaving the exhaust ports. When fresh air is mixed with hot exhaust gases, oxidation is increased, reducing the concentration of hydrocarbons and carbon monoxide and converting them into harmless carbon dioxide and water.

2 All vehicles with a 3.8L V6 engine utilize a ''managed air'' thermactor system, which diverts thermactor air either upstream to the

exhaust manifold check valve or downstream to the rear section check valve and dual bed catalyst.

3 An air control valve is used to direct the air upstream or downstream. An air bypass valve is used to dump air to the atmosphere. The two valves are combined into a single unit on the 3.8L V6 engine (see illustration).

4 Early four-cylinder engines are equipped with an air injection system called Pulse Air or Thermactor II (see illustration). This design uses natural pulses present in the exhaust system to pull air into the xhaust manifold and/or catalyst through pulse air valves. The pulse air valve is connected to the exhaust manifold and/or catalytic converter with a long tube and to the air cleaner or silencer with a hose.

Checking

Air supply pump

5 Check and adjust the drivebelt tension (refer to Chapter 1).

6 Disconnect the air supply hose at the air bypass valve inlet.

7 The pump is operating satisfactorily if air flow is felt at the pump outlet with the engine running at idle, increasing as the engine speed is increased.

8 If the air pump doesn't pass the above tests, replace it with a new or rebuilt unit.

Combination air bypass/air control valve

9 Clearly label, then disconnect the hoses from the combination valve outlets (see illustration).

4.1 An exploded view of the managed air thermactor system used on the 3.8L V6 engine

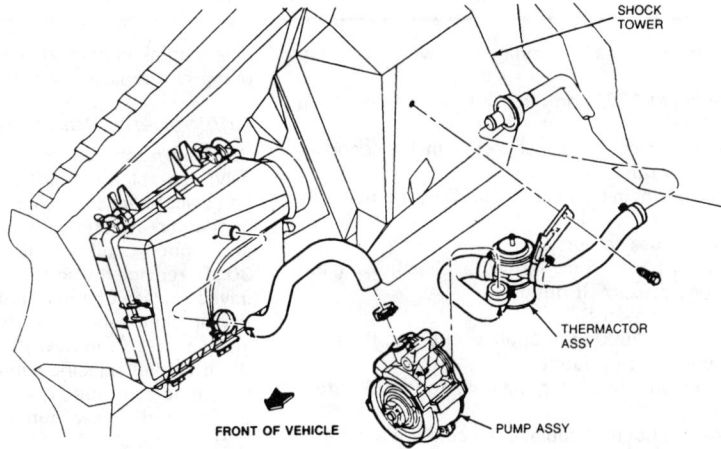

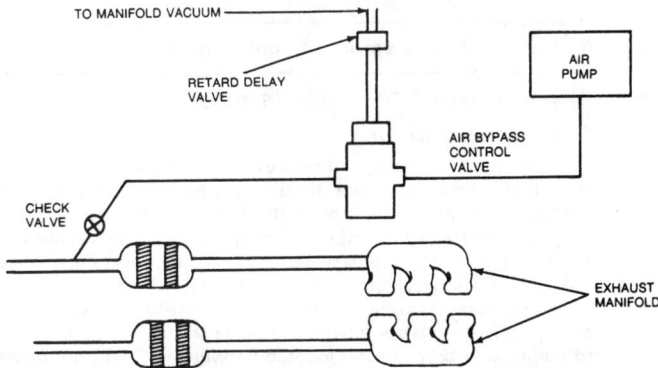

SHOCK TOWER

THERMACTOR ASSY

FRONT OF VEHICLE

PUMP ASSY

TO MANIFOLD VACUUM

RETARD DELAY VALVE

AIR PUMP

AIR BYPASS CONTROL VALVE

CHECK VALVE

EXHAUST MANIFOLD

4.3 A schematic of the thermactor system used on the 3.8L V6 system

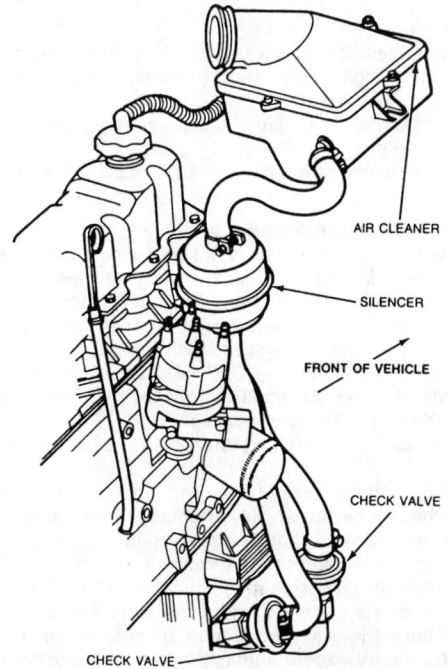

AIR CLEANER

SILENCER

FRONT OF VEHICLE

CHECK VALVE

CHECK VALVE

4.4 The Pulse Air or Thermactor II system used on early vehicles with a four-cylinder engine

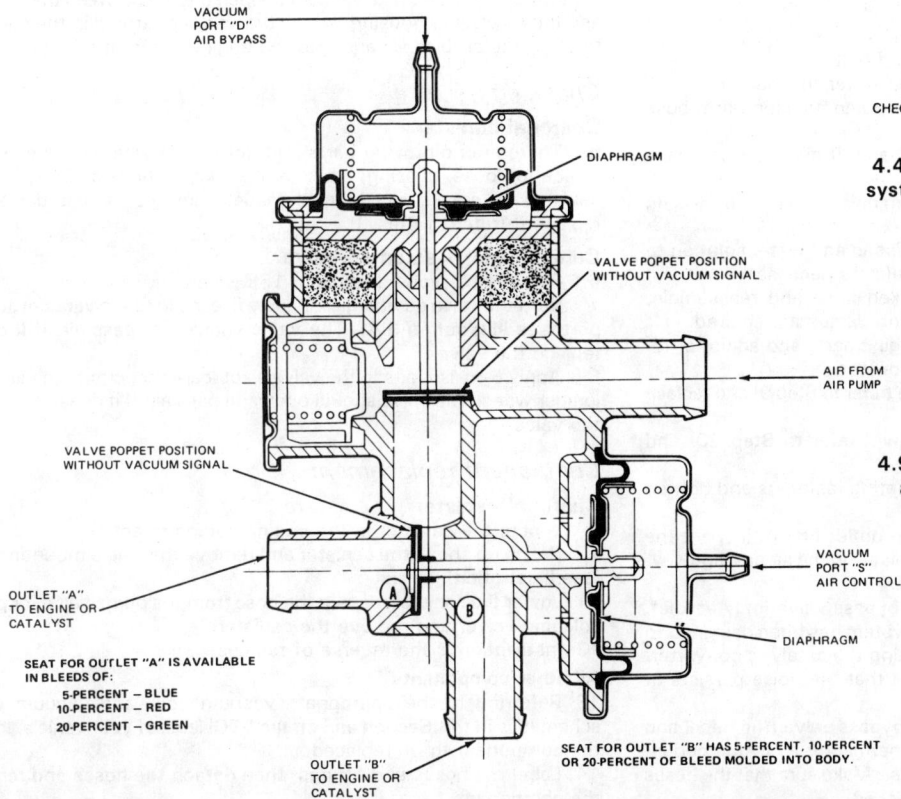

VACUUM PORT "D" AIR BYPASS

DIAPHRAGM

VALVE POPPET POSITION WITHOUT VACUUM SIGNAL

AIR FROM AIR PUMP

VALVE POPPET POSITION WITHOUT VACUUM SIGNAL

4.9 A cutaway of the combination air bypass/air control valve unit

VACUUM PORT "S" AIR CONTROL

OUTLET "A" TO ENGINE OR CATALYST

DIAPHRAGM

SEAT FOR OUTLET "A" IS AVAILABLE IN BLEEDS OF:
5-PERCENT – BLUE
10-PERCENT – RED
20-PERCENT – GREEN

OUTLET "B" TO ENGINE OR CATALYST

SEAT FOR OUTLET "B" HAS 5-PERCENT, 10-PERCENT OR 20-PERCENT OF BLEED MOLDED INTO BODY.

10 Disconnect the vacuum hose from the combination valve and plug the hose.
11 With the engine running at 1500 rpm, verify that air flows from the bypass vents.
12 Unplug and reconnect the vacuum hose at port D, then disconnect and plug the hose attached to port S.
13 Verify that vacuum is present in the hose to port D by momentarily disconnecting it.
14 Reconnect the vacuum hose to port D.
15 With the engine running at 1500 rpm, verify that air is flowing out of outlet B with no air flow present at outlet A.
16 Attach a length of hose to port S.
17 With the engine running at 1500 rpm, apply vacuum to the hose and verify that air is flowing out of outlet A.
18 Reconnect all hoses. Be sure to unplug the hose to Port S before reconnecting it.
19 If all conditions above are not met, replace the combination valve with a new one.

Check valve
20 Disconnect the hoses from both ends of the check valve.
21 Blow through both ends of the check valve, verifying that air flows in one direction only.
22 If air flows in both directions or not at all, replace the check valve with a new one.
23 When reconnecting the valve, make sure it is installed in the proper direction.

Thermactor system noise test
24 The thermactor system is not completely noiseless. Under normal conditions, noise rises in pitch as the engine speed increases. To determine if noise is the fault of the air injection system, detach the drivebelt (after verifying that the belt tension is correct) and operate the engine. If the noise disappears, proceed with the following diagnosis. **Caution:** *The pump must accumulate 500 miles (vehicle miles) before the following check is valid.* Reinstall the drivebelt (Chapter 1).
25 If the belt noise is excessive:
   a) Check for a loose belt and tighten as necessary (refer to Chapter 1).
   b) Check for a seized pump and replace it if necessary.
   c) Check for a loose pulley. Tighten the mounting bolts as required.
   d) Check for loose, broken or missing mounting brackets or bolts. Tighten or replace as necessary.
26 If there is excessive mechanical noise:
   a) Check for an overtightened mounting bolt.
   b) Check for an overtightened drivebelt (refer to Chapter 1).
   c) Check for excessive flash on the air pump adjusting arm boss and remove as necessary.
   d) Check for a distorted adjusting arm and, if necessary, replace the arm.
27 If there is excessive thermactor system noise (whirring or hissing sounds):
   a) Check for a leak in the hoses (use a soap and water solution to find the leaks) and replace the hose(s) as necessary.
   b) Check for a loose, pinched or kinked hose and reassemble, straighten or replace the hose and/or clamps as required.
   c) Check for a hose touching other engine parts and adjust or reroute the hose to prevent further contact.
   d) Check for an inoperative bypass valve (refer to Step 9) and replace if necessary.
   e) Check for an inoperative check valve (refer to Step 20) and replace if necessary.
   f) Check for loose pump or pulley mounting fasteners and tighten as necessary.
   g) Check for a restricted or bent pump outlet fitting. Inspect the fitting and remove any casting flash blocking the air passageway. Replace bent fittings.
   h) Check for air dumping through the bypass valve (only at idle). On many vehicles, the thermactor system has been designed to dump air at idle to prevent overheating the catalytic converter. This condition is normal. Determine that the noise persists at higher speeds before proceeding.
   i) Check for air dumping through the bypass valve (the decel and idle dump). On many vehicles, the thermactor air is dumped into the air cleaner or the remote silencer. Make sure that the hoses are connected properly and not cracked.
28 If there is excessive pump noise, make sure the pump has had suf-
ficient break-in time (at least 500 miles). Check for a worn or damaged pump and replace as necessary.

Component replacement
29 To replace the air bypass valve, air supply control valve, check valve, combination air bypass/air control valve or the silencer, label and disconnect the hoses leading to them, replace the faulty component and reattach the hoses to the proper ports. Make sure the hoses are in good condition. If not, replace them with new ones.
30 To replace the air supply pump, first loosen the appropriate engine drivebelts (see Chapter 1), then remove the faulty pump from the mounting bracket. Label all wires and hoses as they're removed to facilitate installation of the new unit.
31 If you're replacing either of the check valves on a Pulse Air System (Thermactor II), be sure to use a back-up wrench.
32 After the new pump is installed, adjust the drivebelts to the specified tension (see Chapter 1).

---

5 Fuel evaporative emissions control system

Refer to illustrations 5.2a, 5.2b, 5.4 and 5.10

General description
1   This system is designed to prevent hydrocarbons from being released into the atmosphere, by trapping and storing fuel vapor from the fuel tank, the carburetor or the fuel injection system.
2   The serviceable parts of the system include a charcoal filled canister and the connecting lines between the fuel tank, fuel tank filler cap and the fuel injection system (see illustrations).
3   Vapor trapped in the gas tank is vented through a valve in the top of the tank. The vapor leaves the valve through a single line and is routed to a carbon canister located between the left front wheel well and the front bumper, where it's stored until the next time the engine is started.
4   The canister outlet is connected to an electrically actuated canister purge solenoid (see illustration) that is, in turn, connected to the air cleaner housing. The canister purge solenoid valve is normally closed. When the engine is started, the solenoid is energized by a signal from the ECA and allows intake vacuum to open the line between the canister and the air cleaner housing, which draws vapor stored in the canister through the air cleaner and into the engine where it's burned.

Checking

Charcoal canister
5   There are no moving parts and nothing to wear in the canister. Check for loose, missing, cracked or broken fittings and inspect the canister for cracks and other damage. If the canister is damaged, replace it (refer to Step 9).

Canister purge solenoid valve
6   Remove the valve (see Step 13).
7   With the valve de-energized, apply five in-Hg to the **vacuum source** port (see illustration 5.4). The valve should not pass air. If it does, replace the valve.
8   Apply 9-to-14 volts to the valve electrical connector terminals with jumper wires. The valve should open and pass air. If it doesn't, replace the valve.

Component replacement

Charcoal canister
9   Locate the canister in the engine compartment.
10 Reach up above the canister and remove the single mounting bolt (see illustration).
11 Lower the canister, detach the hose from the purge valve, or purge solenoid valve, and remove the canister.
12 Installation is the reverse of removal.

All other components
13 Referring to the appropriate vacuum hose and vacuum valve schematics in this Section and on the VECI label of your vehicle, locate the component to be replaced.
14 Label the hoses and fittings, then detach the hoses and remove the component.
15 Installation is the reverse of removal.

LH LOWER FRAME RAIL

FRONT OF VEHICLE

FRONT OF ENGINE

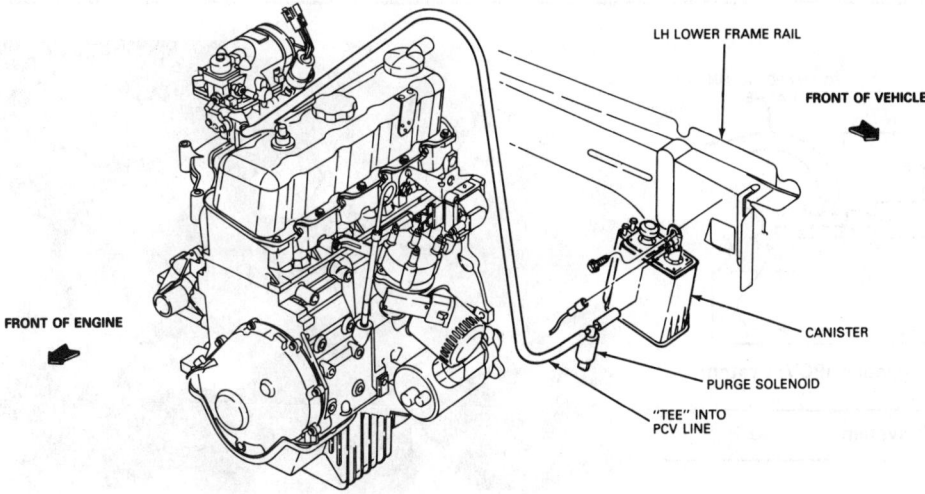

5.2a A typical evaporative canister venting system (four-cylinder engine)

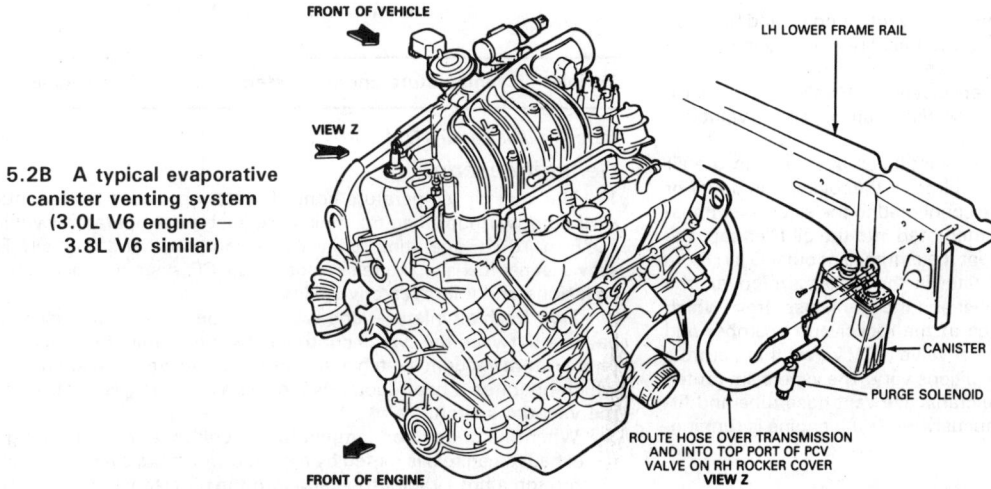

CANISTER

PURGE SOLENOID

"TEE" INTO PCV LINE

5.2B A typical evaporative canister venting system (3.0L V6 engine — 3.8L V6 similar)

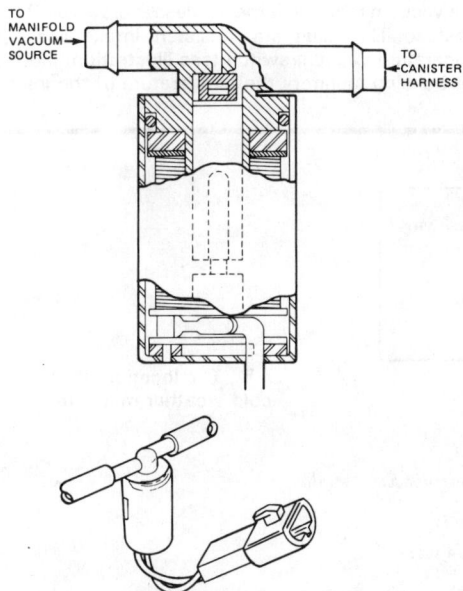

FRONT OF VEHICLE

VIEW Z

LH LOWER FRAME RAIL

CANISTER

PURGE SOLENOID

ROUTE HOSE OVER TRANSMISSION AND INTO TOP PORT OF PCV VALVE ON RH ROCKER COVER
VIEW Z

FRONT OF ENGINE

ROUTE TUBE INBOARD OF PCV HOSE BETWEEN THROTTLE BODY AND RH ROCKER COVER

THROTTLE BODY

PCV HOSE

VIEW Z

TO MANIFOLD VACUUM SOURCE

TO CANISTER HARNESS

5.4 A typical canister purge solenoid

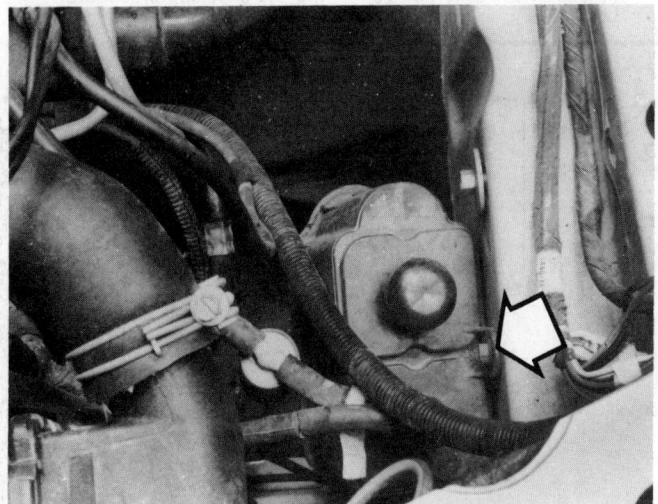

5.10 To remove the canister, remove the single mounting bolt (arrow), then clearly label and detach the vent hoses

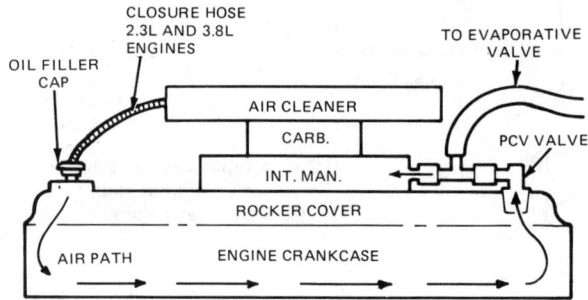

6.1   A typical Positive Crankcase Ventilation (PCV) system

6   Positive Crankcase Ventilation (PCV) system

Refer to illustration 6.1

General description

1   The Positive Crankcase Ventilation (PCV) system **(see illustration)** cycles crankcase vapors back through the engine, where they are burned. The valve regulates the amount of ventilating air and blow-by gas to the intake manifold and prevents backfire from traveling into the crankcase.

2   The PCV system consists of a replaceable PCV valve, a crankcase ventilation filter (integral with the oil filler cap on some vehicles, separate on others) and the connecting hoses.

3   The air source for the crankcase ventilation system is in the air cleaner. Air passes through the PCV filter (in the rocker arm cover or the oil filler cap) and through a hose connected to the air cleaner housing. On vehicles with a PCV filter integrated into the oil filler cap, the cap is sealed at the opening to prevent the entrance of outside air. From the oil filler cap, or separate PCV filter in the rocker arm cover, the air flows into the rocker arm chamber and the crankcase, from which it circulates up into another section of the rocker arm chamber and finally enters a spring loaded regulator valve (PCV valve) that controls the amount of flow as operating conditions vary. The vapors are routed to the intake manifold through the crankcase vent hose tube and fittings. This process goes on continuously while the engine is running.

Checking

4   Checking procedures for the PCV system components are included in Chapter 1.

Component replacement

5   Component replacement involves simply installing a new valve or hose in place of the one removed during the checking procedure.

7.4   The temperature vacuum switch, or TVS, and vacuum motor (arrows) on the four-cylinder engine (the cold weather modulator, or CWM, is on the inside of the air cleaner housing next to the TVS)

7   Inlet air temperature control system (four-cylinder engine)

Refer to illustrations 7.4 and 7.5

General description

1   The inlet air temperature control system provides heated intake air during warmup, then maintains the inlet air temperature within a 70°F to 105°F operating range by mixing warm and cool air. This allows leaner fuel/air mixture settings for the CFI system, which reduces emissions and improves driveability.

2   Two fresh air inlets — one warm and one cold — are used. The balance between the two is controlled by intake manifold vacuum, a temperature vacuum switch and a time delay valve. A vacuum motor, which operates a heat duct valve in the air cleaner, is controlled by the vacuum switch.

3   When the underhood temperature is cold, warm air radiating off the exhaust manifold is routed by a shroud which fits over the manifold up through a hot air inlet tube and into the air cleaner. This provides warm air for the CFI, resulting in better driveability and faster warmup. As the underhood temperature rises, a heat duct valve is gradually closed by a vacuum motor and the air cleaner draws air through a cold air duct instead. The result is a consistent intake air temperature.

4   A temperature vacuum switch **(see illustration)** mounted on the air cleaner housing monitors the temperature of the inlet air heated

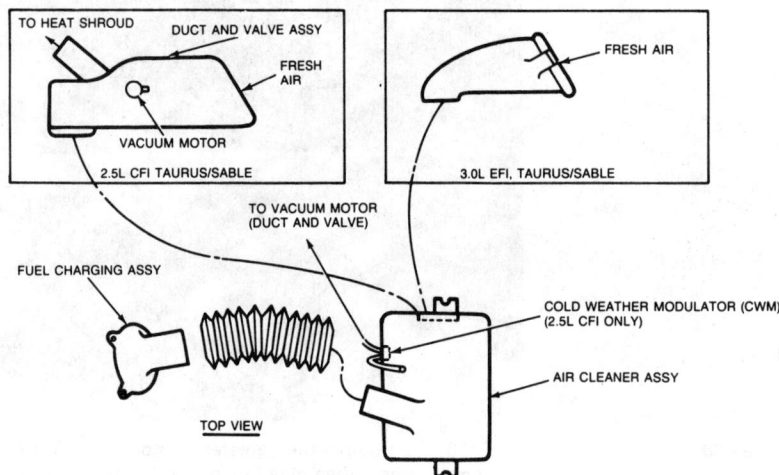

7.5   The location of the cold weather modulator

by the exhaust manifold. A bimetal disc in the temperature vacuum switch orients itself in one of two positions, depending on the temperature. One position allows vacuum through a hose to the motor; the other position blocks vacuum.

5   The vacuum motor itself is regulated by a cold weather modulator (CWM), mounted next to the temperature vacuum switch inside the air cleaner housing assembly **(see illustration)**, which provides the motor with a range of graduated positions between fully open and fully closed.

Checking

Note: *Make sure that the engine is cold before beginning this test.*

6   Always check the vacuum source and the integrity of all vacuum hoses between the source and the vacuum motor before beginning the following test. Don't proceed until they're okay.

7   Apply the parking brake and block the wheels.

8   Detach, but don't remove, the air cleaner housing and element (see Chapter 4).

9   Turn the air cleaner housing so the vacuum motor door is visible. The door should be open. If it isn't, it may be binding or sticking. Make sure that it's not rusted in an open or closed position by attempting to move it by hand. If it's rusted, it can usually be freed by cleaning and oiling the hinge. If it fails to work properly after servicing, replace it.

10   If the vacuum motor door is okay but the motor still fails to operate correctly, check carefully for a leak in the hose leading to it. Check the vacuum source to and from the bimetal sensor and the time delay valve as well. If no leak is found, replace the vacuum motor (see Step 26).

11   Start the engine. If the duct door has moved or moves to the "heat on" (closed to fresh air) position, go to Step 15.

12   If the door stays in the "heat off" (closed to warm air) position, place a finger over the bimetal sensor bleed. The duct door must move rapidly to the "heat on" position. If the door doesn't move to the "heat on" position, stop the engine and replace the vacuum motor (see Step 26). Repeat this Step with the new vacuum motor.

13   With the engine off, cool the bimetal sensor and the cold weather modulator (CWM) by spraying them with air conditioning system freon (wait for 20 seconds after the liquid contacts the sensor and CWM). **Warning:** *Don't cool the bimetal sensor while the engine is running. If freon is drawn into the intake system, poisonous phosgene gas will be produced. Perform this test only in a well-ventilated area.*

14   Restart the engine. The duct door should move to the "heat on" position. If the door doesn't move or moves only partially, replace the TVS (see Step 18).

15   Start and run the engine briefly (less than 15 seconds). The duct door should move to the "heat on" position.

16   Shut off the engine and watch the duct door. It should stay in the "heat on" position for at least two minutes.

17   If it doesn't stay in the "heat on" position for at least two minutes, replace the CWM (see Step 23) and repeat this Step after cooling the CWM and bimetal again with freon.

Component replacement

Temperature vacuum switch (TVS)

18   Clearly label, then detach both vacuum hoses from the TVS (one is coming from the vacuum source at the manifold and the other is going to the vacuum motor underneath the air cleaner housing).

19   Remove the air cleaner housing cover assembly (see Chapter 1 or 4 if necessary).

20   Pry the TVS retaining clip off with a screwdriver.

21   Remove the TVS.

22   Installation is the reverse of removal.

Cold weather modulator (CWM)

23   Detach the air cleaner housing assembly (see Chapter 1 or 4) and turn it upside down.

24   Locate the CWM, then detach both vacuum hoses and remove the CWM.

25   Installation is the reverse of removal.

Vacuum motor

26   Detach the air cleaner housing assembly (see Chapter 1 or 4) and turn it upside down.

27   Locate the vacuum motor.

28   Detach the vacuum hose and drill out the motor mounting rivet.

29   Remove the motor.

30   Installation is the reverse of removal.

---

8   Catalytic converter

Refer to illustrations 8.1, 8.8, 8.9, 8.10, 8.17 and 8.18

General description

1   The catalytic converter **(see illustration)** is designed to reduce hydrocarbon, carbon monoxide amd nitrogen oxide pollutants in the exhaust. The converter "oxidizes" these components (speeds up the heat producing chemical reaction between the exhaust gas constituents) and converts them to water and carbon dioxide.

2   The converter, which closely resembles a muffler, is located in the exhaust system immediately behind the short elbow shaped section of pipe below the exhaust manifold (you'll need to raise the vehicle to inspect or replace it).

3   **Warning:** *If large amounts of unburned gasoline enter the converter, it may overheat and cause a fire. Always observe the following precautions:*

Use only unleaded gasoline
Avoid prolonged idling
Do not run the engine with a nearly empty fuel tank
Avoid coasting with the ignition turned off

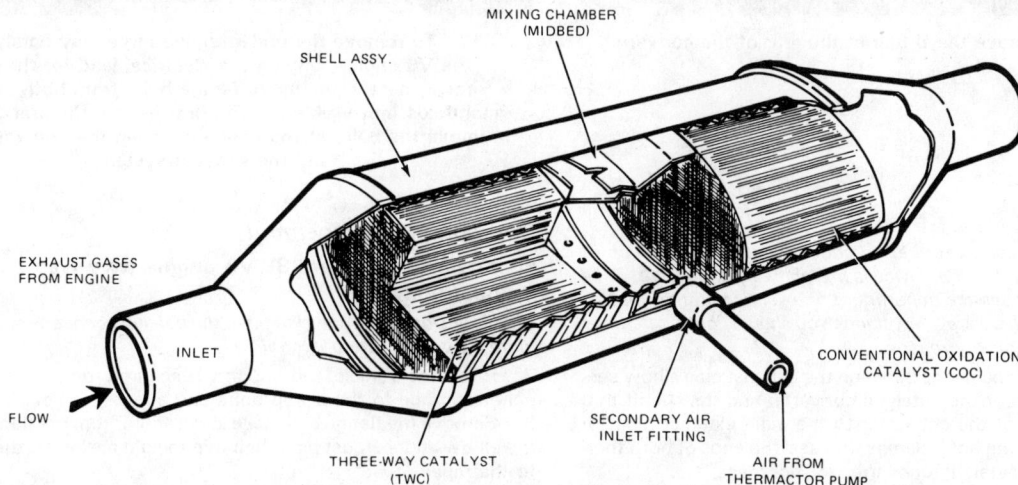

8.1   A typical catalytic converter with a three-way catalyst (reduction of NOx) and conventional oxidation catalyst (reduction of HC and CO)

8.8   To remove the under-body conventional oxidation catalyst/three-way catalyst from the four-cylinder engine or the three-way catalyst from the 3.8L V6, remove the bolts at the forward flange between the converter pipe and the exhaust manifold-to-exhaust system connector pipe . . .

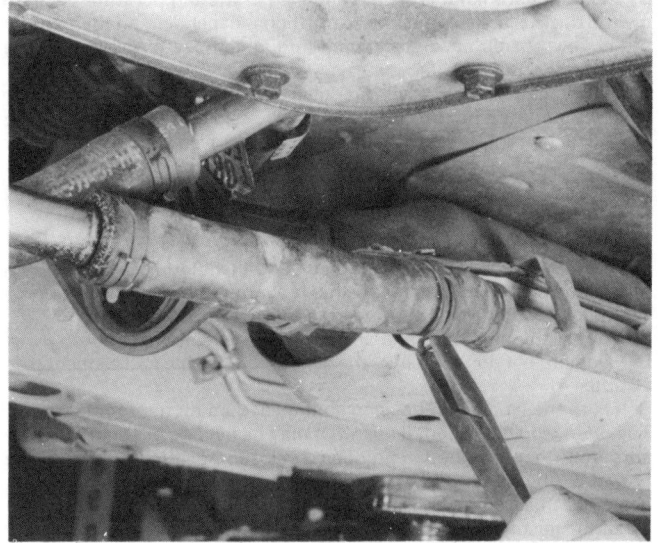

8.9   . . . loosen the hose clamps, detach both thermactor hoses from the inlet pipes . . .

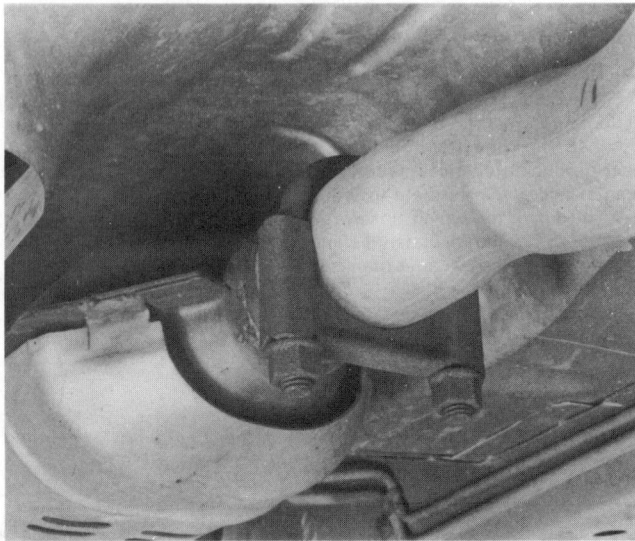

8.10   . . . and remove the U-bolt at the rear of the converter

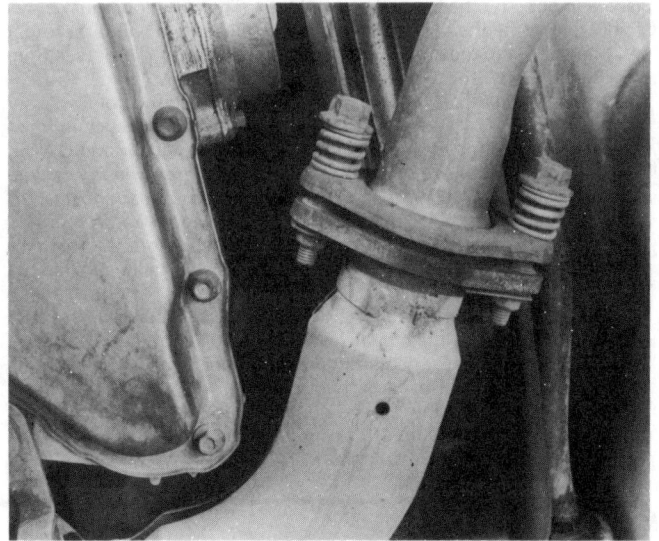

8.17   To remove the under engine three-way catalyst from the V6 engine, unplug the electrical lead for the EGO sensor, detach the upper flange bolts from both exhaust manifolds (not visible in this photo — see Chapter 2), then remove the bolts at the flange between the converter pipe and the exhaust system

Checking

Note: *An infrared sensor is required to check the actual operation of the catalytic converter. Such a device is prohibitively expensive. Take the vehicle to a dealer service department or a service station for this procedure. However, there are a few things you should check whenever the vehicle is raised for any reason.*

4   Check the bolts at the flange between the exhaust pipe elbow section and the front end of the catalytic converter and the U-bolt that secures the rear end of the converter to the main exhaust pipe for tightness. Also check the hose clamps that seal the ends of both thermactor hoses to the catalytic converter for tightness.

5   Check the converter itself for dents (maximum 3/4-inch deep) and other damage which could affect its performance.

6   Inspect the heat insulator plates above and below the catalytic converter for damage and loose fasteners.

Component replacement

Four-cylinder engine/3.8L V6 engine (two-way catalyst, under body)

Warning: *Don't attempt to remove the catalytic converter until the complete exhaust system is cool.*

7   Raise the vehicle and support it securely on jackstands. Apply penetrating oil to the clamp bolts and allow it to soak in.

8   Remove the flange bolts **(see illustration)** from the flange between the elbow and exhaust pipe. Remove the old gaskets if they are stuck to the pipes.

9   Release the hose clamps **(see illustration)** and detach the hoses from the thermactor pipe inlets.

10   Remove the U-bolt **(see illustration)** from the rear joint between the catalytic converter and the main exhaust pipe assembly.

11 Remove the catalytic converter.

12 Installation is the reverse of removal. Be sure to use a new exhaust pipe gasket at the flange.

13 It's always a good idea to inspect and, if necessary, replace the rubber exhaust pipe hangers while the vehicle is raised (see Chapter 4).

14 Start the engine and check carefully for exhaust leaks.

3.0L/3.8L V6 engine (two-way catalyst, under engine)

15 Raise the vehicle and place it securely on jackstands. Apply penetrating oil to the flange bolts.

16 Unplug the electrical lead for the exhaust gas oxygen (EGO) sensor.

17 Remove the flange bolts **(see illustration)** from both ends of the catalytic converter pipe.

18 Remove the catalytic converter pipe **(see illustration)**.

19 Installation is the reverse of removal. Be sure to use new flange gaskets.

20 Start the engine and check for leaks.

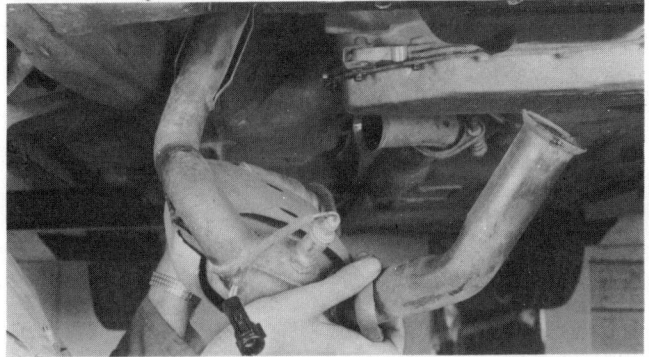

8.18 Carefully lower the catalytic converter pipe from the engine, being careful not to damage either the dual three-way catalyst converters or the EGO sensor

Chapter 7 Part A Manual transaxle

Contents

Specifications

Manual transaxle

Lubricant type
    1986 and 1987 . . . .   Motorcraft Type F or Dexron II
    1988 on . . . .   Motorcraft MERCON automatic transmission fluid
Capacity (approximate) . . . .   6.2 qts

Torque specifications

	Ft-lbs
Shift lever assembly bolt	35 to 50
Speedometer driven gear retainer bolt	4 to 6
Transaxle mount nut	35 to 50
Transaxle-to-engine bolt	25 to 35

---

1 General information

All vehicles covered in this manual are equipped with either a 5-speed manual transaxle or an automatic transaxle. The manual transaxle used on these models is designated the MTX III. All information on the manual transaxle except seal replacement, lubricant level check and mount check and replacement is included in this Part of Chapter 7. Information on the automatic transaxle can be found in Part B.

Due to the complexity, unavailability of replacement parts and the special tools necessary, internal repair procedures for the manual trans-axle is not recommended for the home mechanic. The information contained within this manual will be limited to general information, seal replacement and removal and installation procedures.

Depending on the expense involved in having a faulty transaxle over-hauled, it may be be an advantage to consider replacing the unit with either a new or rebuilt one. Your local dealer or transmission shop should be able to supply you with information concerning cost, availability and exchange policy. Regardless of how you decide to remedy a trans-axle problem, you can still save considerable expense by removing and installing the unit yourself.

2 Manual transaxle lubricant change

1 Raise the vehicle and support it securely on jackstands.
2 Move a drain pan, rags, newspapers and wrenches under the transaxle.
3 Remove the transaxle drain plug, followed by the fill plug, and allow the oil to drain into the pan.
4 After the oil has drained completely, reinstall the drain plug and tighten it securely.
5 Install the fill plug. Using a hand pump, syringe or funnel, fill the transaxle with the correct amount of the specified lubricant.
6 Check the oil level as described in Section 24, Chapter 1, adding more oil as necessary.

3 Shift linkage — removal and installation

Refer to illustration 3.1

Shift lever assembly

1 Use a small screwdriver to pry out the shift knob medallion and remove the shift knob retaining screw **(see illustration)**.
2 Remove the console applique for access and then remove the four boot-to-console screws. Slide the shift boot and knob off the shift lever.
3 Remove the console (Chapter 11).
4 Remove the four shifter-to-floorpan bolts, pry off the two clips retaining the shift cable to the control assembly and use a screwdriver to disconnect the control assembly pivot balls. Be careful not to bend or kink the cables.

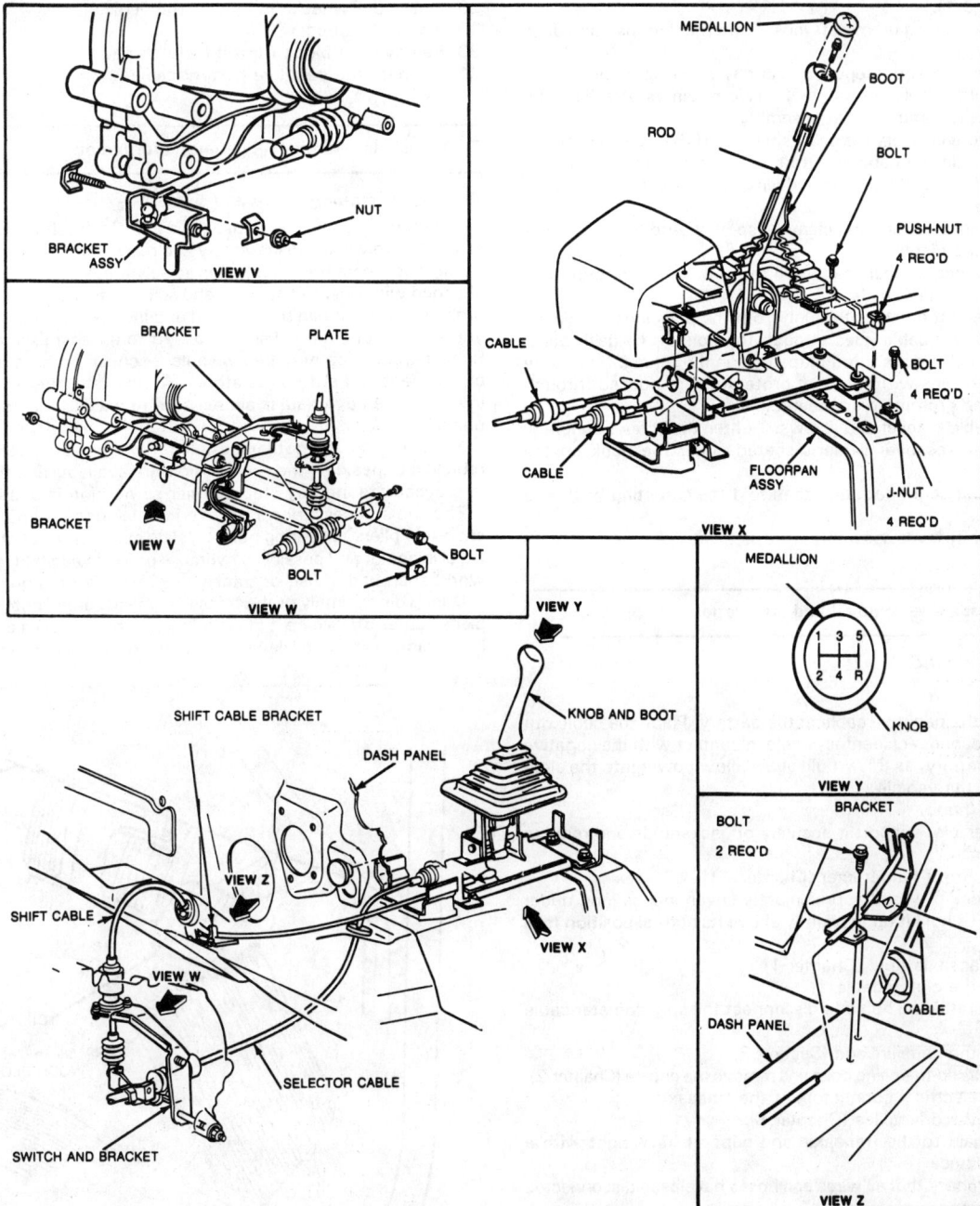

3.1 Shift linkage component layout

5   To install, feed the ends of the cables into the control assembly slots, using the green paint mark of the shifter as a guide. Install the control assembly bolts and tighten them securely.
6   Seat the cable insulators in the shifter slots and secure them with the clips. Use a mallet to seat the clips.
7   Use pliers to snap the cable shifter sockets onto the pivot balls.
8   Install the console.
9   Slide the shift boot and knob assembly onto the shift lever and install the screws.
10 Install the shift knob and screw and snap the applique in place.
11 Install the console applique.

Shift cables and bracket assemblies

12 Remove the console, shifter and boot/knob assembly.
13 Fold the carpet back from the dash panel for access to the cables.
14 Remove the rear seat heater duct.
15 Loosen the two retaining screws and remove the cable bracket **(see illustration 3.1)**.
16 Pull the cable sealing grommets loose from the floor pan and dash panel.
17 Raise the vehicle and support it securely on jackstands.
18 From under the vehicle, remove the two retainers attaching the cables to the switch and bracket assembly.
19 Use a screwdriver to pry the cable sockets off the clamp assembly pivot balls and slide the cable isolators out of the bracket slot.
20 Loosen the two attaching bolts and remove the switch and bracket from the transaxle case.
21 Loosen the nut retaining the clamp assembly onto the input shift shaft and slide the clamp off.
22 In the passenger compartment, pull the shift cables through and remove them from the vehicle.
23 To install, feed the cables through from the passenger compartment. The crossover cable goes through the hole in the dash panel and the selector cable goes through the hole in the tunnel. Make sure the ends of the cables with the boot protectors are pushed through the holes and the grommets are seated.
24 Install the cable bracket and screws. Tighten the screws securely, making sure the crossover cable is seated under the hook on the bracket.
25 Install the rear seat heat duct, then fold the carpeting back into position.
26 Install the shift lever assembly.

4   Manual transaxle — removal and installation

Refer to illustration 4.5

Removal

1   Disconnect the negative cable at the battery. Place the cable out of the way so it cannot accidentally come in contact with the negative terminal of the battery, as this would again allow power into the electrical system of the vehicle.
2   Remove the hood.
3   Raise the vehicle, support it securely on jackstands and remove the front wheels.
4   Remove the front fender liner (Chapter 11).
5   Wedge a block of wood approximately seven inches long under the clutch pedal to hold it up to slightly above its normal position **(see illustration)**.
6   Drain the transaxle fluid (Chapter 1).
7   Disconnect the clutch cable.
8   Remove the retaining bolt and disconnect the speedometer cable (Section 6).
9   Disconnect the shift linkage (Section 3).
10 Remove transaxle-to-engine bolts and remove the engine (Chapter 2).
11 Unplug the electrical connectors at the transaxle.
12 Disconnect the driveaxles (Chapter 8).
13 Secure a chain to the transaxle and support its weight with a suitable lifting device.
14 Make a final check that all wires and hoses have been disconnected from the transaxle.
15 Remove the transaxle mounting nuts.
16 Lift the transaxle from the vehicle.
17 Inspect the clutch components (Chapter 8). In most cases, new

clutch components should be installed as a matter of course if the transaxle is removed.

Installation

18 If removed, install the clutch components (Chapter 8).
19 Lower the transaxle onto the mount studs and install the nuts. Tighten the nuts to the specified torque.
20 Connect the driveaxles.
21 Plug in the electrical connectors.
22 Connect the shift linkage.
23 Connect the speedometer cable and install the retaining bolt. Tighten the bolt to the specified torque.
24 Connect the clutch cable.
25 Install the engine (Chapter 2). Tighten the transaxle-to-engine bolts to the specified torque.
26 Fill the transaxle with the specified fluid.
27 Install the fender liner.
28 Install the wheels and lower the vehicle.
29 Install the hood.
30 Remove the block from the clutch pedal.
31 Connect the negative battery cable.

5   Transaxle overhaul — general information

Refer to illustrations 5.4a and 5.4b

Overhauling a manual transaxle is a difficult job for the do-it-yourselfer. It involves the disassembly and reassembly of many small parts. Numerous clearances must be precisely measured and, if necessary, changed with select fit spacers and snap-rings. As a result, if transaxle problems arise, it can be removed and installed by a competent do-it-yourselfer, but overhaul should be left to a transmission repair shop. Rebuilt transaxles may be available — check with your dealer parts department and auto parts stores. At any rate, the time and money involved in an overhaul is almost sure to exceed the cost of a rebuilt unit.

Nevertheless, it's not impossible for an inexperienced mechanic to rebuild a transaxle if the special tools are available and the job is done in a deliberate step-by-step manner so nothing is overlooked.

The tools necessary for an overhaul include internal and external snap-ring pliers, a bearing puller, a slide hammer, a set of pin punches, a dial indicator and possibly a hydraulic press. In addition, a large, sturdy workbench and a vise or transaxle stand will be required.

During disassembly of the transaxle, make careful notes of how each piece comes off, where it fits in relation to other pieces and what holds it in place. Exploded views are included **(see illustrations)** to show

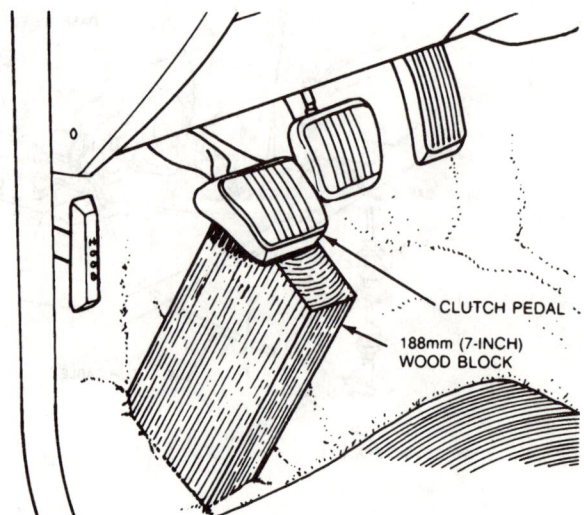

4.5   Support the clutch pedal with a block of wood before removing the transaxle

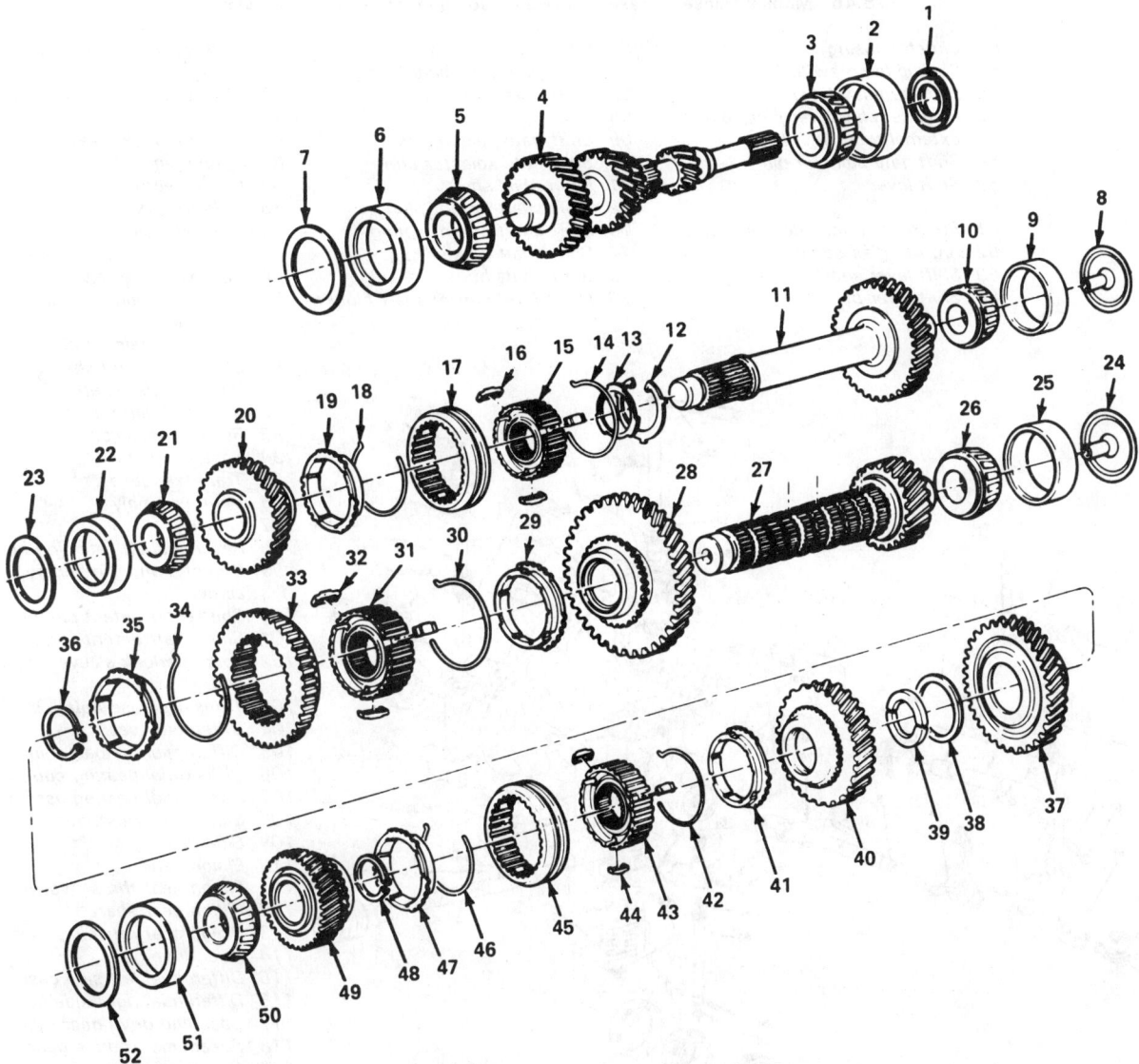

5.4a Manual transaxle shafts — exploded view

1 Input shaft seal assembly	20 5th speed gear	37 2nd speed gear
2 Roller bearing cup	21 5th gear shaft rear bearing	38 2nd/3rd retaining thrust
3 Front input shaft bearing	22 Roller bearing cup	washer
4 Input cluster shaft	23 Bearing preload shim	39 2nd/3rd thrust washer
5 Rear input shaft bearing	24 Mainshaft funnel	40 3rd gear
6 Roller bearing cup	25 Roller bearing cup	41 Synchronizer blocking ring
7 Bearing preload shim	26 Mainshaft front bearing	42 Synchronizer retaining spring
8 5th gear funnel	27 Mainshaft	43 3rd/4th synchronizer hub
9 Roller bearing cup	28 1st speed gear	44 3rd/4th synchronizer hub
10 5th gear front shaft bearing	29 Synchronizer blocking ring	insert
11 5th gear drive shaft	30 Synchronizer retaining spring	45 3rd/4th synchronizer sleeve
12 Synchronizer insert retainer	31 1st/2nd synchronizer hub	46 Synchronizer retaining spring
13 Synchronizer retaining spacer	32 1st/2nd Synchronizer hub	47 Synchronizer blocking ring
14 Synchronizer retaining spring	retaining ring	48 3rd/4th synchronizer ring
15 5th synchronizer	33 Reverse sliding gear	49 4th gear
16 5th syncronizer hub	34 Synchronizer retaining ring	50 Mainshaft bearing
17 5th synchronizer sleeve	35 Synchronizer blocking ring	51 Roller bearing cup
18 Synchronizer retaining spring	36 1st/2nd synchronizer retaining	52 Bearing preload spring
19 Synchronizer blocking ring	ring	

5.4b Manual transaxle case and related components — exploded view

53 Clutch housing
54 Backup lamp switch
55 Reverse relay lever
56 Reverse relay lever pivot pin
57 External retaining pin
58 Shift gate selector pin
59 Shift lever
60 Ball
61 5th/Reverse inhibitor pin
62 3rd/4th bias spring
63 Shift lever shaft
64 Shift lever pin
65 Shift lever shaft seal
66 Shift gate attaching bolts
67 Shift gate plate
68 Selector arm pin
69 Shift gate selector pin
70 Shift gate selector arm
71 Input shift shaft
72 Shift shaft detent plunger
73 Shift shaft detent spring
74 Shift shaft oil seal
75 Shift shaft boot
76 Input fork control shaft block
77 Reverse relay lever actuating spring pin
78 Main shift fork control shaft
79 1st/2nd fork
80 Fork interlock sleeve
81 Spring pin
82 Fork selector arm
83 3rd/4th fork
84 5th shift relay lever
85 Reverse shift relay lever pin
86 5th relay lever pivot pin
87 External retaining ring pin
88 5th fork
89 5th fork retaining pin
90 5th fork control shaft
91 Reverse idler shaft
92 Reverse idler gear bushing
93 Reverse idler gear
94 Case magnet
95 Transaxle case
96 Vent assembly
97 Fill plug
98 Reverse shaft retaining bolt
99 Detent plunger retaining screw
100 Shift shaft detent plunger
101 Shift shaft detent spring
102 Fork interlock sleeve retaining pin
103 Transaxle case bolt
104 Differential seal
105 Differential preload shim
106 Differential bearing cup
107 Differential bearing assembly
108 Side gear thrust washer
109 Side gear
110 Pinion gear
111 Pinion gear thrust washer
112 Pinion gear shaft
113 Pinion gear retaining shaft
114 Final drive gear
115 Differential left side case
116 Differential right side case
117 Case and drive gear rivet
118 Speedometer drive gear
119 O-ring seal
120 Speedometer gear retainer
121 Speedometer gear retainer-to-case seal
122 Speedometer driven gear
123 Case-to-clutch housing dowel
124 Shift gate pawl spring
125 Reverse shift relay lever support bracket
126 Reverse lockout pawl pivot pin
127 5th/Reverse kickdown spring
128 Shift gate plate pawl
129 Ball
130 C-clip
131 Ball
132 Reverse shift relay lever
133 Reverse shift relay spring
134 Transaxle timing window plug
135 Felt washer
136 Clutch release shaft upper bushing
137 Clutch release lever pin
138 Clutch release shaft
139 Clutch release lever

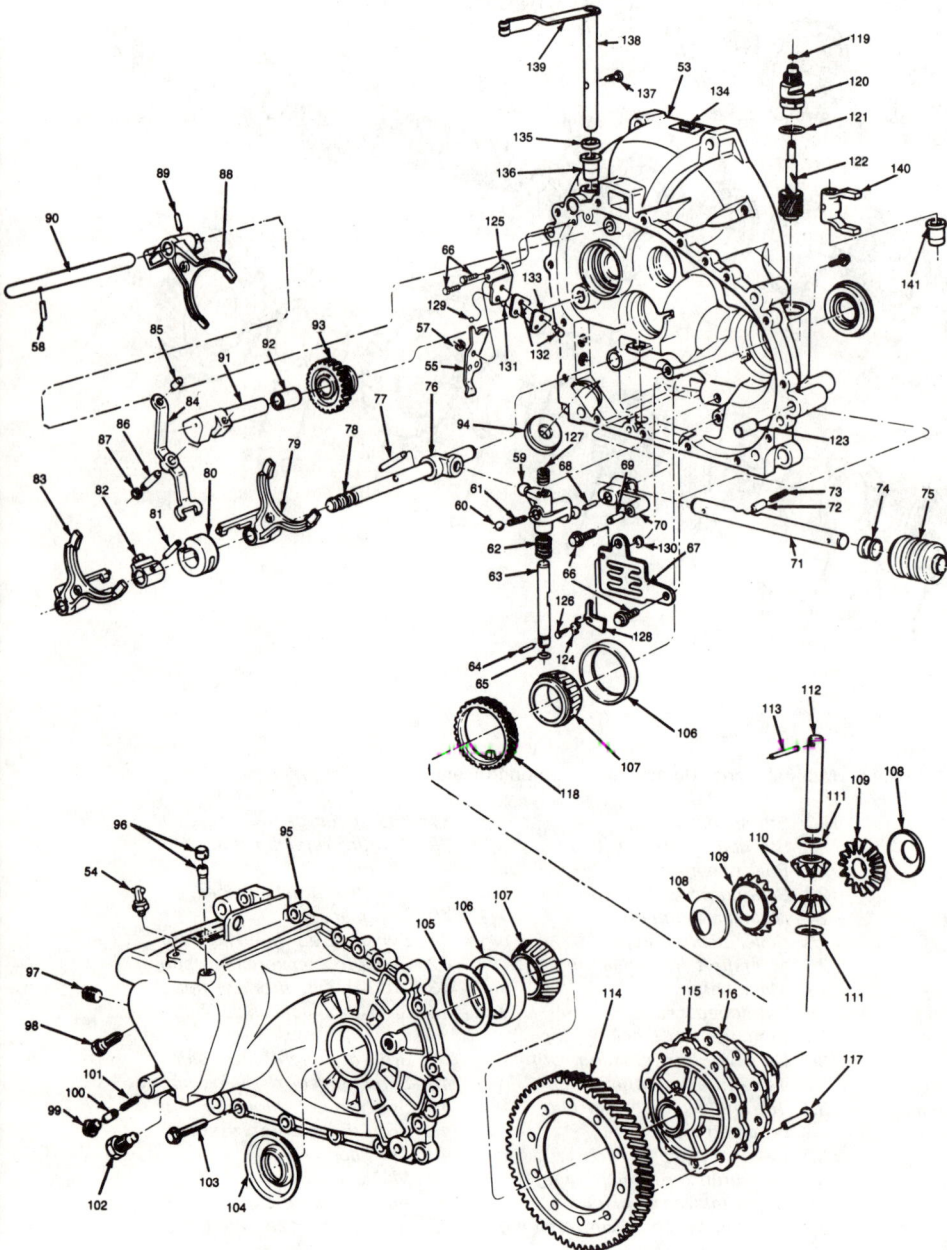

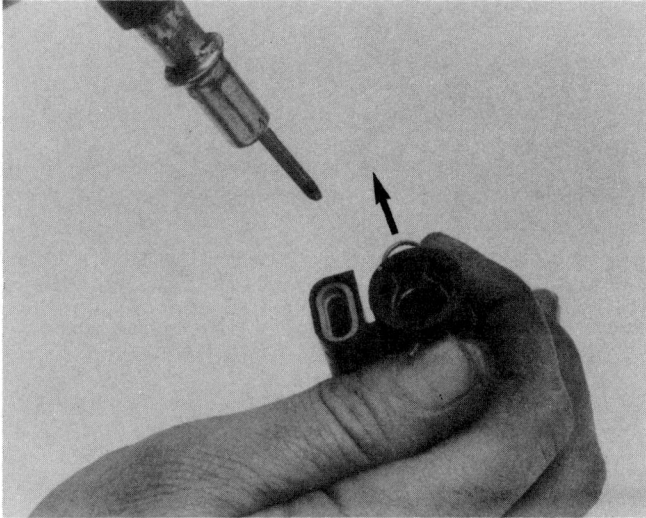

6.4 The speedometer cable retainer clip can be removed by inserting a small screwdriver in the loop at the end and pulling it out in the direction shown (arrow)

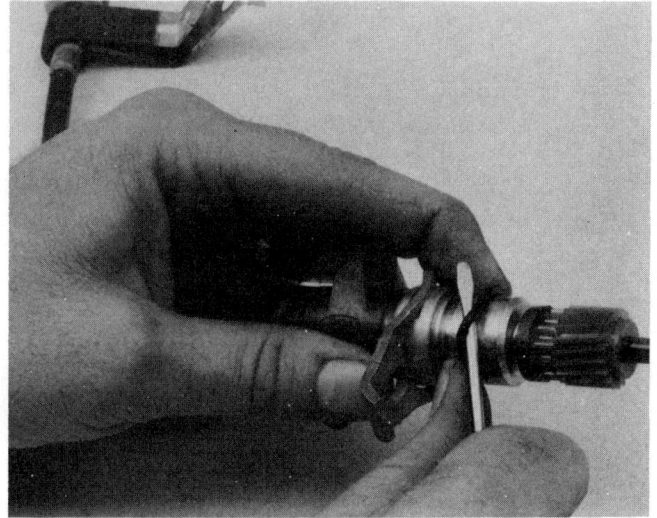

6.5 Insert a small screwdriver under the O-ring, then pull it off

where the parts go — but actually noting how they are installed when you remove the parts will make it much easier to get the transaxle back together.

Before taking the transaxle apart for repair, it will help if you have some idea of what area of the transaxle is malfunctioning. Certain problems can be closely tied to specific areas in the transaxle, which can make component examination and replacement easier. Refer to the *Troubleshooting* section at the front of this manual for information regarding possible sources of trouble.

---

6 Speedometer driven gear O-ring — replacement

Refer to illustrations 6.4 and 6.5

1   Clean off the top of the speedometer retainer.

2   Remove the retaining bolt.

3   Carefully pull up on the cable to withdraw the speedometer retainer and driven gear from the bore.

4   Insert a small screwdriver into the end of the the retaining clip and disconnect the speedometer gear assembly from the cable **(see illustration)**.

5   Use a small screwdriver to remove the O-ring from the groove in the retainer **(see illustration)**.

6   On models so equipped, remove the small O-ring from the stem of the driven gear.

7   Replace the O-ring(s) with new ones.

8   Lightly lubricate the O-ring on the retainer with chassis grease.

9   Insert the driven gear into the transaxle bore and install the retaining bolt. Tighten the bolt to the specified torque.

10 Insert the speedometer cable into the retainer and secure it with the clip.

Chapter 7 Part B   Automatic transaxle

Contents

Specifications

Torque specifications

	Ft-lbs
Neutral start switch bolt	7 to 9
Transaxle-to-engine bolt	
AXOD transaxle	41 to 50
ATX transaxle	25 to 33
Torque converter-to-driveplate nut	23 to 39
Transaxle mount nut	25 to 33
Transaxle mount bracket-to-frame bolt	40 to 50

---

1   General information

The automatic transaxles used on these models are the 4-speed
AXOD and the 3-speed ATX. All information on automatic transaxles
is included in this Part of Chapter 7. Information on the manual transaxle
can be found in Part A.

Due to the complexity, unavailability of replacement parts and the
special tools necessary, internal repair of automatic transaxles is not
recommended for the home mechanic. The information contained
within this manual will be limited to general information, diagnosis,
linkage adjustments and removal and installation procedures.

Depending on the expense involved in having a faulty transaxle overhauled, it may be a better idea to replace it with either a new or rebuilt
one. Your local dealer or transmission shop should be able to supply
you with information concerning cost, availability and exchange policy.
Regardless of how you decide to remedy a transaxle problem, you can
still save considerable expense by removing and installing the unit
yourself.

2   Diagnosis — general

Note: *Automatic transaxle malfunctions may be caused by five general
conditions: poor engine performance, improper adjustments, hydraulic
malfunctions, mechanical malfunctions or malfunctions in the computer or its signal network. Diagnosis of these problems should always
begin with a check of the easily repaired items: fluid level and condition (Chapter 1), shift linkage adjustment and throttle linkage adjustment. Next, perform a road test to determine if the problem has been
corrected or if more diagnosis is necessary. If the problem persists after
the preliminary tests and corrections are completed, additional diagnosis
should be done by a dealer service department or transmission repair
shop.*

Preliminary checks

1   Drive the vehicle to warm the transaxle to normal operating
temperature.
2   Check the fluid level as described in Chapter 1:

Chapter 7 Part B Automatic transaxle

a) If the fluid level is unusually low, add enough fluid to bring the level within the designated area of the dipstick, then check for external leaks (see below).

b) If the fluid level is abnormally high, drain off the excess, then check the drained fluid for contamination by coolant. The presence of engine coolant in the automatic transaxle fluid indicates that a failure has occurred in the internal radiator walls that separate the coolant from the transmission fluid.

c) If the fluid is foaming, drain it and refill the transaxle, then check for coolant in the fluid or a high fluid level.

3 Check the engine idle speed. **Note:** *If the engine is malfunctioning, do not proceed with the preliminary checks until it has been repaired and runs normally.*

4 Check the throttle valve cable for freedom of movement. Adjust it if necessary (Section 6). **Note:** *The throttle cable may function properly when the engine is shut off and cold, but it may malfunction once the engine is hot. Check it cold and at normal engine operating temperature.*

5 Inspect the shift control linkage (Section 5). Make sure that it's properly adjusted and that the linkage operates smoothly.

Fluid leak diagnosis

6 Most fluid leaks are easy to locate visually. Repair usually consists of replacing a seal or gasket. If a leak is difficult to find, the following procedure may help.

7 Identify the fluid. Make sure it's transmission fluid and not engine oil or brake fluid.

8 Try to pinpoint the source of the leak. Drive the vehicle several miles, then park it over a large sheet of cardboard. After a minute or two, you should be able to locate the leak by determining the source of the fluid dripping onto the cardboard.

9 Make a careful visual inspection of the suspected component and the area immediately around it. Pay particular attention to gasket mating surfaces. A mirror is often helpful for finding leaks in areas that are hard to see.

10 If the leak still cannot be found, clean the suspected area thoroughly with a degreaser or solvent, then dry it.

11 Drive the vehicle for several miles at normal operating temperature and varying speeds. After driving the vehicle, visually inspect the suspected component again.

12 Once the leak has been located, the cause must be determined before it can be properly repaired. If a gasket is replaced but the sealing flange is bent, the new gasket will not stop the leak. The bent flange must be straightened.

13 Before attempting to repair a leak, check to make sure that the following conditions are corrected or they may cause another leak. **Note:** *Some of the following conditions (a leaking torque converter, for instance) cannot be fixed without highly specialized tools and expertise. Such problems must be referred to a transmission shop or a dealer service department.*

Gasket leaks

14 Check the pan periodically. Make sure the bolts are tight, no bolts are missing, the gasket is in good condition and the pan is flat (dents in the pan may indicate damage to the valve body inside).

15 If the pan gasket is leaking, the fluid level or the fluid pressure may be too high, the vent may be plugged, the pan bolts may be too tight, the pan sealing flange may be warped, the sealing surface of the transaxle housing may be damaged, the gasket may be damaged or the transaxle casting may be cracked or porous. If sealant instead of gasket material has been used to form a seal between the pan and the transaxle housing, it may be the wrong sealant.

Seal leaks

16 If a transaxle seal is leaking, the fluid level or pressure may be too high, the vent may be plugged, the seal bore may be damaged, the seal itself may be damaged or improperly installed, the surface of the shaft protruding through the seal may be damaged or a loose bearing may be causing excessive shaft movement.

17 Make sure the dipstick tube seal is in good condition and the tube is properly seated. Periodically check the area around the speed sensor for leakage. If transmission fluid is evident, check the O-ring for damage. Also inspect the side gear shaft oil seals for leakage.

Case leaks

18 If the case itself appears to be leaking, the casting is porous and will have to be repaired or replaced.

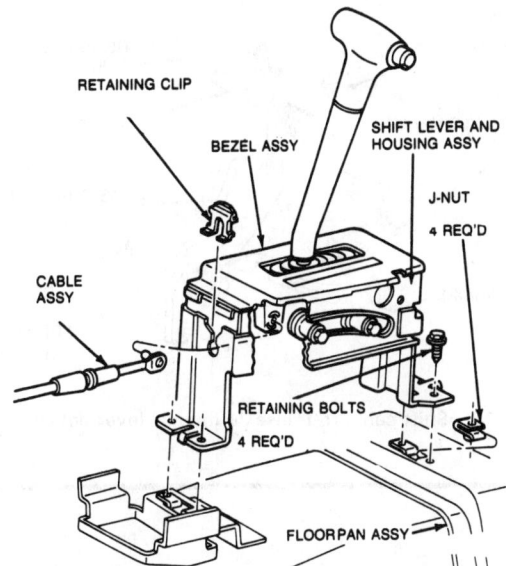

3.4 After removing the retaining clip, disconnect the shift cable, remove the four bolts and lift off the shift lever and housing assembly

19 Make sure the oil cooler hose fittings are tight and in good condition.

Fluid comes out vent pipe or fill tube

20 If this condition occurs, the transaxle is overfilled, there is coolant in the fluid, the case is porous, the dipstick is incorrect, the vent is plugged or the drain back holes are plugged.

3 Automatic transaxle shift linkage — removal and installation

Floor shift

Refer to illustrations 3.4, 3.8 and 3.10

Shift lever and housing

1 Grasp the shift knob securely and pull up to remove it.

2 Remove the center console (Chapter 11).

3 Remove the four screws and lift off the bezel assembly.

4 Pry the retaining clip up with a screwdriver and disconnect the shift cable **(see illustration)**.

5 Remove the four retaining bolts and detach the shift lever and housing from the vehicle.

6 Installation is the reverse of removal. After installation, adjust the linkage (Section 5).

Shift cable

7 Remove the console and disconnect the cable from the retainer.

8 Pull the carpeting back for access and remove the screws securing the cable bracket to the dash panel **(see illustration)**.

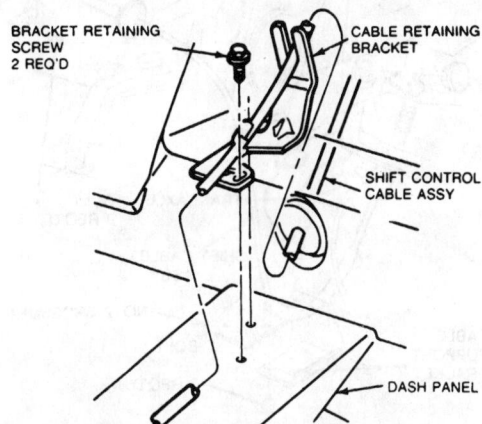

3.8 Pull back the carpet for access to the two cable retaining bracket screws

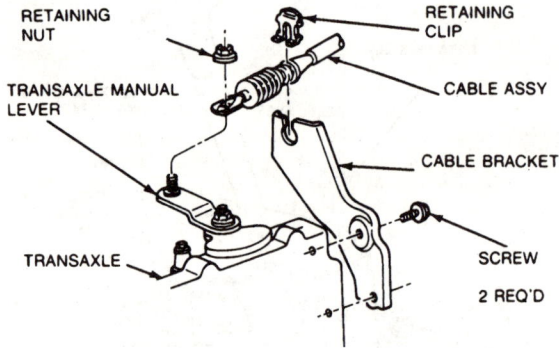

3.10 Shift cable-to-transaxle manual lever details

9 Push the rubber grommet from the floor pan toward the passenger compartment to disengage it.
10 Remove the retaining nut securing the cable to the shift lever at the transaxle, remove the clip and detach the cable (see illustration).
11 Disengage the cable from the bracket and pull it through the dash into the passenger compartment.
12 To install the cable, push the round end through the dash into the engine compartment and install the rubber boot in the body opening.
13 Install the cable bracket and the carpeting.
14 Connect the cable to the shift lever and install the shift knob.
15 Connect the cable to the cable bracket in the engine compartment and install the clip.
16 Place the cable on the transaxle lever and install the nut.
17 Adjust the shift linkage (Section 5).

Column shift
AXOD transaxle
Refer to illustration 3.18
18 Working under the instrument panel, remove the shift control cable

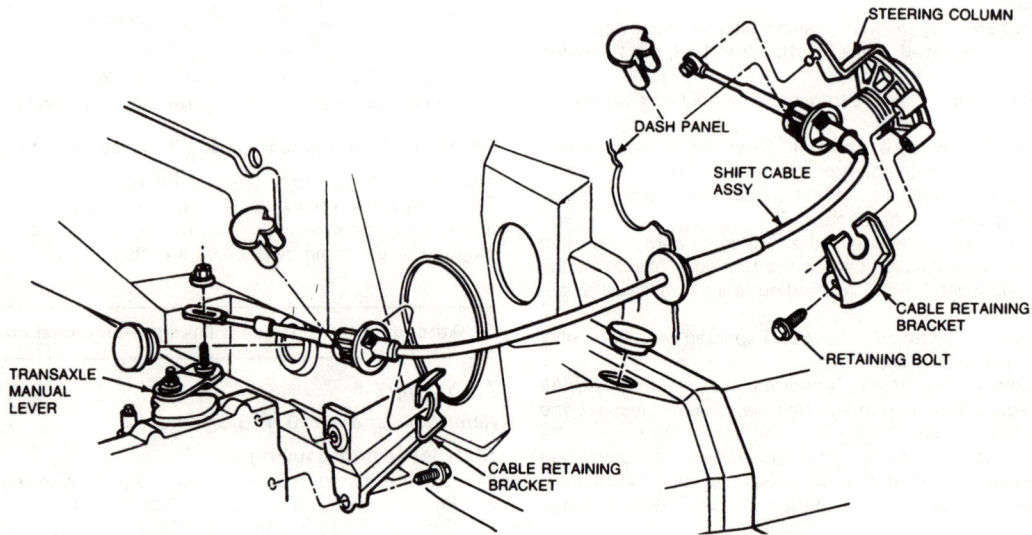

3.18 AXOD column shift cable routing and installation details

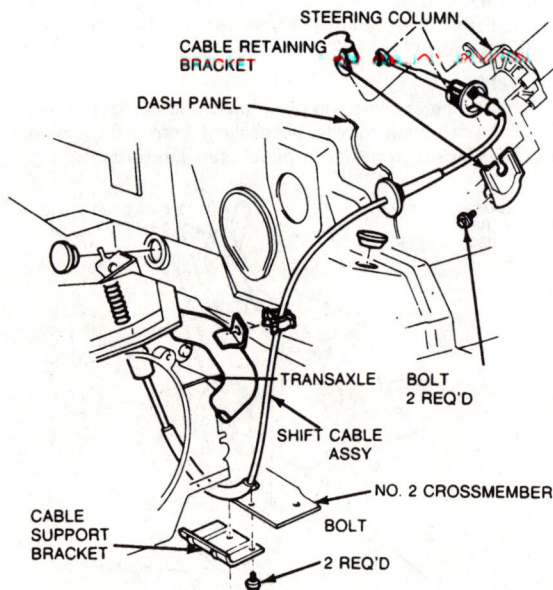

3.28 ATX transaxle column shift cable mounting details

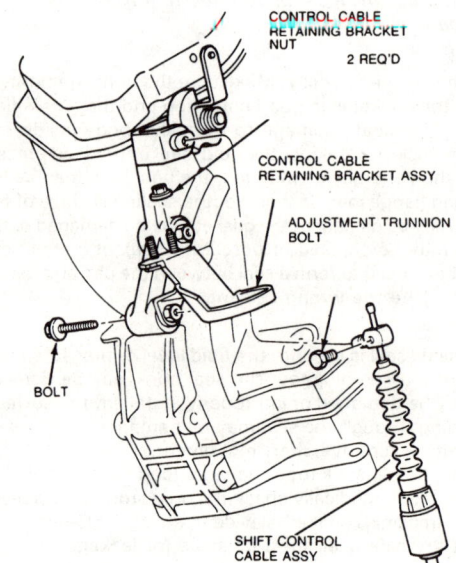

3.31 ATX shift cable-to-transaxle installation details

and bracket from the steering column (see illustration).

19 Pry the plastic cable terminal from the column selector pivot ball, using a screwdriver.

20 Disengage the cable from the retaining bracket on the steering column.

21 Working in the engine compartment, pry the cable bracket from the dash panel.

22 Remove the transaxle lever stud nut.

23 Remove the cable from the transaxle bracket, then pull the cable through into the engine compartment.

24 To install the cable, push it through the dash into the passenger compartment and press the rubber boot securely in place in the dash panel.

25 Working in the engine compartment, engage the cable in the bracket and install the clip. Connect the cable to the transaxle shift lever with the nut loose.

26 In the passenger compartment, install the cable and bracket with the two screws. Tighten the screws securely. Snap the cable plastic terminal onto the selector lever pivot ball on the steering column.

27 Adjust the shift linkage (Section 5).

ATX transaxle

Refer to illustrations 3.28 and 3.31

28 Working under the instrument panel, unbolt the shift cable bracket from the steering column (see illustration).

29 Use a screwdriver to disconnect the cable plastic terminal from the column selector ball and disengage the cable from the bracket.

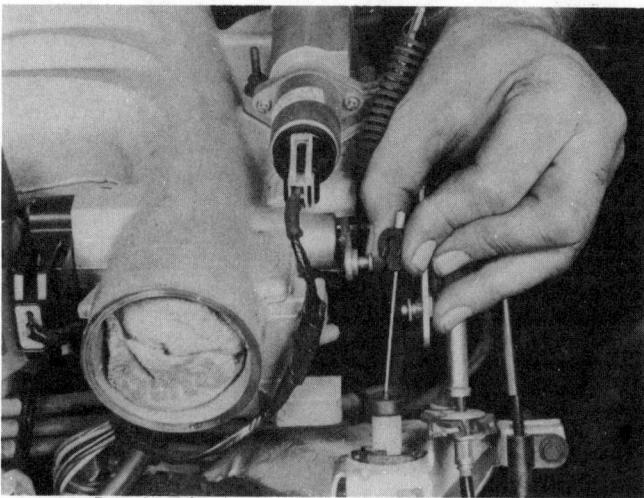

4.5a On the AXOD transaxle, disconnect the TV cable from the throttle lever by lifting it off the lever flange, . . .

4.5b . . . then at the other end, remove the bolt, pull up and disengage the hooked end

30 Working in the engine compartment, pry the cable grommet out of the dash panel.

31 Remove the bolt from the adjustment trunnion on the end of the cable (see illustration).

32 Remove the cable engine support retaining clip.

33 Disengage the cable from the retaining bracket on the transaxle and pull the cable through into the engine compartment.

34 To install the cable, push it through the dash into the passenger compartment, plastic terminal end first.

35 Engage the rubber boot on the cable in the dash panel.

36 Connect the cable to the retaining bracket in the engine compartment.

37 Using a new grommet, install the cable adjustment trunnion on the end of the shift control cable onto the shift lever, with the bolt loose.

38 In the passenger compartment, install the bracket onto the cable. Install the cable and bracket onto the steering column with the two bolts. Tighten the bolts securely.

39 Snap the cable terminal securely to the selector lever on the steering column.

40 Adjust the shift linkage (Section 5) and tighten the shift control cable bolt.

4 Automatic transaxle — removal and installation

Refer to illustrations 4.5a, 4.5b, 4.9, 4.12a, 4.12b, 4.14, 4.17 and 4.20

Removal

1 Disconnect the negative cable from the battery. Place the cable out of the way so it cannot accidentally come in contact with the negative terminal of the battery, as this would again allow power into the electrical system of the vehicle.

2 Remove the hood and left side inner front fender liner (Chapter 11).

3 Remove the air cleaner assembly.

4 On ATX transaxles (four-cylinder models), Remove the timing window plug and rotate the crankshaft until the timing marker on the flywheel lines up with the timing pointer. Mark the crankshaft at the 12 o'clock (TDC) position and then rotate the crankshaft pulley mark to the 6 o'clock (BDC) position.

5 Disconnect the TV linkage (see illustrations).

6 Drain the transaxle fluid (Chapter 1).

7 Remove the starter motor (Chapter 5).

8 Remove the torque converter dust cover.

9 Mark one of the torque converter studs and the torque converter with white paint so they can be installed in the same position (see illustration).

10 Use a large socket and breaker bar on the crankshaft bolt at the front of the engine to lock the engine, preventing it from turning over, then remove the four torque converter nuts. Turn the engine over with the socket and bar for access to each stud nut.

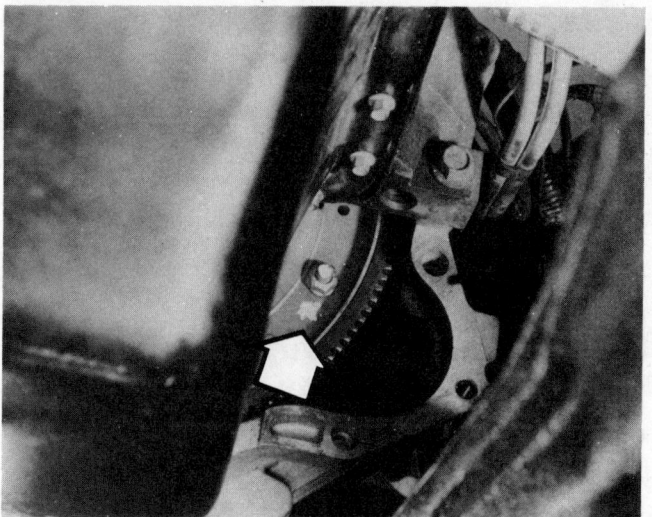

4.9 Mark the torque converter and stud with white paint so it can be reinstalled in the same position

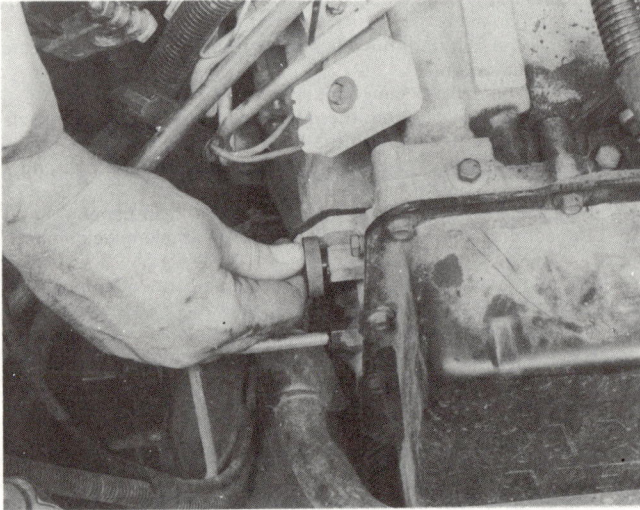

4.12a   Push the special tool into the fitting until it clicks . . .

11 Remove the engine (Chapter 2).
12 Disconnect the fluid cooler lines at the transaxle. On these models, a special tool (available at auto parts stores) is required to disconnect the lines; don't try to unscrew the fitting. Insert the tool into the fitting until a click (indicating the internal retainer has disengaged) is felt and pull the tool and fitting out (see illustrations).
13 Disconnect the speedometer cable.
14 Disconnect the shift linkage (see illustration).
15 Unplug the electrical connectors at the transaxle.
16 Disconnect the driveaxles.
17 Remove the heater coolant tube assembly (see illustration).
18 Secure a chain to the transaxle.
19 Remove the transaxle mount nuts.
20 Connect a hoist to the chain and lift the transaxle out of the engine compartment (see illustration).

Installation

21 Lower the transaxle into place on the mount studs.
22 Install the transaxle mount nuts. Tighten the nuts to the specified torque.
23 Connect the driveaxles.
24 Install the heater coolant tube assembly.
25 Plug in the transaxle electrical connectors.
26 Connect the shift linkage.
27 Connect the speedometer cable.

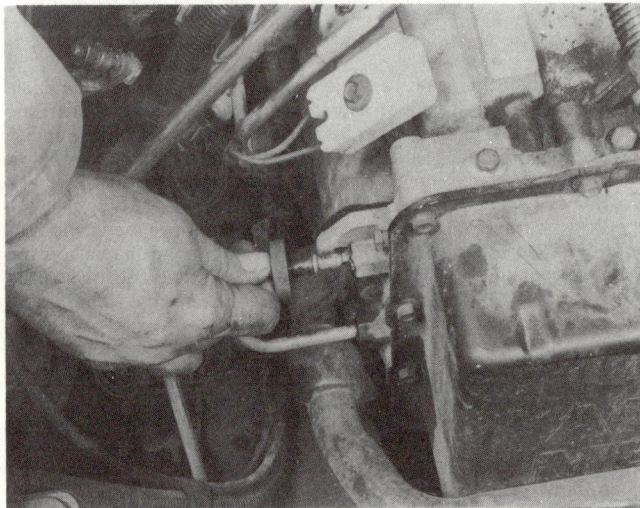

4.12b   . . . and pull the tool and line out of the transmission

4.14   Remove the nut and lift off the shift lever with the linkage still installed — the shaft and lever are keyed so it can only go on one way

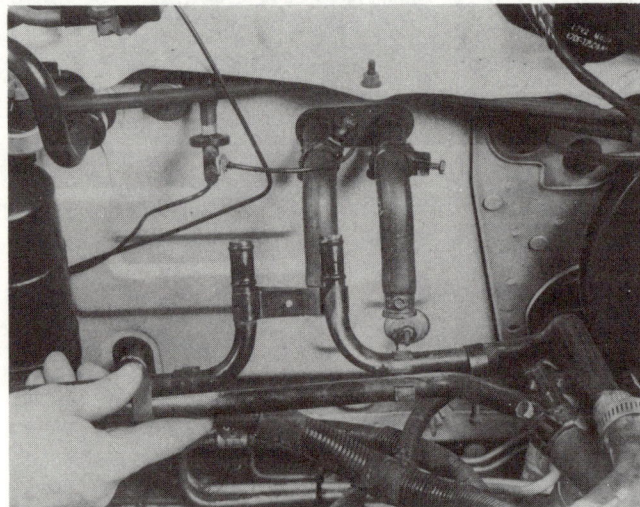

4.17   By removing the heater cooling tube assembly, you will have more room when lifting the transaxle out

4.20   Adjust the position of the hoist on the chain so the transaxle is level before lifting it out

28 Using the special tool, push the cooler lines into the fittings until they click into place.

29 Install the engine (Chapter 2C). When installing the engine on ATX transaxles, the mark made on the crankshaft pulley in Step 4 must be as close to the 6 o'clock position (BDC) as possible.

30 On all models, the white paint mark made on the torque converter and stud during Step 9 must line up. Install the torque converter nuts. Tighten the nuts to the specified torque.

31 Install the torque converter dust cover.

32 Install the starter motor.

33 Connect the TV linkage.

34 Install the air cleaner assembly.

35 Install the front fender liner.

36 Install the hood.

37 Fill the transaxle with the specified fluid (Chapter 1).

38 Adjust the TV linkage.

5 Automatic transaxle shift linkage — adjustment

AXOD transaxle

1 Place the selector lever in the Overdrive position, against the rear stop and have an assistant hold it there during the adjustment process.

2 Working in the engine compartment, loosen the transaxle shift lever-to-cable nut.

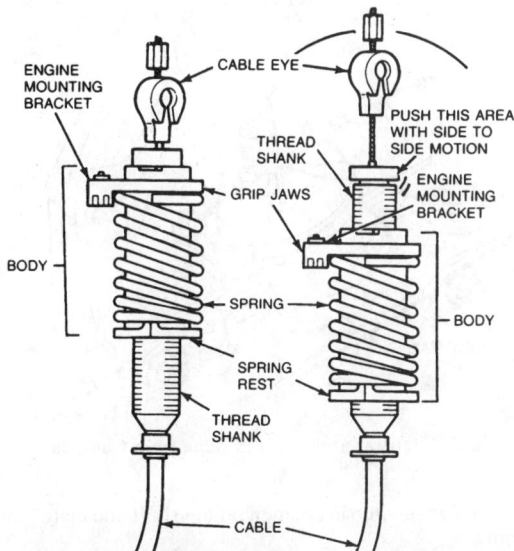

6.3 AXOD TV cable retraction details

6.7 To adjust the ATX transaxle TV control linkage, loosen the bolt on the sliding trunnion block at least one turn, . . .

3 Move the transaxle shift lever to the Overdrive position (the second detent from the rear position) and tighten the nut securely.

4 Check the shift operation in each detent and make sure the engine starts only when the selector lever is in the Neutral position.

ATX transaxle

5 Place the selector lever in the Drive position and have an assistant hold it there during the adjustment process.

6 Working in the engine compartment, loosen the trunnion adjusting bolt located at the end of the shift cable.

7 Move the transaxle shift lever to the Drive position (the second detent from the rear position) and tighten the adjusting bolt securely.

8 Check the shift operation in each detent and make sure the engine starts only when the selector lever is in the Neutral position.

6 Throttle valve (TV) control linkage — adjustment

AXOD transaxle

Refer to illustration 6.3

1 The AXOD TV cable should only require adjustment if the cable, the bracket, the transaxle, the main control assembly or the throttle control assembly have been disconnected or replaced.

2 The TV cable eye must be connected to the throttle control lever link and the cable boot attached to the chain cover.

3 Make sure the threaded shank is retracted all the way with the cable mounted in the the engine bracket. To retract it, hold the spring rest and wiggle the top of the threaded shank while pressing the shank through the spring **(see illustration)**.

4 Connect the end of the TV cable to the throttle body.

5 Rotate the throttle lever to the wide open throttle position and then release it. The threaded shank must move or ''ratchet'' out of the grip jaws. If it does not, check for broken or disconnected components and repeat the procedure.

ATX transaxle

Refer to illustrations 6.7 and 6.9

6 Symptoms of the need for TV linkage adjustment on these models are early or erratic shifts and/or lack of downshifting.

7 With the engine idling at normal operating temperature, loosen the bolt on the sliding trunnion block of the TV control rod assembly at least one turn **(see illustration)**.

8 Remove any corrosion from the control rod and free up the trunnion block so it slides freely.

9 Rotate the TV control lever up, using one finger and light force to make sure the TV control lever is against the internal idle stop **(see illustration)**. Without relaxing the force on the TV control lever, tighten the bolt on the trunnion block securely.

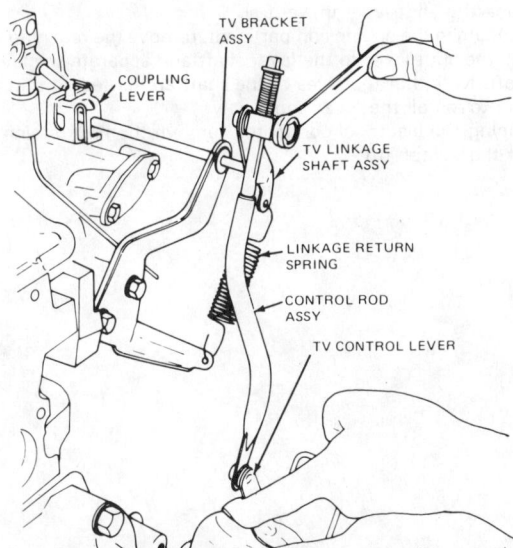

6.9 . . . then, using one finger, rotate the TV control lever at the transaxle up against the internal idle stop and tighten the bolt on the trunnion block

7.2   Pry on the transaxle mount to check for
excessive movement

7   Transmission mount — check and replacement

Refer to illustrations 7.2 and 7.5

1   Remove the left front wheel and the fender liner (Chapter 11).
2   Insert a pry bar or large screwdriver into the opening in the mount
and pry up and down **(see illustration)**.
3   If the mount can be easily moved or if the rubber is cracked, collapsed or separated from the metal backing, replace it with a new one.
4   Support the transaxle with a floor jack and a block of wood.
5   Remove the transaxle nuts and the mount-to-sub frame bolts and
remove the mount **(see illustration)**. It may be necessary to raise the
transaxle slightly with the jack so the mount can be lifted out.
6   Installation is the reverse of removal.

8   Neutral start switch — replacement and adjustment

Refer to illustration 8.6

1   Disconnect the negative cable from the battery. Place the cable
out of the way so it cannot accidentally come in contact with the
negative terminal of the battery, as this would again allow power into
the electrical system of the vehicle.
2   Place the shift lever in Neutral.
3   Working in the engine compartment, remove the retaining nut that
secures the shift lever to the lever shaft and separate the lever from
the shaft. Note that the sides of the shaft are flatted so that it is impossible to install the lever improperly.
4   Unplug the electrical connector, remove the two retaining bolts
and lift the switch off.

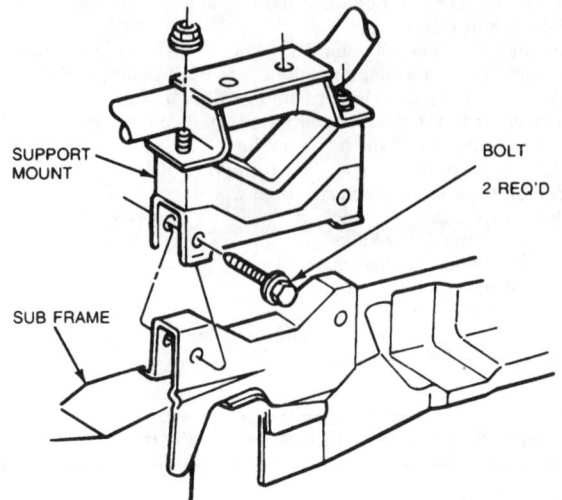

7.5   The transaxle mount is held in place by two bolts

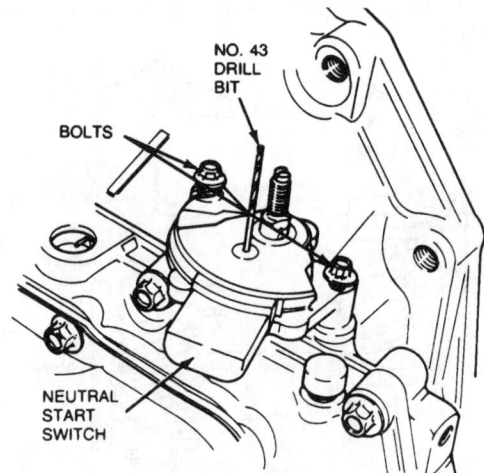

8.6   Neutral start switch adjustment details

5   Place the new switch in position on the shaft and install the bolts
finger tight.
6   To adjust the switch, insert a no. 43 drill bit (0.089-inch) into the
adjustment hole and tighten the bolts securely **(see illustration)**. Note
that the drill cannot be inserted as far into the adjustment hole in any
other gear as it can in Neutral.
7   Connect the negative battery cable.
8   Start the engine in both Park and Neutral to verify that the switch
is properly adjusted.

Chapter 8   Clutch and driveaxles

Contents

Specifications

Driveaxle length (all model years — see illustration 9.15)

4-speed automatic overdrive transaxle
Left side . . . .   18.27 in (463.65 mm)
Right side . . . .   23.58 in (598.55 mm)
3-speed automatic overdrive transaxle
Left side . . . .   22.80 in (578.75 mm)
Right side . . . .   20.09 in (510.05 mm)
Manual transaxle
Left side . . . .   21.24 in (539.05 mm)
Right side . . . .   21.63 in (549.05 mm)

Torque specifications   Ft-lbs
Pressure plate-to-flywheel bolts . . . .   12 to 24
Clutch release lever-to-shaft bolt . . . .   30 to 40
Link shaft support bearing-to-bracket bolts . . . .   16 to 23
Hub (axle) nut . . . .   180 to 200
Wheel lug nuts . . . .   80 to 105

1   General information

Refer to illustrations 1.4a and 1.4b

All vehicles with a manual transaxle have a single dry plate, diaphragm spring type clutch. The clutch plate has a splined hub which allows it to slide along the splines on the input shaft. The clutch and pressure plate are held in contact by spring pressure exerted by the diaphragm spring in the pressure plate.

During gear shifting, the clutch pedal is depressed, which operates a cable, pulling on the release lever so the throwout bearing pushes on the diaphragm spring fingers, disengaging the clutch.

The clutch pedal incorporates a self-adjusting device which compensates for clutch wear. A spring in the clutch pedal arm maintains tension on the cable and the adjuster pawl grabs a ratcheting mechanism when the pedal is depressed and the clutch is released. Consequently the slack is always taken up in the cable, making adjustment unnecessary.

Power from the engine passes though the clutch and transaxle to the front wheels by two driveaxles, on vehicles equipped with a 4-speed automatic overdrive transmission **(see illustration)**. Vehicles equipped with a manual or 3-speed automatic overdrive transmission use a driveaxle on the left side and a link shaft and driveaxle on the right side **(see illustration)**. The driveaxles are nearly equal in length. The driveaxles consist of three sections: the inner splined ends which are held in the differential by clips or springs, two constant velocity (CV) joints and outer splined ends which are held in the hub by a nut. The CV joints are internally splined and contain ball bearings which allow them to operate at various lengths and angles as the suspension is compressed and extended. The CV joints are lubricated with special grease and are protected by rubber boots which must be inspected periodically for cracks, holes, tears and signs of leakage, which could lead to damage of the joints and failure of the driveaxle.

It should be noted that the terms used in this manual to describe various clutch components may vary somewhat from those used by parts vendors. For example, such terms as clutch disc, pressure plate and release bearing are used throughout this Chapter. An auto parts store or dealer parts department, however, might use the terms clutch plate, clutch cover and throwout bearing, respectively, for the above parts. The important thing to keep in mind is that the terms are interchangeable — they mean the same thing. **Warning:** *Dust produced by clutch wear and deposited on clutch components contains asbestos, which is hazardous to your health. DO NOT blow it out with compressed air and DO NOT inhale it. DO NOT use gasoline or petroleum-based solvents to remove the dust. Brake system cleaner should be used to flush the dust into a drain pan. After the clutch components are wiped clean with a rag, dispose of the contaminated rags and cleaner in a covered container.*

2 Clutch operation — check

Other than to replace components with obvious damage, some preliminary checks should be done to diagnose clutch problems.
  a) With the engine running and the brake applied, hold the clutch pedal 1/2-inch from the floor and shift back-and-forth between First and Second gear several times. If the shifts are smooth, the clutch is releasing properly. If they aren't, the clutch is not releasing completely. Check the pedal, cable, lever and throwout bearing.
  b) To check clutch ''spin down time'', run the engine at normal idle speed with the transmission in Neutral (clutch pedal up — engaged). Disengage the clutch (pedal down), wait several seconds and shift the transmission into Reverse. No grinding noise should be heard. A grinding noise would indicate component failure in the pressure plate or clutch disc (assuming that the transaxle is in good condition, of course).

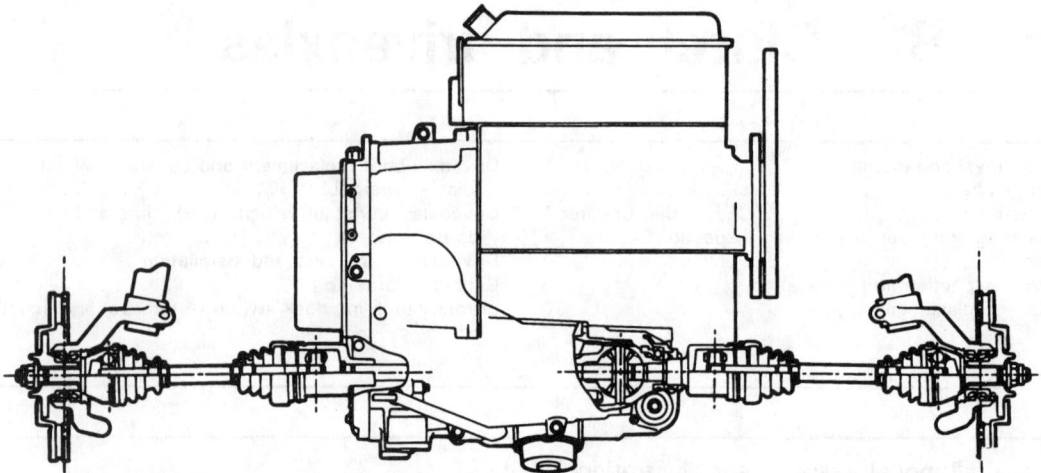

1.4a   Driveaxle arrangement — vehicles equipped with a 4-speed automatic overdrive transaxle employ two nearly equal length driveaxles

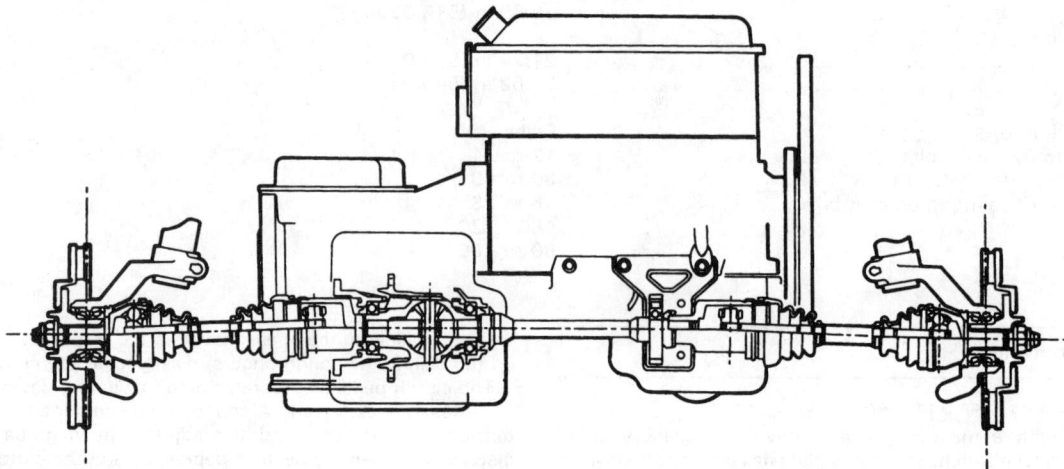

1.4b   Driveaxle arrangement — vehicles equipped with a manual or 3-speed automatic overdrive transaxle also utilize two nearly equal length driveaxles, but an interconnecting link shaft couples the right side driveaxle to the transaxle

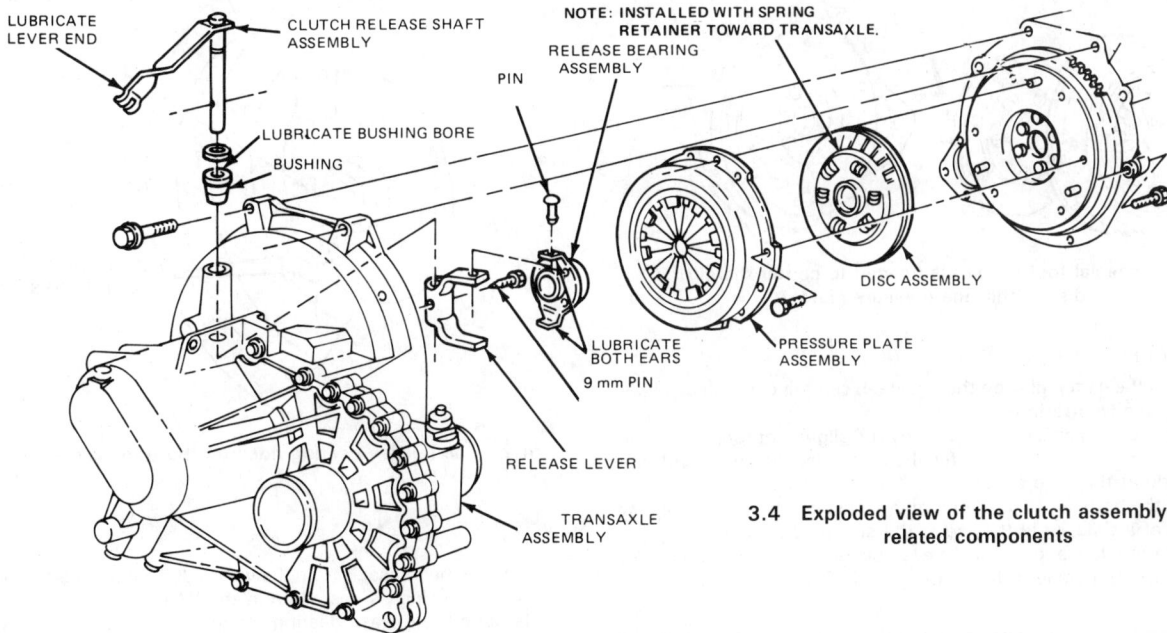

3.4 Exploded view of the clutch assembly and related components

c) A clutch pedal that's binding is most likely caused by a faulty clutch cable or dry clutch release shaft bushing. Lubricate the bushing with SAE 10W-30 motor oil. Check the cable where it enters the housing for rust and corrosion. If it looks good, lubricate the cable with penetrating oil. If pedal operation improves, the cable is worn out and should be replaced.

3 Clutch — removal, inspection and installation

Refer to illustrations 3.4, 3.9 and 3.11

Warning: *Dust produced by clutch wear and deposited on clutch components contains asbestos, which is hazardous to your health. DO NOT blow it out with compressed air and DO NOT inhale it. DO NOT use gasoline or petroleum-based solvents to remove the dust. Brake system cleaner should be used to flush the dust into a drain pan. After the clutch components are wiped clean with a rag, dispose of the contaminated rags and cleaner in a covered container.*

Removal

1   Remove the transaxle from the vehicle (Chapter 7, Part A).
2   Use a center punch to mark the position of the pressure plate assembly on the flywheel so it can be installed in the same position.
3   Loosen the pressure plate bolts a little at a time, in a criss-cross pattern, to avoid warping the cover.
4   Remove the bolts and detach the pressure plate and clutch disc from the flywheel **(see illustration)**.
5   Handle the clutch carefully, trying not to touch the lining surface, and set it aside.

Inspection

6   Inspect the friction surfaces of the clutch plate, pressure plate and flywheel for signs of uneven contact, indicating improper installation or damaged clutch springs. Also look for score marks, burned areas, deep grooves, cracks and other types of wear and damage. If the flywheel is worn or damaged, remove it and take it to an automotive machine shop to see if it can be resurfaced (if it can't, a new one will be required). If the flywheel is glazed, rough it up with fine emery cloth.
7   To see how worn the clutch disc is, measure the distance from the rivet heads to the lining surface. There should be at least 1/16-inch of lining above the rivet heads. However, the clutch disc is ordinarily replaced with a new one whenever it's removed for any reason (due to the relatively low cost of the part and the work involved to get to it). Check the lining for contamination by oil or grease and replace the

clutch disc with a new one if any is present. Check the hub for cracks, blue discolored areas, broken springs and contamination by grease or oil. Slide the clutch disc onto the input shaft to make sure the fit is snug and the splines are not burred or worn.
8   Remove and inspect the release bearing and release lever as described in Section 4.
9   Check the flatness of the pressure plate with a straightedge. Look for signs of overheating, cracks, deep grooves and ridges. The inner end of the diaphragm spring fingers should not show any signs of uneven wear. Replace the pressure plate with a new one if its condition is in doubt **(see illustration)**.
10 Make sure the pressure plate fits snugly on the flywheel dowels. Replace it with a new one if it fits loosely on the dowels.

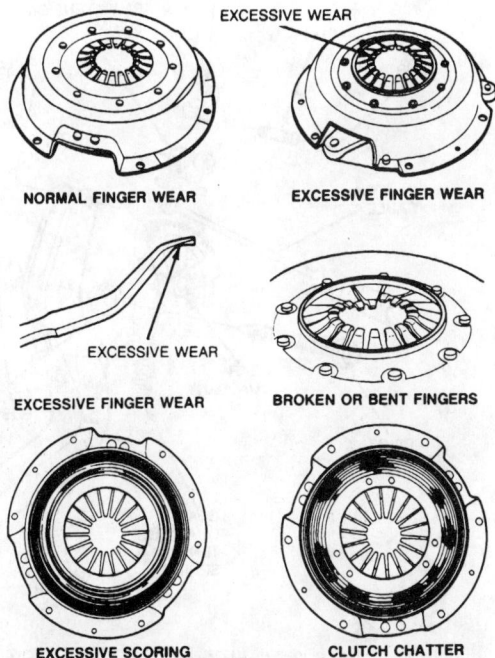

3.9 Replace the pressure plate if excessive wear is noted

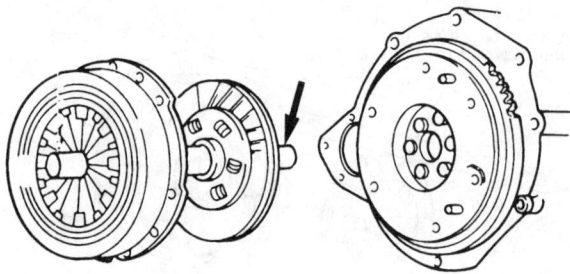

3.11 A special tool (arrow) is needed to center the clutch disc within the pressure plate

Installation

11 Position the clutch disc on the flywheel, centering it with an alignment tool **(see illustration)**.
12 With the clutch disc held in place by the alignment tool, place the pressure plate in position on the flywheel dowels, aligning it with the marks made at the time of removal.
13 Install the bolts and tighten them in a criss-cross pattern, one or two turns at a time, until they're at the specified torque.
14 Install the release lever and release bearing (refer to Section 4).
15 Install the transaxle (refer to Chapter 7, Part A).

---

4   Clutch release bearing and lever — removal, inspection and installation

---

Refer to illustration 4.2
Warning: *Dust produced by clutch wear and deposited on clutch components contains asbestos, which is hazardous to your health. DO NOT blow it out with compressed air and DO NOT inhale it. DO NOT use gasoline or petroleum-based solvents to remove the dust. Brake system cleaner should be used to flush the dust into a drain pan. After the clutch components are wiped clean with a rag, dispose of the contaminated rags and cleaner in a covered container.*

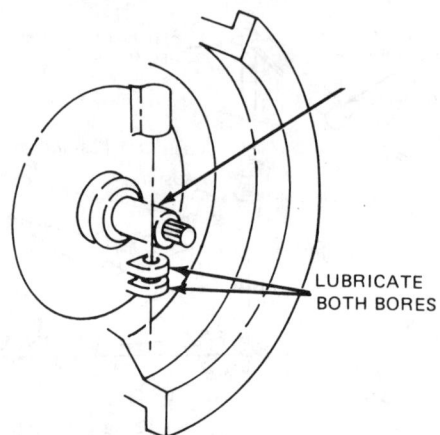

LUBRICATE BOTH BORES

4.2   The release bearing rides on the transaxle extension

Removal

1   Remove the transaxle from the vehicle (Chapter 7, Part A) and clean the clutch housing as described in the Warning above.
2   Remove the release bearing retaining pin from the release lever and slide the bearing off the transaxle extension **(see illustration)**.
3   To remove the release lever from the shaft, remove the lever-to-shaft bolt. Pull the shaft up through the clutch housing and lift out the lever **(see illustration 3.4)**.

Inspection

4   Check the lever arms and shaft for excessive wear and galling.
5   Inspect the bearing for damage, wear and cracks. Hold the center of the bearing and spin the outer race. If the bearing doesn't turn smoothly or if it's noisy, replace it with a new one. It's common practice to replace the bearing with a new one whenever a clutch job is performed, to decrease the possibility of a bearing failure in the future.

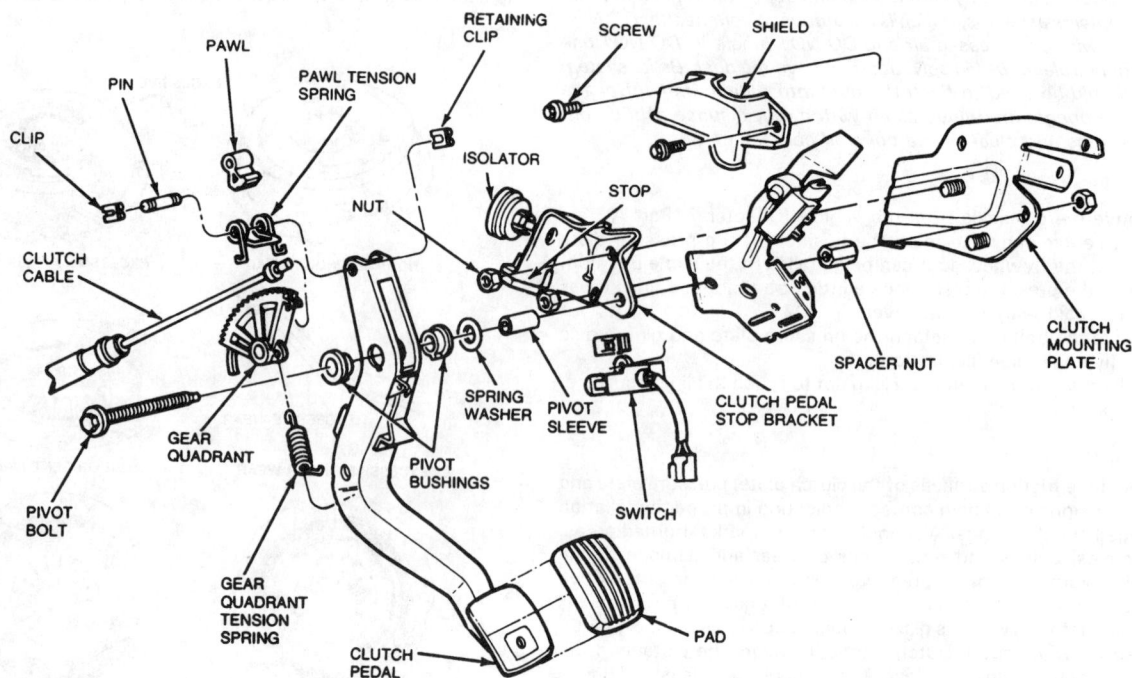

RETAINING CLIP — SCREW — SHIELD — PAWL — PAWL TENSION SPRING — PIN — ISOLATOR — NUT — STOP — CLIP — CLUTCH CABLE — CLUTCH MOUNTING PLATE — SPACER NUT — PIVOT BOLT — GEAR QUADRANT — SPRING WASHER — PIVOT SLEEVE — PIVOT BUSHINGS — CLUTCH PEDAL STOP BRACKET — SWITCH — GEAR QUADRANT TENSION SPRING — CLUTCH PEDAL — PAD

5.2   Exploded view of the clutch pedal, self-adjuster mechanism and related components

Installation

6   Wipe the old grease from the release bearing if the bearing is to be reused. Do not clean it by immersing it in solvent; it's sealed at the factory and would be ruined if solvent got into it. Fill the cavities and coat the inner surface, as well as the transaxle extension with high temperature multi-purpose grease.

7   Lubricate the release shaft bushings, position the release lever in the clutch housing and slide the shaft down through the lever and into the bottom bushing. Install the lever-to-shaft bolt and tighten it to the specified torque. Lubricate the release lever arms where they contact the bearing with high temperature multi-purpose grease.

8   Slide the release bearing onto the transaxle extension and position it in the release lever arms with the ears on the bearing straddling the lever arms. Insert the locating pin through the top ear and into the release lever.

9   Work the clutch release shaft lever by hand to verify smooth operation of the release bearing and shaft.

5   Clutch cable — removal and installation

Refer to illustrations 5.2, 5.3 and 5.8

Removal

1   Remove the left side under dash panel.

2   Pull the clutch pedal to the rear and support it against the bumper stop so that the adjuster pawl is released from the gear guadrant (**see illustration**).

3   Remove the air cleaner assembly for access to the clutch cable. Pull the clutch cable from the clutch release lever with a pair of pliers. Grab the cable end, not the cable itself (**see illustration**).

4   Pull the cable and housing through the insulator on the transaxle (**see illustration 5.3**).

5   Loosen the front clutch pedal shield screw, remove the rear screw and swing the shield up and out of the way. Tighten the front screw to hold the shield up (**see illustration 5.2**).

6   With the pawl released from the gear quadrant, rotate the quadrant forward and unhook the cable. The quadrant is under spring tension — don't let it snap back into position.

7   Pull the cable from the clutch pedal assembly and push it through the firewall to the engine compartment.

Installation

8   Insert the cable through the firewall from the engine compartment side (**see illustration**).

9   Working under the dash, guide the cable through the insulator on the pedal stop bracket (**see illustration 5.2**). Lift up on the clutch pedal, release the pawl and rotate the quadrant forward. Hook the cable end into the quadrant.

10   Swing the shield back into place and tighten the two screws.

11   Route the cable through the insulator on the transaxle housing.

12   Have an assistant pull back on the clutch pedal and hold it there. Connect the cable to the clutch release lever.

13   Depress the clutch pedal a few times to adjust the cable.

14   Install the under dash panel.

15   Install the air cleaner assembly.

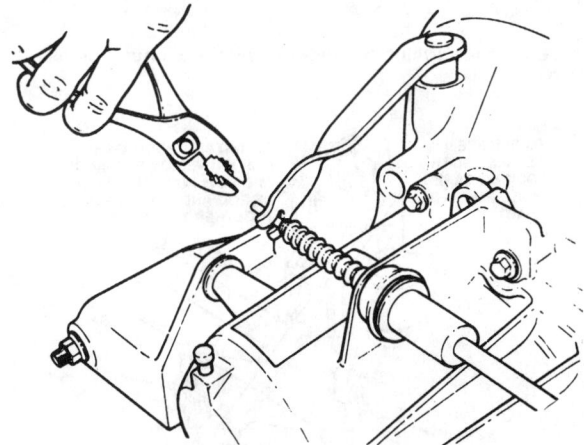

5.3 **Disconnect the clutch cable from the release lever with a pair of pliers**

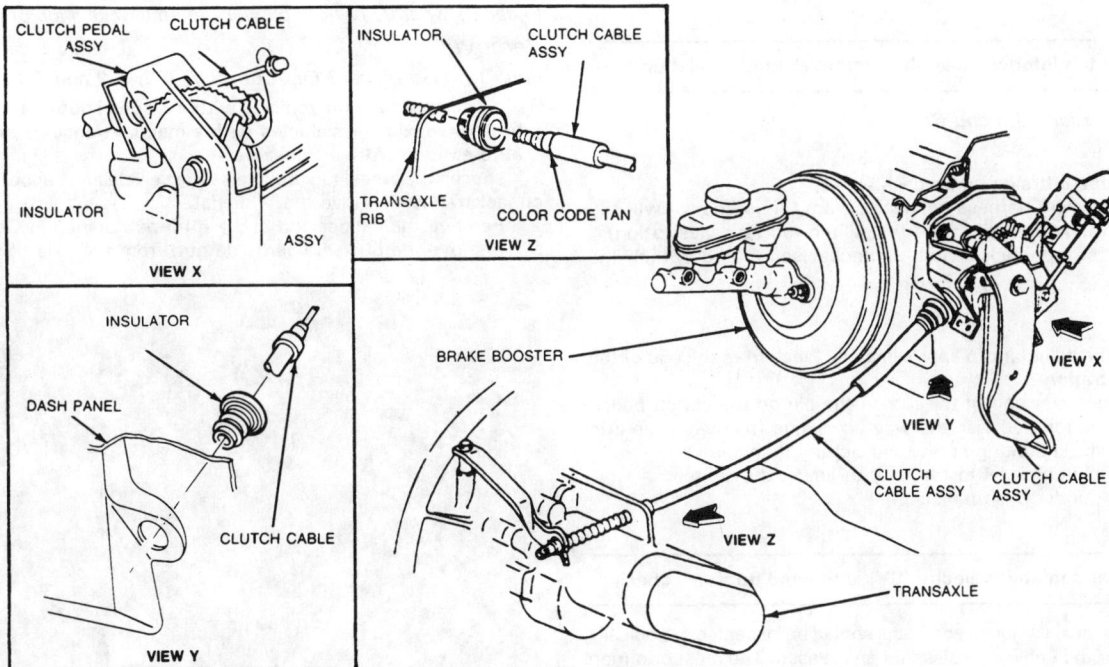

5.8 **Clutch cable installation details**

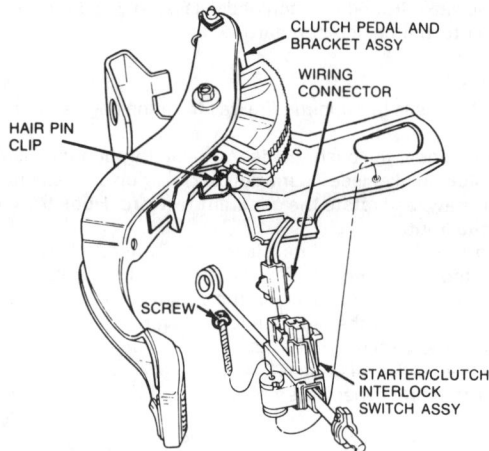

6.3   Starter/clutch interlock switch mounting details

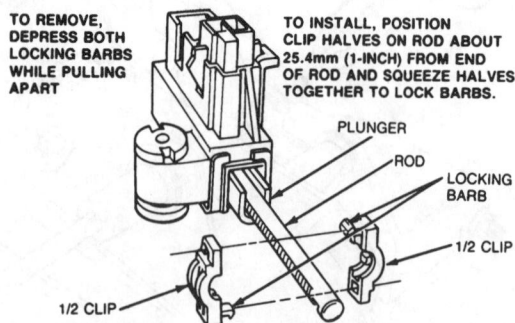

6.5   If the engine doesn't crank over when the ignition key is turned and the clutch pedal is fully depressed, separate the adjuster clip and reposition it closer to the switch

6   Starter/clutch interlock switch — removal and installation

Refer to illustrations 6.3 and 6.5

Removal

1   Remove the left side under dash panel.
2   Detach the wire harness connector from the interlock switch.
3   Remove the hairpin clip from the switch rod **(see illustration)**.
4   Remove the interlock switch-to-bracket screw and detach the switch.

Installation

5   Position the adjuster clip approximately 1 inch from the end of the rod **(see illustration)**.
6   Install the eyelet end of the rod on the pin on the clutch pedal.
7   With the clutch pedal all the way up, swing the switch up into place. Install the mounting screw and tighten it securely.
8   Push the clutch pedal to the floor to adjust the switch.
9   Install the under dash panel.

7   Driveaxles, constant velocity (CV) joints and boots — check

1   The driveaxles, CV joints and boots should be inspected periodically and whenever the vehicle is raised for any reason. The most common symptom of driveaxle or CV joint failure is knocking or clicking noises when turning.
2   Raise the vehicle and support it securely on jackstands.
3   Inspect the CV joint boots for cracks, leaks and broken retaining bands. If lubricant leaks out through a hole or crack in the boot, the

CV joint will wear prematurely and require replacement. Replace any damaged boots immediately (Section 9). It's a good idea to disassemble, clean, inspect and repack the CV joint whenever replacing a CV joint boot, to ensure that the joint is not contaminated with moisture or dirt, which would cause premature CV joint failure.
4   Check the entire length of each axle to make sure they aren't cracked, dented, twisted or bent.
5   Grasp each axle and rotate it in both directions while holding the CV joint housings to check for excessive movement, indicating worn splines or loose CV joints.
6   If a boot is damaged or loose, remove the driveaxle as described in Section 8. Disassemble and inspect the CV joint as outlined in Section 9. **Note:** *Some auto parts stores carry "split" type replacement boots, which can be installed without removing the driveaxle from the vehicle. This is a convenient alternative; however, it's recommended that the driveaxle be removed and the CV joint disassembled and cleaned to ensure that the joint is free from contaminants such as moisture and dirt, which will accelerate CV joint wear.*

8   Driveaxles — removal and installation

Warning: *Whenever any of the suspension or steering fasteners are loosened or removed they must be replaced with new ones — discard the originals and don't reuse them. They must be replaced with new ones of the same part number or of original equipment quality and design. Torque specifications must be followed for proper reassembly and component retention.*

Caution: *Whenever both the right and left driveaxles are removed at the same time, the differential side gears must be supported so they don't fall into the case (manual and 3-speed automatic overdrive transaxles only). A wooden dowel, approximately 15/16-inch in diameter, inserted into each side gear will work. If this precaution is not heeded and the side gears do drop, the differential will have to be removed from the transaxle to realign the gears (which will necessitate towing the vehicle to a Ford dealer service department or a repair shop). Also, this procedure requires a special puller and adapters to install the driveaxle in the hub (due to the interference fit designed into the mating splines on the axle and in the hub). The use of the correct Ford factory tool is highly recommended if available. However, an alternative tool can be fabricated from a bearing puller and materials available at a hardware store. Read the entire procedure before beginning any work to decide whether or not you want to undertake a job of this nature.*

Removal

Refer to illustrations 8.6a, 8.6b, 8.7, 8.8, 8.9 and 8.11

Right driveaxle only on vehicles with a 3-speed automatic transaxle, both driveaxles on vehicles with a manual transaxle or a 4-speed automatic overdrive transaxle

1   Loosen the wheel lug nuts, raise the vehicle and support it securely on jackstands. Remove the wheel(s).
2   Remove the caliper and brake rotor as outlined in Chapter 9.
3   Remove the hub retainer (axle nut) from the axle (if you have a

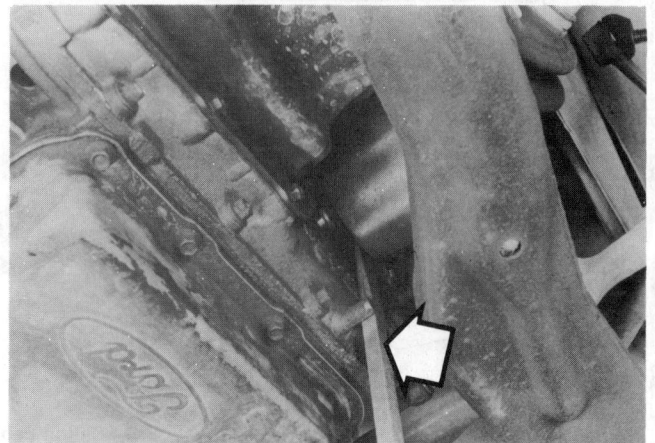

8.6a   Use a large screwdriver or pry bar (arrow) to carefully pry the CV joint out of the transaxle

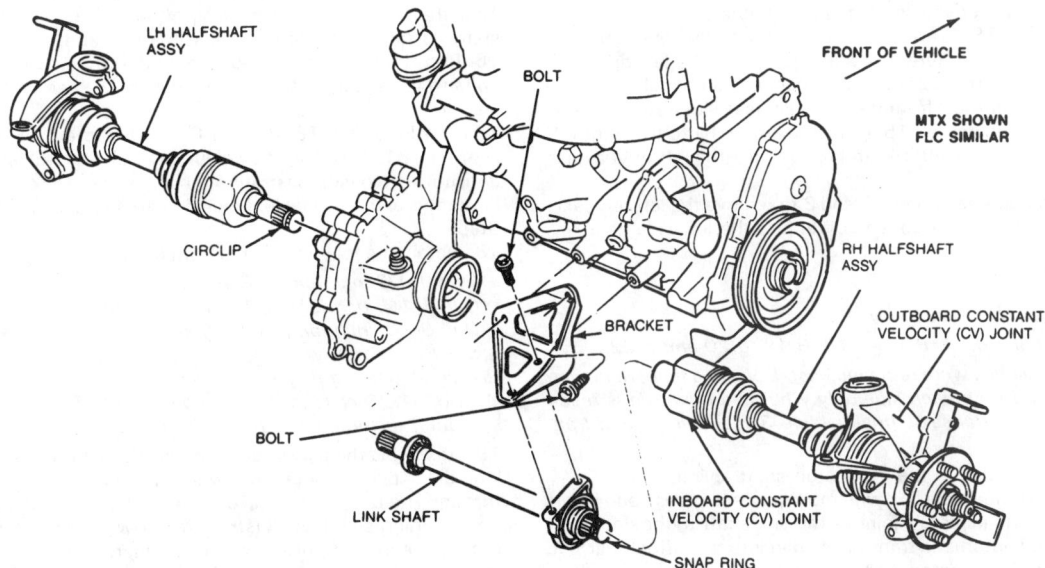

LH HALFSHAFT ASSY

BOLT

FRONT OF VEHICLE

MTX SHOWN FLC SIMILAR

CIRCLIP

RH HALFSHAFT ASSY

OUTBOARD CONSTANT VELOCITY (CV) JOINT

BRACKET

BOLT

LINK SHAFT

INBOARD CONSTANT VELOCITY (CV) JOINT

SNAP RING

8.6b Driveaxle and link shaft installation details (manual and 3-speed automatic overdrive transaxles only)

3-speed automatic transaxle equipped vehicle and both driveaxles are being removed, work on the right one first). Place a pry bar between two of the wheel studs to prevent the hub from turning while loosening the nut.

4   Remove the brake hose support bracket-to-strut bolt.

5   Remove the lower control arm-to-steering knuckle bolt and separate the control arm from the knuckle (refer to Chapter 10).

6   Using a large screwdriver or pry bar, pry the inboard CV joint assembly from the transaxle **(see illustration)**. On 3-speed automatic and 5-speed manual transaxles (right side only), unbolt the link shaft support bearing from the bracket **(see illustration)**. Slide the shaft out of the transaxle. Be careful not to damage the case or the oil pan. Suspend the axle with a piece of wire — don't let it hang, or damage to the outer CV joint may occur.

7   Push the driveaxle out of the hub with a gear puller **(see illustration)**.

8   Once the driveaxle is loose from the hub splines, pull out on the strut/knuckle assembly and guide the outer CV joint out of the hub. Remove the support wire and carefully detach the driveaxle (or link shaft/driveaxle assembly) from the vehicle **(see illustration)**.

9   If both driveaxles are being removed, insert a snug fitting wooden dowel (15/16-inch diameter) into the right hand differential side gear (not necessary on 4-speed overdrive transaxles) **(see illustration)**, then repeat the procedure in Steps 1 through 8 to remove the left driveaxle. Support the left side gear also.

8.7   A gear puller can be used to push the driveaxle out of the hub — DO NOT hammer on the axle! (the puller jaws are hooked behind the hub flange; as the screw is tightened, force is applied to the end of the driveaxle to push it out)

8.8   After the driveaxle has been pushed out of the hub, pull out on the strut/knuckle assembly and free the stub shaft from the hub

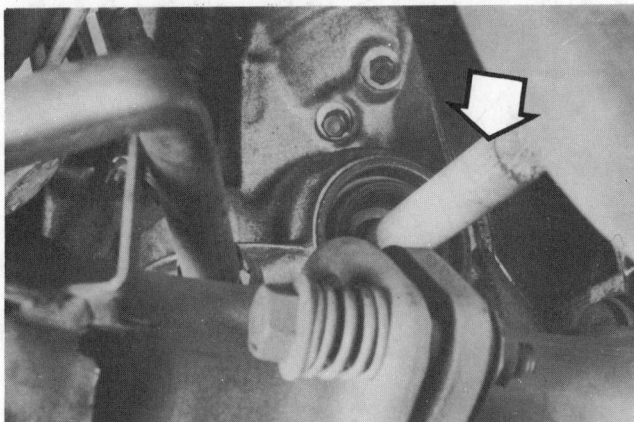

8.9   If both driveaxles are being removed, insert a wooden dowel (arrow) into the differential side gear to keep the gears from falling into the case (except on 4-speed automatic overdrive transaxles)

Left driveaxle on vehicles with a 3-speed automatic transaxle
10   Remove the right driveaxle as described above.
11   Using Ford tool T81P-4026-A or a narrow screwdriver inserted through the right hand differential side gear, drive the left driveaxle stub shaft out of the left differential side gear just far enough to unseat the circlip on the stub shaft from the side gear **(see illustration)**. Insert a snug fitting wooden dowel (15/16-inch diameter) into the right differential side gear to prevent it from falling when the left driveaxle is removed.
12   Follow the procedure in Steps 7 and 8 to remove the left driveaxle from the vehicle. Insert a wooden dowel into the left side gear.

Installation (both driveaxles)
Refer to illustrations 8.14, 8.17, 8.18, 8.19, 8.20 and 8.22
Note: *If both driveaxles were removed, install one at a time, removing the wooden dowel from each side only when the driveaxle is ready for insertion into the transaxle (manual and 3-speed automatic transaxles only).*

13   Install a new circlip on the inner stub shaft splines.
14   Coat the differential seal lips with multi-purpose grease and insert the stub shaft of the inner CV joint or the link shaft (right side only, manual or 3-speed automatic transaxles only) into the differential side gear until the shaft is seated and the circlip snaps into place **(see illustration)**.

15   Pull out on the strut/knuckle assembly and insert the outer CV joint stub shaft into the hub (make sure the splines are aligned). Push the shaft as far into the hub as possible by hand.
16   Bolt the link shaft support bearing to the bracket and tighten the bolts to the specified torque (manual and 3-speed automatic transaxles only).
17   Use Ford tool T81P-1104-C with adapters T83P-1104-BH and adapter T81P-1104-A (if available) to pull the stub shaft into the hub until it's seated **(see illustration)**, then proceed to Step 24. If the special Ford tools aren't available, fabricate a tool as described in the following Steps.
18   Obtain the following items from a hardware store **(see illustration)**:
   Two 1-1/2 inch long 5/8-inch pipe unions
   One 1-1/4 inch long 5/8-inch pipe coupler
   One 3-1/2 inch long by 5/16-inch diameter bolt and nut
   Small and large washers
   A small bearing puller
   Two 4-1/2 inch long Grade 8 bolts (the correct diameter and thread pitch to thread into the puller holes)
19   Assemble the pipe coupler to one pipe union. Insert the 3-1/2 inch long 5/16-inch diameter bolt, with a small washer under the bolt head, through the coupler and union, then install the large washer and nut on the union side **(see illustration)**. Now thread the remaining union onto the exposed portion of the coupler.
20   Grind the ends of each 4-1/2 inch long bolt to a point and thread them into the bearing puller. It may be necessary to install spacers be-

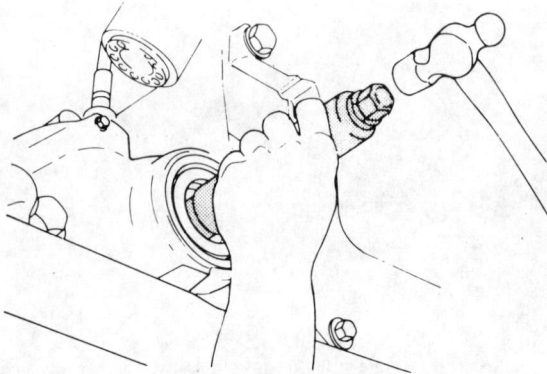

8.11   Driving the left driveaxle out of the differential side gear with Ford tool number T81P-4026-A (a narrow screwdriver may be used to in place of the special tool if extreme care is taken)

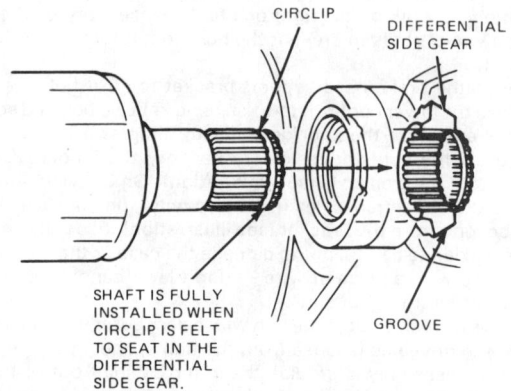

8.14   The inner CV joint stub shaft is completely seated when the circlip on the shaft snaps into the groove in the differential side gear

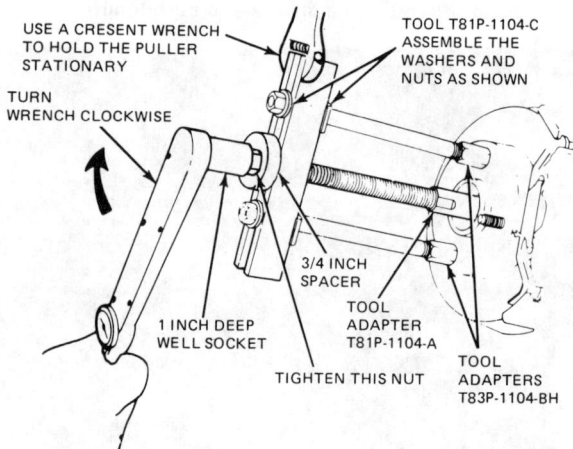

8.17   Using the special Ford tool to pull the stub shaft into the hub

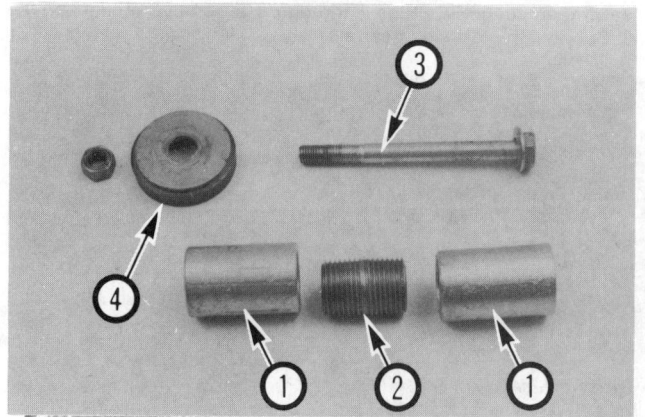

8.18   The hardware required to construct the center portion of the homebuilt driveaxle installation tool

1 Pipe unions (5/8-inch)   3 5/16 x 3-1/2 inch bolt
2 Pipe coupler   4 Washers

tween the bearing puller halves so the bolts will straddle the raised portion of the hub flange **(see illustration)**.

21 Place the previously assembled tubular portion of the tool through the bearing puller, into the hub, and thread it onto the end of the stub axle with a pair of pliers. Although the thread pitch is not exactly the same, the pipe union metal is relatively soft in comparison to the axle, so no damage to the axle threads will occur. Be sure the union goes on straight and don't overtighten it. The large washer should bear against the puller.

22 Thread the two bolts through the bearing puller until they contact the hub flange. They must be exactly perpendicular to the flange, or the bolts will "walk" when tightened **(see illustration)**.

23 Tighten the bolts 1/2-turn at a time, alternating between the two, until the stub axle is pulled into the hub.

24 Remove the tool and install the axle washer and a *new* nut. Tighten the nut to the specified torque while preventing the hub from turning by placing a screwdriver between two wheel studs.

25 Pry down on the lower control arm and insert the balljoint stud into the steering knuckle. Install a *new* pinch bolt and tighten it to the specified torque (Chapter 10).

26 Install the brake rotor and caliper (Chapter 9).

27 Install the brake hose support bracket bolt.

28 Install the wheel and lug nuts and lower the vehicle. Tighten the lug nuts to the specified torque.

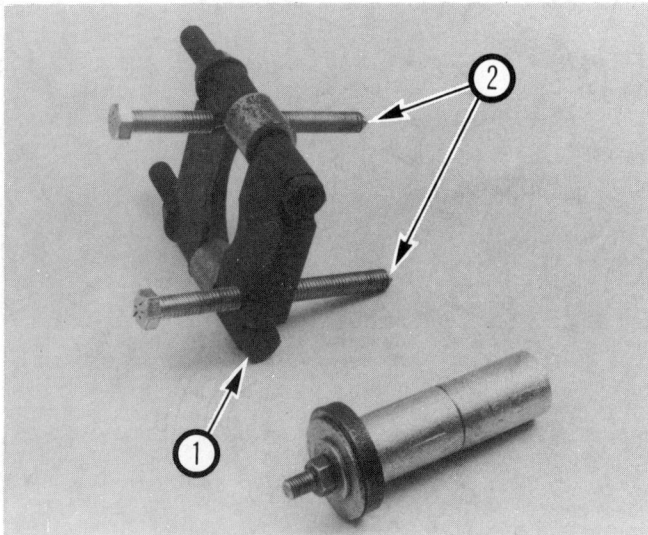

8.19 Thread the coupler into a pipe union and install the bolt and washers as shown, then thread the other pipe union into the coupler

8.20 The completed center portion and the bearing puller with the modified bolts and spacers (use Grade 8 bolts to prevent bending)

1 *Bearing puller*   2 *4-1/2 inch bolts*

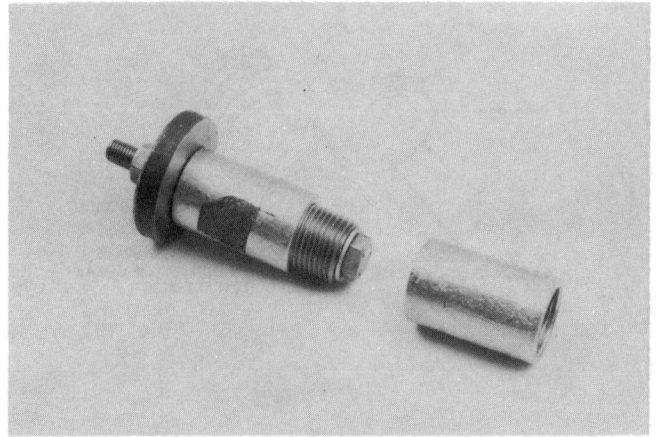

8.22 Thread the center portion of the tool onto the driveaxle stub shaft and slowly tighten the two puller bolts, a little at a time, until the shaft is completely seated in the hub

9 Driveaxle boot replacement and constant velocity (CV) joint — overhaul

Note: *If the the CV joints are worn, indicating the need for an overhaul (usually due to torn boots), explore all options before beginning the job. Complete rebuilt driveaxles are available on an exchange basis, which eliminates much time and work. Whichever route you choose to take, check on the cost and availability of parts before disassembling the driveaxle.*

Preparation

Refer to illustration 9.2

1 Remove the driveaxle (Section 8)

2 If the right side driveaxle on a manual or 3-speed automatic transaxle equipped vehicle is being worked on, mount the link shaft in a vise with wood. Separate the driveaxle from the link shaft by tapping it off with a brass punch **(see illustration)**. Be careful not to let the driveaxle fall on the floor after it has come off.

3 Place the driveaxle in a vise lined with wood so as not to mar the shaft.

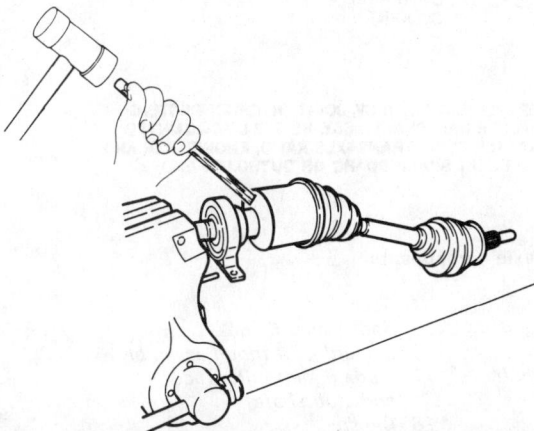

9.2 Separate the driveaxle from the link shaft with a brass punch and hammer

BOOT GROOVE

CRIMPED CAN

OUTER RACE

FILL WITH 125 GRAMS (4.4 OUNCES) OF GREASE (FOR ASSEMBLY)

FILL WITH 125 GRAMS (4.4 OUNCES) OF GREASE (FOR ASSEMBLY)

CONVENTIONAL BOOT (G K N DESIGN)

FILL WITH 100 GRAMS (3.5 OUNCES) OF GREASE (FOR ASSEMBLY)

BOOT GROOVE

TRI-LOBE BOOT (T AND C DESIGN)

OUTER RACE

FILL WITH 70 GRAMS (2.5 OUNCES) OF GREASE (FOR ASSEMBLY)

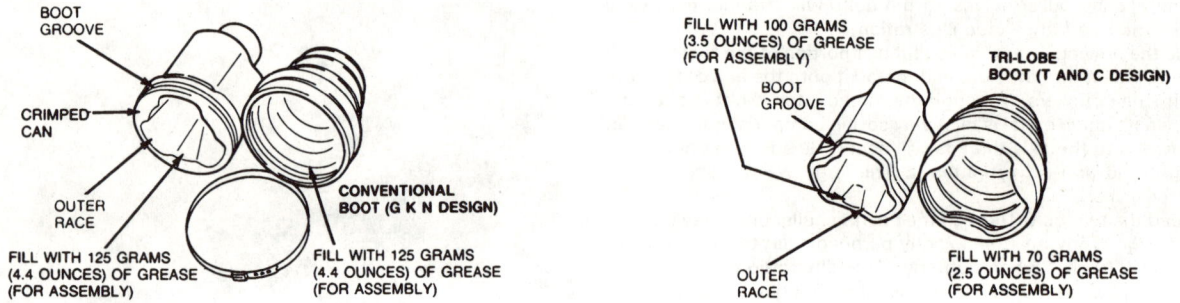

9.4   The two styles of inner CV joints

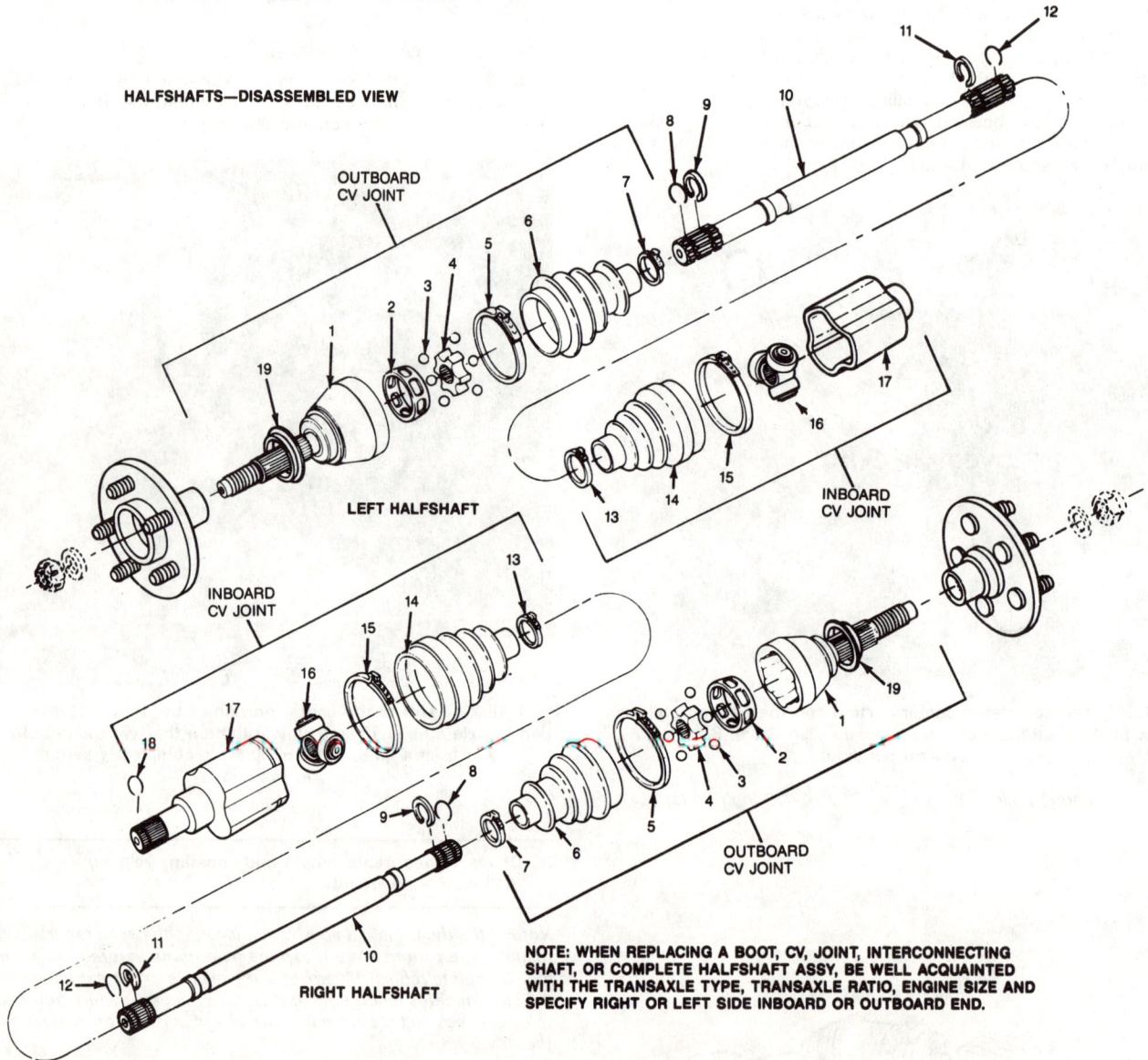

HALFSHAFTS—DISASSEMBLED VIEW

OUTBOARD CV JOINT

LEFT HALFSHAFT

INBOARD CV JOINT

INBOARD CV JOINT

OUTBOARD CV JOINT

RIGHT HALFSHAFT

NOTE: WHEN REPLACING A BOOT, CV, JOINT, INTERCONNECTING SHAFT, OR COMPLETE HALFSHAFT ASSY, BE WELL ACQUAINTED WITH THE TRANSAXLE TYPE, TRANSAXLE RATIO, ENGINE SIZE AND SPECIFY RIGHT OR LEFT SIDE INBOARD OR OUTBOARD END.

9.5a   Exploded view of the driveaxle components

1 Outboard joint outer race and stub shaft	7 Boot clamp (small)	14 Boot
2 Ball cage	8 Circlip	15 Boot clamp (large)
3 Balls (six)	9 Stop ring	16 Inboard joint tripod assembly
4 Outboard joint inner race	10 Interconnecting shaft	17 Inboard joint outer race and stub shaft
5 Boot clamp (large)	11 Stop ring	
6 Boot	12 Circlip	18 Circlip
	13 Boot clamp (small)	19 Dust seal

9.5b Snap-ring pliers should be used to remove both the
inner and outer retaining rings

9.11 Before installing the CV joint boot, wrap the axle
splines with tape to prevent damage to the boot

Inner CV joint and boot

Refer to illustrations 9.4, 9.5a, 9.5b, 9.11, 9.12, 9.15, 9.16 and 9.17

Disassembly

4 **Note:** *There are two types of inner CV joints* **(see illustration).** *Although they are similar in design, the parts are not interchangeable. The repair procedure, however, is the same for both.* Cut off the boot seal retaining clamps and slide the boot towards the center of the driveaxle. Mark the tri-pot housing and the driveaxle so it can be returned to its original position, then slide the housing off of the spider assembly.

5 Mark the spider assembly and the shaft. Remove the spider assembly from the axle by first removing the inner retaining ring and sliding the spider assembly back to expose the outer retaining ring. Remove the outer retaining ring and slide the joint off the driveaxle **(see illustrations).**

6 Use tape or a cloth wrapped around the spider bearing assembly to retain the bearings during removal and installation.

7 Remove the spider assembly from the axle.

8 Slide the boot off the axle.

Inspection

9 Clean old grease from the housing and spider assembly. Carefully disassemble each section of the spider assembly, one at a time, and clean the needle bearings with solvent. Inspect the rollers, spider cross, bearings and housing for scoring, pitting or other signs of abnormal wear, which will warrant the replacement of the inner CV joint.

Reassembly

10 Apply a coat of CV joint grease to the inner bearing surfaces to hold the needle bearings in place when reassembling the spider assembly. Pack the housing with half of the grease furnished with the new boot and place the remainder in the boot.

11 Wrap the driveaxle splines with tape to avoid damaging the boot, then slide the boot onto the axle **(see illustration).**

12 Install the spider bearing with the chamfer facing the stop ring **(see illustration).**

13 Install a new circlip on the end of the shaft, slide the spider bearing against the circlip and seat the stop ring in the groove.

14 Install the tri-pot housing.

15 Seat the boot in the housing and axle seal grooves, then adjust the axle to the proper length **(see illustration).**

16 With the axle set to the proper length, equalize the pressure in the

9.12 When reinstalling the spider
bearing assembly, the chamfered inner
diameter must face in (toward the
stop ring)

9.15 The driveaxle must be set to the proper length

AXOD = 4-speed automatic overdrive transaxle
MTX = manual transaxle
ATX = 3-speed automatic overdrive transaxle

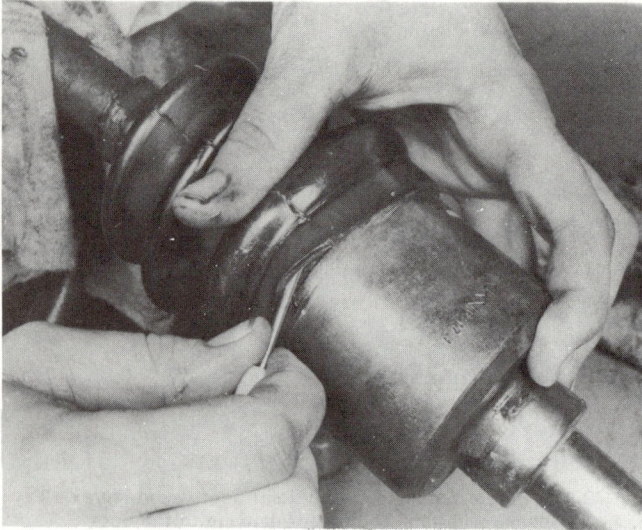

9.16   Equalize the pressure inside the boot by inserting a
small screwdriver between the boot and the outer race

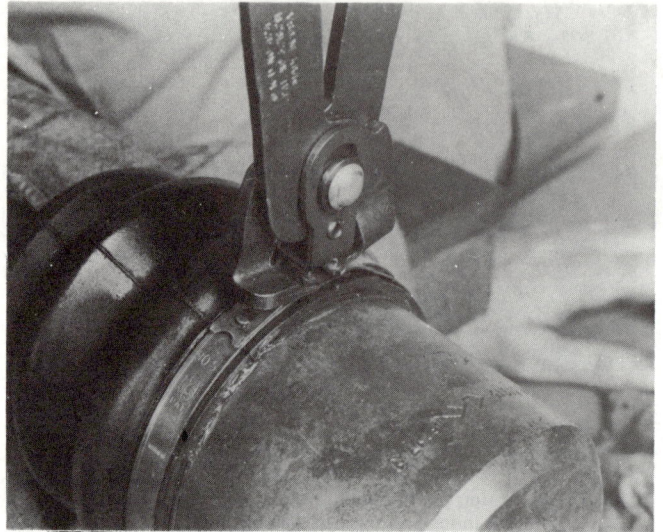

9.17   Securing the boot clamp with the special pliers
(available at auto parts stores)

9.21   Dislodge the CV joint assembly with a brass drift
and hammer (be careful not to let the joint fall!)

9.23   Tilt the inner race far enough to allow ball removal — a
brass punch can be used if the inner race is difficult to move

9.24   If necessary, pry the balls out with a screwdriver

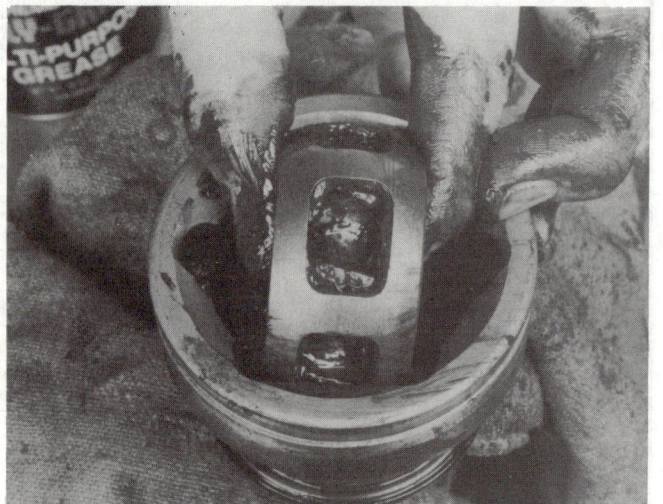

9.25   Tilt the inner race and cage 90-degrees, then align
the windows in the cage with the lands and rotate the
cage and inner race up and out of the outer race

boot by inserting a blunt screwdriver between the boot and the housing (see illustration). Don't damage the boot with the tool.

17 Install the boot clamps. A pair of special clamp-crimping pliers are used to tighten the clamp. The pliers are available at most auto parts stores (see illustration).

18 Attach the driveaxle to the link shaft (right side only, 3-speed automatic transaxles.)

19 Install the driveaxle (or driveaxle/link shaft assembly) as described in Section 8. Be sure to install a new circlip on the inner stub axle.

Outer CV joint and boot
Refer to illustrations 9.21, 9.23, 9.24, 9.25, 9.26, 9.27a, 9.27b, 9.29, 9.30, 9.31 and 9.35

Disassembly
20 Follow the procedure in Steps 2 and 3 of this Section.

21 Cut the boot retaining clamps and slide the boot back off the outer race. With a **brass drift** positioned on the **inner race**, dislodge the CV joint assembly from the axle (see illustration). A lot of force will be required, as the inner race must overcome a circlip on the axleshaft. Do not let the CV joint assembly fall.

22 Mount the outer joint assembly in a vise lined with wood.

23 Press down on the inner race far enough to allow a ball bearing

to be removed. If it's difficult to tilt, tap the inner race with a brass drift and a hammer (see illustration).

24 Pry the balls from the cage, one at a time, with a blunt screwdriver or wooden tool (see illustration).

25 With all of the balls removed from the cage and the cage/inner race assembly tilted 90-degrees, align the cage windows with the outer race lands and remove the assembly from the outer race (see illustration).

26 Remove the inner race from the cage by turning the inner race 90-degrees in the cage, aligning the inner lands with the cage windows and rotating the inner race out of the cage (see illustration).

Inspection
27 Clean the components with solvent to remove all traces of grease. Inspect the cage and races for pitting, score marks, cracks and other signs of wear or damage. Shiny, polished spots are normal and will not adversely affect CV joint performance (see illustrations).

Reassembly
28 Install the inner race in the cage by reversing the technique described in Step 25.

29 Install the inner race and cage assembly in the outer race by reversing the removal method used in Step 25. The beveled edge of the inner race splined area must face out after it's installed in the outer race (see illustration).

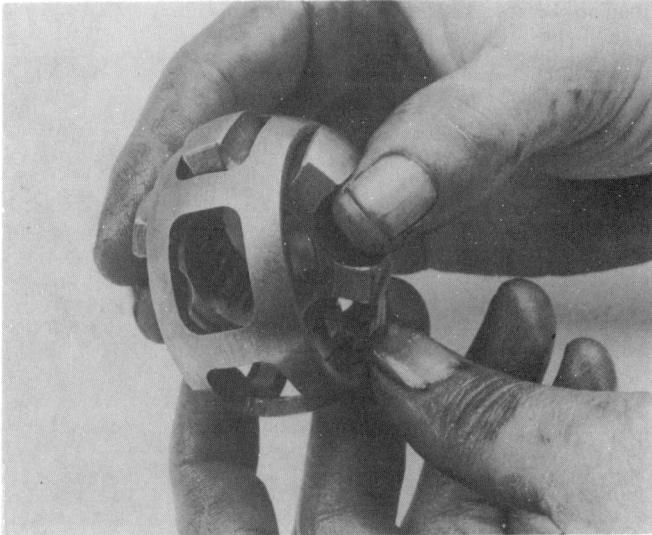
9.26 Align the inner race lands with the cage windows and rotate the inner race out of the cage

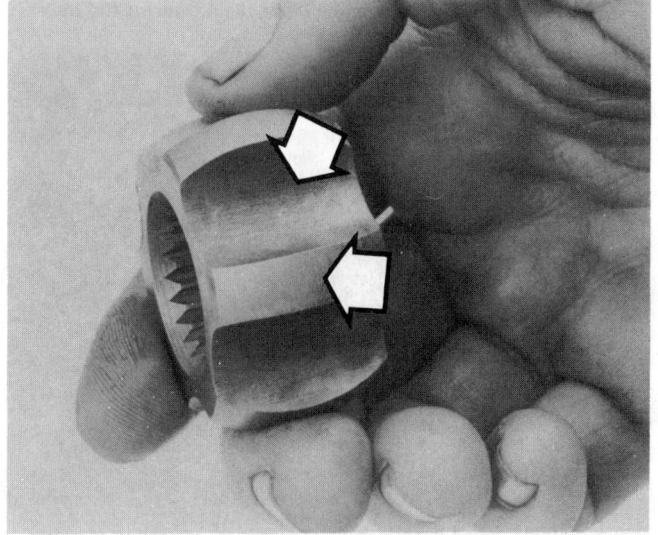
9.27a Check the inner race lands and grooves for pitting and score marks

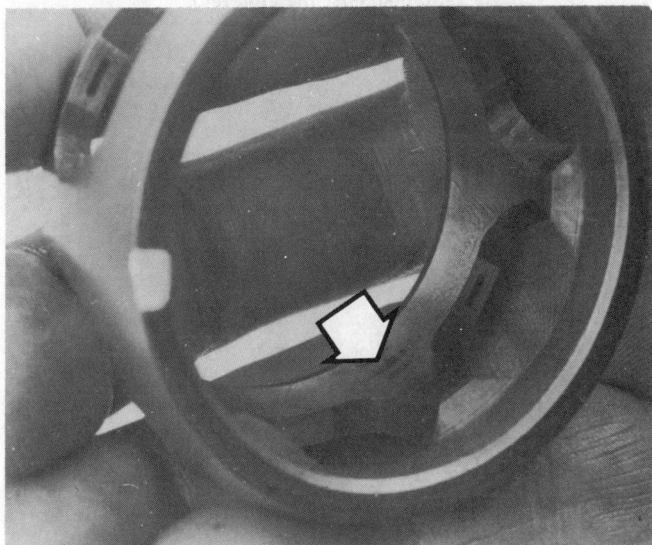
9.27b Check the cage for cracks, pitting and score marks (shiny spots are normal and don't affect operation)

9.29 The beveled edge of the inner race (arrow) must face out when assembled

9.30   Align the cage windows and the inner and outer race grooves, then tilt the cage and inner race to insert the balls

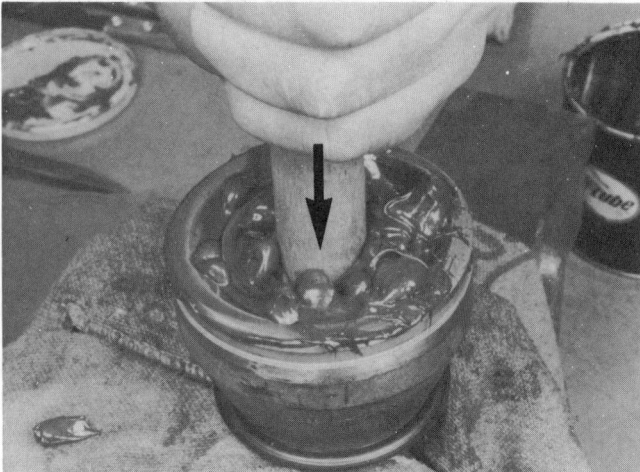

9.31   Apply grease through the splined hole, then insert a wooden dowel (approximately 15/16-inch diameter) through the splined hole and push down — the dowel will force the grease into the joint

10.2   Carefully pry the old seal out of the housing with a screwdriver

30   Press the balls into the cage windows **(see illustration)**.
31   Pack the CV joint assembly with the supplied lubricant through the inner splined hole. Force the grease into the bearing by inserting a wooden dowel through the splined hole and pushing it to the bottom of the joint. Repeat this procedure until the bearing is completely packed **(see illustration)**.
32   Install the boot on the axleshaft as described in Step 11. Apply a liberal amount of grease to the inside of the axle boot.
33   Install a new stop ring and position it in the groove in the axleshaft.
34   Install a new circlip on the end of the axleshaft.
35   Position the CV joint assembly on the axleshaft, aligning the splines. Using a brass or plastic tip hammer, drive the CV joint onto the axleshaft until it seats against the stop ring **(see illustration)**.
36   Adjust the driveaxle length and install the boot. Refer to Steps 15 through 17.
37   Assemble the driveaxle and the link shaft (right side only, 3-speed automatic transaxles only).
38   Install the driveaxle as described in Section 8.

10   Differential seals — replacement

Refer to illustrations 10.2 and 10.3
Caution: *Whenever both the right and left driveaxles are removed at*

9.35   Line up the splines of the inner race with the axleshaft splines, then tap the CV joint assembly onto the shaft with a brass or plastic hammer until the inner race is seated against the stop ring

10.3   Drive the new seal into the transaxle housing with a large socket (arrow) or piece of pipe — be careful not to cock the seal in the bore

the same time, the differential side gears must be supported so they don't fall into the case (except on 4-speed automatic transaxles). A wooden dowel, approximately 15/16-inch in diameter, inserted into each side gear will work. If this precaution is not heeded and the side gears do drop, the differential will have to be removed from the transaxle to realign the gears (which will necessitate towing the vehicle to a Ford dealer service department or a repair shop).

1   Refer to Section 8 and remove the driveaxle.

2   Pry the seal from the transaxle case with a large screwdriver or pry bar **(see illustration)**. Be careful not to damage the case.

3   Coat the outer edge of the new seal with oil or grease, then position it in the bore and carefully drive it in with a hammer and large socket (if a socket isn't available, a section of pipe will also work) **(see illustration)**.

4   Lubricate the seal lip with moly-base grease, then install the driveaxle (Chapter 8).

Chapter 9   Brakes

Contents

Specifications

Brake fluid type . . . . See Chapter 1

Disc brakes

Brake disc thickness
  Standard . . . . 0.945 in (24.0 mm)
  Minimum* . . . . 0.896 in (22.75 mm)
Brake disc thickness variation limit (1-inch from edge) . . . . 0.0005 in (0.013 mm)
Brake disc runout limit . . . . 0.003 in (0.076 mm)
Minimum brake pad thickness . . . . See Chapter 1

Refer to marks stamped on the disc (they supersede information printed here).

Drum brakes

Standard drum diameter
  Sedan . . . . 8.85 in (225 mm)
  Wagon . . . . 9.84 in (250 mm)
Maximum drum diameter
  Sedan . . . . 8.924 in (226.5 mm)
  Wagon . . . . 9.909 in (251.5 mm)
Out-of-round limit . . . . 0.005 in (0.127 mm)
Minimum brake lining thickness . . . . See Chapter 1

Torque specifications   **Ft-lbs**

Front brake caliper mounting pins . . . . 18 to 25
Brake hose-to-caliper bolt
  Front . . . . 30 to 40
  Rear . . . . 8 to 11
Brake pedal pivot bolt nut . . . . 10 to 20
Master cylinder-to-booster nuts . . . . 13 to 25
Power brake booster nuts . . . . 12 to 22
Rear brake caliper pinch bolts . . . . 23 to 26
Wheel cylinder bolts . . . . 9 to 13
Wheel lug nuts . . . . See Chapter 1

1 General information and precautions

General information

All models are equipped with disc type front and drum type rear brakes which are hydraulically operated and vacuum assisted.

The front brakes feature a single piston, floating caliper design. The rear drum brakes are leading/trailing shoe types with a single pivot.

The front disc brakes automatically compensate for pad wear during usage. The rear drum brakes also feature automatic adjustment.

Front drive vehicles tend to wear the front brake pads at a faster rate than do rear drive vehicles. Consequently, it's important to inspect the brake pads frequently to make sure they haven't worn to the point where the disc itself is scored or damaged.

All models are equipped with a cable actuated parking brake which operates the rear brakes.

The hydraulic system is a dual line type with a dual master cylinder and diagonally split hydraulic circuits. In the event of brake line or seal failure, half the brake system will still operate. The system also incorporates a pressure control valve (two on wagon models) that reduces the pressure to the rear brakes in order to limit rear wheel lockup during hard braking.

Precautions

Use only DOT 3 brake fluid.

The brake pads and linings contain asbestos fibers, which are hazardous to your health if inhaled. When working on brake system components, carefully clean all parts with denatured alcohol or brake cleaner. Don't allow the fine dust to become airborne.

Safety should be paramount when working on brake system components. Don't use parts or fasteners that aren't in perfect condition and be sure that all clearances and torque specifications are adhered to. If you're at all unsure about a certain procedure, seek professional advice. When finished working on the brakes, test them carefully under controlled conditions before driving the vehicle in traffic. If a problem is suspected in the brake system, don't drive the vehicle until the fault is corrected.

2 Brake pads (front) – replacement

Refer to illustrations 2.4a through 2.4j

Warning: *Disc brake pads must be replaced on both front wheels at the same time – never replace the pads on only one wheel. Also, the dust created by the brake system contains asbestos, which is harmful to your health. Never blow it out with compressed air and don't inhale any of it. An approved filtering mask should be worn when working on the brakes. Do not, under any circumstances, use petroleum-based solvents to clean brake parts. Use brake cleaner or denatured alcohol only! When servicing the disc brakes, use only high quality, nationally recognized brand-name pads.*

1   Remove the cap from the brake fluid reservoir, siphon off about two-thirds of the fluid into a container and discard it.

2   Loosen the wheel lug nuts, raise the vehicle and support it securely on jackstands. Remove the front wheels.

3   Check the brake disc carefully as outlined in Section 4. If machining is necessary, follow the procedure in Section 4 to remove the disc.

4   Follow the step-by-step illustrations, beginning with 2.4a, for the actual pad replacement procedure. Be sure to stay in order and read the information in the caption under each illustration.

5   Once the new pads are in place and the caliper pins have been installed and properly tightened, install the wheels and lower the vehicle to the ground. **Note:** *If the brake hose was disconnected from the caliper for any reason, the brake system must be bled as described in Section 11.*

6   Fill the master cylinder reservoir(s) with new brake fluid and slowly pump the brakes a few times to seat the pads against the disc.

7   Check the fluid level in the master cylinder reservoir(s) one more time and then road test the vehicle carefully before driving it in traffic.

2.4a   Using a large C-clamp, push the piston back into the caliper bore just enough to allow the caliper to slide off the disc easily – note that one end of the clamp is on the flat area near the brake hose fitting and the other end (screw end) is pressing on the outer pad

2.4b   Remove the two caliper pins (arrows) that hold the caliper to the steering knuckle (this will require a special socket)

2.4c   Rotate the bottom of the caliper up and off the brake disc (support the caliper with a piece of stiff wire – DO NOT let it hang by the rubber hose)

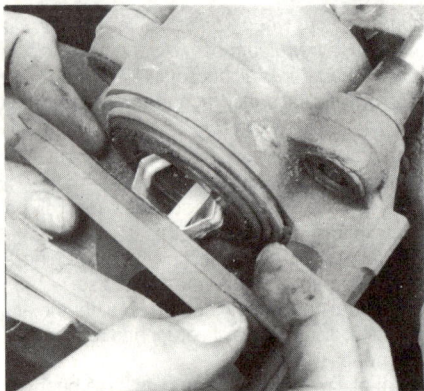

2.4d   Pull the inner brake pad straight
out of the caliper piston

2.4e   Push the outer pad towards the
piston to dislodge the locating lugs from
the caliper frame, then apply firm
pressure to remove the pad

2.4f   Push the piston into the cylinder
bore to provide room for the new pads
to fit over the disc – use a block of wood
and a C-clamp, but don't use excessive
force or damage to the plastic piston
will result

2.4g   The brake pads are marked as to
which side of the vehicle they must be
installed on – don't mix them up

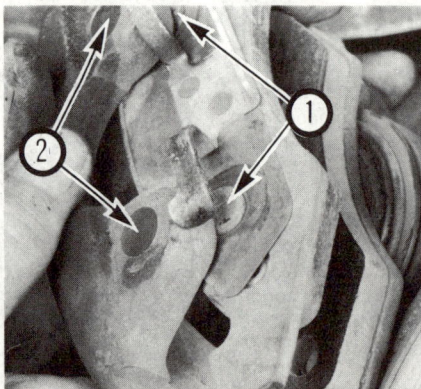

2.4h   To install the new pads in the
caliper, carefully push the inner pad
retaining clips straight into the piston
until the brake pad backing plate rests
on the piston face – slide the outer pad
into the caliper as shown (be sure the
locating lugs on the pad [1] seat in the
mounting holes in the caliper frame [2])

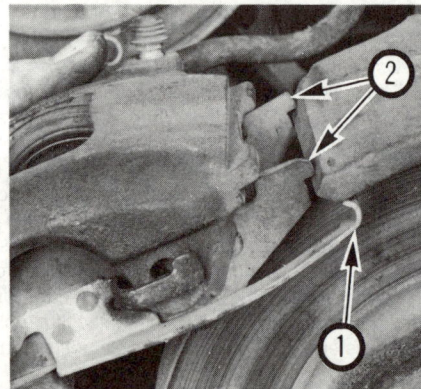

2.4i   Position the anti-rattle spring on
the outer pad (1) under the upper arm of
the steering knuckle, with the notches in
the upper edge of both pads resting on
the upper arm of the knuckle (2), then
rotate the caliper down until the notches
in the opposite end of the pads seat
against the lower arm of the steering
knuckle (make sure the brake hose is
not twisted)

2.4j   Apply silicone grease to the caliper
pins and to the inside of the pin
insulators and insert the pins through
the caliper housing into the steering
knuckle arms (tighten them by hand
first, then to the specified torque)

3.4   Removing the brake hose inlet
fitting bolt (be sure to use new copper
washers on each side of the fitting to
prevent fluid leaks)

3.8   With the caliper padded to catch
the piston, use compressed air to force
the piston out of the bore – make sure
your fingers are out of the way!

3   Disc brake caliper (front) – removal, overhaul and installation

Warning: *Dust created by the brake system contains asbestos, which is harmful to your health. Never blow it out with compressed air and don't inhale any of it. An approved filtering mask should be worn when working on the brakes. Do not, under any circumstances, use petroleum-based solvents to clean brake parts. Use brake cleaner or denatured alcohol only!*

Note: *If an overhaul is indicated (usually because of fluid leakage) explore all options before beginning the job. New and factory rebuilt calipers are available on an exchange basis, which makes this job quite easy. If it's decided to rebuild the calipers, make sure that a rebuild kit is available before proceeding. Always rebuild the calipers in pairs – never rebuild just one of them.*

Removal

Refer to illustration 3.4

1   Remove the cap from the brake fluid reservoir, siphon off two-thirds of the fluid into a container and discard it.
2   Loosen the wheel lug nuts, raise the front of the vehicle and support it securely on jackstands. Remove the front wheels.
3   Using a large C-clamp, push the piston back into the caliper bore **(see illustration 2.4a).**

4   Remove the brake hose inlet fitting bolt and detach the hose **(see illustration).** Have a rag handy to catch spilled fluid and wrap a plastic bag tightly around the end of the hose to prevent fluid loss and contamination.
5   Remove the two mounting bolts and detach the caliper from the vehicle (refer to Section 2 if necessary).

Overhaul

Refer to illustrations 3.8, 3.9, 3.10, 3.11a, 3.11b, 3.15, 3.16, 3.17 and 3.18

6   Refer to Section 2 and remove the brake pads from the caliper.
7   Clean the exterior of the caliper with brake cleaner or denatured alcohol. **Warning:** *Never use gasoline, kerosene or petroleum-based cleaning solvents.* Place the caliper on a clean workbench.
8   Position a wooden block or several shop rags in the caliper as a cushion, then use compressed air to remove the piston from the caliper **(see illustration).** Use only enough air pressure to ease the piston out of the bore. If the piston is blown out, even with the cushion in place, it may be damaged. **Warning:** *Never place your fingers in front of the piston in an attempt to catch or protect it when applying compressed air, as serious injury could occur.*
9   Carefully pry the dust boot out of the caliper bore **(see illustration).**
10   Using a wood or plastic tool, remove the piston seal from the groove in the caliper bore **(see illustration).** Metal tools may cause bore damage.
11   Remove the caliper bleeder screw, then remove and discard the insulators from the caliper ears. Discard all rubber parts **(see illustrations).**

3.9   Carefully pry the dust boot out of the caliper

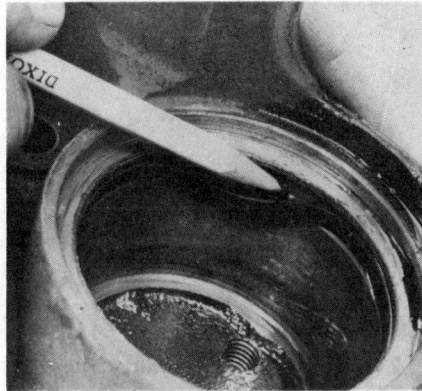

3.10   To avoid damage to the caliper bore or seal groove, remove the seal with a plastic or wooden tool – a pencil works well

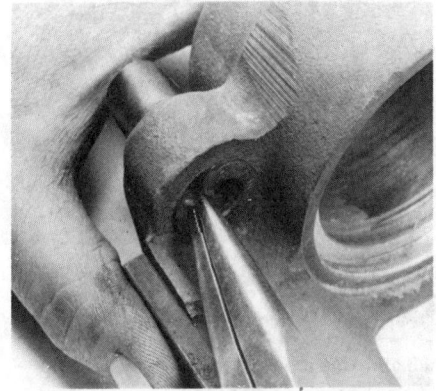

3.11a   To remove a caliper pin insulator, grab it with a pair of needle nose pliers, twist it and push it through the caliper frame

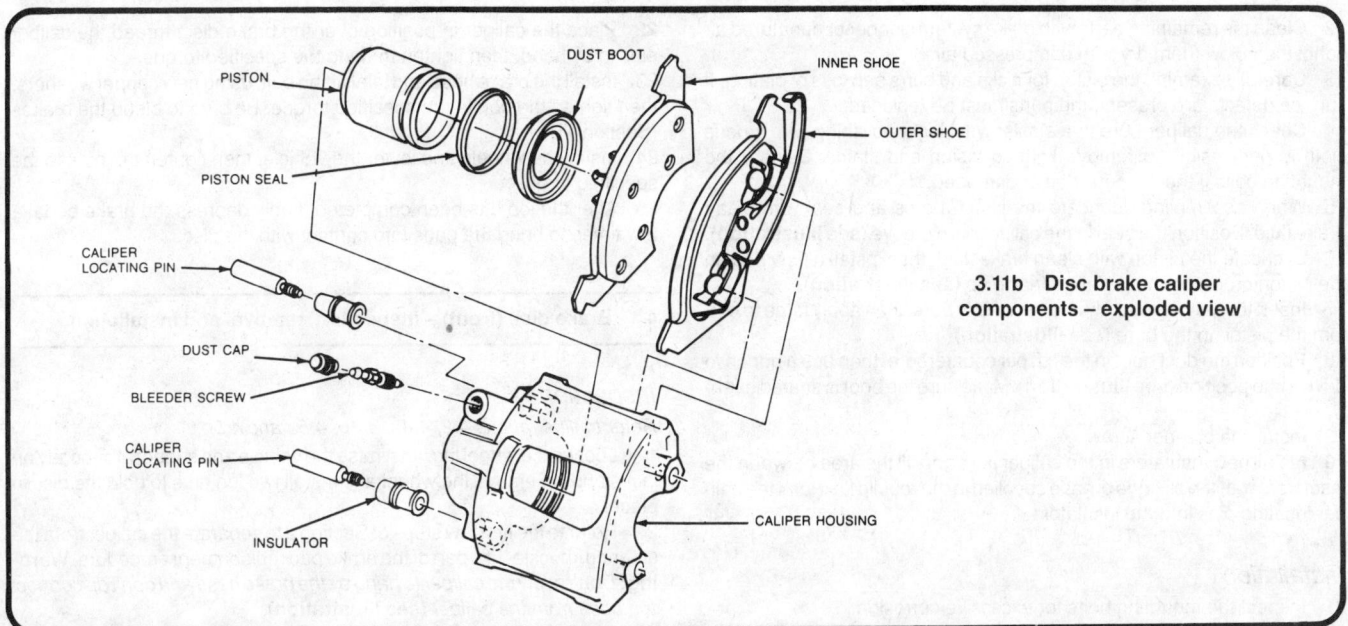

3.11b   Disc brake caliper components – exploded view

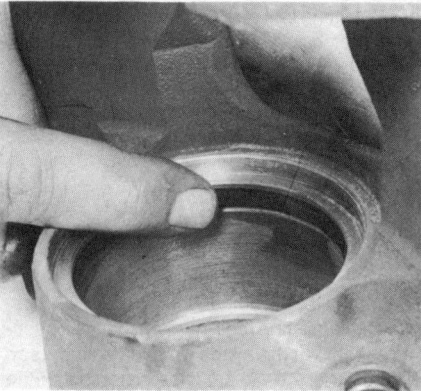

3.15   Position the seal in the caliper bore, making sure it isn't twisted

3.16   Stretch the new boot over the top of the piston, making sure it rests in the piston groove – the flange must be nearest to the top of the piston

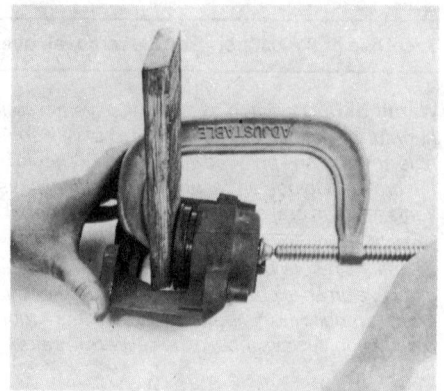

3.17   Install the piston squarely in the caliper bore, then push it in by hand as far as possible (it may be necessary to use a C-clamp and a block of wood to bottom the piston in the bore – work slowly, making sure the piston does not become cocked – it should slide in with very little resistance)

3.18   Use a punch to carefully seat the dust boot

4.2   Suspend the caliper with a piece of wire whenever you have to reposition it – don't let it hang by the brake hose!

4.4a   With two lug nuts installed to hold the brake disc in place, check the disc runout with a dial indicator – if the reading exceeds the maximum allowable runout limit, the disc will have to be machined or replaced

12   Clean the remaining parts with brake system cleaner or denatured alcohol then blow them dry with compressed air.

13   Carefully examine the piston for nicks and burrs and loss of plating. If surface defects are present, the parts must be replaced.

14   Check the caliper bore in a similar way. Light polishing with crocus cloth is permissible to remove light corrosion and stains. Discard the mounting bolts if they're corroded or damaged.

15   When assembling, lubricate the piston bores and seal with clean brake fluid. Position the seal in the caliper bore groove (see illustration).

16   Lubricate the piston with clean brake fluid, then install a new boot in the piston groove with the flange facing up (see illustration).

17   Insert the piston squarely into the caliper bore, then apply force to bottom the piston in the bore (see illustration).

18   Position the dust boot in the caliper counterbore, then use a punch to drive it into position (see illustration). Make sure the boot is seated evenly.

19   Install the bleeder screw.

20   Install new insulators in the caliper ears and fill the area between the insulators with the silicone grease supplied in the rebuild kit. Push the caliper locating pins into the insulators.

Installation

21   Inspect the mounting bolts for excessive corrosion.

22   Place the caliper in position over the brake disc, thread the caliper pins in by hand, then tighten them to the specified torque.

23   Install the brake hose and inlet fitting bolt, using new copper washers, then tighten the bolt to the specified torque. Be sure to bleed the brakes (Section 11).

24   Install the wheels and lower the vehicle, then tighten the nuts to the specified torque.

25   After the job has been completed, firmly depress the brake pedal a few times to bring the pads into contact with the disc.

---

4   Brake disc (front) – inspection, removal and installation

---

Inspection

Refer to illustrations 4.2, 4.4a, 4.4b, 4.5a and 4.5b

1   Loosen the wheel lug nuts, raise the vehicle and support it securely on jackstands. Remove the wheel and install two lug nuts to hold the disc in place.

2   Refer to the first few steps of Section 2 to separate the caliper from the steering knuckle – it's part of the brake pad replacement procedure. **Warning:** *Don't allow the caliper to hang by the brake hose and don't disconnect the hose from the caliper* (see illustration).

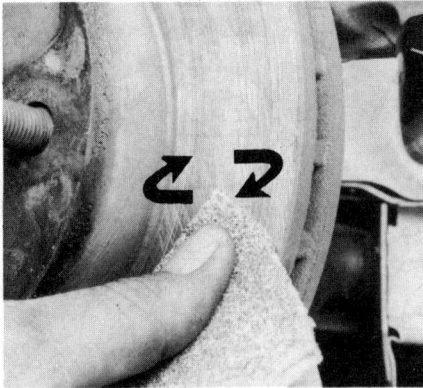

4.4b   Using a swirling motion, remove the glaze from the disc with emery cloth or sandpaper

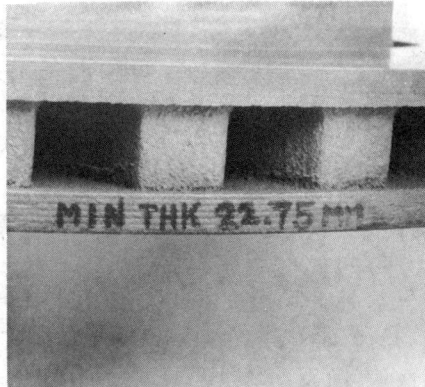

4.5a   The minimum allowable disc thickness is stamped on the edge of the disc

4.5b   A micrometer is used to measure disc thickness

5.2   A hammer and chisel can be used to remove the grease cap from the hub/drum assembly

5.3   After the cotter pin, nut lock and nut have been removed, pull the drum out to dislodge the outer wheel bearing – be careful not to drop the bearing

5.6a   Remove glaze from the drum surface with emery cloth or sandpaper

3   Visually inspect the disc surface for score marks and other damage. Light scratches and shallow grooves are normal after use and may not be detrimental to brake operation. Deep score marks – over 0.015-inch (0.38 mm) – require disc removal and refinishing by an automotive machine shop. Be sure to check both sides of the disc.

4   To check disc runout, attach a dial indicator to the steering knuckle and locate the stem about 1/2-inch from the outer edge of the disc (**see illustration**). Set the indicator to zero and turn the disc. The indicator reading should not exceed 0.003-inch (0.076 mm). If it does, the disc should be resurfaced by an automotive machine shop. **Note:** *Professionals recommend resurfacing of brake discs regardless of the dial indicator reading (to produce a smooth, flat surface that will eliminate brake pedal pulsations and other undesirable symptoms related to questionable discs). At the very least, if you elect not to have the discs resurfaced, de-glaze the brake pad surface with medium-grit emery cloth (use a swirling motion to ensure a non-directional finish)* (**see illustration**).

5   The disc should never be machined to a thickness under the specified minimum allowable thickness, which is stamped onto the edge of the disc itself (**see illustration**). The disc thickness can be checked with a micrometer (**see illustration**).

Removal and installation

6   Remove the two lug nuts which were put on to hold the disc in place and detach the disc from the hub.

7   Installation is the reverse of removal.

5   Brake drum (rear) – removal, inspection and installation

Removal

Refer to illustrations 5.2 and 5.3

1   Loosen the wheel lug nuts, raise the rear of the vehicle and support it securely on jackstands. Block the front wheels, then remove the rear wheel.

2   Remove the grease cap, cotter pin, nut lock and retaining nut (**see illustration**).

3   Grasp the brake drum and pull it out far enough to dislodge the outer bearing and washer (**see illustration**). If the drum is stuck, loosen the brake adjuster star wheel as described in Section 6, Steps 7 through 9.

4   Remove the outer wheel bearing.

5   Pull the hub/drum assembly off the spindle.

Inspection

Refer to illustrations 5.6a and 5.6b

6   Check the drum for cracks, score marks, deep grooves and signs of overheating of the shoe contact surface. If the drums have blue spots, indicating overheated areas, they should be replaced. Also, look for grease or brake fluid on the shoe contact surface. Grease and brake fluid can be removed with denatured alcohol or brake cleaner, but the brake shoes must be replaced if they are contaminated. Surface glazing, which is a glossy, highly polished finish, can be removed with mediumgrit emery cloth (**see**

5.6b The maximum allowable diameter is cast into the drum

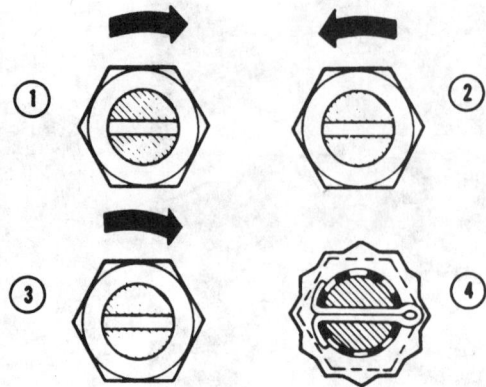

5.9 Rear wheel bearing adjusting procedure

1	While rotating the drum, tighten the nut to 17 to 25 ft-lbs	3	1986 and 1987 vehicles: tighten the nut to 10 to 12 in-lbs; 1988 and later vehicles: tighten the nut to 24 to 28 in-lbs
2	Loosen the nut 1/2-turn	4	Install the nut lock and a new cotter pin

illustration). **Note:** *Professionals recommend resurfacing the drums whenever a brake job is done. Resurfacing will eliminate the possibility of out-of-round drums. If the drums are worn so much that they can't be re-surfaced without exceeding the maximum allowable diameter (cast into the drum)* **(see illustration)**, *then new ones will be required.*

Installation

Refer to illustration 5.9

7   While the hub/drum assembly is off the vehicle, it's a good idea to clean, inspect and repack or, if necessary, replace the rear wheel bearings. Refer to Chapter 1 for rear wheel bearing service.

8   Place the hub/drum assembly on the spindle, install the outer wheel bearing and washer and push the assembly into place.

9   Install the retaining nut and washer and tighten the nut to the initial specified torque while rotating the drum. Back off the adjusting nut 1/2-turn, then tighten the nut to the final torque **(see illustration)**.

10   Install the nut lock, cotter pin and grease cap. Be careful not to damage the grease cap.

11   Install the wheel, lower the vehicle and tighten the lug nuts to the specified torque.

6   Brake shoes (rear) – replacement

Refer to illustrations 6.5a through 6.5p, 6.8, 6.9a and 6.9b

Warning: *The brake shoes must be replaced on both rear wheels at the same time – never replace the shoes on only one wheel. Also, brake system dust contains asbestos, which is harmful to your health. Never blow it*

out with compressed air and don't inhale any of it. Do not, under any circumstances, use petroleum-based solvents to clean brake parts. Use brake cleaner or denatured alcohol only. Whenever the brake shoes are replaced, the return and hold-down springs should also be replaced. Due to the continuous heating/cooling cycle that the springs are subjected to, they lose their tension over a period of time and may allow the shoes to drag on the drum and wear at a much faster rate than normal. When replacing the rear brake shoes, use only high quality, nationally recognized brand-name parts.

1   Siphon off about two-thirds of the brake fluid from the master cylinder reservoir into a container, then discard it.

2   Loosen the wheel lug nuts, raise the rear of the vehicle and support it on jackstands. Block the front wheels and remove the rear wheels from the vehicle.

3   Refer to Section 5 in this Chapter and remove the brake drums.

4   Carefully inspect the brake drums as outlined in Section 5 of this Chapter. Also inspect the wheel cylinder for fluid leakage as described in Chapter 1.

5   Follow the step-by-step illustrations (6.5a through 6.5p) for the actual shoe replacement procedure. Be sure to stay in order and read the information in the caption under each illustration.

6.5a   Before removing any internal drum brake components, wash them off with brake cleaner and allow them to dry – position a drain pan under the brake to catch the residue – DO NOT USE COMPRESSED AIR TO BLOW THE BRAKE DUST FROM THE PARTS!

6.5b   Depress and turn the spring retainers then remove the hold-down springs and pins

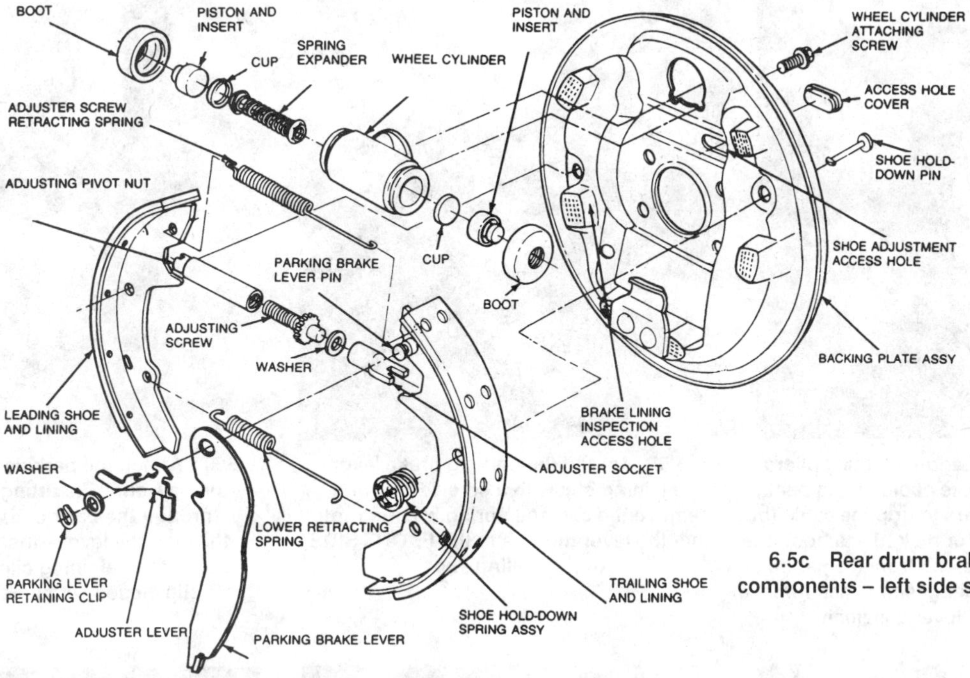

6.5c Rear drum brake components – left side shown

Labels:
BOOT
PISTON AND INSERT
CUP
SPRING EXPANDER
WHEEL CYLINDER
PISTON AND INSERT
WHEEL CYLINDER ATTACHING SCREW
ACCESS HOLE COVER
SHOE HOLD-DOWN PIN
SHOE ADJUSTMENT ACCESS HOLE
ADJUSTER SCREW RETRACTING SPRING
ADJUSTING PIVOT NUT
PARKING BRAKE LEVER PIN
ADJUSTING SCREW
WASHER
CUP
BOOT
SHOE ADJUSTMENT ACCESS HOLE
BACKING PLATE ASSY
LEADING SHOE AND LINING
WASHER
PARKING LEVER RETAINING CLIP
ADJUSTER LEVER
LOWER RETRACTING SPRING
PARKING BRAKE LEVER
BRAKE LINING INSPECTION ACCESS HOLE
ADJUSTER SOCKET
SHOE HOLD-DOWN SPRING ASSY
TRAILING SHOE AND LINING

6.5d Slide the entire assembly down far enough to disengage the top of the shoes from the wheel cylinder, . . .

6.5e . . . then tilt the shoes to lift them past the shoe retaining plate

6.5f Unhook the lower retracting spring from the leading brake shoe

6.5g Spread the bottom of the brake shoes apart and remove the adjusting screw, then the adjusting screw retracting spring – the adjuster lever and leading brake shoe may now be removed

6.5h   Use a pair of diagonal cutting pliers to pull the parking brake cable spring back, then squeeze the pliers to grip the cable (but be careful not to cut or nick it) – unhook the parking brake cable end from the parking brake lever on the trailing shoe, then remove the shoe and lever assembly

6.5i   Spread the parking brake lever retaining clip with a screwdriver and remove the clip and spring washer (note that the lever mounts to the FRONT SIDE of the trailing shoe)

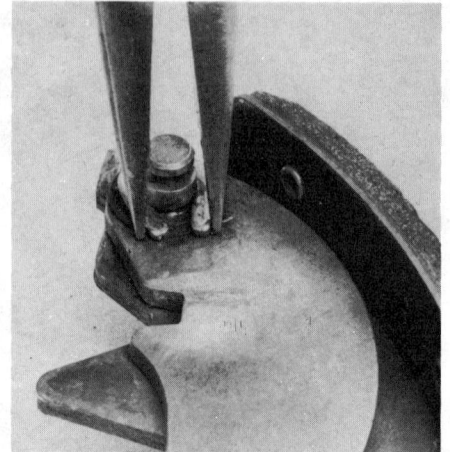

6.5j   Attach the parking brake lever to the new shoe, inserting the pivot pin through the back of the shoe, then through the lever – install the spring washer and retaining clip and crimp the clip closed with a pair of pliers

6.5k   Lubricate the brake shoe contact areas with high-temperature brake grease

6.5l   Install the parking brake cable in the lever, hook the lower retracting spring between the two shoes and slide the shoes down on the shoe retaining plate

6.5m   Install the trailing shoe hold-down pin, spring and retainer, then insert the adjuster screw assembly into the trailing shoe as shown (be sure the correct letter is facing up, depending on the side of the vehicle you are working on)

6.5n   Position the adjuster lever on the parking brake lever pivot pin, . . .

6.5o   . . . then install the new leading shoe, hold-down pin, spring and retainer – stretch the adjuster screw retracting spring and hook it in the notch on the adjuster lever

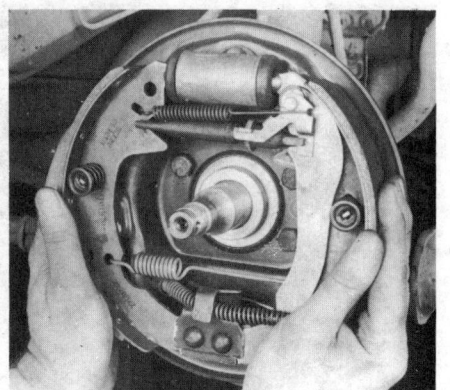

6.5p   Wiggle the brake shoe assembly on the backing plate to center it (make sure your hands are clean before doing this)

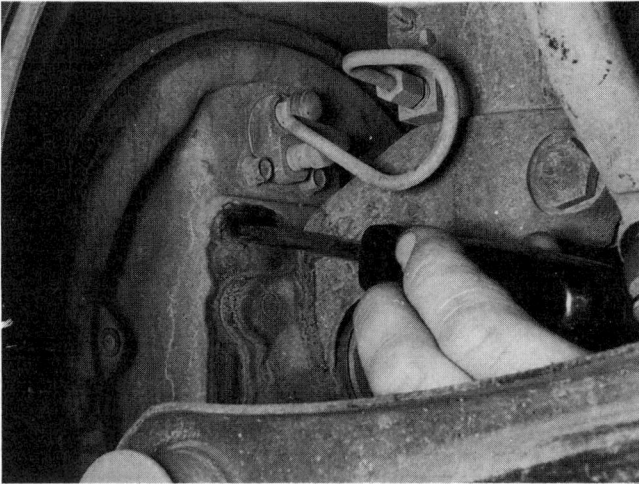
6.8   Turn the star wheel on the adjuster screw assembly until the brake shoes drag on the drum, . . .

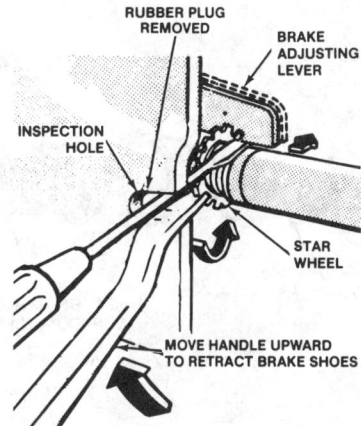
RUBBER PLUG REMOVED
BRAKE ADJUSTING LEVER
INSPECTION HOLE
STAR WHEEL
MOVE HANDLE UPWARD TO RETRACT BRAKE SHOES

6.9a   . . . then back off the wheel with a screwdriver and brake tool while holding the lever away from the wheel until the brake shoes just slightly drag on the drum (the drum must still be able to rotate freely)

6   Once the new shoes are in place, install the hub/drum assembly as outlined in Section 5.

7   Remove the rubber plug from the brake backing plate.

8   Insert a narrow screwdriver or brake adjusting tool through the adjustment hole and turn the star wheel until the brakes drag slightly as the drum is turned (see illustration).

9   Turn the star wheel in the opposite direction until the drum turns freely. Keep the adjuster lever from contacting the star wheel or it won't turn (see illustrations).

10   Repeat the adjustment on the opposite wheel.

11   Install the plugs in the backing plate access holes.

12   Install the wheels and lower the vehicle. Tighten the lug nuts to the specified torque.

13   Adjust the parking brake as described in Section 12 of this Chapter.

14   Top up the master cylinder with brake fluid and pump the pedal several times. Lower the vehicle and check brake operation before driving the vehicle in traffic.

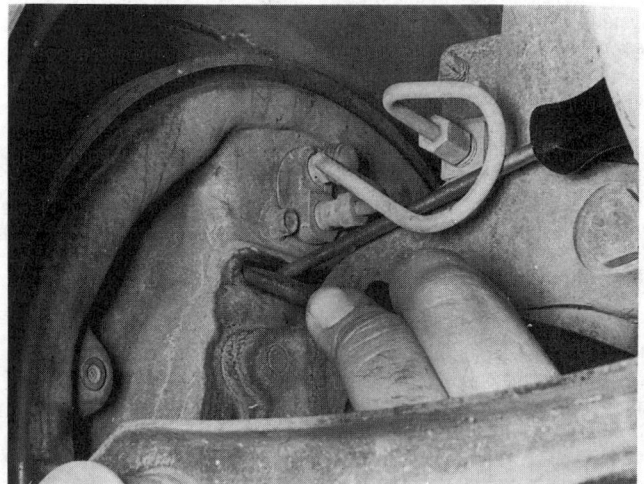
6.9b   Two small screwdrivers may also be used to adjust the brakes

7   Wheel cylinder – removal, overhaul and installation

Note: *If an overhaul is indicated (usually because of fluid leakage or sticky operation) explore all options before beginning the job. New wheel cylinders are available, which makes this job quite easy. If it's decided to rebuild the wheel cylinder, make sure that a rebuild kit is available before proceeding. Never overhaul only one wheel cylinder - always rebuild both of them at the same time.*

Removal

Refer to illustration 7.4

1   Raise the rear of the vehicle and support it securely on jackstands. Block the front wheels to keep the vehicle from rolling.

2   Remove the rear hub/drum (Section 5) and the brake shoe assembly (Section 6).

3   Remove all dirt and foreign material from around the wheel cylinder.

4   Disconnect the brake line (see illustration). Don't pull the brake line away from the wheel cylinder.

5   Remove the wheel cylinder mounting bolts.

6   Detach the wheel cylinder from the brake backing plate and place it on a clean workbench. Immediately plug the brake line to prevent fluid loss and contamination.

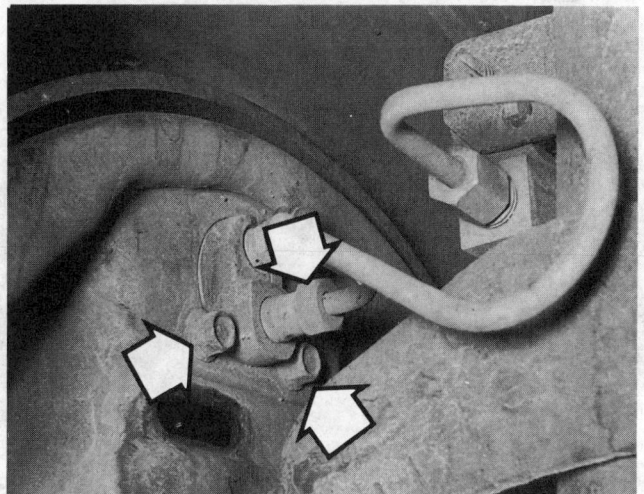
7.4   Unscrew the brake line fitting, then remove the two wheel cylinder bolts (arrows)

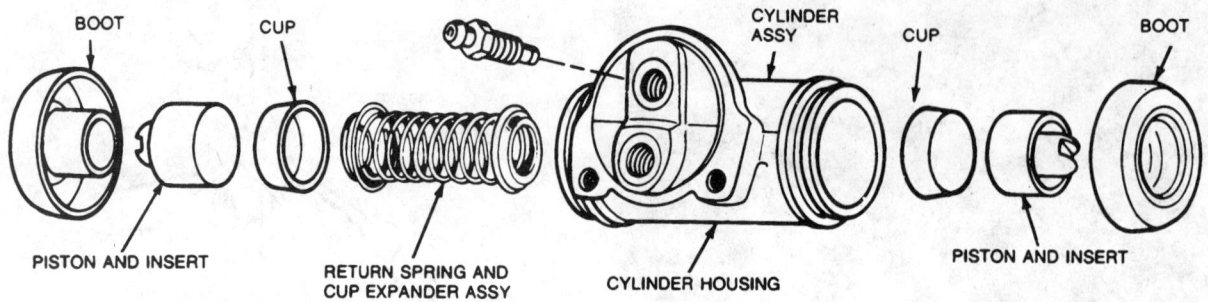

7.7   Wheel cylinder components – exploded view

Overhaul

Refer to illustration 7.7

7   Remove the bleeder valve, cups (seals), pistons, boots and spring assembly from the wheel cylinder housing **(see illustration)**.
8   Clean the wheel cylinder with brake fluid, denatured alcohol or brake system cleaner. **Warning:** *Do not, under any circumstances, use petroleum based solvents to clean brake parts!*
9   Use compressed air to remove excess fluid from the wheel cylinder and to blow out the passages.
10   Check the cylinder bore for corrosion and score marks. Crocus cloth can be used to remove light corrosion and stains, but the cylinder must be replaced with a new one if the defects cannot be removed easily, or if the bore is scored.
11   Lubricate the new cups with brake fluid.
12   Assemble the brake cylinder components. Make sure the cup lips face in.

Installation

13   Place the wheel cylinder in position and install the bolts.
14   Connect the brake line, install the brake shoe assembly and the brake drum. Adjust the wheel bearing as described in Section 5.
15   Bleed the brakes (Section 11).

---

8   Master cylinder – removal, overhaul and installation

Warning: *Do not attempt to rebuild the master cylinder if the vehicle is a 1990 model with the Anti-Lock Brake System (ABS). See section 18.*

Note: *Before deciding to overhaul the master cylinder, check on the availability and cost of a new or factory rebuilt unit and also the availability of a rebuild kit.*

Removal

Refer to illustration 8.2

1   Place rags under the brake line fittings and prepare caps or plastic bags to cover the ends of the lines once they are disconnected. **Caution:** *Brake fluid will damage paint. Cover all body parts and be careful not to spill fluid during this procedure.*
2   Unscrew the tube nuts at the ends of the brake lines where they enter the master cylinder. To prevent rounding off the flats on these nuts, a flare-nut wrench, which wraps around the fitting, should be used **(see illustration)**.
3   Pull the brake lines away from the master cylinder slightly and plug the ends to prevent contamination.
4   Disconnect the brake warning light switch electrical connector, remove the two master cylinder mounting nuts and detach the master cylinder from the vehicle.
5   Remove the reservoir cap, then discard any fluid remaining in the reservoir.

Overhaul

Refer to illustrations 8.7, 8.8, 8.9, 8.10 and 8.14

6   Mount the master cylinder in a vise with the vise jaws clamping on the mounting flange.
7   Depress the piston and remove the snap-ring with a pair of snapring pliers. **(see illustration)**.

8.2   Disconnect the electrical connector, unscrew the four hydraulic fitting tube nuts, then remove the two mounting nuts (arrows) to detach the master cylinder

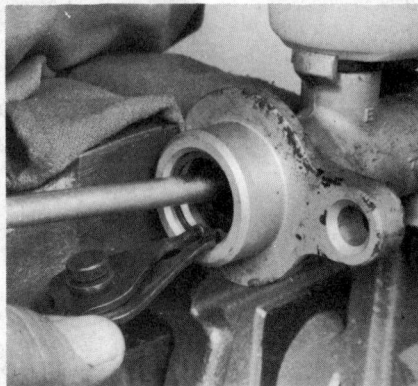

8.7   Use a Phillips screwdriver to push the primary piston into the cylinder, then remove the snap-ring

8.8   Remove the primary piston assembly from the cylinder

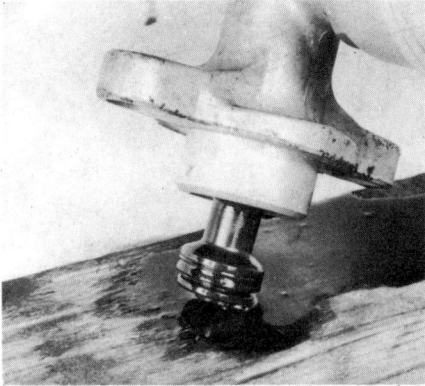

8.9   Tap the master cylinder against a block of wood to eject the secondary piston assembly

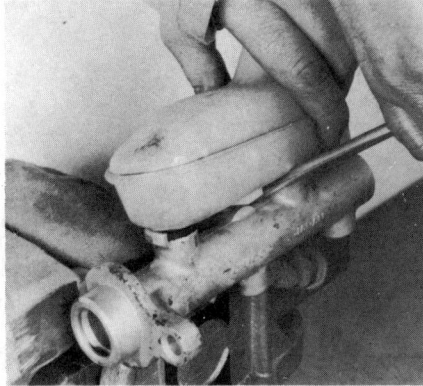

8.10   If it's necessary to remove the fluid reservoir (to replace leaking seals or a broken reservoir), gently pry it off with a screwdriver

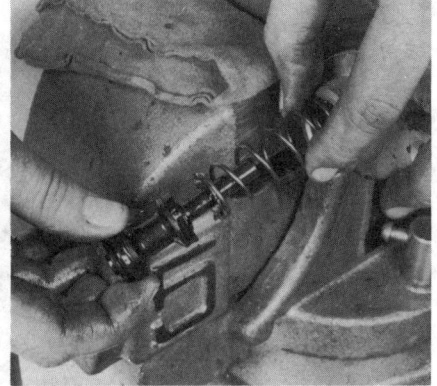

8.14   Coat the secondary piston with clean brake fluid and install it in the master cylinder, spring end first

8   Remove the primary piston assembly from the cylinder bore (see illustration).

9   Remove the secondary piston assembly from the cylinder bore. It may be necessary to remove the master cylinder from the vise and invert it, carefully tapping it against a block of wood to expel the piston (see illustration).

10   If fluid has been leaking past the reservoir grommets, pry the reservoir out of the cylinder body with a screwdriver (see illustration). Remove the grommets.

11   Inspect the cylinder bore for corrosion and damage. If any corrosion or damage is found, replace the master cylinder body with a new one, as abrasives cannot be used on the bore.

12   Lubricate the new reservoir grommets with silicone lubricant and press them into the master cylinder body. Make sure they're properly seated.

13   Lay the reservoir on a hard surface and press the master cylinder body onto the reservoir, using a rocking motion.

14   Lubricate the cylinder bore and primary and secondary piston assemblies with clean brake fluid. Insert the secondary piston assembly into the cylinder (see illustration).

15   Install the primary piston assembly in the cylinder bore, depress it and install the snap-ring.

16   Inspect the reservoir cap and diaphragm for cracks and deformation. Replace it if it's damaged.

17   Note: Whenever the master cylinder is removed, the complete hydraulic system must be bled. The time required to bleed the system can be reduced if the master cylinder is filled with fluid and bench bled (refer to Steps 18 through 25) before the master cylinder is installed on the vehicle.

18   Insert threaded plugs of the correct size into the cylinder outlet holes and fill the reservoirs with brake fluid. The master cylinder should be supported in such a manner that brake fluid will not spill during the bench bleeding procedure.

19   Loosen one plug at a time, starting with the rear outlet ports first (closest to the booster), and push the piston assembly into the bore to force air from the master cylinder. To prevent air from being drawn back into the cylinder, the appropriate plug must be replaced before allowing the piston to return to its original position.

20   Stroke the piston three or four times for each outlet to ensure that all air has been expelled.

21   Since high pressure is not involved in the bench bleeding procedure, an alternative to the removal and replacement of the plugs with each stroke of the piston assembly is available. Before pushing in on the piston assembly, remove one of the plugs completely. Before releasing the piston, however, instead of replacing the plug, simply put your finger tightly over the hole to keep air from being drawn back into the master cylinder. Wait several seconds for the brake fluid to be drawn from the reservoir to

the piston bore, then repeat the procedure. When you push down on the piston it will force your finger off the hole, allowing the air inside to be expelled. When only brake fluid is being ejected from the hole, replace the plug and go on to the other port.

22   Refill the master cylinder reservoirs and install the diaphragm and cap assembly.

Installation

23   Carefully install the master cylinder by reversing the removal steps, then bleed the brakes (refer to Section 11).

---

9   Brake pressure control valve(s) – removal, installation and adjustment

---

Sedan

Removal

Refer to illustrations 9.2 and 9.3

1   Raise the rear of the vehicle and support it securely on jackstands.

2   Remove the valve bracket from the lower suspension control arm (see illustration).

9.2   The brake pressure control valve lower mounting bracket is bolted to the left side rear suspension control arm – a special Torx driver is required to remove the bolt

9.3   Brake pressure control valve mounting details

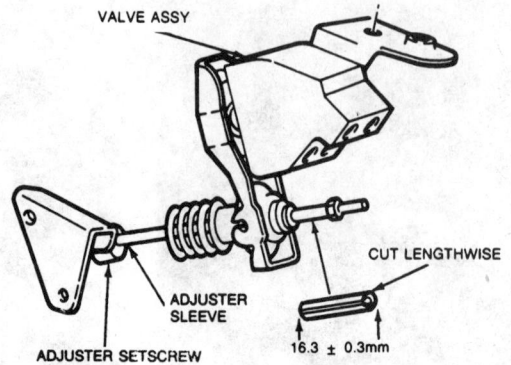

9.10   The brake pressure control valve is adjusted by placing a piece of rubber or plastic tubing between the operating rod upper nut and the lever, then moving the adjuster sleeve so it's seated in the pocket of the lower mounting bracket (this must be done with the vehicle at normal ride height)

3   Mark the positions of the four hydraulic lines at the valve **(see illustration)** and unscrew the tube nuts, using a flare-nut wrench if available. Carefully pull the lines out of the valve.
4   Remove the two bolts that hold the valve to the floor pan, then detach the valve from the vehicle.

Installation

5   Position the valve on the floor pan and install the two mounting bolts, tightening them securely.
6   Connect the valve bracket to the lower suspension arm, install the retaining bolt and tighten it securely.
7   Insert the brake lines into the valve. Start the tube nuts by hand, being careful not to cross-thread them, then tighten them securely, preferably with a flare-nut wrench.
8   Bleed the brakes following the procedure outlined in Section 11.

Adjustment
Refer to illustration 9.10

9   Lower the vehicle and bounce the vehicle a few times to set the suspension at normal ride height.
10   Cut a piece of 1/4-inch I.D. hose or tubing to a length of 16.3 mm and slit it down the side **(see illustration)**.
11   Slide underneath the rear of the vehicle and loosen the valve adjuster setscrew **(see illustration 9.10)**.
12   Using the piece of tubing as a spacer, install it on the upper end of the operating rod. Move the adjuster sleeve up or down, if necessary, so that it rests in the pocket of the mounting bracket on the lower suspension arm. Tighten the adjuster sleeve setscrew securely. Any further adjustments must be left to a Ford dealer service department.

Station wagon
Refer to illustration 9.15

13   Place rags under the master cylinder and prepare caps or plastic bags to cover the ends of the lines once they are disconnected.
14   Loosen the tube nut (either primary or secondary, depending on the valve to be removed) where it enters the pressure control valve, using a flare-nut wrench if one is available.
15   Unscrew the pressure control valve from the master cylinder **(see illustration)**. Plug the open port in the master cylinder to prevent excessive fluid loss and contamination.
16   Installation is the reverse of the removal procedure. Be sure to bleed the brakes following the procedure described in Section 11.

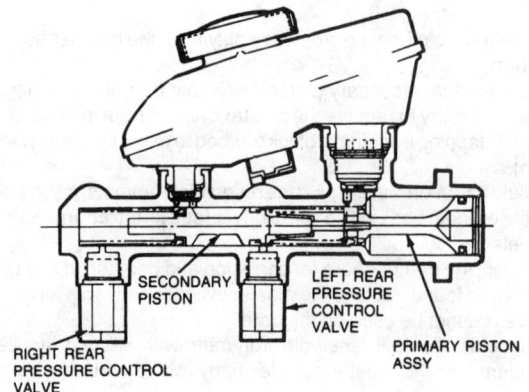

9.15   The brake pressure control valves on station wagon models are screwed into the master cylinder

---

10   Brake hoses and lines – inspection and replacement

Inspection

1   About every six months, with the vehicle raised and supported securely on jackstands, the rubber hoses which connect the steel brake lines with the front and rear brake assemblies should be inspected for cracks, chafing of the outer cover, leaks, blisters and other damage. These are important and vulnerable parts of the brake system and inspection should be complete. A light and mirror will be helpful for a thorough check. If a hose exhibits any of the above conditions, replace it with a new one.

Replacement
Rubber hose
Refer to illustration 10.3

2   Clean all dirt away from the ends of the hose.
3   Disconnect the brake line from the hose fitting using a back-up wrench on the fitting **(see illustration)**. Be careful not to bend the frame bracket or line. If necessary, soak the connections with penetrating oil.
4   Unbolt the hose bracket from the strut assembly.
5   Remove the U-clip from the female fitting at the bracket **(see illustration 10.3)** and remove the hose from the bracket.
6   Disconnect the hose from the caliper, discarding the copper washers on either side of the fitting block.

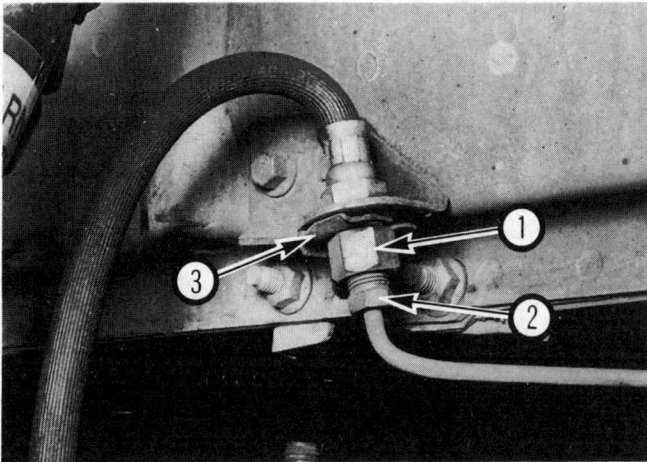

10.3 To disconnect a brake hose from the brake line fitting, place a backup wrench on the hose fitting (1) and loosen the tube nut (2) with a flare-nut wrench – remove the U-clip (3) to detach the hose from the frame bracket

7   Using new copper washers, attach the new brake hose to the caliper.
8   Pass the female fitting through the frame bracket. With the least amount of twist in the hose, install the fitting in this position (use the paint stripe on the hose to help determine twist). **Note:** *The weight of the vehicle should be on the suspension, so the vehicle should not be raised while positioning the hose.*
9   Install the U-clip in the female fitting at the frame bracket.
10   Attach the brake line to the hose fitting using a back-up wrench on the fitting.
11   Mount the brake hose bracket to the strut assembly.
12   Carefully check to make sure the suspension or steering components don't make contact with the hose. Have an assistant push on the vehicle and also turn the steering wheel from lock-to-lock during inspection.
13   Bleed the brake system as described in Section 11.

Metal brake lines

14   When replacing brake lines, be sure to use the correct parts. Don't use copper tubing for any brake system components. Purchase steel brake lines from a dealer or auto parts store.
15   Prefabricated brake line, with the tube ends already flared and fittings installed, is available at auto parts stores and dealers. These lines are also bent to the proper shapes.
16   If prefabricated lines aren't available, obtain the recommended steel tubing and fittings to match the line to be replaced. Determine the correct length by measuring the old brake line (a piece of string can usually be used for this) and cut the new tubing to length, allowing about 1/2-inch extra for flaring the ends.
17   Install the fitting over the cut tubing and flare the ends of the line with a flaring tool.
18   If necessary, carefully bend the line to the proper shape. A tube bender is recommended for this. **Warning:** *Do not crimp or damage the line.*
19   When installing the new line, make sure it's securely supported in the brackets and has plenty of clearance between moving or hot components.
20   After installation, check the master cylinder fluid level and add fluid as necessary. Bleed the brake system as outlined in Section 11 and test the brakes carefully before driving the vehicle in traffic.

11   Brake hydraulic system – bleeding

Refer to illustration 11.8
Warning: *Wear eye protection when bleeding the brake system. If the fluid comes in contact with your eyes, immediately rinse them with water and seek medical attention.*

1   Bleeding the hydraulic system is necessary to remove any air that manages to find its way into the system as a result of removal and installation of a hose, line, caliper or master cylinder. Use only the specified fluid in this system or extensive damage could result. It will probably be necessary to bleed the system at all four brakes if air has entered the system due to low fluid level, or if the brake lines have been disconnected at the master cylinder.
2   If a brake line was disconnected only at one wheel, then only that caliper (or wheel cylinder) must be bled.
3   If a brake line is disconnected at a fitting located between the master cylinder and any of the brakes, that part of the system served by the disconnected line must be bled.
4   Remove any residual vacuum from the power brake booster by applying the brake several times with the engine off.
5   Remove the master cylinder reservoir cover and fill the reservoir with brake fluid. Reinstall the cover. **Note:** *Check the fluid level often during the bleeding operation and add fluid as necessary to prevent the level from falling low enough to allow air bubbles into the master cylinder.*
6   Have an assistant on hand, as well as a supply of new brake fluid, an empty clear plastic container, a length of 3/16-inch clear plastic or vinyl tubing to fit over the bleeder screw and a wrench to open and close the bleeder screw.
7   Beginning at the right rear wheel, loosen the bleeder screw slightly, then tighten it to a point where it's snug but can still be loosened quickly and easily.
8   Place one end of the tubing over the bleeder screw and submerge the other end in brake fluid in the container **(see illustration)**.

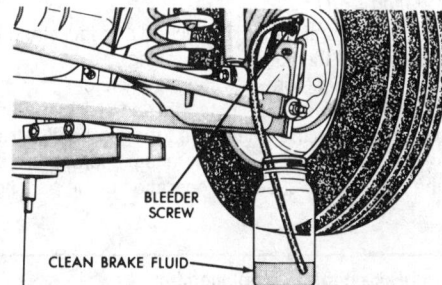

11.8   When bleeding the brakes, a hose is connected to the bleeder screw and then submerged in brake fluid – air will be seen as bubbles in the container and hose (all air must be removed before continuing to the next wheel)

9   Have an assistant pump the brakes a few times to get pressure in the system, then hold the pedal down.
10   While the pedal is held down, open the bleeder screw until brake fluid begins to flow. Watch for air bubbles to exit the submerged end of the tube. When the fluid flow slows after a couple of seconds, tighten the screw and have your assistant release the pedal.
11   Repeat Steps 9 and 10 until no more air is seen leaving the tube, then tighten the bleeder screw and proceed to the left front wheel, the left rear wheel and the right front wheel, in that order, and perform the same procedure. Be sure to check the fluid in the master cylinder reservoir frequently.
12   Never use old brake fluid. It contains moisture which will deteriorate the brake system components.
13   Refill the master cylinder with fluid at the end of the operation.
14   Check the operation of the brakes. The pedal should feel solid when depressed, with no sponginess. If necessary, repeat the entire process. **Warning:** *Do not drive the vehicle if you doubt the effectiveness of the brake system.*
15   If any difficulty is experienced in bleeding the hydraulic system, or if an assistant is not available, a pressure bleeding kit is a worthwhile investment. If connected in accordance with the instructions, each bleeder screw can be opened in turn to allow the fluid to be pressure ejected until it is clear of air bubbles without the need to replenish the master cylinder reservoir during the process.

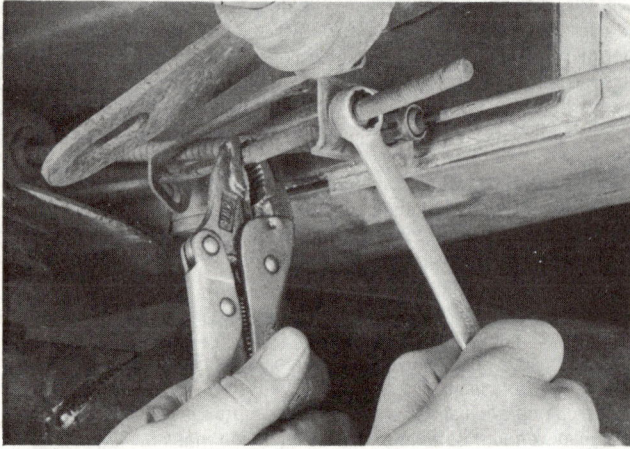

12.3   With a pair of locking pliers clamped to the end of the adjuster rod to prevent it from turning, turn the adjusting nut until the rear brakes drag slightly, then back off the nut until the brakes don't drag when the rear wheels are turned

12   Parking brake – adjustment

Refer to illustration 12.3

1   Raise the vehicle and support it securely on jackstands. Block the front wheels to prevent the vehicle from rolling.
2   Make sure the parking brake is completely released.
3   Working under the vehicle, tighten the adjusting nut until the rear brakes drag slightly when the wheels are turned **(see illustration)**. Turn the nut in the opposite direction until there is no perceptible drag.
4   Lower the vehicle and check the operation of the parking brake.

13   Parking brake cables – replacement

1   Raise the rear of the vehicle and support it securely on jackstands. Release the parking brake completely.

Front cable
Refer to illustrations 13.3 and 13.6

2   Loosen the parking brake cable adjusting nut **(see illustration 12.3).**
3   Disconnect the front cable from the rear cable at the cable connector on the left side of the vehicle **(see illustration)**.

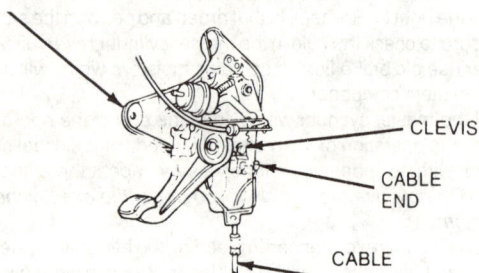

13.6   Unhook the cable end from the clevis, then disconnect the cable housing from the parking brake bracket

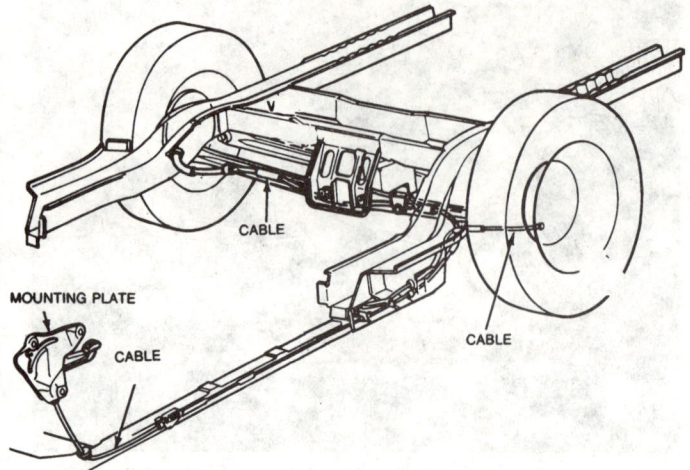

13.3   Parking brake cable routing diagram (sedan model shown, wagon similar)

4   Depress the tangs on the cable retainer at the body bracket (just ahead of the cable connector) and push the cable and housing through the bracket.
5   Push the grommet up through the floor pan.
6   Working inside of the vehicle, remove the left side kick panel, then pull the carpet from the panel. Disconnect the cable end from the clevis **(see illustration)**.
7   Depress the tangs on the cable housing retainer and pull the cable down through the parking brake pedal bracket.
8   Working under the vehicle, pull the cable assembly out through the floor pan hole.
9   Installation is the reverse of the removal procedure. Be sure to adjust the cable following the procedure described in Section 12.

Rear cables
Refer to illustration 13.13

10   Remove the parking brake cable adjusting nut **(see illustration 12.3).**
11   Remove the rear wheel and brake drum/hub assembly (refer to Section 5).
12   Disconnect the end of the parking brake cable from the parking brake lever **(see illustration 6.5h).**
13   Depress the tangs on the cable housing retainer and push the cable through the brake backing plate **(see illustration)**.

13.13   Depress the tangs on the cable housing retainer (arrows) and push the retainer through the backing plate

14.3   Parking brake pedal installation details

1	*Release cable*	3	*Parking brake light switch*
2	*Parking brake cable*	4	*Mounting bolts*

14   Depress the tangs on the retainer at the body side rail bracket (next to the adjuster) and push the cable through.

15   Left cable only: Disconnect the rear cable from the front cable at the cable connector **(see illustration 13.3),** then pull the cable through the side rail bracket.

16   Right cable only: Cut the retaining straps from the suspension lower arms and remove the cable bracket screw at the crossmember, then remove the cable from the vehicle.

17   Installation is the reverse on the removal procedure. Be sure to adjust the cable as outlined in Section 12.

---

14   Parking brake pedal – removal and installation

Refer to illustration 14.3

1   Release the parking brake completely.

2   Back off the adjusting nut to remove all tension from the cables (refer to Section 12).

3   Disconnect the release cable from the pedal assembly **(see illustration)**.

4   Unplug the electrical connector from the parking brake switch. Disconnect the vacuum hose from the vacuum motor if the vehicle is equipped with an antomatic brake release.

5   Remove the three pedal mechanism mounting bolts.

6   Disconnect the parking brake cable, then depress the tangs on the cable housing, pushing the housing through the pedal bracket.

7   Remove the pedal assembly.

8   To install the pedal assembly, reverse the removal procedure and adjust the parking brake cable as outlined in Section 12.

---

15   Brake pedal – removal and installation

Removal

1   Disconnect the negative battery cable from the battery.

2   Remove the under-dash panel and unplug the wiring connector at the brake light switch.

3   Disconnect the brake pedal from the power brake booster pushrod by removing the retaining clip and washer and sliding the pushrod off the pedal pin.

4   Remove the nut and pivot bolt from the top of the pedal.

5   The brake pedal, spacer and bushings can now be removed from the bracket.

Installation

6   Use new bushings and lubricate the bushings, spacer, bolt and all friction parts with a light coat of engine oil.

7   Place the pedal, bushings and spacer in position and slide the pivot bolt into place. Note that it should be installed with the head on the right side of the bracket.

8   Tighten the nut and attach the booster pushrod and brake light switch to the pedal.

9   Operate the brake pedal several times to ensure proper operation.

10   Connect the wire harness to the brake light switch and install the under-dash cover. Connect the battery.

---

16   Power brake booster – removal, installation and adjustment

1   The power brake booster unit requires no special maintenance apart from periodic inspection of the vacuum hose and the case.

2   The brake booster is not serviceable. If a problem develops, install a new or factory rebuilt unit.

Removal

Refer to illustration 16.3

3   Remove the nuts attaching the master cylinder to the booster and carefully pull the master cylinder forward until it clears the mounting studs. Be careful – don't bend or kink the brake lines **(see illustration)**.

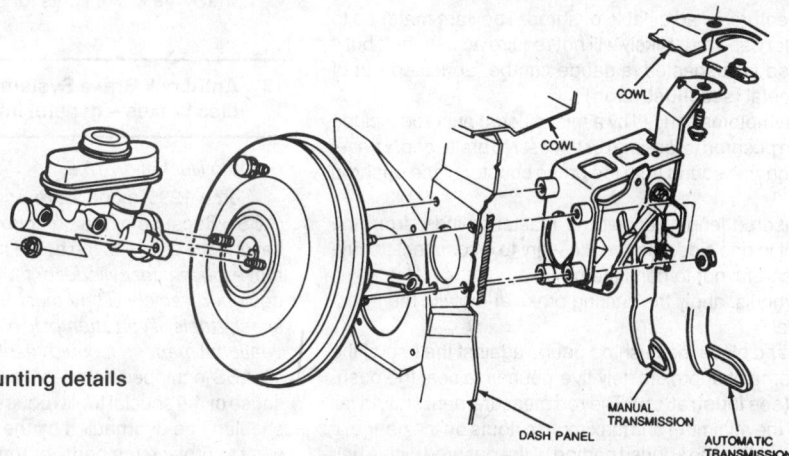

16.3   Power brake booster mounting details

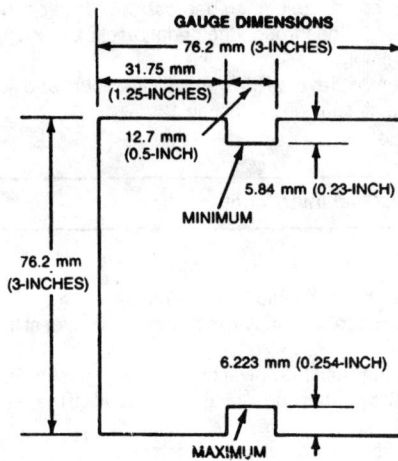

16.11   Power brake booster pushrod gauge template

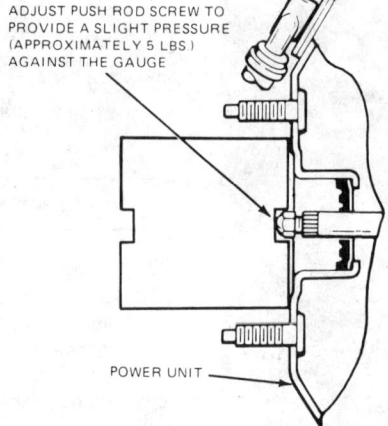

16.15   Checking the pushrod length (the pushrod is factory preset and most likely will never need adjusting)

17.2   Unplug the wiring connector (1), remove the retaining clip (2) and nylon washer (3), then slide the booster pushrod off the pedal pin just enough to allow switch removal

4   Disconnect the vacuum hose where it attaches to the power brake booster.

5   Working in the passenger compartment under the steering column, unplug the wiring connector from the brake light switch, then remove the pushrod retaining clip and nylon washer from the brake pedal pin. Slide the pushrod off the pin **(see illustration 17.2)**.

6   Also remove the nuts attaching the brake booster to the firewall.

7   Carefully detach the booster from the firewall and lift it out of the engine compartment.

Installation

8   Place the booster into position on the firewall and tighten the mounting nuts. Connect the pushrod and brake light switch to the brake pedal. Install the retaining clip in the brake pedal pin.

9   Attach the master cylinder to the booster. Tighten the nuts to the specified torque.

10   Carefully check the operation of the brakes before driving the vehicle in traffic.

Adjustment

Refer to illustrations 16.11 and 16.15

11   Some boosters feature an adjustable pushrod. They are matched to the booster at the factory and most likely will not require adjustment, but if a misadjusted pushrod is suspected, a gauge can be fabricated out of heavy gauge sheet metal **(see illustration)**.

12   Some common symptoms caused by a misadjusted pushrod include dragging brakes (if the pushrod is too long) or excessive brake pedal travel accompanied by a groaning sound from the brake booster (if the pushrod is too short).

13   To check the pushrod length, unbolt the master cylinder from the booster and position it to one side. It isn't necessary to disconnect the hydraulic lines, but be careful not to bend them.

14   Block the front wheels, apply the parking brake and place the transaxle in Park or Neutral.

15   Start the engine and place the pushrod gauge against the end of the pushrod, exerting a force of approximately five-pounds to seat the pushrod in the power unit **(see illustration)**. The rod measurement should fall somewhere between the minimum and maximum cutouts on the gauge. If it doesn't, adjust it by holding the knurled portion of the pushrod with a pair of pliers and turning the end with a wrench.

16   When the adjustment is complete, reinstall the master cylinder and check for proper brake operation before driving the vehicle in traffic.

---

17   Brake light switch – removal and installation

Removal

Refer to illustration 17.2

1   Remove the under-dash panel.

2   Locate the switch near the top of the brake pedal and disconnect the wiring harness **(see illustration)**.

3   Remove the pushrod retaining clip and nylon washer from the brake pedal pin and slide the pushrod off far enough for the outer hole of the switch to clear the pin. Now pull up on the switch to remove it.

Installation

4   Position the switch so it straddles the pushrod and the slot on the inner side of the switch rests on the pedal pin. Slide the pushrod and switch back onto the pin, then install the nylon washer and retaining clip.

5   Reconnect the wiring harness.

6   Install the under-dash panel.

7   Check the brake lights for proper operation.

---

18   Anti-Lock Brake System (ABS) and rear disc brakes – general information

Refer to illustration 18.2

Some 1990 models are equipped with an Anti-Lock Brake System (ABS). Because of the complexity of ABS, most service procedures are beyond the scope of the home mechanic. **Warning:** *Do not attempt to remove the master cylinder or the Hydraulic Control Unit (HCU) on an ABS-equipped vehicle. They must be bled by a new procedure that requires special tools. If you attempt to bleed the master cylinder or HCU in the conventional manner, it could result in a spongy brake pedal.*

ABS-equipped vehicles have rear disc brakes **(see illustration)**. Because of the special tools required to service rear disc brake calipers, they shouldn't be overhauled by the home mechanic. However, if you simply want to replace the pads, or remove the calipers or discs to take them to a dealer for servicing, the following Sections will show you how.

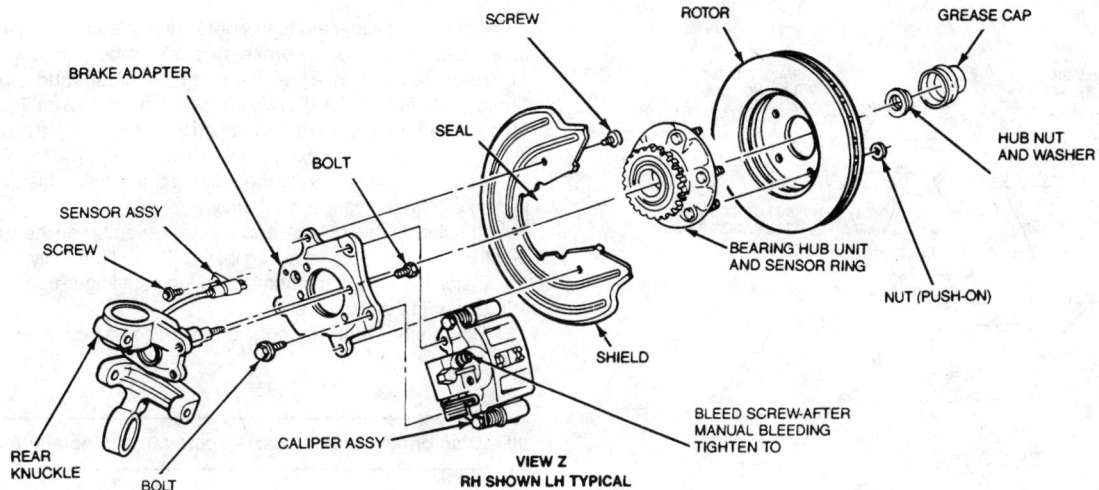

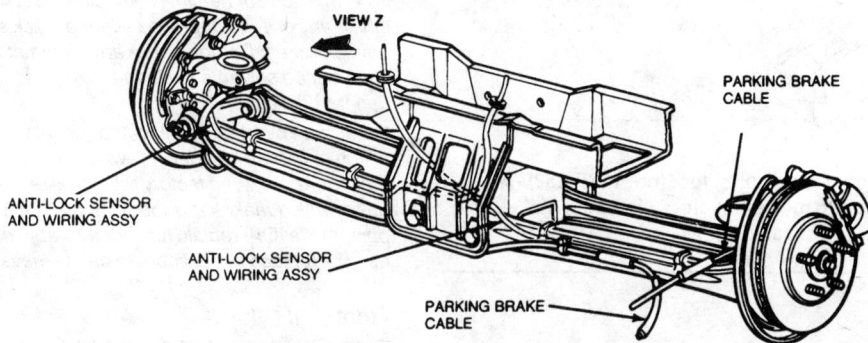

18.2   Rear disc brake components – exploded view

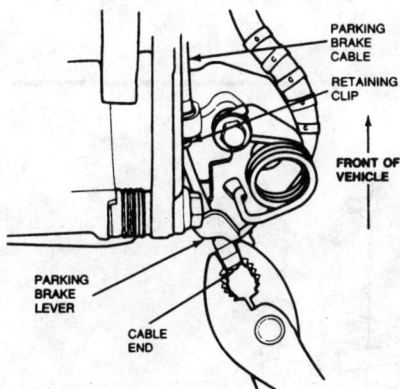

19.4   Remove the retaining clip from the parking brake

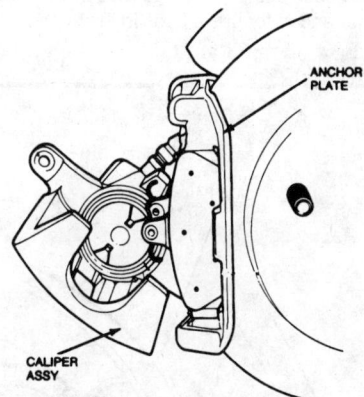

19.6   Rotate the caliper away from the disc to remove the brake pads

19   Brake pads (rear) – replacement

Refer to illustrations 19.4, 19.6 and 19.8

Warning: *Disc brake pads must be replaced on both rear wheels at the same time – never replace the pads on only one wheel. Also, the dust created by the brake system may contain asbestos, which is harmful to your health. Never blow it out with compressed air and don't inhale any of it. An approved filtering mask should be worn when working on the brakes. Do not, under any circumstances, use gasoline or petroleum-based solvents to clean brake parts. Use brake system cleaner or denatured alcohol only!*

Note: *When servicing the disc brakes, use only high-quality, nationally-recognized, name-brand parts.*

1   Raise the vehicle and support it securely on jackstands.
2   Remove the rear wheel.
3   Remove the bolt that attaches the brake hose bracket to the shock absorber bracket **(see illustration 20.2)**.
4   Remove the retaining clip from the parking brake cable at the caliper **(see illustration)**.
5   Hold the slider pin hex heads with an open-end wrench and remove the upper pinch bolt **(see illustration 20.4)**.
6   Rotate the caliper away from the brake disc **(see illustration)**.

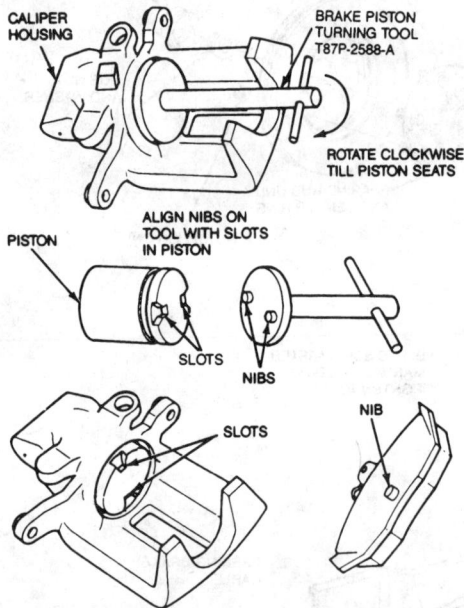

19.8   Using a brake piston turning tool (no. T87P-2588-A or equivalent), rotate the piston clockwise until it's seated

7   Remove the inner and outer brake pads.

8   Use the special factory brake piston turning tool (no. T87P-2588-A), or a pair of large snap-ring pliers, to rotate the piston clockwise until it's seated. Make sure the slots on the piston are positioned so they'll engage with the nibs on the back of the brake pad **(see illustration)**.

9   Install the inner and outer brake pads in the anchor plate.

10   Rotate the caliper assembly onto the disc and into position on the anchor plate. Make sure the brake pads are properly installed.

11   Remove the residue from the pinch bolt threads and apply one drop of Threadlock and Sealer (EOAZ-19554-A) or equivalent. Install the pinch bolts and tighten them to the specified torque while holding the slider pins with an open end wrench.

12   Attach the cable end to the parking brake lever. Install the cable retaining clip on the caliper assembly.

13   Position the brake hose and bracket assembly on the shock absorber bracket and install the retaining bolt. Tighten it securely.

14   Install the wheel and tighten the lug nuts finger-tight.

15   Lower the vehicle.

16   Tighten the wheel lug nuts to the specified torque.

---

20   Disc brake caliper (rear) – removal and installation

Warning: *Dust created by the brake system may contain asbestos, which is harmful to your health. Never blow it out with compressed air and don't inhale any of it. An approved filtering mask should be worn when working on the brakes. Do not, under any circumstances, use gasoline or petroleum-based solvents to clean brake parts. Use brake system cleaner or denatured alcohol only!*

Note: *If an overhaul is indicated (usually because of fluid leaks, a stuck piston or broken bleeder screw) explore all options before beginning this procedure. New and factory rebuilt calipers are available on an exchange basis, which makes this job quite easy. If it's decided to rebuild the calipers, make sure rebuild kits are available before proceeding. Always rebuild or replace the calipers in pairs – never rebuild just one of them.*

Removal

Refer to illustrations 20.2 and 20.4

1   Raise the vehicle and support it securely on jackstands.

2   Detach the brake hose from the caliper assembly **(see illustration)**.

3   Remove the retaining clip from the parking brake at the caliper. Disengage the parking brake cable end from the lever arm **(see illustration 19.4).**

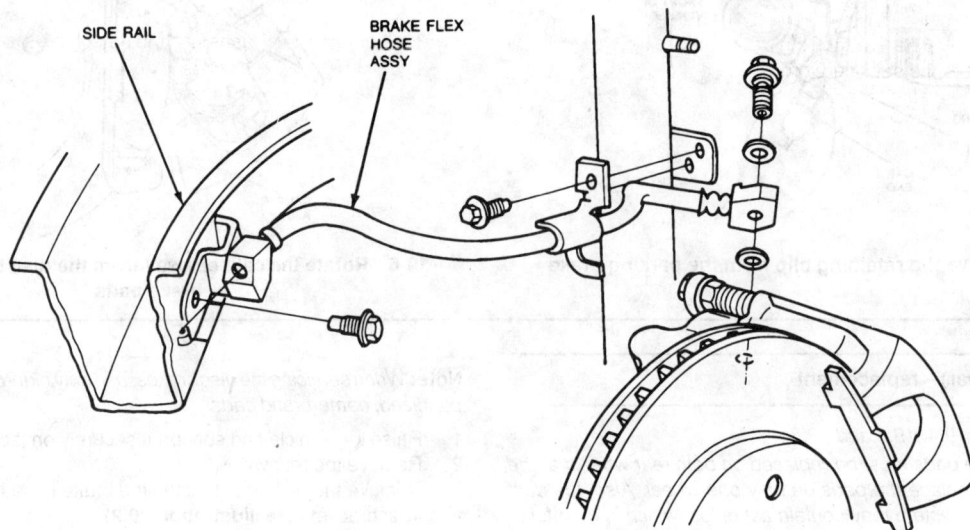

20.2   Brake hose bracket and brake hose-to-caliper bolt locations

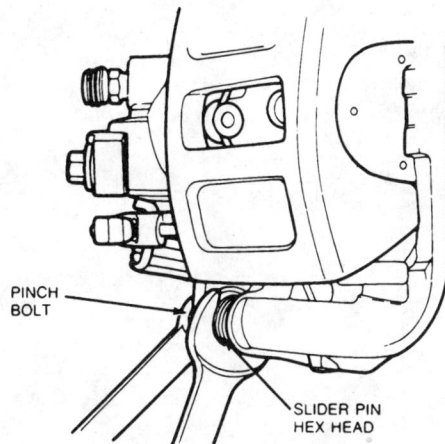

20.4 Hold the slider pin hex heads with an open-end wrench and remove the pinch bolts (this illustration shows the lower pinch bolt being removed)

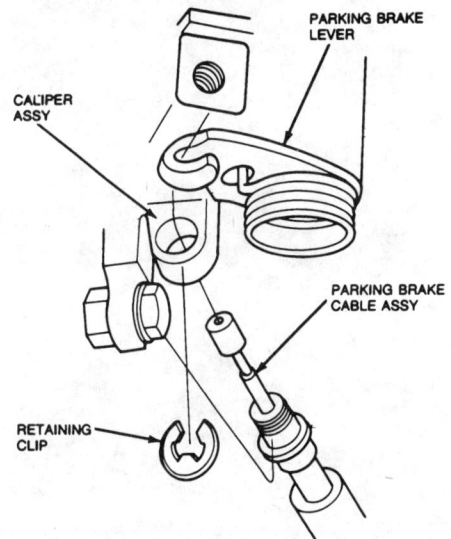

20.11 Attach the cable end to the parking brake lever and install the cable retaining clip on the caliper assembly

4   Hold each slider pin hex-head with an open-end wrench and remove the pinch bolt **(see illustration)**.
5   Detach the caliper assembly from the anchor plate.
6   Remove the slider pins and boots from the anchor plate.

Installation

Refer to illustration 20.11

7   Apply Silicone Dielectric Compound (D7AZ-19A331-A) or equivalent to the inside of the slider pin boots and to the slider pins.
8   Position the slider pins and boots in the anchor plate.
9   Position the caliper assembly on the anchor plate. Make sure the brake pads are correctly installed.
10   Remove the residue from the pinch bolt threads and apply one drop of Threadlock and Sealer (EOAZ-19554-A) or equivalent. Install the pinch bolts and tighten them to the specified torque while holding the slider pins with an open-end wrench.
11   Attach the cable end to the parking brake lever. Install the cable retaining clip on the caliper assembly **(see illustration)**.
12   Using new crush washers, attach the brake hose to the caliper. Tighten the retaining bolt to the specified torque.
13   Bleed the brake system (see Section 11).

14   Install the wheel and tighten the lug nuts finger-tight.
15   Lower the vehicle.
16   Tighten the wheel lug nuts to the specified torque.

21   Brake disc (rear) – inspection, removal and installation

Inspection

Refer to Section 4 – the inspection procedure for the rear disc is the same as the one for the front disc.

Removal and installation

1   Remove the caliper (see Section 20), but don't disconnect the brake hose.
2   Support the caliper with a piece of wire so the brake hose isn't stretched or twisted.
3   Remove the upper and lower anchor plate-to-brake adapter mounting bolts and detach the anchor plate **(see illustration 18.2)**.
4   Remove the two push-nuts and detach the disc from the hub **(see illustration 18.2)**.
5   Installation is the reverse of removal.

Chapter 10   Suspension and steering systems

Contents

Specifications

Torque specifications

Front suspension

	Ft-lbs
Strut upper mounting nuts	22 to 32
Strut-to-steering knuckle pinch bolt	70 to 95
Damper shaft nut	35 to 50
Control arm-to-frame pivot bolt nut	
1986	40 to 55
1987 on	70 to 95
Steering knuckle-to-balljoint pinch bolt nut	40 to 55
Tension strut-to-control arm nut	70 to 95
Tension strut-to-frame nut	70 to 95
Subframe mounting bolts	65 to 85

Rear suspension — sedan

Strut upper mounting nuts	19 to 26
Strut-to-spindle pinch bolt	55 to 81
Control arm-to-spindle nut	
1986	52 to 74
1987 on	42 to 57
Control arm-to-frame nut	
1986	52 to 74
1987 on	45 to 65
Tension strut-to-spindle nut	52 to 74
Tension strut-to-frame nut	52 to 74

Rear suspension — wagon

Upper arm-to-spindle nut	150 to 190
Upper arm-to-frame bolt	70 to 95
Lower arm-to-spindle bolt/nut	60 to 86
Lower arm-to-frame bolt/nut	40 to 55
Tension strut-to-frame bolt/nut	40 to 55
Tension strut-to-lower arm bolt/nut	40 to 55

Steering system

Steering wheel-to-steering shaft nut	
1986	50 to 62
1987	35 to 50
1988 on (bolt)	23 to 33
Intermediate shaft-to-steering column shaft nuts	15 to 25
Intermediate shaft-to-steering gear input shaft pinch bolt	30 to 38
Steering gear mounting bolt nuts	85 to 100
Tie-rod end-to-steering knuckle*	35 to 47
Wheel lug nuts	80 to 105
Power steering pump-to-mounting bracket bolts	30 to 45

Tighten to the minimum specified torque, then align the next castellation in the nut with the cotter pin hole.

1   General information

The front suspension is a MacPherson strut design. The steering knuckle is located by a lower control arm and both front control arms are connected by a stabilizer bar, which also controls fore-and-aft movement of the control arms.

The rear suspension on sedan models also utilizes MacPherson struts. Lateral movement is controlled by two parallel control arms on each side, with longitudinally mounted tension struts between the body and the rear spindles. Body lean is controlled by a stabilizer bar.

The rear suspension on wagon models is comprised of upper and lower control arms (one each per side), coil springs, tension struts (one per side), shock absorbers, spindles and a stabilizer bar.

The rack-and-pinion steering gear is located behind the engine/trans-axle assemby on the subframe and actuates the steering arms, which are integral with the steering knuckles. All models covered by this manual are equipped with power steering. The steering column is connected to the steering gear through an articulated intermediate shaft. The steering column is designed to collapse in the event of an accident.

Note: *These vehicles use a combination of standard and metric fasteners on the various suspension and steering components, so it would be a good idea to have both types of tools available when beginning work.*

Warning: *Whenever any of the suspension or steering fasteners are loosened or removed they must be replaced with new ones — discard the originals and don't reuse them. They must be replaced with new ones of the same part number or of original equipment quality and design. Torque specifications must be followed for proper reassembly and component retention.*

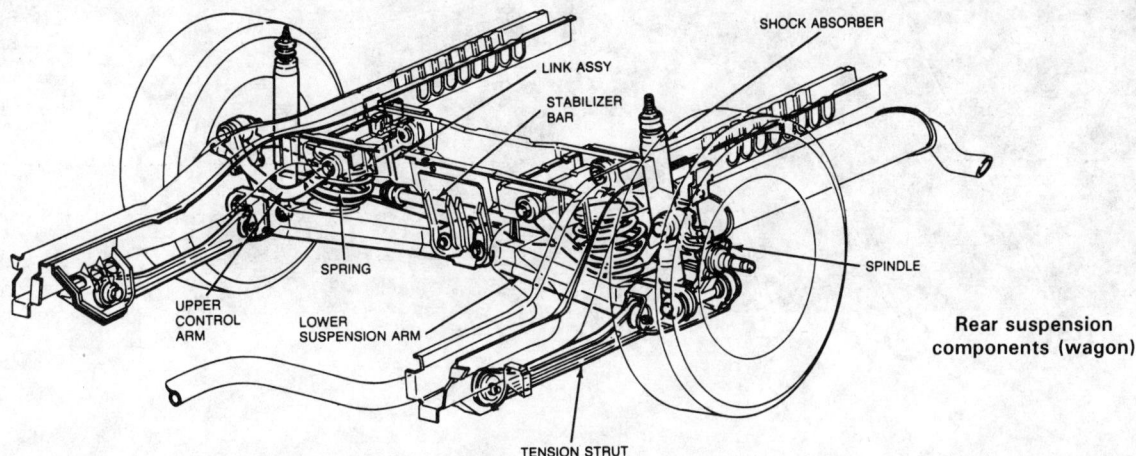

Rear suspension components (wagon)

244

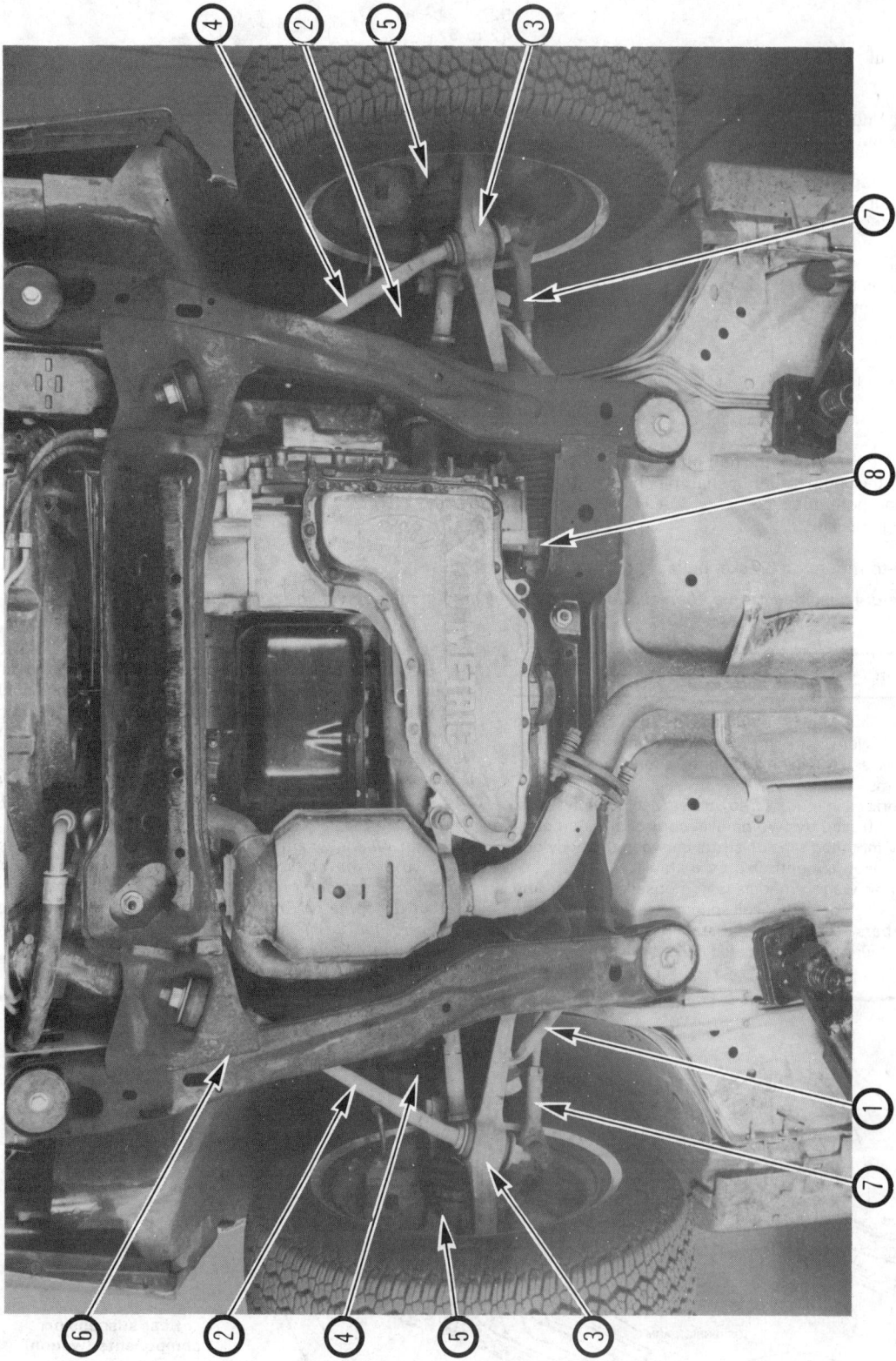

Front suspension and steering components

1 Stabilizer bar
2 Tension strut
3 Control arm
4 Strut/shock absorber and coil
  spring assembly
5 Steering knuckle and hub assembly
6 Subframe
7 Tie-rod end
8 Steering gear

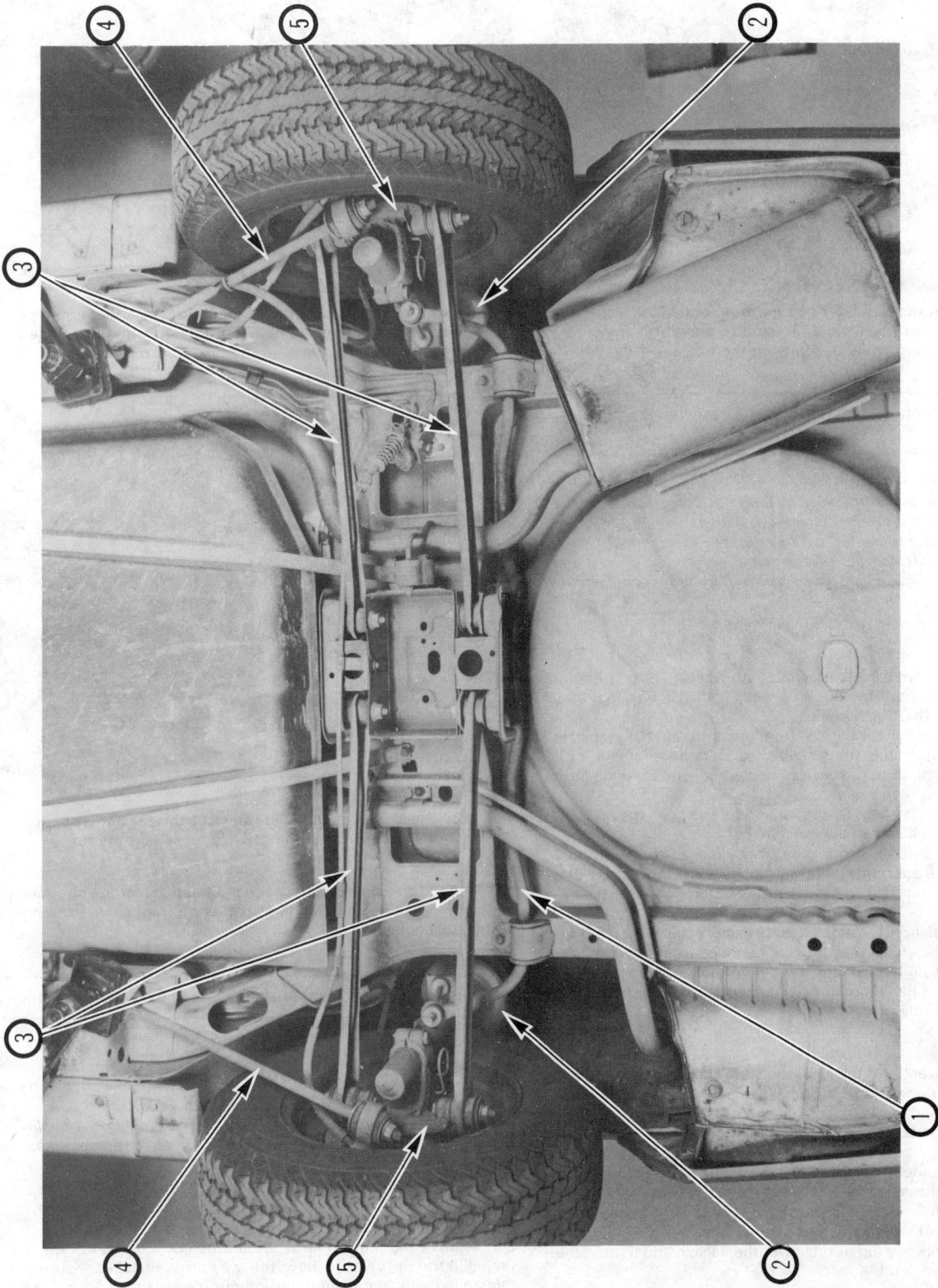

Rear suspension components (sedan)

1 Stabilizer bar
2 Strut/shock absorber and coil
  spring assembly
3 Control arms
4 Tension strut
5 Spindle

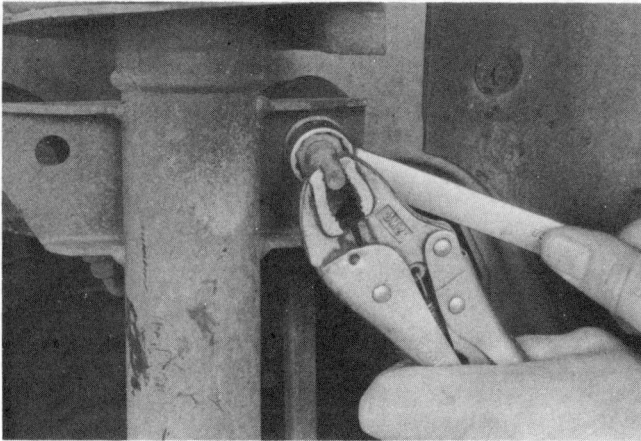

2.2   To loosen the stabilizer bar link from either the strut
bracket or the bar itself, hold the stud to prevent it from
turning while unscrewing the nut

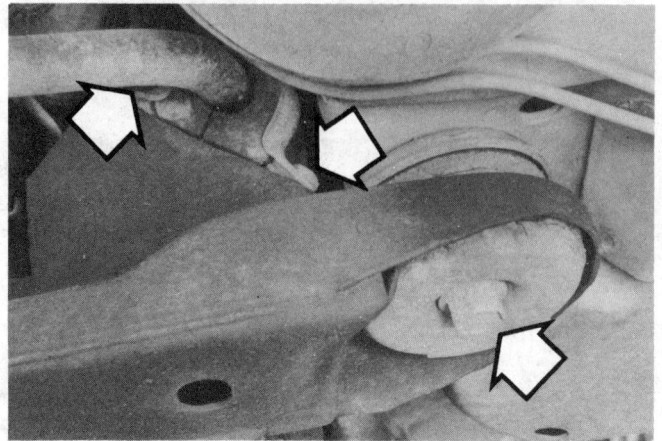

2.4   The stabilizer bar bracket bolts (upper arrows) can be
removed after the subframe bolts (lower arrow) have been
unscrewed and the subframe lowered for clearance

2   Front stabilizer bar, link and bushings — removal and installation

Refer to illustrations 2.2 and 2.4

Warning: *Whenever any of the suspension or steering fasteners are loosened or removed they must be replaced with new ones — discard the originals and don't reuse them. They must be replaced with new ones of the same part number or of original equipment quality and design. Torque specifications must be followed for proper reassembly and component retention.*

Note: *This procedure requires two floor jacks.*

Removal

1   Loosen the front wheel lug nuts from both wheels. Raise the front of the vehicle and support it securely on jackstands placed behind the subframe. Remove the front wheels.

2   Disconnect the stabilizer bar link from the strut and the stabilizer bar **(see illustration)**. If only the stabilizer bar is to be removed, or if the link isn't damaged, it isn't necessary to disconnect it from the strut bracket.

3   Remove the steering gear-to-subframe nuts and push the steering gear up off of the subframe (see Section 25).

4   Place a floor jack under each side of the rear of the subframe. Remove the two rear subframe bolts and slowly lower the jacks a little at a time until the stabilizer bar bracket bolts are accessible **(see illustration)**.

5   Remove the stabilizer bar bracket bolts and pry the U-brackets off the bushings. The bushings may now be removed from the stabilizer bar, if desired, without removing the bar from the vehicle. If it is necessary to remove the bar, carefully guide it out from between the subframe and the body.

Installation

6   Clean the stabilizer bar in the area where the bushings ride. Position the bar on the subframe and fit the bushings over the bar in their approximate locations.

7   Push the U-brackets over the bushings and install the bolts, tightening them securely.

8   Raise the subframe until it contacts the floorpan, then install the subframe bolts, tightening them to the specified torque.

9   Attach the stabilizer bar link to the strut bracket (if it was completely removed) and the bar. Tighten the nuts securely.

10   Install the wheels and lug nuts. Lower the vehicle and tighten the nuts to the specified torque.

3   Balljoints — check and replacement

The balljoints on this vehicle are not replaceable separately. The entire control arm must be replaced if the balljoints are worn out. Refer to

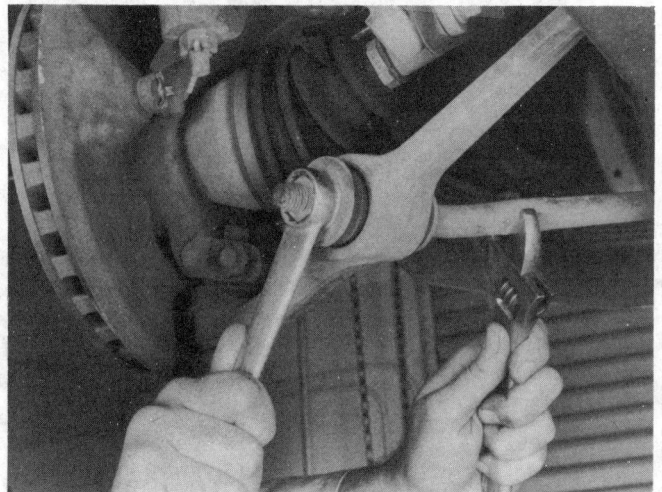

4.2   Place a wrench on the flats of the tension strut to
prevent it from turning while loosening the nut

the *Steering and suspension check* in Chapter 1 for the checking procedure. Refer to Section 5 in this Chapter for front control arm removal and installation.

4   Front tension strut and bushings — removal and installation

Refer to illustration 4.2

Warning: *Whenever any of the suspension or steering fasteners are loosened or removed they must be replaced with new ones — discard the originals and don't reuse them. They must be replaced with new ones of the same part number or of original equipment quality and design. Torque specifications must be followed for proper reassembly and component retention.*

1   Loosen the wheel lug nuts on the side that is to be dismantled. Raise the vehicle and support it securely on jackstands. Remove the wheel.

2   Remove the tension strut-to-control arm nut and dished washer **(see illustration)**. Notice how the washer is installed — it must be reinstalled with the dished portion curling away from the bushing.

3   Remove the tension strut-to-subframe nut.

4   Remove the control arm to subframe nut and bolt (see Section 5).

5   Pull outward on the strut/shock absorber assembly to separate the control arm from the subframe, then move the assembly to the rear just far enough to slip the control arm off the tension strut. **Caution:** *Be careful not to pull the strut/shock assembly too far out or to the*

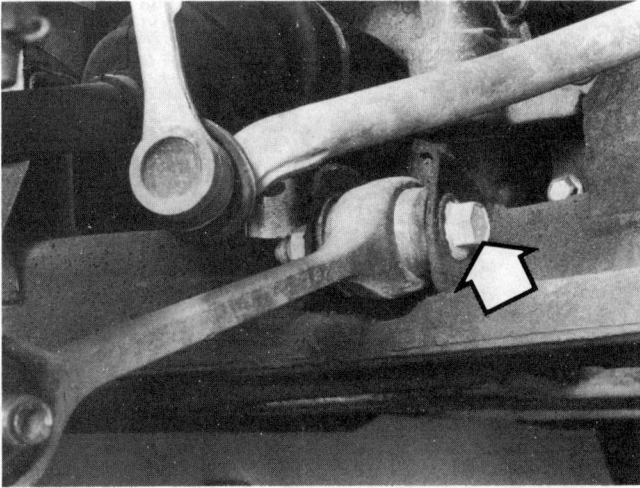

5.3   The control arm is attached to the subframe by a
large pivot bolt (arrow) — before tightening this bolt, make
sure the control arm is at a normal ride height angle

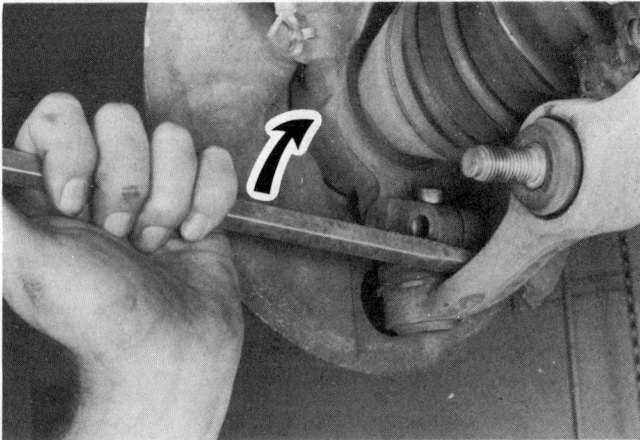

5.5   Pry the balljoint stud out of the steering knuckle

5.4   Remove the balljoint pinch bolt (arrow) from the steering
knuckle — a punch may be used to drive the bolt out

3   Remove the bolt and nut from the inner control arm pivot (see
illustration).
4   Remove the balljoint pinch bolt and nut from the steering knuckle
(see illustration). Spread the joint slightly with a screwdriver or pry bar.
5   Pry the control arm down to separate it from the steering knuckle
(see illustration).
6   Pull the control arm off the tension strut and remove it from the
vehicle.

Inspection

7   Check the control arm for distortion and the bushings for wear,
damage and deterioration. Replace a damaged or bent control arm with
a new one. If the inner pivot bushing or tension strut bushings are worn,
take the control arm assembly to a dealer service department or a repair
shop, as special tools are required to replace them. If the balljoint is
worn or damaged, the control arm must be replaced.

Installation

8   Place the control arm balljoint stud into the steering knuckle. Note
that the notch in the balljoint stud must be aligned with the hole in
the knuckle before the pinch bolt is inserted. Using a new pinch bolt
and nut, insert the bolt from the front of the steering knuckle and tighten
the new nut to the specified torque.
9   Push the stabilizer bar spacer into the rubber insulator in the control
arm from the front side. Swing the control arm into position over the
tension strut end.
10 Install the control arm pivot bolt and tighten the nut to the specified
torque.
11 Install the tension strut-to-control arm washer and nut (with the
dished portion of the washer facing away from the rubber bushing).
Tighten the nut to the specified torque.
12 Install the wheel and lug nuts, lower the vehicle and tighten the
lug nuts to the specified torque.

rear, as damage to the driveaxle inner CV joint may occur.
6   Pull the tension strut out of the subframe, noting how the washers
and bushings are installed. Inspect the bushings for hardness and cracking, replacing them if necessary.
7   If the tension strut bushings in the control arm are in need of
replacement, refer to Section 5 for the control arm removal procedure,
then take the control arm to a Ford dealer service department or an
automotive machine shop to have the new bushings installed.
8   Installation is the reverse of the removal procedure.. Be sure to
tighten all of the fasteners to the specified torque.

5   Front control arm — removal, inspection and installation

Refer to illustrations 5.3, 5.4 and 5.5

Warning: *Whenever any of the suspension or steering fasteners are
loosened or removed they must be replaced with new ones — discard
the originals and don't reuse them. They must be replaced with new
ones of the same part number or of original equipment quality and
design. Torque specifications must be followed for proper reassembly
and component retention.*

Removal

1   Loosen the wheel lug nuts on the side to be dismantled, raise the
front of the vehicle, support it securely on jackstands and remove the
wheel.
2   Remove the tension strut-to-control arm nut and dished washer
(see illustration 4.2).

6   Front strut/shock absorber and coil spring assembly — removal and installation

Refer to illustration 6.2

Warning: *Whenever any of the suspension or steering fasteners are
loosened or removed they must be replaced with new ones — discard
the originals and don't reuse them. They must be replaced with new
ones of the same part number or of original equipment quality and
design. Torque specifications must be followed for proper reassembly
and component retention.*

Removal

1   Loosen the wheel lug nuts. Raise the vehicle and support it securely
on jackstands, then remove the front wheel.
2   Loosen, but do not remove the three strut upper mounting nuts

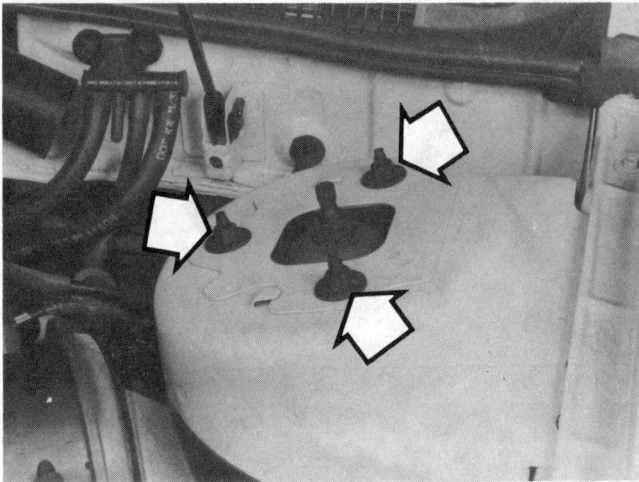

6.2   The strut upper mounting nuts (arrows) are on top of
the shock tower in the engine compartment

7.3   Install a spring compressor and compress the spring
until there is no pressure being exerted on the bearing and
seat assembly

from the shock tower (see illustration).
3   Remove the steering knuckle following the procedure described
in Section 8.
4   Disconnect the stablizer bar link from the bracket on the strut (see
illustration 2.2).
5   Remove the three upper strut mounting nuts from the shock tower
while supporting the strut/spring assembly so it doesn't fall (see illustration 6.2).
6   Carefully guide the strut and spring assembly out of the wheel well.
If the strut/shock absorber assembly is to be replaced, go on to Section 7 and remove the coil spring.

Installation

7   To install the strut, place it in position with the studs extending
up through the shock tower. Install the nuts and tighten them finger
tight.
8   Install the steering knuckle, tightening all fasteners to the specified
torque.
9   Connect the stabilizer bar link to the strut assembly, install the nut
and tighten it securely.
10 Tighten the three upper strut-to-shock tower mounting nuts to the
specified torque.
11 Install the wheel and lower the vehicle. Tighten the lug nuts to
the specified torque.

7   Front strut/shock absorber assembly — replacement

Refer to illustrations 7.3, 7.4, 7.5 and 7.6

1   If the struts exhibit the telltale signs of wear (leaking fluid, loss
of dampening capability) explore all options before beginning any work.
The strut/shock absorber assemblies are not serviceable and must be
replaced if a problem develops. However, strut assemblies complete
with springs may be available on an exchange basis, which eliminates
much time and work. Whichever route you choose to take, check on
the cost and availability of parts before disassembling the vehicle.
Warning: *Disassembling a strut is dangerous — be very careful and
follow all instructions or serious injury could result. Use only a high
quality spring compressor and carefully follow the manufacturer's instructions furnished with the tool. After removing the coil spring from
the strut assembly, set it aside in a safe, isolated area (a steel cabinet
is preferred).*
2   Remove the strut and spring assembly following the procedure
described in Section 6. Mount the strut assembly in a vise with the
jaws of the vise clamping onto the stabilizer bar link bracket.
3   Following the tool manufacturer's instructions, install the spring
compressor (which can be obtained at most auto parts stores or equipment yards on a daily rental basis) on the spring and compress it sufficiently to relieve all pressure from the spring seat (see illustration).

7.4   After the spring has been compressed, remove the
damper shaft nut — use a socket and a ratchet or breaker
bar to keep the damper shaft from turning

7.5   Remove the bearing and seat assembly

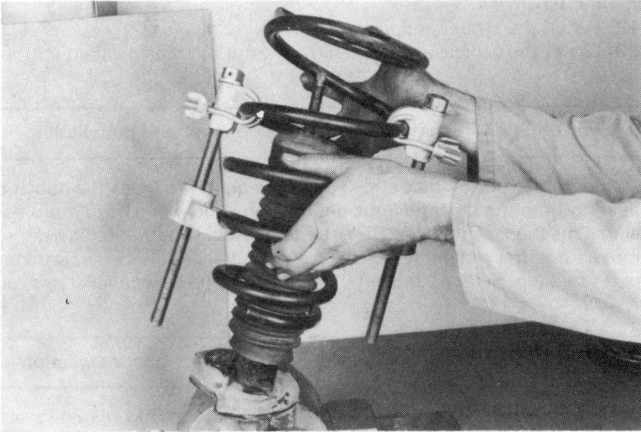

7.6 Remove the compressed spring assembly — use extreme care when handling the spring

8.3 Loosen the strut-to-knuckle pinch bolt (arrow)

This can be verified by wiggling the spring.

4   Loosen the damper shaft nut while using a socket wrench on the shaft hex to prevent it from turning **(see illustration)**. Remove the nut and upper concave washer.

5   Lift the bearing and seat assembly and upper mount off of the damper shaft **(see illustration)**. Inspect the bearing in the spring seat for smooth operation and replace it if necessary.

6   Carefully remove the compressed spring assembly and set it in a safe place, such as inside a steel cabinet **(see illustration)**. **Warning:** *Never place your head near the end of the spring!*

7   Slide the dust boot, washer and the rubber jounce bumper off the damper shaft.

8   Assemble the strut beginning with the jounce bumper, dust boot, washer and spring, then the spring seat and bearing cap top mount assembly. Note that the larger concave washer is installed below the mount.

9   Install the damper shaft nut and tighten it to the specified torque.

10 Install the strut and spring assembly on the vehicle as outlined in Section 6.

---

8   Steering knuckle and hub assembly — removal and installation

Refer to illustrations 8.3, 8.8, 8.9 and 8.10

Warning: *Whenever any of the suspension or steering fasteners are loosened or removed they must be replaced with new ones — discard the originals and don't reuse them. They must be replaced with new ones of the same part number or of original equipment quality and design. Torque specifications must be followed for proper reassembly and component retention. Dust created by the brake system contains*

asbestos, which is harmful to your health. Never blow it out with compressed air and don't inhale any of it. Do not, under any circumstances, use petroleum-based solvents to clean brake parts. Use brake cleaner or denatured alcohol only.

Note: *This procedure requires a special puller and adapters to install the driveaxle in the hub. Refer to Chapter 8 and read the driveaxle removal and installation procedure carefully before beginning this operation, to decide whether or not you want to undertake a job of this nature. Included in Chapter 8 are instructions to fabricate an alternative to the special Ford tool.*

Removal

1   Loosen the wheel lug nuts, raise the vehicle and support it securely on jackstands. Remove the wheel.

2   Remove the brake caliper and support it with a piece of wire as described in Chapter 9. Separate the brake disc from the hub.

3   Loosen, but do not remove the strut-to-steering knuckle pinch bolt **(see illustration)**.

4   Separate the tie-rod from the steering knuckle arm as outlined in Section 29.

5   Remove the balljoint pinch bolt and nut from the steering knuckle **(see illustration 5.4)**. Using a large pry bar, pry the balljoint stud out of the steering knuckle **(see illustration 5.5)**.

6   Loosen but do not remove the upper strut-to-shock tower nuts.

7   Push the driveaxle out of the hub as described in Chapter 8. Support the driveaxle with a piece of wire.

8   Mark the relationship of the strut to the steering knuckle **(see illustration)**. This will simplify reassembly.

9   Remove the strut-to-steering knuckle pinch bolt. Apply penetrating oil to the strut-to-knuckle joint. Spread the pinch joint slightly with a screwdriver or pry bar **(see illustration)**.

8.8 Mark the relationship of the strut to the steering knuckle

8.9 Spread the pinch joint slightly with a screwdriver

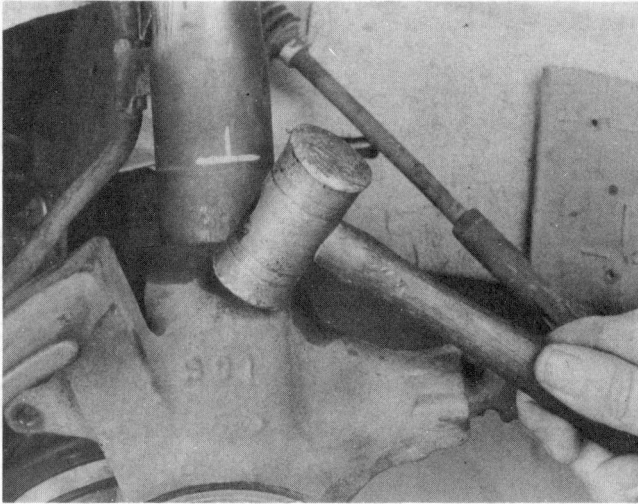

8.10 If the steering knuckle won't easily slide off the strut, tap on it with a brass, lead or shot-filled hammer — be careful not to hit the strut

10 Wiggle the knuckle and hub assembly off the strut. If it is stuck, gently tap the assembly off the strut with a brass, lead or shot-filled hammer, supporting it with your other hand to prevent it from falling when it comes off the strut **(see illustration)**.

Installation

11 Position the knuckle and hub assembly on the end of the strut, aligning the blade on the strut with the pinch joint in the knuckle. The previously applied alignment marks can be used to accomplish this.
12 Install a new strut-to-steering knuckle pinch bolt. Don't tighten it at this time.
13 Install the driveaxle in the hub (refer to Chapter 8).
14 Pull down on the control arm and insert the balljoint stud into the steering knuckle. Note that the notch in the balljoint stud must be aligned with the hole in the knuckle before the pinch bolt is inserted. Install a new pinch bolt from the front and tighten the new nut to the specified torque.
15 Tighten the strut-to-knuckle pinch bolt to the specified torque.
16 Tighten the upper strut-to-shock tower nuts to the specified torque.
17 Attach the tie-rod to the steering knuckle arm as described in Section 29.
18 Place the brake disc on the hub and install the caliper as outlined

in Chapter 9.
19 Install the wheel and lug nuts.
20 Lower the vehicle and tighten the lug nuts to the specified torque.

9 Front hub and bearing assembly — removal and installation

Due to the special tools and expertise required to press the hub and bearing from the steering knuckle, this job should be left to a professional mechanic. However, the steering knuckle and hub may be removed and the assembly taken to a local dealer service department or repair shop. Refer to Section 8 for steering knuckle and hub removal.

10 Rear stabilizer bar and bushings — removal and installation

Warning: *Whenever any of the suspension or steering fasteners are loosened or removed they must be replaced with new ones — discard the originals and don't reuse them. They must be replaced with new ones of the same part number or of originmal equipment quality and design. Torque specifications must be followed for proper reassembly and component retention.*

1 Loosen the rear wheel lug nuts, raise the rear of the vehicle and support it securely on jackstands. Block the front wheels and remove the rear wheels.

Sedan models

Refer to illustrations 10.2 and 10.3

2 Remove the stabilizer bar link lower nuts, washers and bushings **(see illustration)**.
3 Unbolt the stabilizer bar brackets from the floorpan **(see illustration)**. Remove the bar from the vehicle.
4 Inspect the bracket and link bushings for wear, hardness and cracking and replace them if necessary. Be sure to inspect the link upper bushings as well.
5 Installation is the reverse of the removal procedure.

Wagon models

Refer to illustration 10.6

6 Remove the stabilizer bar bracket-to-lower control arm bolts and nuts **(see illustration)**.
7 Remove the stabilizer bar link-to-body bracket bolts and nuts and remove the bar from the vehicle.
8 Slide the bushings and link assemblies off the bar and inspect them for deterioration. Replace any worn-out parts.
9 Installation is the reverse of the removal procedure.

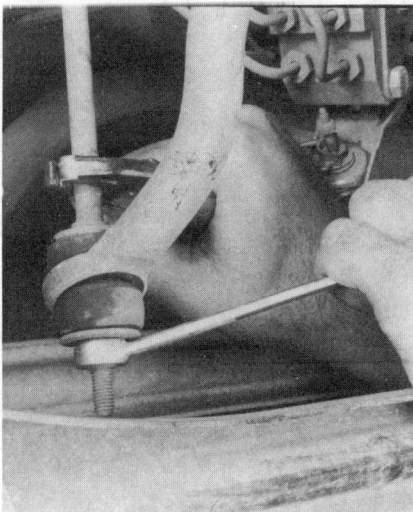

10.2 Hold the stabilizer bar link with a pair of locking pliers to prevent it from turning while removing the nut

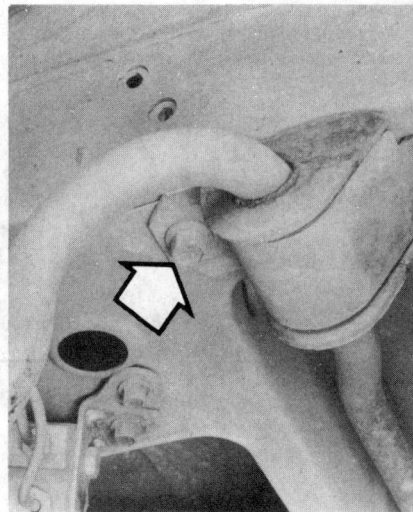

10.3 Remove the bracket bolt (arrow) and swing the stabilizer bar down to disengage the bracket from the frame

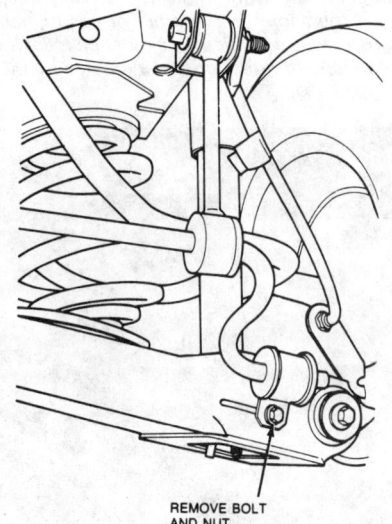

REMOVE BOLT AND NUT

10.6 Rear stabilizer bar mounting details — wagon models

11 Rear strut/shock absorber and coil spring assembly (sedan) — removal and installation

Refer to illustrations 11.1, 11.5, 11.6, 11.11 and 11.14

Warning: *Whenever any of the suspension or steering fasteners are loosened or removed they must be replaced with new ones — discard the originals and don't reuse them. They must be replaced with new ones of the same part number or of original equipment quality and design. Torque specifications must be followed for proper reassembly and component retention.*

Removal

1   Open the luggage compartment and remove the side trim panel from the appropriate side. Loosen, but do not remove the three strut-to-shock tower nuts **(see illustration)**.
2   Loosen the wheel lug nuts, raise the rear of the vehicle and support it securely on jackstands. Block the front wheels and remove the rear wheel.
3   Disconnect the stabilizer bar from the stabilizer bar link, then unbolt the bushing bracket from the floorpan (Section 10).
4   Remove the brake pressure differential control valve lower mounting bracket from the control arm by removing the bolt (see Chapter 9).
5   Unbolt the brake hose from the bracket on the strut **(see illustration)**.
6   To provide additional slack in the brake line, remove the bolt securing the line to the frame **(see illustration)**.
7   Loosen, but do not remove the spindle-to-strut pinch bolt.
8   Remove the tension strut-to-spindle nut, washer and bushing (Section 14) then move the strut/spindle assembly to the rear far enough to free the tension strut from the spindle.
9   Remove the spindle-to-strut pinch bolt.
10 Using a screwdriver, spread the pinch joint slightly to loosen the bond between the spindle and strut **(see illustration 8.9)**.
11 Gently tap the spindle off the strut, using a hammer and punch **(see illustration)**. If it is stubborn, spray some penetrating oil where the spindle and strut meet. Be careful not to bend or kink the brake line.
12 Remove the three upper mounting nuts from inside the luggage compartment, separate the strut from the spindle and remove the strut assembly from the vehicle.

Installation

13 Guide the strut/shock absorber and coil spring assembly up into the wheel well, inserting the three mounting studs into the holes in the shock tower. Brace the bottom of the strut on the spindle so it doesn't fall, then install the three mounting nuts finger tight.
14 Push the spindle down, align the the blade on the back side of the strut with the pinch joint slot on the spindle and insert the strut into

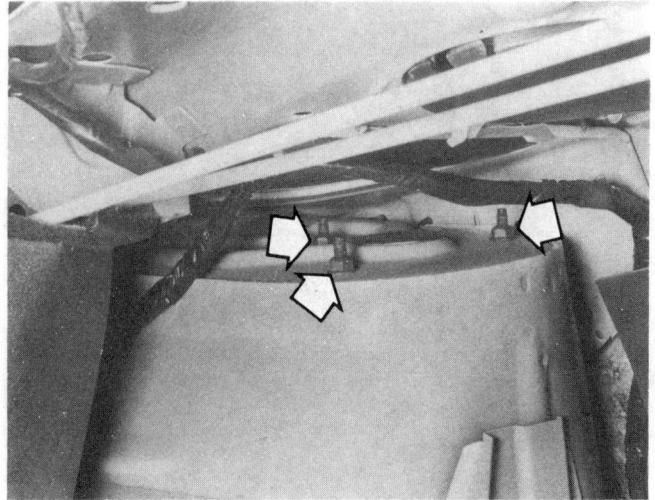

11.1   The three strut-to-shock tower mounting nuts can only be seen after the luggage compartment side trim panel is removed

11.5   The brake hose is fastened to the strut just behind the brake backing plate

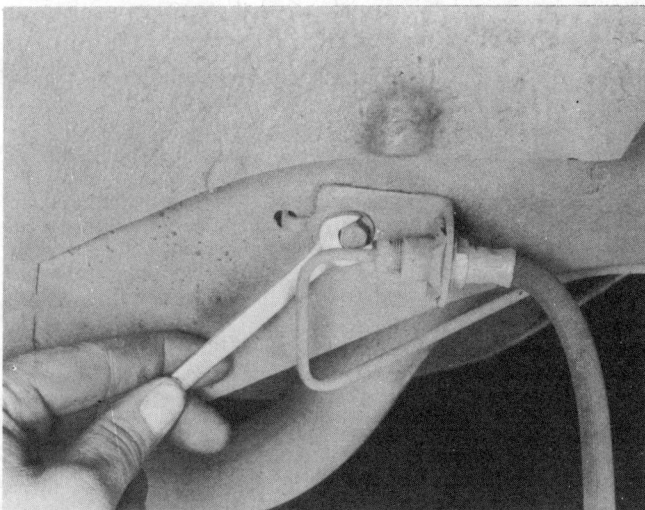

11.6   Unbolt the brake line bracket from the frame to provide additional slack in the line

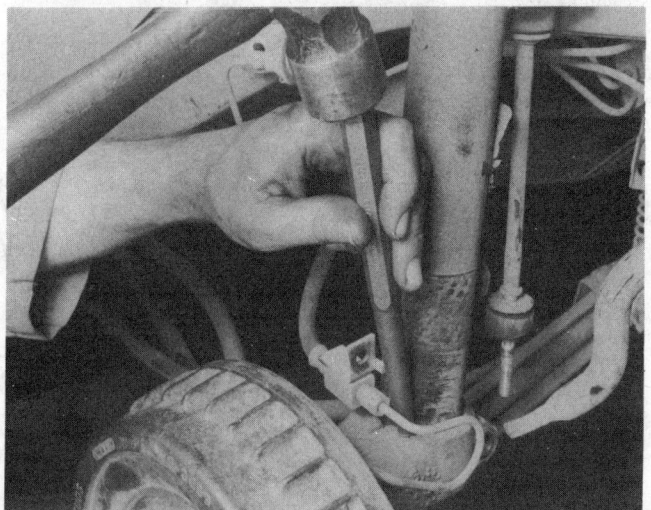

11.11   Tap the spindle down to free it from the strut

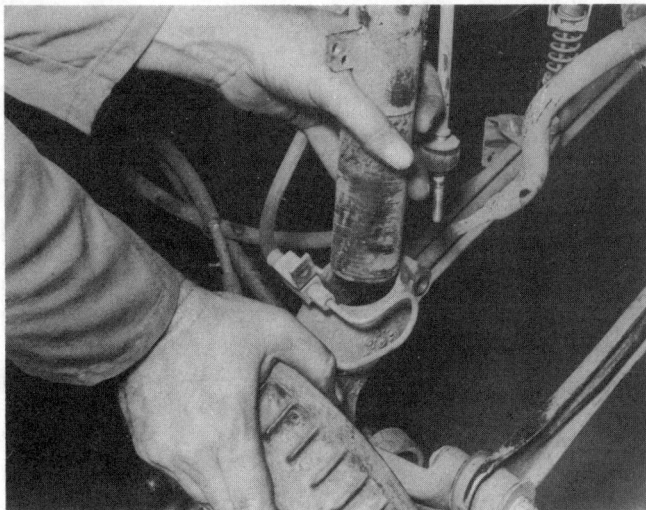

11.14   Push down on the spindle and insert the strut into the pinch joint — a little penetrating oil on the strut tube will help

the spindle (see illustration). Install the pinch bolt, but don't tighten it at this time.
15   Pull the strut to the rear and insert the tension strut into the spindle. Install the bushing, washer and nut, tightening it to the specified torque.
16   Tighten the spindle-to-strut pinch bolt to the specified torque.
17   Connect the brake line bracket to the frame, tightening the bolt securely.
18   Connect the other brake hose bracket to the mounting bracket on the strut and tighten the bolt securely.
19   Insert the stabilizer bar link into the bar, position the stabilizer bar bracket on the floorpan and install the bolt, tightening it securely.
20   Install the stabilizer bar link bushing, washer and nut. Tighten the nut securely.
21   Install the wheel and lug nuts then lower the vehicle. Tighten the nuts to the specified torque.
22   Tighten the three upper mounting nuts to the specified torque and install the luggage compartment side trim panel.

12   Rear strut/shock absorber assembly (sedan) — replacement

Refer to Section 7 for the rear strut/shock absorber assembly replacement procedure, as it is identical to the procedure for the front strut assembly.

13   Rear control arms (sedan) — removal and installation

Refer to illustrations 13.2, 13.3, 13.6a and 13.6b
Warning: *Whenever any of the suspension or steering fasteners are loosened or removed they must be replaced with new ones — discard the originals and don't reuse them. They must be replaced with new ones of the same part number or of original equipment quality and design. Torque specifications must be followed for proper reassembly and component retention.*

Removal

1   Loosen the wheel lug nuts, raise the rear of the vehicle and support it securely on jackstands. Block the front wheels and remove the rear wheel.
2   Remove the control arm-to-spindle nut and push the bolt in as far as possible (see illustration).
3   Mark the relationship of the toe adjuster wheel to the control arm inner mounting bracket (see illustration). This will ensure that the toe adjustment will be returned to the same setting.
4   Remove the inner mounting bolt and nut while supporting the con-

13.2   Remove the control arm-to-spindle nut(s) and push the bolt(s) in as far as possible, then slide the control arm(s) off the bolt(s) — the bolt(s) can't be removed unless the strut is partially removed from the spindle

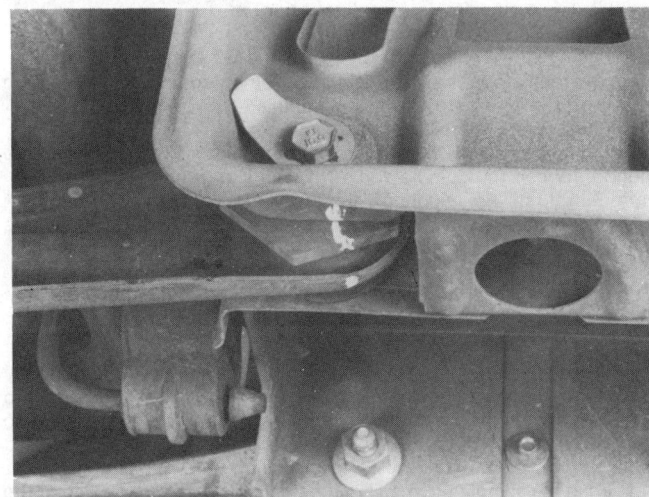

13.3   Mark the relationship of the toe adjuster wheel to the inner mounting bracket if one of the rear control arms must be removed

trol arm. Be careful — the edges on the stamped control arms are very sharp.
5   Remove the control arm from the vehicle.

Installation

6   If installing either left side control arm or the front right side control arm, position the arm with the offset facing up and the flanged side toward the rear, then install the new inner mounting bolt finger tight. If the right side rear control arm is being installed, the offsets must also face up, but the flanged side must face the front of the vehicle (see illustrations).
7   Insert a new control arm-to-spindle bolt through the control arm and spindle from the inside. Install a new nut and washer and tighten the nut hand tight.
8   Place a jack under the spindle and raise it to simulate normal ride height.
9   Check to see that the alignment marks on the toe adjuster wheel are lined up properly, then tighten the inner mounting bolt to the specified torque.
10   Tighten the outer nut to the specified torque.
11   Install the wheel and lug nuts, then lower the vehicle to the ground.

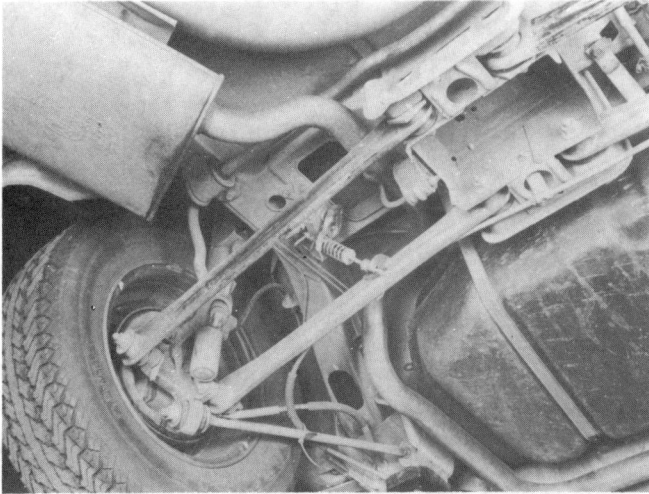

13.6a   The flanged side (sharp edge) of the control arms must face to the rear and the offsets must face up when installing the left side control arms

13.6b   When installing the right side control arms, the offsets must also face up, but the flanges must face each other

14.3   Remove the tension strut-to-spindle nut — a large wrench can be used to prevent the strut from turning

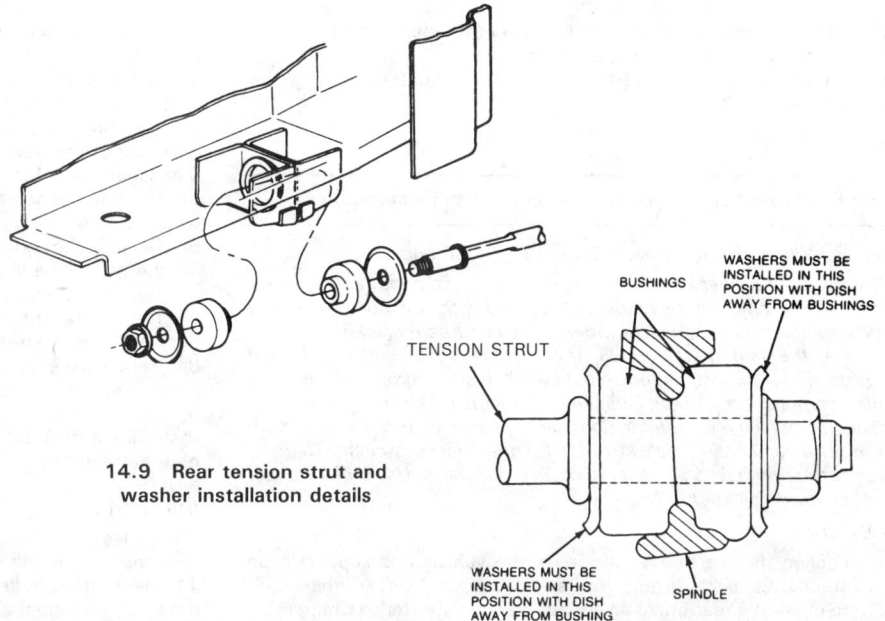

14.9   Rear tension strut and washer installation details

Tighten the lug nuts to the specified torque.
12 Have the rear wheel alignment checked by a dealer service department or an alignment shop.

14   Rear tension strut and bushings (sedan) — removal and installation

Refer to illustrations 14.3 and 14.9

Warning: *Whenever any of the suspension or steering fasteners are loosened or removed they must be replaced with new ones — discard the originals and don't reuse them. They must be replaced with new ones of the same part number or of original equipment quality and design. Torque specifications must be followed for proper reassembly and component retention.*

Removal

1   From inside the trunk, loosen but don't remove the upper strut-to-shock tower nuts **(see illustration 11.1)**.
2   Loosen the wheel lug nuts, raise the vehicle and support it securely on jackstands. Block the front wheels and remove the rear wheel.
3   Remove the large tension strut-to-spindle nut **(see illustration)**. Use a wrench on the flat area of the tension strut to prevent it from turning. Note the washer and bushing arrangement.
4   Remove the large tension strut-to-body nut, washer and bushing. Again, keep the strut from turning by holding it with a wrench on the flat portion. Keep the front bushings separate from the rear bushings — they are different (the rear bushings have indentations in them).
5   Have an assistant pull the spindle/strut assembly toward the rear of the vehicle. At the same time, pull the tension strut from the front mount and remove it from the vehicle.

Installation

6   Check the rubber bushings for cracks and wear. Replace them if necessary.
7   Place the concave washers and inner bushings on the ends of the tension strut, with the dished portion of each washer toward the center.
8   Insert the tension strut (with inner washers and bushings in place) into the spindle. Have an assistant pull the spindle/strut assembly back and insert the front of the tension strut into the body mount.
9   Install the outer bushings, washers and new nuts on the ends of the tension strut, with the dished portions of the washers facing away from the bushings **(see illustration)**. Raise the spindle with a floor jack to simulate normal ride height, then tighten the nuts to the specified torque.

15.4a   The brake backing plate is attached to the spindle by four bolts

15.4b   Hang the brake assembly from the spring with a piece of wire — don't let it hang by the brake hose!

10 Install the wheel and lug nuts and lower the vehicle to the ground. Tighten the lug nuts to the specified torque.

11 Tighten the upper strut-to-shock tower mounting nuts to the specified torque.

15   Rear wheel spindle (sedan) — removal and installation

Refer to illustrations 15.4a, 15.4b, 15.5, 15.6 and 15.9

Warning: *Whenever any of the suspension or steering fasteners are loosened or removed they must be replaced with new ones — discard the originals and don't reuse them. They must be replaced with new ones of the same part number or of original equipment quality and design. Torque specifications must be followed for proper reassembly and component retention. Dust created by the brake system contains asbestos, which is harmful to your health. Never blow it out with compressed air and don't inhale any of it. Do not, under any circumstances, use petroleum-based solvents to clean brake parts. Use brake cleaner or denatured alcohol only.*

Removal

1   Loosen the wheel lug nuts, raise the vehicle and support it on jackstands. Block the front wheels and remove the rear wheel.

2   Remove the rear brake drum/hub assembly (refer to Chapter 9).

3   Unbolt the brake hose support bracket from the strut (**see illustration 11.5**).

4   Remove the four bolts that secure the brake backing plate to the spindle. Detach the backing plate and rear brake assembly from the spindle and suspend it with a piece of wire from the spring. It isn't necessary to remove the parking brake cable from the backing plate (**see illustrations**).

5   Loosen, but don't remove the spindle-to-strut pinch bolt (**see illustration**).

6   Remove the control arm-to-spindle nuts, then slide the control arms off the bolts (**see illustration**).

7   Remove the tension strut rear nut. Use a wrench on the flats of the rod to prevent it from turning. Remove the washer and rubber bushing (**see illustration 14.3**).

8   Remove the previously loosened spindle-to-strut pinch bolt while supporting the spindle so it doesn't fall.

9   Pull the spindle to the rear far enough to clear the tension strut, then slide it off the strut (**see illustration**). The control arm bolts can now be replaced.

Installation

10 Inspect the tension strut bushings for cracks, deformation and signs of wear. Replace them if necessary.

11 Place the spindle on the tension strut end, then push it up onto the strut, aligning the gap in the pinch joint with the blade on the strut.

15.5   Loosen the strut-to-knuckle pinch bolt (arrow)

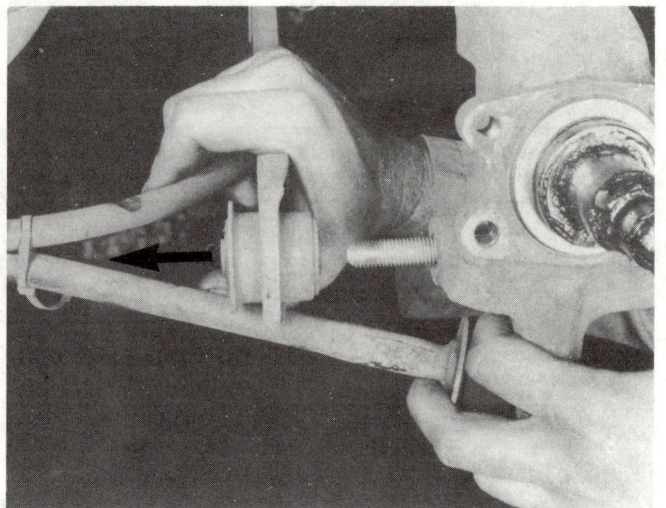

15.6   Push the control arm off the mounting bolt

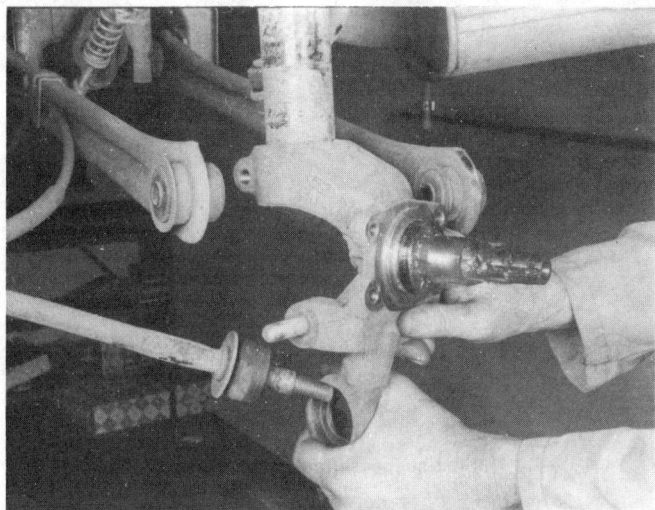

15.9 The spindle can be removed from the strut/shock absorber once it has been disconnected from the tension strut

Insert a new spindle-to-strut pinch bolt and tighten it finger tight.
12 Install the outer tension strut bushing, washer and a new nut. Don't tighten the nut at this time.
13 Install the control arms onto the spindle bolts. Tighten the nuts by hand.
14 Place a jack under the spindle and raise it to simulate normal ride height.
15 Tighten the spindle-to-strut bolt to the specified torque.
16 Tighten the large tension strut nut to the specified torque.
17 Tighten the control arm nuts to the specified torque.
18 Attach the brake backing plate to the spindle and tighten the four bolts securely.
19 Bolt the brake hose bracket to the strut. Be careful not to damage the line when bending it back into place.
20 Install the rear brake drum/hub assembly (Chapter 9).
21 Install the wheel and lug nuts.
22 Lower the vehicle and tighten the lug nuts to the specified torque.

16 Rear shock absorbers (wagon) — removal and installation

Refer to illustrations 16.2 and 16.4
Removal
1 Remove the rear compartment access panels.
2 Loosen, but do not remove the shock absorber upper mounting nut **(see illustration)**. If it is rusted or extremely tight, apply some penetrating oil and allow it to soak in for a few minutes. It may also be necessary to clamp a pair of locking pliers onto the damper shaft to prevent it from turning.
3 Loosen the wheel lug nuts, raise the rear of the vehicle and support it securely on jackstands. Block the front wheels and remove the rear wheel.
4 Position a floor jack under the lower control arm and raise it slightly (just enough to support some of the weight). Remove the two shock absorber lower mounting nuts from the underside of the lower control arm **(see illustration)**.
5 Remove the shock absorber upper mounting nut and remove the shock from the vehicle.

Installation
6 Inspect the rubber bushings for hardness, cracks and other signs of general deterioration. Replace all worn out parts.
7 Place the concave washer and rubber bushing onto the damper shaft and guide the shock into place, inserting the damper shaft into the hole in the frame. Compress the shock and position the lower end on the lower control arm. Install the nuts, tightening them securely.
8 Install the upper rubber bushing, washer and nut. Tighten the nut

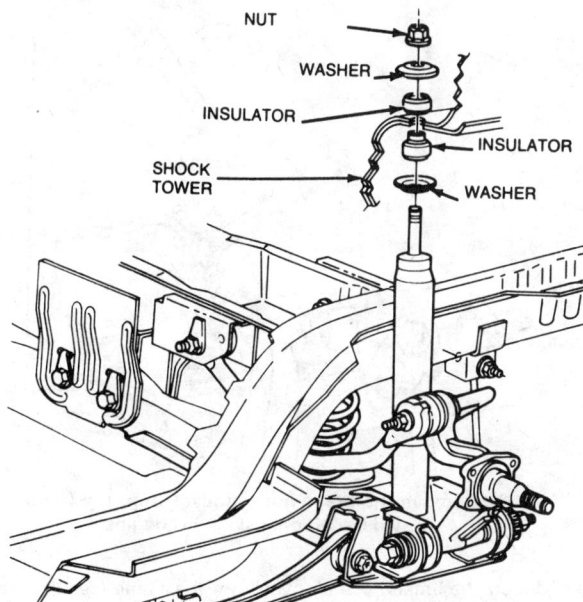

16.2 Rear shock absorber installation details (wagon)

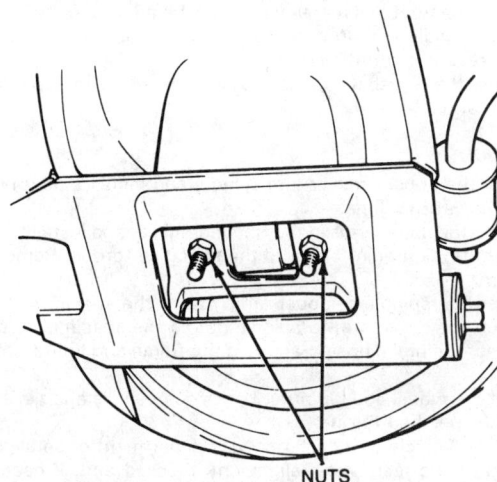

16.4 The shock absorber lower mounting nuts are located on the underside of the lower control arm (wagon)

securely.
9 Install the wheel and lug nuts. Lower the vehicle and tighten the nuts to the specified torque.

17 Rear suspension upper arms (wagon) — removal and installation

Refer to illustrations 17.3 and 17.4
Warning: *Whenever any of the suspension or steering fasteners are loosened or removed they must be replaced with new ones — discard the originals and don't reuse them. They must be replaced with new ones of the same part number or of original equipment quality and design. Torque specifications must be followed for proper reassembly and component retention.*
Removal
1 Loosen the wheel lug nuts, raise the rear of the vehicle and support it securely on jackstands. Block the front wheels and remove the rear wheel.
2 Position a floor jack under the lower suspension arm and raise it to simulate normal ride height.

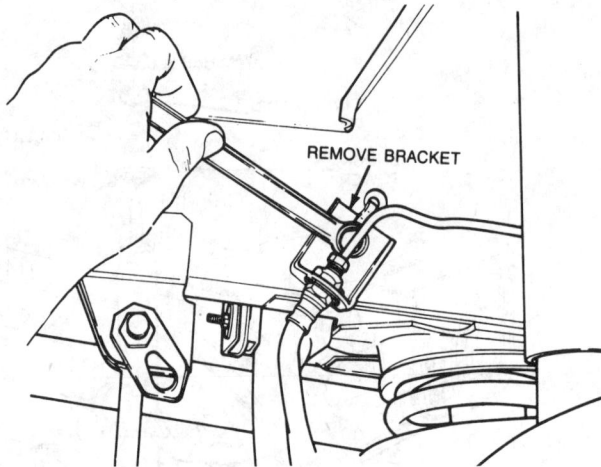

17.3   Remove the brake hose bracket from the frame to provide additional slack in the line

3   Unbolt the brake hose bracket from the frame (see illustration).
4   Loosen, but do not remove the upper arm-to spindle nut (see illustration).
5   Loosen, but do not remove the lower arm-to-spindle nut.
6   Remove the front and rear upper arm-to-frame pivot bolts and nuts.
7   Tilt the spindle and drum brake assembly out and wire it to the frame to prevent it from falling.
8   Remove the nut that retains the upper arms to the spindle and detach the arms.

Installation

9   Attach the upper arms to the spindle and install a new nut. Do not tighten it at this time.
10   Position the upper arms in the frame brackets and install the pivot bolts and nuts, tightening them to the specified torque. Remove the safety wire.
11   Tighten the spindle-to-upper arms nut to the specified torque.
12   Tighten the lower arm-to-spindle nut to the specified torque.
13   Connect the brake hose bracket to the frame and tighten the bolt securely.
14   Install the wheel and lug nuts. Lower the vehicle and tighten the nuts to the specified torque.
15   Drive the vehicle to a dealer service department or an alignment shop to have the rear wheel alignment checked and, if necessary, adjusted.

18   Rear coil spring (wagon) — removal and installation

Refer to illustration 18.9
Warning: *Whenever any of the suspension or steering fasteners are loosened or removed they must be replaced with new ones — discard the originals and don't reuse them. They must be replaced with new ones of the same part number or of original equipment quality and design. Torque specifications must be followed for proper reassembly and component retention.*

Removal

1   Loosen the wheel lug nuts, raise the rear of the vehicle and support it securely on jackstands. Block the front wheels and remove the rear wheel.
2   Position a floor jack under the outer end of the suspension lower arm and raise it to simulate normal ride height.
3   Unbolt the brake hose bracket from the frame (see illustration 17.3).
4   Unbolt the stabilizer bar bracket from the suspension lower arm (see Section 10).
5   Remove the shock absorber lower mounting nuts (see Section 16).
6   Remove the bolt securing the parking brake cable to the lower arm.
7   Remove the tension strut-to-lower arm bolt and nut (see Section 20).
8   Wire the upper arm and drum brake/spindle assembly to the frame

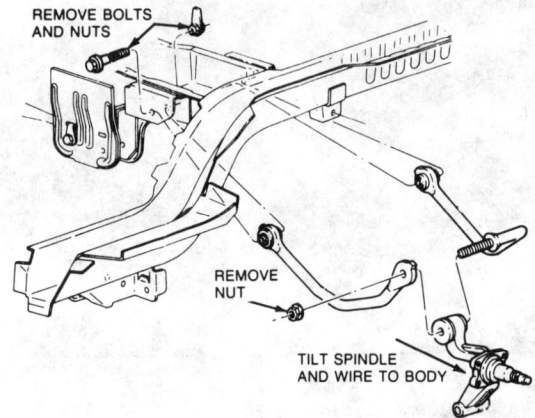

17.4   Upper suspension arm installation details

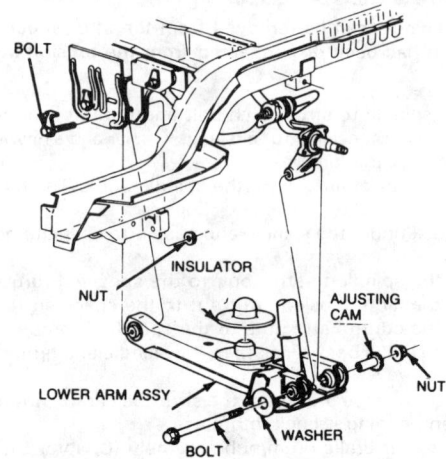

18.9   Suspension lower arm installation details (wagon)

to prevent it from dropping down.
9   Mark the relationship of the adjusting cam to the rear of the suspension lower arm. This will ensure correct rear wheel alignment after reassembly. Remove the lower arm-to-spindle nut, bolt, adjusting cam and washers (see illustration).
10   Slowly lower the floor jack until all of the spring tension is released, then remove the spring and lower insulator from the lower arm.

Installation

11   Inspect the spring insulators for damage and replace them if necessary. Check the spring for distortion and heavy nicks, which will warrant replacement. Push the spring seat into the lower arm.
12   Place the upper insulator on top of the coil spring and set the spring in the pocket in the lower arm.
13   Raise the lower arm into position while guiding the coil spring into the upper pocket in the frame.
14   Remove the wire holding the upper arm and spindle out of the way. Install the lower arm-to-spindle bolt, washers, adjusting cam and nut with the bolt head toward the front of the vehicle, but don't tighten it yet.
15   Install the tension strut, but do not tighten the bolts yet.
16   Install the shock absorber lower mounting nuts, tightening them securely.
17   Attach the stabilizer bar bracket to the lower arm and tighten the bolt securely.
18   Connect the parking brake cable bracket to the lower arm and tighten the bolt securely.
19   Position the brake line bracket on the frame and install the mounting bolt, tightening it securely.
20   Raise the lower arm to simulate normal ride height, then tighten all of the fasteners to the specified torque. **Note:** *Before tightening the*

lower arm-to-spindle nut and bolt, make sure the alignment marks on the adjusting cam and lower arm are lined up.

21 Install the wheel and lug nuts. Lower the vehicle and tighten the nuts to the specified torque.

22 Drive the vehicle to a dealer service department or an alignment shop to have the rear wheel alignment checked, and if necessary, adjusted.

19 Rear suspension lower arm (wagon) — removal and installation

Refer to illustration 19.3

Warning: *Whenever any of the suspension or steering fasteners are loosened or removed they must be replaced with new ones — discard the originals and don't reuse them. They must be replaced with new ones of the same part number or of original equipment quality and design. Torque specifications must be followed for proper reassembly and component retention.*

Removal

1 Loosen the wheel lug nuts, raise the rear of the vehicle and support it securely on jackstands. Block the front wheels and remove the rear wheel.

2 Following the procedure described in Section 18, remove the coil spring.

3 Remove the lower arm-to-frame nut and bolt and lower the arm from the vehicle **(see illustration)**.

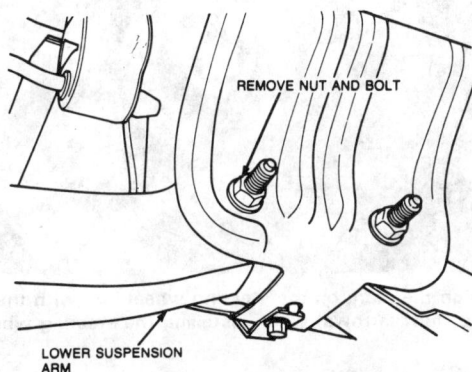

19.3 Remove the lower arm-to-frame pivot bolt and nut

Installation

4 Position the lower arm in the mounting bracket and install the bolt and nut, with the bolt head facing the front of the vehicle. Don't tighten the nut completely at this time.

5 Install the coil spring (Section 18).

6 With the lower arm still raised to simulate normal ride height, tighten the lower arm-to-frame nut and bolt to the specified torque.

7 Install the wheel and lug nuts and lower the vehicle. Tighten the nuts to the specified torque.

20 Rear tension strut (wagon) — removal and installation

Refer to illustration 20.2

Warning: *Whenever any of the suspension or steering fasteners are loosened or removed they must be replaced with new ones — discard the originals and don't reuse them. They must be replaced with new ones of the same part number or of original equipment quality and design. Torque specifications must be followed for proper reassembly and component retention.*

Removal

1 Loosen the wheel lug nuts, raise the rear of the vehicle and support it securely on jackstands. Block the front wheels and remove the rear wheel.

2 Place a floor jack under the lower arm and raise it to simulate normal

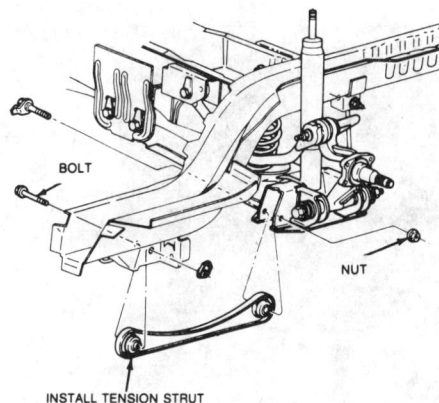

20.2 Tension strut installation details (wagon)

ride height. Remove the tension strut-to-lower arm nut and bolt **(see illustration)**.

3 Remove the tension strut-to-frame nut and bolt and remove the tension strut from the vehicle.

Installation

4 Position the tension strut in the frame bracket and install the bolt and nut, but don't tighten them at this time.

5 Swing the rear of the tension strut up into the lower arm and install the bolt and nut, tightening the nut to the specified torque.

6 Tighten the tension strut-to-frame bolt to the specified torque.

7 Install the wheel and lug nuts and lower the vehicle. Tighten the nuts to the specified torque.

8 If the tension strut has been replaced with a new part, it would be a good idea to drive the vehicle to an alignment shop to have the rear wheel alignment checked and, if necessary, adjusted.

21 Rear wheel spindle (wagon) — removal and installation

Warning: *Whenever any of the suspension or steering fasteners are loosened or removed they must be replaced with new ones — discard the originals and don't reuse them. They must be replaced with new ones of the same part number or of original equipment quality and design. Torque specifications must be followed for proper reassembly and component retention.*

Removal

1 Loosen the wheel lug nuts, raise the rear of the vehicle and support it securely on jackstands. Block the front wheels and remove the rear wheel.

2 Place a floor jack under the lower arm and raise it to simulate normal ride height.

3 Remove the brake drum. Remove the four brake backing plate bolts, lift the brake assembly off the spindle and hang it by a piece of wire **(see illustrations 15.4a and 15.4b)**.

4 Remove the pivot bolts and nuts retaining the suspension upper arms to the frame **(see illustration 17.4)**.

5 Mark the position of the adjusting cam to the rear of the suspension lower arm. This will ensure correct rear wheel alignment upon reassembly. Remove the lower arm-to-spindle nut, bolt, adjusting cam and washers **(see illustration 18.9)**.

6 Remove the spindle from the vehicle, along with the two suspension upper arms.

7 Remove the suspension arms-to-spindle nut and detach the arms from the spindle.

Installation

8 Attach the upper arms to the spindle and install the nut, but don't tighten it yet.

9 Position the spindle/upper arm assembly onto the lower arm. Install the lower arm-to-spindle bolt, washers, adjusting cam and nut, with the bolt head toward the front of the vehicle, but don't tighten it yet.

10 Install the pivot bolts through the upper arms and frame, then install the nuts, but do not tighten the bolts at this time.

11 Make sure the floor jack is supporting the suspension at approx-

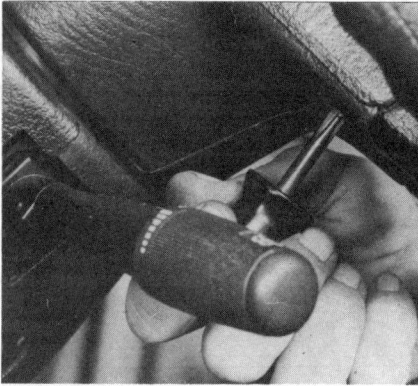

23.2   The horn pad is attached to the steering wheel by two screws

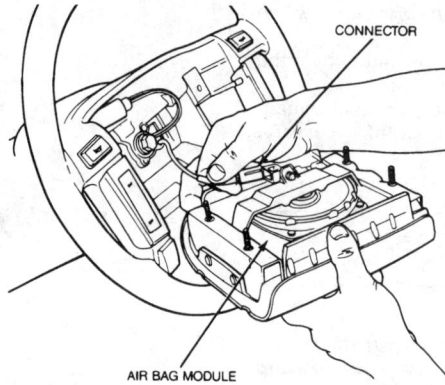

23.3   To remove the airbag from the steering wheel, remove the four retaining nuts, lift the module off the wheel and detach the air bag wire harness from the air bag module

23.4   Remove the steering wheel mounting nut/bolt

imately the normal ride height. Tighten the suspension upper arm pivot bolts to the specified torque.

12   Tighten the upper arm-to-spindle nuts to the specified torque.

13   Check to see that the alignment marks on the adjusting cam and lower arm are lined up, then tighten the lower arm-to-spindle nut to the specified torque.

14   Install the backing plate/brake shoe assembly to the spindle and tighten the four bolts to the specified torque.

15   This would be a good time to clean and repack the rear wheel bearings. Refer to Chapter 1.

16   Install the wheel and lug nuts. Lower the vehicle and tighten the nuts to the specified torque.

22   Steering system – general information

All models are equipped with power assisted rack-and-pinion steering. The steering gear is bolted to the subframe and operates the steering arms via tie-rods. The inner ends of the tie-rods are protected by rubber boots which should be inspected periodically for secure attachment, tears and leaking lubricant.

The power assist system consists of a belt-driven pump and associated lines and hoses. The power steering pump reservoir fluid level should be checked periodically (Chapter 1).

The steering wheel operates the steering shaft, which actuates the steering gear through universal joints and the intermediate shaft. Looseness in the steering can be caused by wear in the steering shaft universal joints, the steering gear, the tie-rod ends and loose retaining bolts.

23   Steering wheel – removal and installation

Refer to illustrations 23.2, 23.3, 23.4 and 23.6

Removal

1   Disconnect the cable from the negative battery terminal.

2   On pre-1990 vehicles, remove the two screws securing the horn pad to the steering wheel. Grasp the pad assembly at the top two corners and pull it straight back off the steering wheel **(see illustration)**. On 1990 models, remove the four airbag module retaining nuts and lift the module off the steering wheel.

3   On pre-1990 vehicles, unplug the wire harness connector and remove the horn pad. On 1990 models, unplug the airbag wire harness from the airbag module and remove the module **(see illustration)**. Unplug the cruise control wire harness from the steering wheel, if equipped.

4   Remove the steering wheel mounting nut (bolt on the 1988 models) **(see illustration)**.

5   Pull the steering wheel straight back off the steering shaft. A steering wheel puller is not required.

23.6   Align the mark on the steering wheel hub with the mark on the shaft (arrows) when installing the steering wheel

Installation

6   Align the index mark on the steering wheel hub with the mark on the shaft and slip the wheel onto the shaft **(see illustration)**. Install the mounting nut or bolt and tighten it to the specified torque.

7   Plug in the electrical connector and install the horn pad.

8   Connect the negative battery cable.

24   Intermediate shaft – removal and installation

Refer to illustrations 24.1a and 24.1b

Warning: *Whenever any of the suspension or steering fasteners are loosened or removed they must be replaced with new ones – discard the originals and don't reuse them. They must be replaced with new ones of the same part number or of original equipment quality and design. Torque specifications must be followed for proper reassembly and component retention.*

1   From under the dash, mark the relationship of the intermediate shaft to the steering column shaft. Remove the two nuts and the retainer that connect the intermediate shaft to the steering column shaft **(see illustrations)**.

2   Remove the three nuts holding the primary boot to the inner dash panel, then peel the boot back from the panel.

3   Raise the vehicle and support it securely on jackstands. From under the vehicle, push the secondary boot away from the steering gear and mark the relationship of the intermediate shaft to the steering gear input shaft, using white paint or a sharp scribe. Remove the intermediate shaft-to-steering gear input shaft pinch bolt and pry the

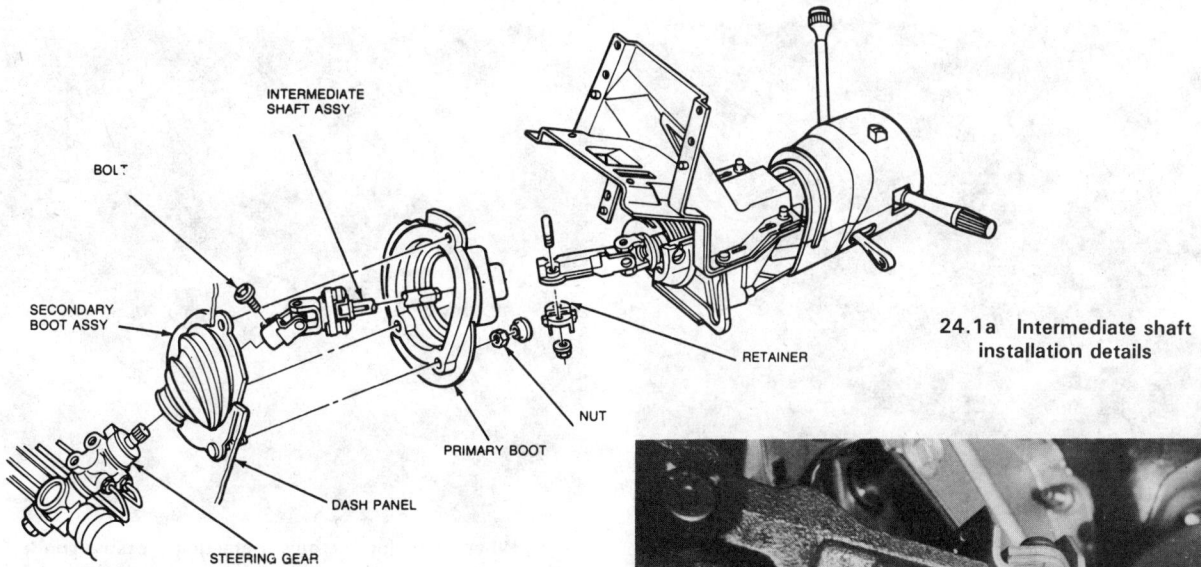

INTERMEDIATE
SHAFT ASSY

BOLT

SECONDARY
BOOT ASSY

RETAINER

NUT

PRIMARY BOOT

DASH PANEL

STEERING GEAR

**24.1a   Intermediate shaft
installation details**

intermediate shaft off the steering gear.
4   Remove the intermediate shaft from inside the vehicle.
5   Installation is the reverse of the removal procedure. Be sure to align the match marks on the shafts and tighten the pinch bolt and the two intermediate shaft-to-steering column shaft nuts to the specified torque.

25   Steering gear – removal and installation

Refer to illustration 25.9
Warning: *Whenever any of the suspension or steering fasteners are loosened or removed they must be replaced with new ones – discard the originals and don't reuse them. They must be replaced with new ones of the same part number or of original equipment quality and design. Torque specifications must be followed for proper reassembly and component retention.*

1   Disconnect the cable from the negative battery terminal.
2   Turn the ignition key to the Run position to unlock the steering wheel.
3   Remove the left side under-dash panel.
4   Remove the three nuts securing the steering column boot to the inside of the firewall. Pull back on the boot to expose the intermediate shaft.
5   Mark the intermediate shaft, the steering gear input shaft and the

24.1b   Remove the two nuts (arrows) and push out the retainer to disconnect the intermediate shaft from the steering column shaft

steering column shaft so they can be reassembled in the same relative positions. Remove the intermediate shaft (Section 24).
6.   Remove the heat shield from the subframe. Disconnect the pressure and return lines from the steering gear and allow the fluid to drain into a container.
7   Loosen the lug nuts on both front wheels. Raise the vehicle and support it securely on jackstands. Apply the parking brake and remove the front wheels.
8   Separate the tie-rod ends from the steering knuckle arms. Refer to Section 29.
9   Remove the two steering gear mounting bolts/nuts from under the subframe (**see illustration**).

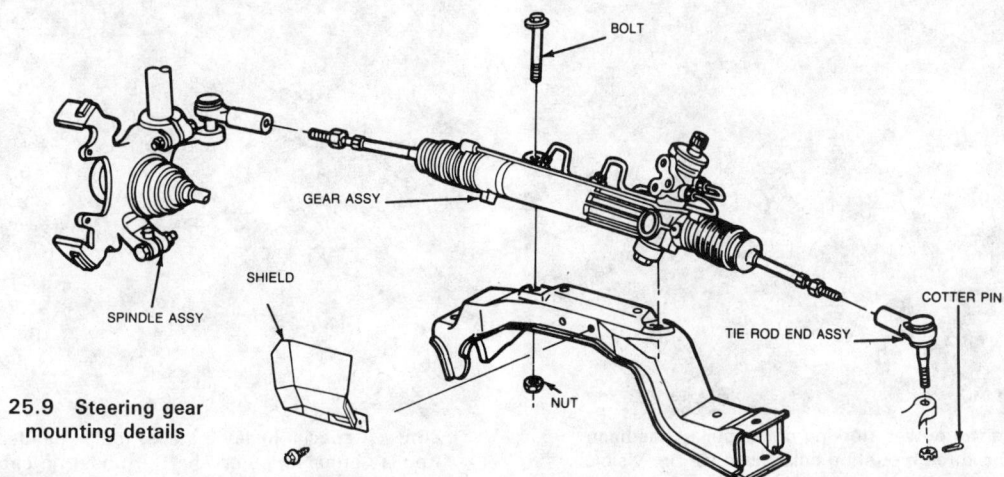

BOLT

GEAR ASSY

SPINDLE ASSY

SHIELD

NUT

TIE ROD END ASSY

COTTER PIN

**25.9   Steering gear
mounting details**

26.3 A special puller is required to remove the power steering pump pulley

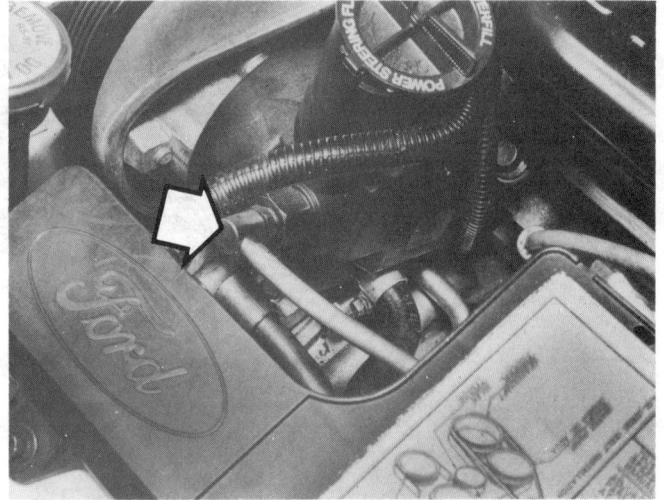

26.4 When removing the power steering pressure line (arrow), a backup wrench should be used on the pump body fitting — the return hose is connected to the pump with a hose clamp

10 Push the steering gear up to dislocate the mounting bolts from the holes, then rotate the gear forward to bring the input shaft out of its hole in the firewall.
11 Carefully guide the steering gear out the left side wheel well.
12 Installation is the reverse of the removal procedure. Be sure to tighten the mounting nuts to the specified torque. Bleed the power steering system following the procedure outlined in Section 28.

26 Power steering pump — removal and installation

Refer to illustrations 26.3, 26.4, 26.5 and 26.8

Removal

1 Disconnect the cable from the negative terminal of the battery.
2 Place a drain pan under the power steering pump. Remove the drivebelt (see Chapter 1).
3 Using a special power steering pump pulley remover, remove the pulley from the pump (see illustration).
4 Remove the pressure and return hoses from the back side of the pump and allow the fluid to drain (see illustration). Plug the hoses to prevent contaminants from entering.
5 Remove the pump mounting bolts (see illustration) and lift the pump from the vehicle, taking care not to spill fluid on the painted surfaces.

Installation

6 Position the pump in the mounting bracket and install the bolts. Tighten the bolts securely.
7 Connect the hoses to the pump. Tighten the fittings securely.
8 Press the pulley onto the pump shaft using a special pulley installer tool (see illustration). Push the pulley onto the shaft until the front of the hub is flush with the end of the shaft, but no further.
9 Install the drivebelt.
10 Fill the power steering reservoir with the recommended fluid and bleed the system following the procedure described in Section 28.

27 Power steering pump reservoir — replacement

Refer to illustrations 27.2a, 27.2b, 27.3, 27.4, 27.5 and 27.7

1 Remove the power steering pump from the vehicle (see Section 26) and place it in a vise, clamping it only by one of the mounting bolt ears.
2 Remove the high pressure line fitting and remove the valve and spring (see illustrations).
3 Wiggle the reservoir off the pump body (see illustration).

26.5 Once the power steering pump pulley has been removed, the three mounting bolts (arrows) are visible

26.8 A special pulley installer tool is needed to push the pulley onto the pump shaft — under no circumstances should the pulley be hammered onto the shaft, as this would damage the pump (this special tool is available at tool stores and some auto parts stores)

27.2a Unscrew the high pressure line fitting, ...

27.2b ... then remove the valve and spring, noting the direction in which it is installed

4   Remove the O-ring from the pump body, clean the groove and install a new O-ring **(see illustration)**. Make sure it is completely seated, with no twists in it.

5   Apply a coat of petroleum jelly to the O-ring and the O-ring contact surface on the inner diameter of the reservoir **(see illustration)**.

6   Push the new reservoir onto the pump body, aligning the holes for the high pressure line fitting.

7   Install two new O-rings on the high pressure line fitting **(see illustration)**, coat them with petroleum jelly and install the spring, valve and fitting in the pump body. Tighten the fitting securely.

8   Install the pump (Section 26), fill the reservoir with the recommended fluid (Chapter 1) and proceed to bleed the power steering system as described in Section 28.

28 Power steering system — bleeding

1   Following any operation in which the power steering fluid lines have been disconnected, the power steering system must be bled to remove all air and obtain proper steering performance.

2   With the front wheels in the straight ahead position, check the power steering fluid level and, if low, add fluid until it reaches the Cold mark on the dipstick.

3   Start the engine and allow it to run at fast idle. Recheck the fluid

27.3   Work the reservoir off the pump body

27.4   Stretch the new O-ring over the pump body and seat it in the groove, making sure it isn't twisted

27.5   Coat the O-ring and the inner diameter of the reservoir with petroleum jelly

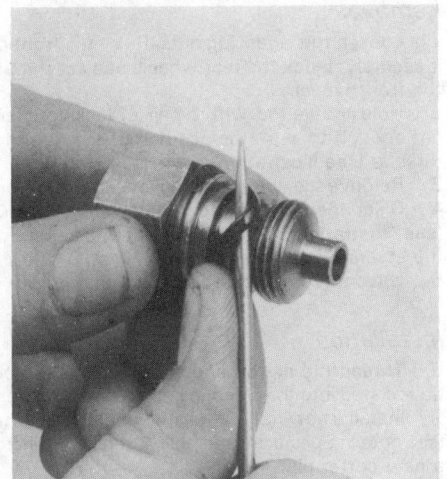

27.7   Install new O-rings on the high pressure fitting

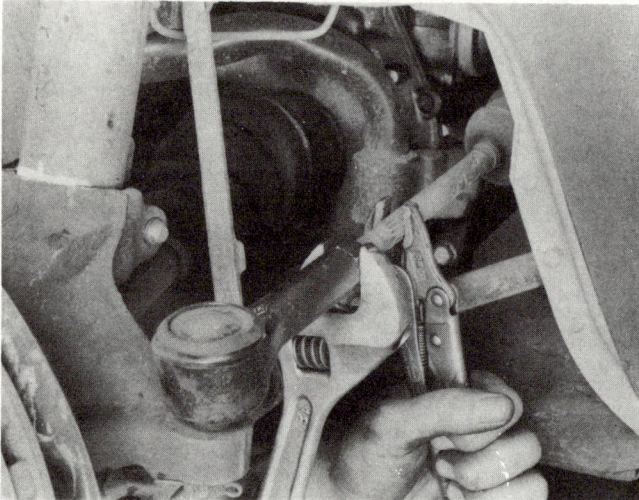

29.2a   Hold the tie-rod with a pair of locking pliers (clamped onto the serrated portion of the tie-rod) and loosen the jam nut

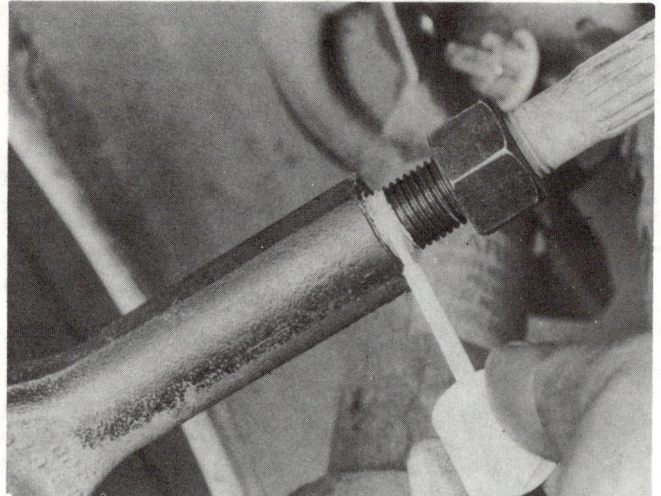

29.2b   Use white paint to mark the position of the tie-rod end on the tie-rod

level and add more if necessary to reach the Cold mark on the dipstick.
4   Bleed the system by turning the wheels from side-to-side, without hitting the stops. This will work the air out of the system. Keep the reservoir full of fluid as this is done.
5   When the air is worked out of the system, return the wheels to the straight ahead position and leave the vehicle running for several more minutes before shutting it off.
6   Road test the vehicle to be sure the steering system is functioning normally and noise free.
7   Recheck the fluid level to be sure it is up to the Hot mark on the dipstick while the engine is at normal operating temperature. Add fluid if necessary (see Chapter 1).

29.4   Use a two-jaw puller to detach the tie-rod end from the spindle arm (notice that the nut has been loosened, but not removed — this will prevent the components from separating violently)

29   Tie-rod ends — removal and installation

Refer to illustrations 29.2a, 29.2b and 29.4
Warning: *Whenever any of the suspension or steering fasteners are loosened or removed they must be replaced with new ones — discard the originals and don't reuse them. They must be replaced with new ones of the same part number or of original equipment quality and design. Torque specifications must be followed for proper reassembly and component retention.*

Removal

1   Loosen the wheel lug nuts. Raise the front of the vehicle, support it securely, block the rear wheels and set the parking brake. Remove the front wheel.
2   Hold the tie-rod with a pair of locking pliers and loosen the jam nut enough to mark the position of the tie-rod end in relation to the threads **(see illustrations)**.
3   Remove the cotter pin and loosen the nut on the tie-rod end stud.
4   Disconnect the tie-rod from the steering knuckle arm with a puller **(see illustration)**. Remove the nut and separate the tie-rod end from the steering kunckle.
5   Unscrew the tie-rod end from the tie-rod.

Installation

6   Thread the tie-rod end on to the marked position and insert the tie-rod stud into the steering knuckle arm. Tighten the jam nut securely.
7   Install a new nut on the stud and tighten it to the specified torque (see note in Specifications table at the beginning of this Chapter). Install a new cotter pin.
8   Install the wheel and lug nuts and tighten the lug nuts to the specified torque.
9   Have the alignment checked by a dealer service department or an alignment shop.

30   Steering gear boots — replacement

Warning: *Whenever any of the suspension or steering fasteners are loosened or removed they must be replaced with new ones — discard the originals and don't reuse them. They must be replaced with new ones of the same part number or of original equipment quality and design. Torque specifications must be followed for proper reassembly and component retention.*

1   Loosen the lug nuts, raise the vehicle and support it securely on jackstands. Remove the wheel.
2   Referring to Section 29, loosen the tie-rod end jam nut and separate the tie-rod end from the steering knuckle.
3   Remove the steering gear boot clamps and slide the boot off the tie-rod.
4   Before installing the new boot, wrap the threads and serrations on the end of the steering rod with a layer of tape so the small end of the new boot isn't damaged.
5   Slide the new boot into position on the steering gear until it seats in the groove in the steering rod and install new clamps.
6   Remove the tape and install the tie-rod end (Section 29).
7   Install the wheel and lug nuts. Lower the vehicle and tighten the lug nuts to the specified torque.

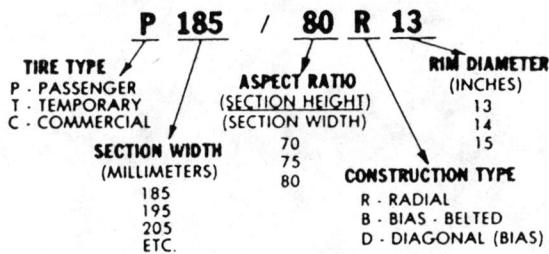

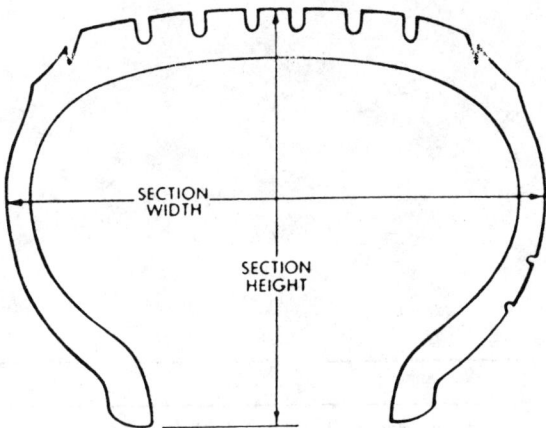

31.1 Metric tire size code

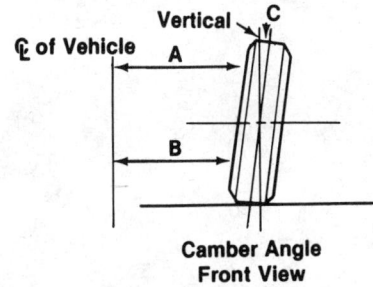

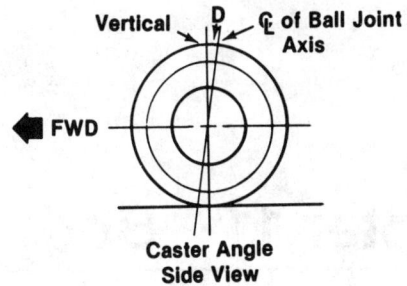

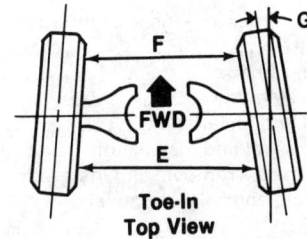

32.1 Front end alignment details

A minus B = C (degrees camber)
E minus F = toe-in (measured in inches)
G = toe-in (expressed in degrees)

31 Wheels and tires — general information

Refer to illustration 31.1

All vehicles covered by this manual are equipped with metric-sized fiberglass or steel belted radial tires **(see illustration)**. Use of other size or type of tires may affect the ride and handling of the vehicle. Don't mix different types of tires, such as radials and bias belted, on the same vehicle as handling may be seriously affected. It's recommended that tires be replaced in pairs on the same axle, but if only one tire is being replaced, be sure it's the same size, structure and tread design as the other.

Because tire pressure has a substantial effect on handling and wear, the pressure on all tires should be checked at least once a month or before any extended trips (see Chapter 1).

Wheels must be replaced if they are bent, dented, leak air, have elongated bolt holes, are heavily rusted, out of vertical symmetry or if the lug nuts won't stay tight. Wheel repairs that use welding or peening are not recommended.

Tire and wheel balance is important in the overall handling, braking and performance of the vehicle. Unbalanced wheels can adversely affect handling and ride characteristics as well as tire life. Whenever a tire is installed on a wheel, the tire and wheel should be balanced by a shop with the proper equipment.

32 Front end alignment — general information

Refer to illustration 32.1

A front end alignment refers to the adjustments made to the front wheels so they are in proper angular relationship to the suspension and the ground. Front wheels that are out of proper alignment not only affect steering control, but also increase tire wear. The only front end adjustment possible on the vehicle toe-in **(see illustration)**.

Getting the proper front wheel alignment is a very exacting process, one in which complicated and expensive machines are necessary to perform the job properly. Because of this, you should have a technician with the proper equipment perform these tasks. We will, however, use this space to give you a basic idea of what is involved with front end alignment so you can better understand the process and deal intelligently with the shop that does the work.

Toe-in is the turning in of the front wheels. The purpose of a toe specification is to ensure parallel rolling of the front wheels. In a vehicle with zero toe-in, the distance between the front edges of the wheels will be the same as the distance between the rear edges of the wheels. The actual amount of toe-in is normally only a fraction of an inch. Toe-in adjustment is controlled by the tie-rod end position on the inner tie-rod. Incorrect toe-in will cause the tires to wear improperly by making them scrub against the road surface.

Camber is the tilting of the front wheels from the vertical when viewed from the front of the vehicle. When the wheels tilt out at the top, the camber is said to be positive (+). When the wheels tilt in at the top the camber is negative (–). The amount of tilt is measured in degrees from the vertical and this measurement is called the camber angle. This angle affects the amount of tire tread which contacts the road and compensates for changes in the suspension geometry when the vehicle is cornering or travelling over an undulating surface.

Caster is the tilting of the front steering axis from the vertical. A tilt toward the rear is positive caster and a tilt toward the front is negative caster.

As stated in the first paragraph, the only adjustment possible is toe-in. However, camber and caster should be measured and checked against factory service specifications, to determine if any front end components are bent or worn out.

Chapter 11   Body

Contents

Specifications

Torque specifications

	Ft-lbs
Hood latch bolt	7 to 10
Hood hinge bolt	7 to 10
Door hinge-to-liftgate bolt	13 to 20
Liftgate hinge bolt	5 to 8
Liftgate latch-to-roof bolt	12 to 20
Front bumper isolator and bracket bolt	16 to 25
Rear bumper isolator and bracket bolt	
1988 sedan	7 to 11
All others	16 to 25
Door window glass retaining nut	3 to 5
Door window glass adjusting nut and bolt	5 to 8

1   General information

These vehicles have a "unibody" layout, using a floor pan with front and rear frame side rails which support the body components, front and rear suspension systems and other mechanical components.

Certain components are particularly vulnerable to accident damage and can be unbolted and repaired or replaced. Among these parts are the body moldings, bumpers, the hood and trunk lids and all glass.

Only general body maintenance practices and body panel repair procedures within the scope of the do-it-yourselfer are included in this Chapter.

2   Body — maintenance

1   The condition of the vehicle's body is very important, because the resale value depends a great deal on it. It's much more difficult to repair a neglected or damaged body than it is to repair mechanical components. The hidden areas of the body, such as the wheel wells, the frame and the engine compartment, are equally important, although they don't require as frequent attention as the rest of the body.

2   Once a year, or every 12,000 miles, it's a good idea to have the underside of the body steam cleaned. All traces of dirt and oil will be removed and the area can then be inspected carefully for rust, damaged

brake lines, frayed electrical wires, damaged cables and other problems. The front suspension components should be greased after completion of this job.

3   At the same time, clean the engine and the engine compartment with a steam cleaner or water soluble degreaser.

4   The wheel wells should be given close attention, since undercoating can peel away and stones and dirt thrown up by the tires can cause the paint to chip and flake, allowing rust to set in. If rust is found, clean down to the bare metal and apply an anti-rust paint.

5   The body should be washed about once a week. Wet the vehicle thoroughly to soften the dirt, then wash it down with a soft sponge and plenty of clean soapy water. If the surplus dirt is not washed off very carefully, it can wear down the paint.

6   Spots of tar or asphalt thrown up from the road should be removed with a cloth soaked in solvent.

7   Once every six months, wax the body and chrome trim. If a chrome cleaner is used to remove rust from any of the vehicle's plated parts, remember that the cleaner also removes part of the chrome, so use it sparingly.

3   Vinyl trim — maintenance

Don't clean vinyl trim with detergents, caustic soap or petroleum-based cleaners. Plain soap and water works just fine, with a soft brush to clean dirt that may be ingrained. Wash the vinyl as frequently as the rest of the vehicle.

After cleaning, application of a high quality rubber and vinyl protectant will help prevent oxidation and cracks. The protectant can also be applied to weatherstripping, vacuum lines and rubber hoses, which often fail as a result of chemical degradation, and to the tires.

4   Upholstery and carpets — maintenance

1   Every three months remove the carpets or mats and clean the interior of the vehicle (more frequently if necessary). Vacuum the upholstery and carpets to remove loose dirt and dust.

2   Leather upholstery requires special care. Stains should be removed with warm water and a very mild soap solution. Use a clean, damp cloth to remove the soap, then wipe again with a dry cloth. Never use alcohol, gasoline, nail polish remover or thinner to clean leather upholstery.

3   After cleaning, regularly treat leather upholstery with a leather wax. Never use car wax on leather upholstery.

4   In areas where the interior of the vehicle is subject to bright sunlight, cover leather seats with a sheet if the vehicle is to be left out for any length of time.

5   Body repair – minor damage

See color photo sequence

Repair of minor scratches

1   If the scratch is superficial and does not penetrate to the metal of the body, repair is very simple. Lightly rub the scratched area with a fine rubbing compound to remove loose paint and built up wax. Rinse the area with clean water.

2   Apply touch-up paint to the scratch, using a small brush. Continue to apply thin layers of paint until the surface of the paint in the scratch is level with the surrounding paint. Allow the new paint at least two weeks to harden, then blend it into the surrounding paint by rubbing with a very fine rubbing compound. Finally, apply a coat of wax to the scratch area.

3   If the scratch has penetrated the paint and exposed the metal of the body, causing the metal to rust, a different repair technique is required. Remove all loose rust from the bottom of the scratch with a pocket knife, then apply rust inhibiting paint to prevent the formation of rust in the future. Using a rubber or nylon applicator, coat the scratched area with glaze-type filler. If required, the filler can be mixed with thinner to provide a very thin paste, which is ideal for filling narrow scratches. Before the glaze filler in the scratch hardens, wrap a piece of smooth cotton cloth around the tip of a finger. Dip the cloth in thinner and then quickly wipe it along the surface of the scratch. This will en-

sure that the surface of the filler is slightly hollow. The scratch can now be painted over as described earlier in this section.

Repair of dents

4   When repairing dents, the first job is to pull the dent out until the affected area is as close as possible to its original shape. There is no point in trying to restore the original shape completely as the metal in the damaged area will have stretched on impact and cannot be restored to its original contours. It is better to bring the level of the dent up to a point which is about 1/8-inch below the level of the surrounding metal. In cases where the dent is very shallow, it is not worth trying to pull it out at all.

5   If the back side of the dent is accessible, it can be hammered out gently from behind using a soft-face hammer. While doing this, hold a block of wood firmly against the opposite side of the metal to absorb the hammer blows and prevent the metal from being stretched.

6   If the dent is in a section of the body which has double layers, or some other factor makes it inaccessible from behind, a different technique is required. Drill several small holes through the metal inside the damaged area, particularly in the deeper sections. Screw long, self tapping screws into the holes just enough for them to get a good grip in the metal. Now the dent can be pulled out by pulling on the protruding heads of the screws with locking pliers.

7   The next stage of repair is the removal of paint from the damaged area and from an inch or so of the surrounding metal. This is easily done with a wire brush or sanding disk in a drill motor, although it can be done just as effectively by hand with sandpaper. To complete the preparation for filling, score the surface of the bare metal with a screwdriver or the tang of a file or drill small holes in the affected area. This will provide a good grip for the filler material. To complete the repair, see the Section on filling and painting.

Repair of rust holes or gashes

8   Remove all paint from the affected area and from an inch or so of the surrounding metal using a sanding disk or wire brush mounted in a drill motor. If these are not available, a few sheets of sandpaper will do the job just as effectively.

9   With the paint removed, you will be able to determine the severity of the corrosion and decide whether to replace the whole panel, if possible, or repair the affected area. New body panels are not as expensive as most people think and it is often quicker to install a new panel than to repair large areas of rust.

10   Remove all trim pieces from the affected area except those which will act as a guide to the original shape of the damaged body, such as headlight shells, etc. Using metal snips or a hacksaw blade, remove all loose metal and any other metal that is badly affected by rust. Hammer the edges of the hole inward to create a slight depression for the filler material.

11   Wire brush the affected area to remove the powdery rust from the surface of the metal. If the back of the rusted area is accessible, treat it with rust inhibiting paint.

12   Before filling is done, block the hole in some way. This can be done with sheet metal riveted or screwed into place, or by stuffing the hole with wire mesh.

13   Once the hole is blocked off, the affected area can be filled and painted. See the following subsection on filling and painting.

Filling and painting

14   Many types of body fillers are available, but generally speaking, body repair kits which contain filler paste and a tube of resin hardener are best for this type of repair work. A wide, flexible plastic or nylon applicator will be necessary for imparting a smooth and contoured finish to the surface of the filler material. Mix up a small amount of filler on a clean piece of wood or cardboard (use the hardener sparingly). Follow the manufacturer's instructions on the package, otherwise the filler will set incorrectly.

15   Using the applicator, apply the filler paste to the prepared area. Draw the applicator across the surface of the filler to achieve the desired contour and to level the filler surface. As soon as a contour that approximates the original one is achieved, stop working the paste. If you continue, the paste will begin to stick to the applicator. Continue to add thin layers of paste at 20-minute intervals until the level of the filler is just above the surrounding metal.

16   Once the filler has hardened, the excess can be removed with a body file. From then on, progressively finer grades of sandpaper should

be used, starting with a 180-grit paper and finishing with 600-grit wet-or-dry paper. Always wrap the sandpaper around a flat rubber or wooden block, otherwise the surface of the filler will not be completely flat. During the sanding of the filler surface, the wet-or-dry paper should be periodically rinsed in water. This will ensure that a very smooth finish is produced in the final stage.

17 At this point, the repair area should be surrounded by a ring of bare metal, which in turn should be encircled by the finely feathered edge of good paint. Rinse the repair area with clean water until all of the dust produced by the sanding operation is gone.

18 Spray the entire area with a light coat of primer. This will reveal any imperfections in the surface of the filler. Repair the imperfections with fresh filler paste or glaze filler and once more smooth the surface with sandpaper. Repeat this spray-and-repair procedure until you are satisfied that the surface of the filler and the feathered edge of the paint are perfect. Rinse the area with clean water and allow it to dry completely.

19 The repair area is now ready for painting. Spray painting must be carried out in a warm, dry, windless and dust free atmosphere. These conditions can be created if you have access to a large indoor work area, but if you are forced to work in the open, you will have to pick the day very carefully. If you are working indoors, dousing the floor in the work area with water will help settle the dust which would otherwise be in the air. If the repair area is confined to one body panel, mask off the surrounding panels. This will help minimize the effects of a slight mismatch in paint color. Trim pieces such as chrome strips, door handles, etc., will also need to be masked off or removed. Use masking tape and several thicknesses of newspaper for the masking operations.

20 Before spraying, shake the paint can thoroughly, then spray a test area until the spray painting technique is mastered. Cover the repair area with a thick coat of primer. The thickness should be built up using several thin layers of primer rather than one thick one. Using 600-grit wet-or-dry sandpaper, rub down the surface of the primer until it is

very smooth. While doing this, the work area should be thoroughly rinsed with water and the wet-or-dry sandpaper periodically rinsed as well. Allow the primer to dry before spraying additional coats.

21 Spray on the top coat, again building up the thickness by using several thin layers of paint. Begin spraying in the center of the repair area and then, using a circular motion, work out until the whole repair area and about two inches of the surrounding original paint is covered. Remove all masking material 10 to 15 minutes after spraying on the final coat of paint. Allow the new paint at least two weeks to harden, then use a very fine rubbing compound to blend the edges of the new paint into the existing paint. Finally, apply a coat of wax.

6 Body repair — major damage

1 Major damage must be repaired by an auto body shop specifically equipped to perform unibody repairs. These shops have available the specialized equipment required to do the job properly.

2 If the damage is extensive, the body must be checked for proper alignment, or the vehicle's handling characteristics may be adversely affected and other components may wear at an accelerated rate.

3 Due to the fact that all of the major body components (hood, fenders, etc.) are separate and replaceable units, any seriously damaged components should be replaced rather than repaired. Sometimes the components can be found in a wrecking yard that specializes in used vehicle components, often at considerable savings over the cost of new parts.

7 Hinges and locks — maintenance

Once every 3000 miles, or every three months, the hinges and latch assemblies on the doors, hood and trunk should be given a few drops of light oil or lock lubricant. Lubricate the door and trunk locks with spray-on graphite lubricant. The door latch strikers should also be lubricated with a thin coat of grease to reduce wear and ensure free movement.

8 Hood — removal, installation and adjustment

Refer to illustrations 8.2, 8.3 and 8.7

1 Open the hood.

2 Scribe or paint alignment marks around the edges of the hood mounting bolts **(see illustration)**.

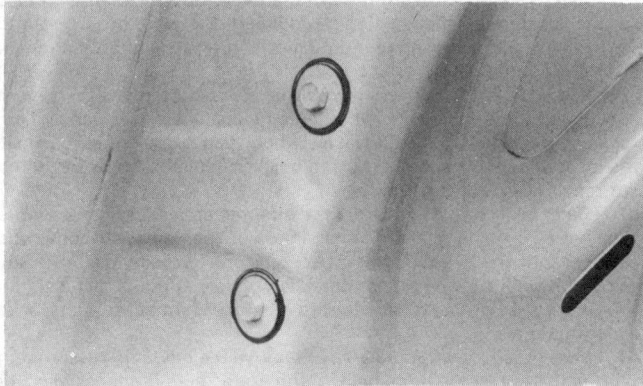

8.2 Scribe or paint alignment marks around the hood mounting bolts before removal so they can be reinstalled in the same position

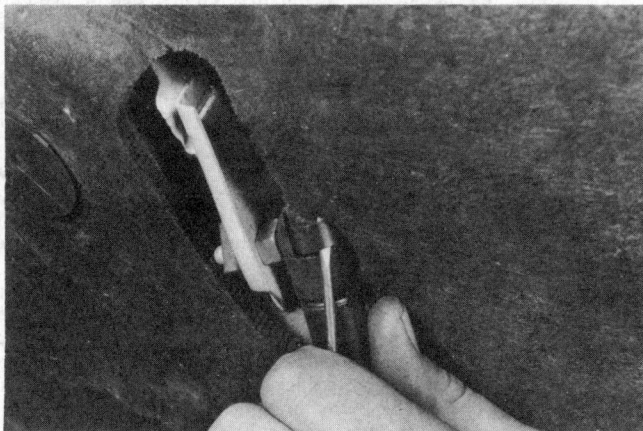

8.3 Use a screwdriver to pry out the retaining clip, then disconnect the hood support strut

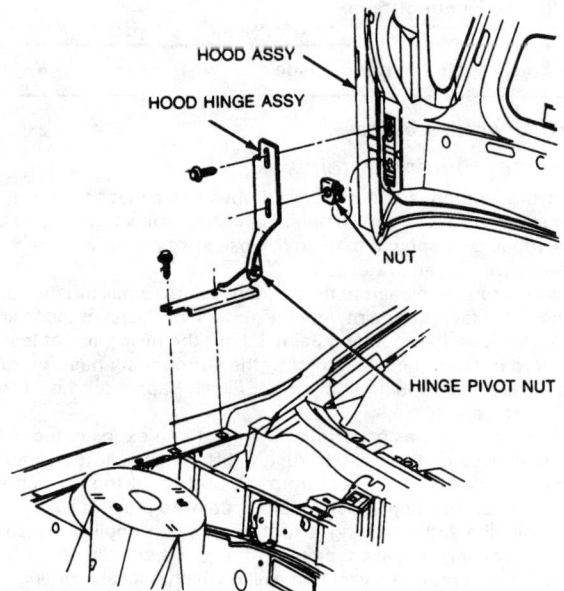

HOOD ASSY

HOOD HINGE ASSY

NUT

HINGE PIVOT NUT

8.7 The hood hinges are slotted to allow small adjustments of the hood position

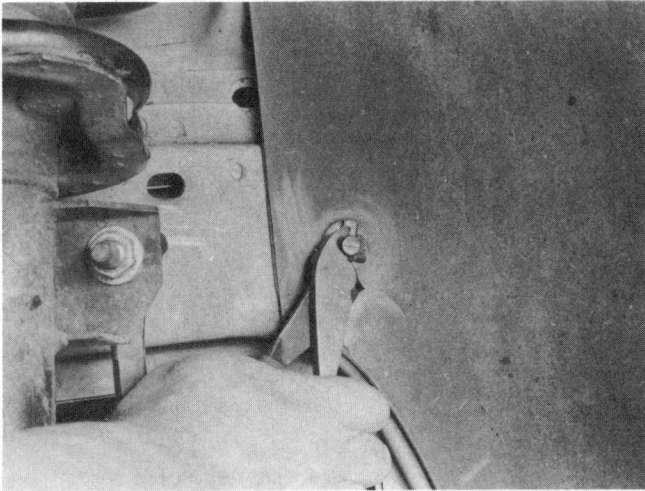

9.2a Use pliers or wire cutters to pull out the center of
each push pin, . . .

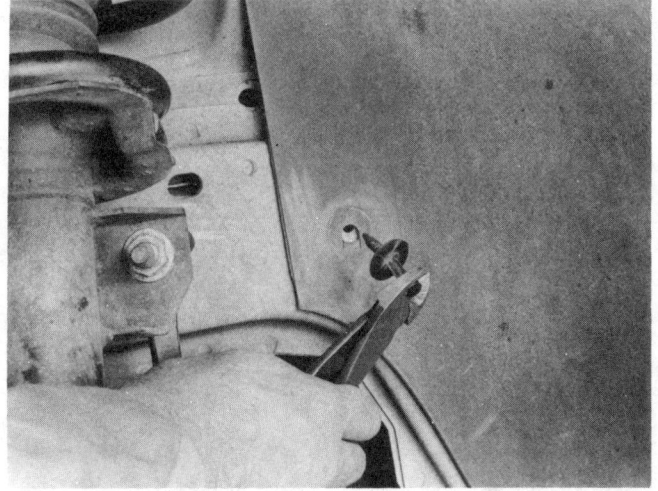

9.2b . . . then pull the push pins out

3   Have an assistant support the hood and use a small screwdriver
to pry off the retaining clip, then disconnect the upper ends of the hood
support struts (see illustration).
4   Remove the hinge assembly-to-hood mounting bolts.
5   Remove the hood.
6   Installation is the reverse of removal.
7   The hood can be adjusted fore-and-aft and side-to-side by loosening
the two hood-to-hinge bolts at each hinge (see illustration). Reposition
the hood and tighten the bolts.
8   To raise or lower the rear of the hood, loosen the hinge-to-body
bolts. Raise or lower the hinge as necessary to make the hood flush
with the surrounding panels. Then tighten the hinge-to-body bolts.

9   Front fender liner — removal and installation

Refer to illustrations 9.2a and 9.2b

1   Raise the front of the vehicle, support it securely on jackstands
and remove the appropriate front wheel.
2   Remove the plastic push pins retaining the fender liner to the
chassis. This is accomplished by disengaging the centers of the pins
with pliers or wire cutters; do not cut them off, just pull them out (see

illustration). Once the centers are disengaged, pull the pins from the
fender liner (see illustration).
3   Remove the four Phillips head screws retaining the fender liner.
4   Grasp the sides of the fender liner securely, detach it from the
fender well and lower it from the vehicle.
5   Installation is the reverse of removal. To install the push pins, insert
them into place and then push the centers in until they lock.

10   Hood release latch and cable — removal and installation

Refer to illustrations 10.1, 10.4 and 10.6

Latch

1   Mark the latch position with paint or a scribe, disconnect the cable,
remove the two retaining bolts and detach the latch (see illustration).
2   Installation is the reverse of removal.

Cable

3   Working in the engine compartment, disconnect the cable at the
latch and retaining clips.
4   Working in the passenger compartment, detach the trim panel by
prying with a screwdriver and remove the two cable release lever re-

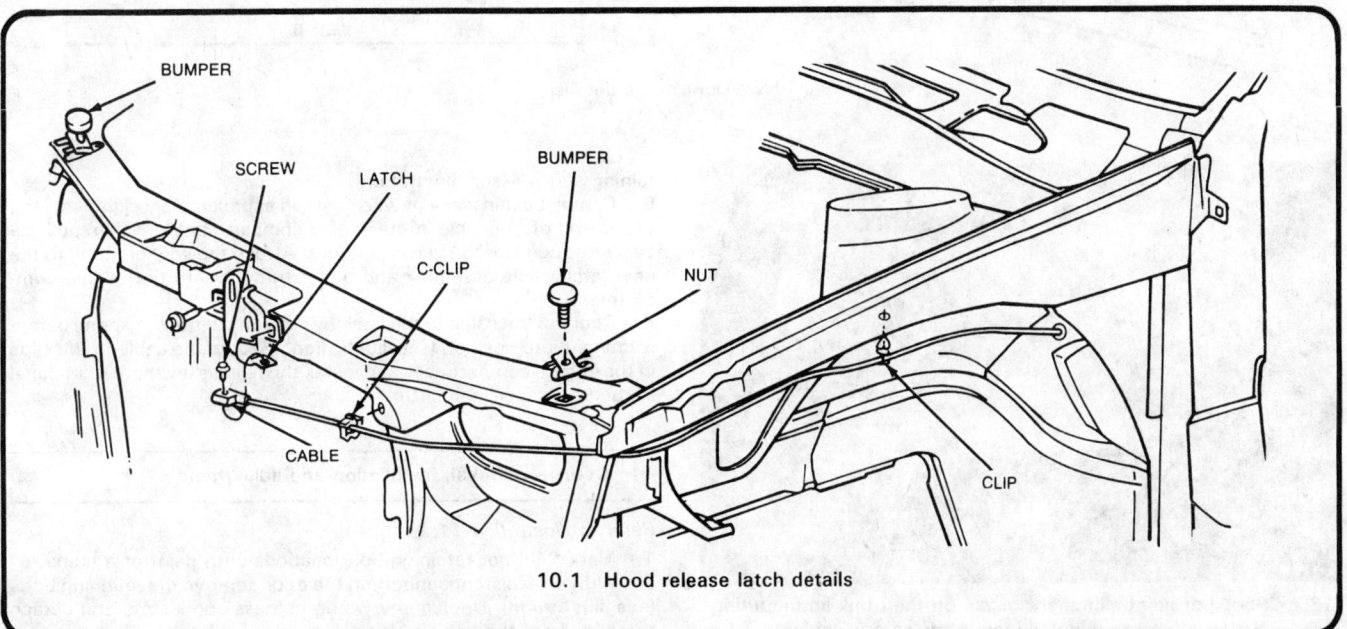

10.1 Hood release latch details

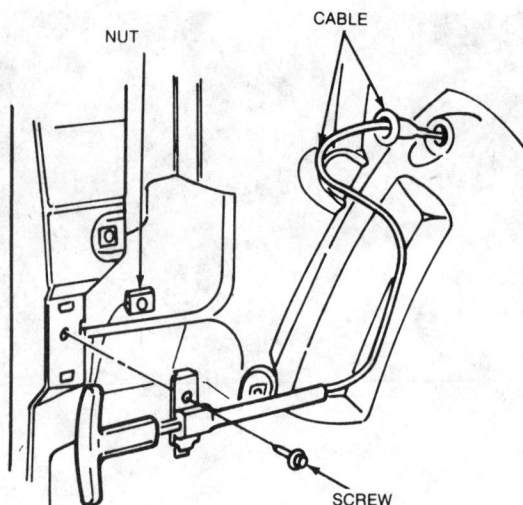

10.4   Cable release lever details

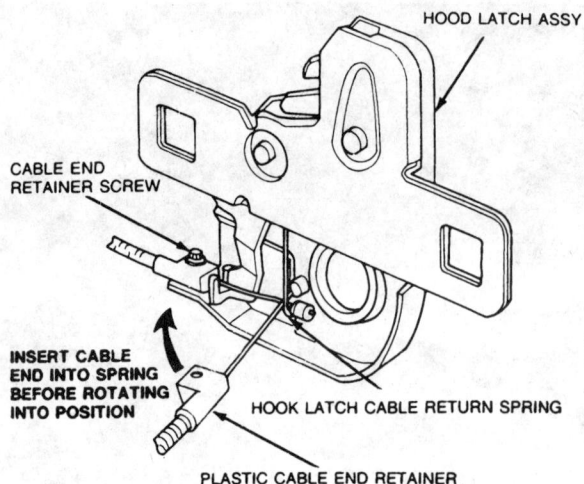

10.6   Cable-to-latch connection details

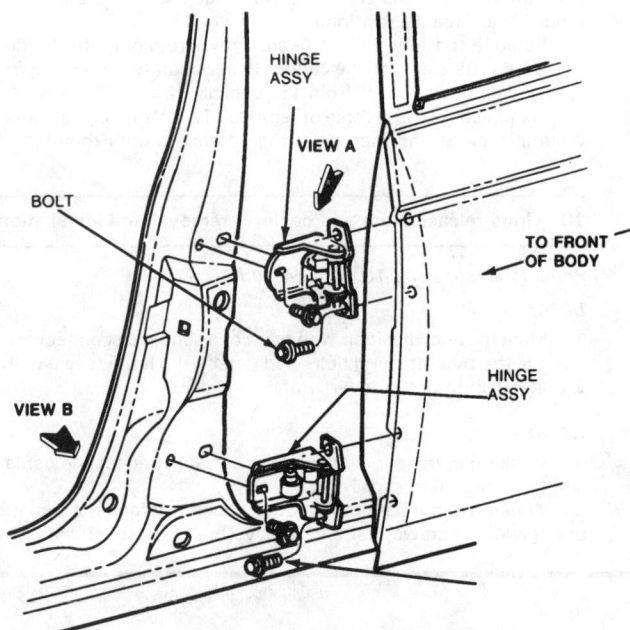

11.2   Door hinge details

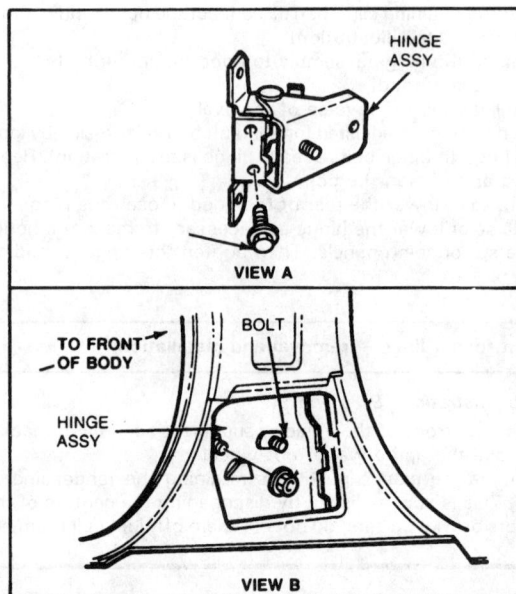

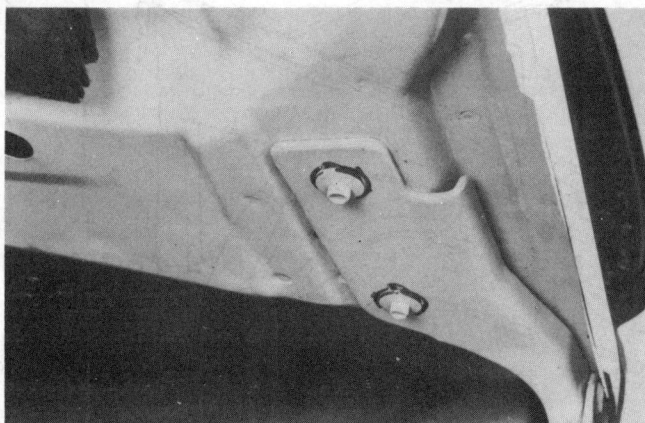

12.2   Scribe or paint alignment marks on the trunk lid mounting flange to ensure reinstallation in the same position

taining screws (see illustration).

5   Connect a thin piece of wire or string approximately eight feet long to the end of the cable in the engine compartment and then pull the cable through into the vehicle interior. Attach the wire or string to the new latch cable assembly and pull it through into the engine compartment.

6   Connect the cable to the latch by inserting it into the spring before rotating it into position (see illustration). Secure the cable to the clips in the engine compartment and install the release lever and trim panel in the passenger compartment.

11   Door — removal, installation and adjustment

Refer to illustration 11.2

1   Mark the door retaining bolt locations with paint or a marker.
2   With an assistant supporting the door, remove the retaining bolts (see illustration). Unplug any wiring harness connectors and detach the door from the vehicle.

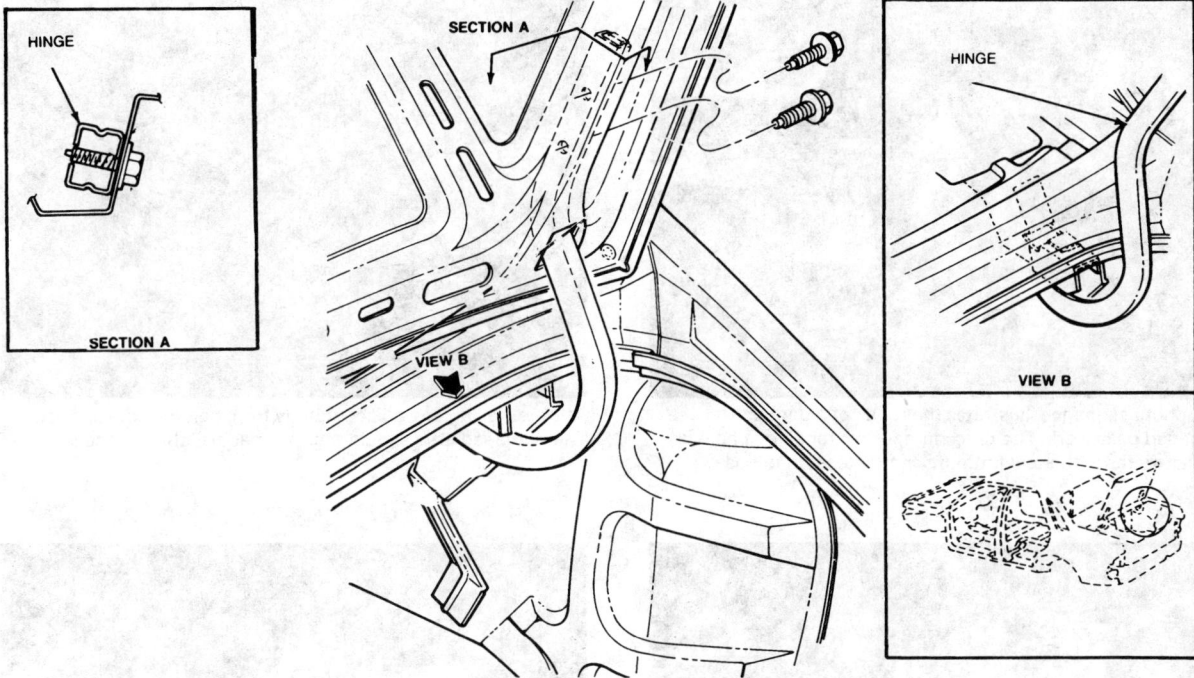

12.6 The trunk lid can be moved slightly to align it with the rear fenders

3   To install, place the door in position and install the bolts finger tight. Adjust the door position until the bolts are in the marked positions and tighten the bolts securely.
4   The door hinges are enlarged and elongated to provide sufficient adjustment for door alignment. To adjust the door position, loosen the bolts and nuts slightly and move the door to the desired position with a padded pry bar. Tighten the bolts securely, close the door and check for fit. Repeat the procedure until the door fits properly.

12 Trunk lid — removal, installation and adjustment

Refer to illustrations 12.2 and 12.6
1   Open the trunk lid.
2   Scribe or paint alignment marks around the trunk lid hinge bolt flanges **(see illustration)**.
3   Loosen and remove the hinge bolts.
4   Remove the trunk lid.
5   Installation is the reverse of removal.
6   The trunk lid can be shifted fore-and-aft and from side-to-side. The up-and-down adjustment is made by loosening the hinge screws and raising or lowering the trunk lid **(see illustration)**.
7   The trunk lid should be adjusted for an even and parallel fit in the opening. It should also be adjusted up-and-down for a flush fit with the surrounding panels. Care should be taken not to distort or mar the trunk lid or surrounding body panels.

13 Station wagon liftgate — removal, installation and adjustment

Refer to illustration 13.5
1   Open the liftgate and support it in the open position.
2   Unplug any electrical connectors.
3   Mark the position of the hinge screws by scribing around them.
4   Disconnect the upper ends of the liftgate support struts by prying the spring clips off with a small screwdriver.
5   With an assistant supporting the liftgate's weight, remove the hinge-to-liftgate bolts and lower the liftgate from the vehicle **(see illustration)**.

6   To install, place the liftgate in position and install the liftgate bolts in the marked positions. Tighten the bolts to the specified torque.
7   Connect the support struts.
8   The liftgate position can be adjusted by pulling down the headliner and loosening the latch-to-roof bolts **(see illustration 13.5)**. Move the liftgate to the desired position and tighten the bolts to the specified torque. Repeat the procedure until the gap between the liftgate and surrounding panels is even.

14 Bumpers — removal and installation

Refer to illustrations 14.2 and 14.3
1   Raise the vehicle and support it securely on jackstands.

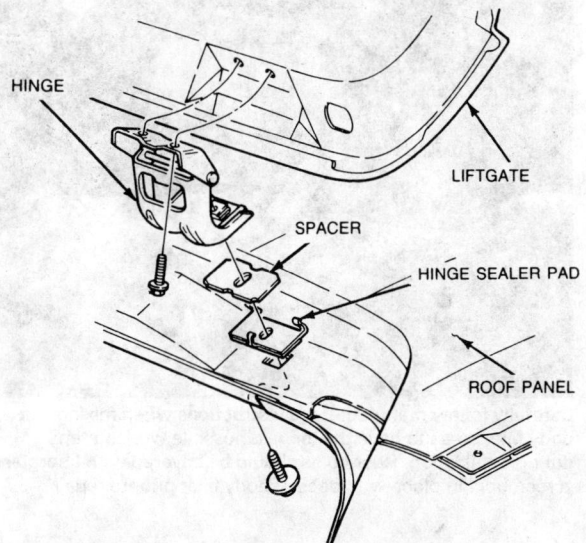

13.5 Liftgate hinge details

This photo sequence illustrates the repair of a dent and damaged paintwork. The procedure for the repair of a hole is similar. Refer to the text for more complete instructions

After removing any adjacent body trim, hammer the dent out. The damaged area should then be made slightly concave

Use coarse sandpaper or a sanding disc on a drill motor to remove all paint from the damaged area. Feather the sanded area into the edges of the surrounding paint, using progressively finer grades of sandpaper

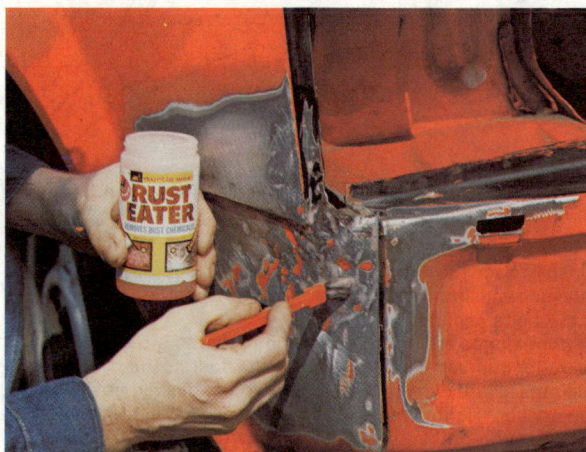

The damaged area should be treated with rust remover prior to application of the body filler. In the case of a rust hole, all rusted sheet metal should be cut away

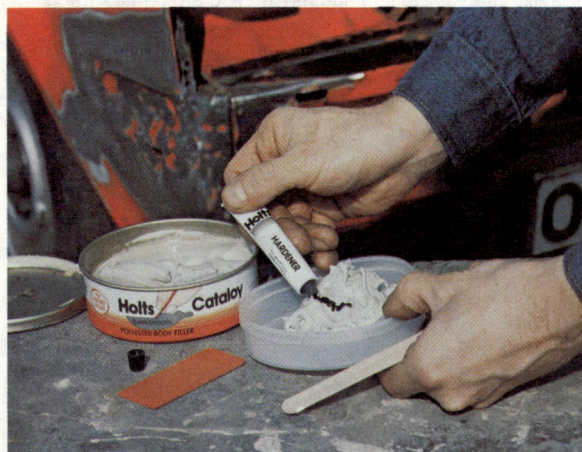

Carefully follow manufacturer's instructions when mixing the body filler so as to have the longest possible working time during application. Rust holes should be covered with fiberglass screen held in place with dabs of body filler prior to repair

Apply the filler with a flexible applicator in thin layers at 20 minute intervals. Use an applicator such as a wood spatula for confined areas. The filler should protrude slightly above the surrounding area

Shape the filler with a surform-type plane. Then, use water and progressively finer grades of sandpaper and a sanding block to wet-sand the area until it is smooth. Feather the edges of the repair area into the surrounding paint.

Use spray or brush applied primer to cover the entire repair area so that slight imperfections in the surface will be filled in. Prime at least one inch into the area surrounding the repair. Be careful of over-spray when using spray-type primer

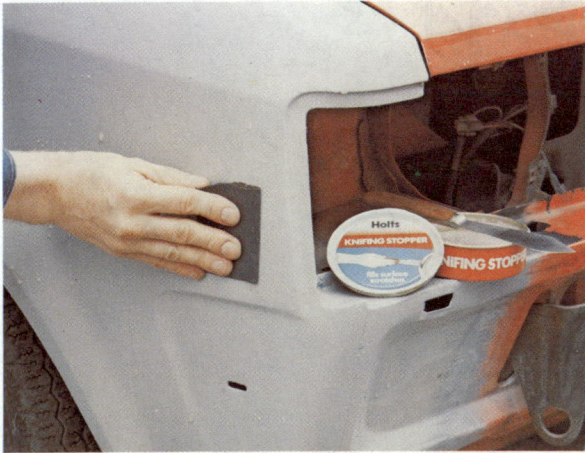

Wet-sand the primer with fine (approximately 400 grade) sandpaper until the area is smooth to the touch and blended into the surrounding paint. Use filler paste on minor imperfections

After the filler paste has dried, use rubbing compound to ensure that the surface of the primer is smooth. Prior to painting, the surface should be wiped down with a tack rag or lint-free cloth soaked in lacquer thinner

Choose a dry, warm, breeze-free area in which to paint and make sure that adjacent areas are protected from over-spray. Shake the spray paint can thoroughly and apply the top coat to the repair area, building it up by applying several coats, working from the center

After allowing at least two weeks for the paint to harden, use fine rubbing compound to blend the area into the original paint. Wax can now be applied

FENDER

FRONT LICENSE
PLATE MOUNTING
BRACKET

FRONT BUMPER

ISOLATOR

BUMPER

RIVET

PUSH PIN

BUMPER

SECTION A

SECTION B

SECTION C

ISOLATOR AND BRACKET

SECTION A

FRONT LICENSE
PLATE MOUNTING
BRACKET

SECTION C

SECTION B

BUMPER

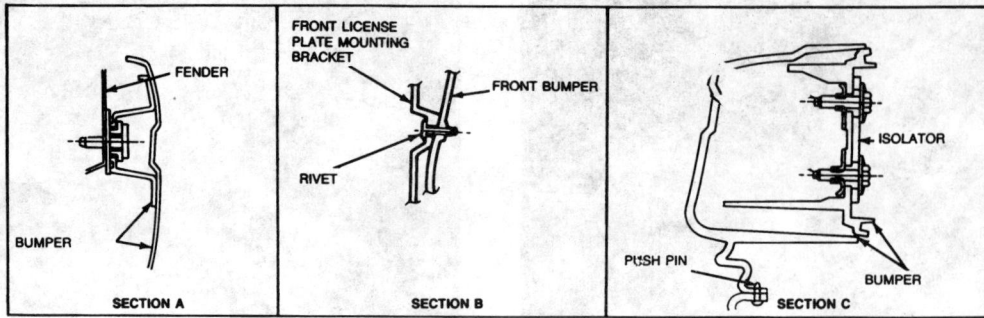

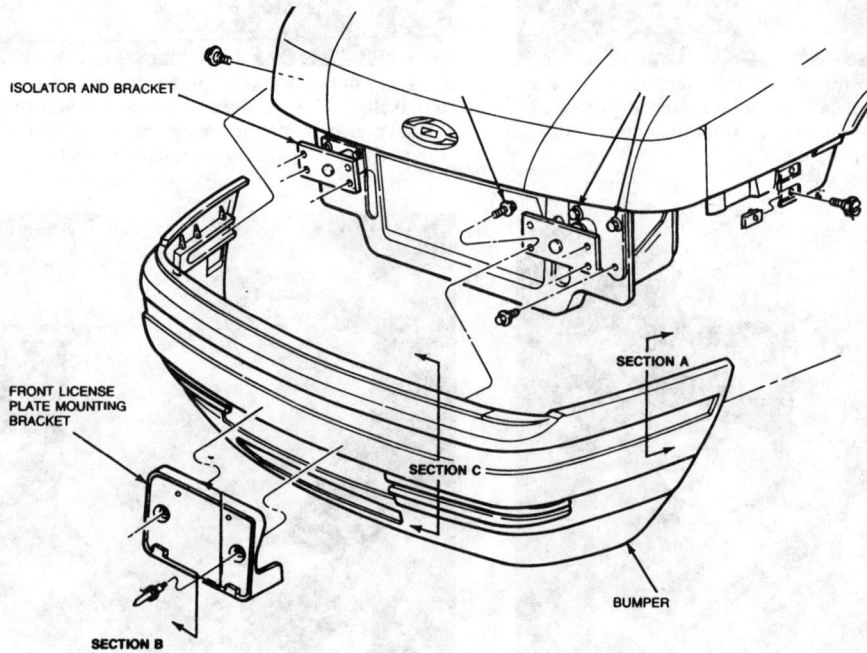

14.2 Front bumper and isolator details

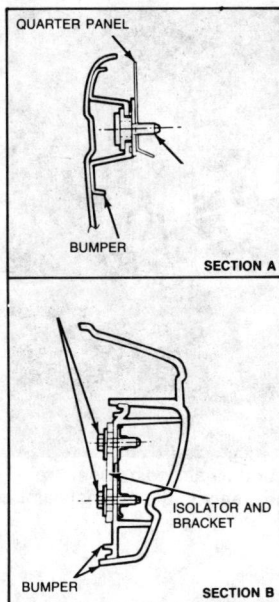

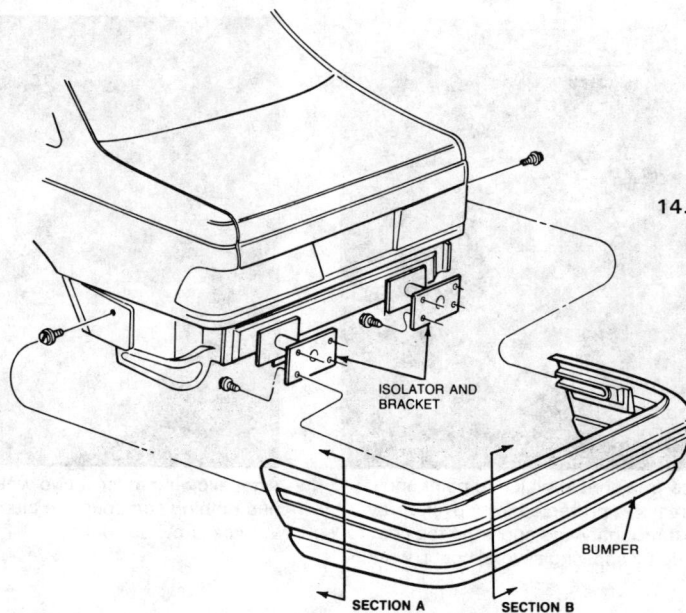

QUARTER PANEL

BUMPER

SECTION A

ISOLATOR AND
BRACKET

BUMPER

SECTION B

14.3 Rear bumper details

ISOLATOR AND
BRACKET

BUMPER

SECTION A

SECTION B

2   Working under the vehicle, remove the bolts retaining the isolater and bracket assemblies to the bumper (see illustration).
3   With the help of an assistant, slide the bumper off the guide bolts on the sides of the body and remove the bumper (see illustration).
4   Installation is the reverse of removal. After installation, tighten the isolator and bracket bolts to the specified torque.

15   Door trim panel — removal and installation

Refer to illustrations 15.2a, 15.2b, 15.3, 15.5a, 15.5b and 15.6

1   Disconnect the negative cable from the battery. Place the cable out of the way so it cannot accidentally come in contact with the negative terminal of the battery, as this would again allow power into the electrical system of the vehicle.
2   Remove the door trim panel retaining screws (see illustrations).
3   On manual window regulator models, pry off the window crank cover, remove the screw and lift off the crank (see illustration). On power regulator models, pry off the control switch assembly and unplug it.
4   Insert a large screwdriver or a pry bar between the door panel and the door and disengage the clips along the bottom.
5   Once the clips are disengaged, swing the door panel out at the

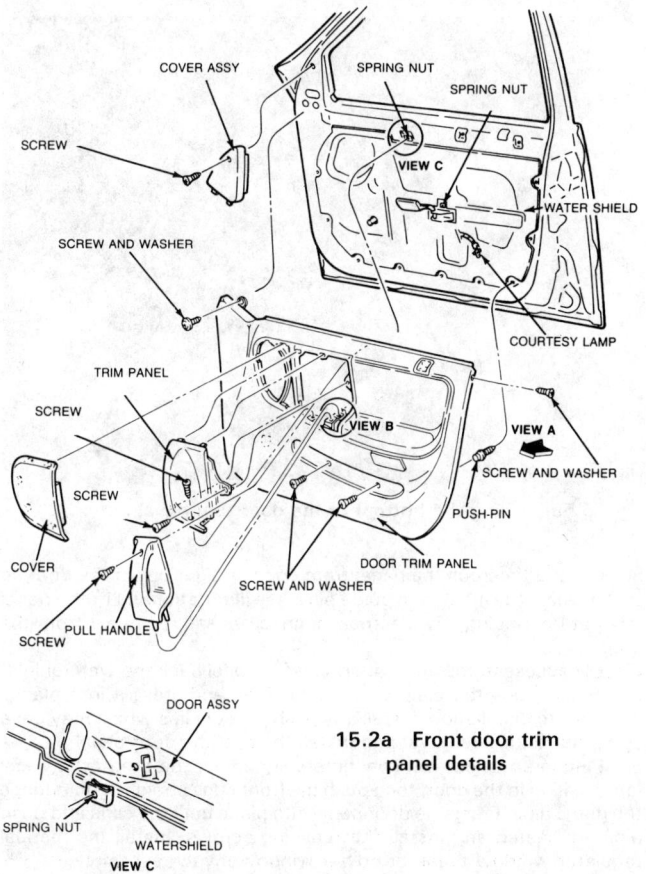

15.2a Front door trim panel details

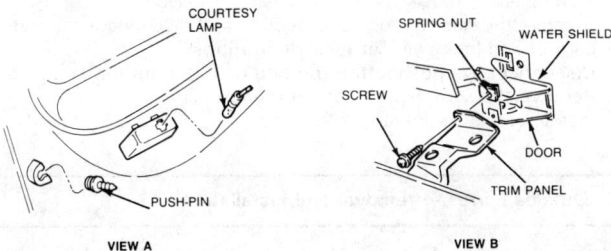

15.2b Typical rear door trim panel details

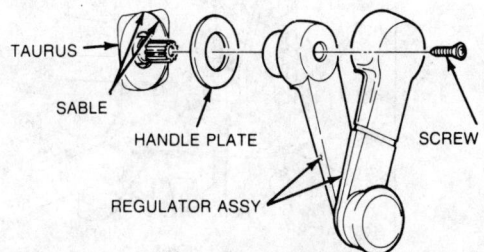

15.3 Manual window crank details

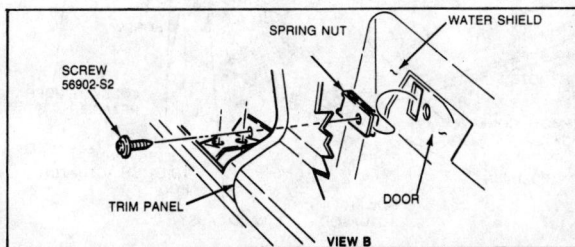

15.5a   Swing the bottom of the door trim panel out . . .

15.5b   . . . and then lift the panel out and up on the top
to clear the guide pins before lifting it off

bottom and then pull the panel front edge straight out of the door so
that it clears the molded-in guide pins (see illustrations). Lift the panel
straight up, unplug any electrical connectors and remove it from the
door.
6   For access to the inner door, carefully peel back the watershield.
To install, place the watershield in position and press it into place.
7   Prior to installation, install any push pins or clips which may have
come out during removal and install them in the door panel.
8   Plug in any electrical connectors and lower the top of the panel
into position in the door, then push the front edge straight in to engage
the guide pins. Press the door panel into place until the clips and push
pins are seated and install the retaining screws. Install the manual
regulator window crank or power window switch assembly.

16   Door latch and remote controls — removal and installation

Refer to illustrations 16.2a and 16.2b
1   Remove the door trim panel (Section 15) and carefully peel back

the watershield.
2   Remove the remote control assembly and disconnect the rod at
the control and lock cylinder (see illustrations).
3   Disconnect the pushbutton rod and handle from the latch.
4   Remove the screws and detach the latch.
5   Installation is the reverse of removal.

17   Outside mirror — removal and installation

Refer to illustration 17.1
1   Remove the door trim panel (refer to Section 15) and sail cover
(see illustration).
2   Remove the mirror mounting stud nuts and detach the mirror and
adjustment cable assembly from the door. Be sure to note the routing
of the adjustment cable before removing the mirror.
3   Installation is the reverse of removal.

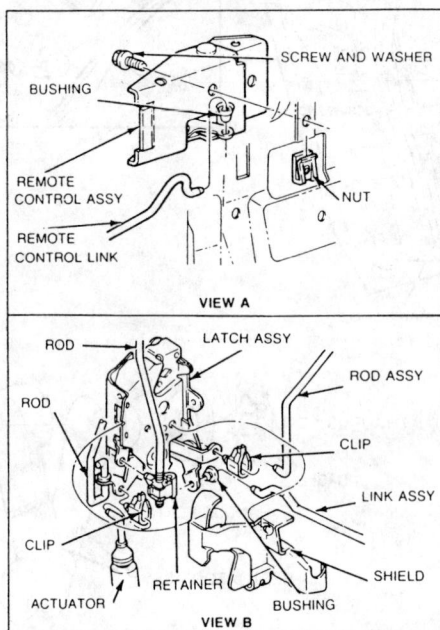

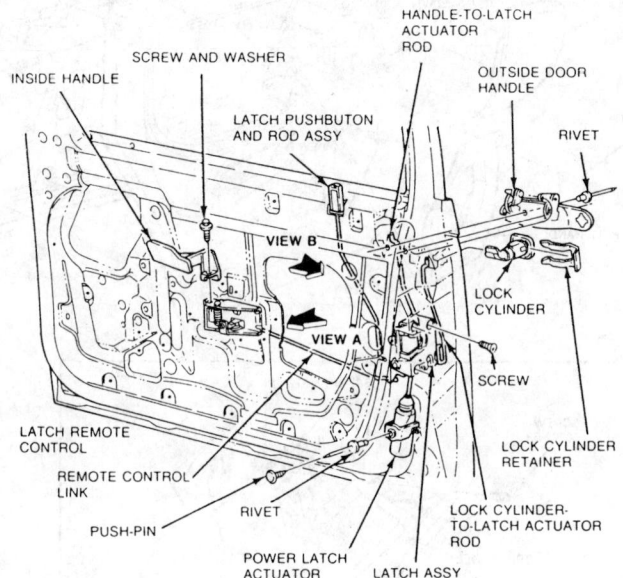

16.2a   Typical front door latch and and remote control details

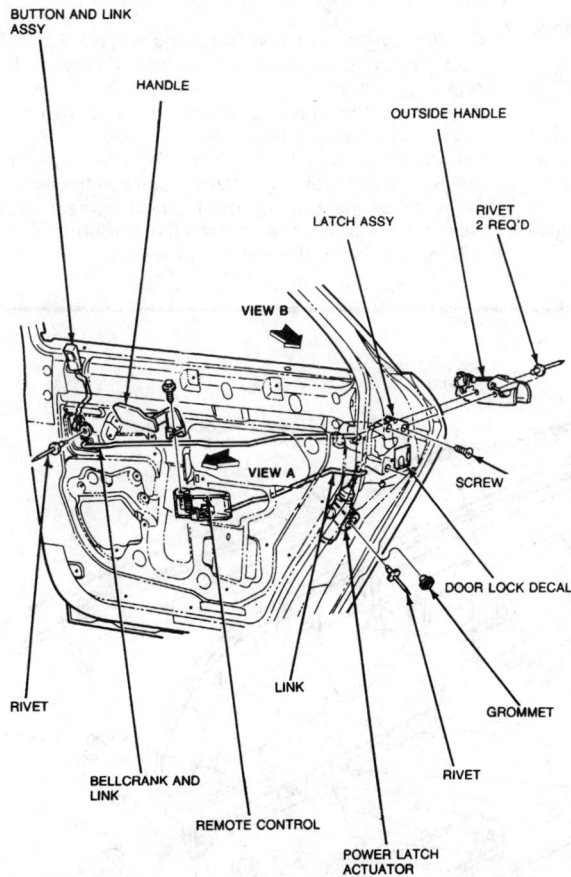

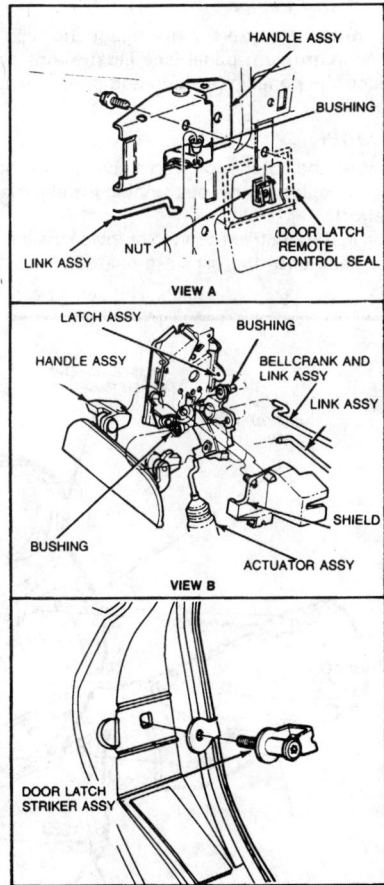

16.2b Typical rear door latch and remote control layout

18 Dashboard finish panels — removal and installation

Refer to illustrations 18.2, 18.4 and 18.11

1 Disconnect the negative cable from the battery. Place the cable out of the way so it cannot accidentally come in contact with the negative terminal of the battery, as this would again allow power into the electrical system of the vehicle.

Steering column opening cover

2 Remove the retaining screws and rotate the steering column opening cover out of the instrument panel (see illustration).
3 Installation is the reverse of removal.

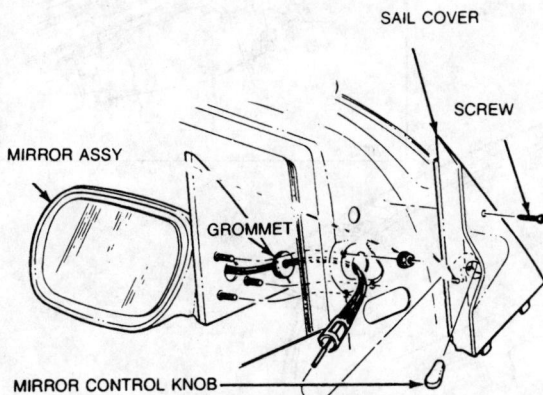

17.1 Outside mirror installation details

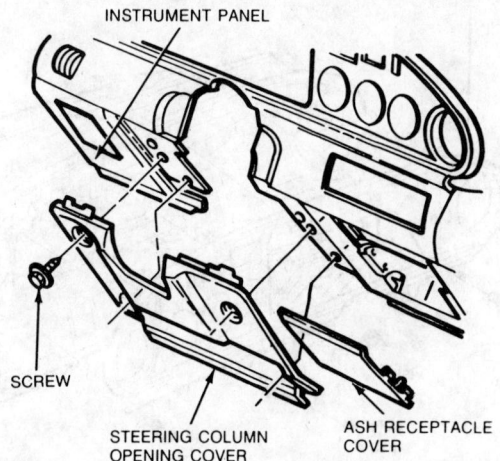

18.2 Steering column opening cover details

Left hand finish panel

4   Carefully pry up at the corners to disengage the clips and remove the panel from the instrument panel (see illustration).
5   To install, place the panel in position and press it into place until the clips are seated.

Radio finish panel

6   Pry gently around the outer edge with a screwdriver until the panel clips are disengaged. Pull the panel out, unplug the electrical connector and lift the panel off.
7   To install, plug in the electrical connector, place the panel in position and press it into place until the clips are seated.

Instrument cluster opening finish panel

8   Remove the torx head retaining screws. Pull off the headlight and heater/air conditioner control knobs and remove the headlight switch retaining nut.
9   Remove the steering column trim shroud and unplug the steering column electrical connectors.
10   On tilt wheel models, move the wheel to the lowest position.
11   Remove the retaining screws and pull the panel out sharply to disengage the clips. Unplug any electrical connectors and lower the panel from the instrument panel (see illustration).
12   Installation is the reverse of removal.

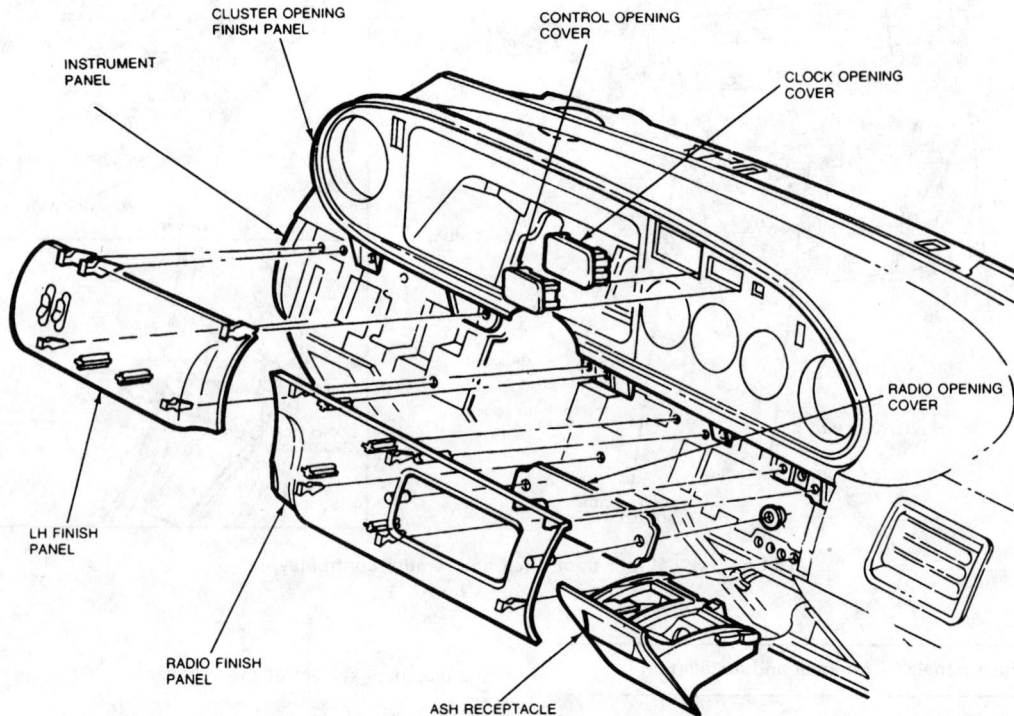

18.4   Dashboard finish panel component layout

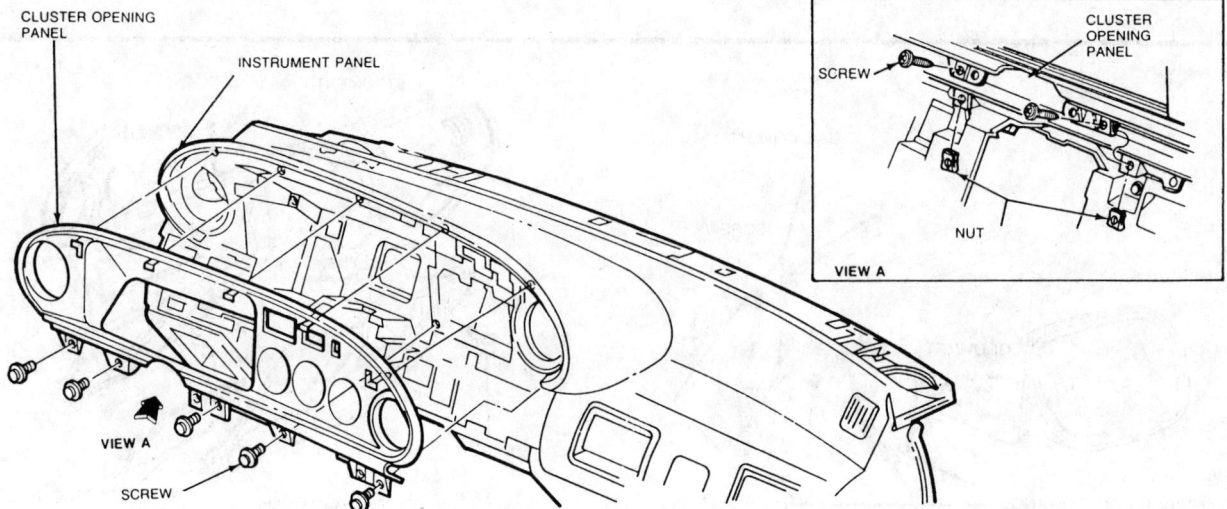

18.11   Instrument finish panel details

19 Center console — removal and installation

Refer to illustrations 19.1 and 19.8

1986 and 1987 models

1   Use a small screwdriver to pry out the two plug buttons from the base of the front of the console and remove the two attaching screws (see illustration).

2   Use a small screwdriver to pry out the gearshift opening panel.

3   Remove the console-to-front floor bracket screw(s) (floor mounted manual transmission and column mounted automatic transmission-equipped models have one screw, floor mounted automatic transmission-equipped models have two).

4   Snap out the rear access panel and remove the three console-to-floor bracket attaching screws.

5   Move the shift lever on floor-mounted models fully to the rear, slide the console to the rear and lift up for access to the electrical connector.

6   Unplug the electrical connector and lift the console from the vehicle.

7   Installation is the reverse of removal.

1988 models

8   Open the armrest door, remove the two hinge-to-door retaining screws and lift the door off (see illustration).

9   Pry off both of the hinge covers for access to the armrest base-to-mounting bracket attaching bolt.

10 Remove the bolt and lift off the console base and the armrest base assemblies.

11 Installation is the reverse of removal.

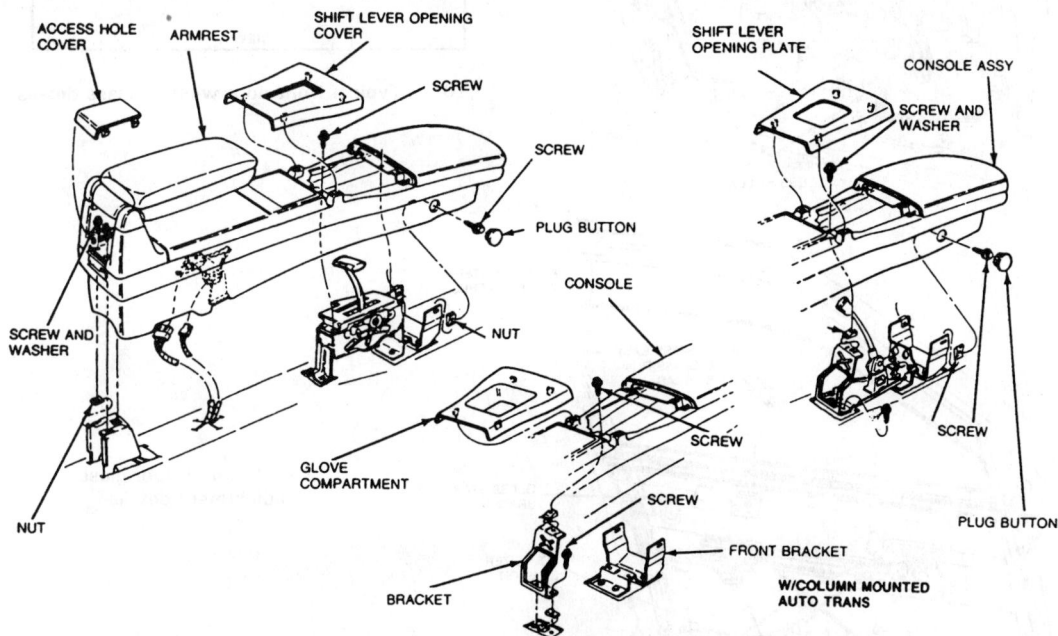

19.1   Center console details (1986 and 1987 models)

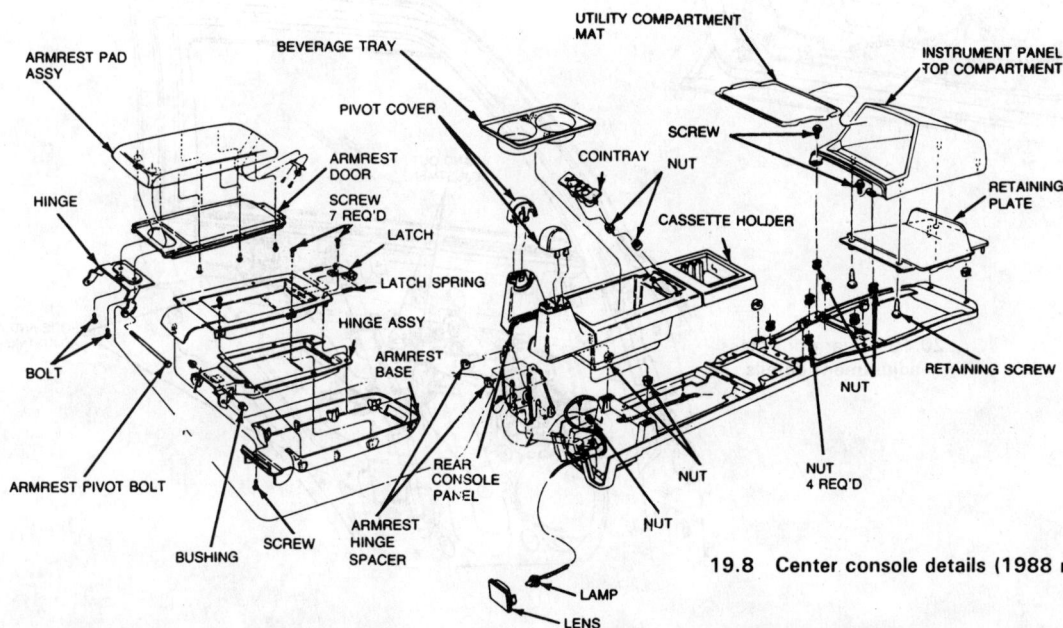

19.8   Center console details (1988 models)

VIEW A

RIVET REMOVAL
ACCESS HOLES

OUTER GLASS RETAINER
2 REQ'D

SPACER
2 REQ'D

DOOR GLASS

REGULATOR
C-CHANNEL

RIVET

VIEW A

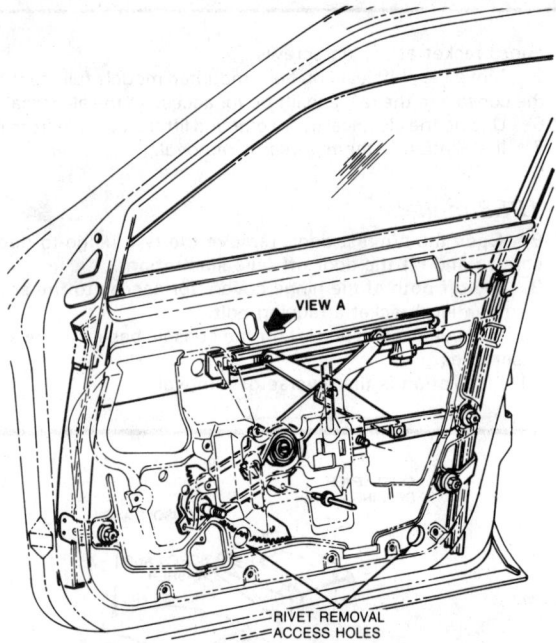

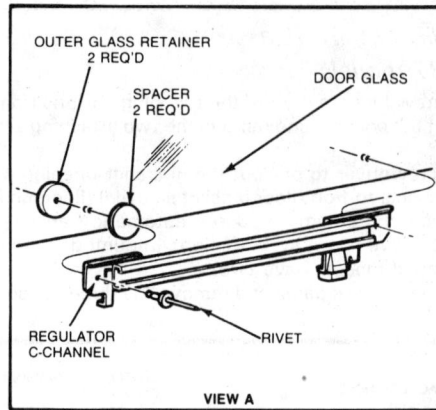

20.3   Typical front door window glass details

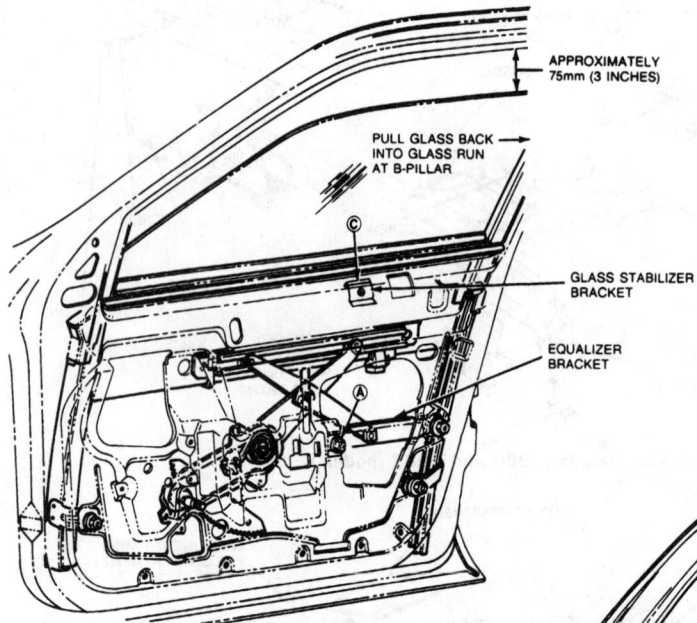

APPROXIMATELY
75mm (3 INCHES)

PULL GLASS BACK
INTO GLASS RUN
AT B-PILLAR

GLASS STABILIZER
BRACKET

EQUALIZER
BRACKET

20.12   Front door glass
adjustment details

IN AND OUT
ADJUSTMENT

FORE AND AFT
ADJUSTMENT

20.16   Rear door glass
adjustment details

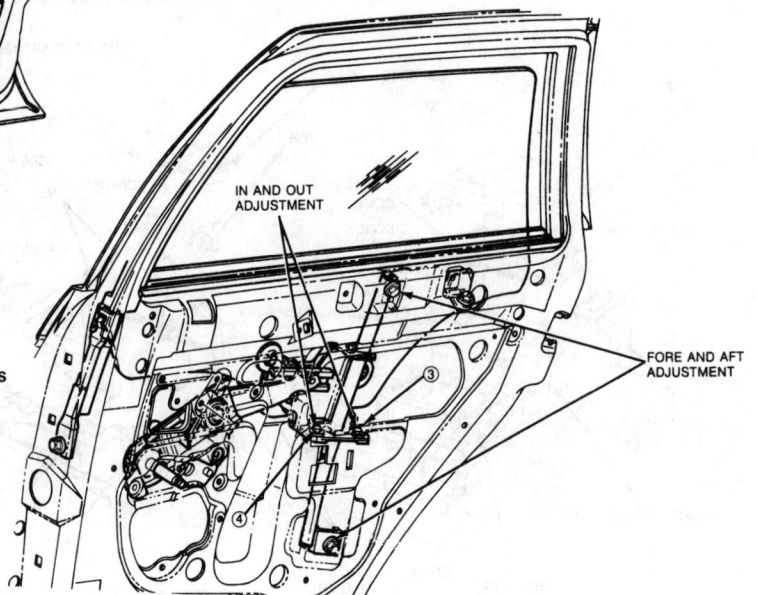

20 Door window glass — removal, installation and adjustment

Refer to illustrations 20.3, 20.12 and 20.16

Removal

1   Remove the door trim panel and watershield (Section 15).
2   Pull the inner door weatherstripping from the door flange.
3   On front doors, lower the glass for access to the two glass-to-retaining bracket rivets **(see illustration)**.
4   Insert a wood block between the door outer panel and the glass bracket and use a punch and hammer to remove the bracket-to-glass retaining rivet center pins. Drill out the rivets with a 1/2-inch drill bit.
5   On front doors, loosen the door glass stabilizer retaining nut. Remove the glass by tipping it forward and then lifting it from the door through the door belt opening toward the outside.
6   On rear doors, remove the glass stabilizer screw and the bracket. Lift the glass up through the door belt moulding and remove it from the door.

Installation

7   Make sure the plastic spacers and retainer are installed on the glass.
8   Lower the glass into position in the door.
9   Position the glass in the bracket and secure it with rivets. Alternatively, 1/4-inch by 1-inch long screws with nuts can be used to secure the glass to the bracket. Tighten the nuts to the specified torque.
10 Install the door weatherstripping.

Adjustment

11 Lower the glass approximately two to three inches from the full up position.

Front door

12 Loosen the adjustment nuts, and with the door open, put your hands on both sides of the glass and pull it back into the B-pillar glass run as far as possible **(see illustration)**.
13 Tighen nut and washer A (in illustration 20.12), apply downward pressure on the equalizer bracket and then tighten nut B.
14 Set the door glass stabilizer so that it is touching the glass slightly and then tighten nut C to the specified torque.
15 Cycle the glass several times to make sure it fits properly, adjusting as necessary.

Rear door

16 To initially set the glass to the window opening, loosen the adjusting bolts and push it forward into the B-pillar and tighten nut number 1, followed by 2, 3 and 4 **(see illustration)**.
17 The glass can be adjusted in and out and fore and aft after loosening the appropriate adjustment bolts.

21 Automatic shoulder harnesses – general information

Many late model vehicles are equipped with automatic front seat shoulder harnesses. They are termed automatic because you don't have to buckle them – the shoulder harness automatically positions itself when the door is closed and the key is turned on. An emergency release lever allows the harness to be manually removed for exit in an emergency. **Warning:** *Be sure to fasten the manual seatbelt as well. The automatic shoulder harness will not work properly unless the seatbelt is fastened.*

Most systems have a warning light and buzzer that indicate the emergency lever has been pulled up, releasing the shoulder harness. Also, if you disconnect any wires or remove any automatic shoulder harness components when performing repair procedures on other vehicle components, be sure to reinstall everything and check the harness for proper operation when the repairs are complete.

Since the automatic shoulder harness is operated by several electric switches and is computer controlled, diagnosis and repair must be done by a dealer service department. Do not jeopardize the safety of front seat occupants – if the automatic shoulder harness malfunctions, or you have questions regarding the proper use or operation of the system, contact a dealer service department.

Chapter 12 Chassis electrical system

Contents

1 General information

Warning: *To prevent electrical shorts, fires and injury, always disconnect the cable from the negative terminal of the battery before checking, repairing or replacing electrical system components.*

The chassis electrical system of this vehicle is a 12-volt, negative ground type. Power for the lights and all electrical accessories is supplied by a lead/acid-type battery which is charged by the alternator.

This chapter covers repair and service procedures for various chassis (non-engine related) electrical components. For information regarding the engine electrical system components (battery, alternator, distributor and starter motor), see Chapter 5.

2 Electrical troubleshooting — general information

A typical electrical circuit consists of an electrical component, any switches, relays, motors, fuses, fusible links or circuit breakers, etc. related to that component and the wiring and connectors that link the component to both the battery and the chassis. To help you pinpoint electrical circuit problems, wiring diagrams are included at the end of this book.

Wiring color code

When referring to the wiring diagrams, use the following alphabetical code to determine the color of the wires you are checking:

B Black	LG Light green	T Tan
BR Brown	N Natural	W White
DB Dark blue	O Orange	Y Yellow
DG Dark green	P Purple	(H) Hash*
GY Gray	PK Pink	(D) Dot*
LB Light blue	R Red	

Note: *The presence of a tracer on the wire is indicated by a secondary color followed by a ''H'' for hash or a ''D'' for dot. A stripe is understood if no letter follows.*

Before tackling any troublesome electrical circuit, first study the appropriate wiring diagrams to get a complete understanding of what makes up that individual circuit. Trouble spots, for instance, can often be isolated by noting if other components related to that circuit are operating properly. If several components or circuits fail at one time, chances are the problem is in a fuse or ground connection because several circuits are often routed through the same fuse and ground connections.

Electrical problems usually stem from simple causes such as loose or corroded connectors, a blown fuse, a melted fusible link or a bad relay. Visually inspect the condition of all fuses, wires and connectors in a problem circuit before troubleshooting it.

The basic tools needed for electrical troubleshooting include a circuit tester, a high impedance (10 K-ohm) digital voltmeter, a continuity tester and a jumper wire with an inline circuit breaker for bypassing electrical components. Before attempting to locate or define a problem with electrical test instruments, use the wiring diagrams to decide where to make the necessary connections.

Voltage checks

Perform a voltage check first when a circuit is not functioning properly. Connect one lead of a circuit tester to either the negative battery terminal or a known good ground.

Connect the other lead to a connector in the circuit being tested, preferably nearest to the battery or fuse. If the bulb of the tester lights up, voltage is present, which means that the part of the circuit between the connector and the battery is problem free. Continue checking the rest of the circuit in the same fashion.

When you reach a point at which no voltage is present, the problem lies between that point and the last test point with voltage. Most of the time the problem can be traced to a loose connection. **Note:** *Keep in mind that some circuits receive voltage only when the ignition key is in the Accessory or Run position.*

Finding a short circuit

One method of finding shorts in a circuit is to remove the fuse and connect a test light or voltmeter in its place. There should be no voltage present in the circuit. Move the wiring harness from side-to-side while watching the test light. If the bulb goes on, there is a short to ground somewhere in that area, probably where the insulation has rubbed through. The same test can be performed on each component in the circuit, even a switch.

Ground check

Perform a ground test to check whether a component is properly grounded. Disconnect the battery and connect one lead of a self-powered test light, known as a *continuity tester*, to a known good ground. Connect the other lead to the wire or ground connection being tested. If the bulb goes on, the ground is good. If the bulb does not go on, the ground is not good.

Continuity check

A continuity check determines if there are any breaks in a circuit (if it is conducting electricity properly). With the circuit off (no power in the circuit), a self-powered continuity tester can be used to check the circuit. Connect the test leads to both ends of the circuit, and if the test light comes on the circuit is passing current properly. If the light doesn't come on, there is a break somewhere in the circuit. The same procedure can be used to test a switch, by connecting the continuity tester to the power in and power out sides of the switch. With the switch turned on, the test light should come on.

Finding an open circuit

When diagnosing for possible open circuits it is often difficult to locate them by sight because oxidation and/or terminal misalignment are hidden by the connectors. Merely wiggling a connector on a sensor or in the wiring harness may correct the open circuit condition. Remember this if an open circuit is indicated when troubleshooting a circuit. Intermittent problems may also be caused by oxidized or loose connections.

Electrical troubleshooting is simple if you keep in mind that all electrical circuits are basically electricity running from the battery, through the wires, switches, relays, fuses and fusible links to each electrical component (light bulb, motor, etc.) and then to ground, from which it is passed back to the battery. Any electrical problem is an interruption in the flow of electricity to and from the battery.

3 Connectors — general information

Refer to illustrations 3.1, 3.2 and 3.3

Always release the lock lever(s) before attempting to unplug inline type connectors. There are a variety of lock lever configurations **(see illustration)**. Although nothing more than a finger is usually necessary to pry lock levers open, a small pocket screwdriver is effective for hard-

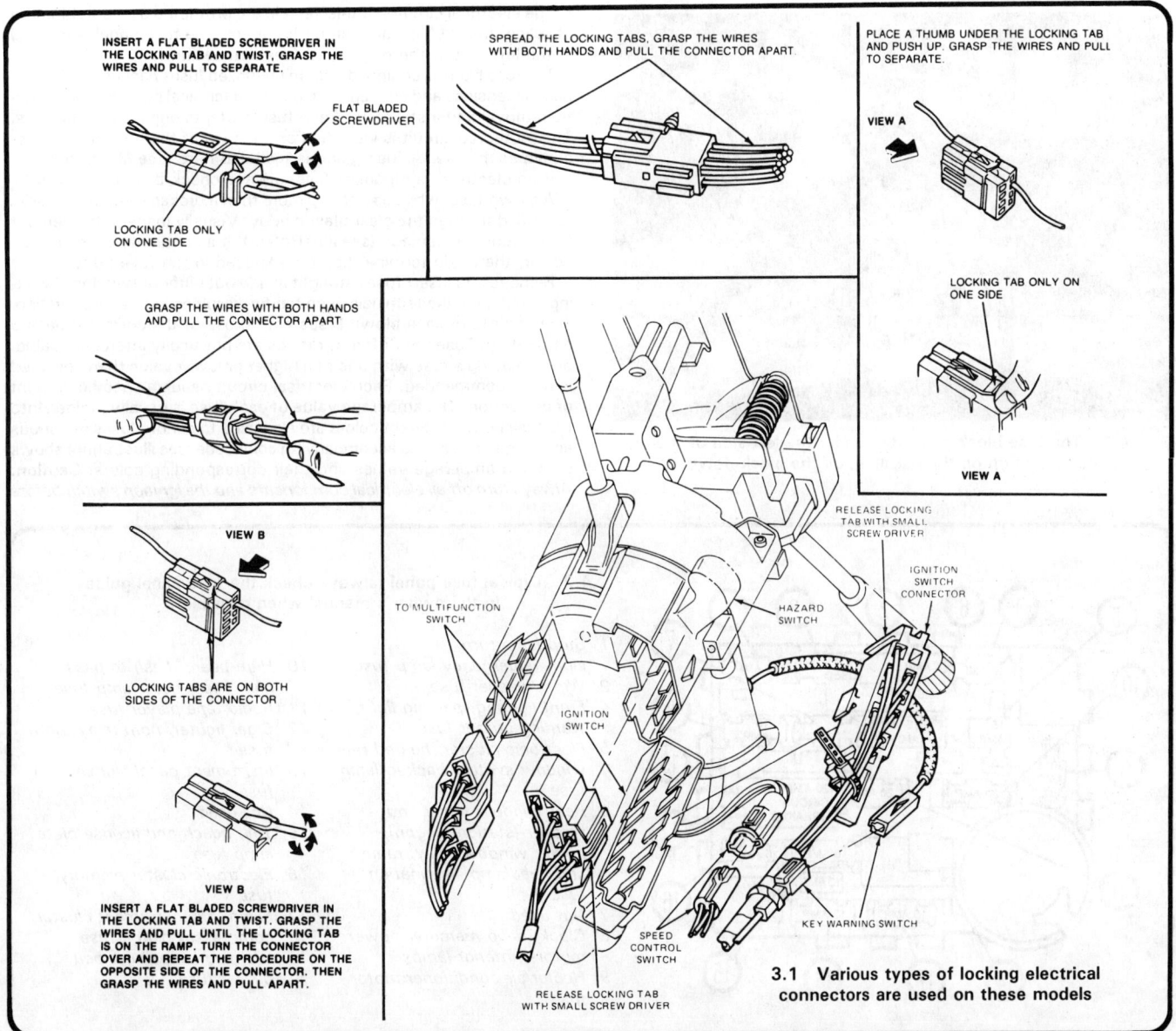

INSERT A FLAT BLADED SCREWDRIVER IN THE LOCKING TAB AND TWIST, GRASP THE WIRES AND PULL TO SEPARATE.

FLAT BLADED SCREWDRIVER

LOCKING TAB ONLY ON ONE SIDE

GRASP THE WIRES WITH BOTH HANDS AND PULL THE CONNECTOR APART

VIEW B

LOCKING TABS ARE ON BOTH SIDES OF THE CONNECTOR

VIEW B

INSERT A FLAT BLADED SCREWDRIVER IN THE LOCKING TAB AND TWIST. GRASP THE WIRES AND PULL UNTIL THE LOCKING TAB IS ON THE RAMP. TURN THE CONNECTOR OVER AND REPEAT THE PROCEDURE ON THE OPPOSITE SIDE OF THE CONNECTOR. THEN GRASP THE WIRES AND PULL APART.

SPREAD THE LOCKING TABS, GRASP THE WIRES WITH BOTH HANDS AND PULL THE CONNECTOR APART.

PLACE A THUMB UNDER THE LOCKING TAB AND PUSH UP. GRASP THE WIRES AND PULL TO SEPARATE.

VIEW A

LOCKING TAB ONLY ON ONE SIDE

VIEW A

RELEASE LOCKING TAB WITH SMALL SCREW DRIVER

IGNITION SWITCH CONNECTOR

HAZARD SWITCH

TO MULTIFUNCTION SWITCH

IGNITION SWITCH

SPEED CONTROL SWITCH

KEY WARNING SWITCH

RELEASE LOCKING TAB WITH SMALL SCREW DRIVER

3.1 Various types of locking electrical connectors are used on these models

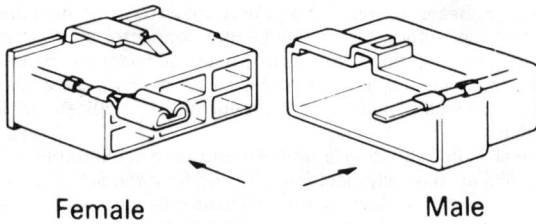

3.2   To distinguish between male and female halves of the connector, look at the terminal pins

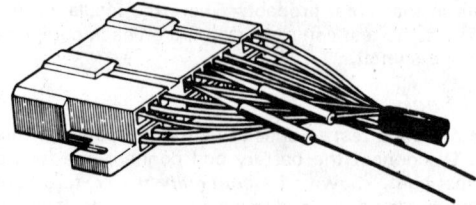

3.3   When checking for continuity or voltage with a circuit testing device, insert the test probe from the wire harness side (rear side of connector)

to-release levers. Once the lock levers are released, try to pull on the connectors themselves, not the wires, when unplugging two connector halves (there are times, however, when this is not possible — use good judgment).

It is usually necessary to know which side, male or female, of the connector you're checking. Male connectors are easily distinguished from females by the shape of their internal pins (see illustration).

When checking continuity or voltage with a circuit tester, insertion

4.1   The fuse block is located under the left side of the dash; pull up on the bar and pull the block down

of the test probe into the receptacle may open the fitting to the connector and result in poor contact. Instead, insert the test probe from the wire harness side of the connector (see illustration).

4   Fuses — general information

Refer to illustrations 4.1, 4.2, 4.4 and 4.6

The electrical circuits of this vehicle are protected by a combination of fuses, fusible links and circuit breakers. The fuse panel is located in the left end of the dashboard (see illustration).

The fuse block is equipped with miniaturized fuses because their compact dimensions and convenient blade-type terminal design allow fingertip removal and installation. Each fuse protects one or more circuits. The protected circuit is identified on the face of the fuse panel cover above each fuse. A fuse guide is included here (see illustration).

If an electrical component fails, always check the fuse first.

A blown fuse, which is nothing more than a broken element, is easily identified through the clear plastic body. Visually inspect the element for evidence of damage (see illustration). If a continuity check is called for, the blade terminal tips are exposed in the fuse body.

Remove and insert fuses straight in and out without twisting. Twisting could force the terminals open too far, resulting in a bad connection.

Be sure to replace blown fuses with those of the correct type and amp rating. Fuses of different ratings are physically interchangeable, but replacing a fuse with one of a higher or lower value than specified is not recommended. Each electrical circuit needs a specific amount of protection. The amperage value of each fuse is usually molded into the fuse body. Different colors are also used to denote fuses of various amperage values. The accompanying color code (see illustration) shows common amperage values and their corresponding colors. Caution: Always turn off all electrical components and the ignition switch before

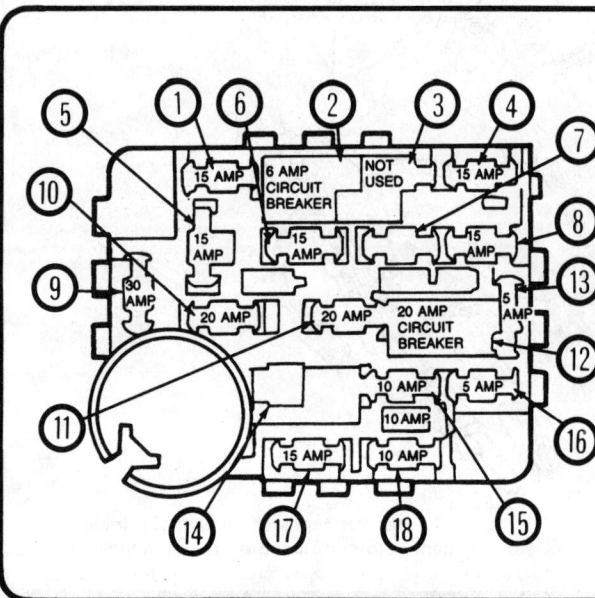

4.2   Typical fuse panel (always check the fuse panel guide in the owner's manual when possible)

1   Stop lamp/turn signal/emergency lamp fuse
2   Wiper/washer fuse
4   Front lighting, parking light, warning buzzer fuse
5   Electronic cluster, heated rear window switch, backup lamp fuse
6   Rear window wiper and washer (station wagon), power window relay, radio and headlamp illumination fuse
7   Not used
8   Clock, radio memory, power mirrors, interior lamps
9   Heater/air conditioner motor fuse
10   High beam, flash to pass, high beam head lamp fuse
11   Radio/tape player fuse
12   Cigar lighter, horn relay, horn fuse
13   Instrument panel illumination fuse
14   Not used
15   Tail, coach and license plate lamp fuse
16   Electronic cluster memory fuse
17   Electronic instrument cluster, compressor clutch fuse
18   Warning lamps/seat belt buzzer fuse

4.4 To test for a blown mini-fuse, pull it out and inspect it visually for an open (1), then with the circuit activated, use a test light across the terminals (2)

Fuse Value Amps	Color Code
4	Pink
5	Tan
10	Red
15	Light Blue
20	Yellow
25	Natural
30	Light Green

4.6 Each fuse amp value has a corresponding color code

replacing a fuse. Never bypass a fuse with pieces of metal or foil. Serious damage to the electrical system could result.

If the replacement fuse immediately fails, do not replace it again until the cause of the problem is isolated and corrected. In most cases, this will be a short circuit in the wiring caused by a broken or deteriorated wire.

5 Fusible links — general information

Refer to illustrations 5.1a, 5.1b and 5.1c

Some circuits are protected by fusible links. These links are used in circuits which are not ordinarily fused, such as the starter circuit (see illustrations). If a circuit protected by a fusible link becomes inoperative, inspect for a blown fusible link.

Although fusible links appear to be of heavier gauge than the wire they are protecting, their appearance is due to thicker insulation. All fusible links are four wire gauges *smaller* than the wire they are designed to protect. The location of the fusible links on your particular vehicle can be determined by referring to the wiring diagrams at the end of this Chapter.

Fusible links cannot be repaired. If you must replace one, make sure that the new fusible link is a duplicate of the one removed with respect to gauge, length and insulation. Original and Ford replacement fusible links have insulation that is flame proof. Do not fabricate a fusible link from ordinary wire — the insulation may not be flame proof. **Warning:** *Do not mistake a resistor wire for a fusible link. The resistor wire is generally longer and is identified by a ''Resistor — don't cut or splice'' warning.*

Charging system fusible link

1 To replace the fusible link in the charging system, proceed as follows:
a) Disconnect the negative cable at the battery.
b) Disconnect the fusible link from the wiring harness or the fusible link eyelet terminal from the battery terminal of the starter relay (on some vehicle applications, the fusible link is looped outside the wire harness).
c) Cut the damaged fusible link and the splices from the wires to which it is attached. Disconnect the feed wire part of the wiring and cut out the damaged portion as closely as possible behind the splice in the harness. If the fusible link wire insulation is burned or opened, disconnect the feed as close as possible behind the splice in the harness. If the damaged fusible link is between two splices (the weld points in the harness), cut out the damaged portion as close as possible to the weld points.
d) Strip the insulation back approximately 1/2-inch.
e) Splice and solder the new fusible link to the wires from which the old link was cut. Use rosin core solder at each end of the new link to obtain a good solder joint.
f) Wrap the splices completely with vinyl electrical tape around the soldered joint. No wires should be exposed (see illustration).

g) Securely connect the eyelet terminals (if any) to the battery stud on the starter relay. **Note:** *Some fusible links (see illustration) have an eyelet terminal for a 5/16-inch stud on one end. When the terminal is not required, use one of the fusible links shown with the insulation stripped from both ends.*
h) Install the repaired wiring as before, using existing clips, if provided.
i) Connect the battery ground cable.
j) Test the circuit for proper operation.

All other fusible links

2 To service any other blown fusible link, use the following procedure:
a) Determine which circuit is damaged, its location and the cause of the open fusible link. If the damaged fusible link is one of three fed by a common 10 or 12 gauge feed wire, determine the specific affected circuit.
b) Disconnect the negative battery cable.
c) Cut the damaged fusible link from the wiring harness and discard it. If the fusible link is one of three circuits fed by a single wire, cut it out of the harness at each splice and discard it.
d) Identify and procure the proper fusible link and butt connectors for attaching the fusible link to the harness.
3 To service any fusible link in a three-link group with one feed:
a) After cutting the open link out of the harness, cut each of the remaining undamaged fusible links close to the feed wire weld.
b) Strip approximately 1/2-inch of insulation from the detached ends of the two good fusible links. Insert two wire ends into one end of a Ford butt connector and carefully push one stripped end of the replacement fusible link into the same end of the butt connector and crimp all three firmly together (see illustration 5.1b). **Note:** *Be very careful when fitting the three fusible links into the butt connector — the internal diameter is a snug fit for three wires. Be sure to use a proper crimping tool. Pliers, side cutters, etc. will not apply the proper crimp to retain the wires.*

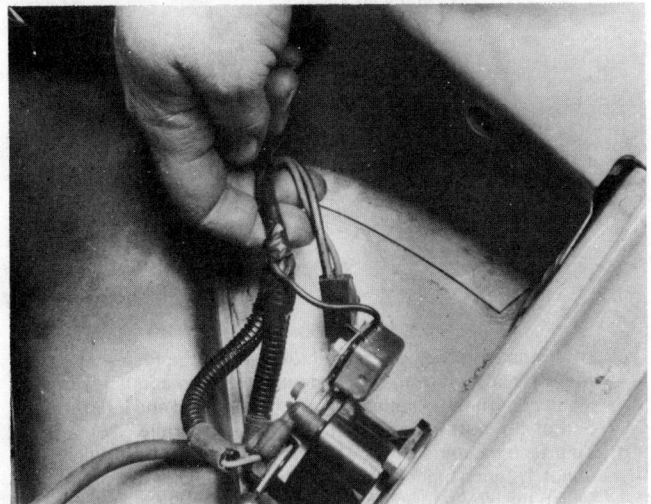

5.1a A typical system in which the fusible links are connected to the starter solenoid

TAPE

REMOVE EXISTING VINYL TUBE SHIELDING
REINSTALL OVER FUSE LINK BEFORE CRIMPING
FUSE LINK TO WIRE ENDS

TAPE OR STRAP

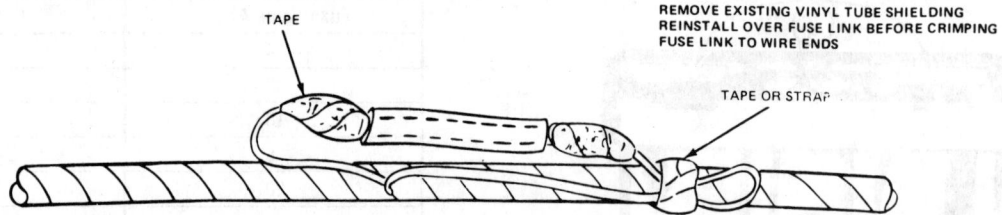

**TYPICAL REPAIR USING THE SPECIAL #17 GA. (9.00" LONG-YELLOW) FUSE LINK REQUIRED FOR THE AIR/COND.
CIRCUITS (2) # 687E AND #261A LOCATED IN THE ENGINE COMPARTMENT**

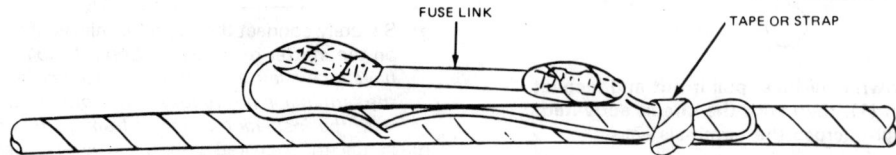

FUSE LINK

TAPE OR STRAP

TYPICAL REPAIR FOR ANY IN-LINE FUSE LINK USING THE SPECIFIED GAUGE FUSE LINK FOR THE SPECIFIED CIRCUIT

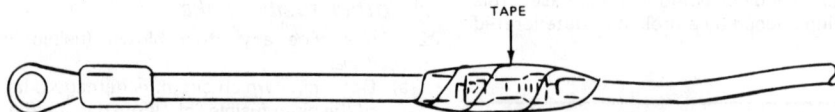

TAPE

TYPICAL REPAIR USING THE EYELET TERMINAL FUSE LINK OF THE SPECIFIED GAUGE FOR ATTACHMENT TO A CIRCUIT WIRE END

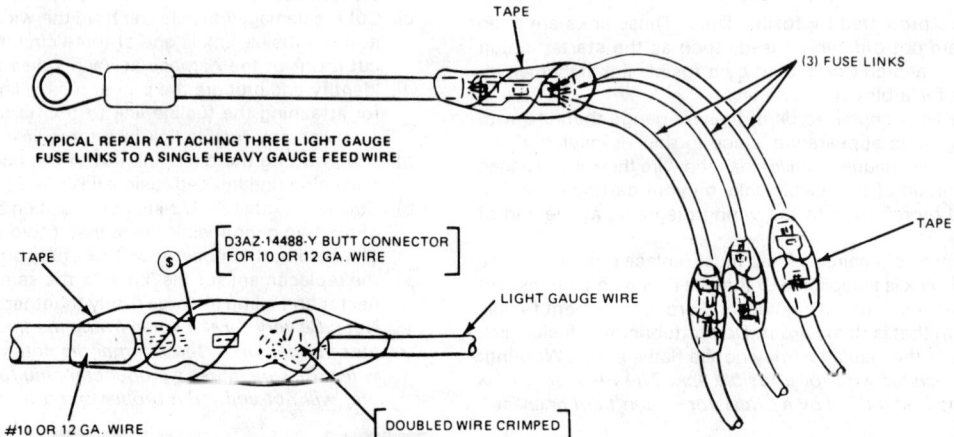

TAPE

(3) FUSE LINKS

**TYPICAL REPAIR ATTACHING THREE LIGHT GAUGE
FUSE LINKS TO A SINGLE HEAVY GAUGE FEED WIRE**

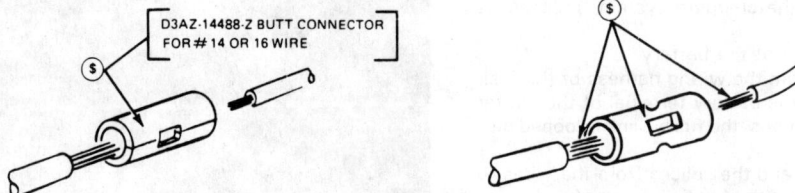

TAPE

TAPE

D3AZ-14488-Y BUTT CONNECTOR
FOR 10 OR 12 GA. WIRE

LIGHT GAUGE WIRE

#10 OR 12 GA. WIRE

DOUBLED WIRE CRIMPED

D3AZ-14488-Z BUTT CONNECTOR
FOR # 14 OR 16 WIRE

5.1b   Fusible link repair details

c) After crimping the butt connector to the three fusible links, cut the weld portion from the feed wire and strip about 1/2-inch of insulation from the cut end. Insert the stripped end into the open end of the butt connector and crimp very firmly.

d) To attach the remaining end of the replacement fusible link, strip about 1/2-inch of insulation from the wire end of the circuit from which the blown fusible link was removed and firmly crimp a butt connector to the stripped wire. Insert the end of the replacement link into the other end of the butt connector and crimp firmly.

e) Using rosin core solder with a consistency of 60 per cent tin and 40 per cent lead, solder the connectors and the wires at the repairs and insulate with electrical tape.

4   To replace any fusible link on a single circuit in a harness, cut out the damaged portion, strip about 1/2-inch of insulation from the two wire ends and attach the appropriate replacement fusible link to the stripped wire ends with two proper size butt connectors. Solder the connectors and wires and insulate with tape.

5   To service any fusible link which has an eyelet terminal on one

**WIRING ASSEMBLY — FUSE LINK
(WITH INSULATION STRIPPED BOTH ENDS)**

D3AZ—14A526-H #14 GA. WIRE — 9.00" ± .50 LENGTH
(GREEN INSULATION)

D3AZ—14A526-J #16 GA. WIRE — 9.00" ± .50 LENGTH
(ORANGE INSULATION) AS REQ'D.

D3AZ—14A526-K #17 GA. WIRE — 9.00" ± .50 LENGTH
(YELLOW INSULATION) AS REQ'D.
(SPECIAL USED WITH AIR CONDITIONING SYSTEM)

D3AZ—14A526-L #18 GA. WIRE — 9.00" ± .50 LENGTH
(RED INSULATION) AS REQ'D.

D3AZ—14A526-M #20 GA. WIRE — 9.00" ± .50 LENGTH
(BLUE INSULATION) AS REQ'D.

**WIRING ASSEMBLY — FUSE LINK
(WITH EYELET TERMINAL AND ONE END STRIPPED)**

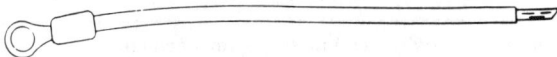

D3AZ—14A526-D #14 GA. WIRE — 9.00" ± .50 LENGTH
(GREEN INSULATION) AS REQ'D.

D3AZ—14A526-E #16 GA. WIRE — 9.00" ± .50 LENGTH
(ORANGE INSULATION) AS REQ'D.

D3AZ—14A526-F #18 GA. WIRE — 9.00" ± .50 LENGTH
(RED INSULATION) AS REQ'D.

D3AZ—14A526-G #20 GA. WIRE — 9.00" ± .50 LENGTH
(BLUE INSULATION) AS REQ'D.

BUTT CONNECTOR — WIRING SPLICE

D3AZ—14488-Y FOR #10 AND 12 GA. WIRE (LOAD CIRCUIT) AS REQ'D.
D3AZ—14488-Z FOR #14 AND 16 GA. WIRE (LOAD CIRCUIT) AS REQ'D.

5.1c Fusible link and connector types

end (like the charging circuit), cut off the open fusible link behind the weld, strip about 1/2-inch of insulation from the cut end and attach the appropriate new eyelet fusible link to the cut stripped wire with an appropriate size butt connector. Solder the connectors and wires at the point of service and insulate with tape.

6   Connect the cable to the negative terminal of the battery.

7   Test the system for proper operation.

6 Circuit breakers — general information

Refer to illustration 6.1

Circuit breakers protect accessories such as the windshield wiper, horn, cigar lighter etc. Circuit breakers are located in the fuse box **(see illustration)**. Refer to the fuse panel guide in Section 4 and the fuse panel guide in your owner's manual for the location of the circuit breakers used in your vehicle.

Because a circuit breaker resets itself automatically, an electrical overload in a circuit breaker protected system will cause the circuit to fail momentarily, then come back on. If the circuit does not come back on, check it immediately.

a) Remove the circuit breaker from the fuse panel.

b) Using an ohmmeter, verify that there is continuity between both terminals of the circuit breaker. If there is no continuity, replace the circuit breaker.

c) Install the old or new circuit breaker. If it continues to cut out, a short circuit is indicated. Troubleshoot the appropriate circuit (see the wiring diagrams at the back of this book) or have the system checked by a professional mechanic.

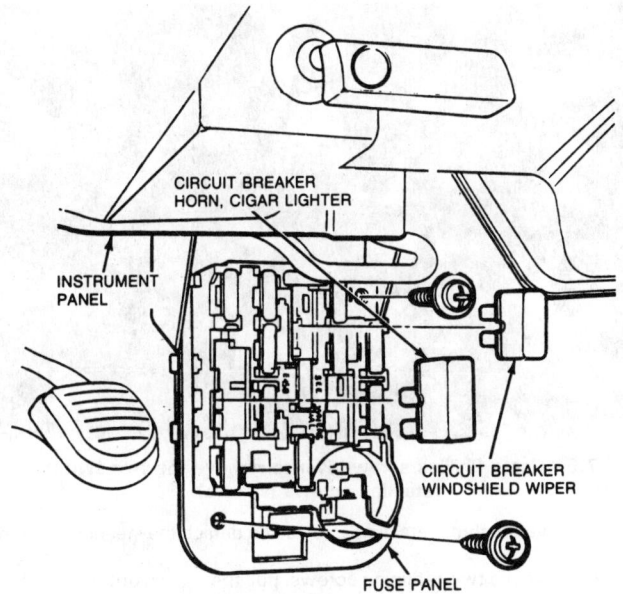

6.1 The circuit breakers plug into the fuse block

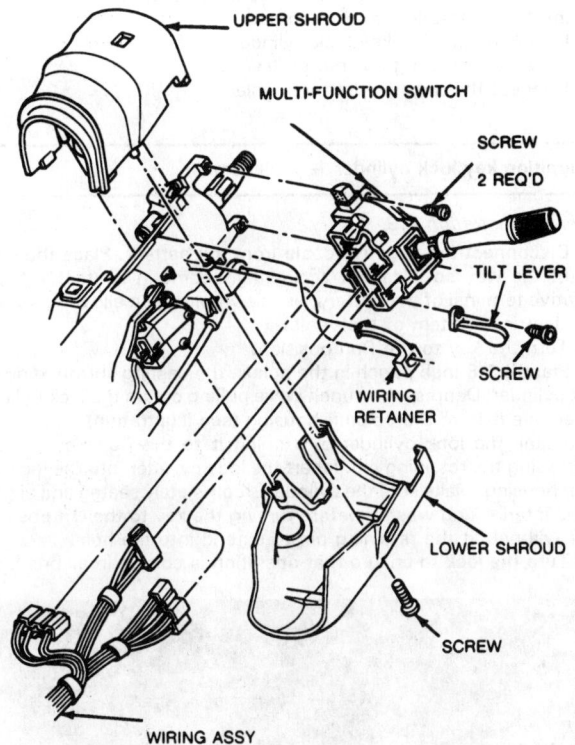

7.2 Multi-function switch component layout

7 Turn signal/hazard/flash-to-pass/dimmer switch (multi-function switch) — replacement

Refer to illustrations 7.2 and 7.5

1   Disconnect the negative cable from the battery. Place the cable out of the way so it cannot accidentally come in contact with the negative terminal of the battery, as this would again allow power into the electrical system of the vehicle.

2   On tilt column models, lower the column to the lowest position, remove the retaining screw and lift off the tilt lever **(see illustration)**.

3   Remove the ignition key lock cylinder (Section 8).

7.5 Use a Phillips screwdriver to remove the two switch retaining screws (arrows)

4   Remove the three retaining screws and detach the steering column shroud.
5   Remove the two retaining screws, pull the switch out, unplug the connector and withdraw the switch assembly from the steering column **(see illustration)**.
6   Plug in the electrical connector, place the new switch in position and install the screws. Tighten the screws securely.
7   Install the steering column shroud.
8   Install the ignition key lock cylinder.
9   Install the steering column tilt lever.
10   Connect the negative battery cable.

8 Ignition key lock cylinder — replacement

Refer to illustration 8.3

1   Disconnect the negative cable from the battery. Place the cable out of the way so it cannot accidentally come in contact with the negative terminal of the battery, as this would again allow power into the electrical system of the vehicle.
2   Turn the key to the Run position.
3   Place a 1/8-inch punch in the hole in the casting surrounding the lock cylinder. Depress the punch while pulling out on the lock cylinder to remove it from the column housing **(see illustration)**.
4   Install the lock cylinder by turning it to the Run position and depressing the retaining pin. Insert the lock cylinder into the lock cylinder housing. Make sure the cylinder is completely seated and aligned in the interlocking washer before turning the key to the Off position. This will permit the retaining pin to extend into the hole.
5   Turn the lock to ensure that operation is correct in all positions.

9.6 Use a small screwdriver to pry out the wiper arm release lever while lifting the arm up to disengage the assembly from the spindle

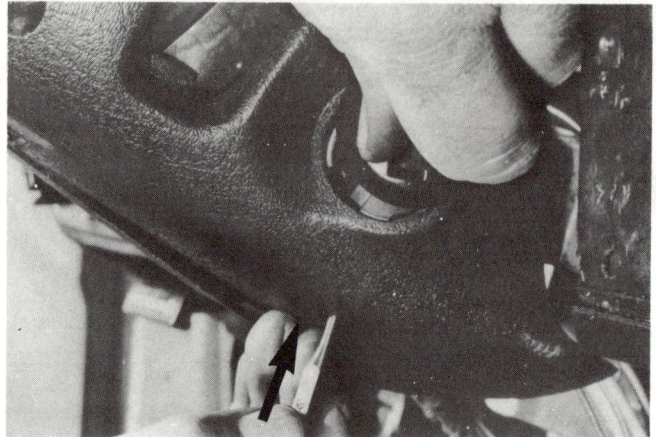

8.3 With the lock cylinder in the Run position, push in on the release lever with a small punch to release the cylinder

9 Wiper/washer switch and motor — replacement

1   Disconnect the negative cable from the battery. Place the cable out of the way so it cannot accidentally come in contact with the negative terminal of the battery, as this would again allow power into the electrical system of the vehicle.

Switch

Windshield wiper

2   The windshield wiper/washer switch is incorporated into the multi-function switch. See Section 7 for the multi-function switch replacement procedure.

Rear wiper

3   Remove the four retaining screws and detach the instrument cluster finish panel by pulling the upper edge out.
4   Unplug the wiring connector, remove the retaining screws (if equipped) and pry the switch out.
5   Installation is the reverse or removal.

Motor

Windshield wiper

Refer to illustrations 9.6, 9.8 and 9.9

6   Remove the left hand wiper arm by prying out the release lever while lifting up on the arm **(see illustration)**.
7   Remove the left hand cowl leaf screen.
8   Disconnect the wiper linkage from the motor arm by lifting up on the clip **(see illustration)**.
9   Unplug the electrical connector, remove the retaining bolts and lift the motor from the engine compartment **(see illustration)**.
10   Installation is the reverse of removal.

Rear wiper

Refer to illustration 9.11

11   Remove the wiper arm assembly **(see illustration)**.
12   Open the liftgate.
13   Unplug the wiring connector, remove the retaining nut, disengage the motor assembly from the liftgate and remove it from the vehicle.
14   Installation is the reverse of removal.

10 Hazard/turn signal flasher — replacement

Refer to illustration 10.2

1   Disconnect the negative cable from the battery. Place the cable out of the way so it cannot accidentally come in contact with the negative terminal of the battery, as this would again allow power into the electrical system of the vehicle.
2   The combination hazard/turn signal electronic flasher unit is mounted under the left side of the instrument panel, above the fuse panel **(see illustration)**.

WIPER LINKAGE DRIVE ARM

CLIP

WIPER MOTOR ARM

NOTE: PUSH THE DRIVE ARM FIRMLY ONTO PIN UNTIL LOCKED IN PLACE.

INSTALLATION

LIFT AND SLIDE CLIP TO REMOVE ARM

REMOVAL

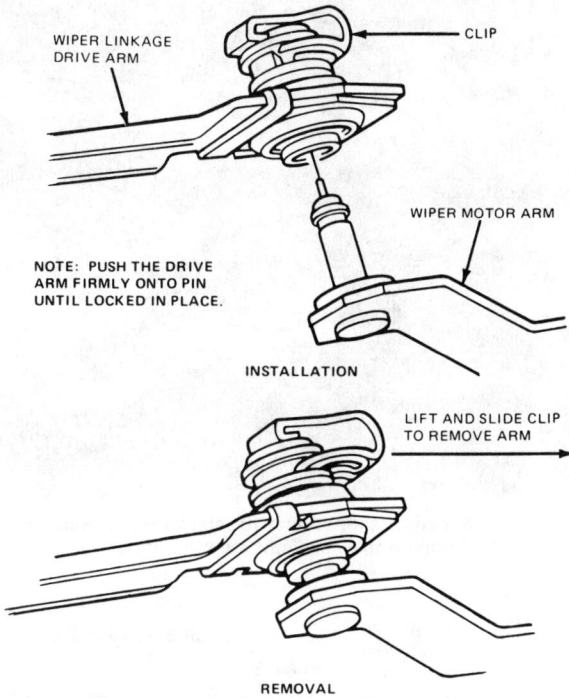

9.8 Wiper linkage connection details

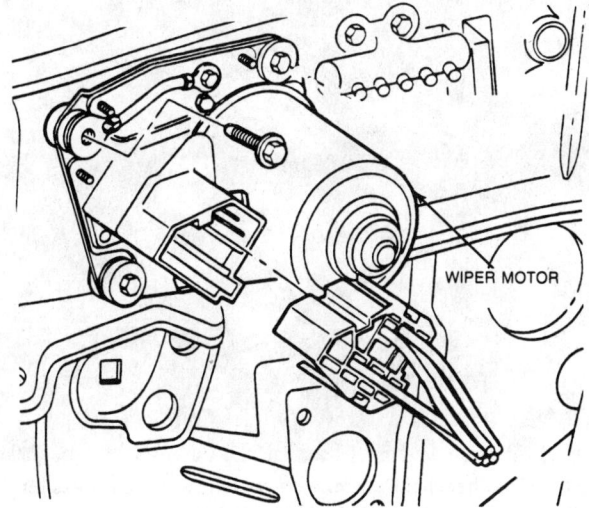

WIPER MOTOR

9.9 Unplug the connector, remove the bolts and lift the wiper motor off

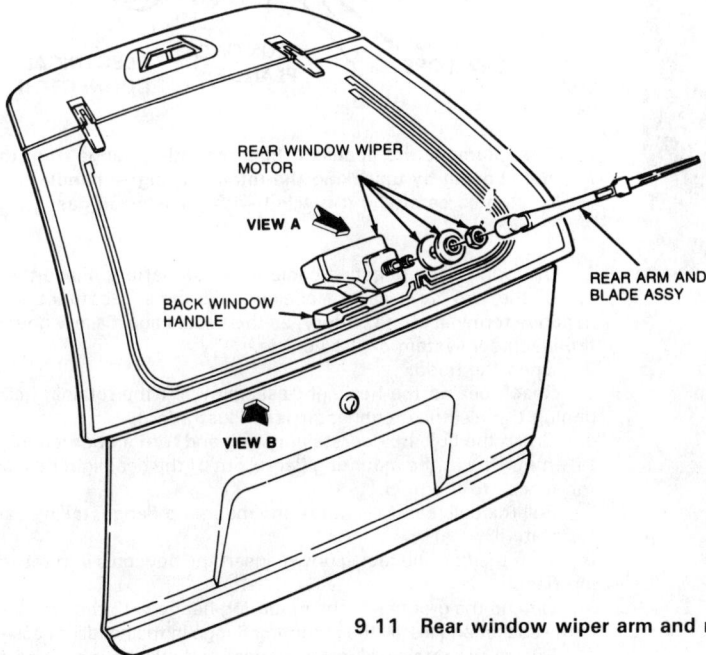

REAR WINDOW WIPER MOTOR

VIEW A

BACK WINDOW HANDLE

REAR ARM AND BLADE ASSY

VIEW B

REAR WINDOW WIPER MOTOR

REAR ARM AND BLADE ASSY

VIEW A

REAR WINDOW WIPER MOTOR ASSY

BACK WINDOW LATCH

VIEW B

9.11 Rear window wiper arm and motor installation details

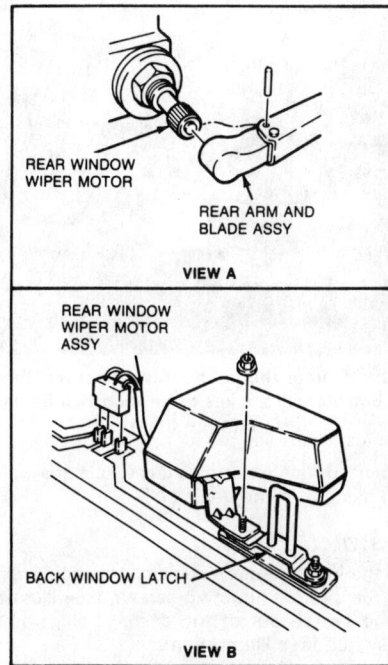

3   Reach up under the instrument panel, grasp the flasher unit securely and disengage it from the mounting clip. Unplug the electrical connector to remove the flasher unit from the vehicle.
4   Installation is the reverse of removal.

11 Headlight switch and dimmer/rheostat — replacement

Refer to illustrations 11.3, 11.4 and 11.7

1   Disconnect the negative cable from the battery. Place the cable out of the way so it cannot accidentally come in contact with the

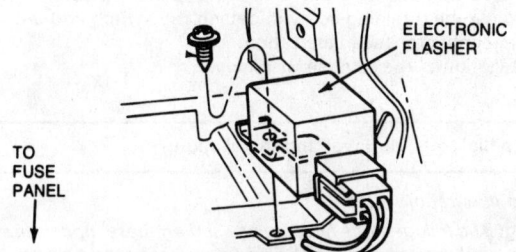

ELECTRONIC FLASHER

TO FUSE PANEL

10.2 The turn signal/hazard flasher unit is mounted under the dash above the fuse block

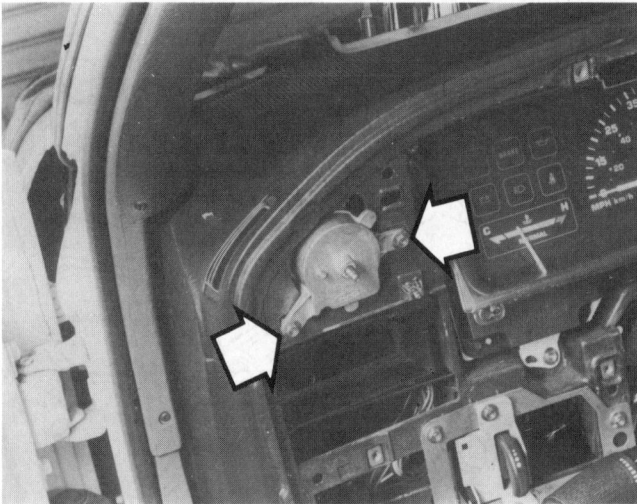

11.3   The headlight switch screws (arrows) are accessible
after removing the finish panel

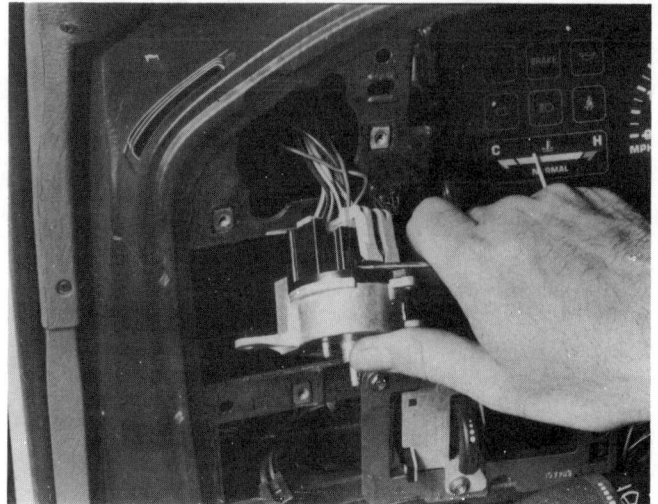

11.4   Use a small screwdriver to release the locking clip
and unplug the headlight switch connector

11.7   The dimmer/rheostat screws (arrows) have a torx
head but a small socket or wrench can be used to
remove them

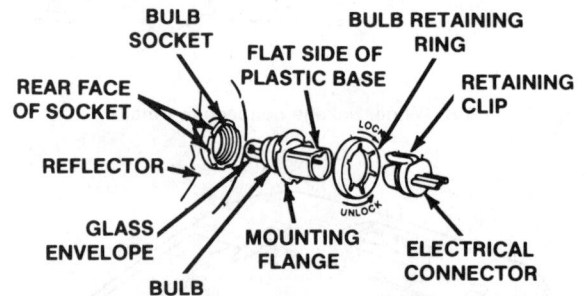

12.3   Remove the headlight bulb mounting flange from the
bulb socket by unlocking the retaining ring — handle the
bulb carefully; it is filled with pressurized gas

negative terminal of the battery, as this would again allow power into
the electrical system of the vehicle.

Headlight switch

2   Remove the instrument cluster finish panel (Chapter 11).
3   Remove the switch mounting screws **(see illustration)**.
4   Rotate the switch out of the dash, unplug the connector and
remove the switch **(see illustration)**.
5   Installation is the reverse of removal.

Dimmer/rheostat

6   Remove the left hand dashboard trim panel (Chapter 11).
7   Remove the retaining screws, detach the switch and unplug the
electrical connector **(see illustration)**.
8   Installation is the reverse of removal.

---

12   Headlights — removal and installation

Refer to illustration 12.3

Warning: *The halogen gas filled bulbs used on these models are under
pressure and may shatter if the surface is scratched or the bulb is
dropped. Wear eye protection and handle the bulbs carefully, touching
only the base whenever possible.*

1   Disconnect the negative cable from the battery. Place the cable
out of the way so it cannot accidentally come in contact with the
negative terminal of the battery, as this would again allow power into
the electrical system of the vehicle.
2   Open the hood.
3   Reach behind the headlight assembly, lift the retaining clip and
unplug the electrical connector **(see illustration)**.
4   Grasp the bulb holder retaining ring and turn it counterclockwise
to remove it. Lift the mounting flange out of the headlight bulb socket
for access to the bulb.
5   Pull the bulb carefully out of the mounting flange, taking care not
to rotate it.
6   With the flat side facing down, insert the new bulb into the mounting flange.
7   Line up the grooves of the mounting flange with the locating tabs
in the socket and install the mounting flange in the headlight assembly.
8   Rotate the retaining ring clockwise to lock the mounting flange
in place.
9   Press the electrical connector into the mounting flange until the
clip snaps into place, locking it.
10   Reconnect the negative cable to the battery.

---

13   Bulb replacement

Front lights

Refer to illustration 13.1

1   Front bulbs on these models are located in the front combination
light housing **(see illustration)**.

*SHOWN FOR REFERENCE, REMOVAL NOT REQUIRED

WIRING ASSEMBLY

HEADLAMP BULB AND SOCKET ASSEMBLY

VIEW B

*HEADLAMP LENS AND BODY ASSEMBLY

SIDE MARKER BULB AND SOCKET ASSEMBLY

*LAMP ASSEMBLY SIDE MARKER

FRONT OF VEHICLE

VIEW B

LAMP ASSEMBLY WIRING ASSEMBLY

VIEW SHOWING INSTALLATION OF WIRING ASSEMBLY TO HEADLAMP ASSEMBLY

TAURUS
LEFT HAND HEADLAMP SHOWN, RIGHT HAND SYMMETRICALLY OPPOSITE

WIRING ASSEMBLY

CORNERING LIGHT BULB AND SOCKET ASSEMBLY

RADIATOR SUPPORT

INNER PARKING LIGHT BULB AND ASSEMBLY SOCKET

WIRING ASSEMBLY

INNER PARKING LIGHT ASSEMBLY

HEADLIGHT LENS AND BODY ASSEMBLY

HEADLIGHT BULB AND SOCKET ASSEMBLY

CORNERING LIGHT LENS ASSEMBLY

PARKING LIGHT BULB AND SOCKET ASSEMBLY

PARKING LIGHT ASSEMBLY

SABLE
RIGHT HAND HEADLAMP SHOWN, LEFT HAND SYMMETRICALLY OPPOSITE

FRONT OF VEHICLE

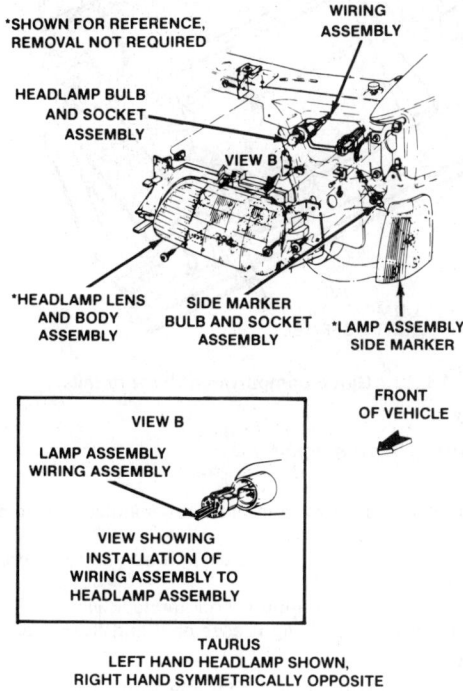

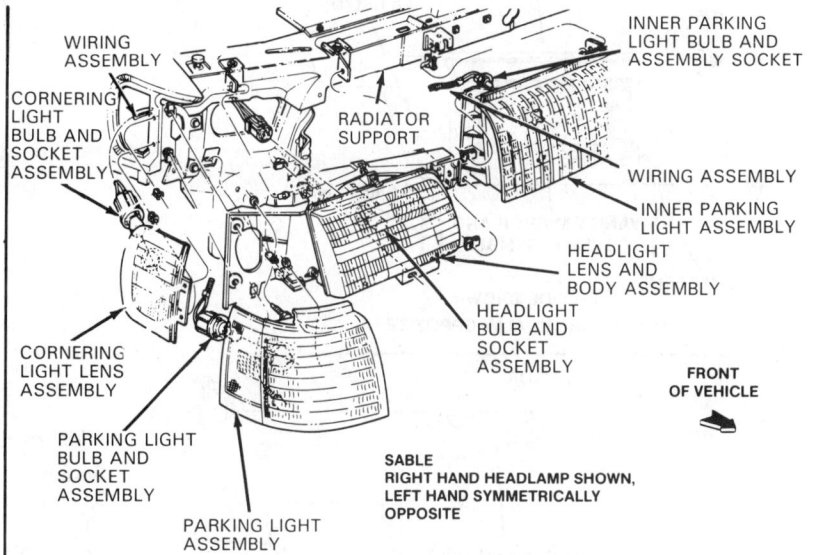

13.1   The front light bulbs are located in the combination light housing — Sable right hand headlight shown; left hand symmetrically opposite

Taurus parking/turn signal light

2   Reaching through the access hole in the radiator support, rotate the bulb socket assembly counterclockwise and disengage it from the housing (**see illustration 13.1**).
3   Remove the bulb from the socket by pressing it in and turning it counterclockwise. Push the new bulb in and turn it clockwise to lock it.
4   Install the socket and bulb in the housing.

Sable parking/turn signal light

5   Remove the two retaining screws and pull the parking light assembly out (**see illustration 13.1**).
6   Grasp the bulb socket and turn it to remove it.
7   Remove the bulb from the socket, then install the new bulb.
8   Place the socket in position and turn it to secure it.
9   Install the light and screws.

Taurus front side marker light

10   Remove the nut and washer from the attaching stud located at the top of the housing and rotate the top of the housing out until the stud tip is clear of the slot in the housing (**see illustration 13.1**).
11   Lift the light up to clear the tabs on the housing and remove it.
12   Twist the bulb socket counterclockwise to remove it. Replace the bulb by pulling it out of the socket and pressing the new one into place.
13   Install the bulb socket, lower the light into the tabs, rotate it into position and install the washer and nut.

Sable cornering light

14   Remove the parking light and bulb as described in Steps 5 and 6, then remove the two retaining screws and lift the cornering light out.
15   Replace the bulb by pulling it out of the socket and pressing the new one into place.
16   Place the cornering light in position and install the retaining screws.
17   Install the parking light.

Interior lights

Instrument cluster bulbs

Refer to illustrations 13.19 and 13.20

18   Remove the instrument cluster (Section 17).
19   Separate the cluster mask from the housing (**see illustration**).
20   The instrument cluster bulbs can be replaced after rotating the holders and lifting them out (**see illustration**). Pull the old bulb out of the holder and press the new one in.

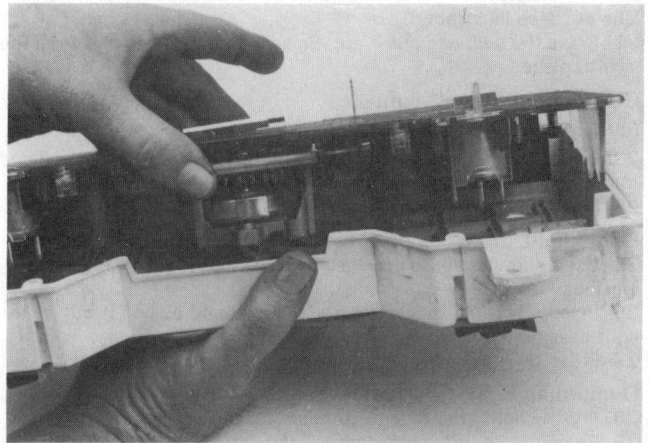

13.19   Separate the instrument cluster from the housing — be careful, the components are fragile

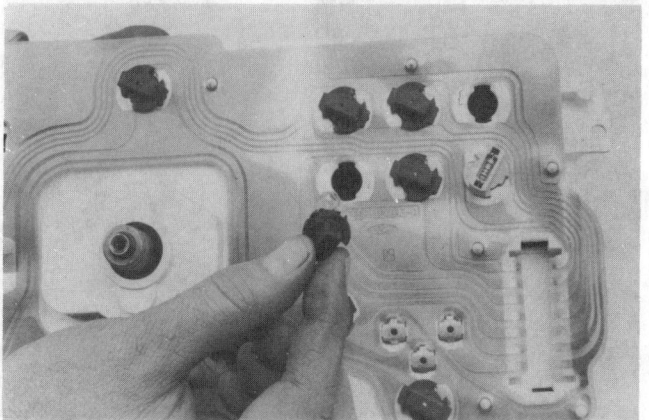

13.20   Rotate the bulb holder until the tabs line up with the notches in the housing, then pull it out

SABLE   VISOR ASSEMBLY   BULB 4 REQ'D

LAMP LENS

VANITY MIRROR AND COVER ASSEMBLY

LAMP LENS

LH SIDE SHOWN
RH SYMMETRICALLY OPPOSITE

TAURUS

VISOR ASSEMBLY   BULB

BULB LENS 2 REQ'D

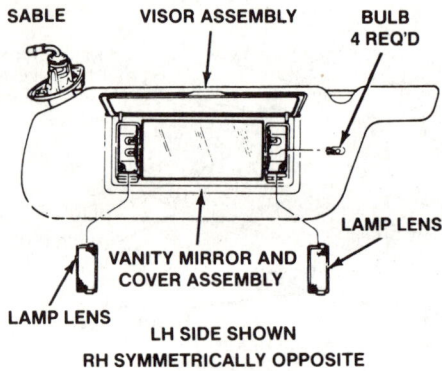

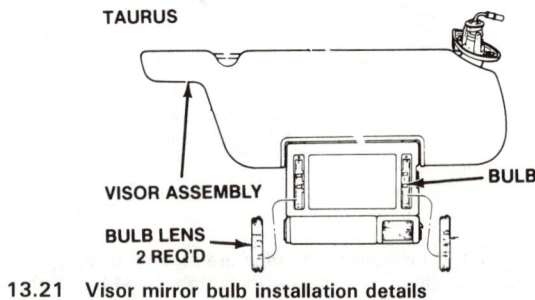

13.21   Visor mirror bulb installation details

Visor mirror light

Refer to illustration 13.21

21 Pull the visor down and use a small screwdriver to pry the bulb lens out **(see illustration)**

22 Grasp the bulb and pull it out. Press the new bulb in and snap the lens in place.

Glove compartment light

Refer to illustration 13.23

23 Open the glove compartment, grasp the bulb with your thumb and forefinger and pull it out of the socket **(see illustration)**.

24 Press the new bulb in.

Dome light

25 Use a screwdriver to pry the lens cover tabs in to release the locking tabs.

26 Relace the bulb by grasping it securely and pulling it out of the light assembly.

27 Press the new bulb into place and install the lens cover.

Dome/map light

28 Pry the light lens tabs in to release them and remove the lens.

29 Remove the retaining screws and lower the dome/map light assembly. Replace the bulbs from the rear of the assembly.

30 Replace the light assembly and lens.

GLOVE COMPARTMENT LIGHT ASSEMBLY

13.23   Glove compartment light details

High-mounted brake light

Sedan

31 Pry off the covers, remove the two retaining screws and lift the light cover off the bracket.

32 Remove the light assembly by pulling it up and toward the front of the vehicle.

33 Remove the bulb by rotating it counterclockwise.

34 Install the new bulb, the light assembly and the cover.

Station wagon

35 Pry the trim panel off the liftgate frame with a small screwdriver.

36 Remove the four cover nuts.

37 From outside the vehicle, pull the light assembly out.

38 Pull the wiring grommet out, unplug the wiring harness and detach the connector clip from the liftgate.

39 Pull the old bulb out of the socket and press the new one in.

40 Connect the light wiring harness and attach the locator to the liftgate.

41 Install the light assembly and cover.

Brake, tail and license plate light

Sedan

Refer to illustration 13.43a, 13.43b and 13.44

42 Open the trunk.

43 Remove the trunk rear panel **(see illustrations)**.

44 Rotate the bulb holders counterclockwise to remove them **(see illustration)**.

45 Rotate the bulbs counterclockwise to remove them from the holders.

46 Installation is the reverse of removal.

Station wagon

Refer to illustration 13.47

47 Remove the light assembly screws and side marker nuts for access to the bulbs **(see illustration)**.

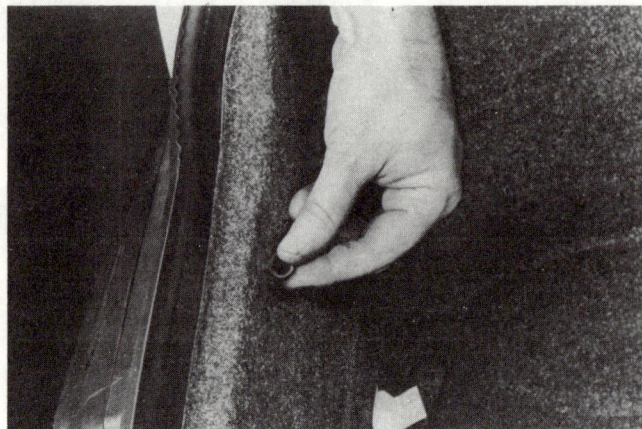

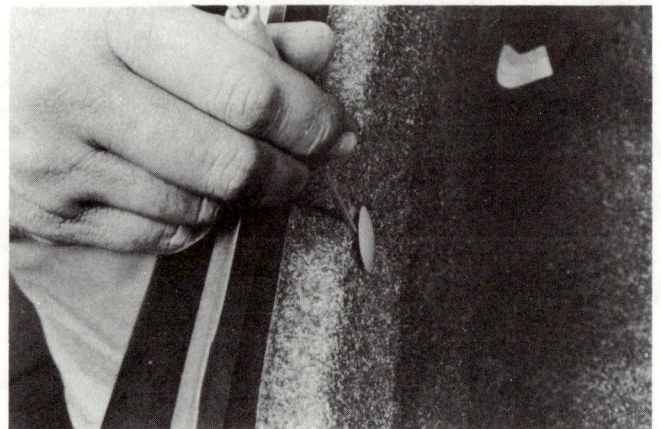

13.43a   Unscrew the tie-down hooks . . .

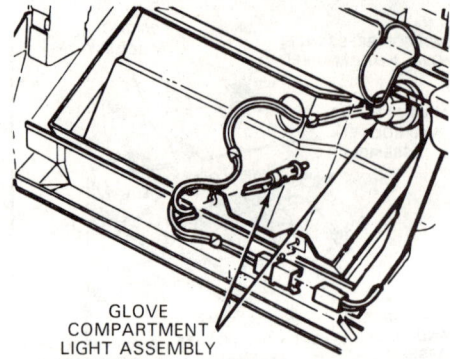

13.43b   . . . and pry out the rear panel clips with a small screwdriver

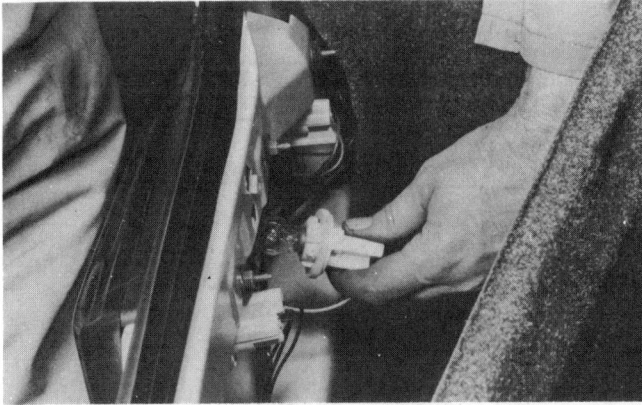

13.44 Rotate the bulb holder counterclockwise and withdraw it from the housing

48 Remove the bulb by grasping it and pulling it from the socket.
49 Press the new bulb into the socket and install the light assembly.

License plate light

Refer to illustration 13.50

50 Remove the light assembly and remove the bulb by grasping it and pulling it from the socket (see illustration).
51 Press the new bulb into the socket and install the light assembly.

14 Radio and speakers — removal and installation

1 Disconnect the negative cable from the battery. Place the cable out of the way so it cannot accidentally come in contact with the negative terminal of the battery, as this would again allow power into the electrical system of the vehicle.

Radio

Refer to illustration 14.3

2 Remove the center dashboard finish panel (Chapter 11).
3 Remove the retaining screws (see illustration).
4 Pull the radio out of the instrument panel, disconnect the antenna and electrical connectors and remove it from the vehicle.
5 Installation is the reverse of removal.

Speakers

Instrument panel mounted

Refer to illustration 14.7

6 Remove the speaker cover.
7 Remove the retaining screws and lift the speaker out (see illustration). Unplug the electrical connector and remove the speaker.
8 Installation is the reverse of removal.

14.3 Remove the screws (arrows) and pull the radio out for access to the electrical and antenna connectors

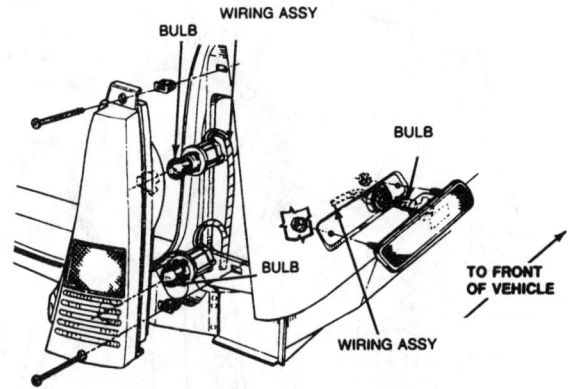

13.47 Station wagon rear light component layout

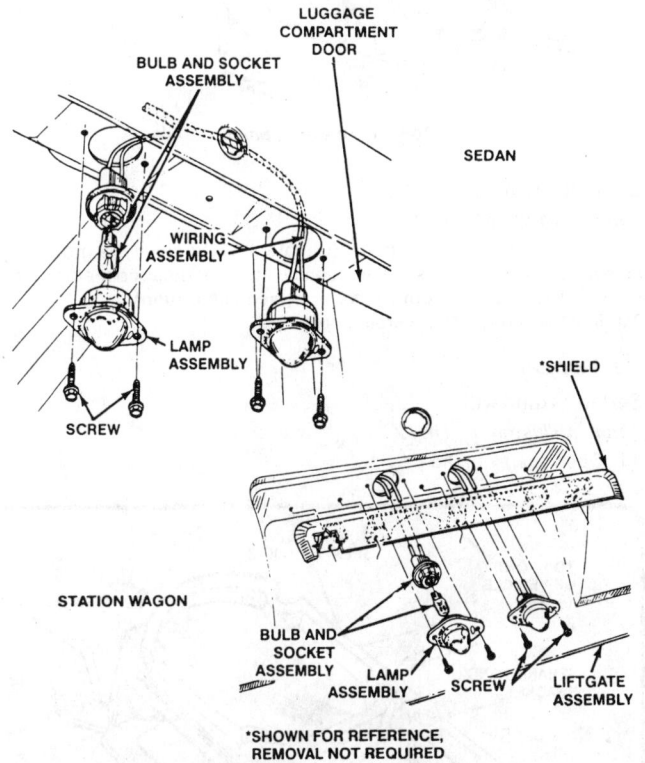

13.50 License plate light details

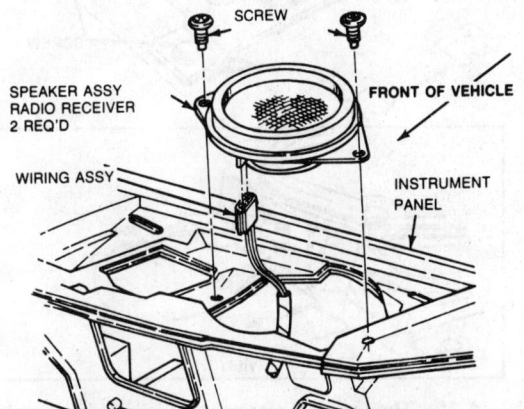

14.7 Instrument panel mounted speaker details

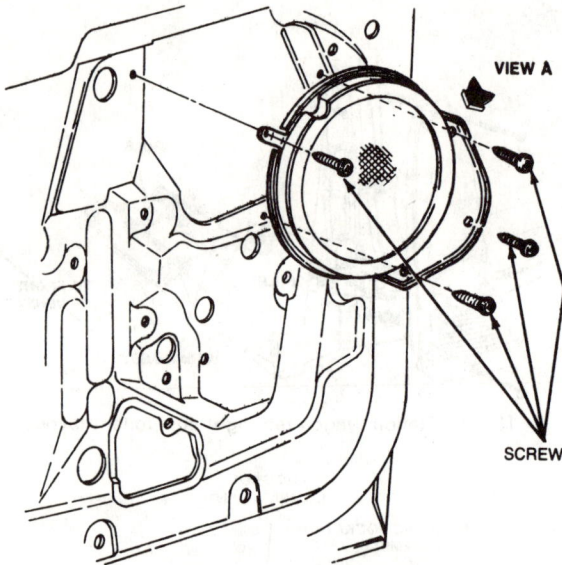

14.9   Door mounted speaker details

Door mounted

Refer to illustration 14.9

9   Remove the door trim panel (Chapter 11). Remove the mounting screws, withdraw the speaker, unplug the electrical connector and remove the speaker from the vehicle **(see illustration)**.

10   Installation is the reverse of removal.

Rear speaker

Sedan (standard)

Refer to illustration 14.12

11   Open the trunk lid.

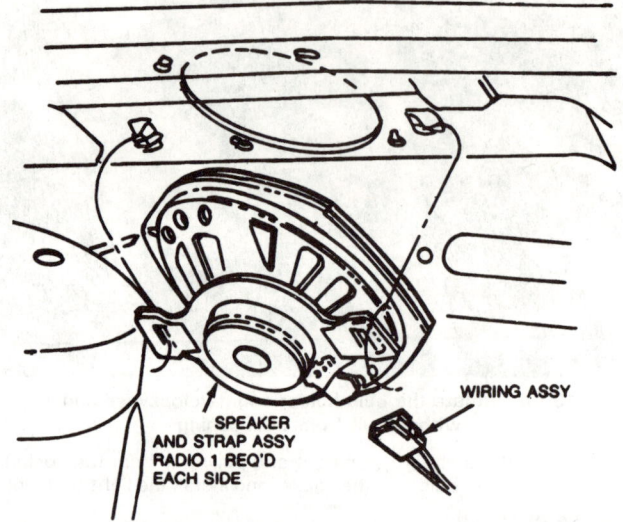

14.12   The sedan standard rear package tray mounted speaker is retained by straps

12   Working in the trunk compartment, unplug the wiring assembly from the speaker **(see illustration)**.

13   Pull on one end of the speaker retaining strap to disengage it from the tab on the package tray and remove the speaker from the vehicle.

14   To install, place the speaker and strap in position with one end of the strap over the tab on the package tray. Pull the opposite end of the strap until it is engaged over the other tab securing assembly.

Sedan (optional)

Refer to illustration 14.16

15   Remove the speaker grille from the package tray.

16   Remove the retaining screws, lift the speaker up and unplug the

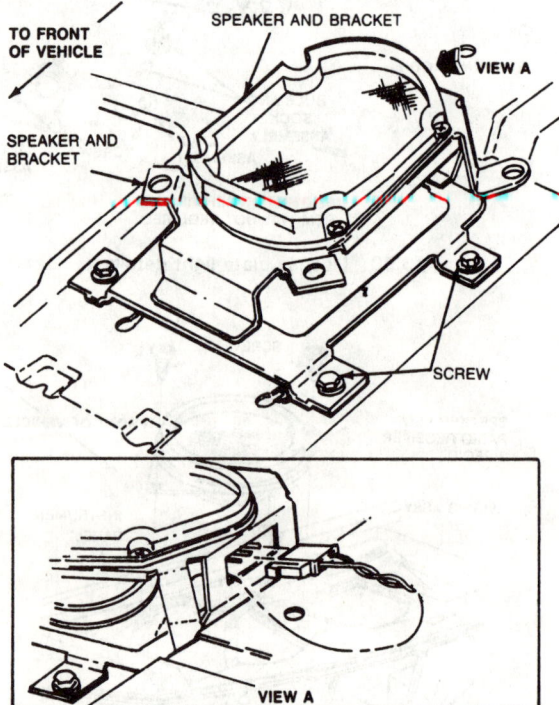

14.16   The optional rear speaker is held in place by screws

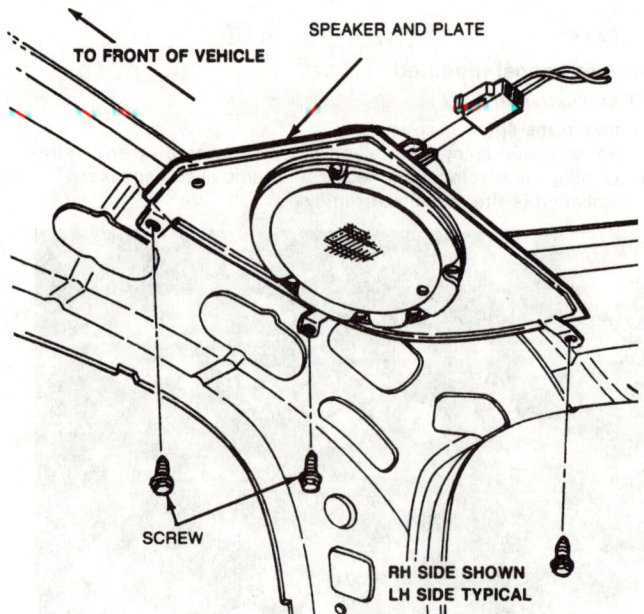

14.19   Station wagon rear speaker mounting details

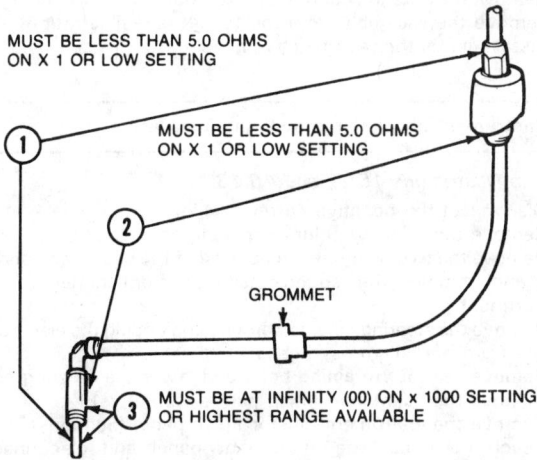

15.1a Checking the resistance between the antenna mast and cable

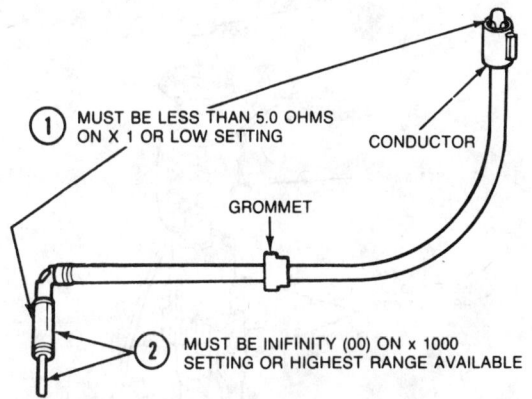

15.1b Checking the resistance between the antenna cable and base

electrical connector. Remove the speaker **(see illustration)**.
17 Installation is the reverse of removal.

Station wagon
Refer to illustration 14.19

18 Remove the rear upper corner trim panel.
19 Remove the three retaining screws **(see illustration)**.
20 Unplug the speaker wires and slide the edge of the speaker bracket our from under the headliner.
21 Installation is the reverse of removal.

15 Radio antenna — check and replacement

Resistance check
Refer to illustrations 15.1a and 15.1b

1 With the antenna cable installed on the vehicle and the cable unplugged from the radio, check the antenna with an ohmmeter at the points shown **(see illustrations)**. If any readings are not as specified, replace the antenna and cable assembly.

Replacement
Refer to illustrations 15.4 and 15.9

2 Push in on the sides of the glove compartment door and move the door all the way down.
3 Unplug the antenna lead from the rear of the radio.
4 Disengage the cable from the clips and retainers under the instrument panel **(see illustration)**.
5 Remove the right front fender liner by pulling out the centers of the plastic clips with pliers. Remove the screws, detach the liner and lower it from the fender well.
6 Unplug the cable from the antenna. On power antennas, unplug the power lead.
7 Pull the antenna cable through the hole in the door hinge pillar and remove it through the fender well.
8 On manual antennas, unscrew the antenna mast with a wrench and remove it from the vehicle.

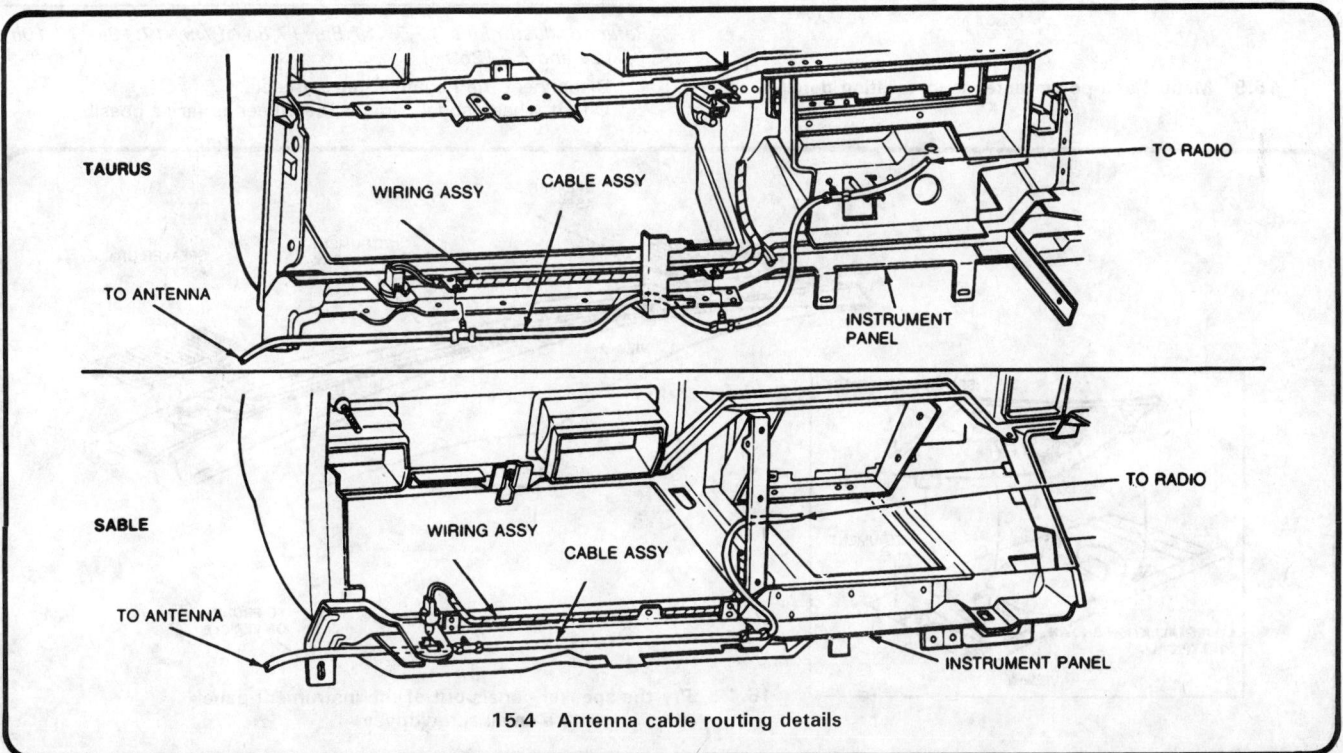

15.4 Antenna cable routing details

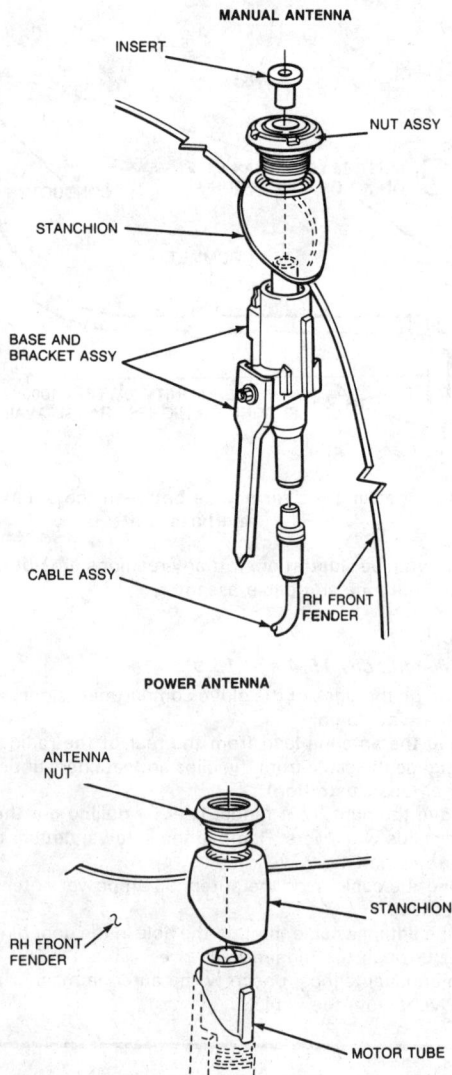

MANUAL ANTENNA

INSERT

NUT ASSY

STANCHION

BASE AND
BRACKET ASSY

CABLE ASSY

RH FRONT
FENDER

POWER ANTENNA

ANTENNA
NUT

STANCHION

RH FRONT
FENDER

MOTOR TUBE

15.9   Manual and power antenna installation details

9   Remove the antenna nut or stanchion nut with a wrench or socket and remove the assembly from the fender **(see illustration)**.
10   Installation is the reverse of removal.

16   Instrument panel — removal and installation

Refer to illustrations 16.12 and 16.13

1   Disconnect the negative battery cable.
2   Remove the steering column opening cover.
3   Remove the two pushnuts on the side of the heater/air conditioner case and remove the sound insulator from under the glove compartment.
4   Remove the steering column shrouds and unplug the electrical connectors from the column switches.
5   Remove the four retaining bolts and lower the steering column.
6   Remove the dashboard finish panels (Chapter 11).
7   Remove the instrument cluster finish panel (Section 17).
8   Reach up under the instrument panel and disconnect the speedometer cable by pressing on the flat of the plastic connector.
9   Open the glove compartment door and depress the side of the bin to allow the glove compartment assembly to swing down.
10   In the passenger compartment, disconnect the electrical, vacuum and cable controls under the instrument panel.
11   In the engine compartment, unplug all of the underhood electrical connectors from the main wiring harness. Disengage the rubber grommet seal from the dash panel and push the harness through into the passenger compartment.
12   Pry out the instrument panel mounted radio speaker grilles **(see illustration)**.
13   Remove the two lower instrument panel-to-cowl retaining bolts **(see illustration)**.
14   Remove the instrument panel brace retaining bolt located under the radio.
15   Remove the three upper instrument panel retaining bolts.
16   Pull the instrument panel back away from the cowl, disconnect any remaining wiring and/or heater/air conditioning connectors and remove the assembly from the vehicle.
17   Installation is the reverse of removal.

17   Instrument cluster — removal and installation

Refer to illustrations 17.7, 17.8a, 17.8b, 17.9, 17.10a, 17.10b, 17.12a and 17.12b

1   Disconnect the negative battery cable.
2   On tilt wheel models, lower the wheel as far as possible.

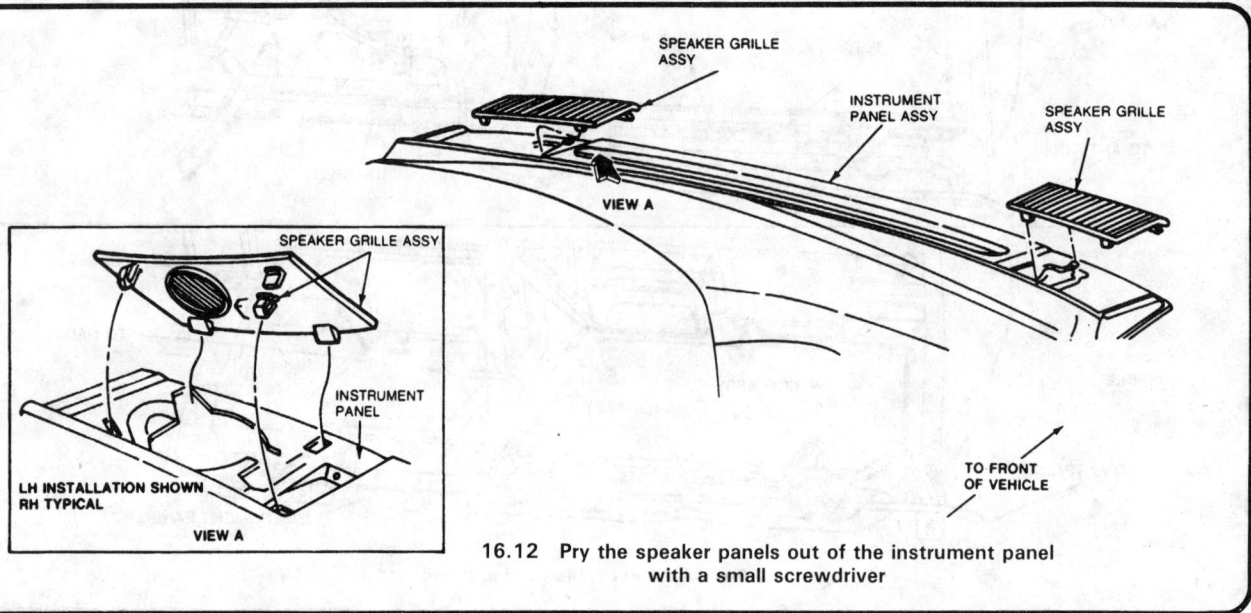

SPEAKER GRILLE
ASSY

INSTRUMENT
PANEL ASSY

SPEAKER GRILLE
ASSY

VIEW A

SPEAKER GRILLE ASSY

SPEAKER GRILLE ASSY

INSTRUMENT
PANEL

LH INSTALLATION SHOWN
RH TYPICAL

VIEW A

TO FRONT
OF VEHICLE

**16.12   Pry the speaker panels out of the instrument panel
with a small screwdriver**

VIEW A

SCREW AND WASHER LOWER CENTER
IP BRACE

BRACE ASSY
IP TO DASH

BOLT AND WASHER

BOLT AND
WASHER

BRACE ASSY IP TO
DASH

BOLT AND
WASHER ASSY

LOWER CENTER
IP BRACE

VIEW B

VEHICLE IDENTIFICATION
PLATE

SCREW
3 REQ'D

INSTRUMENT
PANEL ASSY

Y-NUT
3 REQ'D

VIEW C

VIEW B

U-NUT
1 REQ'D EACH SIDE

VIEW A

BRACE ASSY
IP TO DASH

SCREW
1 REQ'D EACH SIDE

TAURUS INSTALLATION SHOWN
SABLE INSTALLATION SIMILAR

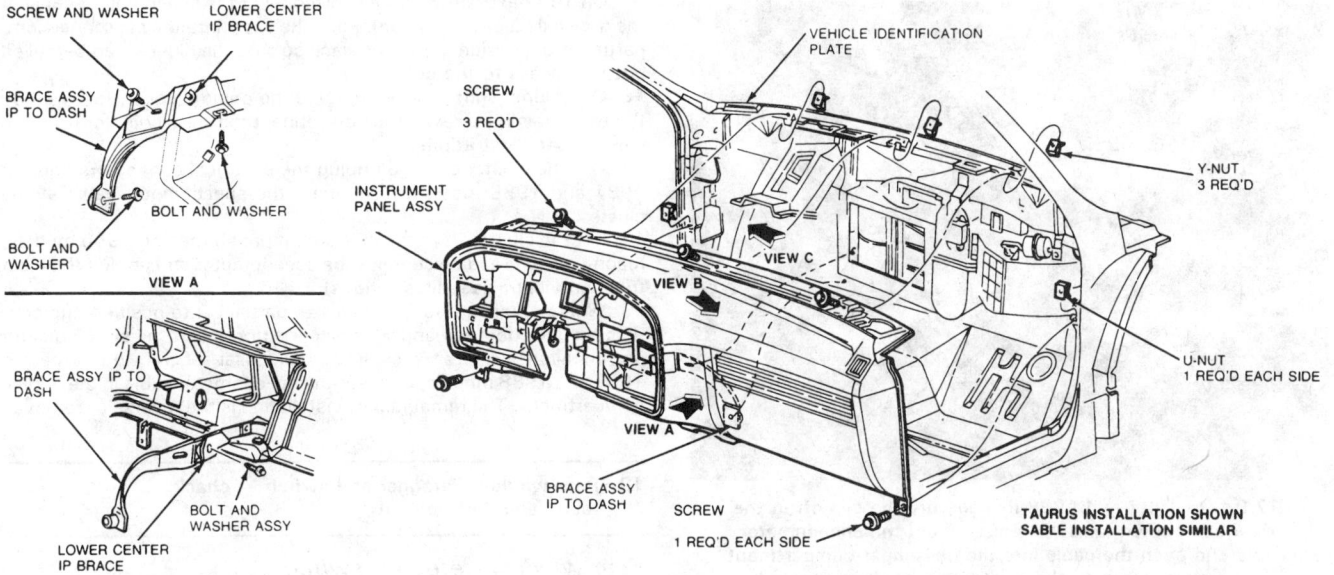

16.13 Instrument panel mounting details

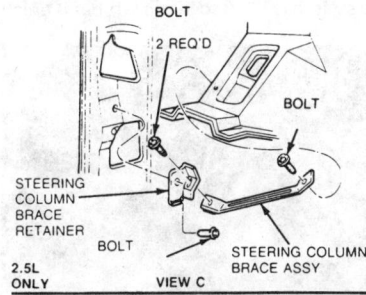

BOLT
2 REQ'D

BOLT

BOLT

STEERING
COLUMN
BRACE
RETAINER

STEERING COLUMN
BRACE ASSY

BOLT

2.5L
ONLY   VIEW C

3   On 1986 models, lower the fuse panel, reach up behind the instrument cluster and disconnect the speedometer cable.
4   On 1987 and 1988 models, remove the ignition lock cylinder (Section 8).
5   Remove the retaining screws and detach the steering column cover.
6   Remove the dashboard finish panels (Chapter 11).
7   Remove the instrument cluster mask retaining screws (see illustration).
8   Remove the odometer reset button (if equipped) and rotate the mask lens out of the instrument panel (see illustrations).

17.7 Instrument cluster mask screw locations (arrows)

17.8a Pull the odometer reset button straight off the stem

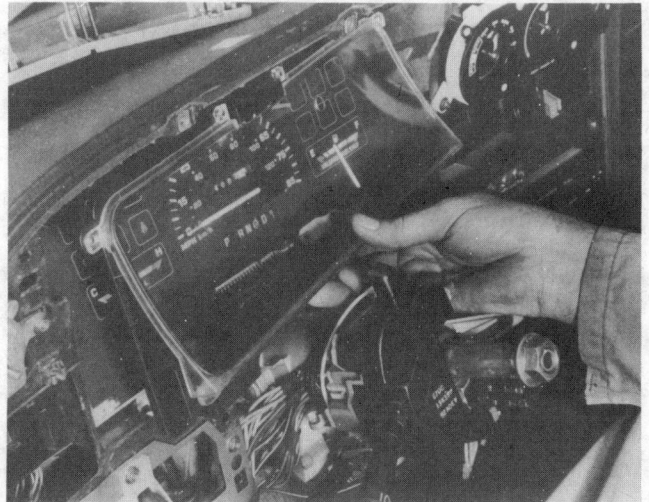

17.8b Grasp the bottom of the mask lens and rotate it up
and out of the dash

17.9   On 1987 and 1988 models, pry the clip off in the direction shown (arrow) to disconnect the speedometer cable and push the cable into the passenger compartment to provide slack so the cluster can be disconnected

9   On 1987 and 1988 models, disconnect the speedometer cable at the transaxle (see illustration). Push the cable into the passenger compartment to provide sufficient slack so that the cluster can be pulled out for access to the connectors.

10   On column shift models, remove the column collar, followed by the two retaining screws, then disconnect the shift indicator from the cluster (see illustrations).

11   Pull the cluster out and unplug the electrical connectors and, on 1987 and 1988 models, disconnect the speedometer cable at the cluster.

12   Lift the cluster from the instrument panel, then on 1986 models, reach behind it and disconnect the speedometer and unplug the electrical connector (see illustrations).

13   When installing, push the cluster partially into position and connect the speedometer and wiring connector. Insert the shift indicator and install the screws. Press the column collar securely into place. On 1987 and 1988 models, connect the speedometer cable in the engine compartment. The remainder of installation is the reverse of removal.

18   Rear window defogger and switch — check, repair and replacement

Rear window defogger switch
Refer to illustration 18.2

1   The rear window defogger switch is located in the left hand finish

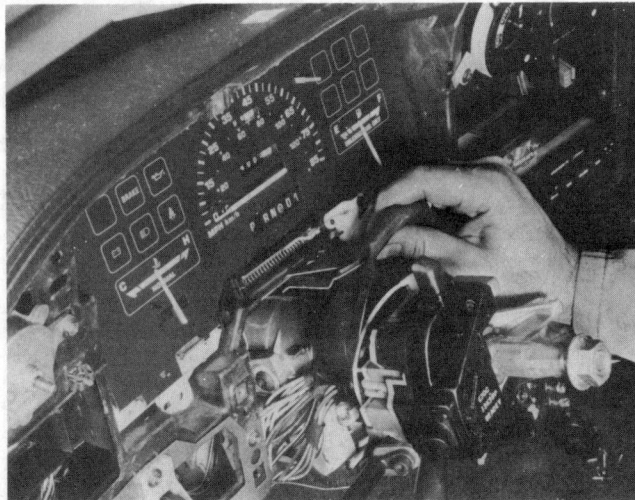

17.10a   Pull the column collar straight out to remove it

17.10b   Remove the screws and rotate the column shift indicator out

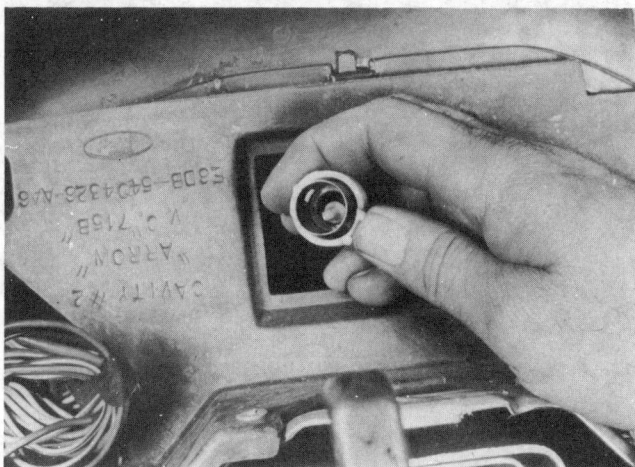

17.12a   Press the cable release with your thumb to disconnect the cable from the speedometer

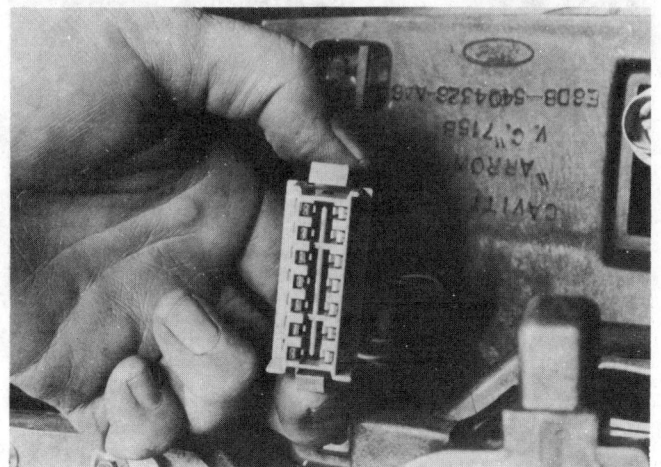

17.12b   To release the electrical connector from the socket in the back side of the instrument cluster, depress the two locking levers and pull on the connector

panel or instrument cluster finish panel. To check it, detach the finish panel from the dashboard, turn it around so that the back is facing you and locate the electrical connector for the defogger switch.

2 Referring to the accompanying terminal guide (see illustration), ground pin G, connect a jumper wire between pins I and B and connect a 12-volt test light between pin L and ground.

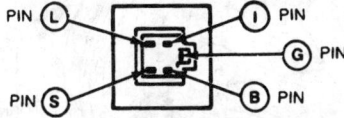

18.2 Terminal guide for checking the rear window defogger switch

3 Apply power to pin B. The test light should not light.
4 Momentarily put the switch in the On position. The test light should come on and stay on after the control returns to the Normal position.
5 The test light should go off under the following conditions:
   a) If the switch is moved to the Off position.
   b) If the power to the ignition Acc terminal is removed, or approximately ten minutes have elapsed.
6 Apply power to the S pin. The test light should come on.
7 If the switch fails any of the above checks, replace it.
8 To replace the switch, unplug the electrical connector and remove the switch from the A/C and heater control assembly.
9 Installation is the reverse of removal.

Rear window defogger grid wire

Check
10 Use a strong light inside the vehicle. Visually inspect the wire grid from the outside. A broken grid wire will appear as a brown spot.
11 Run the engine at idle. Set the control switch to On. The indicator light should come on.
12 Working inside the vehicle with a voltmeter, contact the broad red-brown strips (the "bus") on the sides of the rear window. The meter should read 10-to-13 volts. A lower voltage reading indicates a loose ground wire (pigtail) connection at the grounded side of the glass.
13 Contact a good ground point with the negative lead of the meter. The voltage reading should not change.
14 With the negative lead of the meter grounded, touch each grid line of the heated rear window at its midpoint with the positive lead:
   a) A reading of approximately six volts indicates that the line is good.
   b) A reading of zero volts indicates that the line is broken between the mid-point and the positive side of the grid line.
   c) A reading of 12 volts indicates that the circuit is broken between the mid-point of the grid and ground.

Repair
Refer to illustrations 18.18 and 18.28

Note: *Any break in the grid longer than one inch cannot be repaired. The rear window must be replaced. For breaks less than one inch in length, use the following procedure. You will need to obtain grid repair compound and brown touch-up paint from a Ford dealer.*

15 Bring the vehicle inside a heated garage and allow it to reach room temperature (60°F or above).
16 Clean the entire grid line repair area with glass cleaning solvent. Remove all dirt, wax, grease, oil or other foreign matter. The repair area must be clean and dry.
17 Mark the location of the break on the outside of the window.
18 Using cellulose tape, mask off the area directly above and below the grid break. The break area should be at the center of the mask, and the tape gap must be no wider than the existing grid line (see illustration).
19 If both the brown and silver layers of the grid are broken or missing, apply a coating of the brown touch-up paint across the break area first. Two coats may be necessary to obtain the proper color. Allow the touch-up paint to dry.
20 Apply three coats of the silver grid repair compound. Allow three to five minutes drying time between coats. The coating of the silver grid repair compound should extend at least 1/4-inch on both sides of the break. **Note:** *If the brown layer of the grid is not broken or missing, apply only the silver grid repair compound to the break. Allow the compound to dry for five minutes, then remove the mask.*
21 After removing the mask, check the outside appearance of the grid repair. If the silver repair compound is visible above or below the grid,

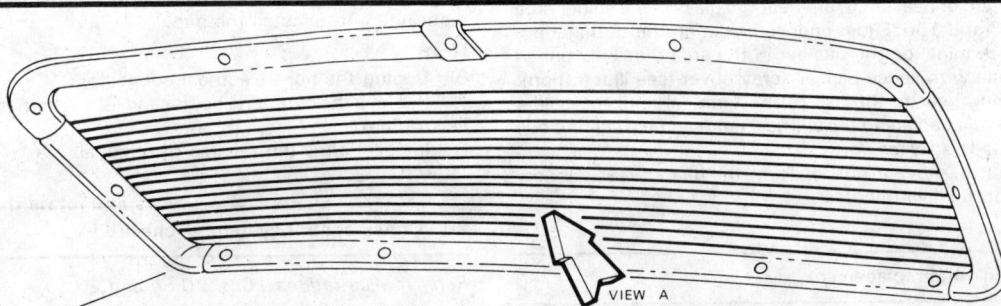

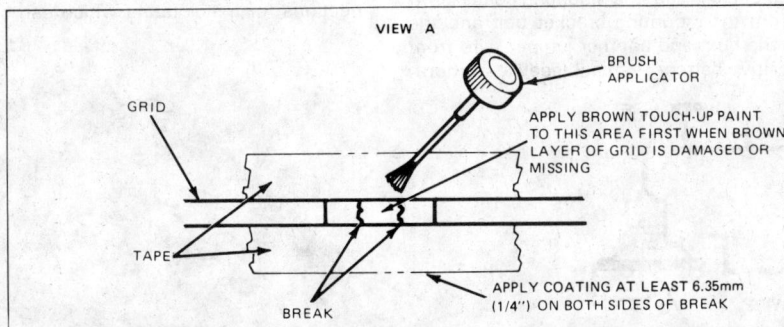

18.18 Rear window defogger grid repair details

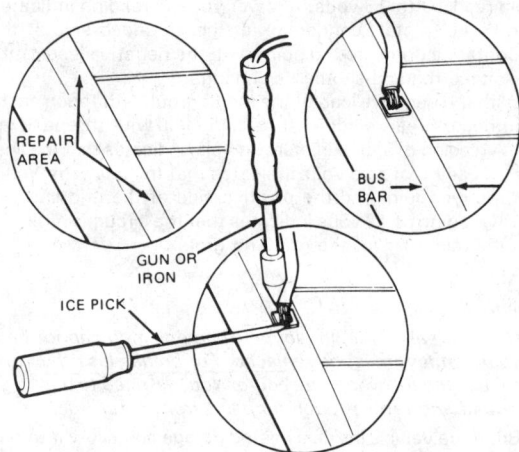

18.28   Position the terminal on the bus bar in the area that was tinned and hold it in place with an ice pick or screwdriver

this excess should be removed. This can be done by placing a single edge razor blade on the glass parallel to the grid and scraping gently towards the grid. **Caution:** *Be careful not to damage the grid line with the razor blade.*

22   The repair coating will air dry in about one minute and can be energized within three to five minutes. Optimum hardness and adhesion occur after approximately 24 hours. At that time, the repair area may be cleaned with a mild window cleaner.

Lead wire terminal service

23   Allow the rear window to warm up to room temperature for a half hour to an hour.

24   Clean the bus bar in the area to be repaired using fine steel wool (3/0 to 4/0 grade).

25   Restore the area where the bus bar terminal was originally attached by applying three coats of grid repair compound. Allow approximately ten minutes drying time between coats.

26   Working as quickly as possible to avoid overheating the glass, tin the bus bar with solder in the area where the terminal will be reattached.

27   Using a heat gun or heat lamp, pre-heat the glass in the solder area to between 120° and 150°F just prior to soldering the terminal on.

28   Position the terminal on the bus bar in the area that was tinned and hold it in place with an ice pick or screwdriver **(see illustration)**.

29   Apply soldering heat to the pad of the terminal until the solder flows. **Note:** *To avoid damaging the bus bar, remove the soldering gun or iron as soon as the solder flows.*

30   Start the vehicle, move it outside, turn the heated rear window on and leave it on for five minutes.

19   Horn — check and replacement

Check

Refer to illustration 19.1

1   If the horn doesn't work, first make sure the mounting bolt is tight. Connect one jumper wire from the mounting bracket bolt and the negative battery terminal to the horn and another jumper wire from the horn terminal and the positive battery terminal **(see illustration)**.

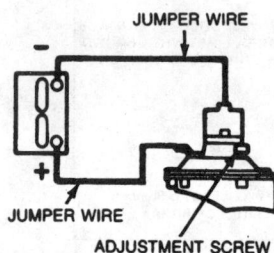

19.1   Horn check diagram (refer to text)

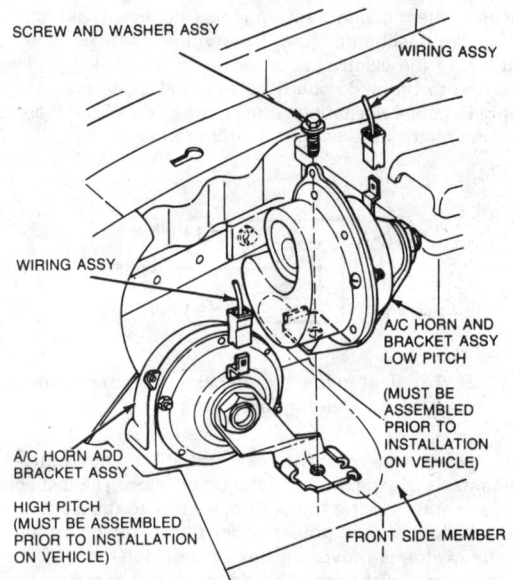

19.7   The horn assemblies are located in the right front corner of the engine compartment

2   If the horn doesn't work and there is no sparking at the battery terminal, disconnect the jumper wires. Turn the adjusting screw counterclockwise between 1/4 and 3/8-turn and then use pliers to keep it from turning by squeezing the housing extrusions. If the horn doesn't work when the wires are reconnected, replace it with a new one.

Replacement

Refer to illustration 19.7

3   Disconnect the negative battery cable.

Horn switch

4   Remove the two screws from the back side of the steering wheel and detach the horn pad.

5   Unplug the horn switch from the steering wheel, plug in the replacement unit and reinstall the pad.

Horn

6   Unplug the horn electrical connector.

7   Remove the mounting bolt(s) and lift the horn from the vehicle **(see illustration)**.

8   Installation is the reverse of removal.

20   Cruise control system — check

Refer to illustrations 20.3, 20.5a and 20.5b

1   Because of the complexity of the cruise control system and the special tool and techniques required, repair should be left to a dealer service department or a repair shop. However, it is possible for the home mechanic to make simple checks of the wiring and vacuum connections for minor faults which can be easily repaired.

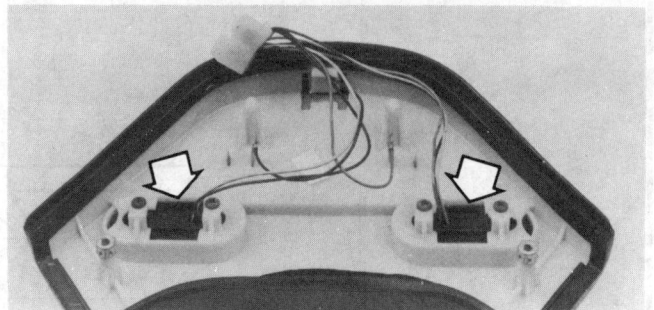

20.3   Check the cruise control switches and wires (arrows) for damage and loose connections

20.5a   Make sure the hose connections to the cruise control unit are tight

20.5b   The cruise control system is operated by vacuum, so check the hoses and valves (arrows) for cracks and loose connections

2   Remove the two retaining screws and lift off the horn pad.
3   Check the cruise control switches and harness for broken wires and loose connections (see illustration).
4   Pull down the fuse box and check the cruise control fuse (Section 4).
5   The cruise control system is operated by vacuum so it is critical that all vacuum switches, hoses and connections are secure. Check the hoses in the engine compartment for tight connections, cracked hoses and obvious vacuum leaks (see illustrations).

21   Power door lock system — general information

Because of the difficulty involved in gaining access to the remote door lock motor, replacement of this component is best left to a dealer service department.

22   Power windows — general information

Because of the difficulty involved in gaining access to the power window motor, replacement of this component should be done by a dealer service department.

LEGEND

WIRE IDENTIFICATION

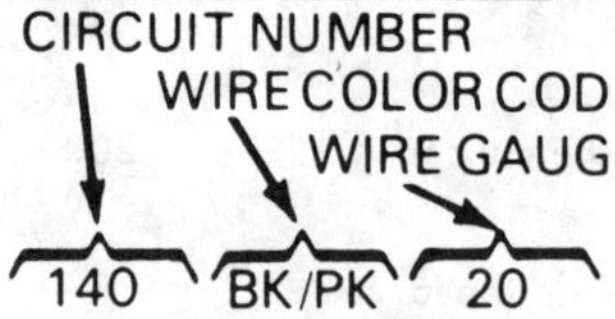

CIRCUIT NUMBER
WIRE COLOR CODE
WIRE GAUGE

140   BK/PK   20

WIRING COLOR CODE
(PRIMARY COLORS)

BLACK	BK
BROWN	BR
TAN	T
RED	R
PINK	PK
ORANGE	O
YELLOW	Y
DARK GREEN	DG
LIGHT GREEN	LG
DARK BLUE	DB
LIGHT BLUE	LB
PURPLE	P
GRAY	GY
WHITE	W
HASH	(H)
DOT	(D)

The presence of a tracer on the wire is indicated by a secondary color followed by an ''H'' for hash or a ''D'' for Dot. A stripe is understood if no letter follows.

Wiring diagram color codes

INDICATOR LAMP SYSTEM

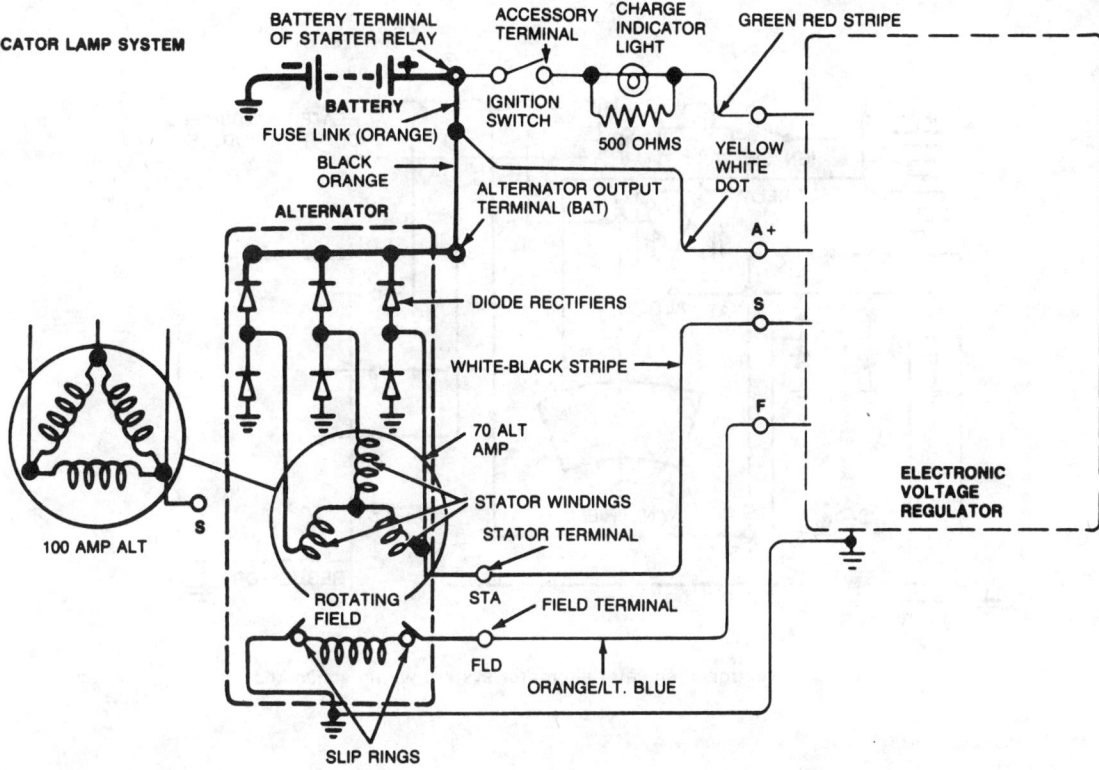

BATTERY TERMINAL OF STARTER RELAY

ACCESSORY TERMINAL

CHARGE INDICATOR LIGHT

GREEN RED STRIPE

BATTERY

IGNITION SWITCH

FUSE LINK (ORANGE)

500 OHMS

YELLOW WHITE DOT

BLACK ORANGE

ALTERNATOR OUTPUT TERMINAL (BAT)

A+

ALTERNATOR

DIODE RECTIFIERS

S

WHITE-BLACK STRIPE

F

70 ALT AMP

STATOR WINDINGS

STATOR TERMINAL

100 AMP ALT

S

ROTATING FIELD

STA

FIELD TERMINAL

FLD

ORANGE/LT. BLUE

ELECTRONIC VOLTAGE REGULATOR

SLIP RINGS

AMMETER SYSTEM

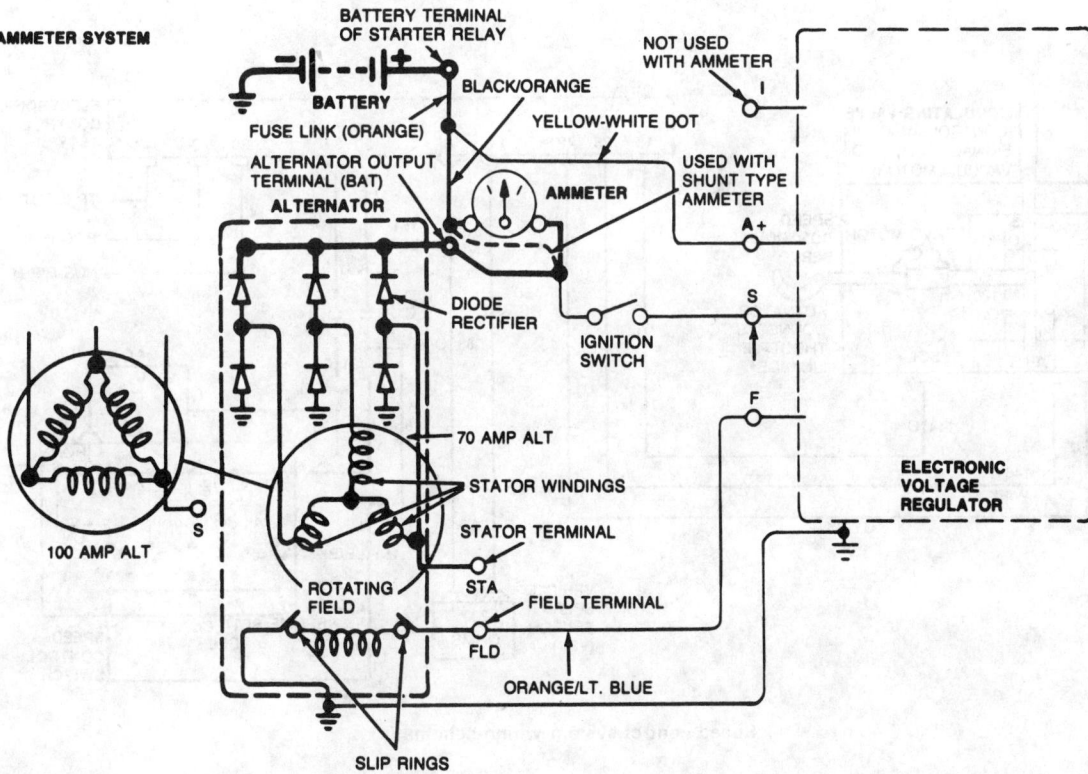

BATTERY TERMINAL OF STARTER RELAY

NOT USED WITH AMMETER

BATTERY

BLACK/ORANGE

I

FUSE LINK (ORANGE)

YELLOW-WHITE DOT

ALTERNATOR OUTPUT TERMINAL (BAT)

AMMETER

USED WITH SHUNT TYPE AMMETER

ALTERNATOR

A+

DIODE RECTIFIER

S

IGNITION SWITCH

70 AMP ALT

F

STATOR WINDINGS

STATOR TERMINAL

100 AMP ALT

S

STA

ROTATING FIELD

FIELD TERMINAL

ELECTRONIC VOLTAGE REGULATOR

FLD

ORANGE/LT. BLUE

SLIP RINGS

Side terminal-type alternator system wiring schematic

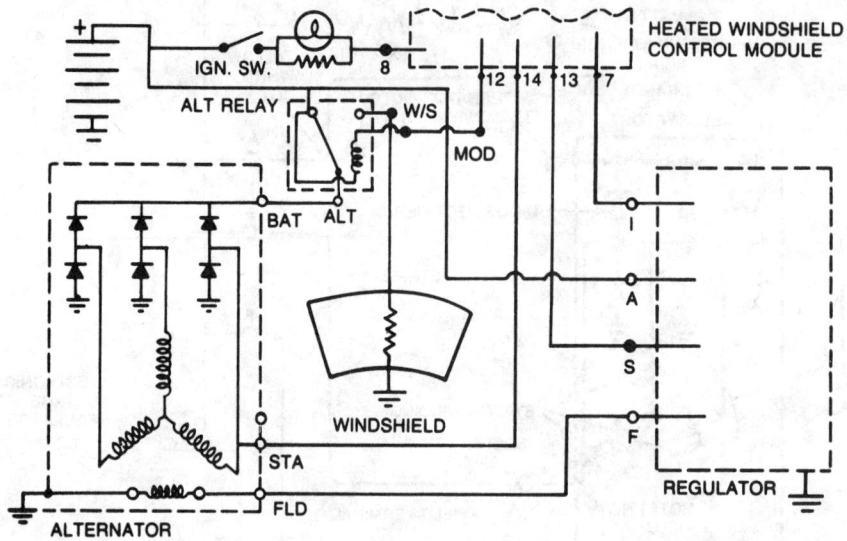

Integral electronic regulator alternator system wiring schematic

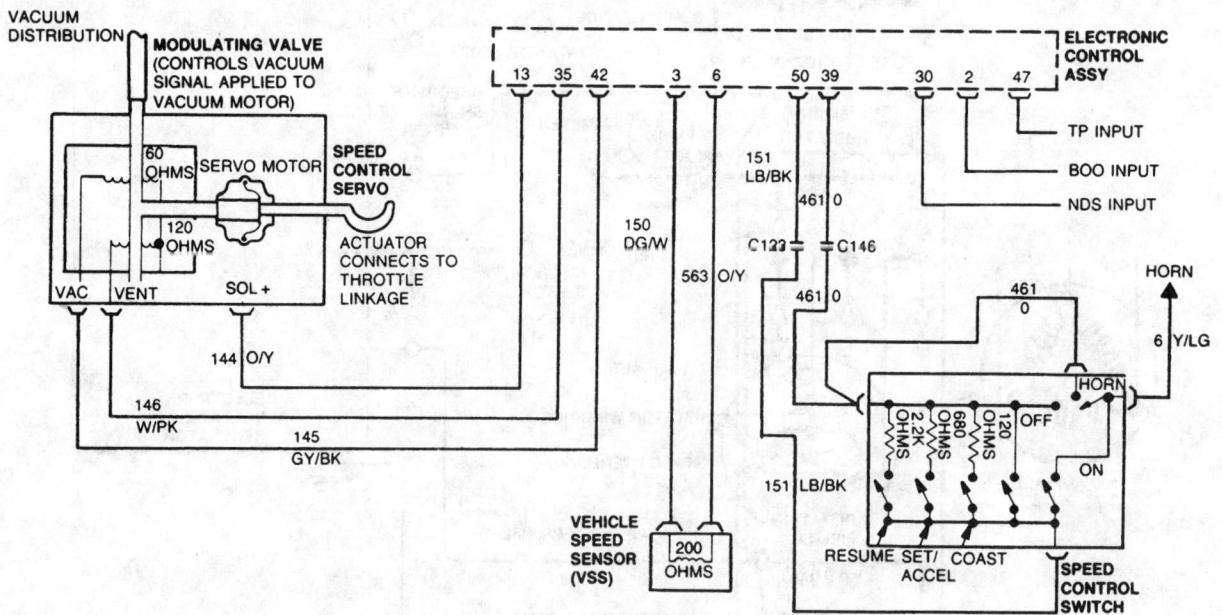

Speed control system wiring schematic

HOT IN ACCY OR RUN

2 FUSE PANEL 6.25A

WIPER SWITCH

WASHER PUMP

LO OFF HI

LO OFF HI

LO OFF HI

WIPER/WASHER CONTROL

C161

941 BK/W

W A F L B H G C C D B C161

65 DG

S141 941 BK/W 941 BK/W C169

56 DB/O

58 W

587 BK/W

590 DB/W

65 DG S140

941 BK/W

LOW WASHER FLUID LEVEL SWITCH CLOSED WITH LOW FLUID LEVEL

993 BR/W

57 BK S119

57 BK S116

57 BK G200

589 O

61 Y/R

SHORTING CONNECTOR C169

82 PK/Y

C144

82 PK/Y

441 BK/W

LOW WASHER FLUID LEVEL INDICATOR

WASHER SWITCH

M

63 R

D5 LG

57 BK S116

57 BK

G200

57 BK S118

57 BK

G201

INDICATOR ASSY WITH OPTIONAL INDICATORS

28 BK/PK

C148 56 DB/O 58 W 61 Y/R 63 R

28 BK/PK 58 W 61 Y/R 63 R

WIPER MOTOR AND SWITCH

1 2

PARKED PARKED

WIPER MOTOR SWITCH

RUN PARKING PARKING

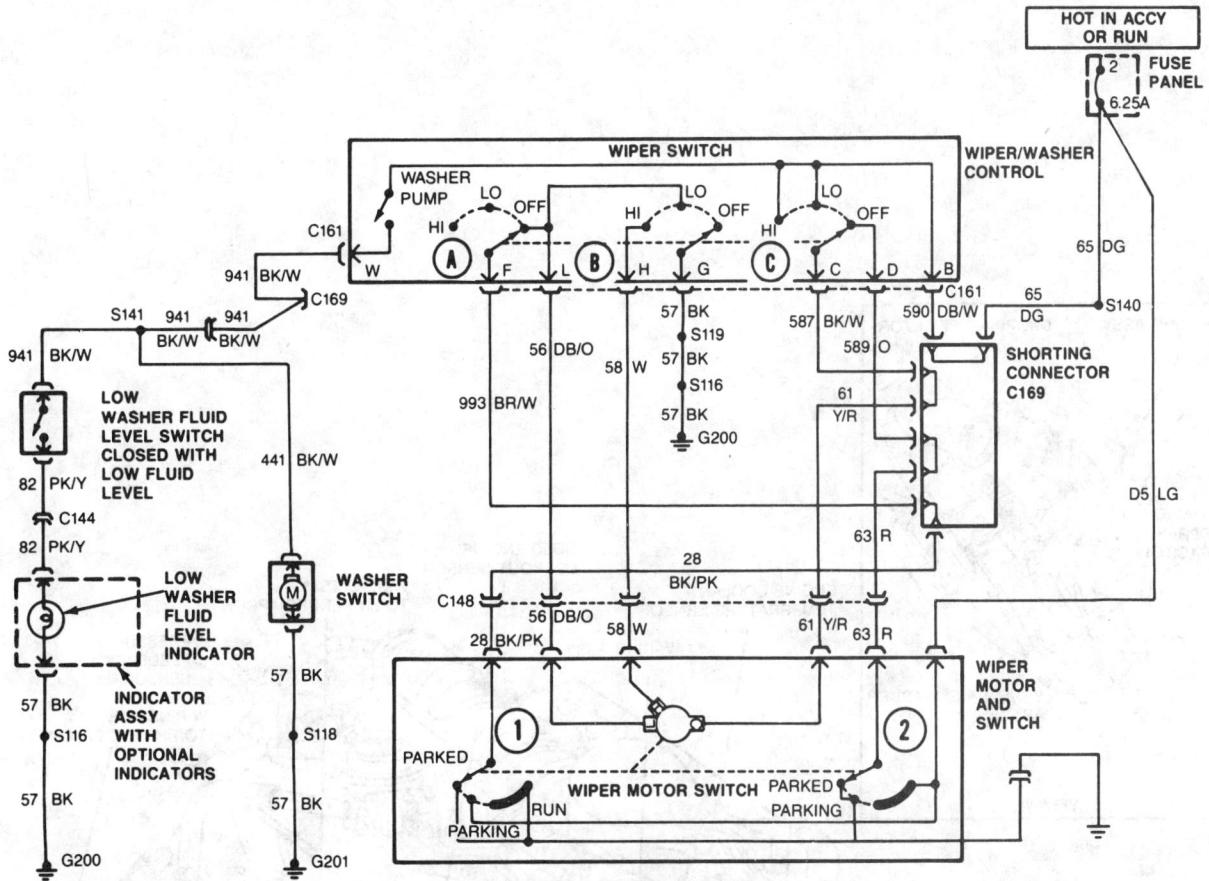

Windshield wiper/washer system wiring schematic

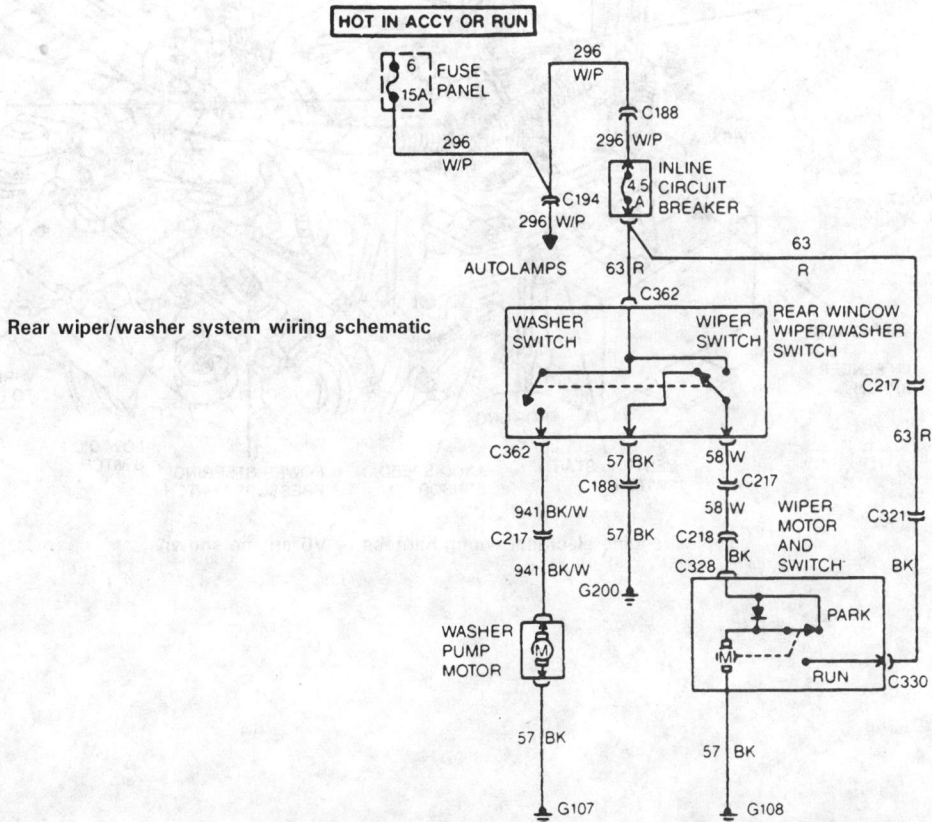

HOT IN ACCY OR RUN

6 FUSE PANEL 15A

296 W/P

C188

296 W/P

INLINE CIRCUIT BREAKER 4.5A

C194

296 W/P

AUTOLAMPS

63 R

C362

63 R

WASHER SWITCH

WIPER SWITCH

REAR WINDOW WIPER/WASHER SWITCH

C217

63 R

Rear wiper/washer system wiring schematic

C362

57 BK

58 W

C188

57 BK

C217

941 BK/W

C217

941 BK/W

WASHER PUMP MOTOR

M

57 BK

G107

58 W

C218

58 W

C328 BK

WIPER MOTOR AND SWITCH

M

C321

BK

PARK

RUN C330

57 BK

G108

G200

WIRING ASSY   DROPPING RESISTOR

TO RADIO
SUPPRESSION
CAPACITOR

SCREW AND WASHER
ASSY

VIEW A

COLD ENGINE
LOCKOUT SENSOR

ENGINE COOLANT
TEMPERATURE SENSOR

WIRING ASSY
TO LH FENDER APRON

WIRING ASSY

PRESSURE
FEEDBACK
SENSOR

WIRING ASSY
TO RH FENDER APRON

COIL ASSY

COOLANT
TEMPERATURE
SENDER

TFI MODULE

WIRING ASSY

OIL PRESSURE
SWITCH

SPEED SENSOR

KNOCK SENSOR

VIEW A

TO FRONT
OF BODY

WIRING ASSY
TO LH FENDER APRON

WIRING ASSY
TO
LH FENDER
APRON

SHORTING
PLUG

NEUTRAL START
SWITCH

AXOD SPEED
SENSOR

POWER STEERING
PRESSURE SWITCH

LOW OIL
SWITCH

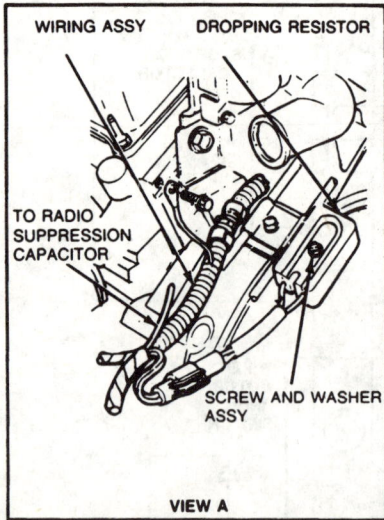

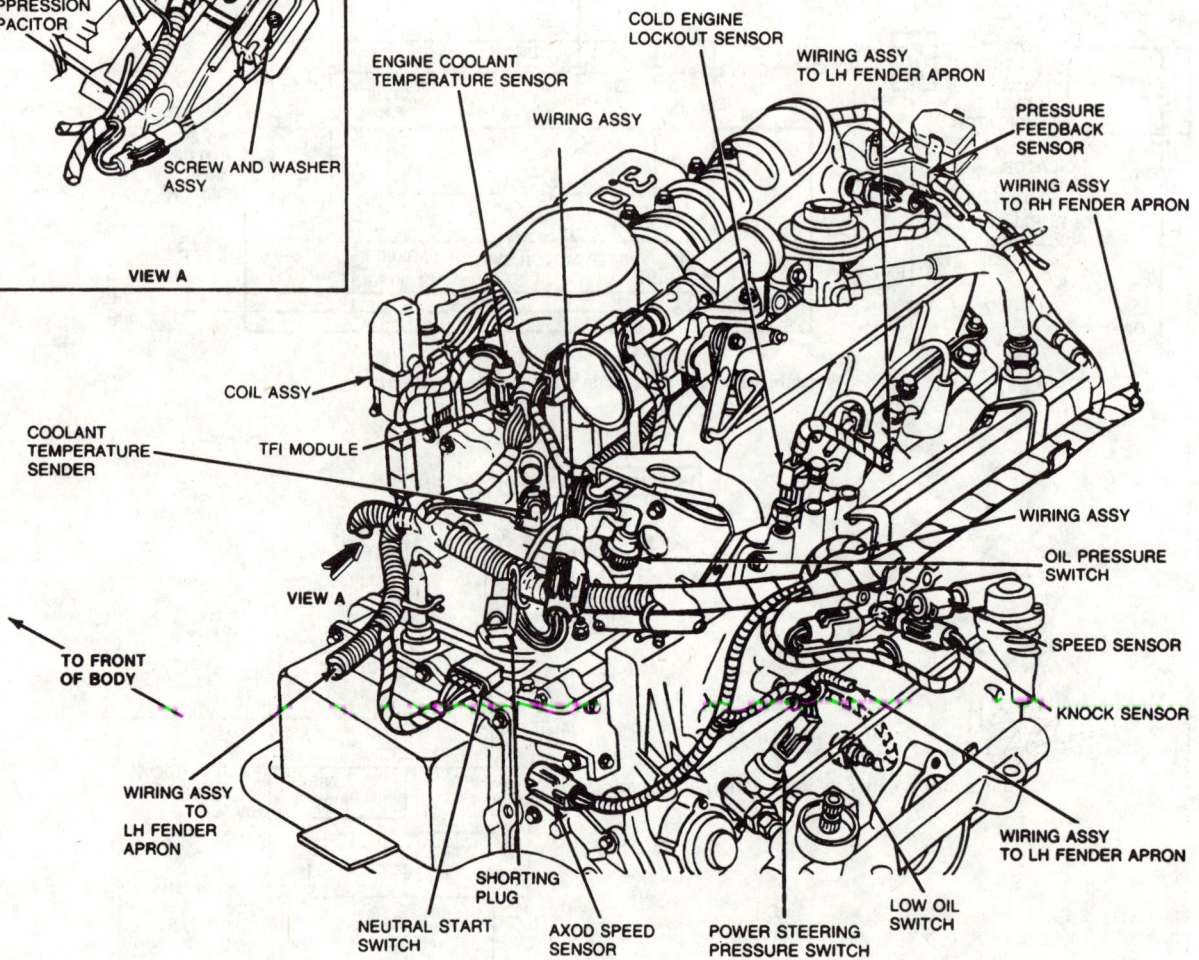

Typical engine electrical wiring harness — V6 engine shown

WIRING ASSY HEADLAMP DIMMER SWITCH JUMPER VIEW E

WIRING ASSY
WIRING ASSY
VIEW D

HEADLAMP SWITCH ILLUMINATION
HEADLAMP SWITCH
DIMMER SWITCH
VIEW C

FLASHER ASSY
VIEW A
SCREW

HEATED REAR WINDOW SWITCH
VIEW B

SUN LOAD SENSOR
WIRING ASSY
TO SPEAKER
WIRING ASSY
TO LH FLOORPAN WIRING ASSY
TO LH FLOORPAN WIRING ASSY
BULB ASSY
TO PARKING BRAKE SWITCH ASSY

VIEW C
VIEW A
TO STOPLAMP SWITCH

WIRING ASSY TO MANUAL A/C CONTROLS
TO INSTRUMENT CLUSTER
TO INTERVAL WIPER CONTROL
TO STEERING COLUMN
WIRING ASSY TO DIAGNOSTIC MODULE

TO CLOCK
WIRING ASSY

TO MANUAL A/C CONTROL
WIRING ASSY TO EATC CONTROL ASSY
VIEW B
VIEW D
VIEW E
TO RADIO
FROM RADIO TO SPEAKERS
TO CHIMES
TO BLOWER MOTOR
WIRING ASSY TO BLOWER MOTOR RESISTOR
TO BLOWER SPEED CONTROL EATC

TO INSTRUMENT PANEL ILLUMINATION
GLOVE COMPARTMENT LAMP
WIRING ASSY GROUND
WIRING ASSY 14401 TO BLEND DOOR ACTUATOR
SCREW 2 REQ'D

TO SPEAKER
WIRING ASSY TO EATC
BULB ASSY

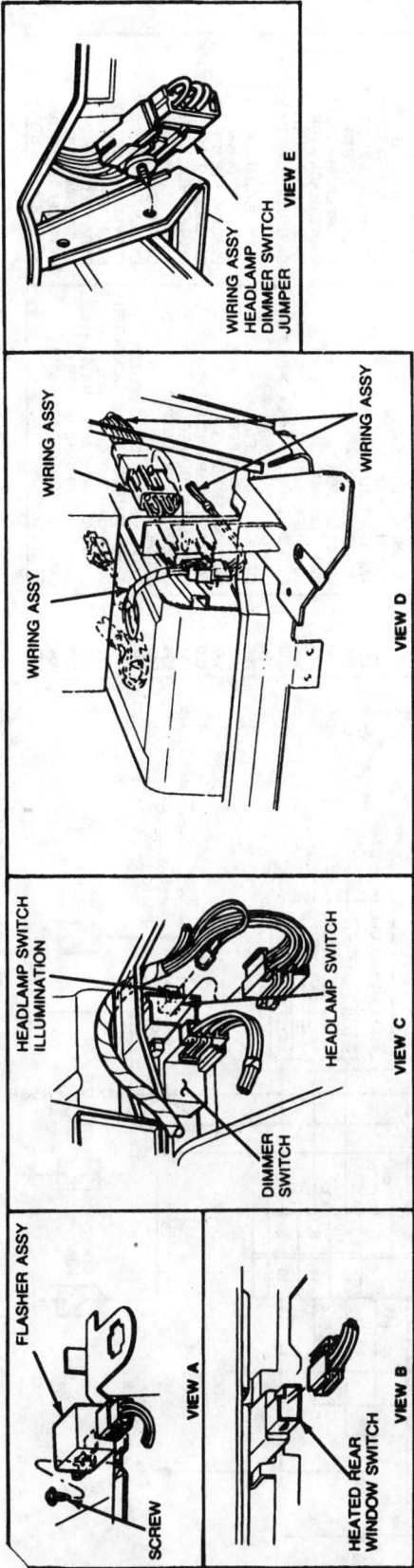

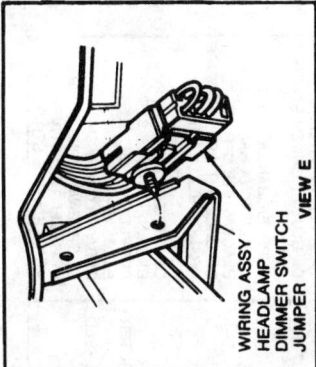

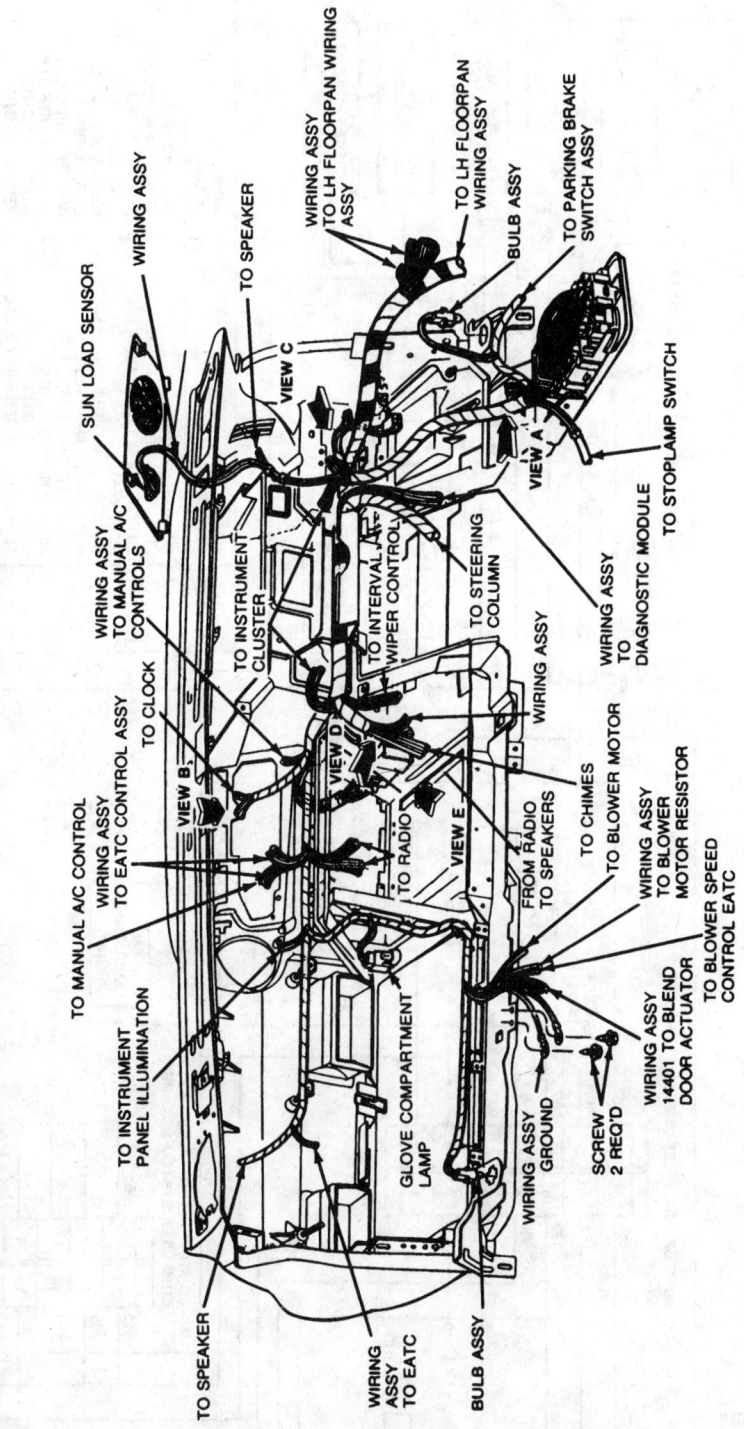

Typical instrument panel wiring harness

ALTERNATOR REGULATOR
SEAT BELT WARNING SENSOR
HIGH BEAM SWITCH
LEFT TURN SIGNAL SWITCH
RIGHT TURN SIGNAL SWITCH
BRAKE WARNING SWITCH

CONNECTOR "B" CLUSTER

RUN SWITCH TO ALT. IND. LAMP

RUN, START AND ACCY

TEMP SENDER

OIL PRESSURE SWITCH

CONNECTOR "C" SPEEDOMETER/TACHOMETER

SPEED SENSOR
TO IGNITION COIL PRIMARY
TACH SELECT FROM ENGINE COMPARTMENT
HEADLAMP SWITCH
RHEOSTAT ASSY
RUN AND ACCY
RUN AND ACCY

SEPARATELY FUSED BATTERY ALWAYS HOT
TO PIN 7 OF CHIME MODULE
RUN ONLY
POWER GROUND
SIGNAL GROUND

LOW OIL LEVEL SENSOR
LOW OIL PROVEOUT
START ONLY
LOW OIL LEVEL TIMER CIRCUIT
RUN ONLY

LAMP OUT MODULE
BRAKE LAMP OUT
TAIL LAMP OUT
HEAD LAMP OUT

WIPER/WASHER SWITCH
RUN AND ACCY
WASHER FLUID LOW SWITCH

CONNECTOR "A" FUEL COMPUTER/SYSTEM SCANNER

OPEN

FUEL FLOW FROM EEC IV MODULE

TO PIN 7 OF CHIME MODULE

LIFT GATE AJAR
DOOR AJAR

WIRE COLOR
WHITE/LT BLUE STRIPE
LT GREEN/WHITE STRIPE
DK GREEN/YELLOW DOT
LT GREEN/BLACK STRIPE
RED/LT GREEN STRIPE
LT BLUE/RED STRIPE
WHITE/PURPLE DOT
YELLOW/WHITE STRIPE
WHITE/RED STRIPE
RED/WHITE STRIPE
BLACK
PINK/YELLOW STRIPE
RED/LT GREEN STRIPE
ORANGE/BLACK STRIPE
YELLOW/RED STRIPE
DK GREEN/WHITE STRIPE
WHITE/BLACK STRIPE
TAN/YELLOW STRIPE
DK BLUE/LT GREEN STRIPE
GRAY
PURPLE/ORANGE HASH
LT BLUE/PINK HASH
BLACK/WHITE STRIPE
DK GREEN/LT GREEN STRIPE
ORANGE/BLACK STRIPE
RED
ORANGE/YELLOW STRIPE
DK BLUE/ORANGE STRIPE
PURPLE/ORANGE STRIPE
BLACK/ORANGE HASH
RED/YELLOW HASH
LT GREEN/PURPLE STRIPE
LT GREEN/RED STRIPE
PURPLE/WHITE STRIPE

CIRCUIT NUMBER	SIGNAL DESCRIPTION
2	RT TURN SIGNAL
3	LT TURN SIGNAL
11	IGN COIL NEG TERMINAL
12	HIGH BEAM
16	SWITCH TO ALTERNATOR LAMP
19	INST PANEL LAMPS FEED
26	LIFT GATE AJAR SWITCH
29	FUEL SENDER TO GAUGE
31	OIL PRESSURE SENDER
39	TEMPERATURE SENDER TO GAUGE
57	POWER GROUND
82	WASHER FLUID LEVEL
130	HEAD LAMP OUT
132	TAIL LAMP OUT
135	BRAKE LAMP OUT
150	SPEED SENSOR
168	PWM ILLUMINATION
183	TONE GENERATOR
205	FUEL SENDER TO FUEL COMPUTER
208	LOW OIL LEVEL
298	EIC RUN ONLY FEED
305	FUEL FLOW FROM EEC-IV
397	TACHOMETER SELECT
450	SEAT BELT WARNING LAMP
484	EIC ILLUMINATION FEED
506	ENGLISH/METRIC OUTPUT
563	SIGNAL GROUND
564	SWITCHES TO FUEL COMPUTER
565	SPEED OUTPUT TO FUEL COMPUTER
627	DOOR AJAR SWITCH
640	SEPARATELY FUSED BATTERY
797	WARNING LAMPS AND GAUGES FEED
904	LAMP TO ALT/REGULATOR (GND)
977	BRAKE WARNING

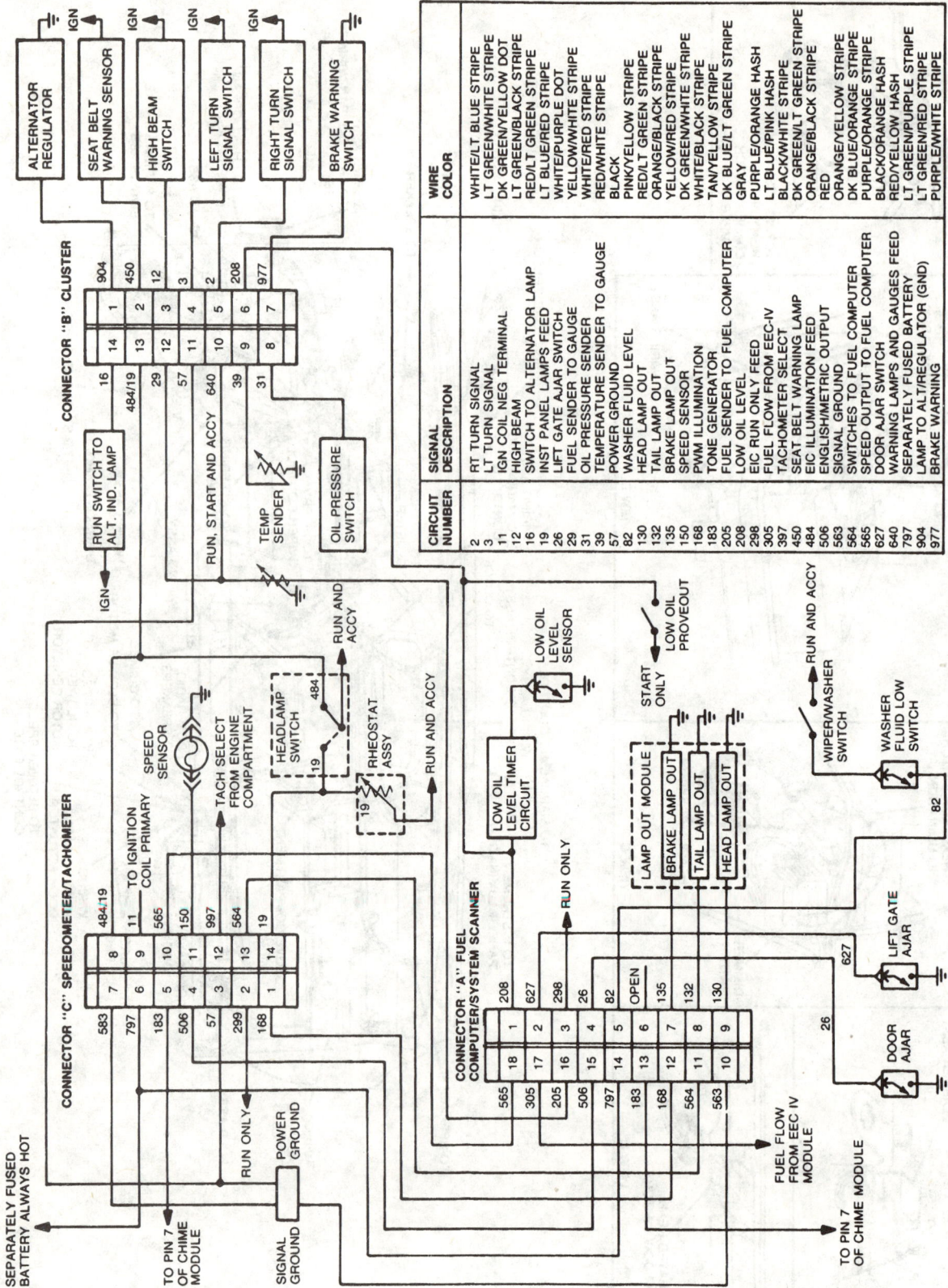

Electronic instrument panel wiring schematic

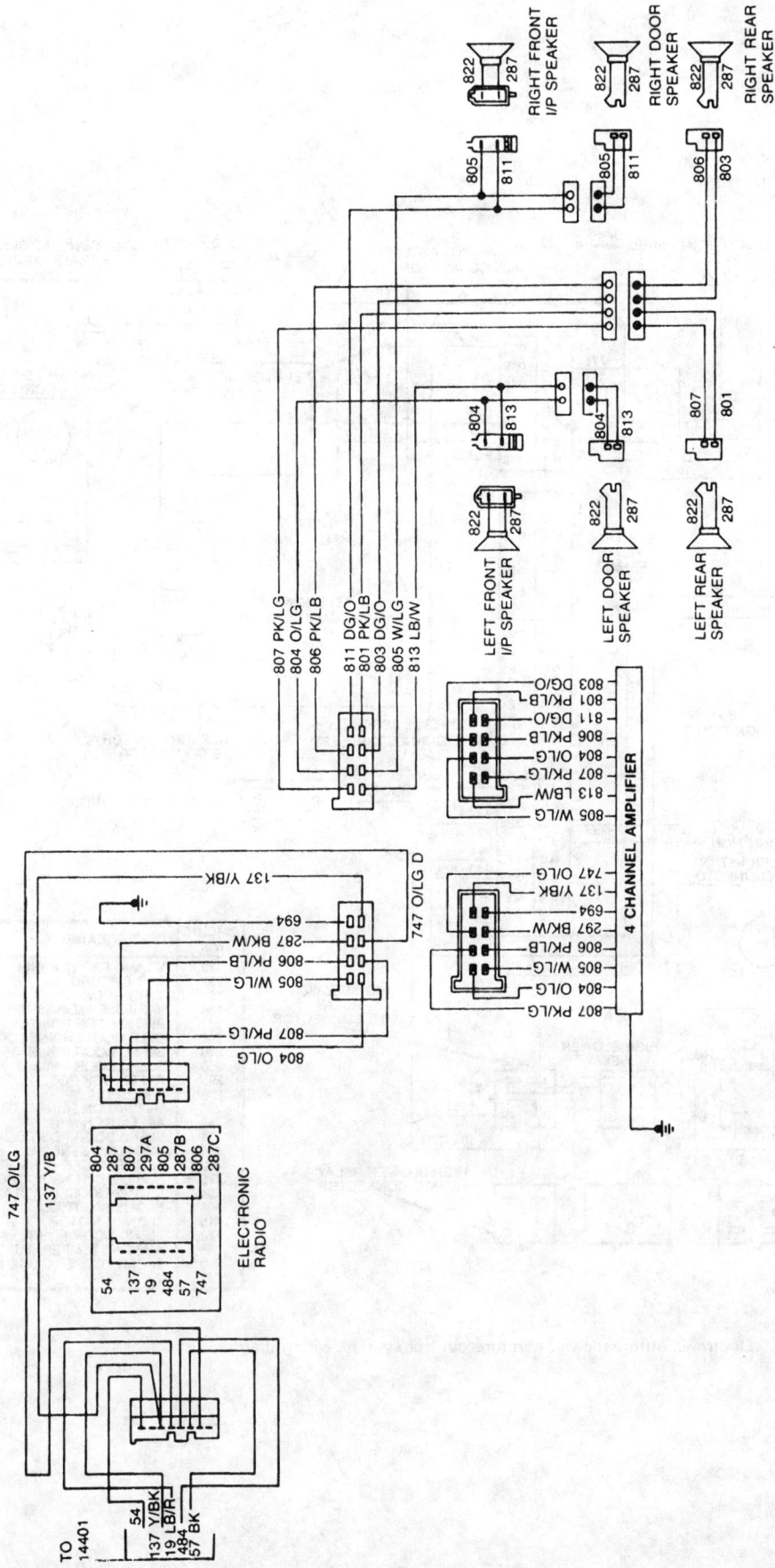

Sound system wiring diagram

RIGHT FRONT I/P SPEAKER
RIGHT DOOR SPEAKER
RIGHT REAR SPEAKER
LEFT FRONT I/P SPEAKER
LEFT DOOR SPEAKER
LEFT REAR SPEAKER

822 287

805 811
805 811
806 803
804 813
804 813
807 801

807 PK/LG
804 O/LG
806 PK/LB
811 DG/O
801 PK/LB
803 DG/O
805 W/LG
813 LB/W

4 CHANNEL AMPLIFIER

803 DG/O
801 PK/LB
811 DG/O
806 PK/LB
804 O/LG
807 PK/LG
813 LB/W
805 W/LG

747 O/LG
137 Y/BK
694
297 BK/W
806 PK/LB
805 W/LG
804 O/LG
807 PK/LG

ELECTRONIC RADIO

804
287
807
297A
805
287B
806
287C

54
137
19
484
57
747

137 Y/BK
694
287 BK/W
806 PK/LB
805 W/LG
807 PK/LG
804 O/LG

747 O/LG D
747 O/LG
137 Y/B

TO 14401
54
137 Y/BK
19 LB/R
484 BK
57 BK

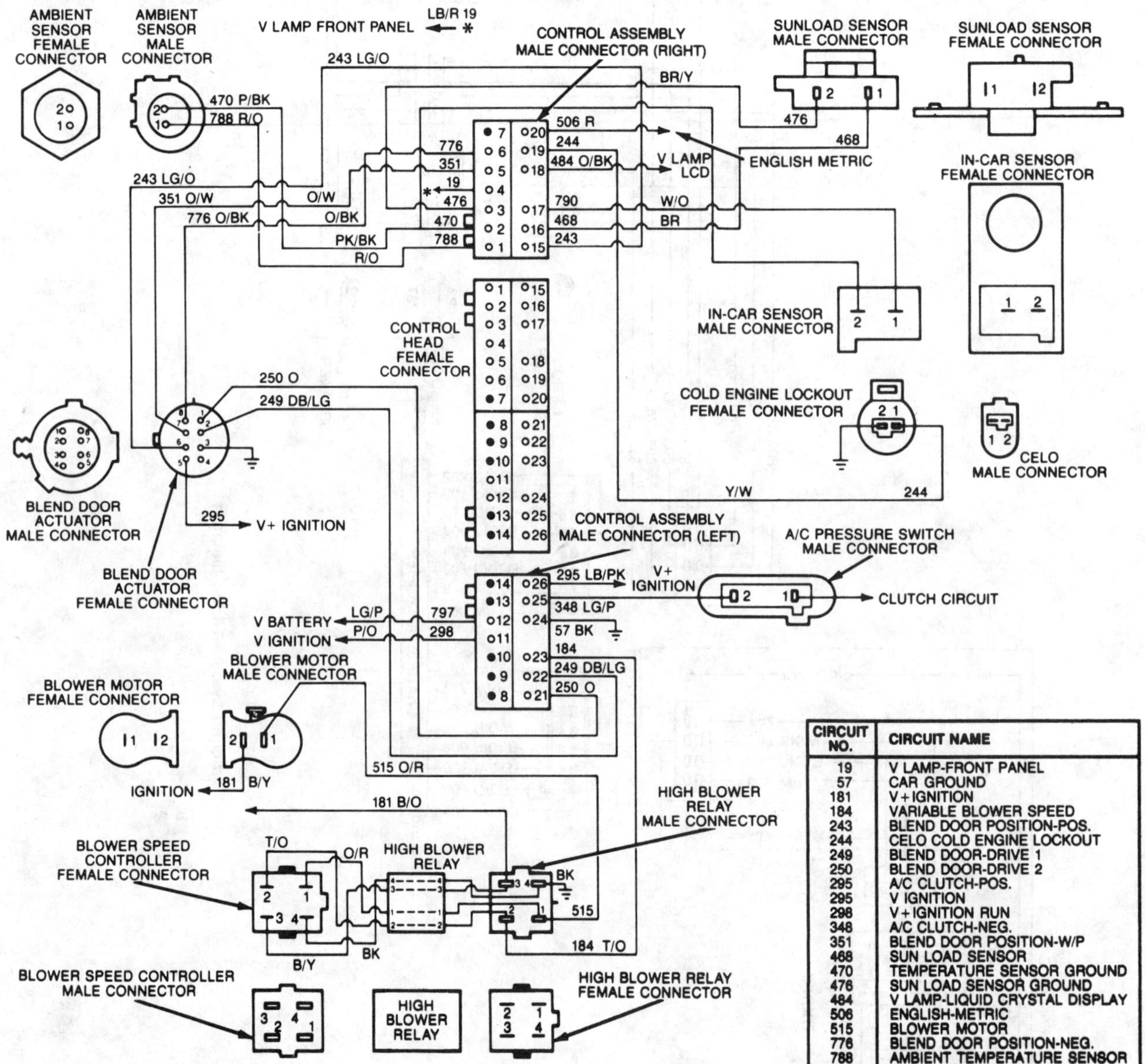

AMBIENT SENSOR FEMALE CONNECTOR

AMBIENT SENSOR MALE CONNECTOR

V LAMP FRONT PANEL ← *   LB/R 19

CONTROL ASSEMBLY MALE CONNECTOR (RIGHT)

SUNLOAD SENSOR MALE CONNECTOR

SUNLOAD SENSOR FEMALE CONNECTOR

243 LG/O

470 P/BK
788 R/O

BR/Y

506 R
244
484 O/BK

V LAMP LCD

476
468

ENGLISH METRIC

IN-CAR SENSOR FEMALE CONNECTOR

243 LG/O
351 O/W
776 O/BK

O/W
O/BK
PK/BK
R/O

776
351
19
476
470
788

7
6
5
4
3
2
1

20
19
18
17
16
15

790
468
243

W/O
BR

IN-CAR SENSOR MALE CONNECTOR

CONTROL HEAD FEMALE CONNECTOR

1
2
3
4
5
6
7
8
9
10
11
12
13
14

15
16
17
18
19
20
21
22
23
24
25
26

COLD ENGINE LOCKOUT FEMALE CONNECTOR

CELO MALE CONNECTOR

250 O
249 DB/LG

BLEND DOOR ACTUATOR MALE CONNECTOR

BLEND DOOR ACTUATOR FEMALE CONNECTOR

295   V+ IGNITION

Y/W   244

CONTROL ASSEMBLY MALE CONNECTOR (LEFT)

A/C PRESSURE SWITCH MALE CONNECTOR

14
13
12
11
10
9
8

26
25
24
23
22
21

295 LB/PK
348 LG/P
57 BK
184
249 DB/LG
250 O

V+ IGNITION

CLUTCH CIRCUIT

V BATTERY
V IGNITION

LG/P   797
P/O   298

BLOWER MOTOR MALE CONNECTOR

BLOWER MOTOR FEMALE CONNECTOR

IGNITION ←   181 B/Y

515 O/R

181 B/O

HIGH BLOWER RELAY MALE CONNECTOR

BLOWER SPEED CONTROLLER FEMALE CONNECTOR

T/O   O/R
HIGH BLOWER RELAY
2 1
4 3
B/Y   BK

3 4
2 1
BK
515

184   T/O

BLOWER SPEED CONTROLLER MALE CONNECTOR

3 4
2 1

HIGH BLOWER RELAY

HIGH BLOWER RELAY FEMALE CONNECTOR

2 1
3 4

CIRCUIT NO.	CIRCUIT NAME
19	V LAMP-FRONT PANEL
57	CAR GROUND
181	V+IGNITION
184	VARIABLE BLOWER SPEED
243	BLEND DOOR POSITION-POS.
244	CELO COLD ENGINE LOCKOUT
249	BLEND DOOR-DRIVE 1
250	BLEND DOOR-DRIVE 2
295	A/C CLUTCH-POS.
295	V IGNITION
298	V+IGNITION RUN
348	A/C CLUTCH-NEG.
351	BLEND DOOR POSITION-W/P
468	SUN LOAD SENSOR
470	TEMPERATURE SENSOR GROUND
476	SUN LOAD SENSOR GROUND
484	V LAMP-LIQUID CRYSTAL DISPLAY
506	ENGLISH-METRIC
515	BLOWER MOTOR
776	BLEND DOOR POSITION-NEG.
788	AMBIENT TEMPERATURE SENSOR
790	IN-CAR TEMPERATURE SENSOR
797	V+BATTERY

Electronic automatic temperature control system wiring diagram

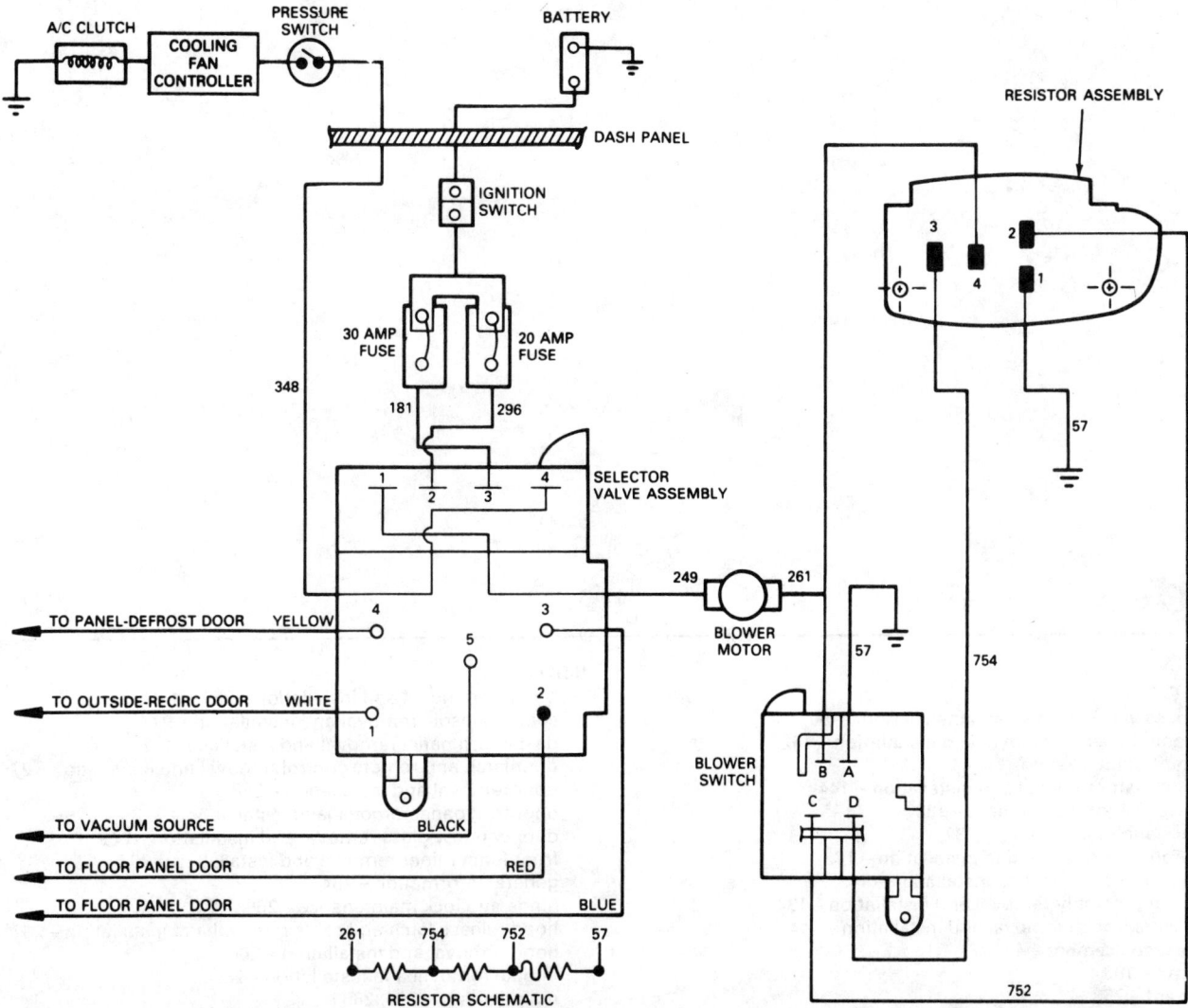

A/C CLUTCH
COOLING FAN CONTROLLER
PRESSURE SWITCH
BATTERY
DASH PANEL
RESISTOR ASSEMBLY
IGNITION SWITCH
30 AMP FUSE
20 AMP FUSE
348
181
296
SELECTOR VALVE ASSEMBLY
TO PANEL-DEFROST DOOR YELLOW
TO OUTSIDE-RECIRC DOOR WHITE
TO VACUUM SOURCE BLACK
TO FLOOR PANEL DOOR RED
TO FLOOR PANEL DOOR BLUE
BLOWER MOTOR
249 261
57
754
752
BLOWER SWITCH
261 754 752 57
RESISTOR SCHEMATIC

MODE SELECTOR SWITCH

TERMINAL	AMPS	MAX AC	NORM AC	VENT	OFF	FLOOR	MIX	DEF
2 — BATTERY 4 — A/C CLUTCH	4	2 + 4	2 + 4	NONE	NONE	NONE	2 + 4	2 + 4
3 — BATTERY 1 — BLOWER	30	1 + 3	1 + 3	1 + 3	NONE	1 + 3	1 + 3	1 + 3

POSITION	CIRCUIT MAKE	AMP
1. LOW	B	—
2. MED. 1	B + D	20
3. MED. 2	B + C + D	25
4. HIGH	B + A + C	35
BLOWER SWITCH		

CIRCUIT NO.	WIRE COLOR	WIRE GA
754	LT GREEN W WHITE HASH	14
752	YELLOW W RED DOT	14
348	LT GREEN W PURPLE HASH	14
296	WHITE W PURPLE STRIPE	14
261A	ORANGE W BLACK STRIPE	12
261	ORANGE W BLACK STRIPE	12
181	BROWN W ORANGE STRIPE	12

Manual air conditioning system schematic

Index

HAYNES AUTOMOTIVE MANUALS

NOTE: New manuals are added to this list on a periodic basis. If you do not see a listing for your vehicle, consult your local Haynes dealer for the latest product information.

ALFA-ROMEO
531 Alfa Romeo Sedan & Coupe '73 thru '80

AMC
694 Jeep CJ – see JEEP (412)
694 Mid-size models, Concord, Hornet, Gremlin & Spirit '70 thru '83
934 (Renault) Alliance & Encore all models '83 thru '87

AUDI
162 100 all models '69 thru '77
615 4000 all models '80 thru '87
428 5000 all models '77 thru '83
1117 5000 all models '84 thru '88
207 Fox all models '73 thru '79

AUSTIN
049 Healey 100/6 & 3000 Roadster '56 thru '68
Healey Sprite – see MG Midget Roadster (265)

BLMC
260 1100, 1300 & Austin America '62 thru '74
527 Mini all models '59 thru '69
*646 Mini all models '69 thru '88

BMW
276 320i all 4 cyl models '75 thru '83
632 528i & 530i all models '75 thru '80
240 1500 thru 2002 all models except Turbo '59 thru '77
348 2500, 2800, 3.0 & Bavaria '69 thru '76

BUICK
Century (front wheel drive) – see GENERAL MOTORS A-Cars (829)
*1627 Buick, Oldsmobile & Pontiac Full-size (Front wheel drive) all models '85 thru '90
Buick Electra, LeSabre and Park Avenue; Oldsmobile Delta 88 Royale, Ninety Eight and Regency; Pontiac Bonneville
*1551 Buick Oldsmobile & Pontiac Full-size (Rear wheel drive)
Buick Electra '70 thru '84, Estate '70 thru '90, LeSabre '70 thru '79
Oldsmobile Custom Cruiser '70 thru '90, Delta 88 '70 thru '85, Ninety-eight '70 thru '84
Pontiac Bonneville '70 thru '86, Catalina '70 thru '81, Grandville '70 thru '75, Parisienne '84 thru '86
627 Mid-size all rear-drive Regal & Century models with V6, V8 and Turbo '74 thru '87
Skyhawk – see GENERAL MOTORS J-Cars (766)
552 Skylark all X-car models '80 thru '85

CADILLAC
Cimarron – see GENERAL MOTORS J-Cars (766)

CAPRI
296 2000 MK I Coupe all models '71 thru '75
283 2300 MK II Coupe all models '74 thru '78
205 2600 & 2800 V6 Coupe '71 thru '75
375 2800 Mk II V6 Coupe '75 thru '78
Mercury in-line engines – see FORD Mustang (654)
Mercury V6 & V8 engines – see FORD Mustang (558)

CHEVROLET
*1477 Astro & GMC Safari Mini-vans all models '85 thru '90
554 Camaro V8 all models '70 thru '81
*866 Camaro all models '82 thru '89
Cavalier – see GENERAL MOTORS J-Cars (766)
Celebrity – see GENERAL MOTORS A-Cars (829)

625 Chevelle, Malibu & El Camino all V6 & V8 models '69 thru '87
449 Chevette & Pontiac T1000 all models '76 thru '87
550 Citation all models '80 thru '85
*1628 Corsica/Beretta all models '87 thru '90
274 Corvette all V8 models '68 thru '82
*1336 Corvette all models '84 thru '89
704 Full-size Sedans Caprice, Impala, Biscayne, Bel Air & Wagons, all V6 & V8 models '69 thru '90
319 Luv Pick-up all 2WD & 4WD models '72 thru '82
626 Monte Carlo all V6, V8 & Turbo models '70 thru '88
241 Nova all V8 models '69 thru '79
*1642 Nova and Geo Prizm all front wheel drive models, '85 thru '90
*420 Pick-ups '67 thru '87 – Chevrolet & GMC, all V8 & in-line 6 cyl 2WD & 4WD models '67 thru '87
*1664 Pick-ups '88 thru '90 – Chevrolet & GMC all full-size (C and K) models, '88 thru '90
*831 S-10 & GMC S-15 Pick-ups all models '82 thru '90
*345 Vans – Chevrolet & GMC, V8 & in-line 6 cyl models '68 thru '89
208 Vega all models except Cosworth '70 thru '77

CHRYSLER
*1337 Chrysler & Plymouth Mid-size front wheel drive '82 thru '88
K-Cars – see DODGE Aries (723)
Laser – see DODGE Daytona (1140)

DATSUN
402 200SX all models '77 thru '79
647 200SX all models '80 thru '83
228 B-210 all models '73 thru '78
525 210 all models '78 thru '82
206 240Z, 260Z & 280Z Coupe & 2+2 '70 thru '78
563 280ZX Coupe & 2+2 '79 thru '83
300ZX – see NISSAN (1137)
679 310 all models '78 thru '82
123 510 & PL521 Pick-up '68 thru '73
430 510 all models '78 thru '81
372 610 all models '72 thru '76
277 620 Series Pick-up all models '73 thru '79
235 710 all models '73 thru '77
720 Series Pick-up – see NISSAN Pick-ups (771)
376 810/Maxima all gasoline models '77 thru '84
124 1200 all models '70 thru '73
368 F10 all models '76 thru '79
Pulsar – see NISSAN (876)
Sentra – see NISSAN (982)
Stanza – see NISSAN (981)

DODGE
*723 Aries & Plymouth Reliant all models '81 thru '88
*1231 Caravan & Plymouth Voyager Mini-Vans all models '84 thru '89
699 Challenger & Plymouth Saporro all models '78 thru '83
236 Colt all models '71 thru '77
419 Colt (rear wheel drive) all models '77 thru '80
610 Colt & Plymouth Champ (front wheel drive) all models '78 thru '87
*556 D50 & Plymouth Arrow Pick-ups '79 thru '88
234 Dart & Plymouth Valiant all 6 cyl models '67 thru '76
*1140 Daytona & Chrysler Laser all models '84 thru '88
*545 Omni & Plymouth Horizon all models '78 thru '89
*912 Pick-ups all full-size models '74 thru '90
*349 Vans – Dodge & Plymouth V8 & 6 cyl models '71 thru '89

FIAT
080 124 Sedan & Wagon all ohv & dohc models '66 thru '75
094 124 Sport Coupe & Spider '68 thru '78
087 128 all models '72 thru '79
310 131 & Brava all models '75 thru '81
038 850 Sedan, Coupe & Spider '64 thru '74
479 Strada all models '79 thru '82
273 X1/9 all models '74 thru '80

FORD
*1476 Aerostar Mini-vans all models '86 thru '88
788 Bronco and Pick-ups '73 thru '79
*880 Bronco and Pick-ups '80 thru '90
014 Cortina MK II all models except Lotus '66 thru '70
295 Cortina MK III 1600 & 2000 ohc '70 thru '76
268 Courier Pick-up all models '72 thru '82
789 Escort & Mercury Lynx all models '81 thru '90
560 Fairmont & Mercury Zephyr all in-line & V8 models '78 thru '83
334 Fiesta all models '77 thru '80
754 Ford & Mercury Full-size, Ford LTD & Mercury Marquis ('75 thru '82); Ford Custom 500, Country Squire, Crown Victoria & Mercury Colony Park ('75 thru '82); Ford LTD Crown Victoria & Mercury Gran Marquis ('83 thru '87)
359 Granada & Mercury Monarch all in-line, 6 cyl & V8 models '75 thru '80
773 Ford & Mercury Mid-size, Ford Thunderbird & Mercury Cougar ('75 thru '82); Ford LTD & Mercury Marquis ('83 thru '86); Ford Torino, Gran Torino, Elite, Ranchero pick-up, LTD II, Mercury Montego, Comet, XR-7 & Lincoln Versailles ('75 thru '86)
*654 Mustang & Mercury Capri all in-line models & Turbo '79 thru '90
*558 Mustang & Mercury Capri all V6 & V8 models '79 thru '89
357 Mustang V8 all models '64-1/2 thru '73
231 Mustang II all 4 cyl, V6 & V8 models '74 thru '78
204 Pinto all models '70 thru '74
649 Pinto & Mercury Bobcat all models '75 thru '80
*1026 Ranger & Bronco II all gasoline models '83 thru '89
*1421 Taurus & Mercury Sable '86 thru '90
*1418 Tempo & Mercury Topaz all gasoline models '84 thru '89
1338 Thunderbird & Mercury Cougar/XR7 '83 thru '88
*344 Vans all V8 Econoline models '69 thru '90

GENERAL MOTORS
*829 A-Cars – Chevrolet Celebrity, Buick Century, Pontiac 6000 & Oldsmobile Cutlass Ciera all models '82 thru '89
*766 J-Cars – Chevrolet Cavalier, Pontiac J-2000, Oldsmobile Firenza, Buick Skyhawk & Cadillac Cimarron all models '82 thru '89
*1420 N-Cars – Pontiac Grand Am, Buick Somerset and Oldsmobile Calais '85 thru '87; Buick Skylark '86 thru '87

GEO
Tracker – see SUZUKI Samurai (1626)
Prizm – see CHEVROLET Nova (1642)

GMC
Safari – see CHEVROLET ASTRO (1477)
Vans & Pick-ups – see CHEVROLET (420, 831, 345, 1664)

(continued on next page)

---

* Listings shown with an asterisk (*) indicate model coverage as of this printing. These titles will be periodically updated to include later model years — consult your Haynes dealer for more information.

Haynes Publications Inc., P.O. Box 978, Newbury Park, CA 91320 • (818) 889-5400 • (805) 498-6703

NOTE: New manuals are added to this list on a periodic basis. If you do not see a listing for your vehicle, consult your local Haynes dealer for the latest product information.

HONDA
138	**360, 600 & Z** Coupe all models '67 thru '75
351	**Accord CVCC** all models '76 thru '83
*1221	**Accord** all models '84 thru '89
160	**Civic 1200** all models '73 thru '79
633	**Civic 1300 & 1500 CVCC** all models '80 thru '83
297	**Civic 1500 CVCC** all models '75 thru '79
*1227	**Civic** all models except 16-valve CRX & 4 WD Wagon '84 thru '86
*601	**Prelude CVCC** all models '79 thru '89

HYUNDAI
*1552	**Excel** all models '86 thru '89

ISUZU
*1641	**Trooper & Pick-up**, all gasoline models '81 thru '89

JAGUAR
098	**MK I & II**, 240 & 340 Sedans '55 thru '69
*242	**XJ6** all 6 cyl models '68 thru '86
*478	**XJ12 & XJS** all 12 cyl models '72 thru '85
140	**XK-E** 3.8 & 4.2 all 6 cyl models '61 thru '72

JEEP
*1553	**Cherokee, Comanche & Wagoneer Limited** all models '84 thru '89
412	**CJ** all models '49 thru '86

LADA
*413	**1200, 1300. 1500 & 1600** all models including Riva '74 thru '86

LANCIA
533	**Lancia Beta** Sedan, Coupe & HPE all models '76 thru '80

LAND ROVER
314	**Series II, IIA, & III** all 4 cyl gasoline models '58 thru '86
529	**Diesel** all models '58 thru '80

MAZDA
648	**626** Sedan & Coupe (rear wheel drive) all models '79 thru '82
*1082	**626 & MX-6 (front wheel drive)** all models '83 thru '90
*267	**B1600, B1800 & B2000 Pick-ups** '72 thru '90
370	**GLC Hatchback (rear wheel drive)** all models '77 thru '83
757	**GLC (front wheel drive)** all models '81 thru '86
109	**RX2** all models '71 thru '75
096	**RX3** all models '72 thru '76
460	**RX-7** all models '79 thru '85
*1419	**RX-7** all models '86 thru '89

MERCEDES-BENZ
*1643	**190 Series** all four-cylinder gasoline models, '84 thru '88
346	**230, 250 & 280** Sedan, Coupe & Roadster all 6 cyl sohc models '68 thru '72
983	**280 123 Series** all gasoline models '77 thru '81
698	**350 & 450** Sedan, Coupe & Roadster all models '71 thru '80
697	**Diesel 123 Series** 200D, 220D, 240D, 240TD, 300D, 300CD, 300TD, 4- & 5-cyl incl. Turbo '76 thru '85

MERCURY
See FORD Listing

MG
475	**MGA** all models '56 thru '62
111	**MGB** Roadster & GT Coupe all models '62 thru '80
265	**MG Midget & Austin Healey Sprite** Roadster '58 thru '80

MITSUBISHI
Pick-up – see Dodge D-50 (556)

MORRIS
074	**(Austin) Marina 1.8** all models '71 thru '80
024	**Minor 1000** sedan & wagon '56 thru '71

NISSAN
*1137	**300ZX** all Turbo & non-Turbo models '84 thru '86
*1341	**Maxima** all models '85 thru '89
*771	**Pick-ups/Pathfinder** gas models '80 thru '88
*876	**Pulsar** all models '83 thru '86
*982	**Sentra** all models '82 thru '90
*981	**Stanza** all models '82 thru '90

OLDSMOBILE
	Custom Cruiser – see BUICK Full-size (1551)
658	**Cutlass** all standard gasoline V6 & V8 models '74 thru '88
	Cutlass Ciera – see GENERAL MOTORS A-Cars (829)
	Firenza – see GENERAL MOTORS J-Cars (766)
	Ninety-eight – see BUICK Full-size (1551)
	Omega – see PONTIAC Phoenix & Omega (551)

OPEL
157	**(Buick) Manta Coupe 1900** all models '70 thru '74

PEUGEOT
161	**504** all gasoline models '68 thru '79
663	**504** all diesel models '74 thru '83

PLYMOUTH
425	**Arrow** all models '76 thru '80
	For all other PLYMOUTH titles, see DODGE listing.

PONTIAC
	T1000 – see CHEVROLET Chevette (449)
	J-2000 – see GENERAL MOTORS J-Cars (766)
	6000 – see GENERAL MOTORS A-Cars (829)
1232	**Fiero** all models '84 thru '88
555	**Firebird** all V8 models except Turbo '70 thru '81
*867	**Firebird** all models '82 thru '89
	Full-size Rear Wheel Drive – see Buick, Oldsmobile, Pontiac Full-size (1551)
551	**Phoenix & Oldsmobile Omega** all X-car models '80 thru '84

PORSCHE
*264	**911** all Coupe & Targa models except Turbo '65 thru '87
239	**914** all 4 cyl models '69 thru '76
397	**924** all models including Turbo '76 thru '82
*1027	**944** all models including Turbo '83 thru '89

RENAULT
141	**5 Le Car** all models '76 thru '83
079	**8 & 10** all models with 58.4 cu in engines '62 thru '72
097	**12 Saloon & Estate** all models 1289 cc engines '70 thru '80
768	**15 & 17** all models '73 thru '79
081	**16** all models 89.7 cu in & 95.5 cu in engines '65 thru '72
598	**18i & Sportwagon** all models '81 thru '86
	Alliance & Encore – see AMC (934)
984	**Fuego** all models '82 thru '85

ROVER
085	**3500 & 3500S** Sedan 215 cu in engines '68 thru '76
*365	**3500 SDI V8** all models '76 thru '85

SAAB
198	**95 & 96** V4 all models '66 thru '75
247	**99** all models including Turbo '69 thru '80
*980	**900** all models including Turbo '79 thru '88

SUBARU
237	**1100, 1300, 1400 & 1600** all models '71 thru '79
*681	**1600 & 1800** 2WD & 4WD all models '80 thru '88

SUZUKI
*1626	**Samurai/Sidekick and Geo Tracker** all models '86 thru '89

TOYOTA
*1023	**Camry** all models '83 thru '90
150	**Carina Sedan** all models '71 thru '74
229	**Celica ST, GT & liftback** all models '71 thru '77
437	**Celica** all models '78 thru '81
*935	**Celica** all models except front-wheel drive and Supra '82 thru '85
680	**Celica Supra** all models '79 thru '81
1139	**Celica Supra** all in-line 6-cylinder models '82 thru '86
201	**Corolla 1100, 1200 & 1600** all models '67 thru '74
361	**Corolla** all models '75 thru '79
961	**Corolla** all models (rear wheel drive) '80 thru '87
*1025	**Corolla** all models (front wheel drive) '84 thru '88
*636	**Corolla Tercel** all models '80 thru '82
230	**Corona & MK II** all 4 cyl sohc models '69 thru '74
360	**Corona** all models '74 thru '82
*532	**Cressida** all models '78 thru '82
313	**Land Cruiser** all models '68 thru '82
200	**MK II** all 6 cyl models '72 thru '76
*1339	**MR2** all models '85 thru '87
304	**Pick-up** all models '69 thru '78
*656	**Pick-up** all models '79 thru '90
787	**Starlet** all models '81 thru '84

TRIUMPH
112	**GT6 & Vitesse** all models '62 thru '74
113	**Spitfire** all models '62 thru '81
028	**TR2, 3, 3A, & 4A** Roadsters '52 thru '67
031	**TR250 & 6** Roadsters '67 thru '76
322	**TR7** all models '75 thru '81

VW
091	**411 & 412** all 103 cu in models '68 thru '73
036	**Bug 1200** all models '54 thru '66
039	**Bug 1300 & 1500** '65 thru '70
159	**Bug 1600** all basic, sport & super (curved windshield) models '70 thru '74
110	**Bug 1600 Super** all models (flat windshield) '70 thru '72
238	**Dasher** all gasoline models '74 thru '81
*884	**Rabbit, Jetta, Scirocco, & Pick-up** all gasoline models '74 thru '89 & **Convertible** '80 thru '89
451	**Rabbit, Jetta & Pick-up** all diesel models '77 thru '84
082	**Transporter 1600** all models '68 thru '79
226	**Transporter 1700, 1800 & 2000** all models '72 thru '79
084	**Type 3 1500 & 1600** all models '63 thru '73
1029	**Vanagon** all air-cooled models '80 thru '83

VOLVO
203	**120, 130 Series & 1800 Sports** '61 thru '73
129	**140 Series** all models '66 thru '74
244	**164** all models '68 thru '75
*270	**240 Series** all models '74 thru '90
400	**260 Series** all models '75 thru '82
*1550	**740 & 760 Series** all models '82 thru '88

SPECIAL MANUALS
1479	**Automotive Body Repair & Painting Manual**
1654	**Automotive Electrical Manual**
1480	**Automotive Heating & Air Conditioning Manual**
482	**Fuel Injection Manual**
299	**SU Carburetors** thru '88
393	**Weber Carburetors** thru '79
300	**Zenith/Stromberg CD Carburetors** thru '76

See your dealer for other available titles

6-1-90

Over 100 Haynes motorcycle manuals also available

---

* Listings shown with an asterisk (*) indicate model coverage as of this printing. These titles will be periodically updated to include later model years — consult your Haynes dealer for more information.

Haynes Publications Inc., P.O. Box 978, Newbury Park, CA 91320 ● (818) 889–5400 ● (805) 498–6703